WITH NRSV COMPARISON

INTERNATIONAL LESSON COMMENTARY

The Standard in
Biblical Exposition

Based on the
International Sunday
School Lessons (ISSL)

Victor®
The Bible Teacher's Teacher

COOK COMMUNICATIONS MINISTRIES
Colorado Springs, Colorado • Paris, Ontario
KINGSWAY COMMUNICATIONS LTD
Eastbourne, England

Victor® is an imprint of
Cook Communications Ministries, Colorado Springs, CO 80918
Cook Communications, Paris, Ontario
Kingsway Communications, Eastbourne, England

THE KJV INTERNATIONAL BIBLE LESSON COMMENTARY

First printing, 2007
Printed in U.S.A.
1 2 3 4 5 6 7 8 9 10   Printing/Year   10 09 08 07

Editor: Daniel Lioy, Ph.D.
Editorial Manager: Doug Schmidt
Cover Design: Ray Moore/Two Moore Design
Cover Photo: ©2000-2005 PhotoSpin, Inc.

ISBN: 0781445027

CONTENTS

SEPTEMBER, OCTOBER, NOVEMBER 2007
GOD CREATED A PEOPLE

UNIT I: GOD CREATED A PEOPLE

UNIT II: GOD'S PEOPLE INCREASED

UNIT III: GOD'S PEOPLE RE-CREATED

DECEMBER 2007, JANUARY, FEBRUARY 2008
GOD'S CALL TO THE CHRISTIAN COMMUNITY

UNIT I: GOD'S CALL AT CHRISTMAS AND BEYOND

UNIT II: THE AWARENESS OF GOD'S INSTRUCTION

UNIT III: GOD SUMMONS US TO RESPOND!

CONTENTS

■

A Word to the Teacher

In Paul's farewell address to the Ephesian elders, he said he had not hesitated to proclaim to them "the whole will of God" (Acts 20:27). Expressed differently, though the apostle used tact and discernment, he never tried to conceal any of the truths associated with the Gospel. This especially included the Father's redemptive purpose and plan through His Son, the Lord Jesus Christ.

As a Sunday school teacher, it is also your privilege to teach the whole counsel of God's Word. Sometimes you will discuss a positive topic, such as the promises the Lord made to His people. On other occasions, you will present a less pleasant theme, such as the judgment of God on the rebellious.

Regardless of the subject matter being taught, your job as a Sunday school teacher is eternally relevant. After all, you are not just giving the students important biblical information. God is also using you to be an agent of change in their lives. This is an awesome responsibility, and one that I know you take seriously.

As you purpose to teach God's Word to your students, take a few moments to think about what He has done and is doing through you. Pray that your students will discover that the Scriptures are as relevant today as they were thousands of years ago. Then, watch in fascination as they discover that the Lord is both merciful and just. May God richly bless you as you share the riches of His truth with your students!

Your fellow learner at the feet of the Master Teacher,
Dan Lioy

USE *THE KJV INTERNATIONAL BIBLE LESSON COMMENTARY* WITH MATERIAL FROM THESE PUBLISHERS

Sunday school materials from the following denominations and publishers follow the International Sunday School Lesson outlines (sometimes known as the Uniform Series). Because *The KJV International Bible Lesson Commentary* (formerly *Tarbell's*) follows the same ISSL outlines, you can use *The KJV International Bible Lesson Commentary* as an excellent teacher resource to supplement the materials from these publishing houses.

Nondenominational:

Standard Publishing—*Adult*

Urban Ministries—*All ages*

Echoes Teacher's Commentary (*Cook Communications Ministries*): *Adult*

Denominational:

Advent Christian General Conference—*Adult*

American Baptist (Judson Press)—*Adult*

Church of God in Christ (Church of God in Christ Publishing House)—*Adult*

Church of Christ Holiness—*Adult*

Church of God (Warner Press)—*Adult*

Church of God by Faith—*Adult*

National Baptist Convention of America (Boyd)—*All ages*

National Primitive Baptist Convention—*Adult*

Progressive National Baptist Convention—*Adult*

Presbyterian Church (U.S.A.) (Bible Discovery Series—Presbyterian Publishing House or P.R.E.M.)—*Adult*

Union Gospel Press—*All ages*

United Holy Church of America—*Adult*

United Methodist Church (Cokesbury)—*All ages*

GOD CREATED THE HEAVENS AND THE EARTH

BACKGROUND SCRIPTURE: Genesis 1:1-25
DEVOTIONAL READING: Psalm 8

KEY VERSES: In the beginning God created the heaven and the earth. And the earth was without form, and void; and darkness was upon the face of the deep. And the Spirit of God moved upon the face of the waters. Genesis 1:1-2.

KING JAMES VERSION

GENESIS 1:1 In the beginning God created the heaven and the earth. 2 And the earth was without form, and void; and darkness was upon the face of the deep. And the Spirit of God moved upon the face of the waters. 3 And God said, Let there be light: and there was light. 4 And God saw the light, that it was good: and God divided the light from the darkness. 5 And God called the light Day, and the darkness he called Night. And the evening and the morning were the first day. 6 And God said, Let there be a firmament in the midst of the waters, and let it divide the waters from the waters. . . . 8 And God called the firmament Heaven. And the evening and the morning were the second day. . . . 10 And God called the dry land Earth; and the gathering together of the waters called he Seas: and God saw that it was good. . . . 12 And the earth brought forth grass, and herb yielding seed after his kind, and the tree yielding fruit, whose seed was in itself, after his kind: and God saw that it was good. 13 And the evening and the morning were the third day. 14 And God said, Let there be lights in the firmament of the heaven to divide the day from the night; and let them be for signs, and for seasons, and for days, and years: 15 And let them be for lights in the firmament of the heaven to give light upon the earth: and it was so. . . . 19 And the evening and the morning were the fourth day. 20 And God said, Let the waters bring forth abundantly the moving creature that hath life, and fowl that may fly above the earth in the open firmament of heaven.. . . 22 And God blessed them, saying, Be fruitful, and multiply, and fill the waters in the seas, and let fowl multiply in the earth. 23 And the evening and the morning were the fifth day. . . .25 And God made the beast of the earth after his kind, and cattle after their kind, and every thing that creepeth upon the earth after his kind: and God saw that it was good.

NEW REVISED STANDARD VERSION

GENESIS 1:1 In the beginning when God created the heavens and the earth, 2 the earth was a formless void and darkness covered the face of the deep, while a wind from God swept over the face of the waters. 3 Then God said, "Let there be light"; and there was light. 4 And God saw that the light was good; and God separated the light from the darkness. 5 God called the light Day, and the darkness he called Night. And there was evening and there was morning, the first day.

6 And God said, "Let there be a dome in the midst of the waters, and let it separate the waters from the waters." . . . 8 God called the dome Sky. And there was evening and there was morning, the second day.

10 God called the dry land Earth, and the waters that were gathered together he called Seas. And God saw that it was good. . . . 12 The earth brought forth vegetation: plants yielding seed of every kind, and trees of every kind bearing fruit with the seed in it. And God saw that it was good. 13 And there was evening and there was morning, the third day.

14 And God said, "Let there be lights in the dome of the sky to separate the day from the night; and let them be for signs and for seasons and for days and years, 15 and let them be lights in the dome of the sky to give light upon the earth." And it was so. . . . 19 And there was evening and there was morning, the fourth day.

20 And God said, "Let the waters bring forth swarms of living creatures, and let birds fly above the earth across the dome of the sky." . . . 22 God blessed them, saying, "Be fruitful and multiply and fill the waters in the seas, and let birds multiply on the earth." 23 And there was evening and there was morning, the fifth day. . . .

25 God made the wild animals of the earth of every kind, and the cattle of every kind, and everything that creeps upon the ground of every kind. And God saw that it was good.

Monday, August 27	Psalm 8	*God the Creator*
Tuesday, August 28	Genesis 1:1-5	*The First Day*
Wednesday, August 29	Genesis 1:6-8	*The Sky*
Thursday, August 30	Genesis 1:9-13	*The First Harvest*
Friday, August 31	Genesis 1:14-19	*The Sun and Moon*
Saturday, September 1	Genesis 1:20-23	*The Birds and Sea Creatures*
Sunday, September 2	Genesis 1:24-25	*The Animals*

BACKGROUND

Three Hebrew terms are used in the Genesis account to speak of God's creative work. The word used in 1:1 means to make something new. There it refers to the creation of the universe from nothing (sometimes referred to by the Latin phrase *ex nihilo*). A different Hebrew term describes the creative action in 1:25. This word means "to fashion." Unlike the previous term, this one indicates the shaping of something that already existed. God first brought the universe into being and then used this material to fashion His creatures. A third term for God's creative work is used in 1:24, which says that the land would *bring forth* living creatures according to their kinds. In the original, it literally means "to cause to come forth."

The Hebrew word for *God* in Genesis 1:1 is *Elohim*, a widely used plural form emphasizing God's majesty and power. The word allows for the Trinity without falling into the trap of polytheism (belief in many gods). We are not told when the triune God began His work, just that it was *in the beginning*. God has always existed (Ps. 90:2). The heavens and the earth, however, had a definite beginning point in time.

In Hebrew speech, pairs of opposites were often used to express totality. In Psalm 139:2, for example, David's phrase *Thou knowest my downsitting and mine uprising* means God knew everything about David. Similarly, the phrase *the heaven and the earth* in Genesis 1:1 means that God created all things—spiritual beings, physical beings, matter, energy, time, and space. In the Genesis account, it's helpful to remember that God is involved in but distinct from His creation. People have often made the mistake of worshiping parts of creation rather than the Creator Himself. We shouldn't try to appreciate a great painting without considering the painter, and neither should we fail to recognize God as the master designer of the universe.

Geness 1:2 reveals that in its early stage, the earth was *without form, and void*, a phrase that translates the rhyming Hebrew words *tohu wabohu*. The idea is that the earth was chaotic, not ordered; and because the earth was barren, God would spend the days of Creation forming and filling it. According to a view called the gap theory, an extended period of time passed between the events of 1:1 and those of 1:2. First, God created the heavens and the earth. Later, as a byproduct of Satan's rebellion against God, the earth was converted to a formless state. Then God re-created it. Those who reject the gap theory declare that the temporarily formless state of the earth need not be considered in negative terms. God simply chose to create by beginning with formless matter and then giving it form. Thus, there was only one creation.

Genesis 1:2 refers to the water on the surface of the earth. Water is shapeless; it is the same all over. Water suggests the formlessness of the earth in its early stage. Moreover, *darkness was upon the face of the deep*. This was so because, according to the events of Creation week, God had not yet brought the sun and the other celestial lights into existence. Meanwhile, the Spirit of God *moved upon* the waters of the earth. The Spirit was like a mother bird brooding over her eggs. Here we see that God was about to bring forth life on His new world. The same Hebrew term rendered *moved upon* in 1:2 is used in Deuteronomy 32:11 to speak of an eagle that hovers over the nest when it stirs up the young. The picture Scripture paints is not one in which God sets the universe in motion and passively allows natural forces to operate, but one in which He is directly involved in every aspect of Creation.

NOTES ON THE PRINTED TEXT

The first verse in Genesis begins with God. Here we learn that before time ever began, He eternally existed. At first, the earth had no shape and was empty. Also, darkness cloaked the surface of the watery deep surrounding this formless mass. Meanwhile, the Spirit of God was moving over the surface of the water (Gen. 1:2). He was active in bringing order out of chaos.

The Son was also involved in the creation of the world. He, along with the Father and the Spirit, eternally preexisted and was the one through whom all things came to be (John 1:1-3). Indeed, the Word is the source of all life, whether material or spiritual in nature (1:4). Moreover, all things—whether visible or invisible—were created through the Son and for Him, and are held together in Him (Col. 1:16-17). He both made the universe and sustains it by His powerful command (Heb. 1:2-3).

The biblical account reveals that the universe has not always existed and that it did not come into existence through natural and impersonal forces; instead, God created the heavens and the earth in a miraculous way. For instance, Genesis 1:3 indicates that the one true and living God simply issued His command—*Let there be light*—and it was so. Since it is not until the fourth day of creation that God brings the sun into existence (1:14–19), the light present during the first three days did not correspond to what is presently known. The *light* mentioned in 1:3 contrasts sharply with the *darkness* noted in 1:2. God's provision of light is the first step in the process of bringing order out of chaos and making the earth hospitable for humans.

During the third day of creation, as God reflected on the light He had commanded into existence, He concluded that it was *good* (1:4). In this case, the light served God's benevolent purposes, especially in enabling humanity to fulfill its divinely ordained role in the world. From a broader biblical perspective, light is conducive for life—

especially in terms of promoting, enhancing, or producing such—and thus meets with God's approval. The divine is so sovereign in His rule that He even makes the darkness conform to His will (Ps. 104:19–26). For example, in the creation account He *divided the light from the darkness* (Gen. 1:4). In this context, light and darkness, while distinct from one another, coexist together in harmony. In later biblical usage, they become mutually exclusive and incompatible entities (see John 1:5; 1 John 1:5–7).

According to Genesis 1:5, God identified the light as *Day* and the darkness as *Night*. Also, the first day of creation was marked by the passage of *evening* and *morning*. In fact, six of the seven days are closed out in this way and parallel the Hebrew manner of reckoning time. The idea is that night (which is between evening and morning) ends the day. Then, with the appearance of dawn's first light, a new day begins, along with the new creative possibilities it brings.

During the second day of creation, the Lord commanded a *firmament* (1:6) into existence. This vault-like space separated waters under the expanse from the waters above the expanse (1:7). Next, God called the firmament *Heaven* (1:8), which included what we know today as the sky; and with that the second day of creation ended.

During the third day of creation, the Lord commanded the water under the expanse to be gathered to one place, which in turn enabled dry ground to appear (1:9). The Creator-King called the dry ground *Earth* (1:10) and the water *Seas*. What He saw was good, especially in helping to foster and sustain life on the newly formed planet. As the third day of creation continued to unfold, the Lord effortlessly commanded the land to produce vegetation. The result was that the soil burst forth with all kinds of grass, seed-bearing plants, and fruit-bearing trees (1:11). Every aspect of this occurred as God intended. He regarded the fertility of the planet's vegetation to be *good* (1:12) because it produced and enhanced life, especially in providing food for air and land creatures, most notably humans (see 1:29–30). Thus ended the third day of creation (1:13).

During the fourth day of creation, God commanded lights to appear in the expanse of the heavens for the purpose of separating the day from the night. These celestial luminaries also served as signs to enable people to mark off seasons, days, and years (1:14). There is not a hint of difficulty as God imposed His will on the world He was bringing into existence (1:15). The heavens, as the handiwork of God, declare His glory (Ps. 19:1). Day and night the sun, moon, and stars in the sky silently attest to the Lord's existence (19:2-4). Indeed, since the dawn of time, the world has stood as a visible testimony to God's eternal power and divine nature (Rom. 1:20). Because God has disclosed Himself in creation, all people stand condemned before Him. The condemnation of those who suppress God's truth is justified because ignoring the revelation of God in creation is indefensible.

With respect to God's pristine creation, the *greater light* (Gen. 1:16) refers to the sun, which dominates the daytime sky. The *lesser light* denotes the moon, which is often visible at night. They exist in the expanse of the heavens, along with the stars, because God sovereignly placed them there (1:17). Their presence helps earth's inhabitants move about on the planet and distinguish day from night. Because this is conducive to promoting life on the globe, it is truly good (1:18). Thus ended the fourth day of creation (1:19).

During the fifth day of creation, God decreed that water on the earth teem with aquatic life and that the sky be filled with birds of every kind (1:20). The Lord deemed that such abundance of activity was good (1:21). Indeed, God blessed these earth-dwelling creatures by enabling them to be productive and numerous in their respective realms of existence (1:22). And with that the fifth day of creation ended (1:23). Finally, during the sixth day of creation, God called the land creatures into existence. Whether it was domesticated animals, smaller creeping things, or wild beasts, they all owed their existence to God (1:24). The vastness and diversity of such life was good, according to God's decree (1:25). This included the existence of humankind (1:26-27).

SUGGESTIONS TO TEACHERS

Genesis is the book of beginnings. In this portion of Scripture, we find the beginnings of the material universe, human life, human sin, divine judgment on human sin, covenant promises, and the Israelite tribes—to name just a few. Genesis provides a foundation for a great deal of what we know about life and our Lord. Moreover, from start to finish, Genesis is a book of history, and its historical account is trustworthy because God is its Author.

1. IN THE BEGINNING . . . GOD CREATED. Genesis insists that the universe owes its origin to an intelligent Creator, not an impersonal "force." The origin of all that is may be attributed to the one we call God. Furthermore, all that exists has come into being because of our caring Creator.

2. AND GOD SAW THAT IT WAS GOOD. This planet Earth, and especially human life, are not to be seen as inherently evil. We must not regard our existence as dismal and think that we have to contrive some sort escape from the world. Unlike the pessimists of our day, we should have an optimistic, joyful, and affirming attitude toward God and His creation.

3. AND THERE WAS EVENING AND THERE WAS MORNING. Consider with your class that the Creator measured time. Our sense of history and awareness that our lives are regulated by days, weeks, months, and years of sunrises and sunsets all derived from God's orderly arrangement. This means that our lives are neither endless nor senselessly repetitive.

4. GOD CREATED EVERY LIVING CREATURE. God is the source of life. Scientists might tinker with genes, as in the case of the cloned sheep produced in the

Scottish laboratory in 1997, but only the Creator bestows the ingredients needed for living organisms to survive and thrive.

<table>
<tr><td>

FOR ADULTS

</td><td>

■ **TOPIC:** How Is Creation Possible?

■ **QUESTIONS:** 1. What does it mean that, at the dawn of time, the earth was formless and void? 2. In what sense was the light God command-

</td></tr>
</table>

ed into existence good? 3. What was the firmament that God brought into existence during the second day of creation? 4. How was God, the Creator-King, able to separate the waters from the dry land? 5. What purpose did God assign to the lights He created?

■ **ILLUSTRATIONS:**

Nighttime Experience. I vividly recall the night when, as an adult, I experienced the most wonderful sense of God's creativity I had enjoyed since early childhood. Strangely enough, it happened on the hood of a 1974 Pontiac Catalina. It was an early August night, and the stars were already standing out from a deep, black background. I decided to while away an hour or two just lying on my car hood, watching the sky.

Suddenly, a ball of light streaked across the sky from right to left, high above me; and then another did the same thing. Soon the sky was filled with shooting yellow-red balls of light that seemed impossibly close. I held my breath, my eyes wide open with amazement. "Thank you, Father," I said over and over.

The next day I learned that I had witnessed the annual Perseid meteor shower, named for the constellation Perseus, which is in the area of the sky where the shooting stars appear. According to one expert, Perseus is a beautiful group of stars in the Milky Way galaxy. I cannot speak for the constellation, but its meteor offspring are breathtaking.

Amazingly, we do not have to look to the sky to see God's handiwork in nature. Our world is a living testament to the goodness of God in creation, imperfect though it has become due to the Fall. Whether we are digging dirt, wading in surf, or listening to bird songs, every day brings countless reminders of God's incredible creativity. When the Lord Himself stepped back and saw all that He had made, He declared it to be very good (Gen. 1:31). No one should doubt for a moment that it is.

A Sense of Perspective. Trusting in God may seem simple, but the God whom we trust is greater than we can imagine. William Beebe, the naturalist, told of visits he made to Theodore Roosevelt. According to Henry Sloane Coffin (the former president of Union Theological Seminary), often at Sagamore Hill, the Roosevelt home, Beebe and Roosevelt would go out on the lawn at night, gaze up at the heavens, and wait to see who could detect "the faint spot of light-mist beyond the lower left-hand corner of the Great Square of Pegasus. Then one or the other would recite the following:

"That is the Spiral Galaxy of Andromeda.
It is as large as our Milky Way.
It is one of a hundred million galaxies.
It is 750,000 light-years away.
It consists of one hundred billion suns,
each larger than our sun."

Beebe recalled that Roosevelt would grin at him and say: "Now, I think we are small enough. Let's go to bed."

Back to Basics. To find out what really happened when the Earth was created, engineers spent weeks gathering information, checking and rechecking it, then feeding it into a powerful computer. The great moment came. All was complete. Everyone gathered around. A button was pushed. The great computer whirled into action. Lights flashed. Bells rang. Finally, a typed message emerged: See Genesis 1:1!

■ **TOPIC:** Starting Line

■ **QUESTIONS:** 1. What was the Spirit of God doing at the dawn of time? 2. How is the power of God evident in commanding the light and darkness into existence? 3. In what sense was the sky, water, and land that God brought into existence good? 4. What categories of creatures were brought into existence after the earth was formed? 5. What purpose do the air, land, and sea creatures serve in God's creation?

■ **ILLUSTRATIONS:**

Backyard Guest. "Why did God make that?" The look on his face matched the wonder in his voice. "That" was the largest, ugliest spider ever encountered by my then-four-year-old son. The spider had taken up residency in our yard that summer, moving its mammoth web from place to place. My son kept a keen eye out for it. Although the web was a marvel to look at when the sun glinted on its intricately woven threads, the spider creeping across it was nightmare material.

God, like our backyard guest, has spun an intricate web; but God's weaving of creation is a true marvel. His web still stands, a testimony to the One who made it, a verification that both it and He are *very good* (Gen. 1:31). Unlike our scary guest, God does not stand ready to devour prey. He waits to embrace His children.

It Just Happened. A young man, who prided himself on being an atheist, once came into the study of the famed 17th-century astronomer, Kircher. The young man saw there a very fine working model of the solar system. By turning a handle, the planets could be made to revolve in their respective orbits around the sun.

The young man asked, "Very ingenious, indeed, but who made it?" Kircher replied,

"Oh, no one made it." The young man shot back, "Tell me. I want to know. Who made it?" Kircher quipped, "Nobody made it. It just happened."

The young man began to see the astronomer's point, became annoyed, and remarked, "I see you are trying to be funny." Kircher asked, "Isn't it rather you who are funny? You can't believe that this little model just happened, and yet you can believe that the real sun and moon and stars, and the whole universe came into being without a Maker!"

With fantastic precision and intricacy, our world, as it has for millennia, carries on its macro and micro functions, as we live, love, work, and die here; but what does it all mean? If we have come to believe that the world and its contents are the result of mere chance, then there is no reason to consider its meaning at all. Life exists for no particular reason—it just is, period.

If, however, we have determined that there must be a Creator who purposed to make our world and who put us in it, suddenly there are issues of significance and meaning to consider; and if we believe that the God of the Bible is that Creator, then we can understand, at least in part, His heart and mind concerning His purpose for creation as well as His desire for its eternal future.

Small-Scale Evidence of Grand-Scale Design. Astrophysicist, Hugh Ross, is the founder and president of the organization *Reasons to Believe*. He reports that a group of "Japanese scientists exploring the crystal structure" of a particular enzyme have "discovered nature's own rotary engine." This "tiny motor" is no larger than "ten billionths by ten billionths by eight billionths of a meter" and includes the "equivalent of an engine block, a drive shaft, and three pistons." The biological marvel, which operates at "speeds between 0.5 and 4.0 revolutions per second," represents the "smallest motor that the laws of physics and chemistry will allow."

Moreover, the complexity of such a system within the "tiny enzyme" reflects a "mind-boggling quantity, not to mention quality, of information." Some insist that this information came from "blind chance and random process." But as Ross notes, nothing in existence can "self-program without intelligent input." Indeed, the most plausible explanation is that God, the Intelligent Designer, "structured these molecules and taught them to perform their functions." Furthermore, the weight of scientific evidence indicates that "all living creatures" bear the imprint of "the matchless brilliance and power of a Supreme Creator."

GOD CREATED HUMANKIND

BACKGROUND SCRIPTURE: Genesis 1:26—2:3
DEVOTIONAL READING: Isaiah 40:25-31

2

KEY VERSE: And God said, Let us make man in our image, after our likeness: and let them have dominion over . . . [everything] upon the earth. Genesis 1:26.

KING JAMES VERSION

GENESIS 1:26 And God said, Let us make man in our image, after our likeness: and let them have dominion over the fish of the sea, and over the fowl of the air, and over the cattle, and over all the earth, and over every creeping thing that creepeth upon the earth.
27 So God created man in his own image, in the image of God created he him; male and female created he them. 28 And God blessed them, and God said unto them, Be fruitful, and multiply, and replenish the earth, and subdue it: and have dominion over the fish of the sea, and over the fowl of the air, and over every living thing that moveth upon the earth.

29 And God said, Behold, I have given you every herb bearing seed, which is upon the face of all the earth, and every tree, in the which is the fruit of a tree yielding seed; to you it shall be for meat. 30 And to every beast of the earth, and to every fowl of the air, and to every thing that creepeth upon the earth, wherein there is life, I have given every green herb for meat: and it was so.

31 And God saw every thing that he had made, and, behold, it was very good. And the evening and the morning were the sixth day.

NEW REVISED STANDARD VERSION

GENESIS 1:26 Then God said, "Let us make humankind in our image, according to our likeness; and let them have dominion over the fish of the sea, and over the birds of the air, and over the cattle, and over all the wild animals of the earth, and over every creeping thing that creeps upon the earth."
27 So God created humankind in his image,
     in the image of God he created them;
     male and female he created them.
28 God blessed them, and God said to them, "Be fruitful and multiply, and fill the earth and subdue it; and have dominion over the fish of the sea and over the birds of the air and over every living thing that moves upon the earth." 29 God said, "See, I have given you every plant yielding seed that is upon the face of all the earth, and every tree with seed in its fruit; you shall have them for food. 30 And to every beast of the earth, and to every bird of the air, and to everything that creeps on the earth, everything that has the breath of life, I have given every green plant for food." And it was so. 31 God saw everything that he had made, and indeed, it was very good. And there was evening and there was morning, the sixth day.

HOME BIBLE READINGS

BACKGROUND

Bringing humankind into existence was the final and climactic act of God. Genesis 1:26 begins with the Creator-King decreeing, *Let us make.* There are various explanations for the use of the plural here. Some consider this to be a hint of the Trinity, namely, a plurality within the divine unity of the Father, Son, and Spirit. Another possibility is that the Hebrew signifies either a plural of majesty (for example, the royal "we") or a situation in which God addresses the statement to Himself.

A third group proposes that God and His heavenly angelic court are in view (see Isa. 6:8). In this case, while the latter are included in the statement, it is God who actually brings humankind into existence. It is not clear, however, in what sense the cosmic attendants possess the divine "image" and participate in God's creation activity. Some conjecture that the assembly of heavenly beings governs the world and communicates with humanity under God's royal authority.

Down through the centuries, people have debated what it means for humans to be made in God's image, with the varieties of views stressing either the nature or function of human life. Put another way, the divine likeness is either a special character (or quality) given to humans or a role (or task) entrusted to them. Perhaps a combination of both views should be affirmed, especially that people somehow and in some way bear the image of God in both the material and immaterial aspects of their existence.

This observation surely includes temporal (physical) life and for believers eternal life. Indeed, only the redeemed enjoy fellowship with the Lord as the object of His special love. The discussion about the divine likeness in humanity has also focused on the ability of people to reason, make ethical decisions, and exercise dominion. Possessing high mental abilities and behaving morally concern the nature of human life, while governing the rest of creation deals with the function of human life.

From a New Testament perspective, the spiritual character of the redeemed cannot be ignored. In short, becoming increasingly more like the Messiah is closely connected with bearing the image of God (Rom. 8:29; 2 Cor. 3:18; Eph. 4:22-24; Col. 3:9-10). Even within fallen humanity, though the image of God has been defaced through sin, people still bear the divine likeness to some degree (Gen. 5:1; 9:6; Jas. 3:9), and this sets them apart from the rest of earth's creatures.

The Genesis account indicates that God gave humans the capacity and authority to govern creation as His ruling representatives. Their jurisdiction extended to the fish in the sea, the birds in the sky, and animals on the land (whether small or large, wild or domesticated). The mandate for people to govern the world as benevolent vice-regents of the true and living God is a reflection of His image in them (see Gen. 9:2; Ps. 8:5-8; Heb. 2:5-9). By ruling over the rest of creation in a responsible fashion, people bear witness to the divine likeness placed within humanity. Also, as they mediate God's presence, they make His will a reality on earth.

These statements should not be taken as permission to exploit and ravage either the environment or its inhabitants, including other humans. After all, people are not the owners of creation, but rather stewards who are accountable to their divine owner. While they have jurisdiction over animals and plants (Gen. 1:28-29), they exercise no authority over cosmic entities and forces (Eph. 6:10-12). Moreover, because all people bear the image of God, they have sanctity and innate worth. Correspondingly, they are to be treated with dignity and respect.

NOTES ON THE PRINTED TEXT

In Genesis 1:3—2:3, we have the description of seven event-filled days. In the first six of those days, God created. Then, on the seventh day, He rested. The passages describing each of the six days of creation begin with the phrase *And God said* (1:3, 6, 9, 14, 20, 24). God created with words, and His every command was effective.

Commentators have long noticed that Day 1 seems to correspond to Day 4, Day 2 to Day 5, and Day 3 to Day 6. The first three days were preoccupied with God's forming the earth; and the second three days were taken up with His filling what He had formed. On Day 1, God created day and separated it from night. Later, on Day 4, He created the sun, moon, and stars that shine by day and by night. On Day 2, God made the sky by separating surface water from clouds. Then on Day 5, God created the sea creatures that live in the water and the birds that live in the sky. On Day 3, God separated dry ground and surface water, making land and seas. He also made vegetation. On Day 6, God created animals and humans, both of which live on land and eat vegetation.

After God spoke the living things into existence, He gave them orders. The supremacy of humans over the rest of creation is surely due to the fact that both male and female people are made in the *image* (1:26-27) and *likeness* (1:26) of God. Bearing the divine image is both a privilege and responsibility for humans. With respect to privilege, it indicates that they are at the summit of God's creation. In terms of responsibility, they are stewards serving as God's vice-regents over the aquatic life in the oceans, over the winged creatures that fly through the air, and over all the animals that live on the ground—whether large or small, wild or domesticated (1:26). These truths apply equally to men and women (1:27).

Genesis 2 records a parallel account of God's creation of humankind; but unlike the first one, it focuses narrowly on the first humans and the special place the Lord prepared for them. It says in 2:7 that God formed a man from the dust of the ground. The Hebrew term rendered *formed* was commonly used of a potter's work (for example, see Isa. 45:9). In a sense, the Lord was like potter, and the first man was like a pot made of clay. The Hebrew noun translated *man* (Gen. 2:7) is *adam*. Here and in 2:20 the word could be translated either as *man* or as the name *Adam*. Also, there is a pun in 2:7, since the Hebrew for *man* (*adam*) sounds like and may be related to the Hebrew for *ground* (*adamah*).

In regard to his earthly body, Adam was much like the animals. Both he and they were formed out of the ground (compare 2:7 and 19). Likewise, the man had the breath of life in him just like the animals (compare 1:30 and 2:7). Adam became a *living soul* (2:7) just as the animals were living creatures (1:20, 24)—the same words in Hebrew; yet Adam was also different from the animals because he was made in the image of God (1:27).

The Lord never planned for Adam to be a loner, the only one of his kind (2:18). All along, God intended to make a woman for Adam. Likewise, from the start marriage and the family were part of God's plan. What Adam needed was a helper suitable for him, and none could be found among the existing creatures God had made. The phrase rendered *help meet* (2:20) more literally means "a help as opposite him." Of course, this could only be a woman, not an animal. The man and the woman would correspond to one another. Expressed differently, they would complement and complete each other.

Genesis 2:21 says that God caused a deep sleep to come over Adam, like anesthetic for an operation. The woman was not created from the dust as Adam had been. She was formed from a part of the man himself (2:22). Sharing the same life as Adam, the woman was fully a part of the human race the Lord had started. The woman, like the man, bore the image of God (1:27).

When Adam woke after his operation, God led the woman to him. Genesis 2:23 reveals that Adam was overjoyed to see her. The man recognized that here, finally, was his suitable life partner. In Hebrew, the noun rendered *Woman* (*ishshah*) is as similar to the word for *Man* (*ish*) that's found here as in English. In this way, it reflects the basic similarity between the first two humans. Because men and women are made for each other, a man will leave his parents and be united to his wife and be physically intimate with her (vs. 24). Adam and Eve, the first members of the human race, were husband and wife from their initial moment together and remained united for life. Their marriage set a pattern for the marriages of their descendants.

The Lord not only brought people into existence but also blessed them (1:28). This means He endowed them (and their descendants) with the ability to flourish and be successful in serving as His vice-regents. Humanity's populating the world and bringing it under their control in a responsible fashion would be a testimony to God's blessing on their lives. Part of the divine blessing included people having many children and filling the earth with their descendants. The Lord intended for people to subdue the earth, which included having dominion over all its creatures. People should not hesitate to fulfill the divine mandate, for as Paul explained, every creation of God is good and to be received with thanksgiving (1 Tim. 4:4). Such is the proper response to what has been sanctified by God's decree and by prayer (4:5).

In Genesis 1:29 and 30, God reiterated key truths that He had previously declared. God permitted human beings to eat as food every seed-bearing plant on the earth's surface as well as every tree with seed in its fruit. In addition, God allowed all the animals and birds to eat every green plant (whether grasses or grains) for food. These decrees, along with all of God's other pronouncements, came to pass under His sovereign providence and authority.

When God considered all that He had done, He declared that it was *very good* (1:31). In short, all that was necessary for life to flourish—in the totality of its rich array and diversity—was now in place. With that, the sixth day of creation ended. The earth was originally uninhabitable, being unformed and void (1:2). By the end of the creation week, God had made the planet a most hospitable place to live. In fact, as 2:1 states, the Creator-King had perfectly executed His will by bringing order and harmony to the universe—the heavens, the earth, and everything they contained, including the animate and inanimate entities populating the world.

SUGGESTIONS TO TEACHERS

Why was I born?" "What's the purpose of human existence?" Teenagers, unsure of their identities and feeling alone, may ask the first question. Rabbis, theologians, and philosophers have discussed the second. Both questions reflect a basic human desire to find some meaning to life. Your class members undoubtedly have pondered whether God has any purpose for them. This week's lesson opens this profound topic from the point of view of Genesis 1:26-31.

1. BEING CREATED IN GOD'S IMAGE. Humans have a special relationship to the Creator. Only we are accorded the standing of being made in God's image—that is, given the ability to live caringly and creatively as God does, if we wish to do so. Discuss with your class the meaning of being made in God's image.

2. HAVING DOMINION OVER CREATION. In the creation account, *dominion* does not mean dominating or exploiting; rather, it signifies responsibility. God has given provision enough for all His creation, but holds us accountable to see to it that food enough to sustain everyone is provided and distributed. Likewise, God insists that we protect the environment. We are reminded that we must share this planet and is resources with others, including lesser species, because we are interdependent.

3. LOVING US INTO EXISTENCE. According to the biblical account, our lives are not the result of some cosmic joke, as some people might believe. The caring

Creator made humankind out of the dust of the ground. And yet, while we humans are made from the ordinary stuff that everything else in nature has, people are distinct because they have in them the breath of life from God. This difference between us and the rest of creation is an indication of just how much God has loved us into existence.

4. LEAVING US WITH A PURPOSE. The Creator holds humans responsible to look after planet Earth. Mention the need to treat all nature with care. Christians should properly speak out against ravishing the planet's provisions or plundering its resources.

5. LIVING IN OPENNESS. Round out this lesson by reminding the class that God's intention for us humans is that we live in trust with Him and one another. Note that this involves mutual caring, not domineering by either gender. The man and the woman in a marriage must consider one another as a partner.

FOR ADULTS

■ TOPIC: Why Are We Here?

■ QUESTIONS: 1. In what sense do people bear the image and likeness of God? 2. To what extent do people have dominion over all the creatures of creation? 3. Why is it important to regard both genders as being made in the image of God? 4. In what sense is the blessing of God on people, who bear His image? 5. What did God mean when He commanded people to be fruitful and multiply?

■ **ILLUSTRATIONS:**

Only God Is Great. Louis XIV of France was the monarch who pompously called himself "Louis the Great" and made the famous statement "I am the state!" In his eyes, he had created something grand and glorious and deserved to be exalted. At the time of his death in 1715, his court was the most magnificent in Europe.

To dramatize his greatness, Louis XIV had given orders prior to his death that at the funeral, the cathedral was to be lit by a single candle set above his coffin. When that eventful day arrived, thousands of people packed into the cathedral. At the front lay Louis XIV's body in a golden coffin; and, per his instructions, a single candle had been placed above the coffin. The congregation sat in hushed silence. Then Bishop Massilon stood and began to speak. Slowly reaching down, he snuffed out the candle and said, "Only God is great!"

Massilon recognized that even the greatest human accomplishments are insignificant when compared to the actions of the infinite Creator of the universe. Measured against God's glory, majesty, and greatness, no human can lay claim to greatness. Louis XIV had built a government, but God had created the entire universe!

Made for God. The late Gene Roddenberry, the creator of the award-winning *Star Trek* series, is quoted as pondering the wonders of creation as he wrote the science fiction series set in the 21st century. In particular, he was struck by the conviction he held that no other intelligent forms of life existed in the world overhead. "In fact," stated this television dramatist, "everything about our sun and its planets proclaims *reserved for humanity*. What a lovely educational arrangement for the offspring of our fertile Earth-egg planet!" While God made this planet for us, we are made for God and His purposes.

The Greatest Journey. James Shreeve of the *National Geographic* reported on the scientific investigation being conducted to determine where human beings originated. At one time, the only information researchers had came from the "sparsely scattered bones and artifacts" people "left behind on their journeys." In the past few decades, however, "scientists have found a record of ancient human migration" in the genetic markers of "living people." By comparing the chromosomal data of "people from various populations," scientists can approximate "where and when these groups parted ways in the great migration around the planet."

By culling through the available information, geneticists have determined that "all of humanity" is linked to one man and one woman who lived in Africa thousands of years ago. In fact, the scientific evidence shows that "all the variously shaped and shaded people" living across the planet "trace their ancestry to African hunter-gatherers." Furthermore, research indicates that these early humans "walked out of Africa" and "seeded other lands." Genesis 1:26-27 likewise affirms that everyone originated from a genetic Adam and Eve and that from them sprang the entire human race.

FOR YOUTH	■ **TOPIC:** In Whose Image? ■ **QUESTIONS:** 1. Why is it important to see ourselves as being created in the image of God? 2. How should people treat the animals of creation,

over which people have dominion? 3. What are some ways that God's blessing is evident in the lives of His people? 4. How can people be wise stewards of the natural resources of the earth, over which they have responsibility? 5. What are some of the good things of God's creation for which we can praise Him?

■ **ILLUSTRATIONS:**

A Garden of Eden? Pastor Alvin Stevens heard that little Bridgeville, California, was for sale. The entire town, 80 acres and 25 buildings, Stevens felt, was where the Lord wanted the pastor and his flock to live. Stevens drove the 330 miles north of San Francisco and looked at the land of mist-shrouded forests and trout-filled streams. He saw the place as an ideal spot to raise families and care for the elderly. The asking price was $450,000 with a down payment of $150,000.

Stevens took his dream of buying a Garden of Eden to his congregation at Stonybrook Full Gospel Temple. After a prayer meeting, five of the 70 people agreed to sell their homes and make the down payment. Forty-eight people eventually moved to Eden, a former stagecoach stop that subsequently had become a hippie commune. During the hippies' time, marijuana had grown, and it continued to sprout when Stevens' people arrived. The congregants of Full Gospel Temple found broken toilets and septic tanks, heaps of smelly garbage, and abandoned electrical equipment littering the area. In addition, a high unemployment rate dampened the hopes of the new residents. The newcomers found that the place was not the idyllic spot they'd hope to live in. Their Eden had been spoiled.

What a contrast this situation is to the Genesis account. God created a garden with a wonderful variety of living things. By their act of aggression, humans allowed the garden to deteriorate. No amount of human effort could change that process. Only God's creation was perfect. People simply cannot recreate Eden.

The True Reason for Being Special. Advertisers pandering to youth outdo themselves to make their products more attractive than those of their competitors. For example, when we consider teen fashions, we can see how important it is for adolescents to stand out in a crowd; yet no matter how impressive our clothes, computers, and cars might be, they are nothing compared to the magnificence of God's creation. We need to be careful, lest we lose sight of God's glory in the welter of things that are supposed to make us happy.

The world has a way of dominating our time, and it tries to shape our desires and values; but as Christians, we are wise to step back and ask why God made us. What does He desire of us? Also, how can we strengthen our faith in Him and not be stunted by the world's values? Meditating on God our Creator is a step in the right direction in recognizing the true reason for our being special in His eyes.

Who's the Boss? Humans may have been given dominion over every living thing, but is that really the case with the mosquito? This poor creature has no animal rights activists defending its existence. People swat the tiny insect. Most people feel that the only good mosquito is a dead one!

In defense of the bug, however, researchers have discovered that the creature hunts with its olfactory sense. Floral scents draw the mosquito. Breath and body odors attract the pest. Every time people exhale carbon dioxide, they tell the mosquito that the next meal is near. In fact, these bugs are equipped with CO_2 receptors on their feelers called *palpi* that can detect the gas 50 feet away. Mosquitoes smell this gas and the body odors of humans. In reality, the presence and breath of people are simply the proverbial dinner bell ringing. The little menace is simply obediently responding to the invitation of people. So in reality, people are the boss and have dominion over the creatures of the world—even the mosquito!

ABRAHAM, SARAH, AND ISAAC

BACKGROUND SCRIPTURE: Genesis 15:1-6; 18:1-15; 21:1-8

DEVOTIONAL READING: Isaiah 51:1-5

KEY VERSE: Is any thing too hard for the LORD? Genesis 18:14.

3

KING JAMES VERSION

GENESIS 15:5 And he brought him forth abroad, and said, Look now toward heaven, and tell the stars, if thou be able to number them: and he said unto him, So shall thy seed be. 6 And he believed in the LORD; and he counted it to him for righteousness. . . .

18:11 Now Abraham and Sarah were old and well stricken in age; and it ceased to be with Sarah after the manner of women. 12 Therefore Sarah laughed within herself, saying, After I am waxed old shall I have pleasure, my lord being old also? 13 And the LORD said unto Abraham, Wherefore did Sarah laugh, saying, Shall I of a surety bear a child, which am old? 14 Is any thing too hard for the LORD? . . .

21:1 And the LORD visited Sarah as he had said, and the LORD did unto Sarah as he had spoken. 2 For Sarah conceived, and bare Abraham a son in his old age, at the set time of which God had spoken to him. 3 And Abraham called the name of his son that was born unto him, whom Sarah bare to him, Isaac. 4 And Abraham circumcised his son Isaac being eight days old, as God had commanded him. 5 And Abraham was an hundred years old, when his son Isaac was born unto him. 6 And Sarah said, God hath made me to laugh, so that all that hear will laugh with me. 7 And she said, Who would have said unto Abraham, that Sarah should have given children suck? for I have born him a son in his old age. 8 And the child grew, and was weaned: and Abraham made a great feast the same day that Isaac was weaned.

NEW REVISED STANDARD VERSION

GENESIS 15:5 He brought him outside and said, "Look toward heaven and count the stars, if you are able to count them." Then he said to him, "So shall your descendants be." 6 And he believed the LORD; and the LORD reckoned it to him as righteousness. . . .

18:11 Now Abraham and Sarah were old, advanced in age; it had ceased to be with Sarah after the manner of women. 12 So Sarah laughed to herself, saying, "After I have grown old, and my husband is old, shall I have pleasure?" 13 The LORD said to Abraham, "Why did Sarah laugh, and say, 'Shall I indeed bear a child, now that I am old?' 14 Is anything too wonderful for the LORD?" . . .

21:1 The LORD dealt with Sarah as he had said, and the LORD did for Sarah as he had promised. 2 Sarah conceived and bore Abraham a son in his old age, at the time of which God had spoken to him. 3 Abraham gave the name Isaac to his son whom Sarah bore him. 4 And Abraham circumcised his son Isaac when he was eight days old, as God had commanded him.
5 Abraham was a hundred years old when his son Isaac was born to him. 6 Now Sarah said, "God has brought laughter for me; everyone who hears will laugh with me." 7 And she said, "Who would ever have said to Abraham that Sarah would nurse children? Yet I have borne him a son in his old age."

8 The child grew, and was weaned; and Abraham made a great feast on the day that Isaac was weaned.

HOME BIBLE READINGS

BACKGROUND

Genesis 11:10-26 records a genealogy from Shem, the son of Noah, to Abram (Abraham). We learn that Terah was the father of Abram, Nahor, and Haran (11:26). Haran, who was the father of Lot (11:27), died while the family was still living in Ur of the Chaldeans (11:28). Joshua 24:2 states that during their residency in Ur, the entire household worshiped and served pagan deities.

In the time of Abram, the city of Ur, in the southern most part of what is now Iraq, was an important commercial center with a population of at least 300,000 people. Over 100,000 clay business documents have been found at the site, as well as the remains of an extensive library. Musical instruments and statuettes found in the royal tombs indicate a high level of craftsmanship and cultural standards. The well-educated people of Ur were proficient in mathematics, astronomy, weaving, and engraving.

Walls averaging 30 feet in height protected Ur from intruders. At the heart of the city was the three-tiered ziggurat (a kind of step pyramid) dedicated to the moon god Nanna, the protector of the city. Some two-story homes contained the best comforts available in the ancient world, including a kind of primitive air conditioning. The town's harbor on the Euphrates River brought travelers from all over the world to conduct trade. The gold, silver, and precious stones found in Ur testify to the wealth in the city.

None of these things, however, could reverse the fact that Abram's wife, Sarai, was unable to conceive (Gen. 11:29-30). In the culture of that day, being childless was considered a social disgrace. This circumstance did not change, even when Terah, Abram, Sarai, and Lot left Ur to go to Canaan (11:31). After traveling 600 miles north along the Fertile Crescent trade route, the group arrived in Haran, where they stayed for a time, accumulating possessions and servants (12:5). It was also there that Terah died (11:32).

God next called Abram to leave his country, his people, and his father's household, and go to a land he did not know (Gen. 12:1; 15:7; Neh. 9:7; Acts 7:2-3); in other words, a 75-year-old man was to be lifted out of the familiar and placed in the unfamiliar (Gen. 12:4). In return, God promised to bless him in an unprecedented way. Though Abram was childless, God pledged to make him a great nation with many descendants. The Lord promised to give Abram honor and make him a source of blessing to others. Through Abram's descendants, God would pour out great blessings for all humanity (12:2-3).

The patriarch stepped out in faith and obeyed the divine summons (Gen. 12:4-5; see Heb. 11:8). When he arrived in Canaan, the land was thinly populated by a variety of peoples who had descended from Canaan, the grandson of Noah (10:1, 6). Nomadic tribesman moved through the hill country and valleys. Some urbanization had begun to take place at fortified cities. Generally, the area was far behind the standard of civilization Abram had left behind in Ur. While the patriarch was at Shechem (Gen. 12:6), the Lord appeared to him and promised to give the land of Canaan to his descendants (12:7). God next appeared to Abram while he was in the Negev (13:1). The Lord repeated His promised that Abram's descendants would one day possess the whole of Canaan (13:14-15). God also assured the patriarch that his offspring would be like the dust of the earth in number (13:16).

During the next 10 years, Abram became embroiled in regional politics (chap. 14). He may have begun to wonder whether he would survive much longer and have offspring, as God had promised. Around the time the patriarch was 85, the Lord came to him in a vision at night and told him not to be afraid. Moreover, God pledged to protect him and to reward him in great abundance (15:1). Abram, however, wondered about the value of such blessings when he remained childless. In that day, the desire to have children—especially sons—was great. With no clear understanding of immortality, people believed that children provided the opportunity for a kind of earthly immorality. A son could carry on his father's name and take over the family's possessions.

Abram concluded that he would have to leave his estate to a favored servant, Eliezer of Damascus, rather than to a son of his own (15:2-3). God did not go along with Abram's plan to make Eliezer his heir; instead, the Lord affirmed that a son of Abram's not yet born would become the patriarch's heir (15:4). Furthermore, while Abram looked ahead just one generation, God saw the whole future and knew about the multitude of people who would call Abram their ancestral father.

NOTES ON THE PRINTED TEXT

As a way to assure Abram concerning the divine promise of a son, the Lord led the patriarch out into the darkness of the night and requested that he look upward to the sky. With no pollutants, Abram could see thousands upon thousands of stars on a clear night. With a myriad of stars in view, God said, *So shall thy seed be* (Gen. 15:5). In turn, Abram believed what the Lord had promised, and God credited the patriarch's response of faith as righteousness (15:6). Later, Paul used this passage to demonstrate that people have always been saved by faith, not by works (Rom. 4:1-3, 18-22).

God's covenant with Abram had two main provisions: descendants and land. With the matter of the heir settled, the Lord reminded Abram of His promise of the land to which God had called the patriarch. The people as numerous as the stars would need a place to live, and that place would be Canaan (Gen. 15:7). When Abram asked how he could be sure he would receive the land (15:8), the Lord graciously gave the patriarch the reassurance he sought. God chose to copy a common practice of that time used to confirm special agreements (15:9-17). In human covenants, both parties to the transaction usually passed between the dead animals; but in this case only the Lord did so. Since the fulfillment of the promise depended on God alone, Abram was merely a spectator. God defined the extent of the land He would give. It lay between the river of Egypt (probably one of the seasonal rivers in the Negev) in the south to the Euphrates River in the north. At that time, this land was occupied by at least 10 different people groups (15:18-21).

When Abram was 86 years old, Sarai's Egyptian servant, Hagar, bore the patriarch a son, whom he named Ishmael (chap. 16). Then, when Abram was 99 years old, the Lord established the covenant of circumcision with the patriarch and his descendants. Furthermore, God changed the patriarch's name to Abraham and the name of his wife to Sarah. This was done in conjunction with the Lord's promise to give Abraham many descendants, to make him the father of many nations, and to deed the land of Canaan to his offspring (chap. 17).

Sometime later, the Lord appeared to Abraham in the plains of Mamre to disclose that within a calendar year, Sarah would have the son of promise (18:1-10). At this moment, Sarah was listening at the entrance to a nearby tent. Both she and her husband were advanced in years, and she was well past the age of childbearing (18:11). Thus, when Sarah heard the prediction, she laughed to herself. She found it hard to believe that she would have the pleasure of becoming pregnant and bearing a son (18:12).

The Lord asked Abraham why Sarah laughed in unbelief at the declaration of the divine promise (18:13). Such a response was inappropriate, for nothing was too hard or impossible for God to do on behalf of His people. The Lord was serious in remaining faithful to His pledge that at the appointed time the following year, Sarah would bear the patriarch a son (18:14).

When Abraham was 100 and Sarah was 90 (21:5), God graciously visited Sarah just as He had said He would and did for her what He had promised (21:1). God enabled Sarah to become pregnant and she bore Abraham a son in his old age. The conception and birth occurred at the appointed time (21:2). Abraham named his newborn son *Isaac* (21:3), which means "he laughs." For years Abraham had waited, at times taking matters into his own hands in an attempt to help God give him an heir; but in the end, God worked miraculously to give the patriarch a son through Sarah. The baby's name would be a reminder of how the Lord had proved His faithfulness to the aged parents of their newborn.

In accordance with God's command, Abraham circumcised Isaac when he was eight days old (21:4). Sarah drew attention to the Lord's faithfulness by noting that He, through the birth of Isaac, had brought her the joy of laughter. Moreover, all those who heard the good news of Isaac's birth would signal their joy over the fulfillment of the divine promise (21:6).The gestation and birth of Isaac were followed by his healthy physical maturation. Despite Sarah's advanced age, God enabled her to nurse her son (21:7). These events stood as a testimony to the graciousness and awesome power of the Lord. This was not a make-believe child. Isaac grew physically and eventually was weaned (21:8). In ancient times, infant mortality was high. By the time a child reached the age of two or three, there was a stronger likelihood he or she would survive. For this reason, it was common for children to be weaned at this time. In the case of Isaac, such a milestone called for a great feast, which Abraham gladly held. It was the least he could do to celebrate the maturing of a child the patriarch and his wife had waited so long to have.

Despite Abraham's faults, the New Testament writers held up the patriarch as a model of genuine faith. Paul said that all believers, both Jews and Gentiles, are Abraham's children because they, too, come to God through faith. It was by faith that the Gentiles came to know God, not through their good works, their Jewish heritage, or their obedience to the Jewish law (Gal. 3:6-14). The writer of Hebrews emphasized that Abraham and Sarah believed God in spite of the seeming impossibility of having an heir of their own. That faith enabled the elderly couple to become parents. They believed that the Lord would be faithful in fulfilling His promise of a child through Sarah (Heb. 11:11).

SUGGESTIONS TO TEACHERS

It's possible to read the narrative of Abraham and Sarah on one level as a superbly interesting human drama; but the account of a couple struggling to live through questions and disappointments also relates God's involvement in our history. Surely, every person at some point asks questions like the following: "Does the Lord really keep His word?" "Can I be sure life has meaning?" "Why doesn't God come through the way I'm told He will?"

These are the kinds of questions Abraham and Sarah agonized over during their long period of childlessness. They had reached the point where they were convinced that their chief servant, Eliezer, would be their heir, and that Sarah would never conceive. God seemed to have been playing a nasty trick by promising that the elderly couple would be parents of the ancestor of His chosen people. Accordingly, the thrust of this week's lesson is that God keeps His word.

1. VICTORY OF TRUST. Faith has been described as "in-spite-of confidence in the Lord." Despite misgivings and problems, doubts and delays, a person may trust God to keep His word. Abraham questioned whether God would deliver on His promises of a son. But in spite of everything, Abraham took God at His word and was declared to be in a standing of uprightness before Him. Talk with the class about how hard it is to trust God in some situations. Ask the students to share experiences when faith was not easy, or when their trust was rewarded.

2. TITLE FOR A TERRITORY. God entered into a covenant, promising

Abraham sufficient land to provide for his needs and provision for his descendants. Don't let the lesson at this point get sidetracked into a discussion about modern land claims of the Israelis versus the Palestinians. Instead, focus on God's promise to look after those who are faithful.

3. SNICKERS IN THE TENT. Both Abraham and Sarah laughed in apparent disbelief at the announcement that Sarah would finally have a child. The scene in Genesis 18 where Sarah hears this news and laughs cynically is a humorous touch in the account. The punch line that your students can take to heart is in 18:14, *Is any thing too hard for the Lord?* Discuss the meaning of this question, especially in light of the apparent impossible situations in your church or community.

FOR ADULTS	■ TOPIC: Our Place in the Family! ■ QUESTIONS: 1. Why did God take the time to emphasize to Abraham that he would have innumerable descendants? 2. What is the connec-

tion between Abraham's belief in God's promise and God crediting it to him as righteousness? 3. How did Sarah's ongoing childless condition affect the ability of the couple to rely on God to fulfill His promises to them? 4. How did the Lord's messenger respond to Sarah's laughter? 5. How was God's grace evident in giving Sarah the ability to conceive?

■ **ILLUSTRATIONS:**

From Knowledge to Faith. When Pam chose to become a teacher, she knew she wanted to touch children's lives, just as her mother, who was also a schoolteacher, had. What Pam had not counted on was the fact that some children would seem so untouchable. I recall her saying to me, "I had a student whom I'll call Gary who I can only describe as obnoxious and obstinate. He was so much trouble, I thought I was being specially punished when I had to teach him for both sixth and seventh grade."

Pam had little real faith that Gary would ever change. Pam said, "But he surprised me. To my amazement, he changed when he discerned I was truly trying to care for him, that I was trying to like him as a person. That realization made a genuine difference for our relationship and for him as a person. After he graduated, I saw him at a mall, and he called out to me. We chatted for a while, and I was just floored. I would have sworn he would be one of the kids who would walk the other way if he saw me coming."

Many of us live with Garys every day—people we are sure will never change; and we see situations that look hopeless or impossible. We may know that God is powerful enough to change any life, or any situation, but it is something else altogether to expect such changes. This week's lesson offers a memorable glimpse into the joy that comes when God's people learn to move from knowledge to faith.

God of the Impossible. A number of Christian organizations report that the tendency of individuals in the West toward independence is a threat to the traditional family structure. These agencies note that it is difficult for us to place our lives and our future in the hands of anyone else. Within our control, the outcome might not be an incredible success, but at least it will be predictable and safe; however, our God desires that we instead step into a wonderful world of adventure with Him at the controls.

How can we entrust our existence to God, especially when it seems impossible at times? Nonetheless, the record of Scripture and of our own experiences in following the Lord tell us that He seems to love the word "impossible." He most often does not work through our agenda, and we do not always see Him working in ways we understand; but He asks us to learn to trust His heart. Indeed, this is the first step in becoming a part of His spiritual family.

Risking Because of God's Promise. There is a sign on the wall of a business that reads: "According to the theory of aerodynamics, and as can readily be proven by wind tunnel experiments, the bumblebee is unable to fly. This is because the size of its wings in relation to the size of its body makes flying impossible. But the bumblebee, being unacquainted with these scientific truths, goes ahead and flies anyway and gathers a little honey every day."

Perhaps one problem with the Church today is that its leaders and parishioners can be too practical. We spend so much time and energy finding ways and reasons why something can't be done, rather than trusting the Lord to guide and empower our efforts. It might be prudent for us to unacquaint ourselves with what apparently won't work and reacquaint ourselves with the truths and promises of God's Word. In fact, churches that grow are willing to trust the God of the impossible to be with them as they take the risk of venturing out in faith to try new things for His glory. Moreover, believers who grow are also willing to trust God in this way.

As the children of God, then, let's try to be a riskier people, a more adventurous people. Let us be those who are willing to take on the work God as given us to do without asking whether it can be done, but just doing it. Sure, it's an impractical idea. But whoever said the Church is supposed to be practical?

FOR YOUTH

■ **TOPIC:** Child of Promise

■ **QUESTIONS:** 1. How many descendants did God say Abraham would have? 2. What was Abraham's response to God's declaration regarding his descendants? 3. Why did Sarah initially doubt God's promise of a child? 4. From whom did Sarah receive the ability to conceive? 5. What characterized Sarah's laughter at the birth of Isaac?

■ **ILLUSTRATIONS:**

Commitment Pays Off. Brandon Esip wanted to be chosen to play for New England in a 1997 summer basketball tournament in Belgium. The 17-year-old Bourne, Massachusetts, adolescent practiced for hours every day. Even when sidelined by ankle injuries as a high-school letterman, Esip practiced shooting baskets while hopping on one foot in his backyard. All his commitment eventually paid off as he was chosen to play.

God chose Abraham for a bigger game in life with a far greater promise. He spent years trusting in that promise. Eventually, it paid off as Abraham experienced God's fulfilled promise.

Modern Covenants. Bill needed spending money in high school. Like many young people, he went to work for a national fast-food outlet. The restaurant agreed to pay him the minimum wage to work at the counter and guaranteed him at least 10 hours per week. For his part, Bill agreed to be at the establishment two nights per week. This is a covenant or a contract. Each party enters into an agreement. It is similar to the one made between God and Abraham in connection with the divine promise of a son through Sarah.

Lifetime Promise. In Victor Hugo's *Les Miserables*, Jean Valjean met a dying Fantine, a woman fired from his factory. Jean made a promise to Fantine to look after her daughter, Cosette. Fantine was dumbfounded. It seemed unlikely that anyone would do such a thing. She concluded, however, that God had sent Jean to her.

Perhaps you are like Fantine. You question promises that seem unlikely to be fulfilled. Fantine died trusting Jean to keep his promise. And Jean did indeed remain faithful to his pledge. He adopted Cosette as his own child and looked after her through a turbulent revolution until she was happily wed.

Maybe like Fantine, you have not expected others to keep their promises. You may even be happily surprised when they do. This week's account of Abraham serves as a reminder that God keeps His promises, even those as unlikely as the one made to Abraham and Sarah.

ABRAHAM, HAGAR, AND ISHMAEL

BACKGROUND SCRIPTURE: Genesis 21:9-21
DEVOTIONAL READING: Genesis 16

KEY VERSE: [God said to Abraham,] And also of the son of the bondwoman will I make a nation, because he is thy seed. Genesis 21:13.

4

KING JAMES VERSION

GENESIS 21:9 And Sarah saw the son of Hagar the Egyptian, which she had born unto Abraham, mocking. 10 Wherefore she said unto Abraham, Cast out this bondwoman and her son: for the son of this bondwoman shall not be heir with my son, even with Isaac. 11 And the thing was very grievous in Abraham's sight because of his son. 12 And God said unto Abraham, Let it not be grievous in thy sight because of the lad, and because of thy bondwoman; in all that Sarah hath said unto thee, hearken unto her voice; for in Isaac shall thy seed be called. 13 And also of the son of the bondwoman will I make a nation, because he is thy seed.

14 And Abraham rose up early in the morning, and took bread, and a bottle of water, and gave it unto Hagar, putting it on her shoulder, and the child, and sent her away: and she departed, and wandered in the wilderness of Beersheba. 15 And the water was spent in the bottle, and she cast the child under one of the shrubs. 16 And she went, and sat her down over against him a good way off, as it were a bowshot: for she said, Let me not see the death of the child. And she sat over against him, and lift up her voice, and wept. 17 And God heard the voice of the lad; and the angel of God called to Hagar out of heaven, and said unto her, What aileth thee, Hagar? fear not; for God hath heard the voice of the lad where he is. 18 Arise, lift up the lad, and hold him in thine hand; for I will make him a great nation. 19 And God opened her eyes, and she saw a well of water; and she went, and filled the bottle with water, and gave the lad drink. 20 And God was with the lad; and he grew, and dwelt in the wilderness, and became an archer. 21 And he dwelt in the wilderness of Paran: and his mother took him a wife out of the land of Egypt.

NEW REVISED STANDARD VERSION

GENESIS 21:9 But Sarah saw the son of Hagar the Egyptian, whom she had borne to Abraham, playing with her son Isaac. 10 So she said to Abraham, "Cast out this slave woman with her son; for the son of this slave woman shall not inherit along with my son Isaac." 11 The matter was very distressing to Abraham on account of his son. 12 But God said to Abraham, "Do not be distressed because of the boy and because of your slave woman; whatever Sarah says to you, do as she tells you, for it is through Isaac that offspring shall be named for you. 13 As for the son of the slave woman, I will make a nation of him also, because he is your offspring." 14 So Abraham rose early in the morning, and took bread and a skin of water, and gave it to Hagar, putting it on her shoulder, along with the child, and sent her away. And she departed, and wandered about in the wilderness of Beer-sheba.

15 When the water in the skin was gone, she cast the child under one of the bushes. 16 Then she went and sat down opposite him a good way off, about the distance of a bowshot; for she said, "Do not let me look on the death of the child." And as she sat opposite him, she lifted up her voice and wept. 17 And God heard the voice of the boy; and the angel of God called to Hagar from heaven, and said to her, "What troubles you, Hagar? Do not be afraid; for God has heard the voice of the boy where he is. 18 Come, lift up the boy and hold him fast with your hand, for I will make a great nation of him." 19 Then God opened her eyes and she saw a well of water. She went, and filled the skin with water, and gave the boy a drink.

20 God was with the boy, and he grew up; he lived in the wilderness, and became an expert with the bow. 21 He lived in the wilderness of Paran; and his mother got a wife for him from the land of Egypt.

Monday, September 17	Genesis 16:1-6	*Sarah Deals Harshly with Hagar*
Tuesday, September 18	Genesis 16:7-16	*God Protects Hagar*
Wednesday, September 19	Genesis 21:9-13	*Abraham's Offspring*
Thursday, September 20	Genesis 21:14-16	*Waiting for Death*
Friday, September 21	Genesis 21:17-19	*Water from God*
Saturday, September 22	Genesis 21:20-21	*Ishmael Grows Up*
Sunday, September 23	Genesis 25:12-18	*Ishmael's Descendants*

BACKGROUND

In Galatians 4:21-31, Paul referred to the episode involving Sarah and Hagar in Genesis 21:10. The apostle was dealing with a circumstance in which his readers seemed eager to take upon themselves the burden of keeping the law. Thus Paul determined that an argument based on passages in books of the law would help bring them around to his side (Gal. 4:21). The apostle was combating a group of legalists called Judaizers. They taught that faith in the Messiah was not adequate to be declared righteous by God. Supposedly, obedience to the Old Testament law, or at least parts of it, was also necessary. It seems the legalists used historical and geographical features from the Genesis account in an allegory to support their own position.

The apostle began with the same historical incidents that the legalists presumably began with (4:22-23). Paul noted that Abraham had two sons, one by the slave woman (Hagar) and the other by the free woman (Sarah). The apostle stated that Ishmael was born as the result of human effort. In contrast, Isaac was born as the result of a divine promise. When Paul stated that he was speaking figuratively, he was not implying that the Genesis account was an allegory; rather, he was using this historical episode as the basis for his own allegorical construction (4:24). Expressed differently, he saw in the historically accurate ancient writings a theological meaning that went beyond the narrative itself.

During the Israelites' wanderings in the wilderness, they stopped at Mount Sinai in Arabia (Exod. 19). There God entered into a covenant with them and gave them the law. It was this law that Paul's opponents tried to enforce on the Galatians. The apostle regarded Hagar's literal slavery to be symbolic of the spiritual slavery caused by the law given at Mount Sinai (Gal. 4:24). Paul noted that Hagar also corresponded to the Jerusalem of the apostle's day. The reason is that Jerusalem was the center of the Jewish religion and the hometown of the Judaizers. Paul personified the city of Jerusalem and said she was enslaved with her children, meaning the nonbelieving Jews. They were still in bondage to law because they had not found freedom through faith in the Messiah (4:25; see Rom. 9:30-33).

In contrast, the followers of Jesus are the children of another mother, namely, the Jerusalem that is from above (Gal. 4:26), where the Savior reigns (Heb. 12:22; Rev.

21:2) and where believers have their citizenship (Phil. 3:20; Col. 3:1-3). In Galatians 4:27, Paul quoted from Isaiah 54:1 to show how this heavenly Jerusalem can be said to be the mother of all Christians. Isaiah prophesied of the enslavement of the people of Jerusalem and Judah in Babylon. During that time, Jerusalem would be *barren* (that is, largely empty of people), as Sarah was literally barren before conceiving Isaac.

Furthermore, Isaiah prophesied of a later time when Jerusalem would have many children (that is, would once again have inhabitants). In the same way, the Jerusalem above would have many children; in other words, many people would trust in the Messiah for salvation. This is similar to God's promise to give Abraham many descendants. Gentile and Jewish Christians are the fulfillment of this prophecy. Consequently, the Galatians were like Isaac (namely, the children of promise) and the Judaizers were like Ishmael (Gal. 4:28).

Paul stated in 4:29 that the son born by human effort persecuted the son born by the power of the Spirit (see Gen. 21:9). Likewise, those whom the Spirit had spiritually regenerated were being persecuted by the legalists of the apostle's day (see Acts 13:44-45; 14:2, 19-20). In so doing, the Judaizers violated the will of God. They also failed to see that once the Son of promise had come—namely, Jesus the Messiah—the Mosaic law and covenant were obsolete, outdated, and replaced by the new covenant (Jer. 31:31-34; Heb. 8:7-13). When Sarah saw Ishmael persecuting her son, she urged Abraham to eject Hagar and Ishmael (Gen. 21:10; Gal. 4:30). When the patriarch hesitated, God implied that it would be all right for him to let the mother and adolescent go (Gen. 21:12). Paul wanted his Christian readers to see this as an assurance of them having the authority to expel the Judaizers from their congregation.

Galatians 4:31 contains the apostle's main point in developing the allegory. While the Judaizers may have taught that the Galatians were children of the slave woman unless they obeyed the law, Paul insisted that his readers were already children of the free woman. By God's grace, all who trust in the Messiah are free.

Notes on the Printed Text

From the time the Lord directed Abraham to leave his native country and journey to Canaan, the patriarch was assured that he would have many descendants (Gen. 12:1-3). In turn, they would inherit the promised land (12:7). God's pledge to Abraham was made at various times in the years to come, including after the departure of his nephew, Lot (13:14-17). There were moments, however, when Abraham's faith seemed to falter. For instance, when the patriarch was 86 (16:16), his wife, Sarah, hatched a scheme to enable Abraham to obtain a child through an Egyptian servant named Hagar. If all went according to plan, she would bear Abraham a son, whom he would then adopt as the heir of his estate (16:1-2). As it turned out, however, Sarah's plan quickly went awry.

Sarah's proposal for Abraham to have a child through a surrogate, while reflecting the cultural norms of the day, was an attempt to fulfill God's purposes through human means. Thus, after living in Canaan for a decade, the patriarch was physically intimate with Hagar, who in turn became pregnant. Then, when she began to despise her mistress, Sarah took out her frustration on Abraham. In response, the patriarch told Sarah to do whatever she thought was best with respect to Hagar. The regrettable outcome was that the Egyptian servant fled, after being mistreated by Sarah (16:3-6). The Lord's angel found Hagar near a spring in the wilderness and directed her to return to Sarah. The young mother-to-be was encouraged by the promise that her son, whom she was to name Ishmael, would have an illustrious future. Hagar heeded the divine directive by returning to and remaining in Abraham's family (16:7-15).

Fifteen years later, Sarah gave birth to her own son, whom Abraham named Isaac (21:1-3). The child's birth was an occasion for joy (21:4-7) and the time of his weaning several years later prompted his father to host a large feast (21:8). We can only wonder how Ishmael, who was around 17, must have felt as the festivities in honor of Isaac took place. Perhaps Hagar's adolescent son felt a twinge of jealousy. If so, this would explain why Sarah found Ishmael mocking Isaac in some way (21:9). While the exact nature of the offense is debated among experts, the result of the incident is clear. Sarah was so upset that she did not even refer to Hagar and Ishmael by name. Instead, Sarah talked about them indirectly as *this bondwoman and her son* (21:10). Sarah demanded that Abraham expel them permanently from the family. His wife feared that Ishmael might become a threat to and somehow jeopardize Isaac's future inheritance of the family estate.

Abraham was quite upset by the recent development, perhaps due in part to his love of and concern for Ishmael (21:11). God, however, conveyed to the Abraham (possibly through a dream) not to be so distressed about the adolescent and his mother (21:12). The Lord directed the patriarch to do as Sarah demanded, reassured by the fact that Ishmael—the son of the bondwoman—and his descendants would become a great nation (21:13); nonetheless, the covenantal promises were to be reckoned through Isaac (21:12).

Abraham, having been reassured by God, arose early the next morning and prepared some food. He gave this to Hagar, and strapped an animal skin filled with water on her shoulders. Then the patriarch sent her away with her son, both of whom began to wander aimlessly through the wilderness of Beersheba (21:14). Beersheba was located at the southern end of the land of Canaan. It was there that Abraham and Abimelech (the king of Gerar) made a peace treaty, in recognition of the patriarch's special status and material wealth. The two also swore an oath of mutual assistance (21:22-31). In fact, the name "Beersheba" means either "well of the seven" or "well of the oath."

The few gallons of water in Hagar's animal skin soon ran out in that arid climate. The mother, being filled with despair over the deplorable situation facing her and her son, shoved the adolescent under one of the nearby shrubs (possibly a tamarisk, which thrived in that arid region; 21:15). By this time both of them were weak from dehydration and facing death. Hagar decided to abandon her son, for she could not bear to see him expire.

As she sat across from him about a bowshot (that is, around 100 yards) away, she began to sob uncontrollably. Likewise, Ishmael started to cry (21:16).

We learn from 21:17 that the Lord had not abandoned Hagar and her adolescent son. God's angel called to the mother from heaven and asked why she was troubled. The celestial messenger also directed Hagar not to be afraid, for God was aware of Ishmael's feelings of distress. The mother was told to have her son stand up and lead him on the next part of their journey. They could continue knowing that God would one day make the adolescent into a great nation (21:18).

At this point, the Lord enabled Hagar to see a well of water; and she responded by going over to it, filling her container, and giving Ishmael a drink (21:19). In the years that followed, God's favor rested on Ishmael, the son of Abraham through Hagar. Ishmael lived in the wilderness and became an archer (21:21). This implies that he learned to survive by the expert use of his weapons. Ishmael eventually settled in the Desert of Paran. This arid region was located in the east central part of the Sinai peninsula. According to the custom of the day, Ishmael's mother found a wife for him from her native land of Egypt (21:22). Scripture records that Ishmael did leave behind many descendants, including the 12 rulers God had previously promised (17:20), who formed several nations (25:12-18). Many Arabs today trace their lineage back to Ishmael. Thus, in a sense, the struggle between Ishmael and Isaac continues today in the Arab-Israeli tensions.

SUGGESTIONS TO TEACHERS

It can be hard to believe that God can do all things and is working even when we cannot see Him at work. So we "help" God work out His will. It's like a three year old helping his father paint the house. It may bring us satisfaction seeing our hand in the process. At best, however, it will be messy. At worst, it will have to be done all over again. Instead, we need to leave the task and its accomplishment to the Lord.

1. GOD'S PERFECT TIMING. Timing is often extremely important. When a batter swings just a little too late, he misses the ball. When a driver brakes a few seconds late, she crashes into another car. When travelers arrive at the gate a minute or two late, they get to see their plane departing without them. In instances like these, once the time has passed, the intended result cannot be reclaimed. The God we trust and serve never misses a deadline. His timing is always perfect, even when we think otherwise. God does not work on our timetables but on His own. As our Shepherd, He faithfully watches over us. In fact, He has assumed this responsibility of taking care of us in the best way possible.

2. GOD'S COMMITMENT TO US. Scripture does not promise that believers will avoid all accidents and illness; but the Bible does teach that no trouble can destroy our relationship with God or render His power inoperative. Each step we take, each breath we breathe, we can know that God is with us and that we are under His care. This affirmation of faith rests on what we know about the Lord. God the Creator is aware of every detail of our lives. The Protector's assurance is that He will continue to guide us, regardless of whatever threats might emerge against us in the future. Of course, harm might arise from enemies at home and abroad, or even from within our own families; but because we are people of faith, we have put our trust in God's all-knowing, all-loving care.

3. GOD'S PROTECTION FOR US. Much more than physical protection is in view here. The assaults of the world, the flesh, and the devil are made against our souls, and thus we need God's protection in each of these arenas. It's reassuring to know that nothing escapes the attention of our loving Guardian and Keeper. When the trials of life seem overwhelming, we should fortify our souls, not with wishful thinking, but with truths about God revealed in His Word. We cannot promise people that everything will be all right; but we can reassure them that God's love and care will be there when they need it.

FOR ADULTS

■ **TOPIC:** Dealing with Dissension in the Family!

■ **QUESTIONS:** 1. Why did Sarah want Abraham to expel Hagar and Ishmael? 2. How did Paul apply the episode involving Sarah and Hagar and their respective sons to the apostle's own day? 3. Why did Sarah's demand upset Abraham? 4. How did God reassure Abraham concerning Ishmael? 5. How did God provide for the mother and her son in their time of need?

■ **ILLUSTRATIONS:**

Motivating Factor. A first-grader glowed with delight as she handed a neighbor a spelling test on which a teacher had written in large letters "100%—A Great Job!" The girl said, "I showed this to my Mom and Dad because I knew it would make them happy." It's not hard to imagine the child riding home on the school bus as she beamed with anticipation at the moment her parents would express their approval over a job well done. The daughter's desire to please her mother and father was clearly a strong motivating factor in her life.

This is the same sort of incentive that should be at the heart of our relationship with God. Expressed differently, our desire to please Him should prompt us to try make every effort to do what pleases Him. This includes living at peace with the members of our biological and spiritual families. When out of a desire to bring joy to God, we strive for harmony among the people around us, unity and goodwill are the lasting fruits of our labor.

Expressions of Love. On January 2, 2006, an explosion at the Sago Mine in West Virginia led to the deaths of 12 miners by carbon monoxide poisoning. Rescue crews frantically tried to reach the 12 in time, but their efforts failed. Late the following day, the 12 were found dead. As Martin Toler huddled with the other 11 miners in their attempt to find shelter from the poisonous air, he took out an insurance form he had stuffed in his pocket. He then used a pencil to scribble out in faint sentences a good-bye to his family.

Toler stated that he and the others died peacefully. The note also read, "Tell all I'll see them on the other side. It wasn't bad. I just went to sleep. I love you." Other notes were found, too. And these messages assured family members that the miners had not suffered, that they had gone to sleep. On any scrap of paper they had with them, the miners scratched out their farewells and last "I love you's."

Despite the imminence of their own deaths, the miners were able to find a way of offering some expression of love to their families. These extraordinary displays of grace and selfishness are what help keep families together, rather than split apart in dissension, when times are rough.

Knit with Love. In the March 1996 issue of *Guideposts,* a short article written by Brigitte Weeks was published. The author talked about "knitting sweaters for refugee children" and asked if anyone would like to join her. In an update article appearing a decade later in the magazine, Weeks noted that more than 300,000 sweaters had been made to provide warmth for "children across the country and around the world."

The success of this venture is partly due to the formation of countless knitting groups across the United States. And according to Weeks it's not just the children who have been blessed by this activity. The participants have also benefited by "the warmth and companionship of the knitting groups." For example, one member of a group from Michigan noted that it included a "severely depressed knitter whose tense hands gripped the needles and pulled the stitches tight." Over time as this individual learned to "trust in God's promises never to forsake His children," her "stitches began to relax." Similarly, as we learn to depend more and more on God, we will increasingly relax in His presence and do amazing things in His power to bring Him glory.

FOR YOUTH

■ **TOPIC:** A Great Nation

■ **QUESTIONS:** 1. In what way was Ishmael mistreating Isaac? 2. How did Abraham respond to Sarah's demand to expel Hagar and Ishmael? 3. What future did God have in store for Ishmael? 4. How did Abraham prepare Hagar and Ishmael for their departure? 5. How did God intervene in the lives of the mother and her son?

■ **ILLUSTRATIONS:**

Roots. As a child, John grew up looking at an old photograph of a young man wearing the uniform of a Union Army lieutenant. John's parents told him that he had been named after the man in the picture. At college, John discovered some resources that enabled him to learn about his namesake's regiment and the action that he had seen. As John began to take an interest in his other ancestors, he learned of their role in helping to make their nation great. The biblical account of Abraham and his family traces the roots of God's people from their humble beginnings to the establishment of their great nation in the land of promise.

A Weighty Issue. According to the *Chicago Sun-Times*, a report put out by the International Journal of Pediatric Obesity noted that "nearly half of the children in North and South America will be overweight by 2010." The situation is not much better for the European Union. Recent surveys indicate that if "present trends continue," about "38 percent of all children will be overweight." Similar upward trends are expected for children in "the Middle East and Southeast Asia." It's no wonder that one expert said, "We have truly a global epidemic. . . . It's like the plague is in town."

Is this any way for a society to build a great nation? Obviously not! People of all ages can do their part to moderate their appetites and promote a more balanced, healthy, God-centered lifestyle for the good of all humankind.

Remembering the Key. John Bunyan's classic, *Pilgrim's Progress*, vividly describes the meaning of remembering God's promises—promises like those He made to Abraham, Hagar, and Ishmael. In the story, the two main characters, Christian and Hopeful, traveled to the celestial city. They fell asleep on the grounds of the Giant Despair. After awakening, the two found themselves in the hands of the Giant. They were then taken to Doubting Castle and put, Bunyan says, into a stinking dungeon.

Now what misery and fears possessed their hearts! Could it be, the two asked each other, that someday Giant Despair in one of his fits might lose the use of his limbs, or that he might fail to lock one of those grim doors that held them in? Such hopes failed and their prospects worsened. They were taken out into the yard of the castle and shown bones—allegedly of pilgrims like themselves—whom the Giant in earlier days had pulled to pieces. So also would he do to them in the dungeon.

Then, Bunyan relayed, about midnight on the Saturday evening, Christian and Hopeful began to pray and continued in prayer until near the break of day. A little while before it was dawn, good Christian rose up as a man half-amazed and said, "O what a fool am I, thus to lie in a stinking dungeon when I might as well have my liberty: I have a key in my bosom called Promise, that will, I am persuaded, open my lock in Doubting Castle." "Then," said Hopeful, "that's good news, my brother; pluck it out of thy bosom and try."

And so the two did. The key called "Promise" unlocked the door of the dungeon. Whenever we may be tempted to doubt or give ourselves up for lost, we must remember the key in our pocket. "Promise"—God's sacred assurances given to us in Scripture—unlocks the doors of doubt and despair.

ISAAC AND REBEKAH

BACKGROUND SCRIPTURE: Psalm 100
DEVOTIONAL READING: Genesis 24

KEY VERSE: And I bowed down my head, and worshipped the LORD, and blessed the LORD God of my master Abraham, which had led me in the right way to take my master's brother's daughter unto his son. Genesis 24:48.

5

KING JAMES VERSION

GENESIS 24:34 And he said, I am Abraham's servant. 35 And the LORD hath blessed my master greatly; and he is become great: and he hath given him flocks, and herds, and silver, and gold, and menservants, and maidservants, and camels, and asses. 36 And Sarah my master's wife bare a son to my master when she was old: and unto him hath he given all that he hath. 37 And my master made me swear, saying, Thou shalt not take a wife to my son of the daughters of the Canaanites, in whose land I dwell: 38 But thou shalt go unto my father's house, and to my kindred, and take a wife unto my son. 39 And I said unto my master, Peradventure the woman will not follow me. 40 And he said unto me, The LORD, before whom I walk, will send his angel with thee, and prosper thy way; and thou shalt take a wife for my son of my kindred, and of my father's house: . . . 42 And I came this day unto the well, and said, O LORD God of my master Abraham, if now thou do prosper my way which I go: 43 Behold, I stand by the well of water; and it shall come to pass, that when the virgin cometh forth to draw water, and I say to her, Give me, I pray thee, a little water of thy pitcher to drink; 44 And she say to me, Both drink thou, and I will also draw for thy camels: let the same be the woman whom the LORD hath appointed out for my master's son. 45 And before I had done speaking in mine heart, behold, Rebekah came forth with her pitcher on her shoulder; and she went down unto the well, and drew water: and I said unto her, Let me drink, I pray thee. . . . 48 And I bowed down my head, and worshipped the LORD, and blessed the LORD God of my master Abraham, which had led me in the right way to take my master's brother's daughter unto his son.

NEW REVISED STANDARD VERSION

GENESIS 24:34 So he said, "I am Abraham's servant. 35 The LORD has greatly blessed my master, and he has become wealthy; he has given him flocks and herds, silver and gold, male and female slaves, camels and donkeys. 36 And Sarah my master's wife bore a son to my master when she was old; and he has given him all that he has. 37 My master made me swear, saying, 'You shall not take a wife for my son from the daughters of the Canaanites, in whose land I live; 38 but you shall go to my father's house, to my kindred, and get a wife for my son.' 39 I said to my master, 'Perhaps the woman will not follow me.' 40 But he said to me, 'The LORD, before whom I walk, will send his angel with you and make your way successful. You shall get a wife for my son from my kindred, from my father's house.' . . . 42 "I came today to the spring, and said, 'O LORD, the God of my master Abraham, if now you will only make successful the way I am going! 43 I am standing here by the spring of water; let the young woman who comes out to draw, to whom I shall say, "Please give me a little water from your jar to drink," 44 and who will say to me, "Drink, and I will draw for your camels also"—let her be the woman whom the LORD has appointed for my master's son.' 45 "Before I had finished speaking in my heart, there was Rebekah coming out with her water jar on her shoulder; and she went down to the spring, and drew. I said to her, 'Please let me drink.' . . . 48 Then I bowed my head and worshiped the LORD, and blessed the LORD, the God of my master Abraham, who had led me by the right way to obtain the daughter of my master's kinsman for his son."

Monday, September 24	Genesis 24:1-9	*Wanted: A Wife*
Tuesday, September 25	Genesis 24:10-21	*A Drink for the Camels*
Wednesday, September 26	Genesis 24:22-27	*The Daughter of Bethuel*
Thursday, September 27	Genesis 24:28-32	*A Show of Hospitality*
Friday, September 28	Genesis 24:33-41	*The Errand*
Saturday, September 29	Genesis 24:42-51	*A Wife for Isaac*
Sunday, September 30	Psalm 100	*God's Steadfast Love*

BACKGROUND

Genesis 24 deals with the issue of finding a suitable wife for Isaac. His father, Abraham, did not want him to marry a woman from among their neighbors, the Canaanites, for the latter had no clear knowledge of the true and living God. Abraham did not want his descendants corrupted by heathen idolatry. God Himself would often echo that concern. In the law, God warned that if the Israelites began marrying pagans, they would be ensnared by idolatry (Deut. 7:3-4); but many Israelites did not heed the warning. Even King Solomon allowed his heart to be turned away from God because of the idolatry of his foreign wives (1 Kings 11:4).

Abraham's chief servant worried that the selected woman would not want to travel so far with him to meet Isaac (Gen. 24:39). In that case, the servant wondered whether his master preferred that his son be returned to the land from which Abraham came (24:5). The patriarch, however, insisted that the latter not be done (24:6). Abraham explained that the Lord, the God of heaven, had taken him from his father's household and his native land to establish him in Canaan. The Lord also pledged with a solemn oath to give the promised land to the patriarch's offspring (24:7). Thus, it was there that Isaac was to remain.

Many years before, Abraham believed God's promise of a son through Sarah (15:6); and the patriarch was willing to serve the Lord faithfully and live a blameless life, because Abraham knew Him to be the all-powerful God (17:1). As the patriarch's life drew to a close, he could honestly say to his servant that he had faithfully served the Lord (24:40). Because God Almighty had been so trustworthy and dependable to the patriarch, he could affirm with certainty that the Lord would be with the chief servant on his mission. God would send His angel before the servant to protect and guide him (24:7) as well as ensure that the journey was a success (24:40). The servant's ability to find a wife for Isaac from among Abraham's relatives and his father's family would be a testament to God's blessing on the venture.

In the event that the woman refused to travel back to Canaan with Abraham's servant, he would be freed from the oath (24:8, 41). The patriarch's words gave the chief servant the reassurance he needed to set out on his mission with a caravan of 10 camels bearing all sorts of gifts for the future bride (24:10). The servant journeyed 450 miles to Aram Naharaim (that is, northwest Mesopotamia) and specifically to the town of Nahor. The latter was either Haran or another city nearby.

NOTES ON THE PRINTED TEXT

The issue confronting Abraham was real, but he had a plan. He called his chief servant to him, commissioning the man to go to his relatives and find a wife for Isaac (24:2, 34). The servant may have been Eliezer, whom Abraham had earlier sought to adopt as his heir (15:2). If so, we can see why the patriarch regarded Eliezar so highly. In the course of his assignment from Abraham, this servant displayed good discernment and trust in God.

As the chief servant related his circumstance to the family members of Rebekah, the visitor noted that the Lord had abundantly blessed his master. Indeed, Abraham had become renowned for his material wealth. This included sheep and cattle, silver and gold, male and female servants, and camels and donkeys (24:35). These remarks helped to vouch for the influential status of Abraham.

The patriarch's trust in God was even more noteworthy. Indeed, despite Abraham's faults, the New Testament writers held up him as a model of genuine faith. For instance, the writer of Hebrews emphasized that Abraham believed in God despite the seeming impossibility of having an heir through Sarah (Heb. 11:11). Also, Paul said that all believers, both Jews and Gentiles, are Abraham's spiritual children because they, too, come to God through faith. It was by faith that the sinners came to know God, not through their good works, their heritage, or their obedience to a prescribed set of rules (such as the Jewish law; Gal. 3:6-14).

The chief servant explained that Sarah, the wife of his master, had borne him a son in her old age. Also, it was to this son, Isaac, that the patriarch had given everything that he owned (Gen. 24:36). Sarah died at the age of 127 at Kiriath Arba (namely, Hebron) in Canaan (23:1-2). The rest of chapter 23 records the arrangements Abraham made to secure the burial of his wife in the promised land. The patriarch negotiated the purchase of the cave of Machpelah and the field that went with it. This property represented his first possession of the land in Canaan.

Isaac now remained the only living link between Abraham and his beloved, deceased wife. In the years preceding Isaac's birth, Abraham wondered who would inherit his estate. For a while, it seemed as if Lot would be the heir, but that option was eliminated when Lot moved away from the patriarch and pitched his tents near Sodom (chap. 13). Eliezer of Damascus became the next likely candidate to inherit Abraham's great wealth; but despite Eliezer's admirable qualities, the Lord declared to Abraham that his senior servant would not be the heir to the patriarch's estate (15:2-4). The birth of Ishmael through Sarah's Egyptian servant (chap. 16) meant that he was next in line to receive the family blessing; but he was never a candidate in God's eyes, for the Lord had already designated Isaac as the recipient of the covenant promises and Abraham's estate (17:18-21).

Before Abraham's chief servant left on his mission, the patriarch made him swear an oath. The servant pledged not to acquire a wife for Isaac from among the Canaanites (24:3, 37); instead, the servant was travel to the extended family of the patriarch's father, Terah (11:27), and find a wife for Isaac among these relatives (24:4, 38). To take the oath, the chief servant put his hand under the thigh of Abraham (24:2, 9), possibly near the male organ of procreation. As Abraham faced death, he wanted to ensure the future posterity of his beloved son Isaac. Thus, the patriarch went through a customary practice with his servant that was designed to guard any act of disloyalty. It was a solemn way of saying that if the promise was violated, the person taking the oath called sterility or loss of children upon himself. Moreover, the descendants of Abraham would have the right (and possibly obligation) to avenge the broken vow.

The chief servant expressed his concern to his master about the possibility that Isaac's wife-to-be might not want to relocate to Canaan (24:39). In Abraham's response, he first noted that he had walked faithfully with the Lord for many years. Then, the patriarch stated that God would send His angel with the chief servant and ensure that his journey was a success. Abraham had no doubt that God would lead the servant to Isaac's future wife, someone who was from the patriarch's own clan and family (24:40).

Once the chief servant arrived at the place where Abraham's relatives lived, he had the camels kneel down by the well outside the city. By then it was evening, and the local women were coming out to draw water (Gen. 24:11). The deep faith of the servant is evident in the account. He trusted the Lord and looked to Him for guidance in completing his mission. Abraham's trust in God had profoundly influenced the chief servant, who asked that the sovereign Lord make his journey successful (24:42). In so doing, God would be showing His unfailing covenantal love to Abraham (24:12).

In his prayer, the chief servant described the conditions he hoped God would fulfill. The servant did not want to make a mistake. That is why he looked to the Lord to identify the right woman for Isaac. In this case, the servant noted in his prayer that he was standing beside the local spring, where the young women of the village came to draw water (24:13). The sign from God requested by the servant involved asking one of the girls for a drink of water from her jug (24:43). The servant wanted the young woman whom God had chosen not only to agree to lowering her jar so that the servant could drink, but also to water his master's camels (24:44). If this was the way the encounter unfolded, the servant would know that the Lord had been faithful to Abraham (24:14).

The chief servant related that before he had finished praying in his heart, he saw Rebekah come out (24:45). This young woman was both strikingly beautiful and a virgin (24:16). She performed her tasks quickly, even at a run; and she did not shrink from doing extra work for a visitor. Abraham's servant had planned to ask a young woman to get water for him (24:14); but Rebekah was too quick for him. Before he could address her, she went down into the walk-in well and filled her jar of her own accord. When she came back with the jug on her head or shoulder, the servant met her and asked for a drink

(24:17, 45). She gave it to him and volunteered to fill the nearby water trough for his master's camels (24:18-20, 46).

When the chief servant asked the young woman to what family she belonged (24:47), she explained that she was the daughter of Bethuel, the son of Milcah. Milcah was the wife of Abraham's brother Nahor (24:15; see 24:24, 47). The chief servant, realizing that God had made his journey successful, bowed his head in worship to the Lord (24:26) and praised the God of Abraham for the kindness and faithfulness He had shown the patriarch. The servant was especially grateful that the Lord had led him to the house of one of the patriarch's relatives (24:27). Indeed, God had enabled the servant to meet Rebekah, the future wife of Isaac (24:48).

The rest of the chapter describes the visit of Abraham's servant at Rebekah's home. The girl's father, Bethuel, and brother, Laban, agreed that the matter was from God. They decided to let Rebekah go to the promised land with Abraham's servant, although Laban and Milcah (Rebekah's mother) favored a 10-day delay. Rebekah was willing to forgo the delay. She and Abraham's servant traveled back to Canaan, where Rebekah married Isaac. He not only loved her, but also was comforted by her presence after the death of his mother, Sarah (24:49-67).

SUGGESTIONS TO TEACHERS

Undoubtedly, Abraham's trusted servant learned many lessons from him. Possibly the greatest lesson of all was that of humbly asking God to work on behalf of His people. When we reflect on the life of the patriarch—including the testimony of his servant recorded in Genesis 24—the trust that resulted from a life of communion and communication with God is evident.

1. GOD KNOWS US. At times when life feels confusing and out of control, we may wonder how God is able to understand our prayers. When we read the teachings of the New Testament, we discover that God knows our petitions better than we do ourselves. Even when we are not sure what the right prayers should be or the best method of prayer to use, God actively searches our hearts; and He is able to see the motive of our requests and respond in kind. Indeed, the Spirit intercedes on our behalf in accordance with the Father's will (Rom. 8:26-27).

2. WE CAN DEPEND ON GOD. In this week's lesson text, the chief servant of Abraham is a good model of how we can depend on God and pray to Him concerning every issue in our lives. Perhaps the most important virtue the servant displayed was a view of an awesome God who would work on behalf of anyone who was willing to petition the Lord with his or her requests.

3. WE PRAY TO GOD. The consistent testimony of Scripture is that prayers based upon God's Word and will are petitions that especially please the Lord. Moreover, it seems as if the prayers that God delights most in answering are the ones that begin with an acknowledgment of who He is, are filled with humble cries for help, and end with an affirmation of trust that God will always do what is right.

4. GOD ANSWERS OUR PRAYERS. God's faithfulness to hear our petitions is why many local churches list prayer concerns in their weekly bulletins. It is why every congregational meeting can begin and end in prayer; and it is why some church members believe there is no sweeter sound than someone saying, "I will remember you in my prayers."

FOR ADULTS	■ **TOPIC:** Recognizing the Right Woman ■ **QUESTIONS:** 1. How had the Lord abundantly blessed Abraham? 2. What was the nature of the oath Abraham had his servant swear?

3. How did Abraham respond to the concerns of his servant? 4. What did the servant request from the Lord to let him know that his mission was a success? 5. Why did the servant offer praise to the Lord?

■ **ILLUSTRATIONS:**

A Memorable Couple. Steve Inskeep of *National Public Radio* noted that since 2003, thousands have taken part in the StoryCorps oral history project. It is an opportunity for them to describe their lifetime experiences and accomplishments. The marriage of Danny and Annie Perasa is one inspiring example. They wed in 1978 and remained affectionate toward each other right up to the very end, when Danny succumbed to pancreatic cancer on February 24, 2006. According to Inskeep, regardless of whether the couple was on the radio or in person, their "infectious enthusiasm draws listeners in, making them strain to hear what the couple have to say."

In honor of Annie and Danny's enthusiasm, the StoryCorps oral history project "dedicated its booth in Grand Central Terminal to the Perasas." A specially prepared plaque reads: "This booth is dedicated to Danny and Annie Perasa, who recorded their story here on January 6, 2004. Their humor, heart, eloquence and love will never be forgotten." Their account stands as a witness to the powerful influence a marriage can have when it is founded on unconditional love and undying commitment.

Power in Prayer. When a local community church felt the time was right to move ahead on a building project, the congregation's leaders made plans to develop a monthly prayer calendar for the parish. It was God's faithful answers to prayer that had made the project possible. The church had no desire to move forward without making prayer a priority.

In Philippians 4:6-7, Paul told his friends not to worry about any self-centered concerns. Such anxiety can become all-consuming. It takes our minds off what is important to God and focuses attention on ourselves. We can become self-absorbed, unable to rejoice during hard times or to be gentle with friends and foes alike. When we turn to God and surrender our anxieties to Him, God's peace can reach our innermost parts. Paul did not imply that our burdens will vanish, nor was he talking about a state of mind. In fact, it is an inner peace that can come only from God and is beyond our comprehension.

A Lifetime of Marrying. A Bible-thumping minister named Glynn ("Scotty") Wolfe married 29 times in his life. Apparently, Wolfe didn't read or understand the passage in Genesis where it is reported that God created man and woman to live together caringly, faithfully, and permanently in a lifelong partnership.

Wolfe cast out one wife for eating sunflower seeds in bed and divorced another for using his toothbrush. Wife 29, Linda Essex, was Wolfe's match in that she proudly claimed the record of being the world's most frequently married woman. Her trip to the altar with Wolfe was her 23rd! Wolfe died in June 1997, leaving Linda the opportunity of hunting for husband number 24. God, however, does not intend people and spouses to be throwaway commodities.

FOR YOUTH	■ **TOPIC:** Here Comes the Bride ■ **QUESTIONS:** 1. What kinds of material wealth did Abraham possess?

2. Why did Abraham insist that his son not marry a Canaanite woman? 3. From where was Abraham's servant to find a wife for Isaac? 4. What was the nature of the servant's request to the Lord? 5. How had the Lord led the servant of Abraham on his mission?

■ **ILLUSTRATIONS:**

Unloved. Charlie Brown, the familiar character from the *Peanuts* comic strip, is in love with the little red-haired girl. But it is unrequited love, for Charlie Brown is too shy to even approach her. As a result, the little red-haired girl doesn't even know Charlie Brown is alive.

One day, Charlie Brown and his sister Sally are getting some parcels out the mailbox. Charlie Brown pulls out a letter and asks, "What's this? Is it a love letter from the red-haired girl?" Sally looks at it and says, "No, it's an ad for a tire company." Charlie Brown pulls out another letter and asks, "What's this? A love letter from Peggy Jean?" Sally scans the letter and says, "No, it's an ad from a shoe store." Charlie Brown pulls out a third letter and asks, "What's this? A love letter from the girl I met at the library?" "No," Sally says, "it's an ad for some luggage." Charlie Brown sinks down, leaning up against the mailbox post and sighs, "When you never get any love letters, you have to pretend that everything is a love letter."

We need not go through life as Charlie Brown did. Instead of moaning over feeling unloved by someone of the opposite gender, we can open our eyes to the love of God all around us. We can find it in family and friends, in the beauty and blessings of all creation, and in every act of mercy we witness.

Father of the Bride. In 1991, Steve Martin starred in the remake of the 1950 Spencer Tracy classic titled *Father of the Bride*. The updated film tells the story of George and Nina Banks, who are the parents of young, soon-to-be-wed Annie. George is a nervous father unready to face the fact that his little girl is now a woman. The preparations for the extravagant wedding provide unforgettable comic moments.

Unlike the previously mentioned Hollywood character, Abraham was energized by the prospect of his beloved child, Isaac, finding a suitable mate. Although the search for the right partner involved a lot of patience and discernment, the effort paid off. This holds true for young people today. Rushing impulsively into an ill-advised marriage relationship can lead to many years of unwanted grief. By exercising good judgment now, you can save yourself a lot of agony in the future.

What Do You Believe? July 2007 was the 60th anniversary of a weird crash in Roswell, New Mexico. The site is particularly interesting for individuals preoccupied with UFOs (Unidentified Flying Objects) because of the alleged crash of a flying saucer. A *Time* magazine/Yankelovich poll indicated that 34 percent of Americans believe that intelligent beings from other planets have visited the Earth. Of these, 65 percent believe a UFO crash at Roswell, and 80 percent believe that the U.S. government knows more about extraterrestrials than it chooses to release.

Some scientists assume the existence of intelligent life among the planets. Even if true, most Christian theologians believe that any species simply enlarges God's creativity. Whatever the case may be, our Lord is so powerful that He could lead Abraham's chief servant to the most suitable woman for Isaac to marry. It should also come as no surprise that nothing in the entire universe can limit God's ability to bring about His perfect will for us.

ESAU AND JACOB AS RIVALS

BACKGROUND SCRIPTURE: 1 Corinthians 1:26-31
DEVOTIONAL READING: Genesis 25:19-34

KEY VERSE: And the LORD said unto her, Two nations are in thy womb, and two manner of people shall be separated from thy bowels; and the one people shall be stronger than the other people; and the elder shall serve the younger. Genesis 25:23.

KING JAMES VERSION

GENESIS 25:19 And these are the generations of Isaac, Abraham's son: Abraham begat Isaac: 20 And Isaac was forty years old when he took Rebekah to wife, the daughter of Bethuel the Syrian of Padanaram, the sister to Laban the Syrian. 21 And Isaac intreated the LORD for his wife, because she was barren: and the LORD was intreated of him, and Rebekah his wife conceived. 22 And the children struggled together within her; and she said, If it be so, why am I thus? And she went to enquire of the LORD. 23 And the LORD said unto her, Two nations are in thy womb, and two manner of people shall be separated from thy bowels; and the one people shall be stronger than the other people; and the elder shall serve the younger. 24 And when her days to be delivered were fulfilled, behold, there were twins in her womb. 25 And the first came out red, all over like an hairy garment; and they called his name Esau. 26 And after that came his brother out, and his hand took hold on Esau's heel; and his name was called Jacob: and Isaac was threescore years old when she bare them. 27 And the boys grew: and Esau was a cunning hunter, a man of the field; and Jacob was a plain man, dwelling in tents. 28 And Isaac loved Esau, because he did eat of his venison: but Rebekah loved Jacob.

29 And Jacob sod pottage: and Esau came from the field, and he was faint: 30 And Esau said to Jacob, Feed me, I pray thee, with that same red pottage; for I am faint: therefore was his name called Edom. 31 And Jacob said, Sell me this day thy birthright. 32 And Esau said, Behold, I am at the point to die: and what profit shall this birthright do to me? 33 And Jacob said, Sware to me this day; and he sware unto him: and he sold his birthright unto Jacob. 34 Then Jacob gave Esau bread and pottage of lentiles; and he did eat and drink, and rose up, and went his way: thus Esau despised his birthright.

NEW REVISED STANDARD VERSION

GENESIS 25:19 These are the descendants of Isaac, Abraham's son: Abraham was the father of Isaac, 20 and Isaac was forty years old when he married Rebekah, daughter of Bethuel the Aramean of Paddan-aram, sister of Laban the Aramean. 21 Isaac prayed to the LORD for his wife, because she was barren; and the LORD granted his prayer, and his wife Rebekah conceived. 22 The children struggled together within her; and she said, "If it is to be this way, why do I live?" So she went to inquire of the LORD. 23 And the LORD said to her,

"Two nations are in your womb,
    and two peoples born of you shall be divided;
the one shall be stronger than the other,
    the elder shall serve the younger."

24 When her time to give birth was at hand, there were twins in her womb. 25 The first came out red, all his body like a hairy mantle; so they named him Esau. 26 Afterward his brother came out, with his hand gripping Esau's heel; so he was named Jacob. Isaac was sixty years old when she bore them.

27 When the boys grew up, Esau was a skillful hunter, a man of the field, while Jacob was a quiet man, living in tents. 28 Isaac loved Esau, because he was fond of game; but Rebekah loved Jacob.

29 Once when Jacob was cooking a stew, Esau came in from the field, and he was famished. 30 Esau said to Jacob, "Let me eat some of that red stuff, for I am famished!" (Therefore he was called Edom.) 31 Jacob said, "First sell me your birthright." 32 Esau said, "I am about to die; of what use is a birthright to me?" 33 Jacob said, "Swear to me first." So he swore to him, and sold his birthright to Jacob. 34 Then Jacob gave Esau bread and lentil stew, and he ate and drank, and rose and went his way. Thus Esau despised his birthright.

6

Monday, October 1	1 Corinthians 1:26-31	*God Chose the Least*
Tuesday, October 2	Genesis 24:50-61	*Rebekah Agrees to Marry Isaac*
Wednesday, October 3	Genesis 24:62-67	*Isaac Takes Rebekah as His Wife*
Thursday, October 4	Genesis 25:19-23	*Rebekah's Twins Struggle in the Womb*
Friday, October 5	Genesis 25:24-28	*The Birth of Jacob and Esau*
Saturday, October 6	Genesis 25:29-34	*Esau Sells His Birthright*
Sunday, October 7	Genesis 27:30-40	*Esau's Lost Blessing*

BACKGROUND

Generations (Gen. 25:19) translates the Hebrew noun *toledot*, which is derived from a verb that means "to bear" or "to generate." Nonetheless, in Genesis the phrase introduces more than genealogies. *Toledot* can also contain biographical material as well as summarize a series of important events. The literary importance of this Hebrew noun (which occurs 10 times in Genesis) should not be overlooked, for its repetition throughout the book can help the reader discern how Moses organized and arranged his information.

In particular, *toledot* signals the beginning of a narrative sequence in which the history of an individual or entity is discussed, in some places briefly, while in other places extensively. For instance, 25:12-19 concisely delineates what became of Ishmael and his family line. Then in 25:19—35:29, the history of Isaac and his descendants is traced at length. In the latter passage, the focus is often on Jacob, while in other parts the limelight shifts to Esau.

As each *toledot* section unfolds, the focus of attention increasingly narrows. Genesis begins with God commanding the universe into existence and then zeros in on His creation of humankind. After the account of the worldwide Flood, the aperture closes in on the origins of the Hebrew people, giving particular attention to key events associated with the lives of Abraham, Isaac, and Jacob. This literary development makes sense, for God established His covenant with the patriarchs and their descendants.

According to 25:19-20, Abraham was the father of Isaac, who was 40 years old when he married Rebekah. Genesis 24 (the longest chapter in the book) records how Abraham's chief servant found Rebekah as a wife for Isaac. As the daughter of Bethuel, Rebekah was a near relative of Abraham's family. The text says that Bethuel was an Aramean (or Syrian) from Paddan Aram (see Deut. 26:5), which means "Plain of Aram" or "Field of Aram." This is another name for Aram Naharaim (Gen. 24:10), which literally means "Aram of the two rivers." The reference is to the Euphrates and Tigris rivers in northwest Mesopotamia.

The land of Aram extended from the Lebanon mountain range (on the east) to the Euphrates River (on the west) and from the Taurus mountain range (on the north) to Damascus (on the south). As early as the second millennium B.C., the Arameans began settling what is now called Syria and some parts of Babylon. Eventually, the Arameans formed a loose confederation of encampments and towns.

A comparison of 25:7 and 20 indicates that Isaac married 35 years before Abraham died. Also, a comparison of verses 20 and 26 reveals that Isaac had to wait 20 years—from the time he was 40, when he married Rebekah, until he was 60—before Rebekah gave birth to Esau and Jacob. Moreover, Abraham would have been alive to see the fraternal twins begin to grow up and reach early adolescence.

According to 25:20, Rebekah was the sister of Laban the Aramean. He is first introduced in 24:29-31, where the text relates that he went out to meet the chief servant of Abraham and invited the visitor to lodge at the family home. Laban also played a prominent role in the rest of the account recorded in the chapter. For instance, after the servant rehearsed his encounter with Rebekah, Laban and Bethuel affirmed that the Lord had brought the servant to the area and that God had chosen Rebekah to become Isaac's wife (24:50-51). Also, it was Laban and his mother who suggested that Rebekah stay at least 10 days before leaving her family to marry Isaac (24:55). Years later, Rebekah had Jacob flee to his uncle Laban as a way to escape from Esau, who threatened to kill his twin brother for stealing the family blessing from him (27:43-45).

NOTES ON THE PRINTED TEXT

In Genesis 25:1-11, we read about the final years and the death of Abraham. He lived 35 years after Isaac and Rebekah were married. Abraham also had children through another marriage; but finally, at the age of 175, the patriarch died. Isaac and Ishmael cooperated in burying their father. The mention of Ishmael leads to the mentioning, in 25:12-18, of his descendants and his death at the age of 137. After Abraham's death, the focus of Genesis shifts to the inheritor of God's promises—the patriarch's son, Isaac (25:19).

When Isaac was 40 years old, he married Rebekah (25:20). As the daughter of Bethuel, Rebekah was a near relative of Abraham's family. Rebekah was also the sister of Laban the Syrian. Like Sarah (11:30), Rebekah was childless, and her inability to conceive and bear a son placed the fulfillment of the covenantal promises in jeopardy. A superficial reading of 25:21 might leave the impression that Isaac prayed once or twice and then God answered the patriarch's request; but as was previously noted, two decades passed before the Lord enabled Rebekah to become pregnant. From this we see that it was God's grace that enabled Isaac's wife to conceive.

Perhaps in the interim, as time wore on, Isaac became more and more concerned about his lack of children. Undoubtedly, the Lord was testing Isaac's faith, as He had previously tested Abraham's faith. Indeed, many years earlier the patriarch had waited patiently for Isaac's birth. God knew all along what He would do, but He waited to do it in cooperation with the prayers of such individuals as Isaac and Abraham.

The Lord gave Isaac not one son but two. Prior to their birth, they *struggled together* (25:22) within Rebekah. The Hebrew verb rendered *struggled* suggests an extraordinarily vigorous jostling between the twins. The activity within Rebekah's womb concerned her so much that she wondered why it was happening to her. There also seems to be a hint of discouragement in her question as she despaired over what the activity could mean for the future of her babies.

Understandably, Rebekah decided to ask the Lord for clarification. There is no explanation given as to how Rebekah made her inquiry. One possibility is that she went to a nearby place of worship and consulted some sort of oracle, such as a patriarchal altar (see 12:6-7). First Samuel 9:9 states that in later Israelite history, God's people would go to a seer or prophet to seek the Lord's will. In any case, God disclosed to Rebekah that two nations and peoples were represented by the unborn fraternal twins in her womb. The descendants from one of the children would eventually become stronger than the other. In fact, the offspring of the older child would end up serving the offspring of the younger (Gen. 25:23). In short, the younger son would receive the blessings of the covenant. This turn of events reflected the Lord's will.

The importance of God's statement cannot be overemphasized. In Romans 9, Paul noted that the Lord made His choice regarding the promised line even before the twins were born and before they had done anything good or bad (9:10-11). Perhaps the most difficult sentence to understand is found in 9:13 (see Mal. 1:2-3). Paul was not talking about an emotional or temperamental hatred. This hatred was not absolute, but was relative to a higher choice. Used in this way, the word *hated* (Rom. 9:13) can carry the meaning "loved less." Experts also tell us that in ancient days the word "hate" was often used figuratively. In the present context in regard to the promised line, the phrase *Jacob have I loved, but Esau have I hated* carries the meaning "Jacob I chose, but Esau I rejected." The fact that God did not emotionally "hate" Esau is clear from the fact that the Lord bestowed many temporal blessings on Esau, his family, and his descendants.

As God foretold, Rebekah was carrying twins in her womb (Gen. 25:24). The first child to emerge was reddish all over. Moreover, because his entire body was like a hairy garment, he was named *Esau* (25:25), which possibly means "hairy." When his brother came out, his hand was clutching Esau's heel. Thus the younger twin was named *Jacob* (25:26), which probably means "he grasps the heel." This became a Hebrew idiom for "he deceives." Later in Jacob's life, God renamed him *Israel* (Gen. 32:28; 35:10) as a sign of his spiritual struggle . This is the same name that Jacob's descendants eventually adopted as their political and religious title. Although Jacob was characterized by deceitfulness in his earlier days, by the time he reached the end of his life, he was a person of genuine faith and integrity (Heb. 11:21).

Eventually the fraternal twins reached adulthood. Esau had a reputation for being a skilled hunter. He enjoyed roaming freely in the open fields. In contrast, Jacob was an even-tempered, domesticated person who preferred to live in tents (Gen. 25:27). Because of Isaac's taste for fresh game, he loved Esau more; but Jacob was Rebekah's favorite son (25:28). The displays of favoritism by the parents caused great problems in the home. It deepened the rivalry between the brothers, and eventually broke apart the family.

On one occasion, Jacob was cooking some stew when Esau came in from the open fields. Evidently, his efforts that day to catch fresh game proved futile, leaving him feeling tired and famished (25:29). When Esau spotted Jacob's ready-to-eat red lentil stew, the older brother demanded that his younger twin give him some of it. Esau exclaimed that he wanted a bite of the red stuff because he was starving. Genesis 25:30 says this episode is the reason why Esau was nicknamed Edom, a word in Hebrew that means "red."

Jacob was willing to do what Esau demanded if he deeded over his birthright (25:31). In Bible times it was customary for the firstborn son (whether the child of a legal wife or a concubine) to inherit the rights, or privileges, of the family. This typically included receiving the family name and titles. It also included becoming the leader of the family and the one through whom the line was continued. Further, because a child was the first-born, he usually inherited a double portion of the family estate.

From Esau's shortsighted perspective, the birthright had little immediate value (25:32). Like a skilled hunter who was ready to pounce on his weakened prey, Jacob insisted that Esau swear an oath that he was transferring his inheritance rights (25:33). When Esau agreed to the exchange, Jacob gave his older brother some bread and lentil stew, which Esau promptly consumed before getting up and leaving (25:34). In this way, he treated the family inheritance with contempt.

SUGGESTIONS TO TEACHERS

Esau's life and priorities are a sobering reminder that no one can serve two masters. We will either devote ourselves to the Lord or the things of the world (Matt. 6:24). The devil knows this and works through the allures of the world (1 John 5:19) to draw us away from fellowship with God into fellowship with the world. Thus, we must not be ignorant of the devil's schemes (2 Cor. 2:11), for he uses selfishness, greed, and vain status-seeking to appeal to our sinful natures and seduce us from fellowship with the Father and His Son.

1. WALKING IN RIGHTEOUSNESS. For God's people there are three marks of a genuine relationship with Christ. One is walking in righteousness. Broadly speaking, this means upright living. If we want to be followers of Jesus, we must be willing to live His lifestyle. That means changing any attitude or action that is not in keeping with the example Christ set for us.

2. OBEYING GOD. A second mark of believers should be their obedience to God. Imagine that someone had been pretending to be your friend because that person felt obligated to or was trying to look good in front of others. If you became aware of this, the "friendship" would be meaningless. We must not have that kind of relationship with God, namely, one characterized by legalistically obeying His commands. Our obedience, like Christ's, should come from our love for God, not from just doing what He says we should do. Then others will notice the joy we have in our relationship with the Lord.

3. LOVING GOD'S PEOPLE. A third mark of a genuine relationship with Christ is to love other believers (John 13:35). When Christians demonstrate sacrificial, not self-seeking, love toward each other, they stand out in our "me-first" world. The priority of Christians becomes giving instead of taking. They are encouraging to each other instead of berating. That kind of love should show others the depth of our relationship with the Father through the Son.

■ **TOPIC:** Sibling Rivalry!

■ **QUESTIONS:** 1. What was the significance of the babies struggling within Rebekah's womb? 2. Why was Rebekah's firstborn named Esau? 3. Why was Rebekah's secondborn named Jacob? 4. How did the fraternal twins differ in occupation? 5. What circumstances led up to Esau selling his birthright?

■ **ILLUSTRATIONS:**

United, not Divided. In the April 30, 2004 edition of the *San Jose State University Spartan Daily*, John Myers reported being asked at the last minute to fill in as a judge at the eighth annual Perpetratin' lip-sync/dance competition. What impressed Myers the most were the "steps and strolls" of the African American fraternities. By this he meant the performance of synchronized line dancing punctuated by stomping and clapping.

Myers recalled the routine completed by the Kappa Alpha Psi fraternity. Its members marched in fluid dance steps down the aisle of the auditorium. During this complex routine, they incorporated the use of a cane. "The cane becomes part of the steps," said Alpha English, vice president of Kappa Alpha Psi. "It's a sign of prestige." The steps and strolls unite the chapters, said Ignacio Rios, a member of Sigma Lambda Beta. Imagine how united the members of a church could become if they cooperated just as much in the work of the Lord. There would be no evidence of spiritual "sibling rivalry"!

Honesty at the Tournament. We are used to reports of greed and deceit among athletes. It is refreshing to hear the account of a professional sports figure who refused to give in to self-interest. Davis Love III was competing in the second round in the Western Open in 1994. The golfer knew that good money was riding on his ability to play. When his ball was in the way of another player's putting line, Love moved it. But a couple of holes later, David Love could not recall if he had moved his ball back to its original position. Because he was unsure, he insisted on giving himself an extra stroke.

That extra stroke proved costly. It forced Love to be one of those cut from participating in the tournament. Even if Davis Love had been included and had wound up last, he would have earned $2,000. At the end of the year, he found that he was $590 short of being able to qualify automatically for the 1995 Masters Tournament. His integrity at the Western Open's trials paid a heavy price. David Love knew that he would have to win a tournament in 1995 in order to enter the Masters. Happily, he succeeded in doing so in New Orleans, the week before the Masters, and came in second at the tournament.

Love was asked how he would have felt had he not been able to enter the Masters because of calling a penalty stroke on himself at the Western Open. He replied, "How would I have felt if I'd won the Masters and wondered for the rest of my life if I'd cheated to get in?"

Old Cab Joke. Some years back, veteran utility infielder Frank Duffy of the Boston Red Sox described the sports scene in a pithy line. He could have been speaking for the "Me First" attitudes of many nonsports-types in our society. As he looked around the clubhouse with its collection of selfish players, he made the following famous (or infamous) statement: "25 guys, 25 cabs." Instead of being team-oriented, the players were self-oriented. They all came to the ballpark separately. The 25-cabs saying applies to the way athletes and many of our fellow citizens deceive themselves and others in their efforts to get what they want.

FOR YOUTH

■ **TOPIC:** Costly Stew

■ **QUESTIONS:** 1. How did Jacob respond to Rebekah's childless condition? 2. Why did Rebekah inquire of the Lord concerning her pregnancy? 3. What was the name given to Rebekah's firstborn son? 4. What was the name given to Rebekah's secondborn son? 5. In what way did Esau treat his birthright with disdain?

■ **ILLUSTRATIONS:**

Junk or Jewels? A New York State woman unknowingly allowed her family jewels to be sold for 10 cents at a friend's garage sale. It happened after she took the jewels out of a bank safety deposit box to wear to a wedding. The bank was closed when she got home, so she put the jewels in an old shaving case and stuffed it in another box.

In time, the woman forgot about the jewels, and later she gave the shaving case to a friend who was collecting items for a garage sale. By the time the woman realized what she had done, the precious gems had been sold to an unknown buyer for a dime. In a sense, her pain is similar to Esau's. He too discovered what it's like to realize suddenly that he had lost something of great value.

An Eternal Prize. According to Bill Shaikin of the *Los Angeles Times*, U.S. Speed skater Joey Cheek made Olympic history on February 13, 2006, when he won the men's 500-meter race in Turin, Italy. But even more amazing than this athletic feat was Cheek's announcement minutes after his victory that he would donate his $25,000 gold medal award from the U.S. Olympic Committee. It would go to refugees from the Darfur region of western Sudan so that "children in African refugee camps might have a chance to play sports." He also urged "Olympic sponsors to support the same relief effort."

Cheek's decision is one filled with courage, commitment, and compassion. It stands in contrast to the self-serving, self-focused mindset of someone like Esau. The virtues displayed by Cheek are the same qualities that Paul said should be part of the lives of all believers. In fact, the apostle often used the analogy of a sports race to urge believers to remain focused, single-minded, and undaunted in their devotion to the Savior and His followers. Like an Olympic speed skater, they were to strain to reach the end of the race and receive the eternal, heavenly prize promised to them in Christ.

The Gold Ring. Cory was a college freshman. Through his high school years, he was deeply involved in the youth group in his church. His last two summers before college, he had worked in Christian camps for young children. Because of his outgoing personality, he made friends quickly in college.

One night, following a football game, three fellow students asked Cory to go with them for a late-night snack. When they stopped at a roadside café, one of the boys retrieved a carton of beer from the trunk of the car. When Cory refused to accept a can, the other boys began to pressure him. "Just one drink! What will it hurt? So you've never tried it—you need to know what it's like!"

Cory wanted very much to be accepted. He was about to weaken when he felt the plain, gold ring on the little finger of his right hand. His mother had given it to him the day he left home. His mother said, "Cory, when you are tempted to do something wrong, feel this ring. It will remind you that I am praying for you daily." Cory's resolve was strengthened and he was able to resist the temptation.

ed in the hill country of Canaan, about 12 miles north of Jebus (later Jerusalem) and close to Ai.

The Lord's promise to always be with Jacob was so meaningful to him that he vowed to make Yahweh his God (28:20). Jacob did not ask the Lord for either fame or riches. In a sense, Jacob was establishing a personal relationship with God. Jacob was taking the Lord at His word concerning His promises (see 28:15). The patriarch translated the general promises God had made into specifics relating to his situation. Jacob would trust the Lord to remain with him, protect him on his journey, give him food and clothing, and one day bring him safely back to Canaan (28:20-21). By reiterating the covenantal promises, Jacob claimed them as his own.

Jacob then designated the rough stone column as *God's house* (28:22); in other words, the pillar would serve as a memorial and place for worshiping the Lord. Jacob also pledged to give the Lord one-tenth of his possessions. By this act (evidently a one-time gift), the patriarch expressed his gratitude to God, acknowledged the Lord as his God and King, and declared his willingness to commit everything to the Lord in wholehearted trust. Exactly who Jacob paid his tithe to is not specified in Scripture.

In ancient times, tithing was the practice of giving a tenth of one's income, whether in material goods or money, to God. That it was done by both Abraham (14:18-20) and Jacob (28:22) shows that it was an ancient practice established before the law of Moses prescribed it (Lev. 27:30-33). Throughout Israel's history, the tithe was used to support the priesthood. Also, every third year a special contribution was made for the poor either out of the tithe or in addition to it (Num. 18:21; Deut. 26:12).

SUGGESTIONS TO TEACHERS

While Jacob was in flight, fearing for his life, God spoke to him in a dream. The Lord promised Jacob that He would always be with him, even assuring him that He would look after his descendants. At times, most of us doubt God's presence when something unwelcome occurs in our lives; yet the Lord does not get angry or leave us because our faith wavers. Instead, He indicates to us in many ways that He is always close to us and will guide us like a shepherd.

1. GOD PROVIDES. In life's darkest, fear-inducing moments, the truth that God is our Shepherd and Guide can be reassuring. Just as shepherds provide lush meadows for their sheep to graze and peaceful streams for them to drink from, so the Lord will provide for the needs of His people. God has surely proven Himself to be trustworthy in meeting our needs in the past, and He can be trusted to provide our needs in the future.

2. GOD DELIVERS. Shepherds put their lives on the line to maintain their flock of sheep. To protect and rescue sheep from danger, shepherds were forced to inch out onto risky ledges and to put themselves between wild animals and their sheep. In a sense, our Shepherd has done the same for us today. Jesus put His own life on the line so that our eternal lives might be rescued, and He put Himself between us and the penalty for our sin. Thus, He not only can be trusted for our protection physically, but mentally, emotionally, and spiritually, too.

3. GOD'S INVOLVEMENT. Shepherds realize that a sheep is a fearful, flighty animal that is prone to get lost or harm itself in a multitude of other ways. Therefore, shepherds seek not only to keep their sheep protected, but also to help them sense a degree of contentment in the care of the shepherd. Scripture promises that God's goodness and unfailing love will actually pursue us all the days of our lives, yearning for us to find our contentment in Him.

| **FOR ADULTS** | ■ **TOPIC:** Understanding Our Dreams!
 ■ **QUESTIONS:** 1. Why did Jacob leave Beersheba and set out for Haran? 2. What promises did the Lord make to Jacob as he slept? |

3. Why was Jacob afraid when he woke up from his dream? 4. How did Jacob commemorate what he had experienced at the campsite? 5. What was the nature of the vow that Jacob made to the Lord before he left Bethel?

■ **ILLUSTRATIONS:**

A Special Moment. "There is a specialness to this place that you can feel. With all the history here, I just wanted to be a of part it." The statement came from a Portsmouth, Ohio, man who had taken a day off from work and had driven seven hours to Gettysburg, Pennsylvania, in order to witness the burial of an unknown Civil War soldier whose body had been exposed by the rains and who was finally laid to rest on July 1, 1997.

Jacob might have felt the same way after having a dream in which he encountered God. There was now a specialness to the place where the incident occurred. Perhaps we can look back to times when we sensed the Lord's presence in an unusual way. Even though it may not have involved experiencing a dream as vivid as Jacob's, the experience can be special moment for us from which we draw encouragement and strength to face new challenges in our lives.

Assured of God's Presence. "Why are crying for me? I can't stay with you! Your heavenly Father will always be with you! He loves you more than I ever could." Both frustration and a desire to comfort his little girl could be heard in this father's voice. At 42, he didn't want to leave his young family. Yet, hour by hour, cancer was stealing away the years he had hoped and planned for.

As Janet, now an adult, reflected on that moment decades earlier, she recalled shutting her bedroom door and collapsing in a sea of tears. She had hoped that her father wouldn't hear, but he did. Her father's words often come back to Janet, especially during celebrations of milestones in life in which her father is not physically present—graduations, marriage, the birth of a child, and so on. Janet relates that, in the midst of such loss, one of the greatest gifts we can give to others is the assurance that God is with us and that He will never forsake us, even in our hour of need.

FOR YOUTH	▣ TOPIC: A Dream and a Promise

▣ **QUESTIONS:** 1. What are the details of the ladder, or stairway, that Jacob saw? 2. What promise did the Lord make to Jacob concerning the land? 3. What pledge did God make to Jacob with respect to his future descendants? 4. What did Jacob realize when he awoke from his dream? 5. What did Jacob pledge to do if the Lord watched over him on his journey?

▣ **ILLUSTRATIONS:**

Never Alone. Charles Haddon Spurgeon was one of the greatest of the late nineteenth century preachers in England. In fact, he was called the "Prince of Preachers." He not only proclaimed the Gospel to thousands, but also converted thousands to the Lord with his dynamic preaching. There is another side, however, to Spurgeon's story. Toward the end of his life, he suffered from a sense of isolation because of his political differences with his previous friends; still, he did not feel that God ever abandoned him.

While Jacob was in flight, fearing for his life, God spoke to him in a dream. The Lord promised Jacob that He would always be with Him, even assuring him that He would look after his descendants. God's pledge to always be with His people still holds today. At times, most of us doubt God's presence when something unwelcome occurs in our lives; yet the Lord does not get frustrated and leave us because our faith wavers. Instead, He indicates to us in many ways that He is always close to us.

Reassuring Sound. A large teaching hospital's newborn section had a problem. The crying babies kept each other awake. The newborns needed quiet and sleep, but the distraught staff couldn't seem to find a way of reducing the sound level. Soundproofing the walls and ceiling didn't help to calm the infants. Finally, a staff member experimented with recording the heartbeat of each baby's mother and playing that recording beside the baby's bassinet. The effect was astonishing. The sound that each little one heard even before birth provided the security and comfort that brought calm.

Jacob had not thought much about the Lord until the young man had a strange dream while fleeing to Haran. Unsettled about the past and frightened about the future, he received the message, *I am with thee, and will keep thee in all places whither thou goest* (Gen. 28:15). Like the heartbeat of God, this message brought calm and a sense of relief to the fugitive Jacob. Regardless of our age, we too can draw similar comfort from God's promises to us.

I Have a Dream. On August 28, 1963, civil rights leader Martin Luther King delivered his now famous "I Have a Dream" speech at the Lincoln Memorial in Washington, D.C. King drew attention to the importance of treating all people fairly, regardless of their race, gender, or economic status. He also spotlighted his hope that equity and justice would one day exist for all people across the land. Perhaps the most noteworthy statement was his wish that his "four little children will one day live in a nation where they will not be judged by the color of their skin but by the content of their character."

What are some of your dreams, that is, the ambitions God has placed on your heart? What would the Lord have you do right now to bring about the fulfillment of these Christ-centered desires? Do not be afraid to dream big and achieve great things that bring honor to our Lord!

JACOB AND RACHEL

BACKGROUND SCRIPTURE: Genesis 29
DEVOTIONAL READING: Psalm 91

KEY VERSE: And Jacob served seven years for Rachel; and they
seemed unto him but a few days, for the love he had to her. Genesis 29:20.

KING JAMES VERSION

GENESIS 29:21 And Jacob said unto Laban, Give me my wife, for my days are fulfilled, that I may go in unto her. 22 And Laban gathered together all the men of the place, and made a feast. 23 And it came to pass in the evening, that he took Leah his daughter, and brought her to him; and he went in unto her. 24 And Laban gave unto his daughter Leah Zilpah his maid for an handmaid. 25 And it came to pass, that in the morning, behold, it was Leah: and he said to Laban, What is this thou hast done unto me? did not I serve with thee for Rachel? wherefore then hast thou beguiled me? 26 And Laban said, It must not be so done in our country, to give the younger before the firstborn. 27 Fulfil her week, and we will give thee this also for the service which thou shalt serve with me yet seven other years. 28 And Jacob did so, and fulfilled her week: and he gave him Rachel his daughter to wife also. 29 And Laban gave to Rachel his daughter Bilhah his handmaid to be her maid. 30 And he went in also unto Rachel, and he loved also Rachel more than Leah, and served with him yet seven other years.

31 And when the LORD saw that Leah was hated, he opened her womb: but Rachel was barren. 32 And Leah conceived, and bare a son, and she called his name Reuben: for she said, Surely the LORD hath looked upon my affliction; now therefore my husband will love me. 33 And she conceived again, and bare a son; and said, Because the LORD hath heard that I was hated, he hath therefore given me this son also: and she called his name Simeon. 34 And she conceived again, and bare a son; and said, Now this time will my husband be joined unto me, because I have born him three sons: therefore was his name called Levi. 35 And she conceived again, and bare a son: and she said, Now will I praise the LORD: therefore she called his name Judah; and left bearing.

NEW REVISED STANDARD VERSION

GENESIS 29:21 Then Jacob said to Laban, "Give me my wife that I may go in to her, for my time is completed." 22 So Laban gathered together all the people of the place, and made a feast. 23 But in the evening he took his daughter Leah and brought her to Jacob; and he went in to her. 24 (Laban gave his maid Zilpah to his daughter Leah to be her maid.) 25 When morning came, it was Leah! And Jacob said to Laban, "What is this you have done to me? Did I not serve with you for Rachel? Why then have you deceived me?" 26 Laban said, "This is not done in our country—giving the younger before the firstborn. 27 Complete the week of this one, and we will give you the other also in return for serving me another seven years." 28 Jacob did so, and completed her week; then Laban gave him his daughter Rachel as a wife. 29 (Laban gave his maid Bilhah to his daughter Rachel to be her maid.) 30 So Jacob went in to Rachel also, and he loved Rachel more than Leah. He served Laban for another seven years.

31 When the LORD saw that Leah was unloved, he opened her womb; but Rachel was barren. 32 Leah conceived and bore a son, and she named him Reuben; for she said, "Because the LORD has looked on my affliction; surely now my husband will love me." 33 She conceived again and bore a son, and said, "Because the LORD has heard that I am hated, he has given me this son also"; and she named him Simeon. 34 Again she conceived and bore a son, and said, "Now this time my husband will be joined to me, because I have borne him three sons"; therefore he was named Levi. 35 She conceived again and bore a son, and said, "This time I will praise the LORD"; therefore she named him Judah; then she ceased bearing.

BACKGROUND

After Jacob's encounter with God at Bethel (Gen. 28:10-22), he resumed his journey to the land of the east, which lay between Canaan and Mesopotamia (29:1). For the patriarch, this represented a fresh start, especially in light of the covenantal blessings God had promised to him. Evidently, Jacob did not have to go as far as the town of Haran (located in far northwestern Mesopotamia) before meeting up with the very people whom he had been seeking.

Jacob came upon three flocks of sheep lying in an open field beside a well and waiting to be watered (29:2). In that day, a broad, flat, thick stone with a round hole cut out in the middle covered the mouth of cisterns and wells. This stone in turn was covered by another heavy stone, which typically required several men to roll away. It was the custom for all the flocks to arrive before such a stone was removed. Then, once all the animals had been watered, the stone was rolled back over the mouth of the well (29:3). Jacob learned from shepherds (an occupation shared by both men and women in that culture) that they lived in Haran and that they knew a man named Laban, who was the grandson of Nahor (29:4-5). Jacob also found out that Laban was faring well. In fact, one of his daughters, Rachel, had just arrived with some of Laban's sheep (29:6).

Next, Jacob advised the shepherds to water their flocks and allow the animals to graze some more (29:7); but they explained that they were in the habit of waiting for all the flocks to be assembled before the stone was rolled off the mouth of the well so that the sheep could be watered (29:8). One reason for Jacob's behavior may have been that he disliked seeing workers wasting time; but a more romantic reason is that he wanted some privacy for his first meeting with Rachel.

While the conversation continued, Rachel arrived with her father's sheep, for she was tending them (29:9). Perhaps Jacob could see the beauty of the shepherdess from where he stood. Jacob's father had told him to marry a daughter of Laban (28:2), so Jacob probably guessed that this young woman was the person he had traveled so far to find. The patriarch, being energized by the sight of his cousin, used his own hands to remove the large stone covering the well. This demonstrated his strength to Rachel and enabled Jacob to be of service by watering his uncle's sheep (29:10).

The patriarch not only gave his cousin a customary kiss of greeting, but also wept aloud for joy (29:11). Clearly, this encounter was an emotional one for Jacob. Then, he explained to Rachel that he was a relative of her father and the son of Rebekah. In response, Rachel ran to tell her father. The young woman seems to have been well out in front of him. When Rachel finally reached Laban, she told him about Jacob (29:12). Upon hearing the news, Laban rushed out to meet Jacob, warmly embraced him, gave him a kiss of greeting, and brought him to his house (29:13).

Jacob took the opportunity to relate his situation to his uncle. Upon hearing his nephew's story, Laban openly acknowledged Jacob as being his own flesh and blood (29:14). The traveler had found a new home, where he lodged for the next month; but Jacob didn't lounge around in ease. He quickly began to participate in the routines of Laban's family. Undoubtedly, Jacob had a considerable amount of experience working with his father's sheep and goats. Now he helped take care of his uncle's flocks.

It was Laban who raised the issue of Jacob's wages. Thus far, the uncle had not paid anything to his nephew. Laban realized he could not expect Jacob to work for room and board indefinitely, so the uncle asked his nephew how much he wanted to be paid for his labor (29:15). It seems as if Laban viewed their relationship primarily in economic terms and treated Jacob as a laborer under contract (see 31:38-42). By asking him to name the wages he wanted, Laban probably expected to start a haggling process in the Eastern tradition; but Jacob didn't request money, livestock, or any other wage that could be negotiated. Instead, the patriarch wanted a specific reward, one that he had time to think about and mull over.

Laban the herdsman had two daughters, whom he treated like animals to be bartered in trade. The older daughter was named Leah (which means "cow"), while the younger one was named Rachel (which means "ewe"; 29:16). Leah lacked the kind of beauty people of that day seemed to prize, but the meaning of the Hebrew in 29:17 is uncertain. Views differ as to whether Leah's eyes were plain and dull or tender and delicate. While they may have been appealing in some way, she did not have the exceptional beauty of Rachel, who was gorgeous in both form and appearance. Because Jacob had fallen in love with Rachel, he offered to serve Laban seven years in exchange for the privilege of marrying his younger daughter (29:18). A person could create a lot of wealth in that period of time. Perhaps Jacob made such a generous offer because he had no dowry (or bride price) to give for Rachel. Laban was not so foolish as to reject such an offer, so he agreed to Jacob's terms (29:19).

Notes on the Printed Text

Genesis 29:20 says that Jacob did not seem to mind serving the required period of time for Rachel's hand in marriage. Though it was seven years, it felt like a few days to Jacob because he had such great love for his cousin. Perhaps Jacob felt as if the dowry was rather insignificant in comparison to what he was getting in return—Rachel's hand in marriage. Also, the lengthy engagement gave Jacob and Rachel time to develop their relationship so that they could be as ready as possible for marriage.

At the end of seven years, Jacob told Laban that their contractual agreement had been satisfied. Thus, Jacob wanted to consummate his marriage to Rachel (29:21). In response, Laban invited all the people in the area to celebrate with Jacob at a wedding feast (29:22). Earlier, in 29:19, Laban had responded ambiguously to Jacob. This was a shrewd decision on Laban's part, for he had not explicitly promised to give Rachel to Jacob in marriage; and to Jacob's chagrin, he was not astute enough to discern the vagueness in his uncle's reply.

When evening came, Laban brought his older, veiled daughter (see 24:65), Leah, to Jacob, and he had marital relations with her (29:23). Perhaps the older daughter said little or nothing that night, so that Jacob would not recognize her voice. According to the custom of the time, Laban gave his female servant, Zilpah, to Leah as her maid (29:24). Years earlier, Jacob had capitalized on the blindness of his father, Isaac, in order to deceive him and get the family blessing. Now Laban trumped that feat by using the cover of darkness to pull a fast one over his nephew. In this way, he gave the former trickster a large dose of his own toxic medicine.

We can only guess Rachel's feelings as she found out her father's plan. All her hopes and dreams were being cruelly disrupted by Laban's deceptive scheme. Perhaps he felt compelled to concoct it because he regarded Jacob as a worker who was too valuable to lose. Beyond question, the nephew had enabled Laban's flocks to increase steadily. With respect to Leah, she may have been forced to cooperate reluctantly with her father's plan. Without a doubt, God was using this episode to spiritually prune and mature Jacob.

In the morning, Jacob was shocked to discover that Laban had deceived him (29:25). The uncle's excuse was that local custom did not permit him to marry off a younger daughter before an older one (29:26). Once again, Jacob got into trouble because of rules favoring older children over younger ones. We do not know whether Laban was truly concerned about the custom of marrying the older daughter first; but his underhanded tactics had a long-term corrosive effect on his relationship with his nephew. It would also poison the dynamic between Laban and his two daughters. The Lord used this incident as one of several lessons designed to teach Jacob that it is better to rely on God than to trust in one's own devices.

Laban told Jacob to finish Leah's bridal week. Then, the uncle would give Rachel to her cousin in marriage. Of course, part of the deal was that Jacob had to put in seven more years of service (29:27). Throughout the transaction, Laban operated in a cunning and calculating fashion; and there was nothing Jacob could do about it. Jacob agreed to the terms stipulated by his uncle and received Rachel as his wife (29:28). Laban gave his servant, Bilhah, to his daughter as her personal attendant (29:29). We learn in 29:30 that Jacob loved Rachel more than Leah and willingly labored seven more years for Laban to fulfill their contractual agreement.

Jacob's having two wives inevitably led to rivalry between the sisters, especially over childbearing. Moreover, because Jacob loved Rachel more than Leah, the Lord enabled the latter to become pregnant. Rachel, however, remained childless (29:31). Leah's first pregnancy led to the birth of a son, whom she named *Reuben* (29:32), which means "look, a son." Leah reasoned that the Lord had seen her misery and that having Reuben would cause Jacob to have more love for his mother. Leah's second pregnancy led to the birth of another son, whom she named *Simeon* (29:33), which probably means "one who hears." Leah reasoned that the Lord had heard about her forlorn situation and intervened accordingly.

Leah named her third son *Levi* (29:34), which sounds like and may be derived from the Hebrew for "attached." The mother hoped this most recent childbirth would spur Jacob to bond more closely in affection to his less favored wife. Leah named her fourth son *Judah* (29:35), which sounds like and may be derived from the Hebrew for "praise." This name mirrored Leah's mood. By this time she was overjoyed at God's favorable response to her cry for help. Indeed, it was an occasion for her to give praise to the Lord. At this point, Leah stopped having children.

SUGGESTIONS TO TEACHERS

The biblical account of Laban's underhanded dealings with Jacob doesn't need to be "taught." The details are so vivid and the character traits so obvious that you can almost let this lesson be free-flowing, especially as the students comment on this week's Scripture passage. Nonetheless, consider keeping in mind the following aspects.

1. UNBOUNDED LYING. Begin the teaching time by telling the students the following adage: "Those who cook up stories usually find themselves in hot water." Then ask the class members whether they have experienced the truth of that saying in their lives. Explain that when we tell one lie, it usually leads to more false statements and half-truths.

2. DAMAGED RELATIONSHIPS. There's another adage worth putting forward: "Oh, what a tangled web we weave, when first we practice to deceive!" Explain that at first, the attempt at deception might seem to work; but eventually the twisted knot of lies begins to unravel, and when it does, the faith and trust others had in us usually unravels with it. There may be no worse feeling than to have someone who once loved you and believed in you say, "I'll never trust you again!"

3. TOXIC CONSEQUENCES. Direct the attention of the students to the Scripture lesson text concerning Laban and Jacob. Do not shy away from spotlighting the deceptive way in which the uncle mistreated his nephew and the long-term corrosive effect it had on their relationship. Explain that God certainly did not approve of

Laban's underhanded tactics; nonetheless, the Lord used it as one of several lessons meant to teach Jacob that it is better to rely on God than to trust in one's own devices.

FOR ADULTS	■ **TOPIC:** Dashed Hopes and Fond Wishes! ■ **QUESTIONS:** 1. Why did Jacob agree to serve Laban seven years in order to marry Rachel? 2. Why would Laban trick Jacob by giving him

Leah, rather than Rachel, as his wife? 3. What explanation did Laban offer when Jacob confronted him about his deceit? 4. What new requirement did Laban say Jacob had to fulfill in order to marry Rachel? 5. Why was Jacob so compliant with what Laban required?

■ **ILLUSTRATIONS:**

Relationships and Trust. One of the guiding principles of modern business is this: "Fool me once, shame on you. Fool me twice, shame on me." In other words, it should take only one, hard-won lesson to make us forever wary. If we fail to be sufficiently on our guard after that, it is clearly our own fault.

Not surprisingly, that attitude does not lead to mutually satisfying business partnerships. It makes even less sense when it becomes the guiding principle of our personal lives. It turns once-loving, trusting relationships into bitter disappointments: "I cannot believe she said that about me. I feel so offended!" "You swore you would never do that again. How can I ever believe another of your promises?" "He said he would not tell anybody—and he claimed to be my best friend!" Relationships are built on trust. Once deception enters the picture—a violated confidence, a broken promise, an outright lie—trust is shattered, and the memory of the deceit taints everything that follows.

Pure Greed. John A. Walker, Jr., was a U.S. Navy warrant officer who masterminded one of the most damaging spy rings in American history. He pleaded guilty to various counts of espionage, and received a sentence of life imprisonment with the recommendation that he never be paroled.

Walker had recruited his son, Michael, a 24-year-old Navy yeoman; his brother; and his best friend to sell Navy secrets to the former Soviet Union. Walker's only reason for his treachery was the money. At the convict's sentencing in Baltimore in November 1986, the judge said, "Your motive was pure greed, and you were handsomely paid for your traitorous acts. I look in vain for some redeeming aspect of your character."

Laban's cheating his daughters and their husband did not contribute any redeeming aspects to Laban's character. But God, nonetheless, used this greedy deceitful man for divine purposes.

Ruined Career. On March 3, 2006, former Congressman Randy "Duke" Cunningham was sentenced to eight years and four months in prison. According to Seth Hettena of the *Associated Press*, this is "the longest term meted out to a congressman in decades." Cunningham was found guilty of accepting money and gifts, including a "Rolls-Royce, a yacht, and $40,000 Persian rugs from defense contractors and others in exchange for steering government contracts their way and other favors."

Hettena noted that "Federal prosecutors sought the maximum sentence," while Cunningham's attorneys "asked for mercy." The disgraced former representative from southern California choked up as he addressed the judge and accepted blame for his crimes. Cunningham said, "Your honor, I have ripped my life to shreds due to my actions, my actions that I did to myself." Apparently, U.S. District Judge Larry Burns was convinced by Cunningham's display of remorse, for the federal official spared him from receiving a 10-year maximum sentence. Nevertheless, it's undeniable that Cunningham's acts of duplicity have ruined his career.

■ **TOPIC:** Date and Switch

■ **QUESTIONS:** 1. How did Jacob feel about serving Laban seven years for the privilege of marrying Rachel? 2. In what way did Laban deceive Jacob? 3. How did Jacob feel concerning what Laban had done to him? 4. What did Laban say Jacob had to do in order to secure Rachel's hand in marriage? 5. At first, why was Leah and not Rachel able to conceive and bear children?

■ **ILLUSTRATIONS:**

A Web of Lies. A relative of mine saw a layer of lies created when his daughter was in the third grade. Because she wanted the attention of her classmates, she told them that her mother had been in a serious car accident and that her arm was broken. The child's teacher caught wind of the student's fictional story and instructed the entire class to write get-well cards to the "injured" parent.

The third grader not only had to tell the class how delighted her mother was with the cards they made, but she also had to provide the class with daily reports about her mother's medical progress. It all came crashing down on the girl when her mother happened to go into the garbage to search for a bill she had misplaced. The parent discovered those cards and realized that her daughter was tangled in a web of lies. The mother took her daughter to school to confess and apologize to the girl's teacher and classmates. That confession produced a flood of tears.

The mother actually felt more sorry for her daughter than upset with her. It was a painful lesson for the third grader; but she and her peers learned that lies are like flies. They breed quickly and menace both the person who lied and the people who were lied to.

Far too many Christians are involved in one or more relationships in which they are entangled in a web of deceit. The deceptions may be small or great, but they still do their relationships no good. The best course of action is set these dysfunctional relationships on the right path by dealing honestly and candidly with all forms of pretense and duplicity.

Symbol of Deception. On August 19, 1915, at 3:00 P.M. near the Scilly Isles, the *Nicosian*, a liner converted to a transport, was steaming when a *U-27* surfaced and began to shell the ship. The *Nicosian* sent a distress call over its radio. Before the German submarine could dive, an old rusty steamer, the *Baralong*, appeared.

Believing that an opportunity to sink a second ship existed, the *U-27* did not dive. However, unseen by the Germans, the *Baralong*'s crew hurried to hidden guns. As the ship drew alongside, the Royal Navy ensign suddenly went up the mast and four-inch guns were unveiled. Within minutes, the *U-27* was sunk—a casualty of deception. The *Baralong* was a Q-ship, the British Navy's answer to the German submarine threat. Submariners called Q-ships "Judas ships," naming them for their trickery and deceit.

Like that submarine, some of you may have experienced deception or betrayal by someone you considered harmless or even a friend. Any betrayal is difficult to accept, especially when it comes at the hands of a family member. Jacob learned to think twice in his dealings with Laban.

Ripped Off! Brad was given one dollar by his parents when his family went to the flea market. Walking the aisles, he finally decided to buy a whoopee cushion, convinced of the fun that he would have later with his relatives. The salesman's pitch was persuasive as he promised the 11 year old the lowest price on Cape Cod. Brad accepted the adult's word and bought the novelty with his dollar.

That evening, while Brad and his mother shopped, Brad saw his whoopee cushion at the store for 69 cents. Brad was infuriated, claiming that he had been ripped off. If Brad could feel so cheated at something that cost so little, imagine how Jacob felt when he was tricked by Laban. Jacob's dream of marrying Rachel were foiled, at least for the moment. Jacob would have to give Laban an additional seven years of labor to see the goal of marrying Rachel brought to pass.

ESAU AND JACOB RECONCILED

BACKGROUND SCRIPTURE: Genesis 33
DEVOTIONAL READING: Psalm 133

KEY VERSE: And Esau ran to meet him, and embraced him, and fell on his neck, and kissed him: and they wept. Genesis 33:4.

KING JAMES VERSION

GENESIS 33:1 And Jacob lifted up his eyes, and looked, and, behold, Esau came, and with him four hundred men. And he divided the children unto Leah, and unto Rachel, and unto the two handmaids. 2 And he put the handmaids and their children foremost, and Leah and her children after, and Rachel and Joseph hindermost. 3 And he passed over before them, and bowed himself to the ground seven times, until he came near to his brother. 4 And Esau ran to meet him, and embraced him, and fell on his neck, and kissed him: and they wept.

5 And he lifted up his eyes, and saw the women and the children; and said, Who are those with thee? And he said, The children which God hath graciously given thy servant. 6 Then the handmaidens came near, they and their children, and they bowed themselves. 7 And Leah also with her children came near, and bowed themselves: and after came Joseph near and Rachel, and they bowed themselves. 8 And he said, What meanest thou by all this drove which I met? And he said, These are to find grace in the sight of my lord. 9 And Esau said, I have enough, my brother; keep that thou hast unto thyself. 10 And Jacob said, Nay, I pray thee, if now I have found grace in thy sight, then receive my present at my hand: for therefore I have seen thy face, as though I had seen the face of God, and thou wast pleased with me. 11 Take, I pray thee, my blessing that is brought to thee; because God hath dealt graciously with me, and because I have enough. And he urged him, and he took it.

NEW REVISED STANDARD VERSION

GENESIS 33:1 Now Jacob looked up and saw Esau coming, and four hundred men with him. So he divided the children among Leah and Rachel and the two maids. 2 He put the maids with their children in front, then Leah with her children, and Rachel and Joseph last of all. 3 He himself went on ahead of them, bowing himself to the ground seven times, until he came near his brother.

4 But Esau ran to meet him, and embraced him, and fell on his neck and kissed him, and they wept. 5 When Esau looked up and saw the women and children, he said, "Who are these with you?" Jacob said, "The children whom God has graciously given your servant." 6 Then the maids drew near, they and their children, and bowed down; 7 Leah likewise and her children drew near and bowed down; and finally Joseph and Rachel drew near, and they bowed down. 8 Esau said, "What do you mean by all this company that I met?" Jacob answered, "To find favor with my lord." 9 But Esau said, "I have enough, my brother; keep what you have for yourself." 10 Jacob said, "No, please; if I find favor with you, then accept my present from my hand; for truly to see your face is like seeing the face of God—since you have received me with such favor. 11 Please accept my gift that is brought to you, because God has dealt graciously with me, and because I have everything I want." So he urged him, and he took it.

9

Monday, October 22	Genesis 32:3-12	*Jacob's Prayer*
Tuesday, October 23	Genesis 32:13-21	*Jacob's Presents to Esau*
Wednesday, October 24	Genesis 33:1-4	*The Brothers Wept Together*
Thursday, October 25	Genesis 33:5-11	*The Gift of Reconciliation*
Friday, October 26	Genesis 33:12-15	*Their Separate Ways*
Saturday, October 27	Genesis 33:16-20	*An Altar to God*
Sunday, October 28	Psalm 133	*The Blessedness of Unity*

BACKGROUND

Prior to Jacob's meeting with his elder brother, the patriarch had sent a message to Esau that Jacob wanted to find favor in the sight of his brother (Gen. 32:5). One way to signal this intent was for Jacob, as he approached Esau, to bow toward the ground seven times (33:3). According to ancient records recovered by archaeologists, it was customary to bow this many times when approaching a monarch. Thus, Jacob demonstrated his respect for Esau, who had become a ruler in a region of the south. Jacob was also indicating that he regarded himself to be in a position of subservience to his brother.

Such an attitude of humility had taken two decades to develop in the patriarch. Indeed, throughout most of his life, Jacob had been a struggler. For instance, he pitted himself against Esau and Laban; but those conflicts were just reflections of Jacob's continuing struggle with God over who would control his life. A resolution of the issue occurred in the early morning hours before Jacob's reunion with Esau. The previous night, Jacob had dispatched the entire caravan across the Jabbok River, a main tributary on the Jordan River (32:22-23). Consequently, Jacob was left alone in the camp, which was east of the Jordan and north of the Jabbok rivers. We don't know why the patriarch stayed behind. Perhaps he intended to spend more time in prayer.

That night Jacob had an unusual encounter. Genesis 32:24 says that he wrestled with a mysterious man until daybreak, while 32:30 adds that Jacob had somehow seen God face to face. According to Hosea 12:4, this individual was an angel. Others conjecture this man was the Messiah before His birth at Bethlehem. One possibility is that Jacob wrestled with the angel of the Lord, a figure in the Old Testament who is identified as His messenger but speaks with the authority of God Himself.

In the unfolding episode, Jacob's opponent knocked his hip socket out of joint; nevertheless, the wrestling match continued, and the stranger's identity was about to be exposed by the early morning dawn. Before this could happen, however, the man told Jacob to release him. The patriarch refused to do so until his opponent blessed him (Gen. 32:25-26). In making this request, Jacob evidently suspected something was extraordinary about his adversary.

Next, the man blessed the patriarch by changing his name from Jacob to Israel

(32:27-28). The name *Jacob* pointed to his struggle with people, while the name *Israel* commemorated the wrestling match with the Lord's messenger. The new name signified a new beginning, a new opportunity, a new position, and a new person. Jacob's strength and tenacity would serve God anew, and the Lord would become the God of the patriarch's descendants. Also, it would be from Jacob's new name that the nation descended from him became known as Israel.

Despite Jacob's request, the stranger refused to disclose his name; instead, the man blessed Jacob, who suddenly realized that he had some sort of encounter with God (32:29). We don't know what form this blessing took. Perhaps it was a repetition of the blessings belonging to the Abrahamic covenant. To commemorate the event, Jacob named the place *Peniel* (32:30), which means "face of God." Though the patriarch had seen a manifestation of the Lord and expected to die (see Exod. 33:20; Judg. 13:22), God spared his life.

In terms of who won the wrestling match, the Lord's messenger acknowledged that he had been overcome by Jacob (Gen. 32:28). Nonetheless, Jacob wound up with a damaged hip and could only hold on to his adversary in a desperate embrace. If Jacob had let go in his injured state, God's emissary would have won. The conclusion of the match is a perfect image of Jacob's spiritual relationship with the Lord. The patriarch discovered that his need for the remainder of his life was to rely on the Lord.

As the sun rose, Jacob left Peniel limping because of his hip (32:31). A new day of trust in God dawned for Jacob. It formed the basis of his dependence on the Lord as the encounter with Esau drew closer. As the subsequent narrative of Genesis indicates, Jacob's character was transformed. From now on, he was truly God's servant, and Jacob's descendants, the Israelites, would be given the opportunity to serve the Lord and receive His covenantal blessings.

NOTES ON THE PRINTED TEXT

Apparently on the same morning that God blessed Jacob and gave him a new name, the patriarch saw Esau coming with his 400 men. There could be no mistaking them even at a distance. Jacob did not know Esau's intentions or how the gifts of livestock he had sent had been received (see Gen. 32:13-21). Accordingly, Jacob provided maximum protection for those he loved most. Earlier, when he divided his family into two companies, he evidently had kept all his wives and children in his own company (33:1). Now Jacob put Zilpah and Bilhah with their children in front, and behind them Leah and Rachel with their children (33:2). If Esau attacked, those in the back had the best possibility of escape.

The family members understood the significance of the ranking and how much or how little Jacob favored a particular group. Undoubtedly, it must have been vexing for certain mothers and their children to feel as if they were more expendable than others in the group. Perhaps this sort of favoritism fanned flames of inter-sibling rivalry and jealousy, especially over Joseph (an issue that figures prominently later in the Genesis account). In that time period, ancient Near Eastern society was patriarchal; and someone such as Jacob, as the eldest male in the clan, would have been regarded as the leader of the family. With the privilege of leadership came the responsibility of providing for and protecting the more vulnerable family members. In the present circumstance, Jacob went in front of the entire caravan (33:3).

At the sight of Jacob, Esau became filled with emotion. He ran to Jacob and showered him with signs of affection (33:4). The two-decade interval since the twins had seen each other had brought changes in both of them. Esau's former bitterness had been replaced with a gracious and tender spirit toward his brother. After the tears stopped flowing, the brothers naturally began to catch up on one another's lives. For the first time, Esau met Jacob's wives and children. When the elder twin asked about their identity, Jacob stated that the children were God's gracious gift. As a sign of submission, the patriarch was careful to refer to himself as Esau's *servant* (33:5).

In last week's lesson, we learned Jacob had married two wives. In the years that followed, the Lord's providential intervention led to the birth of the leaders of Israel's future 12 tribes. In turn, they would become God's chosen people, whom He would enable to enter and conquer the promised land. To them the Lord would reveal His glory, and with them He would establish the Mosaic covenant and law (Rom. 9:4). Indeed, they alone would be entrusted with the oracles of God (3:2). Such a bright future was due in part to the Lord's gracious intervention at the reunion of Jacob and Esau. The first members of the patriarch's family to arrive were his two concubines with their children, who bowed low in submission before Esau (Gen. 33:6). Next Leah came with her children, and they bowed down. Finally, Rachel and Joseph appeared and they likewise bowed (33:7).

The previous night, Jacob had selected a gift for his brother Esau. In some contexts, the Hebrew noun rendered *present* (32:13) can refer to the tribute a vassal paid to a monarch. This may be the emphasis in this verse, for earlier Jacob had referred to Esau as his *lord* (32:4) and himself as Esau's *servant*. Jacob picked out 550 animals of different kinds as gifts for the elder twin. Furthermore, Jacob arranged things so that Esau would receive those valuable animals in herds, one after another. Each time Esau received one drove, one of Jacob's servants would deliver a courteous message from their master (32:14-21). Clearly, the patriarch's intent was to build goodwill toward himself before he and his brother met.

After the initial reunion and exchange of introductions were finished, Esau brought up the subject of the herds Jacob had sent him. Of course, the patriarch's servants had told Esau that the animals were gifts; but the elder twin politely inquired to be sure of Jacob's intentions for the flocks and herds. Jacob explained that the droves were meant as presents to ensure the favor of Esau, whom Jacob deferentially referred to as his *lord* (33:8).

After Jacob offered his explanation, a battle of courtesy ensued (which was far better than a real battle; 33:9). Esau declined the generous gift, stating he did not need the animals because he already had many of his own; but Jacob insisted. The patriarch noted that by accepting the gift from his hand, Esau would also be demonstrating that his younger brother had found favor in his sight. Jacob felt that seeing his brother's friendly face and warm acceptance was as if the patriarch had seen the face of God (33:10). Jacob was alluding to the incident at the campsite he had recently left. It was there he had seen God face to face (32:30); and with the favorable encounter with Esau, the patriarch realized that the Lord had answered his prayer for protection (33:11).

Understandably, then, while Jacob remained polite, he also was insistent that his brother accept the present the younger twin had offered. Jacob explained that God had enabled him to materially prosper, so much so that he had all he needed. In 33:11, *blessing* could also be rendered "present." Perhaps the patriarch's gesture toward his brother was his way of making restitution for what he had stolen two decades earlier. Custom also decreed that by receiving the gift, Esau would be confirming his kind intentions toward the giver. Thus, upon Jacob's continued insistence, Esau accepted the gift of animals.

SUGGESTIONS TO TEACHERS

Despite Jacob's fears, his reunion with Esau was joyous. The elder brother evidently was content to forget how Jacob had wronged him. And Jacob had a new attitude of humility toward his brother. Jacob's account should remind us that God seems to delight in choosing the most unlikely persons for His work. God's selection of a once hypocritical shyster like Jacob to be the patriarch of His special community tells us that God also has plans for each of us.

1. EXPERIENCING GOD. Before class, write the following question on a chalkboard or sheet of newsprint: "What things dramatically change a close relationship you have with someone?" Ask the students to write answers under the question. Responses might include moving away, no longer having the same interests, and betrayal. By way of transition into this week's lesson, note that experiencing God should have the greatest impact on all our relationships.

2. CHOOSING RECONCILIATION NOT REVENGE. As you cover the Scripture lesson text, state that when Esau and Jacob finally met, the latter approached his brother humbly yet fearfully. In contrast, Esau's attitude was one of affection. He could have remained bitter over what Jacob had done two decades earlier; but God had so blessed Esau that he no longer seemed to hold a grudge against his younger brother. Instead, he was warm and friendly with Jacob and deeply moved by their long-delayed reunion. Encourage the class members to work for reconciliation in their relationships with others, not revenge.

3. BEING A BLESSING TO OTHERS. Explain to the students that the meeting between Jacob and Esau goes to show that we can start afresh in our relationships with others. Then, end the teaching time by thanking God for coming into the lives of the class members and changing them so wonderfully. Also, ask the Lord to continue to transform them into the image of Christ, with the result that they will be a blessing to others in their relationships.

| **FOR ADULTS** | ■ **TOPIC:** Family Reunion! |

■ **TOPIC:** Family Reunion!

■ **QUESTIONS:** 1. Why did Jacob divide his family before meeting with Esau? 2. What did Jacob initially think the encounter with his brother would be like? 3. What was the significance of Jacob bowing down to the ground seven times as he approached Esau? 4. How did Esau's greeting contrast with that of Jacob? 5. What explanation did Jacob give for the presentation of the flocks and herds?

■ **ILLUSTRATIONS:**

A Changed Life. In the early 1970s, the Watergate scandal toppled President Richard Nixon and his administration. Many of Nixon's aides were convicted of criminal charges and served time in prison. One of those who did was Charles Colson, a former Marine captain who served as the White House special counsel.

In the midst of being disgraced for his dealings in the Nixon White House and being sent to prison, Colson had a life-changing encounter with God, during which he became a devoted follower of Jesus Christ. Colson began to tell fellow inmates about the Savior and organize prison Bible studies.

Since departing from prison, Colson has been a leading voice for Christ not only among believers but also among unbelievers. He has written several best-selling books; and he has founded an effective prison ministry. Colson, who describes himself as a strong-willed and determined person, has determined to serve others in the name of Jesus instead of destroying or deceiving them.

Most of us do not have as interesting a testimony to share as Chuck Colson does, but the change God brings in us and in the way we relate to others is no less important. After Jacob encountered God at the Jabbok River, he faced his brother not with animosity and hatred but with humility and courage. Jacob's encounter with God affected not only his character and identity but also his relationship with others, particularly Esau.

The Bottom Line: Relationship. A friend related an experience that changed his life. As he awakened in his chair on an airliner to the words, "We have a very serious emergency," James suddenly looked toward his eternity. Three engines on the plane had been rendered useless because of fuel contamination, and the remaining one would lose power any second.

James decided to bury his head in his lap and pull up his knees. Then he made what he thought would be his last earth-to-heaven communication: "Oh, Lord, thank You! Life has been wonderful. . . . Oh, Lord, please be with my wife and my children, whom I'll never see again!"

Miraculously, the plane landed and at least one dazed passenger—James—roamed the airport piecing things together. He concluded, "Here is the bottom line: relationship." Nothing else matters. At that moment the family relationships he thought he had cherished went to a much deeper level. God had underscored their importance.

Prayer as ABCs. There is a story told about a Jewish farmer who, through carelessness, did not get home before sunset one Sabbath and was forced to spend the day in the field, waiting for sunset the next day before returning home. Upon his arrival, he was met by a rather perturbed rabbi who chided him for his neglect. Finally, the rabbi asked him, "What did you do out there all day in the field? Did you at least pray?" The farmer answered, "Rabbi, I am not a clever man. I don't know how to pray properly. What I did was simply to recite the alphabet all day and let God form the words for Himself."

When we come to worship, we bring the alphabet of our lives. If our hearts and minds are full of warmth and love toward others—beginning with the members of our family—then those are our letters. Share them with God. It is His task to make the words!

FOR YOUTH

■ **TOPIC:** Family Reunion

■ **QUESTIONS:** 1. What concerns did Jacob have about meeting his brother again? 2. In what way did Esau greet Jacob? 3. What explanation did Jacob offer for the presence of the women and children? 4. Why did Jacob offer so many presents to Esau? 5. Why did Jacob insist on Esau accepting his gift?

■ **ILLUSTRATIONS:**

No Knife or Noose! As the Civil War drew to a close, President Lincoln stood with his little son, Tad, on the steps of the White House listening to a band. One of the soldiers approached with a noose and a knife. He stated that these items were both to be used on Jefferson Davis (the President of the Confederate States of America).

Lincoln told the soldier that reconciliation was hard to effect when one approached with a knife and a noose. His son Tad asked why Davis should not be hanged. Lincoln responded that Davis and all the others should not be hung, and told the boy that he advocated a plan whereby all the rebels would be pardoned and not punished. Lincoln said that revenge was best left up to the Lord.

Lincoln saw an ideal way to resolve a conflict and restore a nation's citizens. Jacob and Esau, likewise, approached each other with open arms, not with a knife and a noose. Their family reunion became an occasion for rejoicing.

A Family Reunion? In 2006, *Madea's Family Reunion* debuted. According to Lions Gate Home Entertainment, the box office hit features a "pistol-packing grandma" who is "planning her family reunion." While doing so, she "must contend with the other dramas on her plate, including the runaway who has been placed under her care, and her love-troubled nieces." One of the most noteworthy taglines in the film is "Learn dignity. Demand respect."

This Hollywood version of a family reunion—which includes scenes of domestic violence, sex, and drug abuse—is a far cry from what we find in our Scripture lesson text. Esau and Jacob don't come after each other with weapons, but reunite in the warmth of God's love. And the virtue of forgiveness, not the vice of revenge, is the basis for their family reunion.

Spoiled Dreams. Near Peniel, the place in the holy land where Jacob had his dream, is a progressive town named Al-Bireh. Al-Bireh happens to be populated by Arabs, and lies within the borders of modern Israel. The forward-looking leaders of Al-Bireh have tried to build good relations with everyone, and had planned to develop a resort. The town had picked up the nickname "The City on the Move."

Then a small group of ultra-orthodox Israelis, the Gush Emunim, moved nearby to start a new settlement. This band of newcomers managed to convince Israeli government authorities to forbid the Arab townsfolk from doing any further construction.

Sadly, the site where Jacob dreamed of a harmonious existence for God's people everywhere has become a location where bitterness and injustice increase. The future for which Jacob was God's instrument now appears bleak in a region where Jacob once lived. Instead of reconciliation, suspicion and strife rule.

JOSEPH'S DREAM

BACKGROUND SCRIPTURE: Genesis 37
DEVOTIONAL READING: Psalm 70

KEY VERSE: And Joseph dreamed a dream, and he told it his brethren: and they hated him yet the more. Genesis 37:5.

KING JAMES VERSION

GENESIS 37:5 And Joseph dreamed a dream, and he told it his brethren: and they hated him yet the more. 6 And he said unto them, Hear, I pray you, this dream which I have dreamed: 7 For, behold, we were binding sheaves in the field, and, lo, my sheaf arose, and also stood upright; and, behold, your sheaves stood round about, and made obeisance to my sheaf. 8 And his brethren said to him, Shalt thou indeed reign over us? or shalt thou indeed have dominion over us? And they hated him yet the more for his dreams, and for his words. 9 And he dreamed yet another dream, and told it his brethren, and said, Behold, I have dreamed a dream more; and, behold, the sun and the moon and the eleven stars made obeisance to me. 10 And he told it to his father, and to his brethren: and his father rebuked him, and said unto him, What is this dream that thou hast dreamed? Shall I and thy mother and thy brethren indeed come to bow down ourselves to thee to the earth? 11 And his brethren envied him; but his father observed the saying. . . .

19 And they said one to another, Behold, this dreamer cometh. 20 Come now therefore, and let us slay him, and cast him into some pit, and we will say, Some evil beast hath devoured him: and we shall see what will become of his dreams. 21 And Reuben heard it, and he delivered him out of their hands; and said, Let us not kill him. . . .

23 And it came to pass, when Joseph was come unto his brethren, that they stript Joseph out of his coat, his coat of many colours that was on him; 24 And they took him, and cast him into a pit: . . . 28 Then there passed by Midianites merchantmen; and they drew and lifted up Joseph out of the pit, and sold Joseph to the Ishmeelites for twenty pieces of silver: and they brought Joseph into Egypt.

NEW REVISED STANDARD VERSION

GENESIS 37:5 Once Joseph had a dream, and when he told it to his brothers, they hated him even more. 6 He said to them, "Listen to this dream that I dreamed. 7 There we were, binding sheaves in the field. Suddenly my sheaf rose and stood upright; then your sheaves gathered around it, and bowed down to my sheaf." 8 His brothers said to him, "Are you indeed to reign over us? Are you indeed to have dominion over us?" So they hated him even more because of his dreams and his words.

9 He had another dream, and told it to his brothers, saying, "Look, I have had another dream: the sun, the moon, and eleven stars were bowing down to me." 10 But when he told it to his father and to his brothers, his father rebuked him, and said to him, "What kind of dream is this that you have had? Shall we indeed come, I and your mother and your brothers, and bow to the ground before you?" 11 So his brothers were jealous of him, but his father kept the matter in mind. . . .

19 They said to one another, "Here comes this dreamer. 20 Come now, let us kill him and throw him into one of the pits; then we shall say that a wild animal has devoured him, and we shall see what will become of his dreams." 21 But when Reuben heard it, he delivered him out of their hands, saying, "Let us not take his life." . . . 23 So when Joseph came to his brothers, they stripped him of his robe, the long robe with sleeves that he wore; 24 and they took him and threw him into a pit. . . .

28 When some Midianite traders passed by, they drew Joseph up, lifting him out of the pit, and sold him to the Ishmaelites for twenty pieces of silver. And they took Joseph to Egypt.

10

Home Bible Readings

Background

The narrative concerning Joseph begins when he was a young man of 17. He and some of his brothers were taking care of his father's flocks (Gen. 37:2). The brothers had done something they shouldn't have while away from home tending the sheep. Joseph saw the wrongdoing and let Jacob know about it. Commentators take different views of Joseph's action. Some censure him, calling him a tattletale, while others commend him, saying he was only acting as any conscientious son should. Although the text doesn't tell us so, the brothers undoubtedly had hard feelings toward their younger sibling because of his reporting of them.

Jacob increased the friction between the older brothers and Joseph by showing his preference for the firstborn of his favorite wife, Rachel. Genesis 37:3 explains that the patriarch loved Joseph more because he was born to his father in his old age. As a matter of fact, Joseph was Jacob's youngest son, next to Benjamin. Jacob showed his favoritism by giving Joseph a special tunic. It's hard to know the exact nature of this outer garment because of the unclear meaning of the Hebrew word that describes it. Differing opinions conjecture that the robe had long sleeves or was richly embroidered. In any case, it distinguished Joseph as the favored son of Jacob and the future ruler over the family.

When Jacob was younger, his mother liked him more than Esau, while Jacob's father preferred Esau. This display of parental favoritism led to threats of murder and to a deep rupture between the fraternal twins. Having seen the damage such preferential treatment can do, Jacob should have known better than to repeat the same mistake among his children. Beyond question, as Joseph wore the ornate robe, it became a source of constant irritation to his siblings. They were reminded that their father loved Joseph best, a realization that fueled resentment and jealousy. The brothers' hatred of Joseph prevented them from being able to speak to him kindly (37:4).

Notes on the Printed Text

The biblical text relates that Joseph experienced two dreams. In the ancient world, people believed that dreams were a window into knowing the future. This sentiment proved to be true in the case of Joseph, for God sent the dreams to show the superior blessings He would give to Rachel's firstborn. After having the dream, Joseph told it to his brothers and in turn their hatred of him intensified (Gen. 37:5). Some commentators allege that Joseph was gloating over his siblings, that his demeanor was arrogant, or that his manner was condescending. There is nothing in the text, however, to support these views.

In the first dream (37:6), Joseph saw himself and his brothers tying up sheaves of grain in the middle of a field. This was a normal harvest scene; but suddenly, Joseph's bundle stood up. Then, his siblings' bundles surrounded Joseph's sheaf and bowed down to it (37:7). The Hebrew verb used here denotes the kind of worship and obeisance servants would give to their master. The brothers correctly interpreted the dream to mean that one day they would bow down to Joseph as their ruler (37:8). This literally happened when Joseph became a ruler in Egypt. As a result of the dream and Joseph's retelling of it, his siblings hatred of him rose a notch higher. Given the existing family dynamics, the response of the brothers is understandable. They may also have been unsettled by what Joseph related, especially if they genuinely wondered whether God was using the dream to disclose what He would do in the future.

In Joseph's second dream, he saw the sun and moon (the parents of the clan) as well as 11 stars (the siblings) bow down to him (37:9). This time Joseph described the dream to his father as well as his brothers. Now even Joseph's indulgent father was upset with his favorite son. He expressed dismay at what he perceived was audacity and rebuked Joseph for it. Jacob accurately interpreted the dream to mean that he, his wife Leah (Joseph's mother, Rachel, had died by this time), and his sons would all bow down to Joseph (37:10). This dream, too, referred to the future when Joseph would be a ruler in Egypt. While Jacob kept in mind and pondered what Joseph said, his brothers grew all the more jealous of him (37:11).

In relating the dreams, Joseph was only telling the truth; but some commentators suggest that he was unwise to mention the dreams and that he was motivated by pride. There are few clues in the text, however, to support this view. Later in the Genesis narrative it is disclosed that Joseph had the ability to interpret dreams. Perhaps, then, he had an inkling of what his first and second dreams meant. Also, while he could have remained silent about the dreams, he chose to tell them. Of course, regardless of whether Joseph should have kept his mouth shut, his brothers were wrong to nurse feelings of jealousy and hatred against him.

Some time after Joseph's dreams, most of Jacob's sons took his flocks about 50 miles north to Shechem (37:12). A desire to get away from Joseph may have been one reason why they traveled so far from their home in the Valley of Hebron; but if so, it did no good, for Jacob sent Joseph after them to find out how they were doing (37:13-14). Neither the father nor his favored son could have known that more than two decades would pass before they laid eyes on each other again.

When Joseph reached Shechem, a man noticed him wandering around the countryside. When the man asked Joseph what he was looking for, he explained that he was in search of his brothers. Joseph requested help from the stranger in finding where the group was grazing the flocks under their care. When the man mentioned overhearing them talk about going on about 15 miles north to Dothan, Joseph left for the place and found his brothers there (37:15-17).

For some time, feelings of ill will toward Joseph had been festering in hearts of his brothers. Thus, when the siblings spotted Joseph from a distance wearing his ornate robe, they hatched a scheme to murder him (37:18). The brothers literally referred to Joseph as "this master of dreams" (37:19). The sarcastic tone of their statement reflected the resentment they felt toward Joseph and the dreams God had given him. The plan involved throwing the younger sibling into a nearby dry cistern.

Jacob's sons agreed to lie about the demise of Joseph. When asked about him, they would claim that a vicious, wild animal had attacked and devoured him. Their uncontrolled jealousy and hatred had brought them to such an intention. They thought they could get away with their scheme because Joseph was away from their father's protection, and there were no witnesses nearby to report their actions. They assumed that by getting rid of their dreaded younger brother, the siblings could prevent his dreams from coming true (37:20). They did not realize that God would use their actions to make the dreams a reality.

Based on Genesis 37:2, some think the sons of Bilhah and Zilpah (namely, Dan, Naphtali, Gad, and Asher; 30:4-13) were the instigators of the murderous plot. When Reuben (the firstborn son of Jacob through Leah) heard the plan, he came to Joseph's rescue by advising his brothers not to take the younger sibling's life (37:21). Rather than harm Joseph and thereby shed innocent blood, Reuben urged the rest to bind Joseph and place him in the cistern, presumably to die of thirst and hunger (37:22).

Reuben secretly planned to help Joseph escape and bring him back unharmed to Jacob. The tide of events, though, would wash away Reuben's good intentions. More effective would have been for him, as the elder son of the group, to put a complete end to the scheme. Despite whatever admirable qualities he had, Reuben previously comprised his integrity and standing in the family by becoming involved in incest with Bilhah, the concubine of his father (35:22). Perhaps the memory of that incident spurred Reuben to make a halfhearted attempt to rehabilitate himself in the situation involving Joseph.

Joseph eventually reached his brothers; but rather than being greeted warmly, the older siblings stripped him of his ornate robe and thus his status. This was the special tunic he wore out of respect for his father (37:23). The brothers, by harming Joseph, dishonored Jacob. After removing Joseph's outer garment, the siblings threw him into a nearby empty cistern. Though there was no water in it (37:24), the underground tank would have been musty and moldy. For health reasons, it would not be a hospitable place to stay for very long.

The callous nature of the brothers is evident as they sat down to eat some food (37:25), seemingly indifferent to Joseph's pleas for mercy (42:21). Sometime during the meal, they spotted a caravan of traders. In ancient times, travel was extremely dangerous. The threat of robbers and wild animals discouraged most people from venturing out alone or even in small groups. For safety on the unmarked roads between Syria and Egypt, caravans such as the one mentioned in this verse were often formed.

The traders spotted by Jacob's sons were carrying spices, balm, and myrrh down to Egypt (37:25). These were goods used in medicine, cosmetics, and preparing the dead for burial. Judah, the fourth son of Jacob and Leah, questioned how he and his siblings would be profited by murdering their brother and hiding his body. All they would gain from such an act was a guilty conscience (37:26). What the group failed to appreciate is that any harm they brought to Joseph would be a moral stain on their lives and an issue God would deal with as the Genesis narrative unfolded.

Judah's face-saving scheme involved not directly laying a hand on Joseph. Instead, they would sell their despised younger brother to the Ishmaelites. Archaeological records indicate that the Egyptians were always open to purchasing slaves, as well as other commodities, from traders such as the Ishmaelites. Judah's plan would not only get rid of Joseph, but also make some money for his brothers at the same time. The group liked Judah's idea and so went along with it (37:27). When the siblings pulled Joseph out of the cistern, he initially may have thought that he would be freed; but perhaps to his dismay, his brothers sold him as slave to the Ishmaelites for 20 pieces of silver. The traders then took him to Egypt (37:28).

SUGGESTIONS TO TEACHERS

Favoritism is the practice of giving unfair preferential treatment to one person or group at the expense of another. This is exactly the case in the family of Jacob. He loved Joseph more than any of his other sons and gave him a special tunic to wear as a symbol of his preference. While this may have helped Joseph to feel special, it infuriated his brothers, who became increasingly resentful of him.

1. THE PRESENCE OF FAVORITISM. Whether we are doing it consciously or not, we may be showing favoritism toward one person at the expense of someone else. Parents, pastors, teachers, bosses, and grandparents are just some of the people who should examine how they are treating others to see if they are playing favorites—and then change that attitude to God's attitude. The Lord, who loves the entire world of people (John 3:16), plays no favorites. In heaven's eyes, no one is overlooked or insignificant.

2. THE LASTING EFFECTS OF FAVORITISM. The effects of favoritism may be hidden for years, especially if those not favored are afraid to voice their feelings. Accumulated hatred and bitterness almost caused Esau to kill Jacob (Gen. 27:41) and certainly motivated Joseph's brothers to sell him as a slave. Anger about preference may produce a *root of bitterness* (Heb. 12:15) that can contaminate families, groups, or even entire communities for a long time.

3. THE POWER OF GOD TO HEAL THE SCARS OF FAVORITISM.

Perhaps you are the one who has been overlooked or ignored; or perhaps you know someone who has been rejected by a parent or superior. God's Spirit can heal even the most damaged person; and all Christians can help heal the victims of favoritism by loving them as God loves. Your friendship may help someone who has been rejected to feel like a person of value.

FOR ADULTS

■ **TOPIC:** Interpreting a Call!

■ **QUESTIONS:** 1. Why did Joseph's brothers harbor so much hatred for him? 2. What was the response of Joseph's brothers to his first dream? 3. What was the response of Joseph's father to his son's second dream? 4. Why would Joseph's brothers want to harm him? 5. What led to Joseph being sold as a slave in Egypt?

■ **ILLUSTRATIONS:**

Eliminating Undue Partiality. "WANTED: Mother. Salary: $00. No retirement, no insurance, no guarantees. Bonuses for a job well done may include a few hugs and kisses. Skills required: Must love children, cats, dogs, hamsters, and fish. Must have nursing experience for kissing 'owies,' and lots of bandages. Must be able to love a kid, even when he's rotten." This tongue-in-cheek advertisement, from *What Kids Need Most in a Mom* by Patricia Rushford, is a good beginning for a never-ending job description. An equally overwhelming one would apply to a father.

Parents know that each child has a "love tank" that requires daily refueling. If this is neglected for any child, his or her "engine" can shut off. The same thing happens in other areas of life when we show undue partiality to particular co-workers, relatives, or even Sunday school students. Pray this week that God would disclose any people in your life to whom you are paying more attention at the expense of others; and consider it part of His call for you to make things right.

Jealousy's Effects. Henry Ford and a business partner named James Couzens started the automobile manufacturing enterprise in 1903 that became known as the Ford Motor Company. Couzens' genius in sales, finance, and administration was key to the success of the new venture. In fact, had it not been for his leadership, the new company would not have survived. Ford was strong in engineering but weak in the areas where Couzens had skills and experience. Many of the well-known policies and practices of the famous car manufacturer were actually Couzens' ideas, though Ford claimed them as his own.

Ford began to grow jealous of Couzens and his brilliant ideas. Finally, in 1917, Ford threw Couzens out after the latter warned that the company would have to do more than produce the Model T. But Ford stubbornly maintained that they should continue manufacturing the same model without introducing any improvements. He even refused to change the color of the Model T from plain black. Ford continued building the same car year after year until he almost ruined his company. In fact, his jealousy cost him dearly, for the Ford Motor Company almost failed due to his actions against Couzens.

Jealous as a Crab. Professional crabbers know that a top on a crab basket is unnecessary. As one crab crawls up to get out of the basket, the others grab at that crab and pull it back down. Joseph's brothers, all evidently lacking in self-esteem, were jealous of their younger sibling. And like a bucket full of crabs, they metaphorically grabbed at him and forced him down. Then, when he continued to outshine them, they chose to eliminate him. Even today, people with low self-esteem can sometimes act like that. Because they do not feel good about themselves, they are prone to be jealous of others. They may even feel tempted to undermine what others are doing in order to make their own accomplishments look better.

FOR YOUTH

■ **TOPIC:** Dreamer in the Pit

■ **QUESTIONS:** 1. What was similar in the two dreams Joseph experienced? 2. Why were Joseph's brothers so resentful of him? 3. What alternative plan did Joseph's brothers adopt? 4. How did Reuben try to intervene on behalf of his brother? 5. Where did the Midianite traders take Joseph?

■ **ILLUSTRATIONS:**

Martin's Mistake. The famous portrait artist, Sir Henry Raeburn, was born in 1756 in Edinburgh, Scotland, into a poor, hardworking family. He showed some artistic ability as a boy and was apprenticed as a goldsmith, but he wanted to paint. Raeburn was able to enroll as a pupil of David Martin, then the most famous portrait painter in Scotland.

Raeburn progressed well as an artist painting miniatures, which were in vogue at the time. He soon became so proficient at producing likenesses of his subjects that Martin became jealous. Martin's resentment grew so intense that he felt he could not protect his own position of being the preeminent painter. Thus, he refused to give Raeburn any further training. Martin thought that by dismissing Raeburn he had forever limited his pupil's ability to succeed. Instead, Martin's move out of jealousy enhanced Raeburn's development. The young artist was freed to develop his own highly original style of portraiture.

Raeburn went to Rome, where he spent two years studying Michaelangelo's masterpiece in the Sistine Chapel. He then returned to Edinburgh in 1787. Much to Martin's disgust, Raeburn soon achieved a position of prominence in the Scottish capital. His famous subjects included Sir Walter Scott and nearly all the great personalities of the late 18th century. Martin's envy served to boost Raeburn to greater heights than he otherwise would have achieved if he had stayed to produce miniatures!

The vengeful act of Joseph's brothers enabled him to rise to prominence, and eventually to save an entire generation of his family from suffering and starvation. Just think of the great things God can do through you, even though you may be the target of jealousy and resentment from others. The key is to trust the Lord for wisdom and strength to do the right thing at all times.

Disillusioned Son. Over a century and a half ago, a German Jewish family's son experienced disillusionment over his father's actions. The family had been pious, practicing Jews, and faithfully followed the synagogue's traditions. When the family moved to another city, the father announced one evening that they would no longer be taking part in the local synagogue's services. Instead, he informed his wife and son that they would begin going to a Lutheran church.

When the lad asked why, the father only offered that it was important to him. Then the son became upset over being torn from his roots and religious practices, and confronted his father to find the reason for the change. The father emphatically said that he wanted to have the business contacts that came from going to the Lutheran congregation. He then scolded his son for not accepting that this move would be profitable for everyone in the family. The son never got over his bitterness.

Later, the young man went to England, and toiled on his writings in the British Museum in London. Today, we know this resentful person as Karl Marx. His atheistic philosophy called Marxism rested on the famous line in his book *Das Kapital*: "Religion is the opiate of the people." A father that failed to provide the spiritual foundations for a boy led to one of the most destructive philosophies in modern times.

Favorites. Upon returning from a shopping trip, John noticed that his brother and sister were each carrying a new Beanie Baby. Without even asking his mother about the trip or how it had gone, John demanded, "And what did you buy me?" Children have a passionate sense of equality and do not want to see any favoritism whatsoever. Joseph's brothers were much like John. Filled with a sense of equality, they simply refused to allow any favoritism. And this nearly led them to commit murder.

JOSEPH'S DREAM COMES TRUE

BACKGROUND SCRIPTURE: Genesis 41:25-45
DEVOTIONAL READING: Psalm 105:16-22

KEY VERSE: And Pharaoh said unto Joseph, Forasmuch as God hath shewed thee all this, there is none so discreet and wise as thou art. Genesis 41:39.

KING JAMES VERSION

GENESIS 41:25 And Joseph said unto Pharaoh, The dream of Pharaoh is one: God hath shewed Pharaoh what he is about to do. 26 The seven good kine are seven years; and the seven good ears are seven years: the dream is one. 27 And the seven thin and ill favoured kine that came up after them are seven years; and the seven empty ears blasted with the east wind shall be seven years of famine. 28 This is the thing which I have spoken unto Pharaoh: What God is about to do he sheweth unto Pharaoh. 29 Behold, there come seven years of great plenty throughout all the land of Egypt: 30 And there shall arise after them seven years of famine; and all the plenty shall be forgotten in the land of Egypt; and the famine shall consume the land; 31 And the plenty shall not be known in the land by reason of that famine following; for it shall be very grievous. 32 And for that the dream was doubled unto Pharaoh twice; it is because the thing is established by God, and God will shortly bring it to pass.

33 Now therefore let Pharaoh look out a man discreet and wise, and set him over the land of Egypt. 34 Let Pharaoh do this, and let him appoint officers over the land, and take up the fifth part of the land of Egypt in the seven plenteous years. 35 And let them gather all the food of those good years that come, and lay up corn under the hand of Pharaoh, and let them keep food in the cities. 36 And that food shall be for store to the land against the seven years of famine, which shall be in the land of Egypt; that the land perish not through the famine. 37 And the thing was good in the eyes of Pharaoh, and in the eyes of all his servants. 38 And Pharaoh said unto his servants, Can we find such a one as this is, a man in whom the Spirit of God is? 39 And Pharaoh said unto Joseph, Forasmuch as God hath shewed thee all this, there is none so discreet and wise as thou art: 40 Thou shalt be over my house, and according unto thy word shall all my people be ruled: only in the throne will I be greater than thou.

NEW REVISED STANDARD VERSION

GENESIS 41:25 Then Joseph said to Pharaoh, "Pharaoh's dreams are one and the same; God has revealed to Pharaoh what he is about to do. 26 The seven good cows are seven years, and the seven good ears are seven years; the dreams are one. 27 The seven lean and ugly cows that came up after them are seven years, as are the seven empty ears blighted by the east wind. They are seven years of famine. 28 It is as I told Pharaoh; God has shown to Pharaoh what he is about to do. 29 There will come seven years of great plenty throughout all the land of Egypt. 30 After them there will arise seven years of famine, and all the plenty will be forgotten in the land of Egypt; the famine will consume the land. 31 The plenty will no longer be known in the land because of the famine that will follow, for it will be very grievous. 32 And the doubling of Pharaoh's dream means that the thing is fixed by God, and God will shortly bring it about. 33 Now therefore let Pharaoh select a man who is discerning and wise, and set him over the land of Egypt. 34 Let Pharaoh proceed to appoint overseers over the land, and take one-fifth of the produce of the land of Egypt during the seven plenteous years. 35 Let them gather all the food of these good years that are coming, and lay up grain under the authority of Pharaoh for food in the cities, and let them keep it. 36 That food shall be a reserve for the land against the seven years of famine that are to befall the land of Egypt, so that the land may not perish through the famine."

37 The proposal pleased Pharaoh and all his servants. 38 Pharaoh said to his servants, "Can we find anyone else like this—one in whom is the spirit of God?" 39 So Pharaoh said to Joseph, "Since God has shown you all this, there is no one so discerning and wise as you. 40 You shall be over my house, and all my people shall order themselves as you command; only with regard to the throne will I be greater than you.

11

Monday, November 5	Genesis 39:1-6a	*In Potiphar's House*
Tuesday, November 6	Genesis 39:6b-10	*Joseph Refuses*
Wednesday, November 7	Genesis 39:11-20	*Revenge*
Thursday, November 8	Genesis 41:1-8	*Pharaoh's Dream*
Friday, November 9	Genesis 41:25-36	*Joseph the Interpreter*
Saturday, November 10	Genesis 41:37-45	*Second-in-Command*
Sunday, November 11	Psalm 105:16-22	*God's Wonderful Works*

BACKGROUND

Once Joseph became the slave of Potiphar, the quality of his character began to show itself. Joseph did not wallow in self-pity, but energetically carried out the tasks set before him (Gen. 39:1-3). Moreover, as 39:2 stresses, the Lord was with Joseph. Although the young man was separated from everyone and everything familiar to him, God helped him to be successful in whatever he did. This enabled Joseph to respond positively to the turn of events in his life. As an experienced leader of men, Potiphar was not long in noticing Joseph's abilities. The official promoted Joseph from common house servant to personal attendant and then to steward of the entire household. In each position, the young man's work was blessed by God. Soon Joseph had Potiphar's complete confidence. Without supervision, Joseph ran everything in the house (39:3-6).

Joseph's smooth sailing eventually became turbulent when Potiphar's wife made bold sexual advances toward the handsome steward. Despite the repeated attempts of Potiphar's wife, Joseph refused to morally compromise. This so vexed Potiphar's wife that she falsely accused Joseph of trying to rape her. Potiphar's response was to commit Joseph to the prison reserved for political detainees—probably the most comfortable facility available (39:7-20). Nonetheless, Joseph's experience was by no means easy. The injustice of his treatment must have wounded him as much as it would anyone; but he remained faithful to God because God remained faithful to him. In particular, the Lord blessed Joseph, which enabled him to gain the favor of the warden and rise to full responsibility over the prison (39:21-23).

While incarcerated, Joseph used his God-given abilities to interpret the dreams of two fellow prisoners, Pharaoh's cupbearer (or food taster) and baker. The baker's dream meant that he would die, while the cupbearer's dream meant that he would be reinstated to his post. Joseph asked the cupbearer to intercede on his behalf with Pharaoh; but when the cupbearer was released from confinement, he forgot about Joseph (40:1-23). Two more years passed before Pharaoh experienced his own dreams. In the first one, he found himself standing on the banks of the Nile River, the source of Egypt's prosperity and power. He saw seven ugly, gaunt cows devour seven fat, healthy-looking cows (41:1-4). In Pharaoh's second dream, he saw seven heads of shriveled and withered grain swallow up seven heads of plump, well-formed grain (41:5-7). The next morning the Egyptian ruler summoned all his priests who were experienced with magic, divination, and soothsaying, but none of them could interpret his dreams (41:8).

The incident triggered the memory of Pharaoh's cupbearer, who recalled his own prior experience with Joseph (41:9-13). This prompted the ruler to order Joseph's immediate release from prison. After he had shaved and changed clothes, Joseph found himself standing before the most powerful man in the known world. Pharaoh's request was straightforward. He needed Joseph to interpret his troubling dreams. The young man stated that while he didn't have any innate ability to do this, God would supply the interpretation the ruler desperately desired (41:14-16). Having this assurance, Pharaoh recounted his dreams (41:17-24).

NOTES ON THE PRINTED TEXT

We can only imagine how clearheaded the Egyptian ruler became as he focused his attention on the lowly, foreign prisoner appearing before him. Joseph explained that both dreams of Pharaoh had the same meaning. The God whom Joseph worshiped and served—despite his years of hardship and isolation—was using him to disclose to Pharaoh what the Lord would soon do (Gen. 41:25). Joseph pointed out that the seven fat cows and the seven plump heads of grain both represented seven years of prosperity (41:26). In contrast, the seven gaunt, ugly cows and the seven withered heads of grain represented seven years of famine (41:27).

Joseph's reference to the *east wind* merits further comment. In the Middle East, a hot wind off the desert often shrivels and destroys crops in agricultural areas such as Israel and Egypt. In Israel, this wind is called the *sirocco* and regularly blows from the east, off the Arabian deserts, in late spring and early fall, with devastating effects (Jer. 4:11-12; Ezek. 19:10-12; Hos. 13:15). Egypt has a similar scorching wind, called the *khamsin*, that blows in from the deserts and wilts crops in the Nile River valley.

By means of the explanation Joseph offered, he clarified the significance of the symbolism in Pharaoh's two dreams. God gave the Hebrew the correct interpretation so that he in turn could make known to the powerful ruler what the Lord was about to do (Gen. 41:28). In this regard, both dreams had identical messages. There would be seven years of abundance in the kingdom (41:29). Then, following the time of plenty, there would be seven years of terrible famine. In fact, it would be so widespread and horrific that all the prosperity would be forgotten and wiped out due to the devastating effects of the famine (41:30).

Egypt (41:29) refers to the country in the northeast corner of Africa. In ancient times, its territory extended from the first waterfall of the Nile River in the south to the Mediterranean Sea in the north (about 650 miles). The only inhabitable areas were the narrow Nile Valley and the broad alluvial Nile Delta through which the long river reached the Mediterranean Sea. Egypt was the home of one of the earliest civilizations. Its culture was rich and complex, having developed over a period stretching from about 3000 B.C. to Roman times.

Joseph's announcement of a kingdom-wide famine posed a real threat to Egypt's dominance on the international scene. A brief episode of drought might be endured without much concern; but the disaster Joseph foretold would be so severe and prolonged that it could decimate the powerful nation situated along the Nile River (41:31). The Hebrew ex-prisoner noted that Pharaoh's experience of two versions of the same dream was God's way of signaling to the ruler that the matter was divinely decreed and would soon occur (41:32).

Because God was sure to act as He had declared through Joseph, the Hebrew urged Pharaoh to take immediate action. In particular, the Egyptian ruler was advised to find someone who was wise and discerning. Such an individual would be aware and informed as well as mature and experienced. This person would also exhibit keen insight and good judgment. Joseph recommended that this even-tempered and morally grounded overseer be placed in charge of a nationwide program (41:33).

Next, Joseph recommended that Pharaoh appoint officials throughout the land to collect one-fifth of the produce harvested during the seven plentiful years (41:34). In ancient Egypt, farming followed a regular cycle. First, the Nile River would flood the land in September, October, and November, providing moisture and a layer of rich soil in which to plant crops. If the Nile did not flood because of low rainfall upstream, famine would follow. After the flood, farmers would plant their crops immediately, before the ground dried out. Then they would harvest the crops in March or April.

Some of the harvest would be given to the town temple for the priests. The rest would be stored in granaries for future use, but a portion was collected as annual taxes by government officials, who carefully counted the harvest. Much of the government's grain went to the pharaoh's storehouses. Thus, the Egyptians would have been used to an official like Joseph collecting grain for Pharaoh; and Scripture says that Joseph used the circumstances of the famine to increase Pharaoh's influence in Egypt (47:23-26).

The commissioners Joseph advised being appointed would have responsibility for gathering all the excess food and grain during the seven years of abundance to come. In turn, the officials—operating under the authority of Pharaoh—were to stockpile these supplies in the royal storehouses located in various cities throughout the realm (41:35). By adopting this strategy, Pharaoh could ensure that there would be enough food to eat when the seven years of famine came. To do otherwise would bring about widespread starvation, resulting in the eventual ruin of the nation. Joseph's proposed course of action was the only way for Egypt to survive the calamity (41:36).

The advice Joseph gave made sense to Pharaoh and all his officials (41:37). As the royal court discussed who should be appointed to oversee the entire operation, Pharaoh openly wondered whether they could find a better person than Joseph, someone in whom resided the spirit of God (41:38). The ruler's rhetorical question expected a negative answer.

Pharaoh took at face value Joseph's earlier statement that God had revealed to him the meaning of the king's dreams (41:16). Pharaoh was convinced that the Hebrew—though a foreigner—was the wisest and most discerning person throughout the entire realm (41:39). Thus, it made sense to appoint the 30-year-old to be the national overseer. In order for Joseph to direct the project, he would manage the household of Pharaoh and have charge over all his officials and inhabitants. They were to submit to the Hebrew's commands. Only the Egyptian ruler would rank higher than Joseph and retain supreme authority (41:40).

It was unusual for Pharaoh to appoint a foreigner for such a vital task as preparing for a famine and to give him so much power in the kingdom. It was especially unusual for the Egyptian ruler to place a relatively young, unknown, and unproven prisoner in an office of such great authority. Only God could have made such an act possible. Joseph had risen from slavery and prison to be the second most powerful person in Egypt, but God's plans for Joseph were just beginning.

To make the appointment official, the Egyptian ruler gave the former Hebrew prisoner the signet ring off his own finger, new clothes, and a chariot. During the seven years of abundance, Joseph married Asenath, the daughter of an Egyptian priest. Also, before the famine came, Asenath bore Joseph two sons, Manasseh and Ephraim (41:41-52). Life was undoubtedly busy and absorbing for Joseph, both personally and professionally. It became even more so as the seven years of drought and hunger began, for Pharaoh directed his starving population to go to Joseph for the food they needed to survive. The famine extended even to Canaan and impacted its inhabitants (41:53-57).

SUGGESTIONS TO TEACHERS

The narrative recorded in Genesis 39—41 puts so much material before you for this week's lesson that you could teach several weeks from these chapters and still not exhaust the possibilities. You'll need to organize your thoughts so as to keep your teaching time focused and your discussion flowing. For today's class period, the following are some of the salient points to keep in mind.

1. WISDOM FROM GOD. The account of Joseph shows us how God gives us wisdom and how we can use that wisdom to help others. Even though he was only 30 when he went before Pharaoh, Joseph was already wise in God's ways, since he had learned to trust God in hard places. We are wise when we trust God through crises. We can then use that godly wisdom to help others—for instance, as we share with a struggling friend what God has done for us.

2. OPPORTUNITIES TO HELP OTHERS. These come when we least expect them. Joseph was brought quickly from prison to the court of Pharaoh. That is why we must walk close to the Lord every day, so we will be ready when He calls us to serve. We must be prepared to alter direction if God suddenly changes our circumstances. Moreover, we never know how far-reaching will be the effects of our sharing godly wisdom. Joseph interpreted Pharaoh's dream correctly and saved Egypt. Later, he saved his own family from starvation. Similarly, people will seek our help in times of need if they have seen God in us.

3. ALL GLORY TO GOD. Pharaoh recognized that God spoke through Joseph. People should notice our humility, acts of kindness, and wise advice as God works through us—but He receives the glory for what we do for Him. Joseph gave God the credit for the correct interpretation of Pharaoh's dream. Likewise, when God gives us wisdom to help others, all the glory belongs to Him.

FOR ADULTS

■ **TOPIC:** A Dream Unfolds!

■ **QUESTIONS:** 1. To whom did Joseph give the credit for the ability to interpret Pharaoh's dreams? 2. What was God signaling by giving Pharaoh two dreams? 3. How did each of Pharaoh's dreams indicate that there would be seven years of plenty? 4. How did each of Pharaoh's dreams indicate that there would be seven years of famine? 5. How did Pharaoh respond to Joseph's advice?

■ **ILLUSTRATIONS:**

A Grand Dream. Isambard Brunel had a dream of building a great ship to sail from England to Australia. In 1857, he lauched the *Great Eastern*. She was 693 feet long, five times the size of any ship afloat! With five gilded and mirrored salons and 800 cabins, she was supposed to be a floating palace. While the predecessor of the modern ocean liner never made much money, she successfully laid the transatlantic cable that ushered in the age of modern instant communication.

Joseph's dreams were greater than Brunel's. Joseph's dreams were of God's power and activity in the adult Hebrew's life and the lives of all those in the world around him. God is also able to unfold similar aspirations in our lives.

Reality Out of Dreams. Joseph's dreams led him to serve. In modern times, another such person was a Canadian physician named Frederick Grant Banting. After World War I, Banting took a job lecturing at Western Ontario Medical School. In the course of time, he had to prepare a lecture on diabetes. Little was known about the dreaded disease. Banting read all the literature he could find on the subject, prepared his lecture, and went to bed. The physician, however, could not sleep. He tossed and rolled as various questions swirled through his mind: *Why is it that some bodies cannot utilize the sugar in their blood? Why does the sugar continue to build up until death occurs? Why? Why? WHY?*

One of the articles Banting had read said that the pancreatic gland of a normal person had large, dark spots on it called "islands," but in a person afflicted with diabetes these "islands" had shrunk to a fraction of their normal size. It must be, thought Banting, that these dark spots have something to do with the disease. Then an idea flashed: Could he take these "islands" off the pancreas of a normal animal, inject a solution from them into a diabetic animal, and prevent or cure the disease?

Early the next morning, the physician asked his superior at the medical school for an assistant and 10 dogs with which to carry out experiments. Though Banting was practically laughed out of the school, he persisted. When his friends heard about it, they begged him not to forsake a great future in surgery for such an outlandish experiment. Nonetheless, Banting persisted in pursuing the idea that arose from his dream. He and his assistant began work on the dogs that the school had supplied. They used the 10; then 25; then 75. Finally, 91 dogs had been killed in the efforts of the researchers to find a cure.

Then, when Banting and his assistant were experimenting on their 92nd dog, something unexpected happened. As the animal lay dying of diabetes, they injected some of the serum. The sugar in its blood began to increase, and a few hours later the dog was up barking and wagging its tail. This was the opening the researchers had been waiting for. Finally, after many heartbreaking failures, Banting was awarded the Nobel Prize in Medicine for his work on diabetes. And today, because of his dream, millions of people with the disease live an almost normal life, instead of expecting an early death.

Modern Josephs. In a large metropolitan area, there is a block known as Welfare Square. In it stands a large silo filled with 19 million pounds of wheat, enough to feed a small city for six months. The grain is there as a reserve to be used in a time of need. A large denominational church, which stores the grain, wants to be able to take care of the poor and needy if the normal channels of distribution ever cease to function. This religious group has taken the experience of Joseph to heart and stored grain. What will you do to help feed the hungry?

FOR YOUTH

■ **TOPIC:** A Dream Come True

■ **QUESTIONS:** 1. What prompted Pharaoh to release Joseph from prison? 2. How did Joseph seek to honor God? 3. What did Pharaoh's dreams mean? 4. What was Joseph's plan for coping with the coming disaster? 5. Why did Pharaoh chose to elevate Joseph to a position of prominence in Egypt?

■ **ILLUSTRATIONS:**

A Fulfilled Dream. Fe Wale, a Presbyterian Filipino pediatrician, directs the Marina Clinic outside of Dumaguete in the southern Philippines. At one point, she was captured by rebels, who insisted that she perform the surgery required to remove a bullet from their leader. They refused to accept the fact that as a pediatrician, the last surgery she had done was in medical school years earlier. So with a prayer, some boiling water, and a makeshift operating table, she successfully performed the operation.

Today Fe Wale's community health workers, wearing identifying T-shirts, are free to work unhampered in the rural areas where many other services have ceased because of the threat of rebel activity. For this saved pediatrician, it is a dream come true. God is also able to make our dreams of service for Him come to pass in His time and in His way.

Wayside Encounter. A rough road winds over the wooded hill that rises above our neighborhood. While walking there with my son, we were alerted by the din of a motorcycle. It soon went silent, and a young man came in sight. He had a satchel slung from his shoulder, and as we approached, it appeared that he was busily picking up beer cans left by others in the thick growth by the roadside.

This person was in military uniform, but, as we learned, acting on his own initiative in an off hour. His purpose was to make the spot, which he had known in childhood, a fit and decent place for recreation. He explained his project to restore disused paths for hikers that intersected the road here and there. After we left him, he mounted his noisy vehicle and tore through the bypaths to test the clearance and the condition of the ground.

For his chance observers, it was a heartening encounter. Here was a young man, barely of voting age, happily and eagerly engaged in a service to the community that nobody expected of him. He was not one of a company of workers recruited under some advertised plan and relying upon the stimulus of the group. He merely hoped that his effort would make things better in the neighborhood and suggest larger action of the sort by the community leaders. It is a reminder that there are young people around us who do not have to be regimented into service, for whom a social need is a direct challenge to be met. Perhaps this could also be true of you!

Suffering Recognized. Legendary professional golfer Chi-Chi Rodriguez finally met Mother Teresa of Calcutta at an airport in the Pacific in August 1997. All of his life Chi-Chi had been impressed by Mother Teresa's care for the poor, especially the suffering children. Chi-Chi himself had grown up in tremendous poverty, the son of a sugarcane cutter. As a boy, Chi-Chi had carried the golf bags of three men for $1.70 a day. Like the woman he admired, he too devotes much of his time to alleviate the suffering of the children of the world, particularly through the youth foundation he established in Clearwater, Florida.

God called Joseph to alleviate the suffering and hunger of his world. And like Chi-Chi and Mother Teresa, Joseph realized he had to act. Will you?

GOD PRESERVED A REMNANT

BACKGROUND SCRIPTURE: Genesis 43:1—45:15
DEVOTIONAL READING: Psalm 85

KEY VERSE: God sent me before you to preserve you a posterity in the earth, and to save your lives by a great deliverance. Genesis 45:7.

KING JAMES VERSION

GENESIS 45:1 Then Joseph could not refrain himself before all them that stood by him; and he cried, Cause every man to go out from me. And there stood no man with him, while Joseph made himself known unto his brethren. 2 And he wept aloud: and the Egyptians and the house of Pharaoh heard. 3 And Joseph said unto his brethren, I am Joseph; doth my father yet live? And his brethren could not answer him; for they were troubled at his presence. 4 And Joseph said unto his brethren, Come near to me, I pray you. And they came near. And he said, I am Joseph your brother, whom ye sold into Egypt. 5 Now therefore be not grieved, nor angry with yourselves, that ye sold me hither: for God did send me before you to preserve life. 6 For these two years hath the famine been in the land: and yet there are five years, in the which there shall neither be earing nor harvest. 7 And God sent me before you to preserve you a posterity in the earth, and to save your lives by a great deliverance. 8 So now it was not you that sent me hither, but God: and he hath made me a father to Pharaoh, and lord of all his house, and a ruler throughout all the land of Egypt. 9 Haste ye, and go up to my father, and say unto him, Thus saith thy son Joseph, God hath made me lord of all Egypt: come down unto me, tarry not: 10 And thou shalt dwell in the land of Goshen, and thou shalt be near unto me, thou, and thy children, and thy children's children, and thy flocks, and thy herds, and all that thou hast: 11 And there will I nourish thee; for yet there are five years of famine; lest thou, and thy household, and all that thou hast, come to poverty. 12 And, behold, your eyes see, and the eyes of my brother Benjamin, that it is my mouth that speaketh unto you.

NEW REVISED STANDARD VERSION

GENESIS 45:1 Then Joseph could no longer control himself before all those who stood by him, and he cried out, "Send everyone away from me." So no one stayed with him when Joseph made himself known to his brothers. 2 And he wept so loudly that the Egyptians heard it, and the household of Pharaoh heard it. 3 Joseph said to his brothers, "I am Joseph. Is my father still alive?" But his brothers could not answer him, so dismayed were they at his presence.

4 Then Joseph said to his brothers, "Come closer to me." And they came closer. He said, "I am your brother, Joseph, whom you sold into Egypt. 5 And now do not be distressed, or angry with yourselves, because you sold me here; for God sent me before you to preserve life. 6 For the famine has been in the land these two years; and there are five more years in which there will be neither plowing nor harvest. 7 God sent me before you to preserve for you a remnant on earth, and to keep alive for you many survivors. 8 So it was not you who sent me here, but God; he has made me a father to Pharaoh, and lord of all his house and ruler over all the land of Egypt. 9 Hurry and go up to my father and say to him, 'Thus says your son Joseph, God has made me lord of all Egypt; come down to me, do not delay. 10 You shall settle in the land of Goshen, and you shall be near me, you and your children and your children's children, as well as your flocks, your herds, and all that you have. 11 I will provide for you there— since there are five more years of famine to come—so that you and your household, and all that you have, will not come to poverty.' 12 And now your eyes and the eyes of my brother Benjamin see that it is my own mouth that speaks to you."

12

BACKGROUND

The famine that afflicted Egypt also plagued the land of Canaan. In turn, this forced Jacob to send his remaining sons (except for Joseph's full brother, Benjamin) to Egypt to buy grain for the family. Such a transaction required them to deal directly with Joseph. After recognizing his brothers and remembering the dream of his youth, the powerful overseer of the land began an elaborate test to see what kind of adults his brothers had become over the years. Joseph started the test by accusing his siblings of being spies and imprisoning them for three days. Joseph then held Simeon as hostage and allowed the other brothers to return to Jacob with food for the family. Joseph also ordered that the money they had brought to buy food be hidden in their sacks of grain. He informed them that to buy more grain and save Simeon, they would have to return before him with Benjamin (Gen. 42:1-20).

Jacob thought he had already lost one of his sons born to Rachel—Joseph. Now the patriarch thought he was in danger of losing his other son born to Rachel—Benjamin—who was probably then in his twenties or early thirties; however, to save the family from starvation, a reluctant Jacob allowed Benjamin to return with his other sons to Egypt. The reformed brothers immediately attempted to return the money that had mysteriously appeared in their grain sacks on the last trip. They also purchased more grain for the family. Then with Simeon returned to them, they all began their journey back to Canaan (42:21—44:3).

The siblings hadn't traveled far before they discovered another phase of Joseph's test. He had again hidden their money in the grain sacks and had hidden his silver cup in Benjamin's grain sack. Joseph's servant accused Benjamin of the crime and offered to let the other brothers go free while he took Benjamin to become Joseph's slave. Instead of saving themselves, the brothers risked their lives by returning to Egypt to plead for Benjamin's freedom. Judah functioned as the spokesperson for the group (44:4-32). After offering a summary and explanation of recent events, Judah concluded by pleading with Joseph to be kept in Egypt as a slave in place of Benjamin. The young man, in turn, would be permitted to return with his other brothers to their home in Canaan (44:33). Judah explained that the alternative would involve him returning to his aged father without Benjamin, and Judah could not bear to witness the devastation Jacob would feel (44:34).

Judah's speech proved that he was not the same man who earlier had come up with the idea of selling Joseph to Midianite traders. It had taken a long time, but the Lord had worked changes in his heart. As Judah was telling about Jacob's sorrow and was offering himself as a substitute for Benjamin, Joseph must have listened with rising emotion. He had wanted to find out if the selfish, vengeful brothers he knew in his youth had changed. By means of his test, Joseph verified that his siblings had not only matured, but also become God-fearing adults. Finally, the overseer could hide his feelings no more. Not for a minute longer could he stand in front of his brothers and pretend to have a merely official interest in them.

NOTES ON THE PRINTED TEXT

Joseph's brothers must have been stunned when they heard him command his Egyptian attendants to leave the room (Gen. 45:1). Probably all along Joseph had been talking to his siblings through an interpreter to disguise the fact that he could understand their Hebrew speech. The tender reunion that was about to occur would be a family matter, and presumably Joseph didn't want any outsiders around to distract him and his brothers. Moses described Joseph's emotional release as so powerful that his weeping could even be heard by the servants who had departed from the area. Somehow, the household of Pharaoh also learned about the incident, perhaps by means of an official report (45:2).

The sons of Jacob were shocked to hear the second-most powerful person in Egypt declare, *I am Joseph* (45:3). For more than 20 years, his siblings thought of Joseph as enslaved or dead. Since meeting Joseph, they never for a moment suspected that the ruler dressed in Egyptian finery and speaking the Egyptian language was their long-lost brother; but there he stood, saying in Hebrew that he was their sibling. Joseph quickly followed up his self-revelation by asking about the father he had not seen for over two decades. Beyond question, this was the concern closest to the heart of the overseer. Thus, he was eager to have more news about his father. Until this point, Joseph would have aroused suspicion by showing too much interest in Jacob.

Joseph's brothers made no reply to his question, for they were still in shock over finding themselves in the presence of their sibling. Evidently, they had not mentioned the name of the brother who—as the cover-up story went—had been killed by an animal (see 42:13; 44:28). Perhaps Joseph's use of his own name convinced them of his true identity. Now they were confused and terrified and undoubtedly wondered if he would eliminate them for what they had done to him. Thinking that perhaps the brothers did not believe he was who he said he was, Joseph called them to him so that they could take a closer look at his face (45:4). Then he repeated his claim to be Joseph, the sibling whom they long ago had sold into slavery. Only Joseph himself could have known the secret that they had mistreated him so shamefully.

Of course, Joseph's brothers were dumbfounded by his revelation. The person they had terribly wronged was now in a position of absolute power over them. He could imprison, enslave, or execute his siblings with just a word. The overseer's emotional outburst only added to their fear of his vengeance; however, like his brothers, he was a different person than the 17-year-old adolescent who was thrown into a cistern. Joseph urged his siblings not to be angry with themselves for their past misdeeds. Ultimately, God had been working in the circumstances that had brought Joseph to Egypt. Though the brothers' actions in the past were despicable, God had used their decisions to place Joseph in a position of authority so that he could rescue Egypt and his own family (45:5).

Joseph explained that the two years of famine that had already passed would extend to seven. (This means that he was now 39 years old.) During this time, the drought would be so severe that neither plowing nor harvesting would occur (45:6). This would be just as true for the family of Jacob as for the entire nation of Egypt. Without immediate assistance and long term help, the Israelite clan would not likely survive. Over the years, Joseph had plenty of time to reflect on the strange turn of events his life had taken. As a person of faith, he could discern God's purposes in what had happened to him. God would use Joseph to preserve a *posterity* (45:7), or remnant, of His people. Joseph's words reminded his brothers of the great peril facing their family and implied that they would be rescued only because God had something special in store for the Israelite clan.

One of the most enduring concepts in Scripture is the *remnant*—a faithful minority who survive a catastrophe or judgment. This notion especially applied to the descendants of Jacob, whom Moses later said had been made a *holy people unto the* LORD *thy God* (Deut. 26:19). *Holy* renders the Hebrew word *qodesh*, which means "separation" or "set apart." In the Old Testament, *qodesh* is frequently applied to the Israelites as God's people. Thus, the descendants of Jacob, as the Lord's upright remnant, were to be separated from sin, impurity, and evil. They were also to be set apart for the sole use of their possessor, Yahweh.

The main point of Joseph's explanation is that ultimately God—not Jacob's sons—was responsible for sending the former Hebrew slave and prisoner to Egypt. Joseph said that the Lord had made him a *father to Pharaoh* (Gen. 45:8). Joseph was speaking figuratively of someone giving others advice, as parents would to their children. In the case of Pharaoh, he relied on Joseph's foresight and prudence. In the years since the Egyptian ruler had appointed him as second-in command, the Hebrew had proven his trustworthiness and dependability. Both the royal household and the entire land of Egypt were in good hands.

Since the first time Joseph's brothers had appeared before him, the overseer had worked out a plan for the family. He would settle them in Egypt. Joseph knew that the Israelite clan had to act quickly in order to survive the famine, which had several more years to go. Thus, he directed his brothers to exhort their father not to delay in relocating the entire family. As reassurance that this was the divinely ordained course of action, Joseph noted that God had made him *lord of all Egypt* (Gen.45:9).

Joseph's plan was to settle the entire Israelite clan—family members, their livestock, and all their possessions—in the land of Goshen (45:10). This region was located in the northeastern section of the Nile River delta. Although the area is not large (about 900 square miles), it was considered some of the best territory in Egypt. With irrigation, it was an excellent site for grazing and for growing certain crops. The Hebrew people were still living in the region at the time of the Exodus, four centuries later. Joseph, as the second-in-command in Egypt, promised to provide the Israelite clan what they needed and would watch over them, especially in the five years of famine that remained. Left on their own in Canaan, Jacob's family would either die from starvation or scatter from the plight of their destitution. Joseph wanted to ensure that the entire group remain together and safe in Egypt (45:11).

Joseph wanted there to be no doubt among his siblings that he truly was their long lost brother. Thus, he dispensed with an interpreter and spoke directly to his brothers (45:12). With the important explanations over, Joseph embraced and wept with his brothers, beginning with the youngest. Benjamin was Joseph's only full brother and the only one innocent in regard to the overseer. Earlier, when Joseph was pretending to be an Egyptian, he must have wanted more than anything to embrace Benjamin and the others. The high ranking official did not have to restrain himself anymore. This mutual display of emotion and the conversation that followed completed the family reunion (45:13-15). Whatever bitterness Joseph may have felt toward his brothers was all gone now. They had nothing to fear from him, for he had forgiven them.

SUGGESTIONS TO TEACHERS

The truth of God's oversight over all that occurred lay at the heart of the reconciliation between Joseph and his brothers. None of them could reverse the wickedness the siblings were guilty of committing against Joseph; but the realization that God can bring good out of evil paved the way for the severed relationship to be restored and rehabilitated. That which was humanly impossible to achieve the Lord sovereignly brought about in His own time and in His own way.

1. IDENTIFYING THE BROTHERS. Joseph's brothers had long since put him out of mind. When they turned up in Egypt to buy food because of the famine back home, they didn't recognize Joseph, for he was dressed in his official uniform as the number two person in the kingdom; but Joseph recognized his siblings.

2. DISPLAYING EMOTION. The biblical text portrays Joseph as an emotional, sensitive man. The moment when he revealed his identity to his brothers is not the first time in the narrative that he cried. He did so briefly, but secretly, when he had Simeon taken from his brothers and held prisoner (Gen. 42:24). Then he showed even more emotion when he first saw his brother Benjamin. So his brothers would not see him cry, he left them and wept by himself for a while in his private room (43:30). Later, he would weep for a long time when he saw and embraced his father Jacob after the passage of more than 20 years (46:29).

3. RESTORING THE RELATIONSHIP. Joseph did not hesitate to welcome his brothers as beloved family members. Be sure to mention the way the Father has restored us to Himself through His Son. In turn, God wants us to mend the broken relationships around us.

4. DISCLOSING GOD'S PURPOSE. Reserve enough teaching time for the key verse of the lesson: *God sent me before you to preserve you a posterity in the earth, and to save your lives by a great deliverance* (45:7). The Lord is in the business of creating newness and of fostering a freshness that takes an unhappy past and ensures that God's purposes will prevail.

FOR ADULTS	■ **TOPIC:** Negative Actions, Positive Results!

■ **QUESTIONS:** 1. Why did Joseph have all the Egyptian attendants leave his presence? 2. Why did Joseph weep so intensely? 3. Why were Joseph's brothers terrified in his presence? 4. What reason did Joseph give for being in Egypt? 5. What plan did Joseph have for the Israelite clan?

■ **ILLUSTRATIONS:**

No Divine Preconditions. The sign on the high-school football team's locker room door read: "Everyone is welcome to play football! To play you must: 1. Give 110%! 2. Be at practice everyday! 3. Have a positive attitude! 4. Listen to your coach!" While the sign said *welcome*, there were preconditions. Joseph welcomed his brothers unconditionally. Expressed differently, there were no preconditions to his offer of reconciliation.

Moreover, despite circumstances that looked less than favorable at first, God accomplished His purposes in Joseph's life; and God's plans for him went beyond his brother's intentions. Sometimes when our plans are frustrated, we feel that God is indifferent or has forgotten us; but we can trust that God loves us and that He has the ability to bring His best out of the worst circumstances.

End of Warring. Over a century ago, Argentina and Chile had each mobilized for war. The relationship between the two neighboring countries in South America had frayed so badly that fighting seemed inevitable. The main area of contention was over the boundary separating the two nations in the Andes mountains. National pride among leaders and people in both countries demanded that the other yield or face invasion and bloody battles.

Then on Easter, in 1900, Bishop Benoventa pleaded for both sides to submit to arbitration, and prayed for a peaceful resolution of the conflict. Thankfully, the heads of government in the two states agreed. And eventually, Argentina and Chile signed a Treaty of Arbitration.

Symbolizing the agreement, both sides melted down their cannons. The tons of metal from the discarded artillery were used to forge a great statue known as *The Christ of the Andes*. It was dedicated on March 13, 1904, and stands in Uspallata Pass, high in the mountain range, on the Argentine-Chilean boundary. In 1937, a tablet was added, bearing in Spanish the inscription: "Sooner will these mountains crumble into dust than Argentines and Chileans break the peace sworn at the feet of Christ the Redeemer."

The Wonder of God's Plan. Jim Elliot, Nate Saint, Pete Flemming, Ed McCulley, and Roger Youderian were martyred in 1956, shortly after they arrived in the jungles of Ecuador to bring the gospel to the Auca Indians. It was a witness that could not be ignored. They were a testimony that faith in God is more precious than life itself. Five years after she watched those martyrdoms, a woman named Dawa became the first Auca Christian. Other conversations followed. Then, 36 years later, the Aucas (also known as the Huaoranis) received their first complete New Testament.

Some wonder if Elliot and his associates could have planned their missionary outreach better and thus worked longer for the Lord; yet God allows some candles to burn fast and brilliantly, while others burn long and steadily. Both are a part of His plan.

FOR YOUTH

■ **TOPIC:** Gotcha!

■ **QUESTIONS:** 1. Why was Joseph concerned about the welfare of his father? 2. Why would Joseph's brothers be bothered by their past decision to sell him into slavery? 3. How did Joseph convince his brothers concerning his identity? 4. How did Joseph come to see God's activity in the experience of being sold as a slave? 5. How was God using Joseph to preserve many lives?

■ **ILLUSTRATIONS:**

Enjoy the Ride. When leaders Mark and Jana set out with their youth group for Pennsylvania from Michigan, they knew the church's bus was not in the best shape. Still, they had not expected to stop dead in bumper-to-bumper traffic on an Ohio interstate exit ramp—on a Sunday morning. There was little the group could do but push the stalled bus onto the shoulder, raise the hood, and pray for help.

Soon a woman on her way to church stopped to find out how she could help. "Well," Mark said, "we need a mechanic." "There's a mechanic in our church," the woman said. "Let me see what I can do." Once at church, the woman interrupted the service to tell the congregation about the group's plight and ask for assistance. She returned to the broken-down bus with a few other churchgoers. "I can repair the bus," one man said. Another pulled Mark aside and said, "I would like to put your group up for the night at our church while you wait for the repair. I would also like to buy your dinner."

That breakdown taught the group important lessons about God's faithfulness. It could have been a time of grumbling and frustration. Instead, they were all reminded that God's purposes exceed our plans, especially as He works to accomplish His will in our lives. We must simply remember whose children we are—and enjoy the ride.

Joyful Reunion. In 1969, Candan Canen Muyan graduated from Elizabeth Forward High School. A few days later, she said goodbye to her "family" (Ellie and Romel Nicolas and their daughter Judy) in Greenrock, Pennsylvania, to fly back to Turkey. Candan had stayed with the Nicolases as part of an American Field Service (AFS) experience. Over the next three decades, Candan and Judy kept in contact. They saw one another in Germany when Candan was married. Still, Candan dreamed of seeing her "family" once again.

Finally, in July 1997, Candan made the trip to the United States. A large Fourth of July family reunion began a week that included bike trails, shopping, amusement parks, family dining, and limousine tours. The Nicolas family wanted to celebrate their reunification after 28 long years. If an American family was able to celebrate so much the return of an adopted AFS daughter's return, imagine what the reunion was like for Joseph and his siblings!

Forgiven and Reunited. In late October 1978, Jefferson Davis was once again made a United States citizen. His citizenship had been removed by a Reconstruction Era congress that wanted to punish the Confederacy. Davis, who had been President of the Confederate States of America, died in 1889. He had been the last confederate leader still ostracized. (General Robert E. Lee had his citizenship restored in 1975.) In finally forgiving and reuniting Davis with his country, President Jimmy Carter said that the nation needed to clear away the guilt, enmity, and recriminations of the past. Joseph must have felt the same as Carter, for Joseph knew that the past must be put aside so that new beginnings can take place.

JACOB BLESSED HIS FAMILY

BACKGROUND SCRIPTURE: Genesis 48:8-21
DEVOTIONAL READING: Psalm 145:1-13

KEY VERSE: Israel said unto Joseph, I had not thought to see thy face: and, lo, God hath shewed me also thy seed. Genesis 48:11.

KING JAMES VERSION

GENESIS 48:11 And Israel said unto Joseph, I had not thought to see thy face: and, lo, God hath shewed me also thy seed. 12 And Joseph brought them out from between his knees, and he bowed himself with his face to the earth. 13 And Joseph took them both, Ephraim in his right hand toward Israel's left hand, and Manasseh in his left hand toward Israel's right hand, and brought them near unto him. 14 And Israel stretched out his right hand, and laid it upon Ephraim's head, who was the younger, and his left hand upon Manasseh's head, guiding his hands wittingly; for Manasseh was the firstborn. 15 And he blessed Joseph, and said, God, before whom my fathers Abraham and Isaac did walk, the God which fed me all my life long unto this day, 16 The Angel which redeemed me from all evil, bless the lads; and let my name be named on them, and the name of my fathers Abraham and Isaac; and let them grow into a multitude in the midst of the earth. 17 And when Joseph saw that his father laid his right hand upon the head of Ephraim, it displeased him: and he held up his father's hand, to remove it from Ephraim's head unto Manasseh's head. 18 And Joseph said unto his father, Not so, my father: for this is the firstborn; put thy right hand upon his head. 19 And his father refused, and said, I know it, my son, I know it: he also shall become a people, and he also shall be great: but truly his younger brother shall be greater than he, and his seed shall become a multitude of nations.

NEW REVISED STANDARD VERSION

GENESIS 48:11 Israel said to Joseph, "I did not expect to see your face; and here God has let me see your children also." 12 Then Joseph removed them from his father's knees, and he bowed himself with his face to the earth. 13 Joseph took them both, Ephraim in his right hand toward Israel's left, and Manasseh in his left hand toward Israel's right, and brought them near him. 14 But Israel stretched out his right hand and laid it on the head of Ephraim, who was the younger, and his left hand on the head of Manasseh, crossing his hands, for Manasseh was the firstborn. 15 He blessed Joseph, and said,
"The God before whom my ancestors Abraham and Isaac walked,
the God who has been my shepherd all my life to this day,
16 the angel who has redeemed me from all harm, bless the boys;
and in them let my name be perpetuated, and the name of my ancestors Abraham and Isaac;
and let them grow into a multitude on the earth."
17 When Joseph saw that his father laid his right hand on the head of Ephraim, it displeased him; so he took his father's hand, to remove it from Ephraim's head to Manasseh's head. 18 Joseph said to his father, "Not so, my father! Since this one is the firstborn, put your right hand on his head." 19 But his father refused, and said, "I know, my son, I know; he also shall become a people, and he also shall be great. Nevertheless his younger brother shall be greater than he, and his offspring shall become a multitude of nations."

13

BACKGROUND

Although Joseph had sent the Egyptians out of the room before he disclosed his identity to his brothers, many outside heard his loud weeping (Gen. 45:2). This roused their interest. At some point they learned that Joseph's brothers had come to him, and they carried the news to the royal palace (45:16). Nine years after receiving his high post, Joseph still enjoyed Pharaoh's favor. As chapter 47 shows, Joseph was in the process of using the nation's grain reserves to make the king tremendously wealthy. Not surprisingly, Pharaoh was kindly disposed toward Joseph. Consequently, the news about the Hebrew overseer's brothers was greeted with pleasure in the royal court.

When Joseph next had an audience with Pharaoh, the matter of his brothers was discussed. Joseph did not even get the opportunity to tell the king about the plan to bring the overseer's family to Egypt before Pharaoh instructed him to do just that. This would be a way for the king to reward his trusted second-in-command for his work (45:17-24). Jacob must have spent the weeks that his sons were away from home worrying about them, especially Benjamin; and the patriarch must have been overjoyed when all 11 returned safe and sound. Initially, though, Jacob was stunned by the news that Joseph was not only alive but also a high official in Egypt. Further persuasion, along with the sight of the carts, animals, and riches, finally convinced Jacob, and he vowed to go to his son in Egypt before the patriarch died (45:25-28).

Chapters 46 and 47 detail the journey of the Israelite clan from Canaan to Egypt. Joseph traveled to meet Jacob in the region of Goshen. After the reunion, Joseph escorted the Israelite caravan to Pharaoh and presented his brothers and father to Egypt's ruler. In keeping with Pharaoh's suggestion, Joseph then provided land and food for the Hebrew immigrants. Joseph himself, though, continued in his government position, saving lives while at the same time enriching Pharaoh.

Chapters 48 and 49 record a deathbed scene. With his last remaining strength, Jacob sat on the edge of his bed and spoke to his sons. They had been called to him because of his final illness (48:1-2). Even Joseph came from his palace with his two boys. Jacob knew death was closing in on him, so he performed the traditional duty of blessing his sons. This meant he divided the inheritance among them and invoked

God's favor upon them. Since Jacob's family was in covenant with the Lord, the belief that their descendants would one day possess the promised land lies behind his words.

The patriarch began his speech by addressing Joseph, telling how almighty God had blessed Jacob long ago at Luz or Bethel (48:3-4; compare 28:10-22). The Lord had promised that Jacob's descendants would become numerous. In light of that blessing, Jacob claimed Manasseh and Ephraim as his own sons. Any other sons Joseph might have would remain Joseph's own. They would not be equal with their uncles, as Manasseh and Ephraim were (48:5-6). In those days, the oldest son usually received twice as much of the inheritance as any other son. Jacob's oldest son was Reuben, but he had proven himself unworthy (35:22). Thus Jacob instead gave the double portion to Joseph by adopting Joseph's sons, Manasseh and Ephraim. Through them, Joseph's descendants would be two tribes, not one.

Next, Jacob mentioned the death and burial of his favorite wife, Rachel, the mother of Joseph and Benjamin. Perhaps Jacob mentioned Rachel to suggest that Manasseh and Ephraim would take the place of any other sons he would have had by Rachel if she had not died early. Finally, Jacob (whom the text begins referring to as Israel) saw two young men he did not recognize. Surely in the 17 years he had spent in Egypt, the patriarch had gotten to know the grandsons, Manasseh and Ephraim; but Israel's eyesight was failing, and he could not easily recognize them (48:7-9). Another possibility is that the patriarch's question was part of the ritual to formally identify the beneficiaries of the covenantal blessings.

NOTES ON THE PRINTED TEXT

Having been told who the two young men were, Israel had them come near. Then he kissed and embraced them (Gen. 48:10). Next, the patriarch admitted that he never anticipated seeing Joseph again. After all, years earlier the older brothers had convinced their father that Joseph was dead. Now the Lord graciously allowed Israel not only to see the face of Joseph but also his children (48:11).

Up until this point, Joseph's two sons probably had been standing by Israel's knees as he blessed them. Scholars think receiving children onto or beside one's knees was a symbol of adoption. At some point, Joseph moved Manasseh and Ephraim away from the knees of their grandfather. Then Joseph bowed down with his face to the ground before the elderly patriarch (48:12). Although Joseph was a high official in one of the most powerful nations of the day in that region of the world, it did not get in the way of him humbly thanking his father for the honor he was showing Joseph in adopting and blessing his two sons.

Joseph's two sons were born to him before the seven years of famine came (41:50). The name of the first son, *Manasseh* (41:51), possibly means "he who brings about forgetfulness" and served as a reminder that God had enabled Joseph to forget all his troubles and the family of his father. The name of the second son, *Ephraim* (41:52), means "to bear fruit" and served as a reminder that God had made Joseph fruitful in the land of his suffering. The names the Hebrew overseer gave his children indicated that he held on to his heritage and faith even while in Egypt.

The Lord honored Joseph's devotion by allowing Jacob to adopt and bless Manasseh and Ephraim. Joseph positioned Ephraim on his right hand, which was across from Israel's left hand. Joseph also placed Manasseh by his left hand and across from Israel's right hand. As Joseph brought his sons closer to their grandfather, the overseer was quite intentional in wanting to maintain this arrangement (48:13). It would allow the firstborn, Manasseh, to receive the greater blessing, in accordance with ancient custom.

Israel, however, broke with tradition by stretching out his right hand and placing it on Ephraim's head. The patriarch deliberately did this, even though Ephraim was the younger son. Next, Israel crossed his hands so that he could place his left hand on Manasseh's head (48:14). Again, this defied conventional wisdom, for Manasseh was the older son. The patriarch's reversal of his hands did not mean that only Ephraim would be blessed. In fact, Israel invoked God's blessing on both young men (48:15-16, 20); but in the providence and sovereignty of God, Ephraim would have the superior blessing.

In the blessing that Israel conveyed to Joseph and his two sons, the patriarch made reference to the covenant-keeping God of Abraham and Isaac. Many years earlier, God came to Abraham in a vision and declared that He was the patriarch's shield of protection as well as the one who would reward him in great abundance (15:1). Later, the Lord referred to Himself as God Almighty and instructed Abraham to serve Him faithfully and live a blameless life (17:1). The testimony of Jacob's grandfather and father was that both of them faithfully lived in the Lord's presence (15:2; 48:15).

As the end of Jacob's life drew closer, he could genuinely affirm that the Lord had been his shepherd (48:15). When Jacob first ventured from Canaan to Paddan-aram, God pledged to watch over him and prosper him (28:10-22). Two decades later, as Jacob prepared to return to Canaan, the Lord promised to be with him (31:3). Before the patriarch's reunion with Esau, Jacob had a life-changing encounter with God's angel (vss. 24-30). Then, as Israel made the journey to Bethel, the Lord appeared to him and spoke reassuringly to him (35:1). Upon Israel's arrival, almighty God again appeared to him and reiterated the covenant promises (35:11-13).

Even in the matter involving Joseph, Israel believed the Lord was sovereignly at work to bring about His will. Indeed, the patriarch was convinced that the Angel sent by God had protected and delivered him from all harm. It may be that Israel thought the divine blessing he was conferring on Joseph's sons would be mediated through this angelic representative. It was Israel's expressed wish that the boys would be identified by the names of Abraham, Isaac, and Israel. An additional implication is that as the Lord enabled Joseph's sons to increase greatly on the earth and become a mighty nation, they would also preserve the honor associated with the names of the patriarchs (48:16).

Joseph was displeased to see that his father placed his right hand on the head of Ephraim, the younger of the two sons. The overseer saw his father's crossing of hands as a mistake and tried to correct it by moving Israel's hand to the head of Manasseh, the older son (48:17). Joseph, perhaps assuming that his elderly and sight-impaired father was unaware of what he was doing, respectfully but straightforwardly explained that Manasseh was the firstborn and thus deserved to receive the greater blessing (48:18); but despite social custom, this was not God's will.

Israel calmly refused to give preferential treatment to Manasseh, Joseph's firstborn. With prophetic insight, the patriarch revealed that the descendants of both young men would become great, but Ephraim's offspring would be greater. In fact, the younger son's descendants would become a multitude of nations (48:19). Centuries later, the tribe of Ephraim did end up being more powerful than the tribe of Manasseh. During the wilderness wandering, the tribe of Manasseh was led by the banner of the tribe of Ephraim. At the time of the divided kingdom, the northern 10 tribes were often collectively called Ephraim.

In blessing Joseph's sons, the patriarch said that the people of Israel would use the names of Ephraim and Manasseh to bless their fellow citizens in the nation (48:20). Perhaps as the grandfather of the two young men put Ephraim ahead of Manasseh, he thought back to the time he had stolen his brother's birthright. Like Ephraim, Jacob had been elevated above his older brother, Esau. Jacob knew from personal experience that sometimes God acts in ways that upset human conventions and ideas.

SUGGESTIONS TO TEACHERS

In our lives, when things do not go according to our predetermined plans, it may be due to the fact that there is a lesson we need to learn, a person we need to meet, or a job only we can do. When God calls, the date books must be set aside. Ultimately, we are travelers with God on a lifelong journey of faith. Thus, His planner (so to speak) takes precedence.

1. HEARING THE CALL OF GOD. What keeps you from hearing someone call you? Distance, language, volume, or the level of anticipation may all be factors. Think of how quickly a mother can hear the soft cry of her child in another room. Obviously, she is tuned in to hear that call; nevertheless, how many times can that same mother call her son to the dinner table before he hears her?

2. HEEDING THE CALL OF GOD. God is calling each one of us. Some of us He is calling to take the first step on a lifelong journey of faith with Him. That step is admitting our sinfulness and accepting His Son, Jesus Christ, as our Lord and Savior. It's the most important first step we can take. For those who have already taken that first step, the journey has only begun. God continues to call, but often we have already scripted our life's journey ourselves and we do not want to heed His summons.

3. HONORING THE CALL OF GOD. What does God ask us to do? Plumbers, accountants, and athletes have been surprised when God called them to enter the ministry or become missionaries; but the Lord may ask us to do simpler things that are also challenging—for instance, sharing the Gospel with someone seated next to us on a bus or inviting a peer at work to go to church with us. Living in faith means continually taking risks, stepping out of the familiar into the unfamiliar. We can learn from other believers how we should respond when God calls. We need to honor His will at all times, no matter the consequences.

FOR ADULTS

■ **TOPIC:** Leaving a Legacy

■ **QUESTIONS:** 1. How did Jacob feel about being able to see Joseph's two sons? 2. What is significant about Joseph bowing in the presence of his father? 3. What difference of opinion did Jacob and Joseph have about which of the sons should receive the blessing of the firstborn? 4. What sort of blessing did Jacob bestow on Joseph's sons? 5. What did Jacob say about the future that awaited the descendants of Manasseh and Ephraim?

■ **ILLUSTRATIONS:**

The Divine Plan for Our Lives. Bob remembers traveling as a child with his father, a regional salesman, to visit accounts throughout southern Illinois. "On those trips, my father relied as much on his date book as he did his map," Bob says. The book was filled with the names and addresses of his customers, directions to their businesses, their purchasing history, and of course, the date of their next appointment. "Without that book," Bob says, "my father would have been out of business in less than a week."

Today, millions in all walks of life hold tightly to their schedulers and planners, both paper and electronic. We use them to map out our future years in advance and plan our days down to the half hour. As a result, our journey through life is often driven by the calendar and the clock.

Sometimes, though, God has other plans for our lives than the ones we so carefully map out. Consider the future of the Israelite clan, especially the two sons of Joseph. He envisioned Manasseh, the firstborn, to receive the primary family blessing from his grandfather; but Jacob bestowed it on Ephraim, the second of Joseph's sons. In this case, God's will went against conventional wisdom and social customs.

A Lasting Legacy. Eli Herring was an outstanding lineman at a nationally recognized university. The 340-pound offensive tackle topped the list in the professional league's draft when he graduated. Herring was also an exceptional student, achieving a 3.5 grade point average his senior year.

The Oakland Raiders made a multimillion dollar offer for this powerful, brainy athlete. Everyone predicted a lucrative career in pro ball for Herring. But then, to everyone's surprise—except to those who knew him well—Herring stated that he would not play on Sundays because of his commitment to his church on that day of each week.

Sunday, of course, is NFL (National Football League) game day. Instead of a contract with the NFL, with Sunday games and the trappings of big money and fame, Herring signed a contract to teach math to high-school students, while keeping his Sundays free for worship. Here is someone who sought to leave a real, lasting legacy for future generations.

Recognizing the Contribution of Others. Every February brings the celebration of Black History Month in the United States. Many educators believe African-American students need to discover and learn their history. Too long, they point out, Americans have seen U.S. history only from a white perspective. Black students have a right to know who and what really shaped their lives in this country.

Black History Month provides an entire community with shared stories and traditions, highlighting the treasures and contributions of various people that might be overlooked. This is important for any group of people.

FOR YOUTH

■ **TOPIC:** Blessed

■ **QUESTIONS:** 1. Why did Joseph position his sons as he did in the presence of Jacob? 2. How had God proven Himself to be faithful to Abraham, Isaac, and Jacob? 3. Why did Ephraim, rather than Manasseh, receive the primary family blessing? 4. How did Joseph try to change what his father was seeking to do? 5. What explanation did Jacob give for his actions?

■ **ILLUSTRATIONS:**

Finding Bounty in Life. The 1994 movie *Blessing* features a cast of characters set on a Wisconsin dairy farm. There's 23-year-old Randi, who's fallen in love with Lyle. He's a restless young man itching to drive the open highways in his Winnebago. Randi, having grown tired of long hours on the family farm, dreams of seeing the ocean. Randi's mother is nearly crippled with arthritis, while her father is burned out and depressed over all the personal and professional challenges he has experienced in his difficult life. Randi also has a 10-year-old brother named Clovis, with whom she is very close.

Intense longings and seemingly unstoppable dreams can be found in each person's life journey. This remains so, despite the harsh realities that seem to contantly pummel them. Viewers learn that existence can be filled with bounty no matter what people go through. This is even more so for believers, who look to God for temporal and eternal blessing.

Remembrances. It began in the fall of 1982, when the concrete foundation of *The Wall* was being poured in Washington, D.C. A U.S. Navy officer walked up to the trench, stood at attention, tossed something into the wet concrete, and saluted. Workmen came over to investigate. The officer said he was giving his dead brother's Purple Heart to the *The Wall*. It was the first official offering.

Every day, the National Park Service collects, catalogs, and stores in a climate-controlled repository the gifts of remembrance left at the Vietnam Veterans Memorial. These have included letters, Bibles, service ribbons, socks, shoes, playing cards, pictures, as well as champagne glasses and booties for weddings and babies that would never occur. Hundreds of these objects are displayed at the Smithsonian National Museum of American History as a memorial. These are remembrances of those who fought from the Delta to Con Thien. As you grow to adulthood, what are some ways you can be a blessing to others that will prompt them to recall your life and work for generations to come?

A Surprising Adventure. Ted Boontheung Rasakham grew up in Laos in southeast Asia. Like everyone else in his family, Ted was a devout Buddhist. His spiritual journey led him to become a Buddhist monk. Then, wartime forced him to flee the country. Ted sought haven across the border in northeastern Thailand. There he languished in a large, crowded refugee camp. During that time, Ted heard the good news about Jesus. Ted was so affected by the Gospel that he turned his life over to the Lord and was baptized as a Christian. Many were upset, but the new convert faithfully agreed to go where God led him.

Eventually, Ted was able to emigrate to the United States. His adventure in faith led him to study for the Christian ministry. After years of hardship and study, Ted was called to the Lao United Church of Christ in Lowell, Texas, the only Laotian congregation in that denomination, and ordained on February 23, 1997, as a Christian pastor. By the guidance and blessing of God, this man discovered that the life of faith can be a surprising adventure.

CALLED TO BELIEVE!

BACKGROUND SCRIPTURE: Luke 1:5-25
DEVOTIONAL READING: Psalm 66:1-4, 16-20

KEY VERSE: And, behold, thou shalt be dumb, and not able to speak, until
the day that these things shall be performed, because thou believest not
my words, which shall be fulfilled in their season. Luke 1:20.

KING JAMES VERSION

LUKE 1:18 And Zacharias said unto the angel, Whereby shall I know this? for I am an old man, and my wife well stricken in years. 19 And the angel answering said unto him, I am Gabriel, that stand in the presence of God; and am sent to speak unto thee, and to shew thee these glad tidings. 20 And, behold, thou shalt be dumb, and not able to speak, until the day that these things shall be performed, because thou believest not my words, which shall be fulfilled in their season. 21 And the people waited for Zacharias, and marvelled that he tarried so long in the temple. 22 And when he came out, he could not speak unto them: and they perceived that he had seen a vision in the temple: for he beckoned unto them, and remained speechless. 23 And it came to pass, that, as soon as the days of his ministration were accomplished, he departed to his own house.

NEW REVISED STANDARD VERSION

LUKE 1:18 Zechariah said to the angel, "How will I know that this is so? For I am an old man, and my wife is getting on in years." 19 The angel replied, "I am Gabriel. I stand in the presence of God, and I have been sent to speak to you and to bring you this good news. 20 But now, because you did not believe my words, which will be fulfilled in their time, you will become mute, unable to speak, until the day these things occur."

21 Meanwhile the people were waiting for Zechariah, and wondered at his delay in the sanctuary. 22 When he did come out, he could not speak to them, and they realized that he had seen a vision in the sanctuary. He kept motioning to them and remained unable to speak. 23 When his time of service was ended, he went to his home.

Monday, November 26	Psalm 66:1-4	*Sing God's Praises*
Tuesday, November 27	Luke 1:5-7	*Righteous before God*
Wednesday, November 28	Luke 1:8-13	*Incense Offering Interrupted*
Thursday, November 29	Luke 1:14-17	*A Ministry Foretold*
Friday, November 30	Luke 1:18-23	*Zechariah Sees a Vision*
Saturday, December 1	Luke 1:24-25	*Elizabeth Conceives*
Sunday, December 2	Psalm 66:16-20	*God Listened to My Prayer*

BACKGROUND

Zechariah and Elizabeth, the parents of John the Baptizer, were both descended from Aaron (Luke 1:5). Levi was the original ancestor of Israel's priests, including those descended from Aaron. The Mosaic legislation, however, made a distinction between Aaronic priests and Levites. Only members of the first group were permitted to offer sacrifices in the tabernacle (Exod. 28; Lev. 8—10). The Levites assisted the Aaronic priests in their responsibilities (Num. 3:5-9; 16:8-9).

Zechariah also belonged to the priestly division of Abijah. This couple pleased the Lord by the way they lived (Luke 1:6). In fact, they consistently walked in the way of righteousness and obeyed all that God had commanded. Nonetheless, despite their blameless lifestyle, they were childless (1:7). In Bible times, children were regarded as God's reward for faithful service (Ps. 127:3-5). Some incorrectly believed the Lord was displeased with and punished those who lacked children. The experience of Zechariah and Elizabeth disproves that theory. From a human perspective, the barren condition of Elizabeth and the advanced age of her and her husband made it highly unlikely that she would ever get pregnant. The inability of this godly couple to have children must have been a deep disappointment for them.

During the reign of David, the Aaronic priests were divided into 24 groups, and Abijah was the leader of the eighth division (1 Chron. 24:10). The priestly groups served in the temple on a rotating basis, with each group ministering for a week twice a year and at the major festivals. Twice a day, before the morning sacrifice and after the evening sacrifice, priests burned incense on the altar in front of the holy of holies in the temple (Exod. 30:7-8). Because there were so many priests (estimated by some to be approximately 18,000 at that time), each priest would get to offer incense at the daily sacrifice only once in his lifetime (if at all) and the opportunity represented the pinnacle of one's ministerial career.

The priests performed a variety of important duties. For instance, they offered gifts and sacrifices for the sins of both themselves and others. The priests also read the law of Moses to God's people and reminded them of their obligation to keep the covenant (Deut. 31:9-13; Neh. 8:2-3). The priests revealed the will of God (Exod. 28:30) and blessed the people (Num. 6:22-26). Moreover, the priests were subject to special laws.

For example, they could not drink wine when they went into the tabernacle (Lev. 10:9). They had to observe the difference between what was holy and what was common (10:10). A priest could only marry an Israelite, and she had to be either a virgin or a widow, not a divorced person (21:7).

NOTES ON THE PRINTED TEXT

The priests used lots to determine who from a certain group would be chosen to burn incense in the temple. Lots were small marked objects like pebbles, sticks, or pieces of pottery. Although the exact method of casting lots remains unclear, some think a priest placed the objects in a jar with a narrow neck. Then when he shook the container, only one piece came out. One day the division of Abijah was on duty, and Zechariah was fulfilling his priestly obligation (Luke 1:8). When the lot was cast, he was chosen to burn incense (1:9). He, along with the other priests, would enter the temple, but they would exit, leaving him alone to perform the offering. While Zechariah performed the ritual, pious Jews stood outside the building to worship and pray (1:10). The smoke drifting upward symbolized the prayers of the devout Jews ascending to the throne of God (Ps. 141:2; Rev. 5:8; 8:3-4).

An angel from the Lord suddenly appeared to Zechariah on the south side of the incense altar, between it and the golden lampstand (Luke 1:11). The right side of the altar would have been regarded as the spot of divine favor (see Ps. 110:1; Mark 16:5). Upon seeing the heavenly being, Zechariah became shocked and terrified (Luke 1:12). A survey of Scripture indicates that being gripped with fear was a common response when messengers from God appeared to people (see Judg. 6:22-23; 13:6, 22; Luke 1:29-20; 2:9). The angel, whose name was *Gabriel* (Luke 1:19), would not leave Zechariah in a state of fear.

Before going any further, the angel from the Lord directed Zechariah not to be afraid. Then the supernatural emissary announced that the prayer of Zechariah had been heard (Luke 1:13). While the priest was offering the sacrifice in the temple, his immediate petition would have been for the nation. But the angel's statement indicates that the long hoped-for desire of Zechariah and Elizabeth would be fulfilled. Possibly this indicates the couple had been praying for the messianic redemption of Israel (see 2:25; 24:21). More likely, however, they had asked God for a child; and the Lord blessed their obedience by granting their deep desire.

The angel declared that Elizabeth's newborn son was to be named *John* (1:13). The Greek noun comes from the Hebrew name *Johanan*, which means "Yahweh has shown favor" or "Yahweh is gracious." This signifies the reason for John's birth, namely, to herald the advent of the Messiah, the gift of God's grace. God's naming John before his birth suggests that the Lord was singling him out for his important work. The angel also declared that Zechariah and Elizabeth would experience great joy over the birth and life of their son, and many others would rejoice with the godly couple at John's birth (1:14). The reason is stated in 1:15. John would "be great in the sight of the Lord." In fact, God would use John to persuade many Israelites to turn to the Lord in faith (1:16).

Instead of consuming and being controlled by wine and other fermented drink, John would be filled with the Holy Spirit, even before his birth. This fact has led some to surmise that John eventually took the vow of a Nazarite (Num. 6:1-4). Those making such a pledge even refrained from ingesting grapes, grape juice, and raisins. In the case of John, however, Luke did not specifically state that he took such a vow. Instead, the emphasis seems to be on John's ascetic lifestyle (see Luke 7:25, 33).

Regardless of one's view on the matter, it's clear that John had a uniquely God-given position. As a prophet in the stature of Elijah (Matt. 11:14; 17:10-13; Luke 7:24-28), John would go as a forerunner before the Lord. John's mission would be to turn the hearts of parents back to their children. He would also persuade disobedient minds to accept godly wisdom (Luke 1:17; see Mal. 3:1; 4:5-6). These two tasks cover all relationships, namely, those involving other people (the horizontal dimension of life) and those involving God (the vertical dimension of life). Furthermore, the Greek verb rendered *to turn* (Luke 1:17) highlights John's task of summoning people to repent, that is, to change the moral and spiritual direction of their lives in preparation for the advent of the Messiah (see 3:1-14; 24:47).

Zechariah, being caught off guard by the angel's announcement, was filled with doubt and asked how he could be sure of what he had been told. When he considered the situation from his limited human perspective, he concluded that it was physically impossible for an elderly man such as himself to become a father, or his wife, who was past the age of childbearing, to become a mother (1:18). The same sort of skepticism overtook Sarah when the Lord revealed that He would enable her to become pregnant through Abraham. The divine promise was made when both of them were advanced in years. In that episode, God declared that nothing He pledged was too difficult for Him to do (Gen. 18:10-14). Likewise, with the situation involving Elizabeth and Zechariah, the Lord was able to fulfill what He had promised.

The angel who appeared to Zechariah announced that his name was *Gabriel* (Luke 1:19), which means "man of God," "God has shown Himself strong," or "God is my hero." The greatness of this messenger from heaven is seen in the fact that Gabriel stood in the presence of the Lord; and because God had sent the angel to announce to Zechariah the good news about John, Zechariah should have believed what he heard. Because the priest had used words to convey his doubt, the Lord would discipline him by preventing him from being able to speak (1:20). Evidently, Zechariah was also unable to hear, for as 1:61-63 indicates, others had to use gestures to communicate with him. He would remain deaf and mute until the time when God fulfilled what He had promised (1:20). This circumstance would also be a sign of assurance that what the angel had declared was true.

It is noteworthy that God broke 400 years of silence by sending Gabriel to a man whose name means "God remembers" (Zechariah). The Lord remembered Zechariah's prayer for a son (1:13), but more than that, He recalled the covenants He made with Abraham and David (Gen. 12:2-3; 2 Sam. 7:12-16; Gal. 3:16-17). Elizabeth's name is also significant in this regard, for it means "God's oath (or covenant)." To speak of her name was to remember that the Lord was a covenant-making, covenant-keeping God. Scripture teaches that the Lord remembers His people, answers their prayers, keeps His promises to them, and sent Jesus to redeem the lost, all because God is gracious.

Under normal circumstances, the priest ministered in the temple for a short period of time and then came out to offer a blessing (see Num. 6:22-27). In the case of Zechariah, the pious Jews waiting outside began to wonder why he seemed to be delayed in the holy place (Luke 1:21). Eventually, the priest did leave the temple, and after he emerged, the people discovered that he was unable to speak to them. The signs he kept gesturing with his hands made this clear and also indicated that he had seen a vision. Expressed differently, while Zechariah ministered in the holy place, he had a supernatural encounter, one involving an angel from the Lord (1:22). In due course, Zechariah's time of service in the temple ended. Then he returned to his home in the hill country of Judea, which was south of Jerusalem (1:23, 39-40).

SUGGESTIONS TO TEACHERS

The personal insights that God gives us through sketches of biblical characters are helpful in assisting us in our own spiritual walk. For instance, we see in snapshots of Zechariah and Elizabeth, their growth in character, their overcoming doubt, and their vibrant faith. The way for us to be pleasing to God seems clear, though we may not always fully understand the ramifications. Specifically, the Lord is pleased when we trust Him fully and obey His Word.

1. UPRIGHTNESS MAKES NO EARTHLY GUARANTEES. Though it is a brilliant testimony to Zechariah and Elizabeth's spirituality, their moral purity and uprightness made no guarantees that their lives would not have its challenges and sorrows. It's important for us to remember that the goal of an upright life is to be pleasing to the Lord, not to obtain relief from our problems. However, God also reminds us that we should not forget all His benefits (Ps. 103:2).

2. GOD'S WAYS MAY, AT FIRST, SEEM DISCONCERTING. Some of our greatest blessings start out as events that scare us or disrupt our normal living routines. True faith looks for the blessing and promise of God in circumstances that first appear frightful or discouraging.

3. GOD OFFERS HIS BLESSINGS. Zechariah and Elizabeth followed the Lord, and He blessed them. We can also expect Him to bless us as we follow Him faithfully. When we say we anticipate God's blessings, we do not mean we set the agenda or make arrogant demands of God. There is a difference between anticipating God's blessings and living as if we deserved to be blessed. Everything the Lord does for us is based on His undeserved favor.

FOR ADULTS

■ **TOPIC:** Surprising Opportunities

■ **QUESTIONS:** 1. What was Zechariah's personal and professional background? 2. What were the people doing outside the temple as Zechariah ministered inside? 3. What announcement did the angel from the Lord make to Zechariah concerning Elizabeth? 4. What ministry awaited John the Baptizer? 5. Why did the angel declare that Zechariah would be unable to speak until John was born?

■ **ILLUSTRATIONS:**

Keeping Our Eyes Open. We had just purchased a house and did not know what the previous owners had planted in the yard. As soon as the ground thawed in the early spring, I placed some lilies in an area under a large bush. To my disappointment, however, only a few survived.

When I later looked around the yard, I noticed some plants beginning to emerge from the ground. The more I looked at them, the more familiar they became. They were lilies, and there seemed to be dozens of them. I decided to take the unexpected opportunity to move some lilies from one spot to another, giving me two areas to grow these fragrant plants. From this experience, I learned that I need to keep my eyes open to the blessings of God that He has provided because He loves me.

Answered Prayer. Zechariah and Elizabeth are not the only ones for whom an answer to their prayer came after a long period of time (Luke 1:13). Clara, an elderly Christian woman, had many unsaved family members for whom she regularly prayed. Year after year, Clara continued petitioning God, yet she never saw one of her prayers answered during her lifetime.

One of these family members was a niece named Shelia, who was only a teenager at the time of Clara's death. Several years after Clara passed away, Shelia, her husband, and their two young daughters moved into a house across the street from a family of Christians. These believers greeted their new neighbors and helped them clear their property so grass could be planted.

Eventually, Shelia became curious about the Christian family's church and asked if she and her family could attend with them. The first time Shelia heard the Gospel, her heart was opened, and she received the gift of salvation. Her husband trusted in Christ soon afterward. Later, Shelia's sister, aunt, uncle, and cousins also were saved in the church. Many months later, Shelia came to realize that the church she and her family members were attending was the very congregation in which her Aunt Clara had prayed faithfully for their salvation.

Keep Moving Forward. Great spiritual leaders throughout history have all had to use faith and perseverance to see the fulfillment of their hopes and prayers. Consider what a few of them have said.

• Don't be afraid to take a big step, if one is indicated. You can't cross a chasm in two small jumps. —*David Lloyd George*

• Even if I knew that tomorrow the world would go to pieces, I would still plant my little apple tree and pay my debts. —*Martin Luther*

• A little faith will bring your soul to heaven; a great faith will bring heaven to your soul. —*Charles Haddon Spurgeon*

FOR YOUTH	■ **TOPIC:** Called to Believe ■ **QUESTIONS:** 1. How did it come about that Zechariah was chosen to minister in the temple? 2. What was Zechariah's initial reaction at the

sight of the angel from the Lord? 3. What sort of lifestyle would characterize John the Baptizer? 4. Why do you think Zechariah initially doubted the announcement of the angel concerning John? 5. How were the people able to figure out that Zechariah had seen a vision in the temple?

■ **ILLUSTRATIONS:**

Overcoming the Tragedy of Death. Jeff Knight served as a youth pastor in Monroe, Washington. His senior pastors were his own parents, until they were killed in an airline crash off the coast of California. Suddenly, Jeff became a father figure to his 17-year-old sister and, along with his wife, co-pastor of the Rock Church.

A year later, Jeff and 40 others from the church traveled to the spot nearest the crash site. They went, not to grieve, but to celebrate the life and ministry of Joe and Linda Knight. Because this son and the congregation made it through their grief by remaining unwavering in their trust in the Lord Jesus, God has enabled them to minister more effectively to others who are hurting. Although Jeff and his wife are young and did not expect to move into leadership so quickly, the church has continued to grow under their direction. They have discovered that faith in the Lord can overcome the tragedy of death.

It Only Gets Better. The great writers of history knew how important it was to take the time to do their best work. Plato wrote the first sentence of his famous *Republic* nine different ways before he was satisfied. Cicero practiced speaking before friends every day for 30 years to perfect his oratorical skills. Noah Webster labored 36 years writing his *Dictionary*, crossing the Atlantic twice to gather material.

Milton rose at 4:00 A.M. every day in order to have enough hours to write his *Paradise Lost*. Gibbon spent 26 years writing the *Decline and Fall of the Roman Empire*. Bryant rewrote one of his poetic masterpieces 99 times before its publication, and it became a classic.

It's important to remember that almost nothing is at its best in the beginning. It is through perseverance, vision, and trust in God's faithfulness that great results come from our efforts to honor His call on our lives.

Who Knows What Will Happen in the End? When Stephanie and Alison first met, they knew that they would be friends forever—at least until a new kid moved to their school. In the spring of their junior year, Steve moved to town. He was so cute that he soon became popular with the whole class. He also had a strong Christian faith and he treated everyone well.

Stephanie and Alison were both friends with Steve, and both wished to be more than friends. However, Steve didn't seem to want to do the "couple-thing"; he just wanted to be friends. When Steve asked Alison to the senior prom, she was ecstatic. On the outside, Stephanie appeared cheerful, but on the inside she felt torn apart. She wondered what was wrong with her. Stephanie never did get asked to the prom, and it was devastating to her. On the one hand, she didn't have a friend to share the misery of not going to the biggest event of the senior year; and, on the other hand, she had to listen continually to Alison's giddy excitement about what this dance might lead to in terms of an ongoing relationship with Steve. Stephanie was miserable.

In spite of her own discouragement, Stephanie knew that God wanted her to remain friendly to both Alison and Steve. Stephanie asked for God's grace to be charitable and not envious. Then, rather than continuing to feel sorry for herself, Stephanie purchased a ticket to a musical concert scheduled to be held on prom night. At least she could celebrate the conclusion of her senior year by choosing an alternate fun activity. While Stephanie was attending the concert, she met Rob, a friend from church, and they enjoyed each other's companionship that evening. Stephanie realized that God had honored her commitment to follow and trust Him completely.

CALLED TO BE A VESSEL!

BACKGROUND SCRIPTURE: Luke 1:26-38
DEVOTIONAL READING: Psalm 40:1-5

2

KEY VERSE: Behold the handmaid of the Lord; be it unto me according to thy word. Luke 1:38

KING JAMES VERSION

LUKE 1:26 And in the sixth month the angel Gabriel was sent from God unto a city of Galilee, named Nazareth, 27 To a virgin espoused to a man whose name was Joseph, of the house of David; and the virgin's name was Mary. 28 And the angel came in unto her, and said, Hail, thou that art highly favoured, the Lord is with thee: blessed art thou among women. 29 And when she saw him, she was troubled at his saying, and cast in her mind what manner of salutation this should be. 30 And the angel said unto her, Fear not, Mary: for thou hast found favour with God. 31 And, behold, thou shalt conceive in thy womb, and bring forth a son, and shalt call his name JESUS. 32 He shall be great, and shall be called the Son of the Highest: and the Lord God shall give unto him the throne of his father David: 33 And he shall reign over the house of Jacob for ever; and of his kingdom there shall be no end. 34 Then said Mary unto the angel, How shall this be, seeing I know not a man? 35 And the angel answered and said unto her, The Holy Ghost shall come upon thee, and the power of the Highest shall overshadow thee: therefore also that holy thing which shall be born of thee shall be called the Son of God. 36 And, behold, thy cousin Elisabeth, she hath also conceived a son in her old age: and this is the sixth month with her, who was called barren. 37 For with God nothing shall be impossible. 38 And Mary said, Behold the handmaid of the Lord; be it unto me according to thy word. And the angel departed from her.

NEW REVISED STANDARD VERSION

LUKE 1:26 In the sixth month the angel Gabriel was sent by God to a town in Galilee called Nazareth, 27 to a virgin engaged to a man whose name was Joseph, of the house of David. The virgin's name was Mary. 28 And he came to her and said, "Greetings, favored one! The Lord is with you." 29 But she was much perplexed by his words and pondered what sort of greeting this might be. 30 The angel said to her, "Do not be afraid, Mary, for you have found favor with God. 31 And now, you will conceive in your womb and bear a son, and you will name him Jesus. 32 He will be great, and will be called the Son of the Most High, and the Lord God will give to him the throne of his ancestor David. 33 He will reign over the house of Jacob forever, and of his kingdom there will be no end." 34 Mary said to the angel, "How can this be, since I am a virgin?" 35 The angel said to her, "The Holy Spirit will come upon you, and the power of the Most High will overshadow you; therefore the child to be born will be holy; he will be called Son of God. 36 And now, your relative Elizabeth in her old age has also conceived a son; and this is the sixth month for her who was said to be barren. 37 For nothing will be impossible with God." 38 Then Mary said, "Here am I, the servant of the Lord; let it be with me according to your word." Then the angel departed from her.

Monday, December 3	Psalm 40:1-5	*God's Wondrous Deeds*
Tuesday, December 4	Luke 1:26-29	*An Unexpected Visitor*
Wednesday, December 5	Luke 1:30-33	*Mary's Son's Future*
Thursday, December 6	Luke 1:34-35	*The Miraculous Conception*
Friday, December 7	Luke 1:36-38	*Nothing Is Impossible!*
Saturday, December 8	Luke 1:39-45	*Elizabeth Blesses Mary*
Sunday, December 9	Luke 1:46-56	*Mary Sings to the Lord*

BACKGROUND

For several hundred years, God's voice through the prophets had been silent in Palestine. The Roman army had nearly crushed the Jews' hopes that the promised Messiah would come to deliver them. Had God forgotten His people? The Jews enjoyed limited political and religious freedom at this time. Roman administrators had appointed the civil and religious leaders of Judea. When small bands of zealots tried unsuccessfully to fight against foreign occupation, the Roman military quickly and brutally subdued their revolts. The average Jew found few reasons to be optimistic about the future.

But when the fullness of time came, God sent the angel Gabriel, whom we learned about in last week's lesson. The word "angel" means "messenger" and is used to identify supernatural beings whom God created to execute His will (Ps. 148:2-5; Col. 1:16). They neither marry nor are given in marriage (Matt. 22:30). In poetic passages, angels are literally called "sons of God" (Job 1:6; 38:7) and "holy ones" (Job 5:1; Ps. 89:5, 7). The two basic divisions of angels are good ones and evil ones. The latter refer to "demons," who rebelled against God.

Within these two divisions, the Bible mentions the following individuals and orders of angels: 1) *Angel of the Lord*. At crucial points in Jewish history, a figure called the Angel of the Lord protected and guided God's people. Many scholars believed this was the Second Person of the Trinity—Jesus Christ. 2) *Angel leaders*. The archangel, or leader of the angels, is Michael. His counterpart among the evil angels, the archdemon, is Satan. God's chief messenger is Gabriel. 3) *Cherubim*. Angels in this order appear to have some human and some animal features, along with multiple faces and wings. The cherubim function as guardians and as bearers of God's throne-chariot. 4) *Seraphim*. Members of this order of angels are possibly more human in appearance, but have six wings. They are servants of God's throne, praising Him and sometimes acting as His agents.

NOTES ON THE PRINTED TEXT

More incredible than Gabriel's announcement to Zechariah and Elizabeth was his message to a young woman in Nazareth (Luke 1:26). The timing of the visit, *the sixth month,* refers back to Elizabeth's five-month seclusion (1:24-

25). The small town of Nazareth was 16 miles west of the southern end of the Sea of Galilee. Located near a major trade route, the village was frequently visited by Roman soldiers and Gentile merchants. Mary was betrothed to a man who was descended from King David, the family from which the prophets had said the Messiah would come (1:27). For Jewish women at this time, betrothal could occur as early as 12 years old, and the betrothal period normally lasted for about a year.

Gabriel appeared to Mary in an undisclosed indoor area, such as the entrance to a room or a house (1:28). The Greek participle translated as *highly favoured* (literally, "one who is favored") draws attention to Mary as the recipient of God's grace. The Vulgate (an early fifth century translation of the Bible into Latin made by Jerome) renders the same word as "full of grace," which gives the incorrect impression that Mary was a source of God's grace to others, rather than someone who received His unmerited blessings. Paul used the same term in Ephesians 1:6, where believers are told that God loved us in Christ *to the praise of his glorious grace that he freely bestowed on us in the Beloved* (NRSV). To be highly favored conveys more than just being shown grace. It is to have grace lavished upon us.

In terms of Mary, God promised to be with her and through her bestow His grace upon many. (The phrase rendered *Blessed art thou among women* [Luke 1:28, KJV] is not found in the earliest Greek manuscripts, so it is omitted from the NRSV.) Mary's understanding of God's grace explains why she was taken aback at Gabriel's greeting. Mary's "why me?" kind of response reflected humility (1:29, 48), but also surprise. Mary seemed more startled by the angel's grace-greeting than his appearance. Mary didn't consider herself particularly special, but God did. Indeed, that's the surprise of grace. And the Lord is still surprising people with His grace. He has told us in His Word that even though we're sinners and undeserving of His grace, we are nonetheless highly favored in Christ.

It was vital for God to send Gabriel to speak with Mary before she became pregnant because she was a virgin and her pregnancy would cause her distress and shame. In addition, she would have no idea who this child was. Gabriel came to prevent any fears and anxieties that Mary might otherwise have felt. The angel also came so that the young woman could prepare for this great event.

Before Gabriel continued his message, he calmed Mary's fears. He had come to bring her good news, not to alarm her (1:30). The angel then told Mary how God was to bless her. She would give birth to a Son and was to call Him *JESUS* (1:31). In Jewish culture, a child's name was supposed to indicate the essence of his or her personality. *Jesus* is the Greek form of the Hebrew name *Joshua*, which means "Yahweh saves" and emphasizes the deliverance of the Lord. Mary's Son would save people from sin and death (Matt. 1:21). It was the hope of every Jewish woman that she might bear the Lord's Messiah. Since Jewish betrothal often took place soon after puberty, Mary was perhaps into her teens when Gabriel disclosed to her that she would be the mother of the promised Redeemer of Israel.

The prophet Isaiah had declared that a virgin would conceive and bear a son (Isa. 7:14). Mary's son would be that child, the absolutely great Messiah of Israel. This miracle was possible because He would also be the *Son of the Highest* (Luke 1:32). Furthermore, He would fulfill what Isaiah had prophesied about the one who would rule on David's throne (Isa. 9:6-7). God had promised David that his kingdom would be established forever (2 Sam. 7:16). In fact, David's descendants reigned over Judah until the Exile (586 B.C.). The angel's reference to the *throne of his father David* (Luke 1:32) meant that God would now restore the broken line of David's succession. Indeed, Gabriel revealed to Mary that her Son would fulfill that promise, most of all as He ruled forever in majestic splendor (1:33).

Mary asked the obvious question. How could she, who had not been physically intimate with any man, become pregnant (1:34)? While Mary's question provides Scripture's best verification for the virginal conception of Jesus, Mary's words also show a strong and thinking mind. She was confident enough in her relationship with God to ask appropriate questions. It's worth noting that both Mary and Zechariah asked Gabriel how God could do the seemingly impossible. The difference in their queries is that Mary asked how it was possible, while Zechariah (in doubt) asked, *Whereby shall I know this?* (1:18). Also, Mary assumed an immediate fulfillment of what Gabriel told her, whereas Zechariah asked for a sign, which Gabriel granted in the form of Zechariah's muteness.

Gabriel anticipated Mary's initial confusion, for the angel was prepared to explain God's message to her. Gabriel said Jesus would need no man to father Him, for the Spirit of God would come upon Mary and act with creative power (1:35). In the Old Testament, the Hebrew counterpart to *overshadow* are the episodes in which the cloud covered the tabernacle when the glory of God descended upon it (for example, Exod. 40:34-35). When the Holy Spirit later came upon Mary, she became the instrument of Jesus' incarnation. Being the *Son of God* (Luke 1:35), Jesus is holy, not because He was dedicated to God, but because He is God.

The Savior's virginal conception and birth, which is essential to Jesus' deity, was likely even foreshadowed in the Garden of Eden. According to Genesis 3:15, God told the serpent that the woman's offspring would crush the serpent's head. This previews Christ's ultimate victory over sin, Satan, and death (see Rom. 16:20). Descendants were usually traced through fathers, but the unique designation of the woman's offspring implies that the Messiah would have no natural father. In fact, in Luke 3:23, the author was careful to qualify that Jesus was only *supposed* (or "thought") to be Joseph's son.

Although Mary had not asked Gabriel for a sign, he pointed toward evidence that God's power was already at work. He mentioned Mary's relative, Elizabeth (not necessarily a cousin), who had long been barren but was now pregnant (1:36). The angel assured Mary that what he said to her would come to pass, for with God nothing is impossible (1:37). Human promises sometimes fail, especially when people lack the resources or inclination to keep them. God, however, always fulfills His word. He always comes through. In this regard, Isaiah noted, *Behold, the LORD's hand is not shortened, that it cannot save* (Isa. 59:1).

Mary's response to Gabriel perhaps helps explain why God had chosen her. Many disturbing questions may have been running through her mind: *Will Joseph believe the unimaginable? What will my friends and neighbors think when they learn I am pregnant? Will I be branded the worst of sinners, rather than God's chosen instrument?* Nevertheless, Mary did not argue with the angel. Instead, she humbly submitted to God when He gave her a responsibility (Luke 1:38). Scripture describes faith as *the substance of things hope for, the evidence of things not seen* (Heb. 11:1). Mary had such faith. Although she did not fully understand Gabriel's message, she accepted God's promise. Faith says, "I will believe the 'impossible' as fact because the Lord says so." We put our faith into action when we obey God in this way.

Mary's compliance with the will of God was buttressed by two assurances Gabriel gave the young woman. The first is, *the Lord is with thee* (Luke 1:28). God often encourages His people by affirming His constant presence with them, particularly when facing something that is hard or challenging (see Hag. 1:13; 2:4; Matt. 28:20; Heb. 13:5). The second assurance is, *with God nothing shall be impossible* (Luke 1:37). From this we see that God will accomplish what He purposes to do in, for, and through us, no matter what the odds or risks. He did with Mary, and He does with us.

SUGGESTIONS TO TEACHERS

This week's lesson concerns the visitation of Gabriel and his dialogue with Mary. We learn about the miraculous way in which the Father would send His Son, Jesus, to become the Savior of the world. This work of redemption would begin with Jesus' birth as a baby into the world that He had created. And Jesus' virginal conception and birth would be through a young woman named Mary.

1. THE ANNOUNCEMENT. Gabriel, who was sent by God to Mary, suddenly appeared to her in her hometown of Nazareth, a city in the region of Galilee. Gabriel's proclamation caused Mary to be perplexed. We, too, are sometimes initially perplexed when we only see the beginning of what God is doing in our lives.

2. THE REASSURANCE. Gabriel comforted Mary with the knowledge that she had found favor with God. As the angel described to Mary what God intended to do, Mary learned that her baby would be be supernaturally conceived within her, that He would reign over the house of Jacob forever, and that His kingdom would never end.

3. THE SURPRISE. We do not have any reason to believe that Mary was, in any way, prepared for Gabriel's visit. To Mary, the angel appeared out of nowhere. Many times the greatest part of our destiny will come to us by way of surprise. It's wonderful to prepare for all that we may anticipate or hope for, but we should always be ready for the unexpected as well.

4. THE EXPLANATION. Gabriel comforted Mary with the knowledge that the all-powerful Lord would do a miraculous thing within her. The angel also gave Mary encouragement to believe the divine declaration when he related that Elizabeth—an older and formerly barren woman—had conceived. God's work in the lives of other believers also encourages us to trust in Him.

FOR ADULTS	■ **TOPIC:** Significance and Purpose

■ **QUESTIONS:** 1. Why was it important for God to send Gabriel to speak with Mary before she became pregnant? 2. In what way is the name of Jesus significant? 3. What connection is there between David and Jesus? 4. How would it be possible for Mary, who was a virgin at the time, to conceive and give birth to the Christ child? 5. Why did the angel mention Elizabeth to Mary?

■ **ILLUSTRATIONS:**

The High Cost of Finding One's Purpose in God. Dietrich Bonhoeffer was a brilliant leader and German pastor. Regrettably, he was also one of the victims of the horrific death-camps during World War II. Prior to being incarcerated for his unrelenting opposition to Hitler's movement, Bonhoeffer was the overseer of a seminary. The significance of his life in influencing countless people for Christ will be remembered by both seminarians and prisoners alike.

One day, after holding a small service for fellow prisoners, Bonhoeffer was taken away. A prisoner wrote that day: "Sunday April 8, 1945. Pastor Bonhoeffer held a little service which reached the hearts of all." He had hardly finished his prayer, when the door opened. Two evil-looking soldiers came in and barked: "Prisoner Bonhoeffer come with us!" The words meant only one thing—the scaffold. As he bid his fellow prisoners goodbye, he said, "For me this is the beginning of a new life, eternal life." For Bonhoeffer, it would be the fulfillment of his oft-quoted life theme, "When Christ calls a man, he bids him come and die."

A Greater Divine Purpose. It wasn't that Paul O'Keeffe particularly liked working with at-risk youth. It's just that those kinds of people seemed to find him. When he worked for a construction company in St. Louis, Missouri, the young men on the crew who were having difficulty seemed to always find him at breaks and lunch-time.

When Paul and his wife, Shirley, relocated to eastern Washington to work in a large aluminum plant, the same scenario happened again. What was there about Paul that seemed to attract the dark moths of society to him? Paul and Shirley were not converted to Christ until their mid-forties. One beautiful part of their testimony was that God graciously swept them into His kingdom on the very same day.

As Paul began to find meaning in his life through his relationship with God, he had many questions about his past. He wondered what it was about him that attracted so many young people to confide in him. For the first time, he began to wonder if that was more than mere coincidence—if it was part of a greater divine purpose. When his Sunday school teacher took every student through a gift-assessment one week, there it was again. It showed that Paul had an aptitude for counseling.

Finally, it all began to make sense to Paul. This natural ability was the predecessor to God's spiritual calling in his life. Paul soon returned to finish his graduate degree and took a job as a high school counselor. Now, more than ever, the teens turn to him for help.

Doing the Lord's Will. The story is told that in ancient times, a king had a huge boulder placed on a well-traveled roadway so it almost blocked the path. The monarch then hid himself and watched to see if anyone would remove the rock.

Many people, including some of the king's wealthiest merchants and courtiers, came to the huge stone and navigated their way around it. Most of them loudly blamed the king for not keeping the roads clear and for having their travel impeded. None of them, however, did anything about getting the huge stone out of the way. Then a peasant came along, carrying a load of vegetables. On approaching the boulder, the peasant laid down his burden and tried to move the stone to the side of the road. After much pushing and straining, he finally succeeded.

As the peasant picked up his load of vegetables to go on, he noticed a purse lying in the road where the boulder had been. The purse was full of gold coins and a note from the monarch indicating that the gold was for the person who removed the boulder from the roadway. The peasant learned what many others never understand: every obstacle we find in our path presents an opportunity to rejoice and be rewarded as we do the Lord's will.

FOR YOUTH
■ **TOPIC:** Called to Be a Servant
■ **QUESTIONS:** 1. In what sense was Mary highly favored by God? 2. What was it about the angel's greeting that troubled Mary? 3. In what sense was Jesus destined to be great? 4. What role would the Holy Spirit serve in the virginal conception and birth of Jesus? 5. How did Mary respond to Gabriel's announcement?

■ **ILLUSTRATIONS:**
Young People Are Still Being Called. When Karin signed up to go to summer camp with her youth group, she was expecting it to be more fun than life-changing. She was

17 years old, and her life was mostly filled with interests in boys, sports, and shopping. She had never once thought about living in a foreign land and doing the work of a missionary.

It was in a corner of the auditorium late one night that Karin received her "call" to serve God through foreign mission service, and the idea scared her terribly. Karin did not even like to eat Chinese take-out, so how could she ever live in southeast Asia? Yet, the sense of her destiny being connected to that region was inescapable. In the following years, Karin saw God make provision and preparation for her in many miraculous ways. She raised her annual support in a very short period of time, and language school seemed to float by with a supernatural grace.

On Karin's first furlough back to her hometown, for her 10-year high school reunion, her friends could not believe how fresh and alive she looked. She was the life of the reunion party. When asked what that extra source of spark and light within her was, Karin took the time to tell how obeying God brings life. Karin had long since learned not to get "preachy" with unbelievers. She merely let the story of God's miraculous love and provision flow from her.

Supernatural Peace in Unexpected Circumstances. When Horatio G. Spafford, the author of the great hymn, "It is Well with My Soul," penned those famous lyrics, we forget the pain that had become their source. You see, some years before its writing, Spafford had sent his family on a trans-Atlantic crossing. During the voyage, the great liner was sunk in a fierce storm. Later, Spafford himself was crossing the Atlantic on the same course that had taken his family. As the ship's captain announced that they were crossing over the site of the famous shipwreck, Spafford leaned over the railing and gazed into the dark waters.

It was at this time of tragedy revisited that God filled Horatio Spafford's heart with a deep peace and joy. Though he knew that in the depths below lay the bodies of his beloved family, the melody in his heart was ringing: "When peace like a river attendeth my way, when sorrows like sea billows roll—whatever my lot, Thou hast taught me to say, It is well, it is well with my soul."

Spafford understood better than most that there is no greater peace that a person can know than to have our lives and our families committed to the purposes of God.

Safe in the Will of God. When Roger Cooke left for Nepal to climb in the Himalayas, his mother was not as frightened as everyone expected her to be. She knew that her son was a very committed Christian. She also knew that he never made big decisions without an assurance that he had prayed and heard from God. When Cooke announced his plans to join the expedition, his mother simply replied: "I'd rather have you on the slopes of Mount Everest, knowing that you are in the will of God, than here in my home, knowing that you're outside that divine will."

CALLED TO PROCLAIM!

BACKGROUND SCRIPTURE: Luke 1:57-80
DEVOTIONAL READING: Malachi 3:1-4

KEY VERSE: And his mouth was opened immediately, and his tongue loosed, and he spake, and praised God. Luke 1:64.

3

KING JAMES VERSION

LUKE 1:67 And his father Zacharias was filled with the Holy Ghost, and prophesied, saying, 68 Blessed be the Lord God of Israel; for he hath visited and redeemed his people, 69 And hath raised up an horn of salvation for us in the house of his servant David; 70 As he spake by the mouth of his holy prophets, which have been since the world began: 71 That we should be saved from our enemies, and from the hand of all that hate us; 72 To perform the mercy promised to our fathers, and to remember his holy covenant; 73 The oath which he sware to our father Abraham, 74 That he would grant unto us, that we being delivered out of the hand of our enemies might serve him without fear, 75 In holiness and righteousness before him, all the days of our life. 76 And thou, child, shalt be called the prophet of the Highest: for thou shalt go before the face of the Lord to prepare his ways; 77 To give knowledge of salvation unto his people by the remission of their sins, 78 Through the tender mercy of our God; whereby the dayspring from on high hath visited us, 79 To give light to them that sit in darkness and in the shadow of death, to guide our feet into the way of peace. 80 And the child grew, and waxed strong in spirit, and was in the deserts till the day of his shewing unto Israel.

NEW REVISED STANDARD VERSION

LUKE 1:67 Then his father Zechariah was filled with the Holy Spirit and spoke this prophecy:
68 "Blessed be the Lord God of Israel,
  for he has looked favorably on his people and
    redeemed them.
69 He has raised up a mighty savior for us
  in the house of his servant David,
70 as he spoke through the mouth of his holy
    prophets from of old,
71 that we would be saved from our enemies and
    from the hand of all who hate us.
72 Thus he has shown the mercy promised to our
    ancestors,
  and has remembered his holy covenant,
73 the oath that he swore to our ancestor Abraham,
  to grant us 74 that we, being rescued from the hands
    of our enemies,
might serve him without fear, 75 in holiness and
    righteousness
  before him all our days.
76 And you, child, will be called the prophet of the
    Most High;
  for you will go before the Lord to prepare his ways,
77 to give knowledge of salvation to his people
  by the forgiveness of their sins.
78 By the tender mercy of our God,
  the dawn from on high will break upon us,
79 to give light to those who sit in darkness and in the
    shadow of death,
  to guide our feet into the way of peace."
80 The child grew and became strong in spirit, and he was in the wilderness until the day he appeared publicly to Israel.

Monday, December 10	Malachi 3:1-4	*A Messenger Is Coming*
Tuesday, December 11	Luke 1:57-61	*Elizabeth Births a Son*
Wednesday, December 12	Luke 1:62-66	*His Name Is John*
Thursday, December 13	Luke 1:67-75	*God Sends a Powerful Savior*
Friday, December 14	Luke 1:76-80	*Preparing the Way*
Saturday, December 15	Luke 3:7-14	*Warnings to the Crowds*
Sunday, December 16	Luke 3:15-20	*A Powerful One Is Coming*

BACKGROUND

Much as the Book of 1 Samuel began with the account of the barren Hannah and her child Samuel, the third Synoptic Gospel opens with the account of the elderly priest, Zechariah, and his barren wife, Elizabeth, who were also blessed with a special child. When the period of gestation ended, Elizabeth gave birth to a son (Luke 1:57). The mother's neighbors and relatives had heard how merciful the Lord had been to her, and they, too, were glad (1:58). Eight days after the child was born, Elizabeth and Zechariah had their infant son circumcised in accordance with the law of Moses (Gen. 17:9-14; Lev. 2:3). The ceremony signified that John belonged to the Lord and the community of His people.

This ceremony was a joyous occasion when family members and friends gathered together. Those present assumed the parents were going to name their newborn after Zechariah, his father (Luke 1:59). Elizabeth, however, objected, saying that the child's name was *John* (1:60). The guests were surprised by the mother's statement, for no one in her or her husband's family was named John (1:61). Those present made gestures to Zechariah to discover what he wanted to name his son (1:62). From this verse it seems likely that Zechariah was deaf as well as mute.

The father asked for a writing tablet, which was probably a board covered with wax that could be written on with a pointed instrument. Zechariah wrote that the child's name was John. This decision amazed the guests, for it broke with the custom of the day (1:63). The angel Gabriel had previously said Zechariah would be mute until his son was born (1:20). After the father indicated what his son's name would be, Zechariah immediately received back his ability to speak. Without hesitation he began to praise God for the birth of John and for the wonderful things the Lord would do through him (1:64).

All the neighbors became filled with awe, for they sensed that something unusual, perhaps even supernatural, had occurred. Moreover, throughout the entire hill country of Judea, the recent series of events became the topic of conversation (1:65). The locals pondered in their hearts what the Lord had in store for John, especially since it was clear that the hand of the Lord was with him (1:66). The latter implies that God's favor, presence, and direction were evident in John's life from the time of his birth.

NOTES ON THE PRINTED TEXT

Luke 1:67 says that John's father, Zechariah, became *filled with the Holy Ghost* and began to prophesy. As the following verses make clear, the elderly father spoke God's will through a song of praise. Zechariah began with a common benediction: *Blessed be the Lord God of Israel* (1:68). The Latin wording at the start of the psalm, which is rendered *blessed be,* has given rise to Zechariah's hymn being called the *Benedictus.*

Zechariah not only enjoined praising God, but also gave reasons for doing so by amassing all the evidence he could remember about God. First, Zechariah praised God because He had turned His face toward His people and set them free. God had broken into the priest's life in such a special way that he could not miss its significance. He equated his experience with God's redemptive purposes for His people. God's saving intervention was the theme of the Old Testament prophecies. They painted glorious pictures of the Messiah's reign over Israel. Zechariah had imbibed deeply of these prophecies. Nothing in his mind superseded his hope of God's coming to redeem His people through the Messiah. In this regard, Gabriel had told Zechariah what John's role would be. He would be filled with the Holy Spirit to bring Israel back to God. John would also *make ready a people prepared for the Lord* (1:17). It's no wonder that Zechariah was excited about what God promised to do through John the Baptizer.

Zechariah thanked God because He had raised up a standard of salvation through David's line. The godly Jews knew that the promised Messiah would be a descendant of King David. Prophecies about the Messiah's Davidic ancestry abound in the Old Testament (2 Sam. 7:12; Ps. 89:3; Jer. 23:5; 33:14). Undoubtedly, Zechariah had these sorts of messianic promises in mind when he made reference to God's *horn of salvation* (Luke 1:69). Zechariah and Hannah used similar terminology when they responded to God's blessing (1 Sam. 2:1; Luke 1:69); however, the image Zechariah had in mind was different from Hannah's. Her vision had to do with being freed from a burden and being able to lift her head up with pride. Zechariah's vision had to do with the power associated with a beast of burden such as an ox, an animal whose horns are indicative of strength. It is clear that the image of a *horn of salvation* in Luke 1:69 referred to the powerful way in which the Father would redeem Israel through His Son, the Messiah.

Zechariah praised God because He had promised long ago through the *holy prophets* (1:70) to provide redemption through the Messiah. Zechariah now saw what had happened in light of his understanding of the messianic prophecies recorded in the Old Testament. Zechariah was thankful, for God had promised salvation from *our enemies* (1:71). Because Israel had suffered so much at the hands of foreign invaders, relief from their oppressing circumstances was uppermost in the minds of God's people. The salvation promised was not in terms of political deliverance, but spiritual liberation from Satan, sin, and death. Indeed, one day the Messiah would usher in a universal reign of peace and justice. It's true that at His first advent, He was rejected and crucified; yet, at His second advent, He will reign in great power and glory.

Zechariah continued to emphasize that what had happened in the amazing birth of John was consistent with all God promised to do for His people. Zechariah was especially thankful for God's *mercy* (1:72), especially His steadfast love through which He fulfilled His promises. The priest also expressed gratitude that the Lord remembered *his holy covenant*. This was in keeping with the *oath which he sware* (1:73) with Abraham, the patriarch. God promised through Abraham that his descendants would possess and dwell in the land that eventually became Israel. In fact, the entire world would be blessed through one of the patriarch's descendants (Gen. 12:1-3; 22:16-18). Through what was about to happen in the lives of John and Jesus, God planned to fulfill His covenant promise to Abraham.

Zechariah was convinced God would rescue His people *out of the hand of [their] enemies* (1:74) so that they could serve Him. Israel's service before God *without fear* was stamped with *holiness and righteousness* (1:75). Zechariah underscored here the character of the Messiah's reign and the purpose of His coming. His ultimate mission was to restore Israel's people to their God-given duty to be holy. Holiness speaks of our relationship with God through faith in Jesus Christ, while righteousness has to do with how we respond to others. We are to serve God *all the days of our life,* striving to be consistent in our witness before the world.

At this point, Zechariah focused his attention on John. He would be a *prophet* (1:76) to prepare the way for the Messiah. John was the forerunner who would tell Israel that the promised Redeemer had arrived in the person of Jesus of Nazareth. John clarified who the Messiah was, what role He would play in the redemption of Israel, and what the people must do in response. When the crowds heard John preach, they recognized that he was indeed *the prophet of the Highest*. The latter expression was a way to refer to the exalted, transcendent God without directly naming Him. First century Jews adopted this convention out of reverence for the divine name. The task of the Lord's prophet was not pleasant, because he was called to expose people's sins. Preparing the way for the Messiah was like road building through mountains and valleys (Isa. 40:3-4).

Most of the Jews had erroneous ideas about the kind of salvation the Messiah would bring. They thought it would be political, not spiritual, in nature. God sent John to teach them the true and correct understanding of spiritual deliverance, which is based on the forgiveness of sins through faith in Christ. The people desperately needed this *knowledge of salvation* (Luke 1:77; see Jer. 31:34), for they were in spiritual darkness. As John went about the difficult task of preparing the people for the advent of the Messiah, the Baptizer would light their path and show them the proper direction to walk. Indeed, though John would cause people to face up to their sinful nature, his message would focus on God's offer of forgiveness, not on condemnation.

Zechariah's song acknowledged that John's life and ministry would be blessed by the *tender mercy of our God* (Luke 1:78). Such steadfast love would be like the dawning of a new day. The priest knew that he himself had received God's grace, and he was overcome by the prospect of God's people being spiritually revived and restored under His merciful hand. John's amazing birth and his preaching of righteousness would be considerable evidence that God had not forgotten His people.

Like the *dayspring from on high*, the Father's mercy made available through His Son would bring light to people living *in darkness and in the shadow of death* (1:79). Like the rising sun, God's unfailing compassion in the Messiah would lead sinners *into the way of peace.* These beautiful words reflect the majesty and glory of Zechariah's proclamation. He was filled with praise because he knew that God was about to do something special for His people through John. The ultimate result of John's ministry would be people making a commitment to repent and accept the salvation freely offered by Jesus.

At the conclusion of Zechariah's song, we learn two main facts concerning John. First, while growing up, he became *strong in spirit* (1:80). This indicates John imbibed his parents' vibrant faith, trust, and hope in the Lord. In fact, from birth John was filled with the Holy Spirit (1:15). Second, John chose a life of seclusion *in the deserts* (1:80), that is, the barren Judean wilderness in the Jordan Valley west of the Dead Sea. This was part of his spiritual preparation for his mission. He was focused on God and His calling. When John began to preach, his desert lifestyle gave power and authenticity to his words (Matt. 3:1-6).

SUGGESTIONS TO TEACHERS

The climax of God's preparation for His Son's entrance into this hostile world came with the preaching of John the Baptist, the herald and forerunner of Jesus. As He often did, God used the unusual and unexpected to manifest His great power. For instance, John was born to a childless couple far past the normal age of childbearing. The response of the priest Zechariah, John's father, to God's amazing grace was Zechariah's submission to the Holy Spirit, who prophesied a thrilling message through him.

1. A VOICE FOR GOD'S SPIRIT. God used Zechariah as a mouthpiece for His Spirit, and God continues to use imperfect messengers through whom to proclaim His good news to a sinful world. God can speak through His people in different ways. Some can share their faith with eloquence, while others have great difficulty speaking. Those who live a consistent Christian life in the world are allowing God's Spirit to manifest divine love through them.

2. A MESSAGE OF HOPE. Zechariah praised God because He was raising up a Savior from the lineage of David, as He had promised. This confirmed the faithful preaching of the prophets of old. God moved to provide salvation for sinners because of His grace, not because of humankind's worthiness. The long centuries of despair for God's people might have caused many of them to think that God had abandoned them. The Spirit reminded them, through Zechariah, that the Lord would keep His promise of a coming Savior because of the covenant He had made with their ancestors. Some believers today may struggle with a sense of hopelessness, convinced that their sins are beyond God's willingness to forgive. The message of hope God has given us to proclaim is that He is able and willing to save sinners because of His great love for them in Christ.

3. A LIGHT IN THE DARKNESS. John came to understand that his role in life was to be transparent so that the Savior might be revealed. John's message of repentance would not be pleasant for people to hear. This remained true, even though the authority of the Spirit of God through which John spoke would seize the hearts of the people. The light of Christ, which shines in the world's darkness of sin, is sufficient to bring conviction upon those who allow it to pierce their hearts. It is always the message that is most important, not the messenger. For instance, John's message was to point the people away from him and to the Lamb of God. Forgiveness of sin would only come after a genuine repentance from sin.

FOR ADULTS	■ **TOPIC:** Life-Changing Events

■ **QUESTIONS:** 1. How was Zechariah able to prophesy words of hope and promise to the people? 2. Why was it important for Zechariah to emphasize that the Savior would be of the lineage of David? 3. What was the *holy covenant* (Luke 1:72) that God had made with His people? 4. What was the message John would proclaim to the people? 5. How can we become more willing to let God speak through us to communicate the good news of salvation to others?

■ **ILLUSTRATIONS:**

Realizing a Dream. Many years ago, Rudy Atwood was the pianist for Charles E. Fuller's radio program the *Old Fashioned Revival Hour*. Atwood's improvisations of hymns and gospel music were fabulous. My family always listened to the *Old Fashioned Revival Hour* on Sunday mornings before we left home for Sunday school and church. Also, my piano teacher knew how fascinated I was by Atwood's playing, for I often would mimic his piano stylings in my limited way.

One day, I read in the newspaper that Atwood and the *Old Fashioned Revival Hour* quartet were coming to the city auditorium for a one-night concert in our southeast Texas city. My heart skipped a beat. My "life-changing dream" was to be able to see Atwood in person and hear him play. My piano teacher knew someone who was instrumental in engaging the quartet for our town, and without my knowing it, made arrangements for me to sit on the stage, in the wings, just a few feet from the piano. I felt as if I was in heaven! At last, I realized my "life-changing dream." But more importantly, God used that opportunity to confirm my calling into Christian ministry.

When Zechariah was chosen to serve in the temple, he, too, realized a dream every priest cherished, but few were able to experience. He did not know that a life-changing event awaited him.

Divine Cultivation. The long winter was over. The farmer, weary from the endless years of raising one crop after another, looked across his fields. The dead, tangled brush was matted on the ground. The earth was packed by the winter rains and snows. Suddenly, the task seemed too great. He refused to plow his fields this year.

On the adjoining farm, the farmer's neighbor stood observing his own fields. He saw the same scene—the dried, matted weeds and the hard earth. But the neighbor also saw, in his mind's eye, the waving, golden grain that would stand proudly on that land as it had season after season through the long years. So the neighbor hitched up his horses and began the arduous task of cultivation. Soon the soil was broken up, the furrows were straightened, and the seed was planted. In the summer, the harvest came as the golden grain waved in the wind.

The calloused, sinful hearts of God's people must have looked like the hard, weed-infested land after a long winter, but God did not walk away. In a manner of speaking, He plowed the field and cultivated the hearts of the people. The coming of John the Baptizer was one way that God prepared them for the coming of His Son.

Where We Are. John Bunyan (1628–1688), author of *The Pilgrim's Progress*, reminds us that Christmas is also a story of redemption: "Christ did not only come into our flesh, but also into our condition, into the valley and shadow of death, where we were, and where we are, as we are sinners." Only then could He whom John the Baptizer announced lead us out of death and into abundant, eternal life.

 For Youth

■ **Topic:** Called to Spread the Word

■ **Questions:** 1. What was the difference between the miracles involved in John's and Jesus' births? 2. What was more important to Zechariah than merely having a son in his old age? 3. As *the prophet of the Highest* (Luke 1:76), what would John do? 4. In what way was John different from Jesus in his growing up years? 5. What can we do to ensure that our role in life is the one God has for us?

■ **Illustrations:**

In the Worst of Times. An old, weathered tombstone stands in a centuries-old cemetery in England. The name chiseled in the stone is unknown, save, no doubt, to the family to which the deceased belonged. Beneath the name and birth and death dates is inscribed this epitaph with a powerful message: "In the worst of times, he did the best of things."

In the worst of times, God prepared a herald for the coming of His Son. The pagan Romans occupied Palestine. God's people lived in physical and spiritual bondage. John was true to God's calling in his life, and "in the worst of times, he did the best of things." How might you fulfill God's call on your life to spread the Gospel?

Paul Revere's Midnight Ride. Every child in the United States should know the account of Paul Revere, the American patriot who, in 1775, carried news to Lexington that the British troops were approaching. He called the people of the countryside to arms. On a borrowed horse, Revere road through the town in the middle of the night, crying out to the sleeping people, "The British are coming! The British are coming!" News had come that General Thomas Gate, the British commander-in-chief of the Massachusetts Bay Colony, had been instructed to enforce order among the colonists. So he ordered his lieutenant to proceed with a detachment of 700 men to destroy the supplies of the colonists in Concord and to arrest the patriot leaders, Samuel Adams and John Hancock.

What if Revere, when he arrived in town on that April night, had walked quietly up to each door, tapped lightly, and apologetically told the occupant that it was rumored that some British soldiers might be moving in their direction? On the contrary, Revere rode through the town shouting at the top of his voice! Lamps were lighted, windows flung open, people poured into the streets, and they were mobilized in moments. Why? It's because Revere heralded impending danger and disaster, and the people responded accordingly.

What Are You Hearing? A man from rural east Texas was visiting his friend in the city of New York. As they walked down a crowded street, the visitor said, "I hear a cricket." "A cricket?" the New Yorker chirped. "No way! You could never hear a cricket in all of this noise! It's the noon hour, and people are all around us. Horns are honking and taxis are squealing around corners. There's no way you could be hearing a cricket!"

"Yes, but I'm sure I do," muttered the east Texan. He walked over to a shrub in a large cement planter by the curb of the street. He dug beneath the leaves and found the cricket he had heard. His friend was astounded. The Texan assured him that his ears were no different from anyone else's. "It simply depends on what you are listening for. Here, let me show you." He took several coins from his pocket and slammed them on the concrete sidewalk. People walking for several yards in both directions stopped and turned their heads. "You see what I mean? It all depends on what you are listening for."

In the desert of Judea, John the Baptizer would listen for the voice of God. John would hear it, and he would spend the rest of his life pointing others to Christ. What are you hearing and sharing with others about the Savior?

CALLED TO REJOICE!

BACKGROUND SCRIPTURE: Luke 2:1-20
DEVOTIONAL READING: Psalm 96:1-6

KEY VERSE: For unto you is born this day in the city of
David a Saviour, which is Christ the Lord. Luke 2:11.

4

KING JAMES VERSION

LUKE 2:1 And it came to pass in those days, that there went out a decree from Caesar Augustus, that all the world should be taxed. 2 (And this taxing was first made when Cyrenius was governor of Syria.) 3 And all went to be taxed, every one into his own city. 4 And Joseph also went up from Galilee, out of the city of Nazareth, into Judaea, unto the city of David, which is called Bethlehem; (because he was of the house and lineage of David:) 5 To be taxed with Mary his espoused wife, being great with child. 6 And so it was, that, while they were there, the days were accomplished that she should be delivered. 7 And she brought forth her firstborn son, and wrapped him in swaddling clothes, and laid him in a manger; because there was no room for them in the inn.

8 And there were in the same country shepherds abiding in the field, keeping watch over their flock by night. 9 And, lo, the angel of the Lord came upon them, and the glory of the Lord shone round about them: and they were sore afraid. 10 And the angel said unto them, Fear not: for, behold, I bring you good tidings of great joy, which shall be to all people. 11 For unto you is born this day in the city of David a Saviour, which is Christ the Lord. 12 And this shall be a sign unto you; Ye shall find the babe wrapped in swaddling clothes, lying in a manger. 13 And suddenly there was with the angel a multitude of the heavenly host praising God, and saying, 14 Glory to God in the highest, and on earth peace, good will toward men.

NEW REVISED STANDARD VERSION

LUKE 2:1 In those days a decree went out from Emperor Augustus that all the world should be registered. 2 This was the first registration and was taken while Quirinius was governor of Syria. 3 All went to their own towns to be registered. 4 Joseph also went from the town of Nazareth in Galilee to Judea, to the city of David called Bethlehem, because he was descended from the house and family of David. 5 He went to be registered with Mary, to whom he was engaged and who was expecting a child. 6 While they were there, the time came for her to deliver her child. 7 And she gave birth to her firstborn son and wrapped him in bands of cloth, and laid him in a manger, because there was no place for them in the inn.

8 In that region there were shepherds living in the fields, keeping watch over their flock by night. 9 Then an angel of the Lord stood before them, and the glory of the Lord shone around them, and they were terrified. 10 But the angel said to them, "Do not be afraid; for see—I am bringing you good news of great joy for all the people: 11 to you is born this day in the city of David a Savior, who is the Messiah, the Lord. 12 This will be a sign for you: you will find a child wrapped in bands of cloth and lying in a manger." 13 And suddenly there was with the angel a multitude of the heavenly host, praising God and saying,

14 "Glory to God in the highest heaven,
and on earth peace among those whom he favors!"

Monday, December 17	Psalm 96:1-6	*Sing a New Song*
Tuesday, December 18	Matthew 1:18b-21	*Joseph and Mary*
Wednesday, December 19	Luke 2:1-5	*Traveling to Bethlehem*
Thursday, December 20	Luke 2:6-7	*Jesus, Firstborn Son*
Friday, December 21	Luke 2:8-14	*Angels Proclaim the News*
Saturday, December 22	Luke 2:15-20	*Shepherds Visit the King*
Sunday, December 23	Psalm 96:7-13	*Judging with God's Truth*

BACKGROUND

Luke 2:1 introduces Jesus' birth by setting it in its historical context. The author mentioned the emperor of Rome, Caesar Augustus. This refers to Octavian, who had established a reputation for being administratively skillful and adroit. As a result of an imperial edict issued by the Roman Senate, Caesar directed that the inhabitants of the empire be registered for the purpose of collecting taxes. The census was not so much to count people as to determine who owed taxes and who could serve in the Roman army (though Jews were not subject to military conscription). This was the first registration taken when Publius Sulpicius Quirinius was governor of the Roman province of Syria (2:2). Caesar relied upon high-level administrators such as Quirinius to ensure that inhabitants throughout the empire journeyed to their home-towns to be registered (2:3). Luke's historical approach underscores the fact that at Jesus' birth, the eternal God invaded temporal human affairs. It also demonstrates that God used secular rulers and events to accomplish His purposes.

Most Bible scholars have concluded that Jesus was born sometime between 8 B.C. and 4 B.C. The following are some of the facts that must be considered: Caesar Augustus was emperor of Rome from 27 B.C. to A.D. 14. (and was succeeded by Tiberius, the Roman emperor at the time that Jesus ministered). One Roman inscription refers to an official who governed Syria sometime in the first decade B.C. and again for a while in the first decade A.D.; this may have been Quirinius. The earliest Roman census we know about (from sources other than the Bible) was conducted in A.D. 6. Since these censuses were probably conducted every 14 years, the *first registration* (2:2, NRSV) would have been in 8 B.C. It may have been delayed, however, a year or more in Palestine. Finally, Jesus may have lived for as long as two years before Herod the Great died in the spring of 4 B.C. (Matt. 2:16, 19). Jesus was about 30 when He began His ministry in A.D. 26 or 27 (Luke 3:23).

NOTES ON THE PRINTED TEXT

The census mentioned in Luke 2:1-2 forced people to go to their hometowns to be registered (2:3). For Joseph, this meant leaving Nazareth, which was situated in lower Galilee roughly halfway between the Sea of Galilee and the

Mediterranean Sea. Nazareth was sufficiently close to the main trade routes of Palestine to maintain contact with the outside world; but its rural setting in a high valley overlooking the Plain of Esdraelon enabled the town to remain somewhat independent and aloof from external influences. Indeed, people from Jerusalem regarded such a frontier town as Nazareth as being on the periphery of Israel's national and religious life (see John 1:46).

To comply with the census, Joseph had to travel about 90 miles—at least a three-day journey—from Nazareth to Bethlehem, the town of his ancestors (and possibly those of Mary). Bethlehem is located on the edge of the Judean desert about seven miles southwest of Jerusalem. The town of Jesus' birth is situated on a high ridge of mountains about 2,500 feet above sea level, near the main road linking Hebron and Egypt. The climate of Bethlehem is somewhat Mediterranean. However, the town's higher elevation moderates the summer temperatures it experiences. This milder climate, along with fertile surrounding hills, makes the area ideal for growing grapes and figs, and for grazing sheep and goats. Bethlehem was the burial place of Rachel, the wife of Jacob (Gen. 35:19). The city was also the setting for much of the Book of Ruth. Bethlehem later became the ancestral home of David, and it was there that Samuel the prophet anointed David as Saul's successor (1 Sam. 16:1, 13; 17:12). King Rehoboam later rebuilt and fortified the city (2 Chron. 11:5-6).

Luke 2:5 says that at the time Joseph made the journey, he was betrothed to Mary. Evidently, she was living with Joseph as his wife, though they had not yet consummated their relationship (Matt. 1:25). Because Mary was almost ready to give birth to Jesus, the trip from Nazareth to Bethlehem was not the best time for her; but there was no way Joseph could delay the journey. Thus, they decided Mary should go with him. In Jewish culture, betrothal was as legally binding as marriage itself. Before the engagement could be finalized, negotiations took place between the groom and the family of the bride. In addition, the groom paid a dowry (usually money or property) to the father of the bride. For a virgin, the period of betrothal typically lasted a year and could be terminated only by divorce. If the groom died during this time, the bride would be regarded a widow. Sexual unfaithfulness during betrothal was considered adultery (Deut. 22:13-21). When the period of betrothal had ended, the groom claimed his bride. After the wedding rituals, the newly married couple could consummate their union.

While Joseph and Mary were in Bethlehem, Mary's pregnancy ended and she delivered her child (Luke 2:6). At this time, Bethlehem likely was overflowing with travelers who sought to register in the census; thus, suitable accommodations were difficult to find. The *inn* (2:7) could have been a reception room in a private home or a space at a public, outdoor shelter, but it was probably not a large building with several individual rooms. The traditional image of an apathetic innkeeper who turned away Joseph and Mary (as well as Jesus) at the door may or may not be accurate. According to tradition, Mary gave birth to her firstborn in a cave that had been made into a stable (2:6). Others, however, think Joseph and Mary stayed in the open courtyard of a crowded home, where there would have been a series of stalls along the walls. Travelers used the stalls as stables and lean-to shelters. Quite possibly, Mary gave birth surrounded by the activity of the courtyard.

Like many peasant children, Mary's son would have been washed in a mixture of water and olive oil, rubbed with salt, and then wrapped in strips of linen. These would be placed around the arms and legs of the infant to keep the limbs protected. (The custom of wrapping infants this way is still practiced in many Middle Eastern countries.) Mary then laid the child in a trough used for feeding animals. Being born in a stable was a humble beginning for one supposed to be the Savior of the world. He would not be the conquering Messiah the nation was anticipating. He would not mobilize the militant Zealots to throw off the Roman yoke. Instead, He came to serve (Mark 10:45), to seek and to save the lost (Luke 19:10).

Mary must have wondered how the angel's words about Jesus could come true (1:32-33). We can be thankful, however, that the Gospel of Luke gives us its distinctive version of Jesus' birth. The third Synoptic Gospel shows us how God stooped to lift fallen humanity. Jesus came as a poor, humble, and homeless baby. Between a humble birth and a debasing (but victorious) death, Jesus lived simply, spoke vividly, and was often in the company of people whom polite society either rejected or ignored (5:27-32; 7:36-50). Because He identified with the lowest, He gives hope today to those who have no other source of hope.

An angel announced the Messiah's birth to ordinary shepherds, not the powerful rulers or religious leaders (2:8). Since shepherds in Bible times lived out in the open and were unable to maintain strict obedience to the law of Moses, they generally were considered to be ceremonially unclean. As a result, they were despised by religious legalists and were typically excluded from temple worship. Custom didn't even allow shepherds to serve as witnesses in legal cases. Interestingly, these shepherds may have been watching over flocks reserved for temple sacrifices in Jerusalem. Why then did God single out these Bethlehem shepherds? Perhaps He wanted to make a point. It's not normally the influential or the elite who catch God's attention, but those who call for help and place their trust in the Lord.

According to 2:9, an angel of the Lord suddenly appeared near or in front of the shepherds and the radiance of God's glory surrounded them. The word *glory*, when applied to God in Scripture, refers to the luminous manifestation of His being. In other words, it is the brilliant revelation of Himself to humanity. This definition is borne out by the many ways the word is used in Scripture. For example, brilliant light consistently went with manifestations of God (Matt. 17:2; 1 Tim. 6:16; Rev. 1:16). Furthermore, the word *glory* is often linked with verbs of seeing (Exod. 16:7; 33:18; Isa. 40:5) and of appearing (Exod. 16:10; Deut. 5:24), both of which emphasize the visible nature of the Lord's glory.

The shepherds were terrified by the sight of the angel; but the heavenly emissary reassured them with good news of a joyous event (Luke 2:10), namely, the birth of Israel's *Savior, Messiah,* and *Lord* (2:11, NRSV). (This combination of terms appears no where else in the New Testament.) The one who eternally existed in regal splendor had been born that night in Bethlehem. Indeed, He who is sovereign and all-powerful would make redemption available to humanity, including the weak and oppressed—even society's outcasts. Military and political leaders during those times were frequently called "saviors"; but Jesus was unique, being the Anointed One of God. The angel encouraged the shepherds to find the Christ child lying in a manger, wrapped snugly in strips of cloth (2:12). In fact, this would be a sign from the Father validating the birth of His Son.

We can imagine the shepherds staring in amazement, trembling and trying to grasp the significance of the angel's announcement. Suddenly, the night sky exploded with the sounds of a vast, heavenly army praising God (2:13). The angels gave glory (or honor) to the Creator and announced peace for all who receive His favor (2:14). In that day, Augustus was hailed as the source and sustainer of peace. Even today, people long for freedom from war as well as to enjoy a state of mental calm and serenity; but true and lasting peace cannot be achieved until individuals experience an ending of hostility with the Father, and this is only possible through faith in the Son (see John 14:27; Rom. 5:1-11).

SUGGESTIONS TO TEACHERS

Perhaps some students in your class think they know all about the birth of Jesus. They may have participated in so many Christmas pageants that they struggle with getting interested in this week's lesson. Your challenge is to help them take a fresh look at what the Bible teaches and to encourage them to rejoice in the coming of God's Son.

1. DATE IN HISTORY. Some occasionally voice doubts about whether an actual person named Jesus really lived. Luke's references to various historical figures clearly show that Jesus was no make-believe person but rather someone who was born at a specific point in time. God did not remain aloof or allow Himself to be considered in the abstract. Instead, the Lord of glory took on flesh and was born in the city of Bethlehem.

2. DEPARTURE TO BETHLEHEM. The harsh realities of the Christmas narrative are sometimes overlooked. At great personal inconvenience, a poor peasant couple was forced to make a long and tiresome journey. The two lived in a turbulent time and were subjected to the dictates of a powerful distant emperor. Augustus ruled through callous local underlings who were backed by a ruthless occupying army. Emphasize to your students that God enabled Mary and Joseph to prevail over their circumstances. Similarly, God can help the class members deal with their problems.

3. DEPRESSING CIRCUMSTANCES. Jesus was born in the most humble of settings. The eternal King did not appear in a grandiose Roman palace, but rather in a dark and dirty place in an obscure corner of the empire. No matter how futile our circumstances might seem, we can find strength in knowing that God cared enough to send His Son to experience life as we know it.

4. DISCLOSURE TO THE SHEPHERDS. Lowly shepherds were the first to learn the momentous news and the first to gaze upon the infant Jesus. From this we see that God sent His Son to even the least significant of humans! No one can rightfully claim that he or she is unimportant to the Lord after hearing that shepherds were Jesus' first audience.

FOR ADULTS

■ **TOPIC:** Reasons to Rejoice

■ **QUESTIONS:** 1. What circumstances forced Joseph and Mary to travel to Bethlehem? 2. Where was Jesus born in Bethlehem and why is that fact important? 3. Why did an angel visit a group of shepherds near Bethlehem? 4. What did the angel tell the shepherds? 5. What was the focus of the angelic chorus?

■ **ILLUSTRATIONS:**

The First Creche. Legend has it that in December of 1223, Francis of Assisi was on his way to preach in the village of Greccio, Italy. As he walked, he pondered how he could bring home to the poor illiterate peasants the real meaning of Christmas. He wanted the account of the Savior's birth to live in their hearts.

Suddenly, Francis had an idea. He would recreate the manger scene for his audience. First, he went to a friend in the village, and between them they fashioned the first creche, or nativity scene. Then, when the peasants came to the church on Christmas eve, they stopped in amazement and fell on their knees in adoration. There they saw a live donkey and ox. They also noticed real people playing the parts of Joseph, Mary, and the shepherds. Moreover, in a crude manger lay a representation of the infant Jesus.

Francis proceeded to tell the onlookers the joyous account of the birth of the Messiah. This enabled the peasants to feel as if they were actually in ancient Bethlehem. This experience also helped them never to forget the message of hope and gladness they heard that night.

Poet's Longing. Thomas Hardy's poem, "The Oxen," describes an old English folk legend in which the oxen are said to kneel in their stalls every Christmas Eve at the stroke of midnight, in memory of Jesus' birth in Bethlehem. At the end of the poem, Hardy imagines someone telling him that in a remote farm, the animals were kneeling that night. If he were invited to see this, the agnostic Hardy said he would "go with the person in the . . . hope that it might be so."

Perhaps you, like the poet Hardy, have wished that there might be some cause for hoping, some reason for worshiping, and some evidence for rejoicing in the truth of the Messiah's birth. Consider again Luke 2:11, *For unto you is born this day in the city of David a Saviour, which is Christ the Lord.*

The Father has come to us in the person of His Son, Jesus. And at the manger, God has reached out to us in love. All of us are residents of this planet where Jesus made His home! This is the reason for hoping, worshiping, and rejoicing.

Good News of Salvation. Did you know that people of other religions also esteem Jesus? Muslims, for example, recognize Jesus as a great prophet and revere Him as *Isa ibn Maryam*—Jesus, the son of Mary, the only woman mentioned by name in the Quran (or Koran). At a time when many Christians deny Jesus' birth to a virgin, Muslims find the account in their holy book and affirm it as true.

"Many Westerners also do not believe Jesus ascended into heaven, but Muslims do," says Seyyed Hossein Nasar, professor of Islamic studies at George Washington University. *Newsweek* magazine says that, according to one recent estimate, alleged visions of Jesus or Mary have occurred some 70 times in Muslim countries since 1985.

It is the Cross, however, that separates Christianity from Islam and all other religions and spiritual traditions. Other religions may celebrate Jesus as a great prophet, but the holy child born in a manger became the holy servant hanging from a tree. This same Redeemer, who was raised from the dead as the holy Son, brings eternal life to all who believe. Here we find the ultimate message of salvation that is Good News to everyone.

■ **TOPIC:** Called to Greet the Messiah

■ **QUESTIONS:** 1. At the time of Jesus' birth, what made the conditions difficult for Mary? 2. How did God move through the actions of others to bring about His will? 3. Why do you think the shepherds were the first to hear the good news of the Messiah's birth? 4. What sign did the angel give to the shepherds to confirm what he had declared? 5. How did the shepherds react to the angel's announcement concerning the baby Jesus?

■ **ILLUSTRATIONS:**
Lost Roots. "Where are you from?" That is one of the most frequently asked questions in a conversation between adults. Many older people grew up in one place, with family roots in a particular town or city. But this isn't true for younger people today. They don't have a strong sense of family roots that links them to one specific place.

A child may have been born in one state, spent his or her preschool years in another state, and then the grade school and middle school years in a third state. Meanwhile, the grandparents live across the country.

Joseph undoubtedly had a sense of family roots and heritage, and that's why Bethlehem was important to him and his family. This reminds us that Jesus knew His background and heritage. We too share in that same heritage, regardless of our past and present life circumstances.

The Gospel: A Best-Kept Secret? If you were to do a computer search on the Internet using the words "best-kept secret," you would get a list that ranges from bed-and-breakfast accommodations to historical biographies and gourmet coffee. One item you likely will not find listed is the good news of salvation through faith in the Messiah.

The Gospel was never intended to be a best-kept secret. Jesus told His first followers to go and proclaim it to the world. That charge has been handed down to us through centuries of believers, and now lies directly in our realm of responsibility. How else are people, whether young or old, going to meet the Messiah who was born in Bethlehem almost 2,000 years ago?

Are we keeping the Gospel to ourselves? Are we afraid that our peers will misunderstand our Good News and call it bad news? Some people who hear our news will reject it—and us. But Jesus has told us not to be afraid of such things, for as He said, *Lo, I am with you alway, even unto the end of the world* (Matt. 28:20).

God's Unseen Purposes. Texas evangelist, James Robison, has a deep heart of compassion for disadvantaged and abused women. His organization has done countless deeds of mercy to help those who have been victimized by the traumas of unwanted pregnancies. Though Robison's organization offers many services, from counseling to crisis-pregnancy support, his concern is not merely the outcome of what he has observed in others. He believes that God has a destiny for others that is often unseen by human eyes.

While others debate the technical aspects of a controversial subject, Robison feels it on a personal level. He'll be the first to tell you how thankful he is that one woman decided to keep a child that was conceived from the pregnancy that resulted from a violent rape. Robison knows that he wouldn't be here today if his mother had chosen otherwise.

CALLED TO WITNESS!

BACKGROUND SCRIPTURE: Luke 2:22-38
DEVOTIONAL READING: Isaiah 49:5-6

KEY VERSE: And Simeon blessed them, and said unto Mary his mother,
Behold, this child is set for the fall and rising again of many in Israel. Luke 2:34.

KING JAMES VERSION

LUKE 2:22 And when the days of her purification according to the law of Moses were accomplished, they brought him to Jerusalem, to present him to the Lord; 23 (As it is written in the law of the Lord, Every male that openeth the womb shall be called holy to the Lord;) 24 And to offer a sacrifice according to that which is said in the law of the Lord, A pair of turtledoves, or two young pigeons.

25 And, behold, there was a man in Jerusalem, whose name was Simeon; and the same man was just and devout, waiting for the consolation of Israel: and the Holy Ghost was upon him. 26 And it was revealed unto him by the Holy Ghost, that he should not see death, before he had seen the Lord's Christ. 27 And he came by the Spirit into the temple: and when the parents brought in the child Jesus, to do for him after the custom of the law, 28 Then took he him up in his arms, and blessed God, and said, 29 Lord, now lettest thou thy servant depart in peace, according to thy word: 30 For mine eyes have seen thy salvation, 31 Which thou hast prepared before the face of all people; 32 A light to lighten the Gentiles, and the glory of thy people Israel. 33 And Joseph and his mother marvelled at those things which were spoken of him. 34 And Simeon blessed them, and said unto Mary his mother, Behold, this child is set for the fall and rising again of many in Israel; and for a sign which shall be spoken against; 35 (Yea, a sword shall pierce through thy own soul also,) that the thoughts of many hearts may be revealed.

NEW REVISED STANDARD VERSION

LUKE 2:22 When the time came for their purification according to the law of Moses, they brought him up to Jerusalem to present him to the Lord 23 (as it is written in the law of the Lord, "Every firstborn male shall be designated as holy to the Lord"), 24 and they offered a sacrifice according to what is stated in the law of the Lord, "a pair of turtledoves or two young pigeons."

25 Now there was a man in Jerusalem whose name was Simeon; this man was righteous and devout, looking forward to the consolation of Israel, and the Holy Spirit rested on him. 26 It had been revealed to him by the Holy Spirit that he would not see death before he had seen the Lord's Messiah. 27 Guided by the Spirit, Simeon came into the temple; and when the parents brought in the child Jesus, to do for him what was customary under the law, 28 Simeon took him in his arms and praised God, saying,

29 "Master, now you are dismissing your servant in
   peace,
  according to your word;
30 for my eyes have seen your salvation,
31 which you have prepared in the presence of all
  peoples,
32 a light for revelation to the Gentiles
  and for glory to your people Israel."

33 And the child's father and mother were amazed at what was being said about him. 34 Then Simeon blessed them and said to his mother Mary, "This child is destined for the falling and the rising of many in Israel, and to be a sign that will be opposed 35 so that the inner thoughts of many will be revealed—and a sword will pierce your own soul too."

5

Monday, December 24	Isaiah 49:5-6	*A Light to All Nations*
Tuesday, December 25	Luke 2:22-24	*The Presentation to God*
Wednesday, December 26	Luke 2:25-26	*The Consolation of Israel*
Thursday, December 27	Luke 2:27-28	*A Sign from the Spirit*
Friday, December 28	Luke 2:29-33	*A Light to the Gentiles*
Saturday, December 29	Luke 2:34-35	*A Sign of Opposition*
Sunday, December 30	Luke 2:36-38	*A Sign of Redemption*

BACKGROUND

Mary and Joseph were careful to fulfill the requirements of the Mosaic law. In the case of Jesus, while He was God's Son, He was not born above the law. Thus it was fitting for Jesus' family to observe its customs. Accordingly, eight days after Jesus' birth, Mary and Joseph had Him circumcised (Lev. 12:3; Luke 2:21). Circumcision symbolized the Jews' unique relationship with God. It was also customary for Jewish boys to be named when they were circumcised. In the case of Mary's firstborn son, she and Joseph named Him *JESUS* (Luke 2:21) in accordance with the directive of the Lord's angel before the Christ child was conceived in Mary's womb (see 1:31).

A woman who had given birth to a male child was considered to be ceremonially unclean for seven days (Lev. 12:2). Then for 33 more days she was not to touch any sacred thing, nor was she to enter the sanctuary (12:4). After 40 days, she was required to go to the temple to be purified in the prescribed manner (Luke 2:22-24). The woman's purification included the offering of a sacrifice. According to Leviticus 12:6, this offering was to be a year-old lamb for a burnt offering and a young pigeon or a dove for a sin offering; but the law also said that if the woman could not afford a lamb, two pigeons or doves would suffice (12:8). Mary evidently chose the second option due to her modest financial situation (Luke 2:24).

According the Mosaic law, the woman's firstborn son was considered holy and thus had to be dedicated to the Lord in service (Exod. 13:2, 11-16; Luke 2:23). This requirement went back to that night in Egypt when the firstborn sons were saved from death by blood applied to the doorposts (Exod. 12:12-13); but since the entire tribe of Levi was chosen for service, a firstborn son could be released from service by a payment of a ransom (Num. 3:11-13; 18:15-16). This act of buying back, or redeeming, the child from God was performed during a presentation ceremony at the temple, probably at the same time as the mother's purification ceremony (Luke 2:22).

A sacrificial offering was the means by which the ransom was paid. In this way, the parents acknowledged that their firstborn belonged to God, who alone had the power to give life. In this special circumstance, however, Jesus was a gift from God to the whole world (John 3:16). Moreover, in the midst of the fulfillment of legal requirements, God put the stamp of approval on His Son with the unusual but blessed ministries of Simeon and Anna.

NOTES ON THE PRINTED TEXT

While Mary and Joseph were at the temple with Jesus (Luke 2:22-24), they met a man named Simeon, whose name means "God has heard" (2:25). From 2:26 we get the impression that he was advanced in years. Throughout his adult life, Simeon had distinguished himself as being *just and devout* (2:25). This means he was morally upright in his behavior and dedicated in his observance of the law. His faithfulness and sincerity in keeping God's ordinances is especially seen in his *waiting for the consolation of Israel*. This phrase refers to Simeon's hope that the Messiah would come and deliver the nation (Isa. 40:1; 49:13; 51:3). Indeed, Simeon loved God so much that he looked with eager anticipation for the comfort the Redeemer would bring to all people.

Simeon was also filled with the Holy Spirit (Luke 2:25). This means Simeon had been given special insight by God's Spirit to recognize the Messiah. The Spirit had also disclosed to Simeon that he would not die until he had seen the Lord's Messiah (2:26). Thus, on the right day and at the right time, the Spirit led Simeon into the temple. This circumstance is just one of several examples in the first two chapters of the second Synoptic Gospel of a promise from God being fulfilled.

The Spirit led Simeon into the temple courts on the day Mary and Joseph brought Jesus there (2:27). Believers have wondered what the nature of the Spirit's work was like among the people of God in the Old Testament era. When all the evidence is taken into consideration, the impression is conveyed that the Spirit mainly came upon selected individuals for specific jobs. Nonetheless, the Hebrew prophets entertained a lively hope that a time was coming when the Spirit of God would be given out more broadly (Isa. 32:15; 59:21; Joel 2:28-29). That hope, which was manifested in upright persons such as Simeon, was fulfilled on the day of Pentecost (Acts 2:14-21).

Because of the special insight Simeon had been given, he immediately recognized Jesus as the Messiah. The reference in Luke 2:27 is to the larger temple area, not to the Most Holy Place. Simeon was either in the court of the Gentiles or the court of women, since Mary was present. Amazingly, the parents allowed the elderly man to hold their son (2:28). Simeon's words of praise concerning the Christ child occurred at the epicenter of the Jewish religion. This implies that, far from being a foreigner and outcast, Jesus was accepted and worshiped by the most pious individuals in Israel.

Simeon's brief prophetic declaration in 2:29-32 is sometimes called the *Nunc Dimittis*, which comes from the opening phrase in Latin, "now dismiss" (in other words, "now permit to die"). In this short refrain, we see the heart of a humble and godly man. Simeon's hymn is a patchwork of passages and themes found in the Book of Isaiah (40:5; 42:6; 46:13; 49:6; 52:9-10). Isaiah's vision of the future included salvation for the Gentiles along with God's chosen people, Israel. We find similar strains in the Minor Prophets as well. Simeon's words were revolutionary and, in some respects, visionary. As a loyal and devout Jew to whom God had given special insight, Simeon recognized that because of the advent of the Messiah, God's redemption would forevermore be available for all people—Jews and Gentiles alike.

Simeon said he was God's *servant* (Luke 2:29), a concept that did not imply a menial, servile existence, but rather privilege and honor in service to the Creator. Moreover, Simeon referred to God as the *Lord*. The latter renders the Greek word *despótes*, which means "master" or "absolute ruler," and from which we get our English term "despot." The divine promise to Simeon had been fulfilled, and now he could die in peace. He explained that he had seen God's salvation (2:30). The idea is that to see Jesus, the Messiah, is to see the deliverance of the Lord (see John 14:9). There is some debate as to whether the phrase *all people* (Luke 2:31) refers to Israel alone or to both Israel and the Gentiles. Verse 32 makes it clear that Simeon included non-Jews as well as Jews. This is a key thematic emphasis of Luke (see Luke 24:47; Acts 10:34-43).

There is also disagreement over the best way to structure Luke 2:32. The KJV sees *light* and *glory* being parallel, or corresponding, ideas; in other words, Jesus is a light to bring revelation to Gentiles and glory to the people of Israel. The NRSV sees *light* as a summary statement that refers to the entire verse. In this case, *revelation* and *glory* would be parallel, or corresponding, ideas; in other words, Jesus is a light for all, but is a revelation for the Gentiles and glory for Israel (Luke 1:78-79; Acts 26:22-23). In either case, the central idea is clear that Jesus makes salvation available to all people. Interestingly, both Mary and Joseph were amazed at what Simeon said about their infant son (Luke 2:33). Simeon's words tell us that in the birth of Jesus, the next stage of redemptive history has begun. Gentiles would experience the same deliverance promised to Jews. Indeed, for all who put their faith in Messiah, God promised to give them eternal life.

After invoking God's blessing upon Joseph and Mary, Simeon prophesied concerning Mary and her son (2:34). Here we find the first hint in the third Synoptic Gospel that Jesus' advent would be accompanied with great difficulty. Perhaps God revealed to Simeon that Joseph would not be alive when the sorrows foretold would come to pass. Although the Scriptures do not give an account for the death of Joseph, no mention is made of him after Jesus began His public ministry. It is generally believed that Joseph died before that time.

The phrase *fall and rising again* emphasizes that Jesus would bring division in the nation. Some would fall (or be judged) and others would rise (or be blessed) because of how they responded to the Messiah (Isa. 8:14-15; Mal. 4:2). Moreover, others see in Simeon's words the fact that Jesus' preaching of repentance would cause many to fall from their self-righteous opinion of themselves to the point where they could recognize their sinfulness and be saved, or exalted, through faith in the Redeemer.

Simeon related that Jesus would be a sign against whom many would speak (Luke 2:34). This is based on the fact that God would appoint the Messiah as the provision for salvation from sin. While some (like Simeon) would receive Him with joy, others (like the religious leaders) would reject Him. As a result, the deepest thoughts of many people (namely, their reasonings and motives) would be exposed by the way they responded to Christ (2:35). Although Jesus came to be the Redeemer of His people, the majority would despise Him. Tragically, despite the glory of the salvation He would freely offer, many of His contemporaries would reject Him as the Messiah.

Simeon mentioned a *sword* piercing *thy own soul*. The remark seems directed specifically to Mary (as opposed to the entire nation of Israel). Simeon's reference to a *sword* (namely, a large, broad, two-edged weapon) is figurative and pictures great pain. The statement probably refers in part to the cross; but Simeon may also have been referring to the pain that all of Jesus' ministry would cause, especially in the opposition He would encounter throughout His ministry. The broader truth is that no one would be able to remain neutral about Christ, and it's still the same today. We must have an opinion about Jesus. Either we are for Him or we are against Him. Either we surrender our lives to Him or we are at war with Him.

SUGGESTIONS TO TEACHERS

Several years ago *Unplug the Christmas Machine* was the startling title that appeared in bookstores. The main idea behind the book was that the day after Christmas, people are no longer caught in the gears and pulled by the levers of a commercialized holiday. This week's lesson may be the first opportunity your students have to pause and recognize the true significance of the Messiah.

1. SIGNIFICANT NAME. Luke 2:21 says that the newborn babe was called *JESUS*. This is the Greek form of *Joshua*, which means "the Lord saves." Take a few moments to discuss what it means to be saved. Be sure to go beyond the pat answers to talk seriously about how Jesus liberates us from relying on violence and revenge, and from living in destructive ways. Likewise, Jesus liberates us to serve others and promote justice. Trusting in Jesus means, for starters, that we recognize Him as our only Redeemer from sin.

2. SACRED OBSERVANCES. Note how Mary and Joseph observed the traditions of their faith both before and after Jesus was born. Our religious practices are also important to us, and they can have a tremendous positive effect on our children. Likewise, regular times of worship are essential to our spiritual health. Have your students discuss some religious traditions they find uplifting.

3. SIMEON'S FULFILLMENT. God lavished His mercy and grace on Simeon by allowing him to see the infant Jesus. From Simeon we learn three important truths. First, Jesus is a gift from God. Second, Jesus is the Messiah promised in the Old Testament. And third, Jesus is a light of salvation and truth to the entire world.

4. SOLEMN PRONOUNCEMENT. Simeon realized that in seeing the infant Jesus, he was privileged to behold the fulfillment of God's promise of the heaven-sent Deliverer. We have a similar opportunity when we look to Jesus with the eyes of faith. We can smile at whatever might happen to us in the future, for we know that in the Messiah we have the hope of eternal life.

FOR ADULTS

■ **TOPIC:** Hearing and Telling Good News

■ **QUESTIONS:** 1. Why was it necessary for Joseph and Mary to bring the infant Jesus to be presented to the Lord in the temple? 2. How did the spiritual qualities Simeon possessed equip him for a unique opportunity? 3. How was Simeon able to be in the right place at the right time? 4. Based on what Simeon said, what was God going to do through the Messiah? 5. How was there both glory and tragedy in Simeon's prophecy concerning the mission of the Savior?

■ **ILLUSTRATIONS:**

Share the News. "I mean it. I *don't* think you should evangelize him!" Her words were hot. She had just gotten off the phone with Mohammad. My caller didn't know that Mohammad, an acquaintance from my college days, was acting the way he always did, brazenly challenging the deeply held beliefs of those to whom he spoke.

I first met Mohammad over two decades ago, when he was on a student visa from Iran. His thick accent and forceful attitude scared the person he called. The same things had scared away others years before. But Mohammad hadn't scared me off. He couldn't resist talking with someone who wouldn't give in to his point of view or walk away in frustration. Eventually, he consented to accepting a Bible from me. I wrote a brief inscription inside.

Mohammad had conveyed to my caller that reading that Bible had prompted him to try to find me. *Great!* I thought. *Perhaps after all these years, he has trusted in the Messiah for salvation!* I listened further. "He said he has studied the Bible thoroughly and for a long time. He's finally made his decision: Christianity is . . . BUNK!" she said incredulously. Mohammad needed prayer then, and he needs prayer now. Christian holidays provide a ready opportunity believers to witness to and pray for those outside the faith.

The People We Know. Sadly, the Good News of the Savior's birth is not at the center of everyone's holiday celebration. Believers need to look around them, perhaps at their most familiar relationships, and see if there are those who need to be pointed to Jesus at this special time of year. Consider the following situations:

• Claire's sister-in-law, Arlene, has never heard the Good News. Claire has been a believer a long time and knows that Arlene needs Jesus' love and forgiveness, but

Arlene often rubs Claire the wrong way. It's far easier or Claire to avoid Arlene than to try to befriend her. But now Claire feels prompted to spend time with Arlene.

• Diane is a housekeeper and has frequent contact with the children of the family for whom she works. For two years, Diane has gone about her business, not mentioning her beliefs, but she has noticed that the 15-year-old son, Shaun, is showing signs that he is seeking spiritual answers to life's questions. Diane's church prints creative and attractive small invitations that announce the upcoming themes of the services. Diane feels God has been prompting her to give an invitation to Shaun and tell him a bit about her church.

• John is a Christian. He had worked at a particular company for two years and then moved on to another position elsewhere. However, John and his former supervisor, Mike, have remained in touch, and from time to time their families have socialized together. John has been sensing that God would like him to take more initiative in this relationship with Mike and become a felt presence of friendship in Mike's life.

True Homage. Susie Hilstrom in *Worldwide Challenge* notes that Audrey Wetherell Johnson (1907–1984) had been raised in England in a Christian home. Under a skeptical tutor in France, however, she came to the conclusion as a young person that she "no longer believed in the bodily resurrection of Jesus, nor in His virgin birth." She penned: "My attitude of agnosticism resulted in months of desperation as I considered the meaninglessness of life without any philosophy in which I could believe."

After returning to England, Wetherell finally arrived at a psychological crisis point. She desperately prayed that God would give her "some philosophy that makes reasonable sense." As a result of her desperate plea, "in a mysterious way that Wetherell could not explain even years later, God met her, and with tears of joy Wetherell worshiped Jesus as Savior and Lord." Later, she became responsible for Bible Study Fellowship, a Christian group that would eventually flourish in over 20 countries with 17,000 leaders. Their continuing goal is to spread the good news of salvation.

FOR YOUTH

■ **TOPIC:** Called to Be Faithful
■ **QUESTIONS:** 1. What kind of person was Simeon? 2. What prophetic message did Simeon share about Jesus? 3. What was Simeon's view of the Messiah? 4. Why could Simeon die in peace after having seen the Messiah? 5. In light of Simeon's prophecy, how would people respond to the Messiah of Israel?

■ **ILLUSTRATIONS:**
Faith on Trial. On March 24, 2006, Bdul Waheed Wafa of the *New York Times* reported that a 41-year-old Afghan, Abdul Rahman, who was born a Muslim, was sentenced to death for converting to Christianity. Under conservative interpretations of Islamic

law, a convert can be executed. But Afghanistan's laws are "silent on the matter," and the country's criminal code does not specifically declare "converting from Islam to Christianity a crime."

Countries in the West made efforts to resolve the case in a way that "honors the universal principle of freedom." One possible compromise involved the court's declaring the defendant mentally ill and allowing him to leave the country in exile. Yet, despite mounting international pressure, the judge presiding over the prosecution initially said he would resist any outside interference. Even the possibility of being executed did not prevent Rahman from telling reporters, "I am not an infidel. I am Christian. I believe in Jesus." Thankfully, an Afghan court eventually decided to dismiss the case against Rahman due to "lack of evidence." After his release from jail, the Italian government granted him asylum in their country.

Filling Father's Shoes. Thomas Watson, Jr., the man who built International Business Machines (IBM) into a computer giant, spent much of his early life worrying about filling his father's shoes. Tortured by self-doubts, Thomas was a depressed child. He was also upset that his sister, Jane, was his father's favorite.

Thomas spent much of his younger years pulling pranks, drinking, dancing, and challenging authority. After a stint in the armed forces, he began to work in the company that his father ran. Thomas succeeded by building the company into what it is today, an industrial powerhouse. At the same time, Thomas has far outgrown the shadow of his demanding father.

Perhaps you also know what it is like to grow up frustrated and unable to live up to the expectations of others. After going to the temple courts, both Joseph and Mary must have left with huge expectations for Jesus. The record of Scripture, though, indicates no frustration of His part. He simply trusted God for the future, and this enabled Jesus to do great things for the Lord. This can also be true of you!

Time to Recognize Jesus' Presence. A researcher named Michael Fortino has made a careful study of hundreds of people across North America for over a year. By using a stopwatch, he has clocked the ways individuals use their time. He has also reported the cumulative effects of these ways. Fortino states that most people spend five years of their lives waiting in lines. Other totals of time include six months sitting at traffic lights, one year searching for misplaced objects, six years eating, eight months opening junk mail, four years doing housework, and two years trying to return telephone calls to people who never seem to be available.

This week will conclude the span of time called the year 2007. Also, we will have a new measure of 365 days to use during 2008. In light of this, let's commit ourselves to recall in each day of the coming year, that Christ lives in us and is a foremost part of our lives.

INSPIRED TO INQUIRE!

BACKGROUND SCRIPTURE: Luke 2:41-52
DEVOTIONAL READING: Psalm 148:7-14

KEY VERSE: And [Jesus] said unto them, How is it that ye sought me? wist ye not that I must be about my Father's business? Luke 2:49.

KING JAMES VERSION

LUKE 2:41 Now his parents went to Jerusalem every year at the feast of the passover. 42 And when he was twelve years old, they went up to Jerusalem after the custom of the feast. 43 And when they had fulfilled the days, as they returned, the child Jesus tarried behind in Jerusalem; and Joseph and his mother knew not of it. 44 But they, supposing him to have been in the company, went a day's journey; and they sought him among their kinsfolk and acquaintance. 45 And when they found him not, they turned back again to Jerusalem, seeking him. 46 And it came to pass, that after three days they found him in the temple, sitting in the midst of the doctors, both hearing them, and asking them questions. 47 And all that heard him were astonished at his understanding and answers. 48 And when they saw him, they were amazed: and his mother said unto him, Son, why hast thou thus dealt with us? behold, thy father and I have sought thee sorrowing. 49 And he said unto them, How is it that ye sought me? wist ye not that I must be about my Father's business? 50 And they understood not the saying which he spake unto them. 51 And he went down with them, and came to Nazareth, and was subject unto them: but his mother kept all these sayings in her heart. 52 And Jesus increased in wisdom and stature, and in favour with God and man.

NEW REVISED STANDARD VERSION

LUKE 2:41 Now every year his parents went to Jerusalem for the festival of the Passover. 42 And when he was twelve years old, they went up as usual for the festival. 43 When the festival was ended and they started to return, the boy Jesus stayed behind in Jerusalem, but his parents did not know it. 44 Assuming that he was in the group of travelers, they went a day's journey. Then they started to look for him among their relatives and friends. 45 When they did not find him, they returned to Jerusalem to search for him. 46 After three days they found him in the temple, sitting among the teachers, listening to them and asking them questions. 47 And all who heard him were amazed at his understanding and his answers. 48 When his parents saw him they were astonished; and his mother said to him, "Child, why have you treated us like this? Look, your father and I have been searching for you in great anxiety." 49 He said to them, "Why were you searching for me? Did you not know that I must be in my Father's house?" 50 But they did not understand what he said to them. 51 Then he went down with them and came to Nazareth, and was obedient to them. His mother treasured all these things in her heart.

52 And Jesus increased in wisdom and in years, and in divine and human favor.

6

Monday, December 31	Psalm 148:7-14	*A Horn for God's People*
Tuesday, January 1	Numbers 9:1-5	*The Passover Feast Instituted*
Wednesday, January 2	Exodus 12:11-14	*First Passover Observed*
Thursday, January 3	Luke 2:41-45	*The Annual Pilgrimage*
Friday, January 4	Luke 2:46-50	*About the Father's Business*
Saturday, January 5	Luke 2:51-52	*Growing Up in Nazareth*
Sunday, January 6	Psalm 148:1-6	*Praise the Lord!*

BACKGROUND

During Jesus' childhood years, He physically matured and became strong (Luke 2:40). With reference to His human nature, Jesus experienced normal development in body, mind, spiritual awareness, and social acceptance. All these things occurred with the perfection that is suited to each phase of life through which He passed (2:40, 52). As Jesus gained knowledge through observation, asking questions, and seeking instruction, He progressively became filled with wisdom (2:40). Jesus' wisdom was more than mere intellectual knowledge. It included the ability to use the knowledge He acquired to the best advantage. Though He did not attend a rabbinical college, the Messiah received a common education, which was primarily religious and which prepared Him for the practical duties of life.

Luke also noted that *the grace of God* was upon Jesus. Because Jesus was human as well as divine, during His earthly life He depended on His heavenly Father for all things, just as we do. Nonetheless, Jesus was sinless, and God's favor upon Him was for reasons unique to His earthly life and ministry. Much of Jesus' growth and development from infancy to adulthood is difficult for us to fathom. Perhaps this is because, as a human being, Jesus was completely unhindered by those sinful influences that affect all of us who are descendants of Adam. Jesus' body and spirit responded to His heavenly Father much as a bud grows into a beautiful and perfect blossom.

NOTES ON THE PRINTED TEXT

When Jesus was *twelve years old* (Luke 2:42), He went with His parents to Jerusalem for the *feast of the passover* (2:41). About the age of 12, a Jewish boy such as Jesus became "a son of the (divine) law" (that is, a *bar mitzvah*), while a Jewish girl became a "daughter of the commandment" (that is, *bas mitzvah*). This meant the children pledged to learn and to obey the commandments of God. Similarly today, Jewish boys and girls spend their twelfth year studying the Torah (a Hebrew word normally translated "law") with rabbis and other Jewish scholars and teachers. After they turn 13, the adolescents are held accountable for knowing and heeding the law. They may also take part in leading religious services, form binding contracts, and testify in religious courts.

Jesus' visit to Jerusalem for Passover is the only account we have about Him between His birth and His baptism. The Passover was celebrated to remind the Jews what God did to free Israel from slavery in Egypt, when the angel of death *passed over* (Exod. 12:27) the Hebrew households and did not kill their firstborn children. The Jewish people in biblical times celebrated the Passover feast annually to remember this event. Many of the elements reminded them of what God had done; but they were also required to dedicate their firstborn children and cattle directly to the Lord. This was a way of giving back to God what the angel of death could have easily taken away.

Luke 2:43-50 reveals that the relationship between Jesus and His parents was not without difficulties. It was a learning experience for Jesus as well as for Joseph and Mary. In the episode under consideration, Joseph and Mary remained in Jerusalem the full seven days of the feast and then started for home, but Jesus stayed behind (2:43). It was not until the parents had walked a day's journey that they realized Jesus was not with them. So the parents started to look for Jesus, but without success (2:44). The parents then turned around and went back to Jerusalem to find Jesus (2:45).

Most likely, the parents traveled to Jerusalem for Passover in a caravan that included their relatives and acquaintances as well as traders taking their goods to sell to the crowds of pilgrims attending the religious festival. Caravans provided some safety for journeys in the Holy Land, since bands of robbers frequently attacked travelers (10:30). A caravan would be a noisy, busy group. If later custom was followed, the women and younger children were positioned at the front of the caravan, followed by the men and older boys. Thus, Joseph or Mary each could have thought Jesus was with the other parent, or that He was traveling with relatives and friends.

Luke did not blame either Jesus or His parents for what had happened. Perhaps from our standpoint, we might assume that Jesus should have told His parents what He was doing. In God's plan, however, the unfolding events served to highlight Jesus' unusual spiritual giftedness. We can well imagine Jesus' thrill and exuberance on His visit to Jerusalem and the temple. This was no ordinary event. Perhaps it was the most dramatic thing that had occurred thus far in His life. Undoubtedly, Jesus followed the inspiration of His heart and the unique genius that was His nature.

Joseph and Mary had traveled with the caravan one day north toward Galilee, and it required a day for them to return to Jerusalem. Then they spent a day searching throughout the city for Jesus. They finally found Him *in the temple* (2:46). Jesus was engaged in dialogue with the teachers of the law. This scene also drew interested observers as well. They were *astonished at his understanding and answers* (2:47).

It's quite possible that these sorts of discussions in the temple occurred on a daily basis. The opportunity to exchange questions and answers drew Jesus' interest. It was highly unusual for the scholars to invite a youth into their theological debates, but Jesus asked such intelligent questions that they included Him. Luke did not record the content of these discussions. Perhaps they concerned matters of rabbinical history and traditions. If so, this would have been more like a gathering of legal experts talking about matters of interest. Jesus, of course, listened and respectfully asked probing questions. He was able to follow the various arguments and, surprisingly, was also able to answer challenging queries put to Him.

The religious experts were taken aback by Jesus' understanding of the law and His ability to answer interpretative questions regarding it. Joseph and Mary were also *amazed* (2:48), but for quite a different reason. At this point, they weren't focusing on Jesus' ability to hold His own among the legal scholars of the day. Instead, Joseph and Mary were concerned for Jesus' well being. Interestingly, when Jesus' parents found Him, it was Mary who addressed Him. There was surprise and frustration in Mary's words. This was the natural response of a mother who temporarily had lost her child.

Joseph and Mary were good parents, but they were not perfect. They were so focused on their search that they didn't understand why Jesus had to be at the temple. Though they could see that the gathered crowd was impressed with Jesus, His parents didn't make the connection between who Jesus was and the sacred place where He was. One fact we learn from this incident is that Joseph and Mary acted like normal parents and they loved their child deeply.

Jesus' answer, as recorded in 2:49, must have cut deeply into the hearts of His parents. In essence, Jesus said, "You just don't understand me." These words, when voiced by a disobedient or rebellious child, are generally a reflection of the nature of that child; but when voiced by *the child Jesus* (2:43), the world's only perfect youth, they were true. In many ways, Joseph and Mary did not comprehend the unique nature of their son (2:50). Later, during Jesus' earthly ministry, His disciples would also fall short of understanding Him (see 9:45; 18:34).

Jesus' answer showed that He had a clear understanding of the relationship between Himself and His heavenly Father. Throughout Jesus' public ministry, He referred to this relationship again and again. Jesus knew that He was one with His Father. For instance, Jesus' statement to Mary, *Did you not know that I must be in my Father's house?* (2:49, NRSV), reveals Jesus' awareness of His status as the Son of God and the realization that His life was on a divine schedule. This is the first clue we find in the Gospels that Jesus was not just an ordinary child from Nazareth. His pilgrimage to Jerusalem was a divinely ordained mission. In fact, Jesus' response to God's call resulted in the Messiah engaging the highest level of learning in the Jewish nation.

Though Joseph and Mary had some awareness of the special relationship Jesus had with God, they did not fully grasp its implications. Jesus needed to talk to His Father. Jesus also needed to learn what His Father expected of Him. In fact, there was no better place to do this than at the temple, the sacred place where God uniquely manifested His presence. Perhaps Mary was for the first time learning what Simeon had told her about her heart being pierced (2:35). Some see this event as the first step in that painful separation. Ultimately, the Lord Jesus' divinely appointed mission would lead to His death on the cross of Calvary.

After the brief visit to Jerusalem and its temple, Jesus returned to Nazareth to live with His parents. Luke 2:51 notes that over the next 18 years, Jesus obeyed His parents. This implies that in every way He submitted to their will. This is perhaps the strangest relationship that a person could ever imagine. How could a perfect individual, who is God incarnate, put Himself under the authority of imperfect human parents? Strange as it may seem, the Bible states that this is what Jesus did. The role of parents is so crucial in God's plans for relationships that Jesus was willing to model that role by being obedient to His earthly parents. Mary, for her part, *kept all these sayings in her heart*. She was a godly woman of great faith and humility. As she watched her son grow into manhood, she recalled the words of the angel and the prophecy of Simeon. No doubt Mary also reflected on the messianic prophecies.

In another concise statement, Luke noted that Jesus continued to develop spiritually, morally, and intellectually. Holiness and humility marked His life. In fact, *wisdom and stature* (2:52) indicate robust spiritual health. From this we see that Jesus wedded truth and conduct. He not only knew the truth, but also lived it. These things were so true in Jesus' life that He *increased . . . in favour with God and men*. What more could be said of anyone than that they pleased God and others? Clearly, Jesus' life with His family bore the stamp of divine and human approval.

SUGGESTIONS TO TEACHERS

We have few details about what happened to Jesus up until the time He began His public ministry. Nevertheless, we can glean much from what is both said and implied in Scripture concerning Jesus' early life. By way of example, the Father, in His wisdom, chose for His Son to be born as an infant and to grow physically, mentally, spiritually, and socially in a normal way, except that He was without sin. Thus, as Jesus increased in God's favor, He modeled the kind of life we should strive to live.

1. LAYING THE FOUNDATION. Jesus did not live a pampered life on earth. For instance, carpentry in ancient times was a physically demanding occupation. Thus, as Jesus learned this trade from Joseph, the Savior developed a strong body in order to handle the demands of the trade. At the same time, Jesus studied the Scriptures in the local synagogue, and God gave Him wisdom to understand the Old Testament. Because Jesus was God's beloved Son and without sin, the Father's unlimited favor was upon Him. Christian parents should seize every opportunity, with God's help, to influence their children for Christ during the early years of their lives.

2. PREPARING FOR MINISTRY. Jesus no doubt looked forward with great anticipation to attending the Passover festival in Jerusalem with His parents. Jesus not only benefited from this experience, but also made an unforgettable impression upon the religious scholars because of the wisdom He displayed in His answers. A consistent exposure to God's Word and Christian teaching will help create a desire in a child's heart to know more about the Lord.

3. WAITING FOR GOD'S TIME. Jesus, at the age of 12, was fully aware of His unique identity. He was also committed to obeying His heavenly Father. Thus, Jesus continued to honor His earthly parents by submitting to them. Jesus' fellow townsfolk became increasingly aware of His dedication to God and desire to obey His commandments. Young people sometimes become impatient in their desire to break away from their home ties; but a loving Christian home atmosphere can help them develop the patience they need to wait for God's leading in their lives.

| **FOR ADULTS** | ■ **TOPIC:** Questions and Answers |

■ **QUESTIONS:** 1. What is the difference between the way in which God's favor was manifested to Jesus and the way it is often shown to us? 2. How might Jesus have anticipated attending the Passover festival with His parents in Jerusalem? 3. In ancient times, what was the spiritual significance of a Jewish boy's twelfth birthday? 4. What caused the teachers of the law to be so impressed with the way Jesus responded to them? 5. What can parents learn from Jesus' childhood regarding the rearing of their own children?

■ **ILLUSTRATIONS:**

Making Adjustments. When Rick and Harriet decided to begin a family, they made some strong commitments to themselves, to each other, and to God. They knew that they must now adjust their lives around the priorities of making sure that their children would know and love Jesus Christ. Rick and Harriet had always been committed to teaching the Bible's stories to their children from their earliest years, but now the parents understood that alone would never be enough. They realized that teaching does not always incorporate proper training, but proper training always incorporates correct teaching. One is knowledge, while the other is lifestyle *and* knowledge. What a joy it became to Rick and Harriet to understand that children nurtured with the proper training would not depart from God's ways when they grow older.

Working 24/7. On a broadcast of *CBS 60 Minutes*, correspondent Lesley Stahl noted that people in the U.S. are working "longer hours than nearly anyone in the developed world." In the case of business professionals and corporate managers, the traditional "40-hour work week is history," being replaced by a new norm—"60- to 80-hour work weeks." Stahl notes that the signs of Americans' "addiction to work are everywhere." Consider rush hour in a busy metropolitan area such as New York. Due to popular demand, the "first train for commuters from the suburbs" into the city was "pushed back to 4:45 A.M." Also, the "Digital Revolution" enables people to use "cell phones, wireless Internet, and handheld computers" to "work anywhere, anytime, 24/7."

Not everyone has adopted this lifestyle. Mike Moody and Jeff Ward once worked "high stress, six-day-a-week jobs as big-city lawyers." But their desire to "spend more time with their wives and children" prompted them to make a drastic change in their professional lives. They now "share a job" as "assistant in-house counsel at Timberland" in Stratum, New Hampshire. According to Stahl, it's a "pretty sweet deal" in which the two "each work three days a week, overlapping on Tuesdays." They also both get a "four-day weekend." Despite their reduced salaries, this work arrangement allows them to keep their priorities straight. They are an example for Christian adults who want to have time for their mates, children, and church family.

The Freedom of Choice. Doug and Dan were fraternal twins; also, their parents were committed Christians and devoted to their church. The father and mother saw to it that their twin boys were in Sunday school and church from the time they were preschoolers. Over the years, the parents watched the personalities of the twins develop. Doug was sensitive, kindhearted, and obedient, while Dan was stubborn, insensitive, and disobedient toward his parents. Often, he had to be disciplined because of his insolence, whereas Doug rarely needed correction. Both boys were exposed to the same parental love and Christian influence.

Dan's teenage years were stormy and defiant, while Doug was solid and consistent in his faith. He loved his brother, Dan, and did all that he could to help him. Doug developed into a dependable, Christian man. He and Dan had a choice before them— to follow their parents' teaching and example or choose their own path. In the case of Jesus, He responded favorably to the teaching of Mary and Joseph.

FOR YOUTH

■ **TOPIC:** Inspired to Inquire!

■ **QUESTIONS:** 1. Why was the Passover festival so important to the Jews in ancient times? 2. How would you describe Jesus' attitude as He listened to the teachers in the temple and asked them questions? 3. How did Joseph and Mary respond to Jesus' absence? 4. How did Jesus respond to the concerns voiced by His parents? 5. In what ways did Jesus grow during His adolescent years in Nazareth?

■ **ILLUSTRATIONS:**

The Master Teacher. The old potter sat at his ancient wheel, pedaling it with his feet to make it spin. Beside him sat a young boy, his face eager and his eyes fastened on the potter's hands. The potter thrust a shapeless lump of clay in the center of the wheel. He felt the texture of the clay and gently began to move his fingers across its surface. Then he stopped the wheel, took the lump from it, and handed it to the lad.

The artisan rose from his stool and motioned for the boy to be seated. Barely able to reach the treadle, the boy began to spin the wheel. He placed the lump on the wheel, but not in the center. The results were disastrous! Patiently, the potter showed his young student the importance of centering the clay on the wheel. Then, step by step, he went through the process of molding a simple vase.

Though the boy's first attempt was quite primitive, he soon learned the basic steps. Because he sat with a master potter, he was well on his way to learning this ancient art. Jesus, as a youth, recognized the men in the temple as wise students of Scripture. He listened to them carefully and thereby grew in wisdom.

Lost! Little Bob was six years old. He had gone with his parents to a large department store in town that had a fabulous toy section. They left him with the toys while they shopped several aisles away. After a while, Bob decided to rejoin his parents. He looked down one aisle and then another, and assumed they had forgotten about him! But Bob knew the way home. He quickly left the store, walked several blocks until he was out of the shopping area, and found the street that led about 10 blocks to his home. An older woman asked Bob whether he was lost, and he blurted, "No! I'm going home!" The woman then asked whether Bob would like for her to walk with him. Bob agreed that it would be nice.

In the meantime, Bob's parents had panicked and notified the police, who began a frantic search through the downtown area. A dozen officers, several squad cars, and a helicopter were dispatched. Meanwhile, Bob's parents decided to drive home to see whether a friend had intercepted Bob and had driven him home. To the parent's great delight and relief, they found Bob sitting in the swing on their front porch with his new friend. Bob's parents' joy at finding him softened their words of correction. Mary and Joseph were "lost from Jesus," but He was not lost, for He was in His Father's house.

The Path to Spiritual Growth. Ben and Ralph were both high school seniors. They had been invited by one of their friends to attend a youth activity at his church. Somewhat reluctantly, they agreed. Many of the young people were their peers in high school. The church youth reached out to Ben and Ralph and made them feel welcome and comfortable by inviting the two to Sunday school.

One day, Ben and Ralph asked for an appointment with the pastor and expressed their desire to trust in Christ. Afterward, they said to the pastor, "We do not come from Christian homes. We do not know anything about the Bible. Would you help us learn how to study it?" The pastor gladly agreed, and began meeting regularly with the two youths. They were eager learners, and the pastor watched them grow spiritually because of their regular exposure to the Word of God. Jesus, as a boy, loved God's Word, and it was reflected in His desire to study and learn its teachings.

Inspired to Love!

Background Scripture: Luke 6:27-36
Devotional Reading: Psalm 37:1-11

Key Verse: Love ye your enemies, and do good,
and lend, hoping for nothing again. Luke 6:35.

KING JAMES VERSION

LUKE 6:27 But I say unto you which hear, Love your enemies, do good to them which hate you, 28 Bless them that curse you, and pray for them which despitefully use you. 29 And unto him that smiteth thee on the one cheek offer also the other; and him that taketh away thy cloke forbid not to take thy coat also. 30 Give to every man that asketh of thee; and of him that taketh away thy goods ask them not again. 31 And as ye would that men should do to you, do ye also to them likewise. 32 For if ye love them which love you, what thank have ye? for sinners also love those that love them. 33 And if ye do good to them which do good to you, what thank have ye? for sinners also do even the same. 34 And if ye lend to them of whom ye hope to receive, what thank have ye? for sinners also lend to sinners, to receive as much again. 35 But love ye your enemies, and do good, and lend, hoping for nothing again; and your reward shall be great, and ye shall be the children of the Highest: for he is kind unto the unthankful and to the evil. 36 Be ye therefore merciful, as your Father also is merciful.

NEW REVISED STANDARD VERSION

LUKE 6:27 "But I say to you that listen, Love your enemies, do good to those who hate you, 28 bless those who curse you, pray for those who abuse you. 29 If anyone strikes you on the cheek, offer the other also; and from anyone who takes away your coat do not withhold even your shirt. 30 Give to everyone who begs from you; and if anyone takes away your goods, do not ask for them again. 31 Do to others as you would have them do to you.

32 "If you love those who love you, what credit is that to you? For even sinners love those who love them. 33 If you do good to those who do good to you, what credit is that to you? For even sinners do the same. 34 If you lend to those from whom you hope to receive, what credit is that to you? Even sinners lend to sinners, to receive as much again. 35 But love your enemies, do good, and lend, expecting nothing in return. Your reward will be great, and you will be children of the Most High; for he is kind to the ungrateful and the wicked. 36 Be merciful, just as your Father is merciful."

7

Home Bible Readings

Monday, January 7	Psalm 37:1-11	*Trust in the Lord*
Tuesday, January 8	Leviticus 19:17-18	*Love Your Neighbor*
Wednesday, January 9	Luke 6:27-28	*Love Your Enemies*
Thursday, January 10	Luke 6:29-30	*Absorb Injustice*
Friday, January 11	Luke 6:31	*Set the Standard*
Saturday, January 12	Luke 6:34-36	*Expect Nothing in Return*
Sunday, January 13	Psalm 37:35-40	*Posterity for the Peaceable*

Background

According to Luke 6:12, Jesus spent the night on a mountainside praying to God. The Messiah's presence on a mountain might be intentionally reminiscent of Exodus 24:12. In this case, though, Jesus was not just a new Moses who was presenting a new law; rather, Jesus utterly transcended Moses as the Lord of the new covenant. While on the mountainside, Jesus selected 12 of His followers for special assignment as apostles. Some experts think the reason He chose 12—the same number as the Israelite tribes—was to indicate that He was creating a new people of God (6:13-16).

After that, Jesus came down from the mountainside with His disciples. It seems reasonable to assume that the level place or plateau on which Jesus stood was in the midst of a more mountainous region (6:17). This observation has prompted some to suggest that the message Jesus delivered in 6:20-49 (traditionally known as the Sermon on the Plain) is an abridgment of the Sermon on the Mount recorded in Matthew 5—7. Admittedly, experts remain undecided about the precise nature of the relationship between these two passages. Be that as it may, all agree there are literary and thematic parallels between the Matthean and Lukan accounts. For example, both Sermons begin with the Beatitudes and end with the lesson on the builders.

Jesus opened Luke's version of His sermon with two lists—the first is a list of blessings and the second is a list of woes (Luke 6:20-26). These lists match up item for item, and together they overturned widely accepted beliefs among Jews in Jesus' day. For example, wealth and social success were considered signs of God's favor, while poverty and hardship were considered signs of divine disfavor; however, too often wealth and social success were achieved by exploiting others. Obviously, God's favor had nothing to do with it. Probably the crowd listening to Jesus' sermon was made up largely of people from the lower classes. If so, perhaps Jesus wanted to assure His hearers that God saw their faith and would eternally reward them.

Notes on the Printed Text

In Luke 6:27-28, Jesus enjoined love for one's enemies. The experts of the day taught others to love their neighbors and hate their enemies (see Lev. 19:18; Pss. 139:19-22; 140:9-11; Matt. 5:43). The idea of hating one's enemies, however, was an extra-biblical injunction maintained by some. It was based on a narrow understanding that a neighbor included only one's fellow citizens. Jesus carried on His ministry in the midst of this intensely prejudiced, exclusivist, and intolerant environment. One of His goals was to tear down the walls that existed between sinners and God. Doing this would enable God's love to flow freely and not be hindered by potential barriers such as nationality, race, party, age, and gender.

Jesus commanded His followers to show kindness to their antagonists (Luke 6:27). Moreover, the disciples were to do good to those who hated them and return blessing for cursing (6:28). Cursing in the New Testament era was really an indirect form of prayer. The idea is that those who cursed called down divine judgment on others. This especially included excommunication from the temple and expulsion from the synagogue (see John 9:22, 34). In addition, Jesus' followers were to pray directly for those who mistreated them. Abuse included spiteful actions as well as malicious speech. When hurt in any of these ways, believers were to be kind and forgiving in return.

A court of law probably would have been the context of Jesus' teaching in Luke 6:29. The implication is that He was not condemning the government's right to prosecute and punish those who were guilty of robbery and violence. Rather, Christ was denouncing a spirit of revenge. To illustrate His point, Jesus said that if a person slapped one of His disciples on the right cheek, the believer was to turn the other cheek so that the person might slap it, if he so desired. The slap on the right cheek would have been a backhanded one, and would have been both an insult as well as an injury. In the ancient Near East, people would have regarded the right side of the face as being more important than the left side. Thus, striking the right side would have been most humiliating and signified public rejection.

Within the context of 6:29, Jesus was indicating that His followers were not to seek restitution (see Isa. 50:6). Thus, for example, if a person chose to sue a follower of Christ with the intention of confiscating his coat, the believer was also to give him his cloak. Likewise, if a person asked one of Jesus' followers for something, the believer was to give it to him. Moreover, if a person wanted to borrow something from a disciple of the Savior, the believer was not to deny the request (Luke 6:30). It would be incorrect to take Jesus' comments as legal prescriptions. For instance, He was not commanding His disciples to give endless amounts of money to everyone who sought it (see Prov. 11:15; 17:18; 22:26). Rather, He was referring to being generous to the poor (see Deut. 15:7-11; Ps. 112:5, 9). The only limit to the believer's response is what love and the Scriptures imposed.

Jesus urged His followers to do for others what they wanted others to do for them (Luke 6:31; see Matt. 7:12). Philosophers have called this truth the Golden Rule. This maxim is found in negative form in the ethical teachings of ancient Greeks, Romans, Jews, Hindus, Buddhists, and Confucianists. Among ancient non-Christian thinkers the Golden Rule went something like this: "Do not do to others what you do not want done to you." This formulation is restrictive in nature and premised on the fear of retaliation. Jesus, however, made the truth a positive obligation, one that was inclusive, not exclusive, in nature. Christ's statement is based on the generosity, forbearance, and forgiveness of God. Believers were to follow the example of their heavenly Father in the hope that others whom they treated kindly would respond with kindness.

Jesus' declaration implied that He did not want His followers to be preoccupied with protecting themselves from outside harm. Rather, He wanted them to concentrate on actively helping others in need. It may be a loving gesture to refrain from killing one's enemy. However, the ultimate act of love is to give one's life for one's enemy (see John 15:13). What Christ said, as articulated in the Golden Rule of Luke 6:31, encapsulated the teaching of the Law and the Prophets (that is, the entire Old Testament; see Exod. 23:4; Lev. 19:18; Deut. 15:7-8; Prov. 24:17; 25:21; Matt. 7:12). Expressed differently, this timeless truth did not do away with and replace the Mosaic law, but rather fulfilled it. The Golden Rule served as an integrating principle for understanding the Old Testament. Although the Golden Rule was not explicitly stated in the Hebrew Scriptures, it was implicitly contained in them and thus was a key to their proper interpretation.

Jesus reasoned that if God's people only loved those who loved them in return, there was nothing commendable or distinctive about that. Indeed, even *sinners* (Luke 6:32) operated in this way. The reference here might be to people who had little, if any, concern for heeding the Mosaic law. In the time of Jesus, such individuals were often regarded with contempt and treated as outcasts. Society might consider the display of mutual love to be normal, customary, and sufficient to fulfill moral expectations. Christ, however, stated that it was ethically inadequate. Merely responding in love to those who have first shown love is equivalent to an exchange of favors (6:33). Jesus called His followers to show God's love without preconditions or self-imposed limitations.

Christ's disciples should not expect to receive any heavenly reward for displays of love that were narrowly focused and conditional in nature, for the most despised people of society—namely, those who made a sizeable profit by collecting taxes from their fellow citizens on behalf of the Roman government—showed love to the same extent (Matt. 5:46). Jesus also said there was nothing uniquely Christlike in greeting only one's brother, for even unsaved people did that. It was unusual to display kindness not only to one's brother but also to one's enemy (5:46-47). Moreover, if believers lent their money or goods only to people from whom they expected to receive an interest payment, there was nothing commendable about that, for sinners did the same thing (Luke 6:34). It was distinctively more godly not only to lend one's possessions to other people, but also to expect to receive nothing in return for one's kindness.

Rather than selfish love, Jesus promoted unselfish love. Toward that end, the Savior reiterated the importance of loving one's enemies, doing good to them, and lending to them, without any expectation of being repaid in kind. The irony in 6:35 is that when

Jesus' followers show love unselfishly, without the motive of getting something in return, they in fact do get something in return. The Most High regards them as the heirs of an eternal, heavenly reward. Also, God considers them to be His spiritual children, for they reflect His grace and kindness to people who are ungrateful and evil.

Christ was stressing that goodwill must not allow itself to be limited by ill will. In fact, those who were genuine children of the Father demonstrated their parentage by their moral resemblance to Him who is love. For example, the person who regarded showing forgiveness as a sign of weakness was hypocritical in asking God to forgive him. Likewise, the person who felt enmity toward others could hardly be an effective peacemaker for the Lord.

God demonstrated His love for sinners by allowing His Son to die for them, even though they were His enemies (Rom. 5:8). The mercy, generosity, and fairness of God is also evident when one realizes that He provides sunshine for all people, regardless of whether they are evil or good. He likewise provides rain for the righteous and the unrighteousness (Matt. 5:45). These truths underscore the universal goodness of the Creator, which is to be the model for the believer's conduct. In short, believers are to be merciful toward others, just as their Father in heaven is merciful (Luke 6:36).

SUGGESTIONS TO TEACHERS

As believers, we still have lapses in showing the love with which Jesus has blessed us. Can we love the people who live around us and work with us, especially those who have been unkind to us, or even other believers who have offended or hurt us in some way? We know we will always encounter situations in which it takes more than our own strength to demonstrate love to others; yet that is just what our Lord requires of us.

1. TO OBEY IS TO HAVE THE RIGHT ATTITUDE. Jesus longs for our loving obedience far more than our absent-minded religious formalities and ceremonies. It's not so much that these activities are unimportant as it is that we have the proper reasons and attitudes for performing them.

2. TO OBEY IS TO HELP OTHERS OBEY. God wants us to go beyond telling and encouraging others to obey Him. He wants us to help others obey Him by obeying Him ourselves and by being an example of obedience.

3. TO OBEY IS TO LOVE GOD. Real obedience cannot happen apart from our love for God. In fact, our obedience demonstrates our love for Him (see John 14:21).

4. TO OBEY IS TO BE GOD-CENTERED. The religious leaders of Jesus' day obeyed God outwardly, but they did so because it would enhance their status among the people. Their obedience was self-centered. Jesus said our obedience should be God-centered, based on our reverence for Him. We're to follow His will, not seek the approval of those who may be watching us.

5. TO OBEY IS TO LIVE BY THE PRINCIPLES BEHIND THE LAW. Jesus' teaching went beyond a ritualistic obedience to the law. He taught that we should obey the "spirit of the law," namely, the principles behind the law and the purpose for which God gave the law to His people.

6. TO OBEY IS TO TRUST GOD. We are not left to our own devices when it comes to obeying God. The Lord, through His Spirit, helps us to obey Him. We cannot obey by ourselves; rather, our obedience comes from God working in us.

FOR ADULTS

■ **TOPIC:** Responding to Opposition

■ **QUESTIONS:** 1. How is it possible for believers to love their enemies? 2. What sorts of things can believers pray for on behalf of those who mistreat them? 3. To what extent are believers to give to others who ask for things from them? 4. Why does God consider it wrong for us to love with preconditions? 5. How has God been merciful to us? How should this influence the way in which we treat our enemies?

■ **ILLUSTRATIONS:**

Love Your Enemies. On the morning of November 8, 1987, Gordon Wilson took his daughter, Marie, to a parade in the town of Enniskillen, Northern Ireland. As Wilson and his 20-year-old daughter stood beside a brick wall waiting for English soldiers and police to come marching by, a bomb planted by terrorists exploded from behind, and the brick wall tumbled down on them.

The blast instantly killed six people and pinned Gordon and Marie beneath several feet of bricks. Gordon's arm and shoulder were severely injured. Unable to move, he felt someone take hold of his hand. It was Marie. "Is that you, Dad?" she asked. "Yes, Marie," Gordon answered. Though her voice was faint, he could hear her over the screams of several people. "Are you all right?" Gordon asked her. "Yes," she said. As Gordon felt his daughter's grip beginning to loosen, again and again he asked if she was all right. Each time she said yes. Finally, Marie said, "Daddy, I love you very much." Those were her last words. Four hours later, she died in the hospital of severe spinal and brain injuries.

Later that evening, a *British Broadcasting Company* reporter requested permission to interview Gordon. After Gordon described what had happened, the reporter asked, "How do you feel about the guys who planted the bomb?" "I bear them no ill will," Gordon replied. "I bear them no grudge. Bitter talk is not going to bring Marie back to life. I shall pray tonight and every night that God will forgive them."

Many asked Gordon, who later became a senator in the Republic of Ireland, how he could say such a thing, how he could forgive such a horrendous act. Gordon explained, "I was hurt. I had just lost my daughter. But I wasn't angry. Marie's last words to me—words of love—had put me on a plane of love. I received God's grace, through the strength of His love for me, to forgive." And for years after this tragedy, Gordon continued to work for peace in Northern Ireland.

Pray for Them Who Despitefully Use You. A woman called the pastor's office, asking the minister to come to her home to pray for her ill husband. The pastor didn't recognize her voice, so he asked her name. "This is Orlean Weathers," she said. "Mrs. Weathers," the pastor said, "I'm sorry, but I don't believe I know you. Have you attended our church?" "Oh, no," she said. "I attend Reverend Morgan's church over on the other side of town." "Well," the pastor responded, "don't you think you ought to call Reverend Morgan to come and pray with your husband?" "No, sir. I couldn't do that," she said. "What my husband has is contagious."

But I Say unto You. In 1777, George Washington's army faced a winter of cold and bleak inactivity on a small mountain near Morristown, New Jersey. The general sensed the restlessness of his men, and so he ordered a stockade built around the encampment immediately. He also doubled the perimeter guard. Work started right away and rumors abounded about how near the enemy might be and whether the stockade would be finished on time.

In the spring, even though the fortifications were not finished, Washington ordered a move. Thinking they were about to be overrun by the enemy, the soldiers did a rapid deployment. Leaving the unfinished fortification, they marched—not to defeat—but to victory over nearby English forces. It was only history that gave the unfinished fort its name: Fort Nonsense.

God, in His inscrutable wisdom, sometimes sends us to do tasks that we don't fully understand, that don't make a lot of earthly sense. But He asks us to work at them, not for the immediate necessity of their completion, but for the good of our character and the good of our souls, especially as He leads us on to higher things.

FOR YOUTH

■ **TOPIC:** Inspired to Love

■ **QUESTIONS:** 1. What is the motivation for believers to love their enemies? 2. What do you think Jesus' meant by the command to turn the other cheek? 3. What does it mean to do to others what we would have them do to us? 4. How is it possible to love others without preconditions? 5. How do believers show that they are God's children?

■ **ILLUSTRATIONS:**

Picture of Love. Chris Carrier of Coral Gables, Florida, was abducted when he was 10 years old. His kidnappers, angry with the boy's family, burned him with cigarettes, stabbed him numerous times with an ice pick, shot him in the head, and left him to die in the Everglades. Remarkably, the boy survived, though he lost sight in one eye. No one was ever arrested.

Finally, 22 years later, a man confessed to the crime. Chris, by then a youth minister at a nearby church, went to see him. He found the man, a 77-year-old ex-convict, frail and blind, living in a Miami Beach nursing home. Chris began visiting often, reading to the ex-convict from the Bible and praying with him. The ministry of Chris opened the door for the man to make a profession of faith in Jesus Christ.

No arrest was forthcoming, for the statute of limitations on the crime was long past. And the statute of limitations had also run out on Chris's hatred and bitterness. He said, "While many people can't understand how I could forgive my kidnapper, from my point of view I couldn't not forgive him. If I'd chosen to hate him all these years, or spent my life looking for revenge, then I wouldn't be the man I am today, the man my wife and children love, the man God has helped me to be."

I studied intently the photograph, in *Leadership Journal*, of Chris holding his kidnapper's hand and praying with him as he lay in a nursing home bed. When I think about the absence of hatred, when I think about the presence of forgiveness, and when I think about Jesus' command to love our enemies, I think about that picture.

I'm Diving In! I recently ran across the anonymous quote, "We're not in this to test the waters; we are in this to make waves." What an excellent idea for the believer who wants to fulfill Jesus' summons to impact this world with His love. We're not called to be like everybody else. We're not called to go with the flow. We are called to be different, to act different, and to talk different. We shouldn't resign ourselves to simply testing the waters. We should do what Steven Curtis Chapman's hit song *Dive* says:

> I'm diving in, I'm going deep in over my head, I want to be
> Caught in the rush, lost in the flow, in over my head, I want to go
> The river's deep, the river's wide, the river's water is alive
> So sink or swim, I'm diving in!

Be Careful! According to legend, one day Francis of Assisi and Brother Leo were out walking together. Suddenly Brother Leo called out, "Brother Francis!"

"Yes, I am Brother Francis," came the reply.

"Be careful, Brother Francis! People are saying remarkable things about you! Be careful."

And Francis of Assisi replied, "My friend, pray to the Lord that I may succeed in becoming what people think I am."

INSPIRED TO PRAY!

BACKGROUND SCRIPTURE: Luke 11:5-13
DEVOTIONAL READING: Psalm 28:6-9

KEY VERSE: And I say unto you, Ask, and it shall be given you; seek, and ye shall find; knock, and it shall be opened unto you. Luke 11:9.

KING JAMES VERSION

LUKE 11:5 And he said unto them, Which of you shall have a friend, and shall go unto him at midnight, and say unto him, Friend, lend me three loaves; 6 For a friend of mine in his journey is come to me, and I have nothing to set before him? 7 And he from within shall answer and say, Trouble me not: the door is now shut, and my children are with me in bed; I cannot rise and give thee. 8 I say unto you, Though he will not rise and give him, because he is his friend, yet because of his importunity he will rise and give him as many as he needeth. 9 And I say unto you, Ask, and it shall be given you; seek, and ye shall find; knock, and it shall be opened unto you. 10 For every one that asketh receiveth; and he that seeketh findeth; and to him that knocketh it shall be opened. 11 If a son shall ask bread of any of you that is a father, will he give him a stone? or if he ask a fish, will he for a fish give him a serpent? 12 Or if he shall ask an egg, will he offer him a scorpion? 13 If ye then, being evil, know how to give good gifts unto your children: how much more shall your heavenly Father give the Holy Spirit to them that ask him?

NEW REVISED STANDARD VERSION

LUKE 11:5 And he said to them, "Suppose one of you has a friend, and you go to him at midnight and say to him, 'Friend, lend me three loaves of bread; 6 for a friend of mine has arrived, and I have nothing to set before him.' 7 And he answers from within, 'Do not bother me; the door has already been locked, and my children are with me in bed; I cannot get up and give you anything.' 8 I tell you, even though he will not get up and give him anything because he is his friend, at least because of his persistence he will get up and give him whatever he needs.

9 "So I say to you, Ask, and it will be given you; search, and you will find; knock, and the door will be opened for you. 10 For everyone who asks receives, and everyone who searches finds, and for everyone who knocks, the door will be opened. 11 Is there anyone among you who, if your child asks for a fish, will give a snake instead of a fish? 12 Or if the child asks for an egg, will give a scorpion? 13 If you then, who are evil, know how to give good gifts to your children, how much more will the heavenly Father give the Holy Spirit to those who ask him!"

8

HOME BIBLE READINGS

Monday, January 14	Psalm 28:6-9	*Answered Prayer*
Tuesday, January 15	Luke 11:1-4	*Teach Us to Pray*
Wednesday, January 16	Luke 11:5-8	*A Friend's Request* ✓
Thursday, January 17	Luke 11:9-12	*Ask and Receive*
Friday, January 18	Luke 18:1-17	*Persistent in Prayer*
Saturday, January 19	Luke 11:13; Acts 2:1-4	*God's Gift of the Holy Spirit*
Sunday, January 20	Psalm 138:1-3	*Praise the Lord!*

BACKGROUND

In Luke 11:1, we learn that one day Jesus was praying in an unnamed spot. When He finished, one of His disciples asked Him to teach the Twelve how to pray, just as John the Baptizer had done for his followers. In that day, Jewish groups typically would express their corporate identity by means of a distinctive prayer. Evidently, the disciples of John the Baptizer had adopted a prayer as their own, and now Jesus' followers requested from Him the opportunity to do something similar.

In response, Jesus outlined a model prayer (11:2-4). Although this is traditionally known as the Lord's Prayer (see also the longer version in Matt. 6:9-13), it more accurately represents how Jesus' followers should approach God. A fuller understanding of what Jesus taught can be obtained by considering both Luke's and Matthew's versions of the Lord's Prayer. We discover that God wants us to address Him in a way that reflects our close, personal relationship with Him. Like a father, God has authority over us, and yet at the same time, loves us and wants to give us the things we legitimately request. Because He lives in heaven, He is transcendent (namely, going beyond our earthly existence) and has the ability to grant our petitions.

The Greek phrase rendered *hallowed be thy name* (Luke 11:2) emphasizes how important it is for us to honor and revere the Lord, as represented by His name. Thus, the initial focus of prayer is not on one's personal needs, but on God's glory. The one who prays also desires that God's rule over His creatures will extend to its fullest bounds and that people on earth will come to obey the Lord as perfectly as do the angels in heaven. Some think that Jesus' reference to the *kingdom* denotes a time when the Messiah will physically rule over the earth. They maintain that the official rejection of Jesus did not negate the promises to Israel regarding the kingdom. Others think that this kingdom refers to Jesus' spiritual rule and that the disciples will someday share close fellowship with Jesus at a future time in this realm.

Perhaps the model prayer Jesus offered prompted some of His disciples to wonder how confident they should be in bringing seemingly small, personal matters to God. Also, if it is permissible for God's spiritual children to make specific requests to Him, then why doesn't He seem to answer all their petitions? These are some of the concerns Jesus addressed in His parable on being persistent in prayer. From this story, they learned that if they prayed, God would answer.

NOTES ON THE PRINTED TEXT

Jesus' parable recorded in Luke 11:5-13 differs from other stories He told in that He made His point by means of contrasts, rather than similarities. In particular, God is not like the friend or the father in these stories, but rather different from them. The parable about the unexpected guest spotlights a typical, though embarrassing, situation in the time of Jesus. It's late at night when a hungry traveler arrives at the home of a friend and requests some food to eat. The friend, however, does not have anything to feed his friend; and since showing hospitality was important in that culture, the friend would feel ashamed if he could not satisfy his guest's request for a meal. This prompts the host to go to a neighbor around midnight to pester him for a loan of three loaves of bread (11:5-6). In a simple Galilean village such as this, in which women baked bread in common courtyards, all the residents would know who had a fresh supply of bread.

The head of the household told his neighbor not to bother him. The former explained that the wooden door was already bolted shut, and he and his children were in bed. Moreover, the homeowner declared that he was unable to get up and give his neighbor anything to eat (11:7). This scene can be better understood with some background information about the typical sleeping arrangements of a home in Jesus' day. The dwelling was probably a peasant's cottage made up of one large room that served the entire family's needs. The bedding was kept in a recessed part of a wall, taken out at night, and spread on reed mats on the floor. The parents would sleep in the center of the room, with the male children positioned on the father's right-hand side and the female children on the mother's left-hand side. Even with a modest-sized family, the father's getting up would have disturbed the whole household, especially any children sleeping closest to him.

As noted earlier, it was a matter of cultural honor for a neighbor to be a good host to visitors. Thus, the host continues to nag his friend for food to give to the hungry traveler. Jesus noted that the inconvenienced fellow would not comply with the request out of friendship; instead, he caves in to the demand because of the neighbor's *importunity* (11:8). Indeed, the worn-down head of the household gives his neighbor not just three loaves of bread, but whatever he requests. The term *anaideia*, which is rendered *importunity*, is used only here in the Greek New Testament. It denotes a lack of sensitivity to what others would consider proper. Such ideas as "shamelessness," "impertinence," and "impudence" are wrapped up in the KJV translation. Other possible renderings include "sheer persistence" and "shameless audacity." The idea is that the neighbor gave his friend as much bread as he needed because the man kept harassing him. In addition, the head of the household possibly wanted to avoid the embarassment that would come from a breach of hospitality (see Prov. 3:27-28).

It would be incorrect to infer from Jesus' story that God will eventually answer our prayers if we keep pestering Him. He is not like a sleepy man who does not want to be troubled and has to be shamed into responding. In reality, our heavenly Father is completely opposite the friend in the house. Jesus' point is that if this man was willing to respond to the pleas of his friend, how much more willing is God to give us the things we really need. He is not reluctant to give us what we ask, but instead is eager to do so. In moments of discouragement or distress, believers can receive consolation and encouragement from God. Although He is the all-powerful and sovereign Lord, they should not be timid or fearful about praying to Him, for Jesus will intercede on their behalf (Heb. 4:14-16; 1 John 2:1). Likewise, believers should not worry about petitioning God in a religiously acceptable manner or framing their words in exactly the proper way, for the Spirit will help them to communicate with God (Rom. 8:26-27).

It thus was fitting for Jesus to encourage His disciples to pray. He stated that when they asked the Father for something, it would be given to them. This meant He delighted to hear and answer their requests. It also meant the disciples were totally dependent on the Lord. The more they looked to God to meet their needs, the less inclined they would be to covet what others had. Whatever Christians sought from God would be found, and whatever door of ministry opportunity they accessed in His will would be opened to them (Luke 11:9). The idea of knocking suggests that a certain urgency should accompany the disciples' praying. The Greek verb tenses used in this verse (present imperatives) indicate continuous action—keep on asking, keep on seeking, and keep on knocking.

The Savior explained that His followers need not fear being rejected or ignored, for God would answer their petitions (11:10). Moreover, Jesus' comments implied that His followers were to persist until the answer came. Perseverance in prayer would produce tangible results, for no prayer went unheard or unanswered by God (see 18:1). The Lord would neither disregard the petitions of His people nor treat them as insignificant. In fact, the prayers of His children were important and would get His personal attention. It would be a mistake to assume from what the Son said that the Father would fulfill unbiblical requests. In that regard, 11:9-10 (see also Matt. 7:7-8) is not a blank check that God issues to people for them to fill in as they please. Before the Lord will answer the requests of believers, they should be seeking to live and pray in His will (see 1 John 5:14-15).

Jesus ultimately intended His comments to encourage, not discourage, His followers to pray. The Savior illustrated His Father's eagerness to fulfill the requests of His children by referring to the sensible practices of all parents. Normally, when children asked for a fish, a reasonable parent would not hand them a water snake, for that would be cruel and insensitive (Luke 11:11). Moreover, if children asked for an egg, they would not get something as inappropriate and harmful as a scorpion (11:12; see Matt. 7:9-10). Similarly, God was not cruel and insensitive toward His children; rather, He was sensible and reasonable in handling their requests.

Human beings, who are fallen and inclined to do evil, understood how to give beneficial and appropriate things to their children. This being true, believers were to consider how much more their heavenly Father would do for them when they brought their requests to Him. He would always give them what was sensible and appropriate to meet their needs for that moment. This would include virtues such as righteousness, purity, and wisdom (Matt. 7:11; Jas. 1:5). Luke 11:13 specifies that the Holy Spirit is the ultimate good gift one can receive from God. From the Spirit believers receive wisdom and guidance to live in a godly manner in a fallen world (see 1 Cor. 2:10-16).

Jesus' teaching unveiled the heart of God. The Savior revealed that the Father was not stingy, selfish, or begrudging. Likewise, His children did not have to grovel and beg as they brought Him their requests. They knew He was a compassionate Father, who understood their needs and cared deeply for them. If human parents could be kind to their children, God, the heavenly Father of believers, was infinitely more considerate in hearing their petitions and meeting their needs. Jesus' teaching serves as a reminder of the true nature of God. He is not a reluctant stranger who has to be coaxed and harassed into bestowing His gifts. He is also not a malicious tyrant who takes vicious glee in playing tricks on others. God is not even like an indulgent grandparent who provides whatever one asks of him. Rather, God is the believer's heavenly Father and the Lord of an eternal kingdom. He is also the one who graciously and willingly bestows the good gifts of His kingdom in answer to prayer (Jas. 1:17).

SUGGESTIONS TO TEACHERS

God longs to give us any and every desire that is in line with His will for our lives. Sometimes, though, we have to wait for these things. Our faith is challenged when the Lord doesn't seem to answer in the way we had hoped or in the timing we had wanted; but our job is to remain faithful, to continue praying, and to keep trusting God no matter what the circumstances look like.

1. RECOGNIZING THE NATURE OF PRAYER. Praying is simply *talking to God*. The act of praying does not change what God has purposed to do. Rather, it is the means by which He accomplishes His will. Talking to God is not a method of creating a positive mental attitude in ourselves so that we are able to do what we have asked to be done. Instead, prayer creates within us a right attitude with respect to the will of God. Prayer is not so much getting God to do our will as it is demonstrating that we are as concerned as He is that His will be done (Matt. 6:10).

2. BEING PERSISTENT IN PRAYER. Perhaps the most unpopular concept regarding the practice of prayer is persistence. Whatever our misgivings about coming before the all-knowing, all-powerful God with the same specific petitions over and over, persistence is scriptural (Luke 18:1-8). God does not become more willing to answer because of perseverance. Rather, the petitioner may become more capable of receiving God's answer to his or her request. Perseverance can clarify in our minds deep-seated desire from fleeting whim. And talking to God about the deepest desires of our heart can prepare our soul to more fully appreciate the answer He gives to our request.

3. HAVING AN ATTITUDE OF GRATITUDE IN PRAYER. Thanksgiving is to be a regular part of our prayer life (1 Thess. 5:18). Thanksgiving is an aspect of praise in which we express gratitude to God. It should spring from an appreciative heart, though it is required of all believers, regardless of their initial attitude. We can thank God for His work of salvation and sanctification, for answering our prayers, and for leading us in the path of righteousness (Phil. 1:3-5; Col. 1:3-5). We can also express gratitude to God for His goodness and unending mercy, and for leading us to spiritual victory in Christ (Ps. 107:1; 1 Cor. 15:57).

■ **FOR ADULTS**

■ **TOPIC:** Finding a Listening Ear

■ **QUESTIONS:** 1. In Jesus' parable, what prompted one friend to go to another friend and request some food? 2. Why was the neighbor initially unwilling to satisfy his neighbor's demand for bread? 3. What eventually persuaded the neighbor to give in to his friend's request? 4. In what way is the Father in heaven unlike the reluctant neighbor? 5. What is the point of Jesus' comparison between earthly fathers and the heavenly Father of believers?

■ **ILLUSTRATIONS:**

An Attentive Benefactor. One day near Christmas, Rod found himself stuck in a long post office line. As he waited, a fragile-looking, middle-aged woman struggled through the front door with a box to mail and shakily approached the post office attendant. The attendant lifted her voice above the crowd and asked, "This woman is not well, and is asking if someone will allow her to go in front of them in line." She turned to the next patron and specifically inquired, "Sir, would you permit this woman to step in front of you?" The man shot back, "No!" The attendant apologized to the woman in disbelief as she struggled out of the lobby in tears.

Rod hurried out to the car as the woman, now weeping openly, was attempting to put her box back inside the vehicle. "Ma'am," Rod said, "I'd be glad to mail this box for you." He took the package, not waiting for her to get cash from her purse, and returned to his spot in line; he sent the box Priority Mail. When Rod came out of the post office, he noticed the car was idling in the handicapped space. The woman motioned for him to come over. Tearfully, she thanked Rod, and spoke about the condition that rarely allowed her to leave home unattended. Rod held her hand and assured her that he was responding from the love of God, and that though she had ventured out alone that day, she was not unattended.

Advanced Answer to Prayer. Oliver Mitchell Sr. is the president of the John E. Mitchell Manufacturing Company in Dallas, Texas. He relates a unique personal account of how God unusually answered a prayer. Oliver was awakened one night in a cold sweat. He had just had a terrible dream in which he was the driver of a car that had run over a small child. The dream was so real to him that he immediately got out of bed and went to his knees, asking God not to allow such a tragedy to happen to him. He remembers the great peace that he received almost immediately and how he went right back to sleep and didn't think about the dream again.

The next day, Oliver was driving his car with four companions to a luncheon across town. Driving at 25 miles per hour, he immediately felt impressed to slam on the brakes. His companions lurched forward, but as they recovered, they looked up just in time to see a diaper-clad toddler run out from between two parked cars. Oliver said his reactions were in direct response to God's prodding.

The Hard Work of Prayer. In *My Utmost for His Highest*, Oswald Chambers makes the following admonishment: "Prayer is a battle; it is a matter of indifference where you are. Whichever way God engineers circumstances, the duty is to pray. Never allow the thought, 'I am no use where I am'; because you certainly can be of no use where you are not. Wherever God has dumped you down in circumstances, pray."

But what if we don't see results? Perhaps we too easily fall into the same trap as the disciple Thomas: "Seeing is believing." We want to know the results of our prayers immediately. According to Chambers, "We won't pray unless we get thrills; that is the intensest form of spiritual selfishness." The author goes on to note that there is "nothing thrilling about a laboring man's work, but it is the laboring man who makes the conceptions of the genius possible; and it is the laboring saint who makes the conceptions of his Master possible."

FOR YOUTH

■ **TOPIC:** Inspired to Pray!
■ **QUESTIONS:** 1. Why did the host feel obliged to feed the hungry traveler? 2. What excuse did the neighbor give for not wanting to help out his neighbor? 3. Why would the neighbor give not just three loaves of bread to his friend, but rather as much as he wanted? 4. What incentive does a believer have to be persistent in prayer? 5. Of what benefit is the Father's gift of the Holy Spirit to believers?

■ **ILLUSTRATIONS:**

Prayers for a Hostage. For seven long years (1985–1991), friends, colleagues, and loved ones brought their petitions to God to deliver Terry Anderson from his captors. Anderson, an *Associated Press* employee, was one of several Americans that Muslims kidnapped in Lebanon and held hostage.

In his book, *Den of Lions*, Anderson says that despite the beatings and deprivation he suffered, his faith in the Lord Jesus remained strong. When Anderson was finally released and asked about his feelings toward his abductors, he said, "I am a Christian. I am required to forgive." After God had answered the petitions of those who prayed for Anderson, as well as Anderson's own prayers for release, the former hostage praised the Lord in churches, on television, and in print.

A Problem with the Radio. As we gathered around my son, Tim's, short-wave radio to listen, four sets of ears were met with blaring static. After months of work, my 14-year-old's project was a disappointment. Even worse, he had to replace the no-good filter with one we ordered through the mail. Less than a week remained until the project fair. Tim said in frustration, "I just don't see how this thing can work out!" I countered, "Maybe there will be time—just enough time. But in case there isn't, are you willing to let this go?" Tim agreed to pray with me. He asked the Lord for His help. But Tim also prayed that God would give him the grace and courage to accept that he might not get his project done.

A postal worker delivered the replacement filter a day before the fair. Within a few hours, Tim tracked down an old—yet very necessary—RF (radio frequency) generator. After buying it, he worked late into the night tuning the radio, until he heard French over the airwaves. Tim then told me that if the radio hadn't worked, it would have been OK, too. He realized God knew best. As if to remind my son of his comment, right after the fair, the new filter went bad. We concluded that our loving God meets our every need—and also has a sense of humor!

The Shortfall That Wasn't. The problem was ordinary enough—a budget miscalculation that was not discovered until late into the fiscal year. Sadly, it was not a minor error for the young church that had carefully budgeted to remodel a building that had recently become their first "permanent" facility.

In the planning process, the budget committee had accidentally double-counted some funds. Consequently, the already financially stretched congregation now faced a $10,000 shortfall. The embarrassed and apologetic budget planners called a congregational meeting and confessed their error. At this point, the threat was very real that the church might lose all that had been invested in transforming the one-time warehouse into a new place of worship.

The committee, however, was prepared to ask the Lord to turn their mistake into a demonstration of His glory and power. They proposed an ambitious, seemingly impossible fund-raising project called the 10K fund. The committee's spokesperson asked the congregants—both young and old alike—to begin praying and then to be willing to do whatever God directed in the way of giving. As these Christians began praying and giving in the way they believed the Lord was leading them, some gave sacrificially, while others experienced unexpected financial windfalls and were able to give from abundance. Amazingly, by the project's deadline, the fund had $10,003 in it!

INSPIRED TO TRUST!

BACKGROUND SCRIPTURE: Luke 12:22-34
DEVOTIONAL READING: Psalm 31:1-5

KEY VERSE: And I say unto you, Ask, and it shall be given you; seek, and ye shall find; knock, and it shall be opened unto you. Luke 11:9.

KING JAMES VERSION

LUKE 12:22 And he said unto his disciples, Therefore I say unto you, Take no thought for your life, what ye shall eat; neither for the body, what ye shall put on. 23 The life is more than meat, and the body is more than raiment. 24 Consider the ravens: for they neither sow nor reap; which neither have storehouse nor barn; and God feedeth them: how much more are ye better than the fowls? 25 And which of you with taking thought can add to his stature one cubit? 26 If ye then be not able to do that thing which is least, why take ye thought for the rest? 27 Consider the lilies how they grow: they toil not, they spin not; and yet I say unto you, that Solomon in all his glory was not arrayed like one of these. 28 If then God so clothe the grass, which is to day in the field, and to morrow is cast into the oven; how much more will he clothe you, O ye of little faith? 29 And seek not ye what ye shall eat, or what ye shall drink, neither be ye of doubtful mind. 30 For all these things do the nations of the world seek after: and your Father knoweth that ye have need of these things. 31 But rather seek ye the kingdom of God; and all these things shall be added unto you. 32 Fear not, little flock; for it is your Father's good pleasure to give you the kingdom. 33 Sell that ye have, and give alms; provide yourselves bags which wax not old, a treasure in the heavens that faileth not, where no thief approacheth, neither moth corrupteth. 34 For where your treasure is, there will your heart be also.

NEW REVISED STANDARD VERSION

LUKE 12:22 He said to his disciples, "Therefore I tell you, do not worry about your life, what you will eat, or about your body, what you will wear. 23 For life is more than food, and the body more than clothing. 24 Consider the ravens: they neither sow nor reap, they have neither storehouse nor barn, and yet God feeds them. Of how much more value are you than the birds! 25 And can any of you by worrying add a single hour to your span of life? 26 If then you are not able to do so small a thing as that, why do you worry about the rest? 27 Consider the lilies, how they grow: they neither toil nor spin; yet I tell you, even Solomon in all his glory was not clothed like one of these. 28 But if God so clothes the grass of the field, which is alive today and tomorrow is thrown into the oven, how much more will he clothe you—you of little faith! 29 And do not keep striving for what you are to eat and what you are to drink, and do not keep worrying. 30 For it is the nations of the world that strive after all these things, and your Father knows that you need them. 31 Instead, strive for his kingdom, and these things will be given to you as well.

32 "Do not be afraid, little flock, for it is your Father's good pleasure to give you the kingdom. 33 Sell your possessions, and give alms. Make purses for yourselves that do not wear out, an unfailing treasure in heaven, where no thief comes near and no moth destroys. 34 For where your treasure is, there your heart will be also."

9

Monday, January 21	Psalm 31:1-5	*Trust God*
Tuesday, January 22	Luke 12:22-24	*Valuable to God*
Wednesday, January 23	Luke 12:25-26	*Worry Won't Help!*
Thursday, January 24	Luke 12:27-28	*Clothed by God*
Friday, January 25	Luke 12:29-31	*God Knows Your Needs*
Saturday, January 26	Luke 12:32-34	*Receive the Kingdom*
Sunday, January 27	Psalm 146:1-7	*Trust God, not Princes*

BACKGROUND

The parable of the rich fool (Luke 12:13-21) forms the context of Jesus' remarks about worrying (12:22-34). Near the midpoint of His journey to Jerusalem, a crowd of many thousands had gathered to listen to Him denounce the hypocrisy of the Pharisees (12:1). At some point, a person asked Jesus to settle a family dispute over an inheritance (12:13). Making such a request of a rabbi was not unusual, for rabbis often served as impartial advisers; but Jesus refused to become involved in the dispute (12:14). Perhaps this surprised those who saw Him as being more insightful and fair than any rabbi they had ever known. While He wouldn't become a judge in the case, He saw that the dispute was rooted in greed. So just as He had warned against hypocrisy (12:1), He now warned against greed (12:15).

Jesus used a parable to illustrate His point (12:16-20). An ambitious man invested all his energy and talents in accumulating wealth. He looked forward to retirement, when he could take life easy and enjoy what he had accumulated; but the man forgot to consider God in his plans. Even though he had barns full of grain and thought he could provide for his every need, his life would end that night. When it came right down to it, he could not control what happened to him. Jesus said everyone who lived like this rich but foolish man would end up the same way (12:21). In contrast, when people invested their energy, talents, and possessions in the divine kingdom, they became *rich toward God.* Indeed, the return on their spiritual investments stretched into eternity.

Jesus was urging His followers to decide who was going to be their real master, for He knew that divided loyalties between God and money would plunge them into spiritual turmoil. Christ also realized that selfishness and greed would leave them spiritually blinded. It would be a mistake to conclude from Jesus' teaching that riches are inherently evil. The Savior was not condemning wealth, but greed and the hoarding of money. Moreover, He viewed the desire to accumulate wealth as a substitute for faith.

NOTES ON THE PRINTED TEXT

Jesus taught that the believer's outlook on life was to be radically different from that of the unsaved. Christians were not to be anxious, for it was counterproductive and prevented them from fully trusting God. Jesus was not condemning proper stewardship and forethought; rather, He was censuring nervousness over the future (Matt. 6:25). In view of that concern, the Savior urged believers not to be panicky about their lives. For instance, the provision of food, drink, and clothes—matters that the unsaved constantly fretted over—were not to preoccupy the thoughts of Jesus' followers (Luke 12:22). This is because there was more to life than these things.

Jesus explained that the lives of believers were of more significance and value than what they wore and ate (Luke 12:23; see Matt. 6:25). We can imagine Him pointing to some wild ravens or crows flying in the sky at that moment. These creatures, which the Jews considered to be unclean (Lev. 11:15; Deut. 14:14), were not involved in planting and harvesting crops. They also did not have storerooms or barns; yet the Father in heaven amply supplied their needs (Luke 12:24; see Matt. 6:26). The point of Jesus' illustration was not advocating idleness, but rather freedom from anxiety. The birds could find the insects they needed to eat everywhere around them—all provided by God. It stood to reason that the person of faith was of more value to God than a bird. This being the case, God would not fail to provide graciously for His people's needs, just as He never failed to provide for the needs of creatures such as birds.

Sadly, the tendency of believers was to be consumed with worry over the most insignificant details of life. Christ declared that being anxious was powerless and useless, and thus a waste of time (Matt. 6:27). Some Bible scholars think Luke 12:25 should be translated as it appears in the KJV, while others think the verse should be rendered as it appears in NRSV. Jesus' point comes through clearly in either translation—worry does not change things. It is not only futile to be anxious about small matters one cannot control, but also the larger matters of life that lie even farther beyond one's control (12:26).

Those who were paranoid about where their clothing, food, and shelter would come from never had any inner peace and rest. Jesus Christ pointed to the lilies of the field (which possibly were representative of all types of wild flowers) and asked His audience to consider how such delicate plants grew. These flowers did not labor to provide protective covering for themselves; yet the great King Solomon in all his splendor had not been clothed as magnificently as the lilies (12:27; see Matt. 6:28-29). To Christ's Jewish audience, Solomon would have been the foremost example of human glory. It stood to reason that the person of faith was more valuable to God than the wild flowers. This being the case, God also would not fail to provide for His people's needs, just as He never failed to clothe the grass of the field.

Next, Jesus stated that the life span of wild grass was very short. One day it was alive and the next day people removed it to burn as fuel (along with wood) in the rounded clay ovens of Palestine. If God was willing to do so much to ensure the growth and development of something as seemingly insignificant as the grass found in a field, would He not do unbelievably more for His people? Jesus assured His listeners that the Lord would provide for the basic needs of His children, individuals who were typically characterized by little faith (Luke 12:28; see Matt. 6:30). Since God abundantly cared for His lesser creatures, it stood to reason that He would care even more for His highest creatures—human beings. That is why it was irrational to worry even in the face of transitoriness and death. The Savior's comments were intended to enhance the confidence of His followers' trust in God.

Since the Lord would always meet His children's needs, they were not to be overly concerned about obtaining such essential items as food, drink, and clothing (Luke 12:29; see Matt. 6:31). The more they remained panicky about these things, the less able they would be to serve the Lord effectively. Likewise, as long as they lived in anxiety, they would miss what true life in Christ was all about. Indeed, worry could become so destructive that it actually became sinful, for a life consumed by anxiety indicated a lack of trust in God and His promises. Jesus stated that the basic necessities of life were constantly preoccupying the thoughts of the nations of the world. Believers, however, were not to be like the unsaved, for the Son promised that the Father would supply His children's needs (Luke 12:30; see Matt. 6:32).

While the unsaved spent their lives seeking after the things of the world, which were destined to pass away, Jesus urged His followers to make seeking God's kingdom and righteousness their foremost and unending priority (Luke 12:31). Some think the emphasis here is mainly prophetic and thus understand Jesus to be referring to the future expansion of God's active reign on earth, the vindication of the upright, and the punishment of the wicked. More likely, the connotation is ethical in nature. This means the principal goal of believers is the establishment of God's rule in their lives and in the lives of the unconverted. Put another way, the highest aim of any disciple is the imputation of Jesus' righteousness to repentant, believing sinners, along with its manifestation in the lives of His people.

Christians need not fear making heavenly concerns their greatest priority, for the Lord would not neglect their needs (Luke 12:31; see Matt. 6:33). When they truly honored God by their faith, He would honor their dependence on Him by supplying their needs. His children might not become wealthy in earthly treasures, but He would ensure they did not lack anything to serve Him effectively. When God had the foremost place in the life of His children, they would turn to Him first for help, fill their thoughts with His desires, make His character the pattern for their behavior, and obey His commandments. In Luke 6:32, Jesus compared His followers to a flock of weak and vulnerable sheep whom the Father in heaven cared for, guided, and protected. In fact, He was well pleased to give them the kingdom. Jesus' teachings about the kingdom show it was both present with Him on earth (Matt. 4:17) and also something that would be completely fulfilled at the end of the ages (13:24-30; 16:28). Jesus revealed that entrance into His kingdom is something that God gives to those who believe (25:34), but (paradoxically) it can cost a person everything he or she has (19:16-24).

Jesus urged His followers to sell their possessions and *give alms* (Luke 12:33) to the poor. Expressed differently, the less attached they were to material riches, the more generous they would be to others in need. The provision of *bags* is a figurative reference to satchels used by business owners for storing money. Earthly treasuries were susceptible to wearing out and being depleted. There was also no guarantee that such temporal wealth would escape being confiscated by thieves or destroyed by cloth-eating moths. In first-century Palestine, the poorer inhabitants made their homes out of mud bricks. Thus, it was easy for thieves to break into these dwellings and steal things. Jesus alluded to this fact to point out how easy it was for people to lose what they owned (Matt. 6:19).

Jesus declared that it was far better to accumulate heavenly treasures, for these were impervious to decay, destruction, and confiscation (Luke 12:33). The reference here is to whatever one does in this life that has eternal value. Likewise, the spiritual riches of God's kingdom could never be devalued, lost, or stolen (Matt. 6:20). The Savior announced that wherever one's treasure was, that was also where his or her aspirations and desires were located (Luke 12:34). Put another way, where people invested their time, talents, and resources was a barometer of what concerned them the most (Matt. 6:21). People who spent their time amassing material wealth had their interests and aims anchored on temporal concerns, whereas people who spent their time amassing spiritual treasures had their interests and aims anchored on eternal concerns.

SUGGESTIONS TO TEACHERS

Fretting and trusting are both chosen patterns of behavior. To build a stronger spiritual "savings account," we must reject fear and choose faith. True security and freedom from worry come from daily, conscious decisions to live in the light that God provides.

1. SERVE GOD, NOT MONEY. Ours is a materialistic society in which most people serve money—whether or not they admit it. They prove that they serve money over God by spending all their waking hours collecting and storing it. And even if they don't somehow lose their money, they will eventually die and leave it behind. It is far better for us to serve our eternal God. Our commitment to Him and to spiritual matters ought to far outweigh our desire for money and what we can buy with it.

2. INVEST IN HEAVEN, NOT IN EARTH. Think eternal. Act eternal. Invest eternal. Be eternal. In the end, nothing will be left except what we've invested for God and the furtherance of His kingdom.

3. PLAN, DON'T WORRY. The old adage says, "Those who fail to plan, plan to fail." Jesus' teaching implied that planning for tomorrow is time wisely invested. In contrast, worrying about tomorrow is time foolishly wasted. Careful planning is thinking ahead about goals and steps and schedules, all while trusting God's guidance. When done well, planning can even help alleviate worry. Worrying, on the other hand, causes us to misplace our trust, and we find it difficult to depend on God. How tragic it is when we let worries about tomorrow affect our present relationship with God!

4. TRUST GOD, NOT YOUR POSSESSIONS. Our possessions will come and go, but our God is here to stay. So let us trust Him exclusively and put our possessions to use for His kingdom.

5. GIVE, DON'T HOARD. Remember that the love of money is a root of all kinds of evil (1 Tim. 6:10). By developing the habit of giving generously to the Lord's work, we prove to God—and to ourselves—that we control our possessions and not the other way around. May we become more fascinated with giving to the kingdom of God and less fascinated with all that we might hoard for ourselves.

| **FOR ADULTS** | ■ **TOPIC:** Combating Anxiety and Worry |

■ **TOPIC:** Combating Anxiety and Worry

■ **QUESTIONS:** 1. Why is it so tempting to worry about our lives? 2. In what sense is life more than the food we eat and the clothes we wear? 3. Why is it pointless to worry about the length of our lives? 4. Why is our heart an accurate indicator of what we treasure most? 5. What is the difference between worry and proper concern for the future?

■ **ILLUSTRATIONS:**

Lessen Your Load. In Noah BenShea's book, *Jacob's Journey: Wisdom to Find the Way, Strength to Carry On*, a rich man comes to Jacob, the baker, and asks him, "When others turn to me for help, what should I say?" "Say, thank you," Jacob replied, toying with a leaf that had fallen from a tree. "What?" said the man. "Why should I say 'thank you'?" His voice grew louder as if to boost his confidence. "What can the poor give me?" "Have you ever met a man whose success is not also a burden?" said Jacob. "Charity allows you to lessen your load. In this way, having less can add to your life!" Now the stranger's voice took a new tone. "I feel like a fool," he said. "No," responded Jacob. "A fool is one who knows too much to learn anything."

Coming Up Empty. Magazine editor, Lewis Lapham, in his book, *Money and Class in America*, tells the story of a chance encounter with a Yale University classmate who had become a New York businessman. The two ran into each other about 30 years after their college graduation, and the businessman immediately began to cry on Lapham's shoulder.

"I'm nothing," the man said. "You understand that, nothing. I earn $250,000 a year, but it's nothing, and I'm nobody." The businessman's despair struck Lapham as being rather grotesque. After all, if the average American family of four earns an annual income in the tens of thousands of dollars, how could this person possibly feel deprived? But when the businessman listed his expenses—a Park Avenue apartment, private school tuitions, taxes, salaries for a maid and a part-time laundress—the total came to $300,400. He was clearly going broke on an income of $250,000 a year!

"As it is," said the businessman, "I live like an animal. I eat tuna fish out of cans and hope that when the phone rings it isn't somebody dunning me for a bill." He might have been pulling down a quarter of a million dollars a year, but according to Lapham, he "had the look of a man who was being followed by the police." He had put his treasures where his heart was, and had come up empty.

Rich toward God. The Marquis de Lafayette was a French general and politician who was extremely rich and fit into the highest French social class. He assisted George Washington in the American Revolution, and then he returned to France and resumed his life as the master of several estates. In 1783, the harvest was a poor one, but the workers of Lafayette's farms still somehow managed to fill his barns with wheat. "The bad harvest has raised the price of wheat," said one of his workers. "This is the time to sell." Lafayette thought about all the hungry peasants in the surrounding villages. Then he said, "No. This is the time to give."

Lafayette had an opportunity to store up treasures for himself, but decided instead to offer his wealth to the poor. This act did not impoverish him, but instead made him rich—rich toward God. Such generosity is good planning for anyone who wants to store up treasures in heaven.

■ TOPIC: Inspired to Trust

■ QUESTIONS: 1. Why do people spend so much time and energy fretting over what they will eat and what they will wear? 2. What was Jesus' point about God's care for the ravens? 3. How does God's care for wild flowers compare to His care for His spiritual children? 4. What does it mean to seek first God's kingdom? 5. Why is it far wiser to store up treasures in heaven rather than on earth?

■ ILLUSTRATIONS:

No Fear of Death. One of my favorite storytellers is the author, Robert Fulghum. He's written several best-selling books, beginning with one called *All I Really Need to Know I Learned in Kindergarten.* More than 15,000,000 copies of his books are in print, in more than 25 languages, and in nearly 100 countries. Needless to say, he has done very well financially.

In an interview with a Christian magazine called *The Door,* Fulghum reports that since his success, people are always saying, "Well, you must have a big house and a big car." And he responds, "No, I have the same house, same car, same friends, same wife." Fulghum admits to being on guard against all kinds of greed, and is committed to trusting in and serving God, not money. Of course, fame is a challenge, Fulghum admits, "and the challenge is to be a good steward with this kind of authority and power—especially with the economics." So one year he did a book tour, and used it to raise $670,000 for a number of good causes. "I don't think I should be given extra credit for doing that," he says. "I think you should think ill of me if I didn't do that."

Death doesn't scare Fulghum. In fact, in one of his books is a picture of the grave he has already picked out, and he likes to visit it. It reminds him to live in a way that is laying up for himself treasures in heaven. And when Fulghum sees the grave, he says to himself, "Don't get lost here. Know where you're going." Those who find ways to trust in and serve God have discovered the right path. They don't have to fear death, for they know where they're going. Their treasure is waiting for them in heaven, not in an earthly bank account, an estate, or in stocks and bonds.

Giving and Storing. Pastor Gary tells how a group of middle-school youth from his church in the northwest part of the United States visited different neighbors to collect food for the local food bank. Of course, an added task was extending an invitation to people to attend pastor Gary's church. In only one hour, the entire group collected more than 760 pounds of food. The youth returned to the church joyful at the generosity of so many people and amazed at what God had accomplished through them.

Then, over pizza, the youth and their parents traded stories. One of the parents told how some youth from the church had knocked on the doors of several lovely homes with nice cars in the driveway where the occupants exclaimed, "We really don't have any extra food to share!" Then one of the other occupants bellowed, "You've got to be kidding!" A teacher friend of pastor Gary calls that "poor talk." In other words, it's when "people of means" pretend they are just getting by.

Giving and seeing that others are fed and taken care of is one of the ways that we can store up for ourselves treasures in heaven.

Ready to Die. In her book, *I Heard the Owl Call My Name*, Margaret Craven tells the story of a cleric's visit to a young minister serving a tribe of Native Americans in British Columbia. The cleric knew and loved this tribe, and enjoyed their feasting and dancing. At the end of his visit he tried to describe his feelings to the minister.

"Always when I leave the village," the cleric said slowly, "I try to define what it means to me, why it sends me back to the world refreshed and confident. Always I fail. It is so simple, yet it is difficult. When I try to put it into words, it comes out one of those unctuous, over-pious platitudes at which clerics are expected to excel." They both laughed. "But when I reach here and see the great scar where the inlet side [of the river] shows its bones, for a moment I know." The minister asked, "What, my lord?" "That for me it has always been easier here, where only the fundamentals count, to learn what every man must learn in this world." "And that, my lord?" "Enough of the meaning of life to be ready to die."

SUMMONED TO LABOR!

BACKGROUND SCRIPTURE: Luke 10:1-12, 17-20
DEVOTIONAL READING: Psalm 78:1-4

KEY VERSE: The harvest truly is great, but the labourers are few: pray ye therefore the Lord of the harvest, that he would send forth labourers into his harvest. Luke 10:2.

KING JAMES VERSION

LUKE 10:1 After these things the Lord appointed other seventy also, and sent them two and two before his face into every city and place, whither he himself would come. 2 Therefore said he unto them, The harvest truly is great, but the labourers are few: pray ye therefore the Lord of the harvest, that he would send forth labourers into his harvest. 3 Go your ways: behold, I send you forth as lambs among wolves. 4 Carry neither purse, nor scrip, nor shoes: and salute no man by the way. 5 And into whatsoever house ye enter, first say, Peace be to this house. 6 And if the son of peace be there, your peace shall rest upon it: if not, it shall turn to you again. 7 And in the same house remain, eating and drinking such things as they give: for the labourer is worthy of his hire. Go not from house to house. 8 And into whatsoever city ye enter, and they receive you, eat such things as are set before you: 9 And heal the sick that are therein, and say unto them, The kingdom of God is come nigh unto you. 10 But into whatsoever city ye enter, and they receive you not, go your ways out into the streets of the same, and say, 11 Even the very dust of your city, which cleaveth on us, we do wipe off against you: notwithstanding be ye sure of this, that the kingdom of God is come nigh unto you. 12 But I say unto you, that it shall be more tolerable in that day for Sodom, than for that city. . . .

17 And the seventy returned again with joy, saying, Lord, even the devils are subject unto us through thy name. 18 And he said unto them, I beheld Satan as lightning fall from heaven. 19 Behold, I give unto you power to tread on serpents and scorpions, and over all the power of the enemy: and nothing shall by any means hurt you. 20 Notwithstanding in this rejoice not, that the spirits are subject unto you; but rather rejoice, because your names are written in heaven.

NEW REVISED STANDARD VERSION

LUKE 10:1 After this the Lord appointed seventy others and sent them on ahead of him in pairs to every town and place where he himself intended to go. 2 He said to them, "The harvest is plentiful, but the laborers are few; therefore ask the Lord of the harvest to send out laborers into his harvest. 3 Go on your way. See, I am sending you out like lambs into the midst of wolves. 4 Carry no purse, no bag, no sandals; and greet no one on the road. 5 Whatever house you enter, first say, 'Peace to this house!' 6 And if anyone is there who shares in peace, your peace will rest on that person; but if not, it will return to you. 7 Remain in the same house, eating and drinking whatever they provide, for the laborer deserves to be paid. Do not move about from house to house. 8 Whenever you enter a town and its people welcome you, eat what is set before you; 9 cure the sick who are there, and say to them, 'The kingdom of God has come near to you.' 10 But whenever you enter a town and they do not welcome you, go out into its streets and say, 11 'Even the dust of your town that clings to our feet, we wipe off in protest against you. Yet know this: the kingdom of God has come near.' 12 I tell you, on that day it will be more tolerable for Sodom than for that town." . . .

17 The seventy returned with joy, saying, "Lord, in your name even the demons submit to us!" 18 He said to them, "I watched Satan fall from heaven like a flash of lightning. 19 See, I have given you authority to tread on snakes and scorpions, and over all the power of the enemy; and nothing will hurt you. 20 Nevertheless, do not rejoice at this, that the spirits submit to you, but rejoice that your names are written in heaven."

10

183

BACKGROUND

The broader context of this week's Scripture passage is Jesus' steady progress toward Jerusalem to die on the cross as an atoning sacrifice for the lost (Luke 9:51). The journey leading up to His divinely appointed end involved Him traveling from one town or village to the next and teaching the residents about the kingdom of God (13:22; 17:11; 18:31; 19:28, 41). The statement that Jesus *set His face* (9:51) to go to the capital was an idiomatic way of indicating the Messiah's steadfast resolve to complete the mission of redemption His Father had given Him (see Isa. 50:7). In short, Jesus came to earth to give His life as a ransom for many, and nothing would deter Him from that end (Matt. 20:28; Mark 10:45).

Along the way, He devoted time and energy to prepare His disciples for His eventual return to heaven. He wanted to ensure they would be able to proclaim the good news of salvation even without Him being physically present. Doing this would require firm, unwavering devotion to Him. In fact, that is why in Luke 9:57-62, Jesus challenged several would-be disciples with the high cost of following Him. Those who wanted to be His followers might have to endure depravation. They had to be willing to set aside all earthly loyalties for the sake of the kingdom and not look back once such a momentous decision was made. The forward look of the divine call to Christian service would settle for nothing less than this.

Previously, Jesus had called and commissioned the Twelve to proclaim the kingdom of God and heal the sick (9:1-2). This mirrored Jesus' own ministry, in which He taught others and restored people to health (for example, 4:16-44). Only the Gospel of Luke records a second episode in which Jesus appointed and dispatched a larger number of followers to be His official delegates. There is a textual problem, however, in 10:1 and 17. Some Greek manuscripts read "seventy" as the number of disciples Jesus chose and commissioned, while other manuscripts put the figure at "seventy-two." These different textual traditions are reflected in the renderings of the KJV and NIV, respectively. Specialists think "seventy-two" is the more difficult reading and has slightly better manuscript support. It is conjectured that some scribes tried to harmonize these verses with several Old Testament passages that refer to groups of 70 people (for example, Num. 11:13-17; Deut. 10:22; Judg. 8:30; 2 Kings 10:1).

In any case, it's clear that Jesus made use of others, in addition to the Twelve, to spread the good news of the kingdom, a decision that foreshadowed the future mission of the church to the nations (Luke 24:47; Acts 1:8). By this time, the Messiah had a large group who followed Him as He journeyed along the way. Understandably, the residents of a modest-sized village would have felt overwhelmed by the sudden appearance of so many people. Thus, Jesus gave advance notice by sending pairs of disciples ahead of Him into every town and place where He intended to journey (Luke 10:1).

Previously, Jesus had dispatched the Twelve in pairs (Mark 6:7). One reason for doing this in both situations might have been the law that a minimum of two witnesses was needed to establish the credibility of a testimony (Deut. 17:6; 19:15). Furthermore, ministering as partners provided companionship and support (Eccl. 4:9-12). This pattern can be seen in the missionary activity of the early church, which included the joint ministries of Peter and John (Acts 3:1; 4:1; 8:14), Paul and Barnabas (11:30; 13:2), Barnabas and Mark (15:39), and Paul and Silas (15:40).

NOTES ON THE PRINTED TEXT

After appointing 70 other disciples (Luke 10:1), Jesus addressed the need for prayer (10:2). From His own ministry experience, He recognized that the multitudes were like fragile, vulnerable sheep without a shepherd (Matt. 9:35-36). Put another way, if the sheep were left to themselves, they could easily get confused and lost. Jesus also realized that people were not being adequately guided by their religious leaders. As in Matthew 9:37-38, Christ's words to the 70 disciples recorded in Luke 10:2 indicated that the harvest of potential converts was abundant, though the workers were few. He instructed His followers to pray to the Father, who was the owner and master of the harvest, for workers to do the spiritual reaping.

As Jesus' sent out His delegation of followers, they would experience opposition and threats from unbelievers. Christ used the metaphor of helpless and defenseless lambs being exposed to ravenous wolves (10:3). The implication is that Jesus was asking His disciples to risk their lives because the work was important. There would be danger and hardship for those invading Satan's territory. Despite this reality, the Savior's followers were commanded to go, trusting God for safety.

As with the Twelve (Luke 9:3; see Matt. 10:9-10; Mark 6:8-9), Jesus' instructions to the larger group of His followers indicated that their mission was important and that they were not to be distracted by lesser concerns (Luke 10:4). In fact, there's a sense of urgency conveyed by Jesus' directives that required His disciples to be frugal and remain focused on the task at hand. This demeanor contrasted with the flamboyant and pretentious manner in which itinerant philosophical teachers of the day conducted themselves. Because the Savior wanted His followers to travel light, He told them not to take a moneybag, traveler's knapsack, or extra footgear (such as sandals). These unnecessary items would have slowed them down. Also, He wanted them to trust God to provide for their needs day by day. Moreover, Jesus forbid His disciples from greeting anyone they met as they traveled along the dusty roads of Palestine (see 2 Kings 4:29). By saying this, the Messiah was not authorizing them to be rude, unfriendly, or antisocial. Instead, Jesus wanted them to hurry along and not squander their time on lengthy traditional greetings. He also directed them to lodge in the homes of those receptive to their ministry.

Upon entering a dwelling, it was customary for a guest to say, "May peace be on this house" (see 1 Sam. 25:5-6). This greeting of peace (equivalent to the Hebrew concept of *shalom* or well-being) was similar to a benediction in which God's blessing was requested (Luke 10:5). The head of the house would show himself to be a peace-loving person by his positive response to the disciples' message. In turn, this determined how the blessing of God was bestowed. Those who refused to welcome the disciples would not have God's peace remain on their household (10:6; see Matt. 10:11-13). As a matter of fact, the forfeiture of such was equivalent to a curse. Jesus told the disciples to stay in one house and accept the provisions offered by their hosts. He barred His disciples to move around from house to house within a town (Luke 10:7; see Mark 6:10; Luke 9:4). Jesus gave this instruction so that the disciples would not insult a host by leaving if they were offered better accommodations elsewhere. Besides, the disciples were to be concerned about their ministry, not their own comfort.

What Jesus said with respect to households visited by His followers also applied equally to entire towns. For example, if the residents of a village welcomed His disciples, this meant they welcomed the message and ministry of the Savior, whom the disciples represented. Jesus told His followers to eat whatever they were served (Luke 10:8). Even if they were offered food not prepared according to the Jewish dietary laws, they were to overlook this (see Acts 10:9-16; 1 Cor. 10:27). After all, the principle focus of the disciples was to heal the sick and proclaim good news of the divine kingdom (see Matt. 10:7-8; Mark 6:12-13; Luke 9:6). Ultimately, the Messiah empowered His disciples to perform miracles of healing (Luke 10:9).

Not all towns would be welcoming. In those places where the residents rejected Jesus' disciples, they were to go to the main road, street corner, or public square of the town and declare that God's condemnation rested on the townspeople for their refusal of His kingdom (10:10). In that day, pious Jews reentering Palestine would cleanse their feet and clothes so as not to pollute the Holy Land with the dust of Gentile territory. Jesus instructed His disciples to use this custom to symbolize the judgment of God on a town's Messiah-rejecting inhabitants. The only remaining responsibility for Jesus' followers was to declare to these towns that the divine kingdom was near. In this case, though, it was not coming to bring salvation but judgment (vs. 11; see Matt. 10:14; Mark 6:11; Luke 9:5; Acts 13:51). Jesus declared that on the day of judgment, these towns would be worse off than Sodom, a city known for its wickedness.

When the larger group of Jesus' followers returned from their mission, they were full of joy and enthusiastically made their report to the *Lord* (Luke 10:17), a title that affirmed Jesus' status and authority as God's agent. As Christ's disciples, they proclaimed the message of the kingdom and even the demons submitted to them. These evil, supernatural beings were the henchmen of Satan; but when the disciples commanded them to depart from their human hosts, the fallen angels obeyed, for Jesus' followers were operating in His name and under His sovereign authority. In 10:18, Jesus declared that Satan and his demonic cohorts had suffered defeat as a result of the ministry of the 70. Expressed differently, because of their faithful service in Jesus' name, they had won a victory against the devil. Moreover, the disciples' expulsion of the demons anticipated the greater defeat of Satan at the hands of Jesus through His redemptive work on the cross.

In 10:19, Jesus told the 70 that He had given them authority to tread or trample on *serpents and scorpions* and to prevail over the full force of the *enemy*. Indeed, nothing at all would harm them. Bible students disagree over how literally to interpret this. Some say Christ was referring to literal protection from poison and satanic power (see Mark 16:8; Acts 28:3-6). Others say the *serpents and scorpions* (Luke 10:19) represent Satan. In any case, while victory over the forces of evil was something to rejoice about, Jesus said it was more significant that the disciples' names were written in heaven (10:20). The biggest triumph we can have over the enemy is to escape his clutches through salvation in Christ.

SUGGESTIONS TO TEACHERS

The Christian faith is different from all other world religions. They all demand that their followers improve themselves through rituals, sacrifice, and good deeds. This human "righteousness" then counts on whether a person becomes a god or achieves some higher level of existence at the end. In contrast, Jesus offers people not some kind of glorified status based on keeping all the rules, but a personal relationship with Him based on faith. He also sends them out to invite others to become His followers.

1. CALLING THE COMMON TYPES. Jesus neither selected the brainiest from the groves of Athens' academe nor the most pious from the precincts of the Jerusalem temple. Jesus bypassed the wealthy from Alexandria and the powerful from Rome. Instead, He chose people from the rank-and-file of society. Remind the class that the Savior calls ordinary persons like us, just as He called fishermen and tax collectors, to do His work.

2. CONFLICTING RESPONSES. The gospel message is empowering to some people and offensive to others. Saved adults must be prepared for both responses. Sometimes the peer at work they thought would laugh them off for talking about Jesus instead listens intently to them. In contrast, the neighbor the adult thought would trust in Christ orders him or her to never again mention God.

3. CONFERRING AUTHORITY. Explain that Jesus conferred extraordinary authority on ordinary people to do His work. Then let your students know that we serve the same Messiah today. He can use anyone, no matter how insignificant he or she might appear to be.

4. COUNTING THE CREW. The 70 weren't drafted or forced into service. Rather, Jesus chose each disciple to serve Him in a special way. Likewise, Jesus wants every member of your class to follow Him and be committed to doing His will. He won't twist their arms to get them to submit. Instead, He wants them to respond willingly to His summons.

FOR ADULTS

■ **TOPIC:** Response Requires Work

■ **QUESTIONS:** 1. Why did Jesus want the 70 to go ahead of Him as His representatives? 2. Why were there so few workers to reap the available spiritual harvest? 3. Under what condition would God's peace rest on a household visited by Jesus' disciples? 4. How were Christ's followers to respond to those who rejected their message and ministry? 5. Why were the 70 filled with joy after their return from their mission?

■ **ILLUSTRATIONS:**

Called to Commitment. The Calvary Chapel association has caught the essence of Jesus' call to His original disciples by training lay persons to live out their Christian commitment. Founded in 1965 by Chuck Smith, Calvary Chapel now claims over 600 congregations in the United States and another hundred worldwide, including the former Soviet bloc. Chuck Smith and his fellow pastors stress strong lay leadership, and they plant new churches by sending these lay people as a small core from parent churches. The leadership often quote the following slogan: GOD DOES NOT CALL THE QUALIFIED; HE QUALIFIES THE CALLED.

Lambs Among Wolves. On March 23, 2006, Bassem Mroue of *ABC News International* reported that U.S. and British forces freed three hostages in rural Iraq. Harmeet Singh Sooden, Jim Loney, and Norman Kember were members of Chicago-based Christian Peacemaker Teams, an organization focused on reducing violence and protecting human rights in conflict zones around the world, including Iraq. According to Mroue, a "kidnapping cell" held the peace activists for four months. The military was able to liberate the captives "based on information from a man captured by U.S. forces only three hours earlier."

Another member of the group, Tom Fox, was found earlier in the month. His captors shot him to death and then "dumped his body on a Baghdad street." Doug Pritchard, the group co-director, stated the deceased would be remembered with tears.

He also said, "Our gladness today is bittersweet by the fact that Tom is not alive to join his colleagues in the celebration." Fox, along with the other three peace activists, represent believers who are willing to make amazing sacrifices in order to promote peace and nonviolence in the name of Christ. They are a living testimony to the truth of Jesus' statement in Luke 10:3, *I send you forth as lambs among wolves.*

Persecution and the Bible. Like the delegation of followers Jesus sent out during His earthly ministry, believers today experience opposition and threats from unbelievers. The American Bible Society reports that today there are "millions of Christians enduring intense persecution" in such far-flung places as the Middle East, the former Soviet bloc, and Asia. Some in the West incorrectly think that "individual cases" are "limited to traditional Islamic states." In reality, incidents of harassment and abuse have been reported in "many parts of Africa, Europe, and even the Americas."

Amid these heart-wrenching situations, the Bible remains the "cornerstone symbol" of the faith of persecuted believers. Indeed, for many the Word of God is "encouragement beyond all else." It's not surprising, then, that the "worldwide pleas for help again and again include requests for more Scriptures." This is one reason why, in the past year alone, an organization such as Cook Communications Ministries International has provided almost 5 million pieces of Christian literature to support the church around the world. They exist to support, promote, and contribute to teaching and applying the Savior's two great commands—loving God and loving one another—by creating and disseminating Christian printed materials and services to people throughout the world.

FOR YOUTH	■ TOPIC: Summoned to Labor ■ QUESTIONS: 1. Why did Jesus send out the 70 in pairs? 2. What did Jesus say His disciples were to pray for from the Lord of the harvest?

3. What did the disciples' greeting of peace signify? 4. What did it mean for the disciples to shake off the dust from their feet? 5. In what sense did Jesus see Satan fall from heaven?

■ **ILLUSTRATIONS:**

Committed. Maura Donohue and Carla Sherred were juniors at Thomas Jefferson High School in Pleasant Hills, Pennsylvania. Both took a day off from school to board buses and ride to Washington, D.C., to participate in an important religious rally. They joined a group at a church at 5:30 A.M. to worship and then ride to the nation's capital. The two said they had a strong passion for their organization's moral cause. Maura and Carla are two youth committed to making a difference in their community.

Jesus called people to become His disciples and commit themselves to His cause.

You also have been called to discipleship. Support it as much as these two young people have chosen to support their religious group's cause.

Healing Attitudes. In April 2000, the *Far East Broadcasting Company* reported how a witch doctor in Uganda had become a Christian. The man had warned Walter Karanja, an engineer who started a church among his co-workers in Masindi, to stop talking about Christ. Finally the witch doctor burst wild-eyed into the church while Karanja was preaching. "Jesus of Walter, do not kill me!" he screamed. When Karanja asked him why he was so afraid, the witch doctor said that he and his followers had hated the church. "I have told them to use their powers to destroy you," he said.

"I know," Karanja replied, "but I am still here." "Why is your power stronger than mine? Why have you and your God not killed me?" the witch doctor asked. Karanja explained that his God, "the God of the universe," is not only all-powerful but also loving. When the man asked to know more, Karanja presented the Gospel to him. The witch doctor became a Christian and changed his name to John. A few days later, he was baptized, and then he burned his witchcraft paraphernalia. News spread quickly, for he had been a prominent and feared leader. Clearly, the Gospel has the power to heal attitudes as well as bodies!

Dealing with Rejection. Natalie struggled with her father, who would never give his full approval. Nothing she did could quite meet his expectations. She earned C's; he demanded B's. She got B's; he wanted A's. She worked and received nearly all A's. Then he asked why she was giving less time to her younger sisters. Natalie kept trying to please her dad.

One Father's Day, Natalie bought a wall plaque for her dad. Its words expressed her love for him. She gave it to him with joy, only to hear his response, "We've got enough junk lying around the house already." Only after some counseling and healing prayer with her pastor could Natalie fully trust that God, her heavenly Father, truly loved her as she was.

He Didn't Deserve Rejection. Rick DeMont had to wait 29 years to receive the justice he deserved. During the 1972 Munich Olympics, at age 16, DeMont won a gold medal in the 400-meter freestyle swim. At least that's what he thought at the time. After a drug test, the International Olympic Committee stripped him of his medal.

What happened? Because of allergies, DeMont had taken medication for asthma. The U.S. authorities knew about and approved his medication, unaware that it broke international rules. For 29 years, DeMont lived with this undeserved rejection. He still does not have his gold medal back. But at least the U.S. Olympic Committee has admitted responsibility and stated its belief that DeMont was innocent of any wrongdoing.

SUMMONED TO REPENT!

BACKGROUND SCRIPTURE: Luke 13:1-9
DEVOTIONAL READING: Psalm 63:1-6

KEY VERSE: I tell you, . . . except ye repent,
ye shall all likewise perish. Luke 13:3.

KING JAMES VERSION

LUKE 13:1 There were present at that season some that told him of the Galilaeans, whose blood Pilate had mingled with their sacrifices. 2 And Jesus answering said unto them, Suppose ye that these Galilaeans were sinners above all the Galilaeans, because they suffered such things? 3 I tell you, Nay: but, except ye repent, ye shall all likewise perish. 4 Or those eighteen, upon whom the tower in Siloam fell, and slew them, think ye that they were sinners above all men that dwelt in Jerusalem? 5 I tell you, Nay: but, except ye repent, ye shall all likewise perish.

6 He spake also this parable; A certain man had a fig tree planted in his vineyard; and he came and sought fruit thereon, and found none. 7 Then said he unto the dresser of his vineyard, Behold, these three years I come seeking fruit on this fig tree, and find none: cut it down; why cumbereth it the ground? 8 And he answering said unto him, Lord, let it alone this year also, till I shall dig about it, and dung it: 9 And if it bear fruit, well: and if not, then after that thou shalt cut it down.

NEW REVISED STANDARD VERSION

LUKE 13:1 At that very time there were some present who told him about the Galileans whose blood Pilate had mingled with their sacrifices. 2 He asked them, "Do you think that because these Galileans suffered in this way they were worse sinners than all other Galileans? 3 No, I tell you; but unless you repent, you will all perish as they did. 4 Or those eighteen who were killed when the tower of Siloam fell on them—do you think that they were worse offenders than all the others living in Jerusalem? 5 No, I tell you; but unless you repent, you will all perish just as they did."

6 Then he told this parable: "A man had a fig tree planted in his vineyard; and he came looking for fruit on it and found none. 7 So he said to the gardener, 'See here! For three years I have come looking for fruit on this fig tree, and still I find none. Cut it down! Why should it be wasting the soil?' 8 He replied, 'Sir, let it alone for one more year, until I dig around it and put manure on it. 9 If it bears fruit next year, well and good; but if not, you can cut it down.'"

11

BACKGROUND

During one episode in which Jesus taught a crowd of thousands about the signs of the times (Luke 12:1, 13, 54), some listeners mentioned an atrocity committed by Pontius Pilate. It was reported that he had massacred a group of Galileans, with the result that some of their blood mixed with the sacrifices they had been offering near the temple in Jerusalem, perhaps during the season of Passover (13:1). There is no other historical record of this event, though it mirrors similar incidents chronicled in the writings of the ancient Jewish historian, Josephus. Pilate was the fifth Roman prefect or governor of Judea (A.D. 26–36) and was notorious for his role in sentencing Jesus to die on the cross. It is generally thought that Pilate was an Italian-born, middle class Roman citizen from the region of Samnium in central Italy.

By all accounts, Pilate was harsh in the way in which he dealt with his Jewish contemporaries. This was due in part to his contempt for their religious convictions. For instance, in one episode the prefect brought into Jerusalem military insignia that bore the image of the emperor. This created a firestorm of protest from the Jewish people, who regarded the effigies as an idolatrous presence that violated their law. Unwavering Jewish resolve in the face of being slaughtered eventually caused Pilate to remove the offensive insignia.

The prefect again incited ill will when he raided the Temple treasury to fund the construction of an aqueduct to bring water to Jerusalem. Pilate used brute force to squash the protests that ensued, which in turn resulted in appalling bloodshed. Later, at the prefect's residence in Jerusalem, he mounted a pair of golden votive shields that were inscribed with the names of Tiberius and himself. The Jewish elite lodged a formal complaint with Tiberius, which prompted him to order the immediate relocation of the shields to Caesarea.

In A.D. 36, Vitellius, the legate of Syria, deposed Pilate, ordering him to appear before the emperor in Rome and explain his actions. Pilate's dismissal from office stemmed from his violent response to a group of Samaritans who had assembled at Mount Gerizim. They did so in anticipation of finding sacred items they believed had been lost from the Samaritan temple (which the Hasmoneans destroyed about a century and a half earlier). The people superstitiously thought Moses had buried these treasures at the foot of the mountain. A Samaritan delegation to Vitellius accused Pilate of cruelly slaughtering innocent lives. Episodes such as these left the prefect with a reputation for being arrogant, vindictive, and easily provoked to anger.

NOTES ON THE PRINTED TEXT

If those listening to Jesus thought they would get a sympathetic response (Luke 13:1), they were mistaken. The Savior declared that the Galileans whom Pilate massacred had not experienced this tragedy because they were worse sinners than their peers (13:2). Jesus then noted to the crowd that unless each of them repented and received eternal life, they faced the prospect of death, namely, eternal separation from God. The word *repent* in 13:3 translates the Greek word *metanoeite*. The term conveys the idea of changing one's mind. In a religious sense, it signifies a turnabout in attitude toward God and life's priorities. Repentance is part of the conversion process. Through the working of the Holy Spirit, sinners come to the point at which they are ready to turn away from sin and place their trust in Christ for salvation.

Jesus brought up another incident in which 18 individuals perished when the tower of Siloam collapsed on them (13:4). This structure was near the reservoir of Siloam and built into the southeast corner of the wall of Jerusalem; however, the precise location of the tower remains unknown. In contrast to the event Jesus previously mentioned, this disaster was an accident beyond anyone's control. It raised the question of whether God was judging the victims for being worse offenders than all the other residents of Jerusalem. As before, in this case Jesus said the answer was no. Moreover, He told the crowd that unless they repented of their sins, eternal condemnation was their end (13:5).

Jesus then told the parable of the spared fig tree. He noted that a Jewish landowner regularly inspected one of the fig trees in his vineyard for fruit (13:6). He complained to the worker who tended the vineyard that after three years, the tree had enough time to become viable and fruitful; yet it remained barren. Some have suggested that the total elapsed time could have been six years, given the fact that it was common practice in Jesus' day for three years to transpire before a farmer even began to look for fruit on a fig tree. Because the one in Jesus' parable remained unproductive, the landowner did not want the tree to continue depleting the soil of nutrients to prolong its growth. Instead, he ordered the worker to cut down the tree (13:7).

Some think Micah 7:1 forms the backdrop of Jesus' parable. This verse records the Lord's lament over Judah's sin, as symbolized by a grove of unfruitful fig trees. Others have noted that the fig tree in Jesus' parable is a variant of the more familiar picture of a vine representing the nation. In fact, there are several places in the Old Testament where Israel is referred to as a vineyard. For example, in Isaiah 5:4 we read that God desired His vineyard (Israel) to bring forth grapes (righteousness); instead, the people brought forth wild grapes (unrighteousness). As a nation ready for exile, Israel's behavior was not pleasing to God. The Father, whom Jesus called *the husbandman* in John 15:1, planted the true vine by sending His Son to dwell among us. Unlike the nation of Israel, the Lord Jesus lived a life of fruitfulness that was pleasing to the Father. For instance, Christ voluntarily offered up His life as the acceptable sacrifice for the sins of the world.

Ancient farming practices are part of the cultural context of Jesus' parable. In Bible times, both city dwellers and villagers were involved in agriculture, and it influenced many facets of the nation's social behavior, law, and religion. Practically every family owned a piece of land in Israel, and many families farmed a small area of their own. Outside the cities, most Israelites lived in villages rather than on farms. The land they cultivated was perhaps miles away from the village and situated near the water supply or on western or northern hillsides, where rainfall was greatest.

The variety of plants cultivated included cereal grains (such as barley and wheat), legumes (such as lentils and peas), and fruit trees (such as grapes, olives, dates, pomegranates, and figs). The conditions in Palestine were not always favorable for the cultivation of crops. The rainy season tended to be short (from mid-October to April) and unpredictable. Also, farm work was made more difficult by the presence of hilly ground and stony soil. To overcome these obstacles, the people terraced the uneven soil to catch rain run-off on the hillsides. Moreover, there were times when certain plants or trees failed to yield any fruit due to diseases, locust attacks, and other pests such as mice, worms, fruit bats, and weeds. These plants or trees were not allowed to remain in the soil. Farmers eventually uprooted or chopped down and burned the ones that yielded worthless fruit.

The sowing of plants took place in the fall. Early autumn rains softened the soil and enabled farmers to till the ground. On larger plots, they used wooden-frame plows pulled by a team of animals (for example, oxen, cows, or donkeys), while on smaller plots, they used hand-held hoes. They would set aside two months to sow cereal grains and two more months to plant legumes and vegetables, and start cultivating grapes in the vineyards. Vines required constant care to keep them productive. For instance, farmers had to gently place vines that had fallen to the ground back into position. They also had to constantly repair trellises and poles supporting the vines and regularly pull the weeds. If farmers did not continuously prune healthy branches and remove dead ones, the plant would not produce a good crop of fruit. The grapes that grew on the plants needed to sufficiently ripen before the farmers could pick them. Otherwise, if they prematurely harvested the fruit, it would taste quite sour.

Produce harvesting occurred in the spring. The farmers would first gather the barley, then the wheat, grapes, and other fruit. Next, the farmers processed the grapes and other fruits. Some of it would be dried in the sun and used to make cakes, but most of it would be used to make wine. People would tread the grapes on a flat, hard surface and allow the juice to run off into a reservoir cut out of rock or made from stones and clay. The juice was then transferred to large jars, which the farmers put in a cool storage place to allow the contents to ferment. To find workers for tilling, sowing, harvesting, and processing, a Jewish landowner would go to the center of town early in the morning and hire those who were waiting there and willing to work. Usually those were the poor people, who depended on someone hiring them each day in order to make enough money to live.

Jesus said that the worker who tended the vineyard petitioned the landowner to give the barren fig tree one more opportunity to bear fruit. Specifically, the worker wanted another year to dig around the tree. His efforts to loosen the soil near the roots would increase the likelihood of the tree obtaining the nutrients it needed to become fruitful. This process would be aided by the presence of manure, which he wanted to toss around the tree as fertilizer (Luke 13:8). The worker hoped that by giving the tree extra time and attention, it would bear fruit during the next growing season; but if it failed to do so, he would accept the landowner's decision to cut down the tree (13:9). The Savior's point is that God, in His grace, does not immediately punish transgressors. Nonetheless, it would be incorrect to assume that His patience and forbearance are a license to sin. Instead, the truth is that the Lord is dealing mercifully with the lost by giving them additional time to repent and receive eternal life (2 Pet. 3:9). While Jesus' parable had immediate application to the people of Israel, the story remains timeless in its relevance to all people throughout history.

SUGGESTIONS TO TEACHERS

In modern life, there is a strong tendency for people to blame others for anything bad that happens, but to take credit for anything good. In God's law court, however, everyone stands or falls on the basis of their own conduct and decisions. God is not swayed by excuses, buck passing, or blame shifting. While it is certainly true that every believer has an obligation to share the Gospel with the lost, in the end, all stand solely responsible for themselves before the Lord.

1. HEEDING THE SAVIOR'S WARNING. Jesus warned the people of His day to guard against twisted and perverted ways of living. He also urged them not to forsake God's upright path. Tragically, while no one wants to be a fool, people keep on doing foolish, destructive things. The problem is that by ignoring God, they fail to realize that wisdom and folly have moral dimensions. Amazingly, an uneducated person may easily surpass an educated person in wisdom, according to God's standards.

2. GETTING RIGHT WITH GOD. What can believers do in a climate of perversion and folly? The only sensible option is for them to turn away from sin in their life and demonstrate the positive values of wisdom represented in the teachings of Jesus, as well as the rest of Scripture. People need to see what wisdom looks like in godly individuals, not just in theory. Christians do not offer simply a better philosophy, but a superior code of wise conduct. The Lord calls His people to repent and do what is right, just, and fair. They seek to avoid the crooked ways of those who mock God. His wisdom is the hallmark of their lives. When our churches are filled with people hungry for learning and doing God's commands, the unbelieving world will take notice.

3. FAITHFULLY PROCLAIMING GOD'S MESSAGE. There are at least two aspects of God's message that He wants us to share with others. First, a part of the message is to tell people that all stand condemned before the Lord because of their sin. Second, we are to tell others that God wants to redeem them from the plight of their sin. We can stress how much God loves all people even though they have rebelled against Him. We can also urge them to repent of their sinful ways and put their faith in Christ for salvation. Regardless of how little or how much response we receive, we should not give up or diminish our efforts.

FOR ADULTS	■ **TOPIC:** Turning Our Lives Around ■ **QUESTIONS:** 1. Why do you think some who were listening to Jesus told Him about the tragedy involving some Galileans? 2. What

assumption had some in the crowd made about the spiritual status of the Galileans who perished at the hands of Pilate? 3. What was the point of Jesus bringing up the incident involving the collapse of the tower in Siloam? 4. What does it mean to repent? 5. What point was Jesus making by telling the parable of the spared fig tree?

■ **ILLUSTRATIONS:**

Last Sermon. According to Bruce Nolan of *Religion News Service*, Billy Graham gave one of his last evangelistic crusades on March 12, 2006, to an enthusiastic crowd of 16,300 in the New Orleans Arena. At 87, Graham looked "frail and tentative" as he "shuffled behind a walker toward the pulpit." Franklin Graham, the elder minister's son, could be seen "gently assisting" his father "into place as flash bulbs sent pulsating light through the arena." There was even an "overflow crowd of 1,500" who watched "outside on jumbo TV screens."

How did Graham's time in the pulpit compare with that of "417 earlier crusades" spanning over six decades? While his "voice has grown thin with the years," attendees could see determination in his "familiar square jaw" and a lifetime of accumulated wisdom reflected in his "swept-back silvery hair." And though the message he gave was "much abbreviated," its focus remained true to what Jesus and the early church proclaimed. The "religious diplomat" spoke on such familiar themes as "repentance, acceptance, and the assurance of salvation through Jesus Christ."

Rescuing the Helpless. The presence of injustice, which concerned those listening to Jesus, has remained a concern for believers down through the centuries. An incident from the life of Amy Carmichael, the Irish missionary to India, serves as a concrete example of what it means to abhor the presence of injustice. Carmichael discovered that some girls were placed in pagan temples to perform sordid acts. The missionary decided to begin a quiet campaign to rescue as many as of them as she could. The following is an excerpt from a biography titled, *Amy Carmichael* by Kathleen White:

> It grieved [Amy] intensely as she unraveled the sordid story of what it meant for [the girls] to be "married to a god." Some of the details were published in *Lotus Buds* and other books, although she left out many of the more harrowing stories. Children might be handed over to the Temple women as a thank offering or for several other reasons. Occasionally, a poor woman might dedicate her child because she could not afford to keep her, or an abandoned child might be picked up by them. Members of the mission and the government were shocked by these startling revelations. Largely through Amy's efforts, it became illegal to "marry" a child to a "god."

FOR YOUTH

■ **TOPIC:** Summoned to Turn Around

■ **QUESTIONS:** 1. What was the nature of the tragedy involving some Galileans? 2. What sort of ruler was Pontius Pilate? 3. Why did Jesus urge the crowd to repent? 4. Why did Jesus imply that it would be incorrect to assign guilt to the people who perished when the tower in Siloam collapsed on them? 5. What are the details of the parable of the spared fig tree?

■ **ILLUSTRATIONS:**

A Faith of Her Own. When Jenna decided to attend college, it was simply a diversion from the life she had been living. Though she had grown up in a Christian home, she had become extremely wayward in her later teen years. Two close encounters with death (each one claiming the life of a friend) convinced Jenna that it was time for a change in her lifestyle. Beginning as a 21-year-old freshman, Jenna found herself searching for the meaning and purpose to her life. As the third semester opened before her, Jenna found herself swimming ever deeper in the dark philosophies of ancient cultures and the religions that dominated them, such as Hinduism and Taoism.

Jenna became more despondent as she searched for the meaning to her existence, but she found no relief in her new-found religions. In her heart, she longed for a relationship with a personal God, not the many divinities of these eastern "—isms." When Jenna found the Messiah of the Jews and Gentiles, she also found the peace that had eluded her for many years. Her repentance brought her once again face to face with a God who is near to those who call upon Him. Jenna's faith had come full circle, but this time it wasn't her parents' faith only. Now she had a deep faith of her own.

A Hard-Learned Lesson. While I was drinking a cup of coffee one morning, Brandon, my five-year-old nephew, walked over to where I was sitting and stood alongside me. He was curious about what was in my cup. I explained to him that I was drinking coffee and cautioned him not to get too close because it was hot. Curiously, he looked at me and said in a childlike manner, "Dat's not hot!" A second warning made him more inquisitive about the matter. Apparently convinced that the coffee was not hot, Brandon quickly struck his index finger into my cup, only to take it out faster than he had put it in. "Ouch," he exclaimed. "Dat's hot!" From that point on, I never had to tell my nephew again about the perils of a hot cup of coffee.

Brandon's initial refusal to heed my warning illustrates the way many young people react when they hear God's message of repentance proclaimed. These adolescents stubbornly refuse to accept the truth. May we not be like them. The Lord wants us to turn away from sin and reorient our lives to following Him.

Never Give Up. For a number of years, several people tried unsuccessfully to create a small electric light that could be used in homes and offices. The famous inventor, Thomas Edison, spent two years searching for a wire that would produce sufficient light when electricity flowed through it. He had people search for filament material in the forests of Japan and the jungles of the Amazon. After thousands of experiments and many failures, he finally discovered a substance that shed good light. Edison's invention of the electric, incandescent lamp would not have occurred if he had given up in frustration somewhere in the process.

Imagine what life would be like if there were no electric lights. Undoubtedly, our world would be very different from what it is today. Consider what the spiritual ramifications would be if we stopped proclaiming the necessity of repentance because we failed to see immediate results from our efforts. Clearly, there would be tremendous eternal loss. That is why we should faithfully relate God's truth to others.

SUMMONED TO BE HUMBLE!

BACKGROUND SCRIPTURE: Luke 14:1, 7-14
DEVOTIONAL READING: Psalm 25:1-10

KEY VERSE: For whosoever exalteth himself shall be abased;
and he that humbleth himself shall be exalted. Luke 14:11.

KING JAMES VERSION

LUKE 14:1 And it came to pass, as he went into the house of one of the chief Pharisees to eat bread on the sabbath day, that they watched him. . . .

7 And he put forth a parable to those which were bidden, when he marked how they chose out the chief rooms; saying unto them, 8 When thou art bidden of any man to a wedding, sit not down in the highest room; lest a more honourable man than thou be bidden of him; 9 And he that bade thee and him come and say to thee, Give this man place; and thou begin with shame to take the lowest room. 10 But when thou art bidden, go and sit down in the lowest room; that when he that bade thee cometh, he may say unto thee, Friend, go up higher: then shalt thou have worship in the presence of them that sit at meat with thee. 11 For whosoever exalteth himself shall be abased; and he that humbleth himself shall be exalted. 12 Then said he also to him that bade him, When thou makest a dinner or a supper, call not thy friends, nor thy brethren, neither thy kinsmen, nor thy rich neighbours; lest they also bid thee again, and a recompence be made thee. 13 But when thou makest a feast, call the poor, the maimed, the lame, the blind: 14 And thou shalt be blessed; for they cannot recompense thee: for thou shalt be recompensed at the resurrection of the just.

NEW REVISED STANDARD VERSION

LUKE 14:1 On one occasion when Jesus was going to the house of a leader of the Pharisees to eat a meal on the sabbath, they were watching him closely. . . .

7 When he noticed how the guests chose the places of honor, he told them a parable. 8 "When you are invited by someone to a wedding banquet, do not sit down at the place of honor, in case someone more distinguished than you has been invited by your host; 9 and the host who invited both of you may come and say to you, 'Give this person your place,' and then in disgrace you would start to take the lowest place. 10 But when you are invited, go and sit down at the lowest place, so that when your host comes, he may say to you, 'Friend, move up higher'; then you will be honored in the presence of all who sit at the table with you. 11 For all who exalt themselves will be humbled, and those who humble themselves will be exalted."

12 He said also to the one who had invited him, "When you give a luncheon or a dinner, do not invite your friends or your brothers or your relatives or rich neighbors, in case they may invite you in return, and you would be repaid. 13 But when you give a banquet, invite the poor, the crippled, the lame, and the blind. 14 And you will be blessed, because they cannot repay you, for you will be repaid at the resurrection of the righteous."

12

199

HOME BIBLE READINGS

Monday, February 11	Psalm 25:1-10	*Prayer of Humility*
Tuesday, February 12	Luke 14:1-6	*Jesus Heals on the Sabbath*
Wednesday, February 13	Luke 14:7-9	*Disgraced at a Banquet*
Thursday, February 14	Luke 14:10-11	*Exalted though Humble*
Friday, February 15	Luke 14:12-14	*The Guest List*
Saturday, February 16	Ephesians 3:1-10	*A Life of Humility*
Sunday, February 17	1 Peter 5:1-5	*Tending the Flock with Humility*

BACKGROUND

Luke 14:1 states that the religious leaders dining at the home of a prominent Pharisee (possibly a synagogue official) were watching Jesus closely to detect any Sabbath-breaking conduct. The Gospels reveal that over the course of Jesus' earthly ministry, the Pharisees and scribes grew increasingly opposed to Him. They envied His popularity, resented His challenges to their traditions, and hated His exposure of their hypocrisy. Undoubtedly, the Jewish leaders wondered whether Jesus had political aspirations and worried about how His increasing influence would affect their control over the people. The Pharisees and scribes allowed their petty concerns to blind them to the truth that Jesus was their Messiah.

The Sabbath regulations the religious leaders wanted Jesus to observe were part of the so-called "tradition of the elders." During the captivity of the Jews in Babylon (605–445 B.C.), there was a renewed interest in the Mosaic law. At that time, an unwritten but highly developed body of teachings and commentary about the law began to develop among the rabbis. The original intention of this tradition was good. The rabbis wanted to prevent violations of the law. They tried to enforce God's Word by setting up humanly devised regulations for all of life, like a hedge around the law. For example, to clarify the commandment to honor the Sabbath and keep it holy (Exod. 20:8; Deut. 5:12), specific rules were developed to tell people which actions were Sabbath-honoring and which were Sabbath-breaking. More and more of these stipulations were devised with each new generation until two centuries after Jesus' death, they were gathered in a written collection called the Mishnah. Even during Jesus' life, the tradition had become so overvalued that it obscured what the law was meant to safeguard.

This fact is evident in the episode under consideration. Luke 14:2 says that a man (either another guest or a bystander) suffering from dropsy was right in front of Jesus. This ailment (also known as edema) involved abnormal swelling of the limbs, which was the result of excessive amounts of fluid accumulating in the cavities and tissues of the body, especially the legs. In Jesus' day, the religious leaders believed restoring someone to health on the Sabbath was work and thus violated their longstanding traditions (see 13:14). Jesus, being aware of this, asked the Pharisees and experts in the interpretation of religious law whether they thought it was legal to heal someone on the Sabbath

(14:3). Would they wind up defending tradition or advocate doing good?

The silence of the legalists indicated they chose the first option, while Jesus approved the second one. Accordingly, the Redeemer took hold of the man, healed him, and sent him away (14:4). Then Jesus turned to the religious leaders and asked which of them did not work on the Sabbath (14:5). After all, if they had a donkey (some manuscripts read "child") or an ox that had fallen into a well on a Sabbath day, they would immediately pull out the person or animal. In short, deeds of mercy were permissible on the Sabbath. Again, Jesus' critics chose to remain silent (14:6), rather than be humiliated by His words of censure (see 13:17).

NOTES ON THE PRINTED TEXT

The focus of Luke 14:1 is Jesus accepting an invitation one Sabbath (perhaps around midday, after a synagogue service) to dine at the house of a leader of the Pharisees. The Jews in Jesus' day felt that a person's lot in life was a measure of God's approval. If a person was wealthy, it was regarded as a sign that God was on his or her side. Oppositely, if a person lived in poverty, it was assumed that person had sinned and was suffering God's judgment. Jews also measured the worth of people by their role in society. The people most respected were the religious leaders (such as the Pharisees and the priests) and the ruling classes. Affluent lay persons and the working middle class were respected, but they were a little lower in the social order and tended to look up to the Pharisees and other religious leaders.

These cultural and social attitudes are evident in the incident recorded in Luke 14:7, which says that the Lord Jesus observed how the guests intentionally chose the places of honor at the table of the prominent Pharisee hosting the meal. In New Testament times, the seating arrangement at gatherings indicated much about the honor and respect extended to those present. At dinner feasts, the closer one sat to the host, the higher the honor. In fact, many Jewish homes had two levels, with honored guests seated on the higher floor. The seat to the right of the host was a place of special honor, with the seat to the left next in rank (see Matt. 20:20-21). Other seats were ranked in descending honor, with the seat on the lower floor and next to the door being the lowest. To be left standing, or seated on the floor, was the humblest position of all. (see Jas. 2:3-4).

To emphasize the importance of humility, Jesus told a parable involving those present receiving an invitation to a wedding feast. He urged them to resist the temptation to recline in the place of honor (Luke 14:8). In that day, meals were not eaten while sitting in upright chairs at a table. Instead, people would recline on their left elbows on the cushioned floor, with their head being closest to the low table and their feet being farthest away. Jesus raised the possibility that the host might ask a guest who had presumptuously taken one of the best spots to vacate it for someone else who was more distinguished or highly respected. Social convention would then require that the person who had been publicly disgraced move to the place of least importance (for example, whatever spot was left at the foot of the table; 14:9).

In that culture, avoiding public embarrassment and shame was important. For that reason the Savior emphasized the wisdom of taking the place of least importance at a banquet. Then, when the host approached, the humble individual would be asked in the presence of all the other guests to move to a more important spot—at the head of the table. As a result, the deferential guest would be honored in front of all those sharing the meal with him or her (14:10). The moral of Jesus parable appears in 14:11. God will humble the proud, who strive to exalt themselves before others. In contrast, God will exalt or honor the humble. This principle, which is repeated elsewhere in Scripture (see Prov. 3:34; 25:6-7; Matt. 18:4; 23:12; Luke 11:43; 18:14; 20:46; Jas. 4:10; 1 Pet. 5:6), was not worldly advice on how to manipulate a situation to make oneself look good. Rather, Jesus was advocating the cultivation of genuine humility among His followers.

Perhaps Jesus was one of those seated in a place of honor near the head of the table. If so, we can imagine Him turning to His host to emphasize the importance of showing unconditional generosity. For instance, when the leader of the Pharisees hosted a dinner or a banquet, Jesus urged him to break with social convention. The goal should not be to invite friends, close family members, other relatives, or rich neighbors (in other words, the powerful and well-to-do), who would feel obliged to extend an invitation in return as a repayment for the display of hospitality (Luke 14:12).

Instead, when planning an elaborate meal, the host was urged to invite people who did not have the means or the ability to reciprocate—*the poor, the maimed, the lame, the blind* (14:13). God would take note of and approve this display of unselfish graciousness. He would also eternally bless His followers for acting in this way. In 14:14, the Greek term rendered *blessed* conveys the idea of endowing someone with productivity or fruitfulness in service to the Lord. Although the kind and caring host would receive no recompense from his or her guests, God would reward him or her at the resurrection of the righteous (Dan. 12:2; John 5:28-29; Acts 24:15). The latter event will occur at the return of Christ, who will sit on His glorious throne and honor those who served others in His name (see Matt. 25:31-46).

Showing hospitality was an important custom in the biblical world. Jews in the Old Testament and Christians in the New Testament were encouraged to be kind to strangers and to take care of the needs of passersby. Hospitality was shown in many ways. The most common was to wash the feet of visitors. This offered much-needed relief to those who traveled long distances over the dusty roads in Israel. It was also common to prepare meals for visitors. This often consumed a great deal of time as hostesses baked bread, cooked meat, and did whatever else was necessary to provide substantial meals for guests. Animals accompanying visitors were also looked after and were given food, water, and shelter. When guests left, they were often given supplies to help them in their travels. This could include food, water, and articles of clothing. The host might even accompany departing visitors for a short distance as they continued their journey. Showing hospitality in a practical way met the physical needs of visitors. It was also crucial for maintaining social relationships.

As far back as the law of Moses, God told His people to give alms (or gifts) to the poor and needy (Exod. 23:11; Deut. 15:7, 11). The prophets of the Old Testament saw alms as a right of the poor. Several prophets warned that when the poor were not taken care of, there was no justice in the land (Isa. 10:1-4; Jer. 5:26-29; Amos 5:12-15). This type of thought led to the idea that righteousness could be obtained through giving alms, and it could also help in obtaining forgiveness of sins. The Pharisees of Jesus' day also believed that almsgiving entitled them to divine favor in moments of trouble. By the time of Jesus' earthly ministry, righteousness and almsgiving were seen as the same thing by many Jews. Jesus encouraged giving to the poor for He said in Matthew 6:2 (NRSV), "*whenever* you give," not "*if* you give"; but Jesus also stressed the need for the right motive. The giver should not take a pious act, such as giving to the poor, and make it a sign of spirituality for others to see.

SUGGESTIONS TO TEACHERS

The only ministry that really matters to God is what is done in a way that pleases Him. It requires Jesus' followers to be humble, generous, and gracious to others. This type of Christian service is not the exclusive entitlement of people who are rich, famous, and powerful. Instead, it is to be extended to all members of society, especially *the poor, the maimed, the lame, [and] the blind* of Luke 14:13.

1. A MATTER OF CONTRASTS. Explain that the word "humble" means to have or show a modest estimate of one's own importance. In contrast, "haughty" means to be arrogantly disdainful of others. Note that Jesus is the premier example of humility, while the religious leaders of His day epitomized haughtiness.

2. A SCRIPTURAL EXAMPLE. Next, state that the footwashing episode recorded in John 13:1-20 is one of the most vivid illustrations in Scripture of humility. Here we read about Jesus dropping to His knees and washing the filthy feet of His beloved disciples. Jesus showed them—and us—the power of Christian service that is offered in unconditional love and generosity. What a memorable example of servanthood the Master demonstrated for us to emulate.

3. A KEY REALIZATION. Point out that it is not easy for us to jettison our pride and humbly express love to others, especially those in need; but since our Lord emphasized it in His teaching and demonstrated it in His life, we can do so as well. Indeed, His love for us empowers us so that we can break free from the kind of pride that demands that we never appear insignificant or vulnerable. He also enables us to care for the needs of others. With the power of Christ operative in our lives, we can do all that pride beckons us not to do.

■ TOPIC: The Necessity of Humility

■ QUESTIONS: 1. What restrictions did the religious leaders in Jesus' day place on activities performed on the Sabbath? 2. Why was Jesus being closely watched by the religious leaders? 3. What motivation did people have for wanting to be seated in places of honor at a feast? 4. Why would being asked to vacate a seat of honor at a banquet be a social embarrassment in the time of Christ? 5. Why would inviting the poor and the crippled to a banquet represent a break with what was normally done in Jesus' day?

■ ILLUSTRATIONS:

A Humble, Devoted Grandmother. Bonny Mulder-Behnia, a correspondent for the *Banner,* tells the story of Terry Hagopian. After her grandson, Anthony, was born, his unwed parents lost custody of him "due to substance abuse." Terry, sensing that the Lord wanted her to "make a long-term commitment to her first grandson," became his "foster-care provider until she could adopt him at age 3."

Anthony is now 9, and his single grandmother ponders whether she's doing all she should for him. "I sense that he's missing out because I'm not physically able to play ball or ride bikes or ice-skate with him," Terry said. "I also feel sad because I'm forced to be the disciplinarian rather than just the grandma who smothers him with love and kisses." Despite the concerns Terry has about the adequacy of her care for Anthony, no one can deny her humble devotion to the task. At an age when many of Terry's peers choose a much easier life, she has intentionally made personal sacrifices for the good of her grandson. She's convinced that "nothing is more important from an eternal perspective."

Billions in Corruption. The mission of the World Bank is to end global poverty. Indeed, over the past six decades, the bank has approved loans in excess of 550 billion dollars. This makes it the "largest and most influential antipoverty institution operating in developing countries." So reported Danielle Knight and Edward T. Pound in *U.S. News & World Report.* In addition, they noted that "kickbacks, payoffs, bribery, embezzlement, and collusive bidding plague bank-funded projects around the world." Moreover, knowledgeable analysts estimate "corrupt practices of one type or another may be associated with more than 20 percent of the funds disbursed by the bank each year."

To his credit, the current president of the World Bank, Paul Wolfowitz, is committed to ending this "cancer of corruption." Since assuming his post in 2005, he indicated that "those who cheat and steal from the bank will be caught and punished." His reason for the anticorruption campaign is that the shameless diversion of "valuable resources" hurts "those the bank is trying to help—the world's desperately poor." His reform efforts include the creation of an "internal rackets squad and a sanctions committee to investigate and punish wrongdoers." And even though "investigating allegations of complex frauds on bank projects around the globe" remains a daunting "uphill fight," the ongoing attempt to clean up the World Bank is imperative, especially given that "across the globe" a "staggering 1.2 billion" people "live on less than $1 a day."

Committed to Giving Back. According to correspondent Ed Bradley of *CBS 60 Minutes*, Tiger Woods is a living golf legend. For over a decade, he has "dominated professional golf so completely that he has changed the game and come to exemplify the pursuit of excellence." Tiger not only has been "ranked number one in the world longer than any other competitor," but also was the youngest golfer "to win 10 major championships." He's a "purposeful, complicated athlete who fiercely guards his private life."

But, as Bradley discovered, there's more to Tiger than golf. In fact, as the once-in-a-generation athlete enters his thirties, he has become as "committed to giving back off the golf course as he is dedicated to his sport." For instance, in February 2006, he opened the first Tiger Woods Learning Center in Anaheim, California, which is "close to where he grew up." The purpose of the center is to give students in fourth through twelfth grades "learning experiences they can't get in their own schools."

Tiger says it was his idea to build the 35,000-square-foot center, which is designed to serve up to 5,000 students from diverse backgrounds each year. He noted, "I wanted something substantial, something bricks and mortar, something that kids could feel and touch and call their own." And what motivated him to spend millions of dollars to make this dream become a reality? According to Tiger, "I guess because I had so many people influencing my life. I wanted to cater this foundation to mentoring and guiding. Because that's ultimately, how I got here." What an amazing display of generosity this is from a star who could be spending everything he earns on himself!

FOR YOUTH

■ **TOPIC:** Summoned to Be Humble
■ **QUESTIONS:** 1. Where did Jesus go to eat on one Sabbath day? 2. Why did the guests pick the places of honor at the banqueting table? 3. What embarrassing situation did Jesus describe to the religious leaders? 4. What would motivate a guest to voluntarily take the lowest place at a banquet? 5. How did Jesus illustrate the importance of showing unconditional generosity to others?

■ **ILLUSTRATIONS:**
Humbly Sharing God's Love. According to Jim Dever of *Evening Magazine,* Akiane Kramarik has been called an "Idaho prodigy" who "paints her mind." The adolescent "started sketching at the age of four and her drawings ended up on the walls, on the furniture, even on her legs." Some consider her "visions of light and sound" to be a miracle. If nothing else, the masterpieces she's created so far are nothing short of amazing, especially at an age when "stick figures would suffice."

Akiane's family has been especially blessed by her paintings. Her mother, Forelli, says at one time she was an atheist. But then she noticed that her daughter "started talking about God." In fact, this adolescent, "with no apparent exposure to Christianity," began "creating Christian thoughts and images." According to Akiane, "God gives me this talent to share with others, to share with others God's love." For instance, she wants people to find hope in her paintings and she tries to draw the attention of people to God.

What becomes of the proceeds from the paintings, which "sell for more than $50,000 apiece"? According to Akiane's parents, while some of the money is being saved for "their daughter's future," the remainder "goes to children's charities and other causes she cares about." Perhaps in the end this is the best way to share the love of God with others—through displays of humble generosity.

Bono on Record. According to Mark Yaconelli, the director of the Youth and Ministry Spirituality Project, Christian megastar Bono began his career in the 1980s as the lead singer for the Irish rock group U2. In the *Christian Century*, Yaconelli noted that the band members "rejected the detached 'cool' that most rock stars sought to embody," and instead endeavored to be sincere and worshipful in the music they sang. Over the next two decades, U2 has become "one of the biggest rock acts in the world."

What has Bono done since becoming an international celebrity? Unlike other stars, who have used their status to grab hold of more fame and fortune, the Christian entertainer has "served as a mouthpiece" for a number of charitable causes that endeavor to reduce disease and poverty in the Third World. This is not a recent development, either. Bono's activism has spanned at least a decade, and he has no plans of stopping anytime soon. He's also a person of deep Christian faith, for whom "prayer and Scripture are critical to his understanding of the world." Bono reflects the kind of humility and generosity that Jesus called for in this week's lesson.

Final Accounting. A group of Christian college students decided to find out what it was like to be homeless. They spent several weekends living among the homeless in Chicago by sleeping out at night on cardboard pallets and scrounging for their food. This incident reminds us that young people generally have a keen sense of helping others. They humbly organize food drives, and walk, run, and swim for charity. They go overseas to build houses, drill wells, and teach people to read. Jesus said these sorts of activities really count with Him. The idea is that by investing our lives in others, we invest in Him. Conversely, by refusing to help others in need, we also refuse to minister to our Savior.

SUMMONED TO BE A DISCIPLE!

BACKGROUND SCRIPTURE: Luke 14:25-33
DEVOTIONAL READING: Psalm 139:1-6

KEY VERSE: Whosoever doth not bear his cross,
and come after me, cannot be my disciple. Luke 14:27.

KING JAMES VERSION

LUKE 14:25 And there went great multitudes with him: and he turned, and said unto them, 26 If any man come to me, and hate not his father, and mother, and wife, and children, and brethren, and sisters, yea, and his own life also, he cannot be my disciple. 27 And whosoever doth not bear his cross, and come after me, cannot be my disciple. 28 For which of you, intending to build a tower, sitteth not down first, and counteth the cost, whether he have sufficient to finish it? 29 Lest haply, after he hath laid the foundation, and is not able to finish it, all that behold it begin to mock him, 30 Saying, This man began to build, and was not able to finish. 31 Or what king, going to make war against another king, sitteth not down first, and consulteth whether he be able with ten thousand to meet him that cometh against him with twenty thousand? 32 Or else, while the other is yet a great way off, he sendeth an ambassage, and desireth conditions of peace. 33 So likewise, whosoever he be of you that forsaketh not all that he hath, he cannot be my disciple.

NEW REVISED STANDARD VERSION

LUKE 14:25 Now large crowds were traveling with him; and he turned and said to them, 26 "Whoever comes to me and does not hate father and mother, wife and children, brothers and sisters, yes, and even life itself, cannot be my disciple. 27 Whoever does not carry the cross and follow me cannot be my disciple. 28 For which of you, intending to build a tower, does not first sit down and estimate the cost, to see whether he has enough to complete it? 29 Otherwise, when he has laid a foundation and is not able to finish, all who see it will begin to ridicule him, 30 saying, 'This fellow began to build and was not able to finish.' 31 Or what king, going out to wage war against another king, will not sit down first and consider whether he is able with ten thousand to oppose the one who comes against him with twenty thousand? 32 If he cannot, then, while the other is still far away, he sends a delegation and asks for the terms of peace. 33 So therefore, none of you can become my disciple if you do not give up all your possessions."

13

Monday, February 18	Psalm 139:1-6 ✓	*You Know Me*
Tuesday, February 19	Luke 14:25-27	*Conditions of Discipleship*
Wednesday, February 20	Luke 14:28-33	*First, Count the Cost*
Thursday, February 21	Luke 18:18-25	*The Rich Ruler's Response*
Friday, February 22	Luke 18:28-30	*Rewards of Discipleship*
Saturday, February 23	Luke 5:1-11	*First Disciples Called*
Sunday, February 24	Acts 9:1-6, 11-16	*Saul Called to Be a Disciple*

BACKGROUND

Part of Jesus' teaching on discipleship included the emphasis in Luke 14:27 of metaphorically carrying one's cross. Jesus did not need to describe the details of crucifixion to His audience. No doubt most of them had seen several, since the Romans had made this mode of death common in Jesus' day. Crucifixion as a means of torture and execution was invented in the East and adopted by the Romans, who used it for slaves and lower-class persons. A victim of Roman crucifixion typically had to carry the crossbeam of his cross to the place of execution. He or someone else would also often carry a tablet citing the charge against him, which was then sometimes nailed to the top of the cross.

At the execution site, the crossbeam would be attached perpendicularly to a longer beam (the stake), at or near the top of it, while it was lying on the ground. The condemned was then nailed to the cross with spikes driven through the wrists and feet. The torso would face forward, but the feet would sometimes be nailed sideways, thus twisting the waist in an unnatural position. A rope was often tied around the victim's chest, knotted between the shoulders, and then tied to the beam behind the body. This was done to prevent the body from falling forward, especially as muscles weakened. Finally, the cross would be lifted and dropped into a hole.

Death was excruciatingly slow and bloody, with the naked victim exposed to the withering heat of the sun by day and temperatures at night dropping to between 40 and 50 degrees Fahrenheit for a spring crucifixion in Palestine. Victims sometimes lasted for two or three days, finally succumbing to death due to poor blood circulation and heart failure. If the crucifiers wanted to make the victim last longer, they would have first outfitted the cross with a block of wood as a seat or a footrest, which would give the victim support and improve circulation. If the crucifiers wanted to shorten the victim's life, they would break his legs with a club to remove his ability to support himself with his legs.

NOTES ON THE PRINTED TEXT

As the Savior's popularity increased, large crowds enthusiastically followed Him while He made His way toward to Jerusalem, where He faced death on a cross (14:25; see 13:22). The implication is that what He said concerning the cost of discipleship was not just directed to the Twelve, but also to the throngs gathered around Him. Many of His disciples had given up everything to follow Him; but Jesus knew that not all those present were true believers. He was headed for Jerusalem and a cross; however, many were tagging along because they thought He was headed for a throne.

Jesus, after turning around to face the large crowds, called them (and us) to a radical consideration of what it means to follow Him. He declared that coming to Him meant hating one's own parents, spouse and children, and siblings. It even meant hating one's own *life* (14:26). It is unlikely that the Savior was advocating literal hatred of one's family, for this would violate the Ten Commandments (compare also a similar saying of Jesus in Matthew 10:37-38). One possibility is that Jesus was speaking rhetorically by using a customary teaching method called hyperbole. This refers to intentional exaggeration to make a point. Jesus frequently spoke in this manner, perhaps to hold His listeners' attention, to touch their imagination, or to show a bit of humor.

Another possibility is that Jesus was speaking comparatively, in the sense of relative value. He was saying that the kingdom of God should take precedence over everything, including one's family. In the New Testament, the contrast between love and hate can also refer to value placed on things by comparison. For example, if we love our lives too much, we will not think of things other than our lives. In essence, that is hating the kingdom of God, because if our minds are on ourselves, they cannot be on God. Conversely, if we have our minds set on Jesus and the divine kingdom, we will not have as much time for selfish pursuits. Thus, in a sense, we will be "hating" our lives here on earth in anticipation of life with the Savior in heaven for eternity.

Next, Jesus declared that those who were not willing to carry their own cross and follow Him could not be His disciples (Luke 14:27). In 9:23, Jesus stated that this had to be done on a daily basis. In both passages, Jesus was speaking metaphorically against the backdrop of being rejected. Put differently, even in the face of denunciation, our allegiance remains with Christ. In a sense, discipleship involves a figurative form of death that is similar to crucifixion. In 9:24-25, we have one of the many paradoxes that arise in Jesus' teaching. He said those who save their life will lose it, while those who lose their life will save it. The cross is not an attractive object, so the natural reaction would be to recoil from it and avoid it; but Jesus said that to seek life by avoiding the cross would in the long run result in spiritual death. Eternal life is of much more value than success, prosperity, or even a long earthly existence. The one who wins without Jesus still loses. The shame of the cross might cause some people to avoid the Redeemer and not want to be identified with Him (9:26); but those who are ashamed of Jesus now will have to face His rejection when He comes in glory.

Jesus used two illustrations (or parables) to explain what He had previously said. In the first one, Jesus mentioned the issue of undertaking a building project, in this case the construction of a watchtower (perhaps to guard a vineyard) or a building on distinct =

a farm. Wise landowners first computed the cost to ensure there were sufficient funds to complete the job (Luke 14:28). Otherwise, once the foundation was laid, there would not be enough money to finish the structure (vs. 29). Then, all who saw this embarrassing spectacle would make the shortsighted owners the object of joking and ridicule (vs. 30).

It's true that salvation is free; but Jesus told people to first count the cost of serving Him before becoming His disciples. Just as a person planning a building project should first make sure he or she can complete the job, Jesus told His followers that they must have a full appreciation of what it demanded of them to be His disciple. One who began to follow Jesus and turned back would not be fit for the kingdom of heaven and would also be ridiculed by the world. Moreover, one must remain/distinct from the world, and the world's wrong ways of thinking, in order to be recognized as a member of God's kingdom. distinct separated

Jesus' second illustration involved one monarch confronting another monarch, whether in a single battle or a drawn-out engagement. Before going to war, though, the ambitious king was wise to determine beforehand whether his small army of 10,000 soldiers would be able to prevail against a larger fighting force of 20,000 combatants (14:31). If the monarch with the smaller army concluded that he could not succeed in such a military engagement, he was prudent to dispatch a representative, while his antagonist was still a long way off, and ask for terms of peace (14:32).

With respect to following Jesus, He wanted potential disciples to consider what they were doing. On the one hand, there is sacrifice involved in committing oneself to Him. On the other hand, to refuse God (the most powerful King) placed one's life in eternal jeopardy. In a sense, Jesus was warning the crowds to opt for peace with the Father through faith in the Son. Doing so included a willingness to give up everything for cause of Christ (14:33). The Greek verb translated *forsaketh* literally means "to say farewell to" or "to take leave of" one's possessions. The idea is that we must not rely on our earthly belongings or who we are, but instead rely on Christ alone both for salvation and for our direction as His disciples.

Jesus was willing to give up everything in order to provide eternal life for us. According to Mark 10:45, by means of His sacrifice on the cross, Jesus paid the price (the *ransom*) to free humanity (the *many,* as opposed to the single life that is being sacrificed) from the bondage of sin and death. The *ransom* He offered is not said to be paid to anyone, but the Greek verb it translates (*lytron*) pictures the price given to release slaves. The irony of prominence in Jesus' kingdom is that the greatest are the servants of others, and Jesus Himself is the ultimate example of that principle in His substitutionary death.

The key to this week's lesson is radical commitment to the kingdom of God. Jesus called the first disciples to complete and absolute surrender of their lives to His lordship. Still today, if we hold on to things in our lives, and even our own lives, we cannot totally abandon ourselves to Jesus as His disciples. In Jesus' day, many people followed Him because He was a dynamic teacher and because He performed amazing miracles. Today, people may belong to church because of a dynamic pastor, or because there are other things they can get out of that congregation. Just as church membership today does not make one a Christian, just being part of the crowd that followed Jesus did not make anyone a disciple. Jesus wants us to understand that to fully experience Him, we must recognize all things are under His control (even good things like family) in order to be totally filled with Him.

Giving up everything to follow Jesus may or may not mean giving up our literal physical possessions. In our modern culture, we often become possessed by our possessions because we think we must have them. Consequently, they occupy more and more of our time and energy; but Jesus told the people of His day that they must give up all of those things in order to be His disciples. The real question, then, is one of priority and focus. There is nothing inherently wrong with having possessions; but the problem comes when the possessions are the main focus of our lives. Jesus declared that wherever our treasure is, there our heart and thoughts will also be (Matt. 6:21). Thus, if our treasure—what we value in life—is the kingdom of God, then naturally our affections and focus will be there. The problem comes when we see our worldly possessions, rather than the kingdom of God, as our treasure.

SUGGESTIONS TO TEACHERS

We live in a culture that craves personal comfort and commends maintaining personal safety. Sadly, the idea of making and honoring long-term commitments is not an ideal upheld by many. It therefore should not surprise us that the demands Jesus places on His followers run counter to popular thinking. The cost of discipleship is often more than most people will pay.

1. RADICAL COMMITMENT. Consider having the students look at both Luke 9:23-26 and 14:25-33. Start with Jesus' words about His messiahship. He warned that He would be a suffering Deliverer, not a popular, conquering hero. His rule would come through sacrificial love and costly caring for others, not through hoarding life. These truths are key to understanding the Savior's life and message.

2. RELUCTANT COMMITMENT. Talk with the students about people they know who seem to be wishy-washy in their commitment to Christ. Also, ask the class why some churchgoers seem energized by the prospect of following Jesus wholeheartedly, while others seem ambivalent or indifferent to the idea.

3. RESOLUTE CROSS-BEARING. Move on to Luke 14:25-27 and discuss the implications of bearing one's cross. Remind the class that there was nothing sentimental or pleasant about carrying a cross in Jesus' time. Then note that self-denial is the idea behind the metaphor. By this Jesus meant a willingness to obey His commands, serve one another, and suffer—perhaps even die—for His sake.

4. REQUISITE COST. Finally, examine the two parables about building a tower and embarking on a military campaign without first considering the cost. Draw the students into some thoughtful conversation about what changes in their lives might be in order or what new priorities they might have to make if they are serious about being Jesus' devoted followers.

<table>
<tr><td>**FOR ADULTS**</td><td>■ **TOPIC:** Becoming Passionate Supporters
■ **QUESTIONS:** 1. Why was it necessary for Jesus' followers to *hate* (Luke 14:26) others in order to be His disciple? 2. What did Jesus</td></tr>
</table>

mean by carrying one's cross as part of the process of being His disciple? 3. What was the point of Jesus' illustration about building a tower? 4. What was the point of Jesus' illustration about one king going to war against another? 5. In what sense must Jesus' disciples give up everything they have to be His followers?

■ **ILLUSTRATIONS:**

In Memorium. I was reading through the newsletter of the seminary where I did graduate studies and noticed the sterling legacies of those who had recently passed away. One believer had enthusiastically served as a Bible school teacher for two decades, and then as a missionary for another two decades. The last years of her life were spent serving in a church in the midwestern United States.

Another Christian served as a missionary for 15 years in Central America. Then, for 12 years, he was a religious professor in a college on the East coast of the United States. He spent most of his later years as a missionary-at-large. Yet another believer began zealously serving the Lord Jesus as a Sunday school teacher and then as a Bible college professor. But the majority of his life was spent serving a small congregation in the southern United States. There he helped to train others to do the work of the ministry.

What is the key to the success of these believers? It's their unwavering commitment to Christ. Their lifelong desire wasn't to become famous, rich, or powerful. Rather, they simply wanted to honor the Lord through their faithful service.

Dying for Christ. In his book, *A Cloud of Witnesses*, Douglas Weaver tells the account of 40 soldiers who were Christians in the Twelfth Legion of the imperial army of Rome. One day, their commanding officer announced an edict issued by Emperor Licinius (A.D. 308–324) "requiring all soldiers to offer sacrifice to the pagan gods." The 40 Christians responded as follows: "You can have our armor and even our bodies, but the allegiance of our heart belongs to Jesus Christ."

The time was mid-winter in A.D. 320. The commanding officer ordered this group of soldiers to march out onto a frozen lake. After they suffered the indignity of having their uniforms stripped off their backs, they were given the ultimatum—"either renounce Christ or die." Slowly, one soldier after another "fell in death." Finally, only one soldier remained standing. As his courage faltered, so did his commitment. He decided to spare his life by stumbling to shore and renounce "his faith in Christ."

All along, an "officer of the guard" watched the unfolding drama and "secretly came to believe in Christ." Upon seeing the last remaining soldier leave the frozen lake, the officer ventured out onto it, "disrobed, and confessed his faith." The following morning, as a new day dawned, 40 lifeless bodies could be seen lying on the icy surface of the lake.

Words of the Commission. For over two centuries, starting with George Washington, the officer's commission in the armed forces of the United States of America has carried almost the same words. The main changes have to do with who originates and signs the document, and where and when the commission is given. But the words otherwise are almost identical for officers' commissions given throughout the nation's long history. The solemn phrases carry heavy responsibilities, as any person who has been commissioned as an officer knows. You pledge to "repose special trust and confidence in your patriotism . . . diligently discharge the duties of (your rank) by doing and performing all manner of things, thereunto belonging . . . to observe and follow such orders and directions . . . This commission is to continue in force indefinitely."

These words could be applied to the commission that Jesus Christ gives each of His followers. Of course, Jesus demands even more. His disciples are to take up their cross and follow Him absolutely.

■ **TOPIC:** Summoned to Be a Disciple
■ **QUESTIONS:** 1. Who was listening to Jesus teach? 2. In what sense did Jesus say His followers had to *hate* (Luke 14:26) others in order to be His disciple? 3. What are some ways that believers today can figuratively carry their cross as they live for Jesus? 4. Why does Jesus compare discipleship to planning things like building a tower and going to war? 5. Why it wrong for believers to rely on their possessions or who they are, rather than on Christ, for salvation?

■ **ILLUSTRATIONS:**
Fan or Follower? A well known religious leader decided to make a stop in a major midwestern city of the United States. It's not surprising that when news spread of his anticipated arrival, many people wanted to see him. One person, in particular, wanted a private audience with the religious leader.

This champion athlete felt that he, of all people, should be given a private audience. After all, the sports figure was known for his physical strength and skill and for the impressive records he had set during his career. Certainly he should have been granted his request. Remarkably, however, the religious leader's staff said he would not be able to meet with the athlete. Perhaps the leader was too busy to fit the athlete into his schedule for the day. Or maybe the leader sensed the athlete was more of a fan who was seeking to boost his own image by being seen with the leader.

When Jesus ministered on earth, there were many people who wanted to see and be seen with Him. But Jesus didn't want fans. Rather, He wanted followers who would commit themselves wholeheartedly to Him!

Demonstrated Understanding. Just before Christmas 1998, former light-heavy-weight boxing champion, Archie Moore, died in San Diego. "The Mongoose" was the only boxer to face both Rocky Marciano and Mohammed Ali. At the funeral Moore was eulogized by George Foreman, a former student who later became a world heavyweight boxing champion, and who is now an ordained minister.

Foreman said, "When I think of Archie Moore, an old proverb comes to mind. Suppose you want to build a tower. First, you sit down and figure the cost. Then you see if you have enough money to finish it. Otherwise, if you lay a foundation and can't complete the building, everyone will make fun of you. In all the years we talked while Archie was teaching me, he made it clear. 'I love God and my family, and I will love you if you work hard.' So Archie laid the foundation, and today he stands as a tower for all athletes, saying, 'If you want it, leave your excuses behind and come get it.'"

Moore and Foreman both understood Jesus' parable regarding priorities. For the Savior's followers, He must come first. No excuses will be accepted.

Tortured for Christ. Richard Wurmbrand is an evangelical minister who spent 14 years imprisoned and tortured in Romania, his homeland, while it was under Communist rule. The horrible experience began in 1945, when the Communists seized control of the country and attempted to regulate the churches to advance their agenda. It was at that time that Wurmbrand began an effective clandestine ministry to his beleaguered fellow Romanians and the occupying Russian soldiers.

In 1948, Wurmbrand was arrested and spent the next three years in solitary confinement. The only persons he saw were his Communist torturers. In 1964, Wurmbrand was released in a general amnesty. Christians in Norway, fearing the grave danger to Wurmbrand should he be imprisoned a third time, negotiated with the Communist authorities for his release from Romania. In May 1966, Wurmbrand testified before a Senate Internal Subcommittee in Washington, D.C. During the hearing, he stripped to the waist to show 18 deep torture wounds covering his body. He is an example of what it means to be a genuine follower of the Lord Jesus Christ.

THE ARK COMES TO JERUSALEM

BACKGROUND SCRIPTURE: 1 Chronicles 15:1–28
DEVOTIONAL READING: Psalm 150

KEY VERSE: David gathered all Israel together to Jerusalem, to bring up the ark of the LORD unto his place, which he had prepared for it. 1 Chronicles 15:3.

KING JAMES VERSION

1 CHRONICLES 15:1 And David made him houses in the city of David, and prepared a place for the ark of God, and pitched for it a tent. 2 Then David said, None ought to carry the ark of God but the Levites: for them hath the LORD chosen to carry the ark of God, and to minister unto him for ever. 3 And David gathered all Israel together to Jerusalem, to bring up the ark of the LORD unto his place, which he had prepared for it. . . . 14 So the priests and the Levites sanctified themselves to bring up the ark of the LORD God of Israel. 15 And the children of the Levites bare the ark of God upon their shoulders with the staves thereon, as Moses commanded according to the word of the LORD. 16 And David spake to the chief of the Levites to appoint their brethren to be the singers with instruments of musick, psalteries and harps and cymbals, sounding, by lifting up the voice with joy. . . .

25 So David, and the elders of Israel, and the captains over thousands, went to bring up the ark of the covenant of the LORD out of the house of Obededom with joy. 26 And it came to pass, when God helped the Levites that bare the ark of the covenant of the LORD, that they offered seven bullocks and seven rams. 27 And David was clothed with a robe of fine linen, and all the Levites that bare the ark, and the singers, and Chenaniah the master of the song with the singers: David also had upon him an ephod of linen. 28 Thus all Israel brought up the ark of the covenant of the LORD with shouting, and with sound of the cornet, and with trumpets, and with cymbals, making a noise with psalteries and harps.

NEW REVISED STANDARD VERSION

1 CHRONICLES 15:1 David built houses for himself in the city of David, and he prepared a place for the ark of God and pitched a tent for it. 2 Then David commanded that no one but the Levites were to carry the ark of God, for the LORD had chosen them to carry the ark of the LORD and to minister to him forever. 3 David assembled all Israel in Jerusalem to bring up the ark of the LORD to its place, which he had prepared for it. . . . 14 So the priests and the Levites sanctified themselves to bring up the ark of the LORD, the God of Israel. 15 And the Levites carried the ark of God on their shoulders with the poles, as Moses had commanded according to the word of the LORD.

16 David also commanded the chiefs of the Levites to appoint their kindred as the singers to play on musical instruments, on harps and lyres and cymbals, to raise loud sounds of joy. . . .

25 So David and the elders of Israel, and the commanders of the thousands, went to bring up the ark of the covenant of the LORD from the house of Obededom with rejoicing. 26 And because God helped the Levites who were carrying the ark of the covenant of the LORD, they sacrificed seven bulls and seven rams. 27 David was clothed with a robe of fine linen, as also were all the Levites who were carrying the ark, and the singers, and Chenaniah the leader of the music of the singers; and David wore a linen ephod. 28 So all Israel brought up the ark of the covenant of the LORD with shouting, to the sound of the horn, trumpets, and cymbals, and made loud music on harps and lyres.

Home Bible Readings

Background

First Chronicles opens with nine chapters of genealogies that stretch from Adam to the time of the return from Babylonian captivity. Then the narrative picks up with the death of Saul, and the rest of 1 Chronicles parallels the contents of 2 Samuel. Second Chronicles covers the same time frame as both books of Kings. Chronicles deals only with the kings who reigned from Jerusalem. The northern kings of Israel are mentioned in passing and only when they have significant contact with the southern kingdom. Chronicles was written to a community of faith that had survived the Babylonian captivity—the worst disaster in Israel's history since enslavement in Egypt. These books, which at first glance seem no more than dusty accounts of temple musicians and minor government bureaucrats, are words of hope for people on the edge of despair.

While the books of Chronicles cover the same time span as the books of Samuel and Kings, Chronicles is much more than a collection of leftovers. The books of Kings showed the Israelites how to evaluate their kings by God's standards; the books of Chronicles showed how vital the house of David and the temple were for the future of God's people. Moreover, Chronicles were originally intended to be books of encouragement for the Jewish exiles freshly back from Babylon. These books taught the importance of the proper worship of God through careful but wholehearted observance of temple rituals. Chronicles championed the descendants of David as the rightful protectors of the priests, Levites, and temple. All the genealogies and lists of officials helped the returned exiles reorganize their national and spiritual lives.

Notes on the Printed Text

The events of 1 Chronicles 15 concern King David transporting the ark of the covenant to Jerusalem. The time was about 997 B.C., which was 13 years after he began his reign as king at Hebron in 1010 B.C. (It wasn't until 1003 B.C. that his reign was acknowledged throughout all Israel.) During that initial period, David conquered Jerusalem from the Jebusites, made the fortress-complex his home, and renamed it the City of David. He also fortified the city from the supporting terraces (or the Millo) to the surrounding walls and had a palace built for himself. Meanwhile,

Joab, the military commander of David's army, supervised the rebuilding of the rest of Jerusalem (11:4-8; 15:1).

At some point, David sensed it was time to relocate the ark of the covenant from Kiriath Jearim, which was a fortified city nine miles north of Jerusalem. After the Philistines returned the ark, it remained in the house of Abinadab at Kiriath Jearim for about two decades (see 1 Sam. 6:19—7:2). Throughout the reign of Saul, David's predecessor, the sacred chest was ignored (1 Chron. 13:1-3). This was regrettable, for the ark was originally intended to be the place where the sovereign Lord met with Israel and provided the people with guidance (see Exod. 25:22). David's proposal to bring the sacred chest to Jerusalem met with the approval of all the Israelites (1 Chron. 13:4).

The plan to move the ark involved bringing it outside Abinadab's house and placing it on a new ox cart. While Abinadab's sons, Uzzah and Ahio, guided the cart, David and a crowd of people danced and sang praises to the Lord; but when the procession came to the threshing floor of Kidon, the oxen stumbled. To prevent the chest from falling, Uzzah reached out and took hold of it; however, the Lord was very angry at Uzzah for doing this and struck him dead right there beside the ark (1 Chron. 13:5-10; see 1 Sam. 6:1-7). Despite David's anger over what God had done (1 Chron. 13:11), the king bore responsibility for the mishap. After all, he violated the instructions recorded in the Mosaic law. To be specific, Levites were supposed to carry the ark on poles inserted through rings permanently attached to the side of the chest (Exod 25:12-14). Also, none of the sacred objects was to be touched, with death being the penalty for violating the injunction (Num 4:5-6, 15). In this regard, Uzzah showed irreverence for God's holy presence by indiscriminately grabbing the ark.

Because of this incident, David decided to temporarily store the ark in the house of a Levite named Obed-Edom, where it remained for three months (1 Chron. 13:13-14; see 15:18, 21, 24). The king also set up a special tent to shelter the ark (15:1). As a result of the previously unsuccessful attempt to move the ark, David decided to do exactly what the Mosaic law commanded. In particular, only Levites were allowed to carry the sacred chest, for the Lord had chosen them to do this and to minister in His presence perpetually (1 Chron. 15:2). The Levites received their priestly status centuries earlier when they distinguished themselves as loyal followers of Moses during the episode involving the golden calf. This incident occurred not long after the Israelites had left Egypt (Exod. 32:28-29; Deut. 33:8-11).

The relocation of the ark of the covenant to Jerusalem was a special occasion. Undoubtedly, time and attention were invested in choosing the site where the chest would be placed. The spot also needed to be prepared for the ark, the vessels and furniture connected with it, and the tent sheltering it. To commemorate this historic event, David summoned all the Israelites to assemble at Jerusalem (1 Chron. 15:3). The king also sent for Aaron's descendants and for the Levites (15:4-10). A total of 862 priests from the tribe of Levi assembled at Jerusalem. The three main divisions were present (descendants of Kohath, Merari, and Gershon), along with three distinct subgroups among the Kohathites (descendants of Elizaphan, Hebron, and Uzziel; 1 Chron. 15:4-10). David summoned six of their leaders (Uriel, Asaiah, Joel, Shemaiah, Eliel, and Amminadab) and the two Aaronic high priests who served during his reign (Zadok and Abiathar). Then, he directed these leaders of the clans of the Levites to consecrate themselves in preparation for transporting the ark. By this David meant they had to go through a set procedure to make them ceremonially clean and acceptable to the Lord (15:11-12). Most likely, this included washing their body and garments and abstaining from sexual relations (Exod. 19:14-15).

David said that after purifying themselves, the Levitical priests would be allowed to carry the sacred chest to the spot the king had designated in Jerusalem (1 Chron. 15:12). The king had learned from his previous attempt to move the ark, how important it was to do exactly what the Mosaic law commanded. David noted that he and the other civil and religious leaders failed to ask God about the proper way to relocate the chest. As a result, the anger of the Lord broke out against the procession (15:13). The Aaronic priests and Levites fully complied with David's injunction to make themselves ceremonially clean (15:14). The descendants of Levi also did exactly what the law said by carrying the ark on poles that rested on their shoulders (15:15).

In ancient times, people used music to commemorate major events in the life of their community and to express their joy on such special occasions. For the Israelites, music was also used to worship the Lord in formal, prescribed ways. This typically involved a choir of singers, choral music, and a full array of instruments, such as lyres, harps, and cymbals. (Like trumpets, the cymbals were not used for musical accompaniment, but to announce the beginning of a song.) Undoubtedly, as the occasion permitted, there was also plenty of spontaneity, in which participants sang and danced with reverence and exuberance to the Lord. This lively medley of elements was evident in David's appointment of Levites to serve as musicians during the transport of the ark to Jerusalem (15:16). Verses 17-24 list the names of those who ministered on that occasion.

Eventually, all the preparations were finalized for the momentous event. A procession from Jerusalem traveled to the house of Obed-Edom to move the ark of the covenant. Those in the entourage included David, the leaders (or elders) of Israel, and the army officers who commanded units of a thousand troops (15:25). Unlike the previous occasion, the king was far more cautious the second time around. Out of reverence for the Lord, David wanted to make sure that nothing went wrong. The Lord gave the Levitical priests the strength they needed to carry the ark of the covenant (15:26). After taking the first six steps, they stopped and waited until David sacrificed a bull and a fattened calf (2 Sam. 6:13). In this way, the king expressed thanks to God that the procession had started. He was also depending on God to bless the journey to Jerusalem with success. By the end of the journey, seven bulls and seven rams were sacrificed (1 Chron. 15:26). In ancient Israel, the presentation of burnt, grain, and peace offerings provided the people with a formal means of approaching the Lord in the place where He manifested His presence (namely, the tabernacle). Also, the sacrifices (both animal and vegetable) helped the covenant community to preserve their holiness and purity before the Lord.

David, the Levites who carried the ark, the singers, and Kenaniah (the music director) were all wearing robes made out of fine linen. The king also wore a linen ephod (15:27). Some think David's garment extended from the waist to the knee (like a skirt). More likely, it resembled a closely fitting, sleeveless vest usually worn by the high priest as part of his ceremonial robes. David, while wearing the linen ephod, was dancing with all his strength before the Lord (2 Sam. 6:14). Meanwhile, the procession accompanying the transport of the ark celebrated the historic event by shouting, blowing rams' horns and trumpets, sounding cymbals, and playing stringed instruments such as lyres and harps (1 Chron. 15:28). When the entourage reached Jerusalem, the ark was put in its place in the middle of the special tent that David had pitched for it. Next, the king worshiped the Lord by sacrificing burnt offerings and fellowship (or peace offerings) in His presence. Once David was finished, he pronounced a blessing over the people in the name of the sovereign Lord. The king then handed to all the men and women in the crowd a portion of bread, a cake of dates (or a portion of meat), and a cake of raisins. After that, all the people returned to their homes (1 Chron. 16:1-3; see 2 Sam. 6:17-19).

SUGGESTIONS TO TEACHERS

There's an old proverb that says "if at first you don't succeed, try, try again." There's also the idea that "practice makes perfect." In the spiritual realm, though, if what we are doing is sinful, it doesn't matter how many times we try. In the eyes of God, we will neither be "perfect" nor "successful" in our attempts. The first thing we must do is adopt a God-honoring approach.

1. A FLAWED APPROACH. The consistent teaching of Scripture is that all people have sinned and fall short of God's glory (Rom. 3:23). The Bible also reveals that if we confess our sins, the Lord is faithful and just to forgive our sins and cleanse us from all unrighteousness (1 John 2:9). The people of God in the Old Testament were aware of these truths, including David. For instance, during the king's first attempt to move the ark of the covenant to Jerusalem, he did not follow the strictures recorded in the law of Moses; and this sin led to the death of at least one Israelite. It also prevented David from fulfilling his plans for three months.

2. A GOD-HONORING APPROACH. Though the king was troubled by the unfortunate turn of events, he came to realize he had transgressed against the Lord. Undoubtedly, it was God's forgiveness and grace that gave David the courage to try again to relocate the sacred chest to Jerusalem. This time, however, he relied on the Lord to make the undertaking a success. The king also made sure that he and all who were with him did everything in accordance with God's Word. Even the priests and Levites sought to minister before the Lord in holiness and purity. God honored their

ephod =

devotion by helping them to carry the ark without any mishaps.

3. ASSURANCE OF GOD'S PRESENCE. We who have trusted in Christ for salvation have the assurance of Scripture that God is always with us and will never forsake us (Heb. 13:5). The Bible teaches us that the Lord is our helper, even in the most difficult of circumstances (13:6). Indeed, He has given us His Spirit as a deposit, guaranteeing our eternal inheritance in the Savior (Eph. 1:14). Moreover, the indwelling Spirit helps us in our weakness and intercedes for us through wordless groans (Rom. 8:26). With the Lord ever present in our lives and eternally on our side, there is nothing that can prevent us from succeeding in all that He calls us to do (8:31). We can give ourselves fully to the work of the Lord, for we know that our Christian service is not in vain (1 Cor. 15:58).

FOR ADULTS

■ **TOPIC:** A Symbol of God's Presence

■ **QUESTIONS:** 1. Why did David feel the need to prepare a place in Jerusalem for the ark of the Lord? 2. Why did David stress that only the Levites could carry the ark of the covenant? 3. Why did the priests and Levites consecrate themselves? 4. What purpose did it serve for the musicians to make a joyful sound while the ark was being transported? 5. What was the significance of the linen ephod that David wore?

■ **ILLUSTRATIONS:**

God's Love in a Baghdad Hospital. Little Ammar, a 9-year-old with terminal leukemia, couldn't smile. His facial nerves were damaged to the point where the muscles just wouldn't work. He was a Muslim child who had been receiving treatment in a Baghdad hospital for four months. One special day, Ammar got the opportunity to hear about Jesus and His love when he received his very own copy of the *Arabic Picture Bible*.

On this same visit to the Children's Teaching Hospital, the team met the administrator, who welcomed them, received his own copy of the *Picture Bible*, and allowed them to distribute *Picture Bibles* to the children in the different wards. When they started giving the books out, everyone wanted a copy. They only had 80 copies that day. The next day they took 120 more. Within a short period of time, all the physicians, nurses, and staff said they wanted their own copy of the *Picture Bible* for their children. The literature became a tangible symbol of God's loving presence.

God's Signature. H.B. London, in his newsletter, *The Pastor's Weekly Briefing*, told about the death of a close friend named Carl Gaede, an outstanding architect. He had won many prestigious awards for his church buildings across the country. Because of his creative skills, he was able to leave his "signature" behind him. People who never knew Gaede personally see his buildings, worship in the sanctuaries he designed, and are blessed by the beauty and uniqueness of those structures.

Our signature is that unique something about us that causes others to remember us. It is the legacy we leave behind us. God the Son left His signature in the world when, in the fullness of time, He stepped out of heaven and, in the form of a little baby, became Immanuel, "God with us." His signature was His everlasting love poured into flesh and blood that never knew sin.

God Is With Me. In an *Upper Room* devotional, Ellen Bergh writes how Amtrak's Coast Starlight train was filled with excited passengers, craning their necks to enjoy the Oregon scenery as the train rolled through green forests. A shining lake gleamed through the trees, and cheerful conversation filled the air.

Suddenly, the light, airy feeling was gone, like a candle blown out in a draft, as the train entered a tunnel. Expecting the sun to reappear quickly, Ellen was uncomfortable as it became even darker. The happy sounds were a thing of the past. Everyone sat in awe of the inky blackness. The longer they traveled in the tunnel, the harder it was to remain calm without any visual cues to reassure them. Even the movement of the train seemed to fall away into pitch darkness. When they came out of the tunnel, laughter and relief filled the compartment.

"My life in Christ is like that unforgettable train ride," Ellen reflects. "Events may plunge me into darkness where I have no clues to sense the Lord's presence. Yet I can trust God is with me even when I can't see what lies ahead."

■ **TOPIC:** God Is With Us!

■ **QUESTIONS:** 1. What had David constructed in Jerusalem? 2. Whom did the Lord choose to carry the ark of the covenant? 3. In what way did the law of Moses prescribe that the ark be transported? 4. Whom did David want to be appointed to serve as musicians? 5. From where did the Levites obtain help to be successful in moving the ark?

■ **ILLUSTRATIONS:**

The Reality of God's Presence. A little boy was afraid to sleep alone. He did not like the darkness, and he could not stand the idea that he was in his room, all by himself. His mother tried to console him by reminding him that he was not alone and that God would be with him to protect him. The little boy thought about this truth for a while. Then he said, "But I need somebody in here who has skin on him!"

God knew that we would be that way and that we could never conceive the fact He is Spirit (John 4:24). The Lord also knew that we could never feel secure with the reality of His presence until His Son appeared in time "with skin on him."

God's Grace. While we must bear some responsibility in obeying God, let's never forget that it is His grace that leads us to safety and fulfillment. It's like the father and his young teenage son who had to carry a large basket of grain into the village market. The father put a long wooden pole through the basket handles and took the short end. He then gave the end that stuck out three or four feet to his son to carry. Though it seemed to the boy that he and his father were carrying the load equally, in reality, the father was carrying the much heavier portion of the weight. Our obedience to God carries a certain weight, but the main load is always shouldered by God.

God Knows What Lies Ahead. Ken Harmon had always wanted to take his family on a road trip through the Colorado Rocky mountains. In fact, he had saved for this trip for almost three years. June finally came and Ken, Sally, and their two children took their rented, 33-foot motor home and left Phoenix, Arizona, for a two-week tour of the majestic high country.

The Harmons had a great trip visiting Colorado's Maroon Bells, Sangre de Christo Mountains, and of course, Rocky Mountain National Park. Soon it was time to head home. As they began their trek west, they had to climb over the Continental Divide one more time. They loved the scenic views of those 10,000-foot-plus mountain highways, but they were certainly thankful that they had a good vehicle to navigate the steep mountain passes.

As the family approached the final pass before crossing the Divide, something inside Sally's mind and heart began to trouble her. She didn't know what it was, but she insisted that Ken pull off at the scenic overlook on the top of the summit. It was lunchtime, so they had their sandwiches and decided to pray together with their children. Again, Sally felt deeply disturbed within. As they prayed, the Harmons could not understand why Sally had felt so insistent about pulling over—what could this mean?

Finally, without any further direction from the Lord, the family started their motor-coach and begin to pull out of the oversized parking lot. Immediately, Ken could tell that something was wrong. As he depressed the brake pedal, it went clear to the floor. He pulled the emergency brake and turned off the engine. Outside, he looked under the front of the vehicle. There, surrounded by a puddle of fluid, Ken could see the broken brake line dripping its final drops. Their brakes were completely gone.

It wasn't until the mobile mechanic fixed their motor home that the reality set in. As the family pulled onto the highway and rounded the first bend, the Harmons could not help notice the five-mile-long, downhill grade with steep cliffs on almost every turn. All of them trembled silently as they realized what God, through the inner witness of instruction to Sally, had saved them from.

GOD'S COVENANT WITH DAVID

BACKGROUND SCRIPTURE: 1 Chronicles 17:1-27
DEVOTIONAL READING: Psalm 78:67–72

KEY VERSES: I took thee from the sheepcote, even from following the sheep, that thou shouldest be ruler over my people Israel: And I have been with thee whithersoever thou hast walked, and have cut off all thine enemies from before thee, and have made thee a name like the name of the great men that are in the earth. 1 Chronicles 17:7-8.

KING JAMES VERSION

1 CHRONICLES 17:1 Now it came to pass, as David sat in his house, that David said to Nathan the prophet, Lo, I dwell in an house of cedars, but the ark of the covenant of the LORD remaineth under curtains. . . . 3 And it came to pass the same night, that the word of God came to Nathan, saying, 4 Go and tell David my servant, Thus saith the LORD, Thou shalt not build me an house to dwell in: . . . 6 Wheresoever I have walked with all Israel, spake I a word to any of the judges of Israel, whom I commanded to feed my people, saying, Why have ye not built me an house of cedars? 7 Now therefore thus shalt thou say unto my servant David, Thus saith the LORD of hosts, I took thee from the sheepcote, even from following the sheep, that thou shouldest be ruler over my people Israel: 8 And I have been with thee whithersoever thou hast walked, and have cut off all thine enemies from before thee, and have made thee a name like the name of the great men that are in the earth. 9 Also I will ordain a place for my people Israel, and will plant them, and they shall dwell in their place, and shall be moved no more; neither shall the children of wickedness waste them any more, as at the beginning, 10 And since the time that I commanded judges to be over my people Israel. Moreover I will subdue all thine enemies. Furthermore I tell thee that the LORD will build thee an house. 11 And it shall come to pass, when thy days be expired that thou must go to be with thy fathers, that I will raise up thy seed after thee, which shall be of thy sons; and I will establish his kingdom. 12 He shall build me an house, and I will stablish his throne for ever. 13 I will be his father, and he shall be my son: and I will not take my mercy away from him, as I took it from him that was before thee: 14 But I will settle him in mine house and in my kingdom for ever: and his throne shall be established for evermore. 15 According to all these words, and according to all this vision, so did Nathan speak unto David.

NEW REVISED STANDARD VERSION

1 CHRONICLES 17:1 Now when David settled in his house, David said to the prophet Nathan, "I am living in a house of cedar, but the ark of the covenant of the LORD is under a tent." . . .

3 But that same night the word of the LORD came to Nathan, saying: 4 Go and tell my servant David: Thus says the Lord: You shall not build me a house to live in. . . . 6 Wherever I have moved about among all Israel, did I ever speak a word with any of the judges of Israel, whom I commanded to shepherd my people, saying, Why have you not built me a house of cedar? 7 Now therefore thus you shall say to my servant David: Thus says the LORD of hosts: I took you from the pasture, from following the sheep, to be ruler over my people Israel; 8 and I have been with you wherever you went, and have cut off all your enemies before you; and I will make for you a name, like the name of the great ones of the earth. 9 I will appoint a place for my people Israel, and will plant them, so that they may live in their own place, and be disturbed no more; and evildoers shall wear them down no more, as they did formerly, 10 from the time that I appointed judges over my people Israel; and I will subdue all your enemies.

Moreover I declare to you that the LORD will build you a house. 11 When your days are fulfilled to go to be with your ancestors, I will raise up your offspring after you, one of your own sons, and I will establish his kingdom. 12 He shall build a house for me, and I will establish his throne forever. 13 I will be a father to him, and he shall be a son to me. I will not take my steadfast love from him, as I took it from him who was before you, 14 but I will confirm him in my house and in my kingdom forever, and his throne shall be established forever. 15 In accordance with all these words and all this vision, Nathan spoke to David.

Monday, March 3	Psalm 78:67-72	*God Chose David*
Tuesday, March 4	1 Chronicles 17:1-6	*No House for God*
Wednesday, March 5	1 Chronicles 17:7-10	*God's House for David*
Thursday, March 6	1 Chronicles 17:11-15	*A House of Ancestors*
Friday, March 7	1 Chronicles 17:16-19	*Great Deeds of God*
Saturday, March 8	1 Chronicles 17:20-22	*A House of Israel*
Sunday, March 9	1 Chronicles 17:23-27	*The House of David*

BACKGROUND

Prophets such as Nathan were people who communicated messages from God, often in times of crisis that involved divine judgment or deliverance (or both). The Lord commissioned these individuals (both men and women) to be His spokespersons. In turn, they conveyed His declarations in a written, dramatic, or oral form. The messages of the prophets could contain elements of proclamation (namely, forthtelling) or prediction (namely, foretelling). The importance of those who served in this capacity is evident by the fact that the word "prophet" occurs over 300 times in the Old Testament and almost 125 times in the New Testament.

An examination of Deuteronomy 13:1-5 and 18:15-22 surfaces at least five indicators by which true prophets of God could be confirmed. They had to be Israelites, speak in the name of the Lord, foretell both the near as well as the distant future, announce signs and wonders, and make declarations that agreed with previous revelations from God. It would be incorrect to assume that they were robots who mechanically mouthed God's words. Instead, when the Lord spoke through His prophets in various portions and in diverse ways, He did so without excluding their human intelligence, individuality, literary style, personal feelings, or any other human factor.

NOTES ON THE PRINTED TEXT

In time, David's palace was completed and he was able to move into it (1 Chron. 17:1). This was possible because the Lord had brought peace to the land (2 Sam. 7:1). Inasmuch as Israel's king had relief from all his enemies, he had the opportunity to step back and think about what had happened to him up to this point in his life and career. He openly shared his concerns to a trusted advisor in the royal court, Nathan the prophet. David lamented the fact that while he lived in a palace made from cedar, the ark of the Lord's covenant sat in the middle of a tent (1 Chron. 17:1; see 2 Sam. 7:2). The king felt as if this large disparity was unacceptable and had to be remedied. The logical solution was for him to oversee the building of a temple in Jerusalem.

We learn from 1 Chronicles 17:1 that Nathan was a true prophet of the Lord whose ministry encompassed the reigns of David and Solomon. Scripture highlights three particular episodes involving Nathan: his declaration of the Lord's promise to David of a perpetual dynasty (2 Sam. 7; 1 Chron. 17); his announcement that God would punish David for his sin involving Bathsheba and Uriah (2 Sam. 12); and his intervention on behalf of Solomon in his efforts to succeed David as king (1 Kings 1). Nathan also penned historical accounts about the reigns of David and Solomon (1 Chron. 29:29; 2 Chron. 9:29). Moreover, Nathan was pivotal in establishing the playing of music in the worship liturgy used at the temple (2 Chron. 29:25). Though a true spokesperson for the Lord, Nathan was far from perfect and could make mistakes. For instance, when David voiced his desire to build a temple to house the ark of the covenant (1 Chron. 17:1), Nathan misspoke when he encouraged the king to do whatever he had in mind. While it's true that the Lord was with David, it was not God's will for him to build a shrine for the ark (vs. 2; see 2 Sam. 7:3).

That night, Nathan received a revelation from the Lord (1 Chron. 17:3). Perhaps God's word came in a vision while the prophet was awake; or it might have been in a dream while Nathan slept. Whatever the case, God referred to David as His servant, which in itself was a great honor. The Lord stated that the king would not be the person to build a temple in Jerusalem (17:4; see 2 Sam. 7:4-5). One reason is that David was too busy waging wars in an effort to expand and consolidate his kingdom (1 Kings 5:3). A second reason is that while fighting many battles, he had become defiled due to all the bloodshed that resulted (1 Chron. 22:8; 28:3). Expressed differently, his being a person of violence, rather than of peace, disqualified (but not necessarily condemned) him. While David would not have the privilege of honoring the Lord by building a shrine in the nation's capital, the plans and provisions he made for its construction helped his son, Solomon, successfully complete the endeavor (22:2-5; 28:2).

There is one Hebrew term, which is usually rendered "house," that lies at the heart of chapter 17. The same word refers to David's palace (17:1), the temple of the Lord (17:4-6), and the dynasty of David (17:10). In brief, the king saw his own palace and desired to build a temple for God; but the Lord declared that He would build a dynasty for David and enable his son, Solomon, to build a shrine in Jerusalem. Notice this play on words in 17:5. The Lord declared that He had not lived in a *house* from the time He liberated the Israelites from Egypt to the day of David's reign. Instead of confining Himself to one location, God traveled with the Israelites as they moved the tabernacle from one place to the next during their 40 years of wandering. Then, after the chosen people settled in Canaan, the Lord never censured any of their leaders, whom He appointed to shepherd the Israelites, for not building a *house* (17:6) made from cedar. Instead, the higher priority was for Israel's judges to watch over those whom God had entrusted to their care.

Nathan was to refer to God as the one who commanded heaven's armies. The all-powerful Lord had taken an obscure shepherd named David and made him the leader of the Israelites, the divinely chosen people (17:7). David did not lobby for this position or do anything noteworthy to receive the honor of being the Lord's servant-king; rather, it was the grace of God that led Him to direct Samuel to anoint David as Israel's next monarch (1 Sam. 16:12-13) and for the entire nation to confirm him as their shepherd-leader (1 Chron. 11:1-2). The path to kingship was neither straightforward nor easy. Regardless, even in the darkest moments, the Lord was with David wherever he went and defeated his enemies right in front of his eyes. And now God pledged to make the name of Israel's king one of the most famous in the world (17:8; see 2 Sam. 7:8-9). God's aim was to establish a place for His people, Israel, and to settle them in Canaan. He wanted them to live there permanently and not be disturbed anymore (1 Chron. 17:9). From the time God chose His people right up until the days of the judges, violent groups oppressed the Israelites; but with the establishment of David as king, the Lord would subdue all His people's enemies (17:10) and give His people rest (2 Sam. 7:11).

First Chronicles 17:10-12 (see 2 Sam. 7:11-13) records the establishment of God's covenant with David, which amplifies and confirms the promises of His covenant with Abraham (Gen. 12:1-3; 17:4-8, 16). Although the word *covenant* is not specifically stated in 1 Chronicles 17, it is used elsewhere to describe this occasion (2 Sam. 23:5; Pss. 89:3, 28, 34; 132:11-12), and the promises associated with it have enduring significance. Clearly, the issues of 1 Chronicles 17 are of immense theological importance. They concern not only the first coming of the Messiah, but also the Savior's eternal rule on the throne of David (see Isa. 9:6-7; 11:1-5; Jer. 23:5-6; Luke 1:32-33).

In particular, the Lord declared that He would build a dynastic house for David (1 Chron. 17:10). When the time came for the king to die, God would raise up one of his sons to succeed him. Solomon, of course, is the person who became Israel's next ruler and for whom the Lord established the Davidic dynasty (17:11). God would let Solomon build a temple for God's *name* (2 Sam. 7:13). In the Old Testament, God's *name* stood for His presence in the tabernacle or temple, often represented by a visible "cloud" around the Holy Place. According to the Lord's express declaration to David and Solomon, the temple was to serve as the dwelling place for His name (see 1 Kings 9:3). That is how God dwelt with the Israelites.

David did not have to worry whether his kingdom would endure after his death, for the Lord pledged to establish the throne of Solomon's dynasty permanently (1 Chron. 17:12). The New Testament reveals that God's promises to David are fulfilled in the Messiah. He keeps the conditions of the covenant perfectly (Heb. 4:15), serves as the Mediator of the covenant (9:15), and promises to return as the conquering King (Matt. 24:29-31). God pledged to establish an intimate, Father-son relationship with David's descendants, beginning with Solomon (1 Chron. 17:13). When a Davidic king did wrong, the Lord would punish him, just as parents discipline their rebellious children (2 Sam. 7:14). God's punishment of David's successors would culminate in the loss of land and temple (see 1 Kings 9:6-9); yet the Lord would never withdraw His loyal love from David's dynastic successors. In contrast, God rejected David's predecessor, Saul, and his dynasty (1 Chron. 17:13) because Saul was unfaithful to the Lord. To be specific, Israel's first king failed to heed God's commands and even consulted a medium, rather than direct his inquiries to God (10:13-14; see 1 Sam. 28:7).

The Lord declared through Nathan that He would make sure David's son, Solomon, and his descendants ruled God's chosen people and kingdom permanently. Indeed, the Davidic dynasty would endure forever (1 Chron. 17:14). God's promise to establish forever the throne of David would not fail (2 Sam. 7:16), being one day fully realized in the Messiah (see Jer. 33:14-26; Mic. 5:2-5). God, who promised to do great things for David, has also done great things for us through Christ. Because we trust in Him, our sins are totally forgiven and we look forward to a glorious future with God in heaven. Nathan told David all that the Lord had revealed to him in his vision (1 Chron. 17:15; see 2 Sam. 7:17). Nathan, whose name means "[God] has given," proved to be a necessary and helpful gift from God to David. Indeed, throughout Nathan's career, he displayed wisdom in his counsel and bravery in his confrontation of injustice.

SUGGESTIONS TO TEACHERS

After building a palace for himself, David felt ashamed that he allowed the ark of God to remain in a tent. He dreamed of erecting a suitable temple to honor God and house the ark. When God denied him the plan to build a temple, David had to live with disappointment. But God also gave David a promise that He would remember Israel's king. This week, have your class reflect on facing the challenges of (1) living with disappointment, and (2) relying on the Lord's promises to us.

1. DAVID'S DREAM AND DECISION. What finer thought than to build a beautiful temple! David's motive was noble and his plan was commendable. Sometimes, our intentions seem to fit in with what we imagine God would approve. But for various reasons, we are disappointed and not able to fulfill what we hoped to do. Some in the class may wish to share episodes of disappointment and how they dealt with them.

2. NATHAN'S DARING DISCLOSURE. It took courage to stand up to the king, but God's spokesman, Nathan, didn't flinch. Informed by God that David would not be permitted to erect a temple, Nathan risked David's displeasure and told him the news that God said, "No!" Going against the wishes and interests of powerful personalities is not easy or pleasant, but prophetic voices must speak up for God. The Church is called to be such a prophetic voice in these times!

3. DAVID'S DISAPPOINTMENT AND DEDICATION. To his credit, David accepted Nathan's message in which God turned down the temple building project. David's trust in God remained undiminished despite the disappointment he must have felt. A dedication to the Lord in which confidence in God continues, regardless of circumstances, is the only way to handle disappointment.

4. GOD'S DECREE AND DOMINION. God covenanted with David that He would remember David forever. God promised David that a son would eventually build the temple and continue his kingdom. David learned to accept the challenge of God's promises. For we who are Christians, God has spelled out the promise of His everlasting love in the person of Jesus Christ. Through the Cross and resurrection of this King, God has covenanted with us.

5. GOD'S DESIRE TO BLESS US. We may rely on God to remember us and to fulfill His plans. God may also be trusted to bless us, regardless of our current problems. Perhaps we will be blessed by seeing someone we have been teaching really grasp what God is about, or by seeing someone advance whom we helped get a job, or by seeing a positive report from a missions agency we have supported for years.

<table>
<tr><td>

FOR ADULTS

</td><td>

■ **TOPIC:** Covenanting

■ **QUESTIONS:** 1. What prompted David to desire to build a temple for the Lord? 2. Why did Nathan counter his original statement to David

</td></tr>
</table>

regarding the building of a temple? 3. Why did God not want David to build a temple for Him? 4. How would God use David to bring peace and stability to Israel? 5. What sort of future awaited the dynasty of David?

■ **ILLUSTRATIONS:**

Faith at Work. The renowned talk-show host, Larry King, reported that during one of his hospital stays, he received many letters and gifts. However, the one that touched him the most was a Bible and a note sent by "Pistol" Pete Maravich, the former Louisiana State University and National Basketball Association star.

The note read: "Dear Larry, I'm so glad to hear that everything went well with your surgery. I want you to know that God was watching over you every minute, and even though I know you may question that, I also know that one day it will become evident to you . . . because He lives."

The following week, Pete Maravich died of a heart attack. Larry King says he will always remember Pete Maravich not just as a Christian, but as a caring Christian. What a wonderful testimony of a believer who covenanted with God to live for Him!

Use It or Lose It. Janice took piano lessons for 12 years and developed into a promising performer. She planned to teach music someday. Then she went to college. Instead of majoring in music education as she originally intended, Janice became interested in contemporary literature and chose an English major. Extracurricular activities in the drama club and gymnastics took up her spare time. Occasionally, she would sit down at the piano, but found her keyboard skills were not as sharp as they once had been.

Upon graduation, Janice moved to Chicago and found a job. She told herself that she would return to her music as soon as possible, but meanwhile she needed to earn a living. She planned to save to buy herself a piano, but a new car and vacations always consumed what she meant to set aside for the piano. New hobbies, especially golf, attracted her. Soon she devoted nearly all her weekends to sharpening her abilities as a golfer.

Then Janice met a man at a golfing party and eventually married him. When the children came, Janice quit her job for several years, reentering the work force when her last child was in junior high. Meanwhile, she sometimes remarked that she would get back to playing the piano again, but it was always "someday."

On their twentieth wedding anniversary, Janice's husband presented her with a lovely spinet piano. Delighted, Janice sat down to play. To her surprise, the years of no practice had ruined her fingering. Gripping a golf club had done something to one wrist. Her ability to sight-read the music seemed to have diminished. Her playing sounded like the clumsy efforts of a beginning piano student. Looking up at her husband, Janice smiled ruefully, "Well, the old saying is true, I guess: 'Use it or lose it.'"

Let this week's lesson be an opportunity for your students to covenant with God to use their faith and continue progressing in Christian growth. If not, like Janice's piano playing, they risk losing touch with what they once loved.

Cost of Salvation. In his book, *Be Right*, Warren Wiersbe tells how G. Campbell Morgan was trying to explain the concept of "free salvation" to a coal miner, but the man was unable to understand it. "I have to pay for it," he continually insisted. But with a flash of divine insight, Morgan asked, "How did you get down into the mine this morning?"

"Why, it was easy," the man replied. "I just got on the elevator and went down."

Then Morgan asked, "Wasn't that too easy? Didn't it cost you something?"

The man laughed. "No, it didn't cost me anything; but it must have cost the company plenty to install that elevator." Then the miner saw the truth: "It doesn't cost me anything to be saved, but it cost God the life of His Son." That's the nature of God's covenantal love, which we receive by grace through faith in the Messiah.

<table>
<tr><td rowspan="3">FOR YOUTH</td><td>■ TOPIC: God's Special Promise</td></tr>
<tr><td>■ QUESTIONS: 1. Why was David bothered by the fact that the ark of the covenant was housed in a tent? 2. How did Nathan initially</td></tr>
</table>

respond to David's desire to build a temple for the Lord? 3. During the Israelites' years of wandering in the wilderness, where did God manifest His presence to them? 4. From what humble beginnings did David get his start? 5. What are some of the specifics of the covenant that God made with David?

■ **ILLUSTRATIONS:**

Relying on the Promise. Arthur Ashe, a champion American tennis player, acquired AIDS through a blood transfusion at the time he underwent heart surgery. The hospital did not suspect or inspect the unit of H.I.V.-contaminated blood. Ashe did not realize that he was infected with the dread virus until five years later when he suffered numbness, then growing paralysis in his playing arm. The diagnosis was a brain tumor. This stay in the hospital for surgery revealed that he had contracted AIDS from the transfusion during his heart surgery five years earlier. Released from the hospital, the seventh-ranked tennis star had to face rumors about his condition as well as face retirement from playing.

Arthur Ashe resisted the temptation to be angry at the Lord. In 1992, he addressed the students at the Niagara County Community College, and testified how in spite of his AIDS, he could trust God to keep His promises to His people.

Challenge of a Promise. Ricky Hoyt has cerebral palsy. He is confined to a wheelchair. His disability is classified technically as a spastic quadriplegic. He cannot even talk and has to communicate through a voice synthesizer. Nonetheless, Ricky Hoyt has been able to compete in over 600 sports events, including 111 triathlons, a 45-day cross-country odyssey, and nearly 20 Boston Marathons. How? Because of the promise of his father and the way that promise has been kept.

Ricky's father, Dick, is a retired Lt. Colonel who has devoted himself to compete with Ricky to fulfill the dreams of his son. Rick is the heart, but Dick Hoyt is the body. Together they compete. Dick pushes the wheelchair, fulfilling his promise to his boy to let him participate even in big-time marathons. How much more does God fulfill His promises to those who trust him? King David learned this.

Commitment to God's Promise. Habitat for Humanity has provided affordable housing for millions throughout the world. Few know the story of its origins. A young millionaire named Millard Fuller had amassed a fortune by the age of 29, and was able to buy anything he fancied. He discovered that his marriage had collapsed because of his greed and attention only to business. Shocked at having his wife, Linda, leave him, he began to take stock of his life.

Millard located Linda in New York and listened to her tell him that she didn't care about having him buy her things. He heard her describe how her life was barren of meaning with his kind of living. They talked and wept together. Then they knelt and prayed. That night in a hotel room in New York City, the couple promised God and each other that they would dispose of everything they had and commit themselves to helping the oppressed and homeless. The Fullers' promise has resulted in ways they never anticipated, as countless chapters of Habitat for Humanity now exist in North American communities and among the poorest in many developing countries.

God Calls Solomon to Build the Temple

BACKGROUND SCRIPTURE: 1 Chronicles 28:1-28
DEVOTIONAL READING: Psalm 132

KEY VERSE: Take heed now; for the LORD hath chosen thee to build an house for the sanctuary: be strong, and do it. 1 Chronicles 28:10.

KING JAMES VERSION

1 CHRONICLES 28:5 And of all my sons, (for the LORD hath given me many sons,) he hath chosen Solomon my son to sit upon the throne of the kingdom of the LORD over Israel. 6 And he said unto me, Solomon thy son, he shall build my house and my courts: for I have chosen him to be my son, and I will be his father. 7 Moreover I will establish his kingdom for ever, if he be constant to do my commandments and my judgments, as at this day. 8 Now therefore in the sight of all Israel the congregation of the LORD, and in the audience of our God, keep and seek for all the commandments of the LORD your God: that ye may possess this good land, and leave it for an inheritance for your children after you for ever. 9 And thou, Solomon my son, know thou the God of thy father, and serve him with a perfect heart and with a willing mind: for the LORD searcheth all hearts, and understandeth all the imaginations of the thoughts: if thou seek him, he will be found of thee; but if thou forsake him, he will cast thee off for ever. 10 Take heed now; for the LORD hath chosen thee to build an house for the sanctuary: be strong, and do it. . . .

20 And David said to Solomon his son, Be strong and of good courage, and do it: fear not, nor be dismayed: for the LORD God, even my God, will be with thee; he will not fail thee, nor forsake thee, until thou hast finished all the work for the service of the house of the LORD. 21 And, behold, the courses of the priests and the Levites, even they shall be with thee for all the service of the house of God: and there shall be with thee for all manner of workmanship every willing skilful man, for any manner of service: also the princes and all the people will be wholly at thy commandment.

NEW REVISED STANDARD VERSION

1 CHRONICLES 28:5 "And of all my sons, for the LORD has given me many, he has chosen my son Solomon to sit upon the throne of the kingdom of the LORD over Israel. 6 He said to me, 'It is your son Solomon who shall build my house and my courts, for I have chosen him to be a son to me, and I will be a father to him. 7 I will establish his kingdom forever if he continues resolute in keeping my commandments and my ordinances, as he is today.' 8 Now therefore in the sight of all Israel, the assembly of the LORD, and in the hearing of our God, observe and search out all the commandments of the LORD your God; that you may possess this good land, and leave it for an inheritance to your children after you forever.

9 "And you, my son Solomon, know the God of your father, and serve him with single mind and willing heart; for the LORD searches every mind, and understands every plan and thought. If you seek him, he will be found by you; but if you forsake him, he will abandon you forever. 10 Take heed now, for the LORD has chosen you to build a house as the sanctuary; be strong, and act." . . .

20 David said further to his son Solomon, "Be strong and of good courage, and act. Do not be afraid or dismayed; for the LORD God, my God, is with you. He will not fail you or forsake you, until all the work for the service of the house of the LORD is finished. 21 Here are the divisions of the priests and the Levites for all the service of the house of God; and with you in all the work will be every volunteer who has skill for any kind of service; also the officers and all the people will be wholly at your command."

BACKGROUND

The building of the temple is a major theme of 1 and 2 Chronicles. Although David did not build the Jerusalem shrine, he made extensive preparations for its construction before he died. For instance, he appointed some of Israel's foreign residents to cut blocks of limestone for the sanctuary. He also supplied a large amount of the iron for the nails that would be needed for the doors in the gates and for the clamps. He provided more bronze than could be weighed and more cedar logs than could be counted (1 Chron. 22:2-4). There was also a seemingly endless supply of gold and silver (22:14). Moreover, at Solomon's disposal would be many stonecutters, masons, carpenters, and an innumerable array of other artisans skilled in using a wide variety of metals (22:15-16).

David wanted to ensure that the temple was so magnificent that it would become famous and be regarded as splendid by the surrounding nations. And yet, while David invested a great deal of effort and resources to ensure the successful building of the shrine, this was not his foremost concern; rather, it was the building of an enduring dynasty founded on wholehearted devotion to the Lord and uncompromising adherence to the Mosaic law. Accordingly, the king prayed that the Lord would give Solomon, who was relatively young and inexperienced (22:5), insight and understanding so that he might obey God's decrees. In fact, the success of the new monarch hinged on him carefully observing all the Lord had commanded (22:12-13).

In Hebrew, the name *Solomon* is similar to *shalom*, the word for *peace* (22:9). Because Solomon's reign would be a time of peace, the Lord had chosen him to build His temple. David quoted to Solomon part of the Lord's promise about the Davidic dynasty found in 17:11-14 (22:10). The latter part of 22:10 implies that David's immediate son foreshadowed the king's later descendant, Jesus Christ, also known as the Son of David (see Matt. 1:1). David also extended his challenge to include other leaders of Israel whose help his son would need to accomplish the construction of the temple (1 Chron. 22:17-18). The king wanted a pledge from all the leaders that they would devote themselves to the Lord and His sanctuary (22:19). David urged them, as he had urged Solomon, simply to begin building (see 22:16). David was convinced that if the leaders and people started the project, the Lord would see that it was completed.

Whereas the meeting with selected officials in 1 Chronicles 22:17-19 seems to have been a private hearing aimed at encouraging Solomon, the assembly in chapter 28 was a public announcement of Solomon's succession to the throne. The leaders whom David assembled in Jerusalem for a final address appear to have been the military, tribal, and cabinet officials described in chapter 27, along with the heroes of David's army (28:1). Even in such a setting, the theme of temple construction dominated David's thinking. David reiterated his longstanding desire to build a temple for the Lord and God's veto of the idea because of the bloodshed in the king's extensive military career (28:2-3). David added that the temple would be a place of rest for the ark of the covenant in comparison to the restlessness of the portable tabernacle. He also referred to the ark as *the footstool of our God* (28:2). The presence of the Lord in some way localized itself over the mercy seat atop the ark (see Exod. 25:22; Num. 7:89; 1 Sam. 4:4; 2 Sam. 6:2; 2 Kings 19:15; Ezek. 10:4).

David next stated how Solomon fit into the plans of God. The Lord, through Jacob, designated Judah as the tribe from which future kings would arise (see Gen. 49:10). God pointed out to Samuel the family of Jesse as the source of the successor to Saul (see 1 Sam. 16:1). The Lord directed Samuel to anoint David as the future king of Israel (16:7, 11-13). First Chronicles 3:1-9 lists 19 sons born to David by seven wives. Solomon was at least the tenthborn, but the Lord chose him to rule on David's throne (28:4-5). Being an Israelite whom God chose was a crucial requirement for a legitimate monarch of Israel (Deut. 17:15). David acknowledged that the kingdom really was not his. The throne Solomon inherited was *the throne of the kingdom of the LORD over Israel* (1 Chron. 28:5). When Israel originally insisted on having a king, the people were rejecting the rule of God over them (see 1 Sam. 8:7). David, however, understood that he ruled as God's representative over the covenant community.

The Lord declared that Solomon would build God's *house* (1 Chron. 28:6) and *courts*. The future temple is called a *house* because it would be permanent in comparison to the movable tent-tabernacle. The house was for God's name (see 22:7-8). God's name represented His attributes, especially His visible glory, which settled on the temple after its dedication (see 2 Chron. 6:20; 7:1). Solomon would build the temple of God and be known as God's son in anticipation of the Son of God who would be born in Bethlehem, the City of David, nearly 1,000 years later (1 Chron. 28:6). The Lord pledged to permanently establish the kingdom of Solomon, if he remained as unswervingly committed as David was to obeying the divine commands and regulations (28:7). The elderly monarch cherished the messianic language of the promises of the Lord that could begin to come true in Solomon if he would govern by the law of God. Solomon needed to remain true to God's Word, even as he had been doing as a young man. At this time, he was probably in his twenties.

First Chronicles 28:8 records David's final instructions to Israel's leaders. The witnesses to the proceedings included God and *all Israel*, the latter referring to the assembly of the Lord's chosen people. David gave the leaders the same mission he had given Solomon. They were to carefully observe everything the sovereign Lord had commanded through Moses. If they did so, they would possess Canaan, which was a *good land*. Next, David stressed to Solomon the conditional nature of the immediate blessings of God on his reign. The young monarch was urged to know God, acknowledge Him, and worship Him alone. When the Lord was the center of Solomon's life, he would be able to serve God with a submissive attitude and a willing spirit. This was the only sensible way to operate, for the Lord knew all the thoughts of every person and the motives for their actions. Solomon had the assurance of knowing that if he sought God, He would be found. Put another way, if the king inquired of the Lord in humility and sincerity, He would hear Solomon's petitions. However, if the king abandoned God, He would permanently reject Israel's ruler (28:9).

The Lord directly emphasized these truths to Solomon when He appeared to the king at Gibeon early in his reign (1 Kings 3:4-15) and later after the temple was built (9:1-9). Tragically, though God remained faithful to His promise to bless Solomon, the king eventually wavered in his commitment. When he grew old, he refused to follow the Lord completely, but instead did what was evil in God's sight. The king's growing apostasy angered the Lord, especially since He had warned Solomon about worshiping false gods. The monarch's refusal to heed the stipulations of the Mosaic covenant would result in the breakup of the kingdom after his death (11:1-13). This historical background information indicates how important David's final words were to Solomon. The aging father wanted his son to take his words of admonition seriously. Solomon had a bright and promising future ahead of him. After all, the Lord had chosen him to build the temple and make it the official sanctuary where the people would worship Him. David wanted Solomon to be confident and energetic as he did the work assigned to him (1 Chron. 28:10).

The elderly monarch also directed the young king to be strong and brave, rather than afraid and discouraged. The reason is that the Lord, Israel's covenant-keeping God, would abide with Solomon, not forsake him. Yahweh would ensure that all the work related to building the temple was finished correctly so it could be used for worshiping Him (28:20). Implicit in David's challenge was his realization that any spiritual weakness, fear, or lack of courage on Solomon's part would prevent the temple construction. Equally implicit was the assumption on David's part that the presence and faithfulness of the Lord would give Solomon strength, peace, and courage to succeed in the work.

David's exhortation to Solomon mirrors what Moses said to Joshua, which indicates that the Lord's presence and power to help had not decreased with time. In particular, the lawgiver urged his successor to be strong and courageous in leading a new generation of God's people into the promised land. Joshua would prosper by remaining faithful to the Lord and heeding His commands. The protégé of Moses had the assurance that God would be with him wherever he went (Deut. 1:37-38; 31:1-8; Josh. 1:1-9). For both Joshua and Solomon, a common goal was to remain morally equitable and upright as they led the heirs of God's covenant promises into a new phase of their existence in Canaan.

In Joshua's day, a new generation of Israelites wholeheartedly supported the nation's leader as he shouldered the task of conquering and settling Canaan. They pledged to obey him just as they had fully obeyed Moses (Deut. 34:9; Josh. 1:16-18). In a similar way, *all Israel* (1 Chron. 29:23) was ready to obey Solomon's every command (28:21). All the royal officials, the army commanders, and David's other sons pledged their loyalty to Solomon as king (29:24). In addition, the various divisions of priests and Levites were ready to carry out their assigned duties in the temple. Moreover, all the skilled workers were prepared to do their work (28:21). If Solomon would commit himself to the Lord and the temple work, no one in Israel would lay a stumbling block in his path.

SUGGESTIONS TO TEACHERS

The death of a long-time or popular leader always is upsetting to those he or she has been serving. If you can remember President John F. Kennedy's assassination, you will recall the grief that the American people felt and the anxiety many in the world experienced over his end. The impending death of David probably produced reactions much like those of the citizens of the United States in November of 1963. However, in the providence of God, a capable leader named Solomon had already been chosen and groomed for the heavy task of leading God's people. Continuity was maintained despite changing times.

1. SOLOMON'S APPOINTMENT AS DAVID'S SUCCESSOR. David knew it was time for him to turn the reins of power over to his son, Solomon. Because the aged monarch was confident of God's wise provision for the Israelites, he entrusted the kingship to Solomon. David was able to leave the leadership of Israel in the hands of a younger generation. How is your congregation preparing to pass on the leadership to the next generation? What specific things can you do to maintain the continuity of the faith?

2. DAVID'S REASSURANCE TO THE PEOPLE. David reassured the Israelites that God's work would not end just because there would be a change in leadership. The king assured them that Solomon would continue what God had called His people to do. In the face of a change in leadership, David brought hope and confidence.

3. OUR UNWAVERING CONFIDENCE IN GOD. As we journey with God on the road of life, He asks us to accept new challenges, such as reaching out to others in need, loving a difficult child or spouse, going the extra mile for a friend, or making decisions full of integrity but lacking in other advantages. Sometimes God directs our steps in gentle nudges, while at other times it is through the stern words of a friend. In every situation, the Lord wants us to be courageous in carrying out our God-given tasks. We can do so, knowing that He is with us every step of the way and will enable us to be successful in what He wants us to do.

<table>
<tr><td>

FOR ADULTS

</td><td>

■ **TOPIC:** Chosen for a Specific Task
■ **QUESTIONS:** 1. Why do you think the Lord chose Solomon to suc-
ceed David as king? 2. Why did God want Solomon to be unswerving

</td></tr>
</table>

in carrying out His commands? 3. What did the leaders of Israel need to do to ensure their ongoing prosperity in Canaan? 4. Why did David want Solomon to acknowledge the Lord as his God? 5. What support would Solomon enjoy from those under his command?

■ **ILLUSTRATIONS:**

Selected to Perform an Important Job. During a broadcast of the popular television program, *MotorWeek*, correspondent Henry Kopacz described how some law enforcement officers learn to drive safely and professionally. The training occurs at the Maryland Police and Correctional Commission's Driver Training Facility in Sykesville. The campus provides "more than just an opportunity to learn how to drive fast for pursuits." Students are given the opportunity to "hone their skills at car control on a closed course." The driving curriculum at the facility recreates real conditions, right "down to every stop sign, railroad crossing, and traffic light."

The staff who teach the curriculum realize they have been selected to perform an important job. Some are "retired from metropolitan police departments," while others bring experience from working in "county and state forces." The administrator of the facility, Al Liebno, believes what the instructors teach students is vital. It's this mind-set that helps explain why the program is so comprehensive. According to Kopacz, when law enforcement officials are "out on the road, they can expect to perform any-thing from traffic stops to high-speed chases." And with the instruction provided at the facility at Sykesville, they learn "exactly what to do."

God has also selected believers to perform key tasks. Indeed, the eternal future of countless unsaved people is at stake, which is why Christians need to take their God-given responsibilities all the more seriously.

Actor Turned Activist. Parkinson's disease (PD) is a disorder that occurs when spe-cific nerve cells (or neurons) in the brain die or become impaired. The symptoms of PD are muscle rigidity and tremor, a slowing of physical mobility, and eventually a loss of physical movement. Other common symptoms include disorders of mood, behavior, thinking, and sensation.

According to the National Parkinson Foundation, PD affects both genders and "shows no social, ethnic, economic, or geographic boundaries." Over 1.5 million Americans have the disease (and there are millions more worldwide), with 15 percent of those being under the age of 50. Medication helps, but allows patients to function for only two or three hours at a time.

In a broadcast appearing on *Dateline*, Katie Couric reported that actor Michael J. Fox is leading the effort to find a cure for PD. In 1998, Fox was "enjoying sit-com success" when he revealed he had the disease. In the years since, he has become a "selfless crusader of scientific research" and an "activist and advocate" for PD. This has involved going to Capitol Hill to testify before "Congress for increased federal funding" and rallying support from both Democrats and Republicans. Fox doesn't regard being diagnosed with PD as a personal loss. If anything, he says the disease has helped to replace "a lot of superficial stuff" in his life with "a lot of deep important stuff," such as "knowledge, understanding, compassion, and . . . humility."

For this "actor turned activist," the battle against PD is a personal calling to which he is wholeheartedly committed. Believers in Christ are also chosen for a specific task, one that has a heavenly focus. They know their efforts will bear fruit for time and eternity.

Serving God with Faith and Courage. Within two months, two of Al and Dellene Stucky's adult children experienced personal tragedy. Michelle was paralyzed from the waist down as a result of a plane crash. Marlyn, hospitalized with acute motor azonal neuropathy, couldn't move at all. Six months later, both were in wheelchairs. Despite their hardships, Michelle and Marlyn, along with their parents, were eager to get back to work. Together, they had been translating the New Testament into the Melpa language of Papua, New Guinea.

Dellene recalls, "Many people thought we were crazy, taking two people in wheelchairs to Papua, New Guinea. It's not wheelchair accessible, let alone an easy place to live. But it's where God wanted us. The Lord performed no end of miracles as we traveled to Los Angeles; Honolulu; Cairns; Australia; and on to Papua, New Guinea. The prayers of God's saints carried us through." It took faith and courage for Michelle and Marlyn to return to their work. Together, they typeset the Melpa New Testament, which was then dedicated and distributed to many people.

FOR YOUTH

■ TOPIC: Called for a Purpose

■ QUESTIONS: 1. What did God pledge to do for Solomon as he began his reign over Israel? 2. What did David urge the leaders of Israel to do? 3. What did David say would happen to Solomon if he forsook the Lord? 5. What would motivate Solomon to be strong and courageous in carrying out his God-given tasks?

■ ILLUSTRATIONS:

Life with a Purpose. Dwight Moody was an evangelist in the second half of the nineteenth century. As a teenager, he was a hard worker and ambitious. It was his dream to become a millionaire. At 17, he moved to Boston and worked in his uncle's shoe store, putting in long hours while still determined to go from rags to riches.

It was then that a Sunday school teacher challenged Moody to commit his life to living in a way that would honor God. This challenge profoundly affected Moody, forcing him to think about a purpose for his life. Thus, on April 21, 1855, through the influence of this teacher, Moody trusted in Christ for his salvation. It was the beginning of a spiritual journey that would end in 1899, but not before Moody himself had stirred up faith in Christ in the hearts of untold numbers of people. God has also called each of us for a purpose and to bring glory to Him.

Called to Lead. Brandon Williams, the running back for Valley High School, stood in the Bible Way Christian Fellowship Church in New Kensington, Pennsylvania, and announced that he would attend the University of Pittsburgh. The January 23, 1997, news conference ended months of recruiting for one of the nation's top 20 running backs. The college won over such finalists as Notre Dame, UCLA, Ohio State, and Syracuse.

Landing Williams was a huge victory for the University of Pittsburgh. The struggling football program had hired a new coach, Walt Harris, in 1997. He guided the team to its first winning season and a Liberty Bowl appearance. However, the team members were largely seniors. The program needed new and younger players to replace many of the departing players. Brandon wanted to be part of that new team and its leadership. That was part of the promise he received from former University of Pittsburgh great and NFL leader, Tony Dorsett, who reminded Brandon that he had watched the rebuilding of a program years earlier.

Brandon is an example of a youth who has been called to lead a new project. Solomon was a similar example. After being chosen by God, he accepted the opportunity to lead the Israelites into a new phase of their existence as a nation.

Believing the Promise. Expeditions now routinely climb Mount Everest. Despite the risks, many people enjoy the challenge. Good health and climbing experience are required. Nevertheless, each individual attempting the trek arrives believing in the promise that this mountain can be conquered with enough effort. David was confident that God would be with His people as Solomon took over as king. The people had to trust in the promises of God recorded in His Word. They also had to remain confident in His abiding presence, for it was only through His power, not their own strength, that they would succeed in doing His will.

FULFILLMENT OF GOD'S PROMISE

BACKGROUND SCRIPTURE: 2 Chronicles 6; Luke 24
DEVOTIONAL READING: Psalm 135:1–5

KEY VERSE: The LORD therefore hath performed his word that he hath spoken: for I am risen up in the room of David my father, and am set on the throne of Israel, as the LORD promised, and have built the house for the name of the LORD God of Israel. 2 Chronicles 6:10.

4

KING JAMES VERSION

2 CHRONICLES 6:12 And he stood before the altar of the LORD in the presence of all the congregation of Israel, and spread forth his hands: 13 For Solomon had made a brasen scaffold, of five cubits long, and five cubits broad, and three cubits high, and had set it in the midst of the court: and upon it he stood, and kneeled down upon his knees before all the congregation of Israel, and spread forth his hands toward heaven,
14 And said, O LORD God of Israel, there is no God like thee in the heaven, nor in the earth; which keepest covenant, and shewest mercy unto thy servants, that walk before thee with all their hearts: 15 Thou which hast kept with thy servant David my father that which thou hast promised him; and spakest with thy mouth, and hast fulfilled it with thine hand, as it is this day.
16 Now therefore, O LORD God of Israel, keep with thy servant David my father that which thou hast promised him, saying, There shall not fail thee a man in my sight to sit upon the throne of Israel; yet so that thy children take heed to their way to walk in my law, as thou hast walked before me. 17 Now then, O LORD God of Israel, let thy word be verified, which thou hast spoken unto thy servant David. . . .

LUKE 24:44 And he said unto them, These are the words which I spake unto you, while I was yet with you, that all things must be fulfilled, which were written in the law of Moses, and in the prophets, and in the psalms, concerning me. 45 Then opened he their understanding, that they might understand the scriptures,
46 And said unto them, Thus it is written, and thus it behoved Christ to suffer, and to rise from the dead the third day: 47 And that repentance and remission of sins should be preached in his name among all nations, beginning at Jerusalem. 48 And ye are witnesses of these things. 49 And, behold, I send the promise of my Father upon you: but tarry ye in the city of Jerusalem, until ye be endued with power from on high.

NEW REVISED STANDARD VERSION

2 CHRONICLES 6:12 Then Solomon stood before the altar of the LORD in the presence of the whole assembly of Israel, and spread out his hands.
13 Solomon had made a bronze platform five cubits long, five cubits wide, and three cubits high, and had set it in the court; and he stood on it. Then he knelt on his knees in the presence of the whole assembly of Israel, and spread out his hands toward heaven. 14 He said, "O LORD, God of Israel, there is no God like you, in heaven or on earth, keeping covenant in steadfast love with your servants who walk before you with all their heart— 15 you who have kept for your servant, my father David, what you promised to him. Indeed, you promised with your mouth and this day have fulfilled with your hand. 16 Therefore, O LORD, God of Israel, keep for your servant, my father David, that which you promised him, saying, 'There shall never fail you a successor before me to sit on the throne of Israel, if only your children keep to their way, to walk in my law as you have walked before me.'
17 Therefore, O LORD, God of Israel, let your word be confirmed, which you promised to your servant David. . . .

LUKE 24:44 Then he said to them, "These are my words that I spoke to you while I was still with you— that everything written about me in the law of Moses, the prophets, and the psalms must be fulfilled."
45 Then he opened their minds to understand the scriptures, 46 and he said to them, "Thus it is written, that the Messiah is to suffer and to rise from the dead on the third day, 47 and that repentance and forgiveness of sins is to be proclaimed in his name to all nations, beginning from Jerusalem. 48 You are witnesses of these things. 49 And see, I am sending upon you what my Father promised; so stay here in the city until you have been clothed with power from on high."

Monday, March 17	Psalm 135:1-5	*Praise for God's Goodness*
Tuesday, March 18	2 Chronicles 6:1-11	*Dedication of the Temple*
Wednesday, March 19	2 Chronicles 6:12-17	*Solomon's Prayer*
Thursday, March 20	2 Chronicles 6:18-31	*Pray toward This Place*
Friday, March 21	2 Chronicles 6:36-39	*Repent and Pray*
Saturday, March 22	2 Chronicles 6:40-42	*God's Promise Remembered*
Sunday, March 23	Luke 24:44-49	*God's Promise Fulfilled*

BACKGROUND

Before David's death in 970 B.C., the kingship had been successfully transferred to his son, Solomon. He in turn firmly secured his control over the throne so that all the tribes of Israel were obedient to him (1 Chron. 29:22-24). Also, the Lord greatly magnified the newly appointed monarch over the nation and bestowed on him greater royal splendor than any king of Israel before him (29:25). Thus, it was God who permitted His chosen people to stand in awe of Solomon and for him to have more wealth and honor than even his father (2 Chron. 1:1).

Early in his reign, Solomon and the representative leaders of Israel went to the high place at Gibeon, for the tabernacle and bronze altar for burnt sacrifices were located there (1 Chron. 21:29; 2 Chron. 1:2-5). Gibeon was about six miles northwest of Jerusalem and functioned as a major center of worship before Solomon built the temple. While at the high place, Israel's king offered sacrifices and prayed to the Lord. Then, that night, God appeared to Solomon and invited him to request anything he wanted. The young monarch asked for wisdom and discernment so he could be effective in leading the chosen people. The Lord not only granted this request, but also made him richer and more famous than any ruler before or after him (2 Chron. 1:7-12).

Second Chronicles 1:14-17 catalogs the riches and possessions of Solomon. In 966 B.C., he used his wealth and power to begin construction on a temple to honor the Lord (2:1). Chapters 2 through 4 detail this massive building project, which was completed seven years later in 959 B.C. (1 Kings 6:37-38). While the design of the Jerusalem shrine bore some resemblance to that of other temples of the day, it was most closely patterned after the tabernacle. In particular, three main areas comprised Solomon's temple: the outer courtyard, the Holy Place, and the Most Holy Place (the latter being cubical in shape).

The king put in the treasuries of the Jerusalem shrine the holy items that belonged to his father David (the silver, gold, and all the objects used in worship; 2 Chron. 5:1). Solomon also relocated the ark of the covenant, the tabernacle, and all the sacred furnishings to the temple (5:4-6). This happened in the twelfth year of his reign (958 B.C.; 1 Kings 8:2). As the priests carried the ark to the temple, Solomon and the elders of Israel sacrificed countless sheep and cattle along the way in thanksgiving (2 Chron.

5:4-6). The king waited nearly a year to transfer the ark so he could do it at the time of the day of Atonement and the Feast of Tabernacles. The blood of the sin offering on the day of Atonement was sprinkled on the atonement cover of the ark. The Feast of Tabernacles celebrated God's blessing on Israel when He took them from a wandering existence to a permanent place to inhabit. The priests placed the ark in the holy place under the wings of the cherubim (5:7). When the priests left the holy place, the cloud of God's glory filled the temple (5:13-14).

NOTES ON THE PRINTED TEXT

Those who assembled with Solomon included all the leaders of the Israelite tribes and their families (2 Chron. 5:2). As they stood before him, he pronounced a blessing over them (6:3). Then he recalled the promise God made with David that his son would build a temple to honor Yahweh. Solomon affirmed that the Lord had fulfilled His pledge to establish the young monarch as Israel's ruler and to enable him to complete the task of building a shrine in Jerusalem to house the ark of the covenant (6:4-11).

Earlier, Solomon had a bronze platform made that was about seven and one-half feet long and wide and four and one-half feet high. He had it placed in the center of the temple's outer courtyard near the altar so that he could be easily seen and heard. Most likely, the platform was erected temporarily for use during the ceremony in which the shrine was dedicated. Here we see that as Solomon officiated over this special occasion, he sought to focus attention on the place of sacrifice. After his initial comments, the king stood with his hands spread out before the altar in front of the entire assembly. Then, he knelt down on his knees and lifted up his hands toward the sky in a gesture signifying prayer (6:12-13; see Exod. 9:29, 33; Ezra 9:5; Isa. 1:15; 1 Tim. 2:8). As the representative and shepherd of God's people, Solomon publicly interceded on their behalf.

In the king's prayer, he affirmed that there was no deity in heaven or on earth like Yahweh, the all-powerful God of Israel. As the Hebrew of 2 Chronicles 6:14 literally says, God is the "one who keeps the covenant and the loyal love." The idea is that He never forgot the covenantal promises He made with His chosen people. He also showed unfailing compassion and favor toward His servants who obeyed His teachings in a wholehearted, sincere manner. These truths were evident in the circumstance involving Solomon and his completion of the temple.

The young monarch acknowledged that the Lord had kept every promise He made to His servant, David (6:15). The past faithfulness of Yahweh toward His chosen people was the basis for Solomon's petition for God's blessing. The king appealed to the Lord to keep the promise He previously made to David, His servant. Specifically, God pledged that David would never fail to have a successor ruling before the Lord on the throne of Israel. The key provision was that David's descendants guarded their behavior and obeyed the Mosaic law, just as he had done throughout his reign (2 Chron. 6:16-17; see 2 Sam. 7; 1 Chron. 17).

In Solomon's prayer, he declared that there was no one who had acted in history as had the God of Israel. He sovereignly directed the long-term course of events so that His covenant promises to His people would be fulfilled. Also, His fidelity was not temporary, and His power was not limited to a particular country or region. These truths are seen in the Lord Jesus, especially His resurrection from the dead. While Luke's account of the Resurrection includes much of the same factual information as the other Gospels, it contains some different elements as well. For instance, while all the Gospel writers mention the women's visit to the tomb, only Luke relates details of Jesus' encounter with the disciples on the road to Emmaus, which was a village about several miles from Jerusalem (24:13). These two devout followers of the Savior were talking about what had happened to Jesus.

Later that evening, Jesus appeared to His disciples and reminded them that while He was previously with them, He told them how the messianic promises recorded in the Old Testament were ordained by God to be fulfilled. The Law, the Prophets, and the Psalms—the three sections of the Hebrew Scriptures—reveal truths about the Redeemer that had to occur. Luke 24:44 affirms that there is a strong interrelationship between the Old and New Testaments. Succinctly put, the triune God brought the universe into existence; humankind sinned, bringing moral and spiritual corruption to themselves and their world; and now the Godhead has made redemption possible through the atoning work of the Son. The divine plan of redemption began at Calvary, continues even now, and will one day be complete when God creates a new heaven and new earth.

At this point, Jesus opened the minds of the disciples to comprehend the Scriptures (Luke 24:45). While the specific texts are not listed in this verse, it's possible they included the many Old Testament passages appearing elsewhere in the Gospel of Luke and the Book of Acts. The threefold thrust of those prophecies was that the Messiah had to die on the cross (see Pss. 22; 31; 69; 118; Isa. 53), rise from the dead on the third day (see Ps. 16:10; 110:1), and have the good news of salvation heralded to the lost (Luke 24:46; see Matt. 28:19; Mark 13:10). Part of the gospel proclamation included an emphasis on repentance for the forgiveness of sins (Luke 24:47). This Hebrew concept included the idea of turning from wrongdoing as a prelude to experiencing the Father's offer of pardon through faith in the Son. Beginning at Jerusalem (the initial center and focus of the Gospel), the followers of the Savior were to announce the Good News to the nations of the world (see Isa. 49:6; Luke 2:32; Acts 13:47). Acts 2 records how all this got started on the day of Pentecost.

Jesus declared to His followers that they were witnesses of all that had occurred (Luke 24:48). The idea of proclaiming all that happened in connection with the Savior is a key concept in the Book of Acts (see 1:22; 2:32; 3:15; 5:32; 10:39, 41; 13:31;

22:15, 20; 26:16). In 1:8, for instance, the risen Lord told His disciples that they and future believers would testify about Him in Jerusalem, in all Judea and Samaria, and to the farthest regions of the earth. They would not do this alone and in their own strength; rather, the Holy Spirit would empower them for effective Christian service.

In Luke 24:29, Jesus referred to the Spirit as the one whom the Son was sending and whom the Father had previously promised to His people. This divine pledge is rooted in such Old Testament passages as Jeremiah 31:31 and Ezekiel 36:26-27. Also, when John prepared the way for the advent of the Messiah, the prophet declared Jesus would baptize people with the Holy Spirit (Luke 3:16). As the disciples heralded the good news, they helped to fulfill what God had promised to do. Moreover, Jesus pledged to clothe His followers with *power from on high* (24:49), which is a reference to the Holy Spirit. He would enable them to bear much fruit by leading many lost people to put their trust in the Redeemer for salvation.

SUGGESTIONS TO TEACHERS

Newspapers and television commercials have inundated us with photos of baby chicks and announcements of egg hunts. And many people seem to celebrate Easter by wearing a pair of cute bunny ears and munching giant chocolate eggs! Your task in this week's lesson is to refocus the attention of your students on the good news of the risen Lord.

1. THE REALITY OF JESUS' RESURRECTION. At the dedication of the newly built Jerusalem temple, Solomon testified to the uniqueness and power of the living God. Similarly, the earliest followers of the Messiah faithfully declared that the Father had raised the Son from the dead. We are not witnesses to the Resurrection in the same sense as Mary Magdalene, Peter, and the Emmaus disciples. Put differently, we are not *eyewitnesses* of the risen Lord; but we have firsthand reports in the New Testament of those who saw Jesus alive from the dead. By comparing these accounts, we can see why it's much more reasonable to conclude that Jesus did indeed rise than that He did not.

2. THE SIGNIFICANCE OF JESUS' RESURRECTION. Over the centuries, many skeptics have tried to disprove the truth of the Resurrection. Some, such as Josh McDowell and Lee Strobel, concluded that the evidence for the Resurrection is far stronger than the evidence against it. And perhaps most conclusive of all is the reality of Jesus manifesting His resurrection life through us. There is no better news than the Resurrection. It means victory over death. It signifies new life that begins now and goes on for eternity.

3. THE POWER OF JESUS' RESURRECTION. The question for us is the following: What are we doing with this great news? We wouldn't keep the news of the birth of a new child or grandchild to ourselves. Neither would we fail to mention that we'd been promoted at work. Are we telling others of the even greater news that Jesus lives? This might be a good time to read Acts 2 to see how the apostles witnessed to the Resurrection once they were clothed with power from on high. Let's recognize their boldness, sense their excitement, and be in awe of their results. We also have the same Spirit empowering us for faithful and effective Christian service. He will enable us to witness to the reality of the Resurrection with the same fervor.

FOR ADULTS	■ **TOPIC:** Whose Promises Can You Trust?

■ **TOPIC:** Whose Promises Can You Trust?

■ **QUESTIONS:** 1. Who was present in the assembly at the dedication of the Jerusalem temple? 2. Why do you think Solomon proclaimed the uniqueness of Israel's God? 3. What covenant promises had God made to David? 4. What prophecies about the Messiah can be found in the Old Testament? 5. What does it mean to be a witness to the reality of the risen Messiah?

■ **ILLUSTRATIONS:**

A Lost Gospel? Matthew, Mark, Luke, and John comprise the four accepted Gospels of the New Testament. But in a book titled, *The Lost Gospel*, Herb Krosney chronicles how another (nonbiblical) version of the life of Jesus was found. It's called the Gospel of Judas, and there's been an international effort to authenticate, conserve, and translate this ancient papyrus document dating to the second century A.D. It is a Coptic copy of an original Greek manuscript.

In the four Gospels of the New Testament, Judas Iscariot is portrayed as the disciple who betrayed Jesus to the Romans for 30 pieces of silver. But in the 66-page codex, a very different Judas emerges. He is shown to be the Messiah's best friend and favorite disciple, the one whom Jesus asks to betray His identity. Supposedly, doing this will bring about the fulfillment of prophecy, the liberation of Jesus' soul from the body that entraps Him, and the soul's ascension to heaven. This revisionist view of Judas depicts him as enabling all of us to find an inner spark within ourselves that will empower us to attain eternity and immortality.

In 180 A.D., an early church leader named Irenaeus (who lived in the city that is now Lyon, France) wrote a condemnation of the Gospel of Judas. Irenaeus knew from the canonical Gospels that the Lord Jesus, not Judas Iscariot, made the ultimate sacrifice for the sins of humankind. And the Messiah alone fulfills the Old Testament promises of salvation (Luke 24:44).

The Limits of Cancer. When my friend's mother was diagnosed with cancer, we were given this poem that tells about spiritual victory in the risen Lord that can be found even in the worst situations. We have since discovered that it was written by Dan Richardson, a believer who, like my friend's mother, eventually lost his battle with cancer. But that did not daunt their spirits or change their eternal destiny with the Lord.

"Cancer is so limited! It cannot cripple love; it cannot shatter hope; it cannot corrode faith; it cannot eat away peace; it cannot destroy confidence; it cannot kill friendship; it cannot shut out memories; it cannot silence courage; it cannot invade the soul; it cannot reduce eternal life; it cannot quench the Spirit; it cannot lessen the power of the Resurrection."

Afraid of God. The picture some people have of God is similar to the view that the German subjects had of their emperor, Frederick William. Legend has it that he was once out walking in a town when he was seen by one of the residents. To his surprise, the man tried to slip quickly inside a doorway in order not to be seen. The emperor roared, "Where are you going?" The man, realizing that he had been spotted, timidly said that he was going into the house. "Your house?" demanded the ruler. Quaking, the man said it wasn't. "Then why are you trying to enter it? You're a burglar, aren't you?"

The man feared that he would be seized and jailed. Deciding that his only hope was to tell the truth, he stammered, "I was trying to avoid you, your majesty." The emperor bristled. "Avoid me. Why?" "Because I fear you, your majesty," replied the now-shaken man. Frederick then grabbed his heavy stick and struck the citizen on the chest, shouting, "You are not supposed to fear me. You are supposed to love me! Now love me, you swine. Love me!"

Thankfully, this isn't God's way. In fulfillment of the Old Testament messianic prophecies, Jesus rose from the dead to provide salvation for those who are alienated and separated from Him because of sin.

FOR YOUTH

■ **TOPIC:** God Keeps Promises

■ **QUESTIONS:** 1. What was the significance of Solomon spreading out his hands toward heaven? 2. How had God remained faithful to His covenant promises? 3. What did Solomon request in his prayer? 4. To whom was repentance and forgiveness of sins to be proclaimed? 5. Why did Jesus emphasize the provision of the Holy Spirit to His disciples?

■ **ILLUSTRATIONS:**

Lives Again. Her remains were excavated by the Association for the Preservation of Virginia Antiquities, the group that owns the Jamestown site. She was discovered in the fall of 1998 by Jamie May as part of an on-going archaeological dig at the historical site. This first lady was Mistress Forrest, the wife of Thomas Forrest. She had come to Jamestown in October 1608, from England. She was accompanied by her maid, Anne Burras. Mistress Forrest died shortly after arriving and was buried naked in an elaborate pinewood coffin. (In those days clothing was considered too valuable to bury with the dead.)

The remains of Mistress Forrest were taken to the Smithsonian Institution for careful examination. Painstaking analysis determined her diet to have been wheat rather than corn. It was also discovered that she was a Caucasian, four feet eight inches tall, and about 35 years old (quite old for that time!). Even her facial features were reconstructed using modern technology. But despite this, Mistress Forrest remains a lifeless mass.

Centuries earlier, others trooped to a burial site to look at the remains of someone who had meant so much to them. His life and words had been indelibly inscribed into their lives. However, instead of gazing at a corpse, they met the risen Lord. In fulfillment of what God promised in the Old Testament, they discovered that Jesus lives forevermore!

A New Beginning. Radical turnarounds command attention. When people known for profanity and immorality, for example, suddenly act differently, others want to know why. Consider the young man who was addicted to drugs. When his friends found out he had successfully stopped his addictive behavior, they wanted to know how it was possible. This gave him an opportunity to tell them how Christ's resurrection had made a difference in his life.

The first-century Christians also experienced a new beginning. Jesus' disciples had forsaken Him when He was arrested and crucified. But after Christ's resurrection, they publicly proclaimed Him as Lord and told people to repent. Jesus can also transform the lives of the students in your class. He can give them the courage to tell their families and friends that He has risen from the dead, just as God promised.

Surprise! A two-year-old girl could hardly wait for Easter to come. She had a new dress to wear and new shoes to go with it, but her father wondered whether she knew the true meaning of the holiday.

"Kara," he asked, "do you know what Easter means?"

"Yes, I do," she smiled.

"What does it mean then?"

With a smile on her face and her arms raised, she cried, "Surprise!"

What better word could there be to describe Easter? No one expected a crucified person to rise from the dead. Even the religious leaders, who put a guard on the tomb, did not do so because they expected a resurrection. The women came that morning to anoint a body, not find an empty grave. No one expected Jesus to be alive, but He was—and He still is! *Surprise!*

JOSIAH RENEWS THE COVENANT

BACKGROUND SCRIPTURE: 2 Chronicles 34
DEVOTIONAL READING: Psalm 119:25–40

KEY VERSE: The king stood in his place, and made a covenant before the LORD, to walk after the LORD, and to keep his commandments, and his testimonies, and his statutes, with all his heart, and with all his soul, to perform the words of the covenant which are written in this book. 2 Chronicles 34:21.

KING JAMES VERSION

2 CHRONICLES 34:15 And Hilkiah answered and said to Shaphan the scribe, I have found the book of the law in the house of the LORD. And Hilkiah delivered the book to Shaphan. . . . 18 Then Shaphan the scribe told the king, saying, Hilkiah the priest hath given me a book. And Shaphan read it before the king. 19 And it came to pass, when the king had heard the words of the law, that he rent his clothes. . . . 25 Because they have forsaken me, and have burned incense unto other gods, that they might provoke me to anger with all the works of their hands; therefore my wrath shall be poured out upon this place, and shall not be quenched. 26 And as for the king of Judah, who sent you to enquire of the LORD, so shall ye say unto him, Thus saith the LORD God of Israel concerning the words which thou hast heard; 27 Because thine heart was tender, and thou didst humble thyself before God, when thou heardest his words against this place, and against the inhabitants thereof, and humbledst thyself before me, and didst rend thy clothes, and weep before me; I have even heard thee also, saith the LORD. . . .

29 Then the king sent and gathered together all the elders of Judah and Jerusalem. . . . 31 And the king stood in his place, and made a covenant before the LORD, to walk after the LORD, and to keep his commandments, and his testimonies, and his statutes, with all his heart, and with all his soul, to perform the words of the covenant which are written in this book. 32 And he caused all that were present in Jerusalem and Benjamin to stand to it. And the inhabitants of Jerusalem did according to the covenant of God, the God of their fathers. 33 And Josiah took away all the abominations out of all the countries that pertained to the children of Israel, and made all that were present in Israel to serve, even to serve the LORD their God. And all his days they departed not from following the LORD, the God of their fathers.

NEW REVISED STANDARD VERSION

2 CHRONICLES 34:15 Hilkiah said to the secretary Shaphan, "I have found the book of the law in the house of the LORD"; and Hilkiah gave the book to Shaphan. . . . 18 The secretary Shaphan informed the king, "The priest Hilkiah has given me a book." Shaphan then read it aloud to the king.

19 When the king heard the words of the law he tore his clothes. . . .

25 "Because they have forsaken me and have made offerings to other gods, so that they have provoked me to anger with all the works of their hands, my wrath will be poured out on this place and will not be quenched. 26 But as to the king of Judah, who sent you to inquire of the LORD, thus shall you say to him: Thus says the LORD, the God of Israel: Regarding the words that you have heard, 27 because your heart was penitent and you humbled yourself before God when you heard his words against this place and its inhabitants, and you have humbled yourself before me, and have torn your clothes and wept before me, I also have heard you, says the LORD." . . .

29 Then the king sent word and gathered together all the elders of Judah and Jerusalem. . . . 31 The king stood in his place and made a covenant before the LORD, to follow the LORD, keeping his commandments, his decrees, and his statutes, with all his heart and all his soul, to perform the words of the covenant that were written in this book. 32 Then he made all who were present in Jerusalem and in Benjamin pledge themselves to it. And the inhabitants of Jerusalem acted according to the covenant of God, the God of their ancestors. 33 Josiah took away all the abominations from all the territory that belonged to the people of Israel, and made all who were in Israel worship the LORD their God. All his days they did not turn away from following the LORD the God of their ancestors.

5

Monday, March 24	Psalm 119:25-32	*Revive Me*
Tuesday, March 25	2 Chronicles 34:1-7	*Josiah Seeks God's Way*
Wednesday, March 26	2 Chronicles 34:8-18	*A Big Discovery*
Thursday, March 27	2 Chronicles 34:19-21	*Josiah Repents*
Friday, March 28	2 Chronicles 34:22-28	*God Hears Josiah*
Saturday, March 29	2 Chronicles 34:29-33	*The Covenant Renewed*
Sunday, March 30	Psalm 119:33-40	*Teach Me*

BACKGROUND

Josiah, one of Judah's most godly kings, was only eight years old when he began to reign in 640 B.C. About 82 years had passed since the northern kingdom of Israel had been conquered by Assyria in 722 B.C. Sixty-one years had elapsed since the Lord had answered King Hezekiah's prayers by destroying the Assyrian army threatening Jerusalem in 701 B.C. Josiah enjoyed a long reign of 31 years, but simple arithmetic shows he died at age 39 (2 Chron. 34:1). A great deal happened in the life of this king, whose tragic end prefigured the fate of the nation.

Josiah's rule followed the short, two-year reign of his father, Amon (33:21). King Amon followed the earlier example of Manasseh by worshiping and sacrificing to idols (33:22). Perhaps his evil example caused some of his own officials to assassinate him after only a couple of years (33:23-24). The Chronicler recorded that Josiah began to seek the Lord in the eighth year of his rule, when he was only 16, and that he was destroying idols and shrines in the Jerusalem area by his twelfth year on the throne (34:3-4). Soon his zeal for destroying idols reached even into the northern territory that had been Israel (34:6-7).

In the eighteenth year of Josiah's reign (622 B.C.), when he was 26, he began to repair the Jerusalem temple (34:8). He delegated the task to three prominent officials in his royal court: Shaphan, who served as a scribe and treasurer to the king, and would have been among one of the highest ranking civil servants; Maaseiah, the governor of Jerusalem; and Joah, the historian who kept the government records. These three men went to Hilkiah, the high priest, and gave him the money that had been collected by the Levites who served as gatekeepers at the Jerusalem shrine (34:9).

The money (literally, silver) was entrusted to the men assigned to supervise the restoration efforts. With some of the money, they paid the workers who did the repairs and renovation (34:10). The remainder of the money was given to the carpenters and masons to purchase chiseled stone for the walls and timber for the rafters and beams, all of which had fallen into disrepair (34:11). Some Levites were put in charge of the laborers of the various trades, while other Levites assisted as secretaries, scribes, and gatekeepers. Together, they ensured that the laborers remained honest and diligent in their work (34:12-13).

Second Chronicles 34:9 states that people from both Judah and Israel contributed money for the restoration effort. When workers removed the money that had been brought to the temple, Hilkiah the high priest discovered what was called the *book of the law of the LORD given through Moses* (34:14). Later, it is called the *book of the covenant* (34:30). That would indicate the scroll contained the laws that the Lord had given to Moses, particularly those recorded in Exodus 19—24; however, the curses Josiah was about to hear seem to have come from Leviticus and Deuteronomy. Thus, what was likely found was either all three books or Deuteronomy, which contains a retelling of the events of the Exodus and a reiteration of God's instructions through Moses.

Hilkiah informed Shaphan about the discovery of the law scroll and gave it to the court secretary (2 Chron. 34:15). Shaphan in turn reported to the king that his officials were doing everything that had been assigned to them (34:16). The scribe specifically mentioned the money that was collected at the temple and had been entrusted to the supervisors of the construction foremen undertaking the repairs (34:17). Shaphan told Josiah that Hilkiah the high priest had given him a scroll containing the Mosaic law. Then the scribe read it out loud before the king (34:18). When Josiah heard what was written in God's Word, he tore his clothes as a sign of mourning and repentance (34:19). The king's great concern suggests he probably heard a passage from the Mosaic law dealing with how God would judge the Israelites if they did not obey His Word. Deuteronomy 28:15-68 is one such passage. In it Moses warned Israel about all the dire consequences that would come upon the people if they rejected the Lord and turned to idolatry.

Josiah next summoned several of his trusted officials and related his concerns. The king ordered the priest and his company to seek an oracle from the Lord about the future of kingdom, including the remnant in Israel and Judah. Josiah figured out that his ancestors had disobeyed the Lord and violated His commands. They thus deserved God's righteous judgment (2 Chron. 34:20-21). Based on what Josiah had heard, he could discern how far the Lord's people had fallen from His holy standards. Judah's king did not offer any excuses. He could see that God's wrath had resulted in the destruction of the northern kingdom and the dispersion of its people. Josiah sensed that the same end would befall Judah. Therefore, he confessed and sought God's will.

Hilkiah and some other court officials left right away and went to talk with Huldah, a previously unnamed prophetess. She was the wife of a court official, Shallum, the keeper of the wardrobe (34:22). She may also have been the prophet Jeremiah's aunt, since Jeremiah had an uncle named Shallum (see Jer. 32:7). Huldah lived in the Second District of Jerusalem, probably a new working-class suburb west of the temple area and inside new walls added by Hezekiah and Manasseh (see 2 Chron. 32:5; 33:14). Josiah wanted to know the implications of the scroll containing the law for himself, for the people, and for the existence of Judah (34:23). Huldah responded first about the people and the place. The prophetess revealed that the Lord would punish Judah, its capital, and its people in accordance with all the curses recorded on the scroll that had been read aloud to Judah's king (34:24). These calamities would happen because the people abandoned the Lord to burn incense and offer sacrifices to pagan deities. God was angered by all the idols they had made. His wrath was so intense that it would blaze against Jerusalem and its temple and not be extinguished (34:25).

Next, Huldah spoke in detail about the future of Judah's king. The prophetess explained that her words were not her own; rather, they came from *the LORD God of Israel* (34:26). Yahweh had taken note of Josiah's tender spirit and responsive heart. In particular, when the king heard that Judah and its people would be completely wiped out, he humbled himself, expressed his despair by tearing his clothes, and wept in repentance before the Lord (34:27). Huldah declared that because Josiah was genuinely distressed by what he had heard, the Lord would not bring His promised judgment until after the king had died and was buried in peace. The officials who received Huldah's message reported what she had said to Josiah (34:28). Since he would meet his death in a losing battle against Egypt, it's appropriate to ask in what sense he was buried in peace. When he died, he was at peace with God and in harmony with his subjects, who loved him and honored him in death (see 2 Kings 23:30; 2 Chron. 35:24-25). Also, his kingdom was still secure and intact.

The king summoned the leaders of the nation and the capital city to lead the populace of Judah in renewing their long-neglected and forgotten covenant with the Lord (2 Chron. 34:29). Josiah then led a royal procession the short distance from the palace to the temple. This group included representatives from all the inhabitants of Judah, the residents of Jerusalem, the priests, and the Levites. In fact, the solemn gathering included the least important to the most important people of the day, for the king knew that spiritual reform had to change everyone (34:30). Josiah's intent was to review the stipulations of the law and urge the leaders and people of Judah to heed them.

The temple was the place where God had pledged to show His presence among His people. It was thus a fitting spot for the king and his subjects to meet and rededicate themselves in service to God. Interestingly, Josiah himself—not Hilkiah the priest, Shaphan the scribe, or Jeremiah the prophet (who served as a spokesperson for God at this time)—read the Book of the Covenant to the assembly. Whether the Book of the Covenant was the same as the Book of the Law (see 34:14-15) or just the part of it detailing the covenant and its attendant blessings and curses is unclear. If the Book of the Law was Deuteronomy, the Book of the Covenant may have been all or parts of chapters 5 through 28. Exodus 24:7 attaches the title *book of the covenant* to Exodus 20—23, a concise statement of Israel's covenant with the Lord.

Josiah and those with him specifically pledged to follow the Lord with all their heart and soul, that is, to observe every aspect of the Mosaic law (2 Chron. 34:31).

The king, along with all the people living in Jerusalem and in the territory of Benjamin, pledged to do this (34:32). In this way, Josiah followed in the steps of Moses (see Exod. 24:3-8), Joshua (see Josh. 24), Samuel (see 1 Sam. 11:14—12:25), and Jehoiada the priest (see 2 Kings 11:17). Josiah also set the stage for later reformers, such as Ezra and Nehemiah (see Neh. 9—10).

In such a huge gathering, there would be tremendous pressure to conform. No one could see into the hearts of others. No one could tell who was sincere and who was hypocritical. Promises would be easy to make in the heat of the moment, but hard to keep when the lure of idolatry beckoned. Nevertheless, Josiah did all he could to bring God's laws into the conscious awareness of the people. The portion of Scripture discovered in the temple was the spark that brought the king and his people to repentance, confession, and commitment to follow the Lord. For the rest of Josiah's rule as king, the people did not turn away from the God of their ancestors (2 Chron. 34:33).

SUGGESTIONS TO TEACHERS

Josiah is a wonderful example of the impact a lifetime of commitment to God and His Word can have on other people. Josiah influenced an entire nation for God and gave them a new beginning of godliness and hope.

1. A HEART FOR GOD. Josiah did not suddenly become a reformer as an adult. His interest in the Lord began during his adolescent years. Josiah lived righteously and used his authority to promote uprightness in his realm. Your students need to realize that long-term spiritual success grows from a heart that has long been interested in God.

2. THIRST FOR GOD'S WORD. When the book of the law was found in the temple, there was never a question in Josiah's mind about whether this occurrence was a good thing. The king wanted to know what the law said and what to do about it. He was horrified to find out how far from the terms of the covenant his nation was living. We also need to respond readily to God's Word. We shouldn't look for loopholes to avoid doing what the Lord wants.

3. SHARING GOD'S WORD. Josiah did not keep God's law to himself. Instead, he eagerly shared it with everyone in his kingdom, for it concerned them. The fact that much of the message was not pleasant did not deter the young king. We need to share the truth of God's Word with others, too. Divine truth is what will change people's lives. We should take advantage of opportunities to use the Bible to help our family and friends deal with the struggles of life.

4. COMMITMENT TO GOD'S WORD. Josiah's reforms took shape when he set an example, and the nation followed it by promising to obey the Lord's covenant. By the time Josiah asked this commitment of his people, he had modeled obedience for a decade. His appeal and example had credibility. The commitment to God's Word that we model will impact our families and our friends. What we model gives credibility to the verbal appeals we make to others in our witness for Christ.

5. OBEDIENCE TO GOD'S WORD. The change in Judah that began with the covenant ceremony in the temple proved to be somewhat genuine and lasting. People in Jerusalem and around the countryside obeyed the law of the Lord day after day and year after year throughout the lifetime of King Josiah. The new beginnings that God gives to us or to those with whom we share Christ start with commitment, but prove themselves real through our obedience over our lifetimes.

FOR ADULTS

■ **TOPIC:** Mending a Broken Relationship

■ **QUESTIONS:** 1. What was the Book of the Law that was found in the temple? 2. Why did Josiah's officials think it was important to tell him about the discovery of the scroll? 3. Why did the Lord plan to judge His people? 4. How had Josiah humbled himself before the Lord? 5. Why did the king think it was important to renew the covenant?

■ **ILLUSTRATIONS:**

The Cost of Renewing Relationships. The adage is true. What we don't know can hurt us. This even applies to our spiritual renewal. The latest edition of *Merriam-Webster's Collegiate Dictionary* says that renewal involves restoring something to freshness or vigor. The process is so thorough that what had become deteriorated is now new.

How can adults experience spiritual renewal, especially in their relationship with God and His people? As this week's lesson indicates, it requires specific, costly steps. This is especially true in terms of the energy spent, the time invested, and the personal sacrifices made. Often, both individual and group activities will help foster spiritual renewal and encourage one to make difficult choices and tough decisions.

Most Christians who have sought to renew their relationship with God would agree that the change, though in their best interests, was not easy. They also would concur that the benefits they obtained were worth the effort.

Wholehearted Obedience. One bitter winter night a traveler on the American frontier came to a broad river that he had to cross to reach the nearest settlement. If he failed, he would freeze to death.

The traveler stepped onto the ice and thought he heard it groan. He got down on his hands and knees to distribute his weight better and started crawling across. Suddenly the man raised his head. He heard singing coming from the wooded bank behind him. Out of the trees burst a horse-drawn sledge loaded with coal. The singing collier did not even see the crawling traveler as he sped past him on the ice. Sheepishly, the man scrambled to his feet and hurried across the river.

Some people obey God as though they are afraid His commands can't support them. In contrast to this way of thinking, Josiah wholeheartedly obeyed God. The promises and commands of the Lord are steadfast and dependable. We thus can obey them with all our hearts.

Landmark Bill. Correspondent Reed Abelson of *The New York Times* reported that in early April 2006, Massachusetts "enacted legislation to provide health insurance for virtually every citizen within the next three years." The landmark bill is the first in the United States requiring "people to buy health insurance if they don't get it at work." The legislation enjoys support from representatives across the political spectrum. Indeed, it was approved by "a Republican governor and a Democrat-dominated House." House Speaker Sal DiMasi compared "the new health law to the Mayflower Compact," which the pilgrims created after landing "on Plymouth Rock in 1620." He noted that the intent of the colonists was to forge a "community of people where laws were made for the common wealth." He says "the new law reflects that original idea."

The notion of a community of people existing in a covenantal relationship mirrors what we find in this week's lesson. Josiah led the officials and populace of Judah to renew their commitment to the Lord and each other, as expressed in the Mosaic Covenant. Then, as now, they realized that a community is benefited most when the basic human needs of everyone are met.

FOR YOUTH

■ **TOPIC:** Mending a Broken Relationship
■ **QUESTIONS:** 1. What characterized the reign of Josiah? 2. Why did the king tear his robes? 3. What were God's people guilty of doing? 4. Why would God let Josiah be buried in peace? 5. Who joined with Josiah to renew the covenant?

■ **ILLUSTRATIONS:**
Relationships Require Commitment. "When I was a boy, my father, a baker, introduced me to the wonders of song," tenor Luciano Pavarotti relates. "He urged me to work very hard to develop my voice. Arrigo Pola, a professional tenor in my hometown of Modena, Italy, took me as a pupil. I also enrolled in a teacher's college. On graduating, I asked my father, 'Shall I be a teacher or a singer?'

"'Luciano,' my father replied, 'if you try to sit on two chairs, you will fall between them. For life, you must choose one chair.' I chose one. It took seven years of study and frustration before I made my first professional appearance. It took another seven to reach the Metropolitan Opera. And now I think whether it's laying bricks, writing a book—whatever we choose—we should give ourselves to it. Commitment: that's the key. Choose one chair." This bit of advice applies even to successfully mending broken relationships. It requires undivided commitment.

The Value of God-Honoring Leaders. Mark R. Watkinson was a minister of the First Baptist Church in Ridleyville, Pennsylvania, and as the shepherd of a dynamic Christian congregation, he was well respected by his flock. Nevertheless, Watkinson did not restrict his influence to his church. Because the struggle between the North and the South was becoming increasingly hostile and religious sentiment was high, Watkinson deeply felt that someone or something had to turn the people's attention back to their Creator.

During this tense political climate in 1861, Watkinson believed the nation needed to be reminded of its spiritual roots. Thus, he wrote a letter to the secretary of the treasury, Salmon P. Chase, noting that the United States coinage omitted any reference to God. Watkinson suggested that a religious motto be inscribed on American coins that would indicate the nation's faith in God.

President Abraham Lincoln's administration enthusiastically welcomed Watkinson's advice, and subsequently, a number of mottoes were considered, including *God Our Trust, Our God and Our Country,* as well as Watkinson's own *God, Liberty, Law.* Finally, Secretary Chase selected *In God We Trust,* which has been printed on United States coinage and currency ever since.

Because of the godly action of one Christian leader, verbal homage is constantly visible to the people of the United States. Indeed, most Americans hold in their hands this sacred statement on a daily basis. Regardless of whether a person subscribes to this creed, these words still boldly indicate how every true Christian should live his or her life.

Leading God's people is not an easy task. Josiah kept the people on God's path, but later they wandered off it. If we are to stay on the Lord's path, we must first have God-honoring leaders like Josiah, and then we must do our part by following that leader and being a good example ourselves.

God's Instructions Are Clear. Pastor Tim, the minister in the novel, *A New Song,* finds himself taking care of the three-year-old son of a hospitalized parishioner. The boy wants to watch videos, but Pastor Tim doesn't have the appropriate device. He considers buying one to pacify the toddler and wonders, "'Do we just plug it in?' He'd never been on friendly terms with high technology, which was always accompanied by manuals printed in Croatian."

When Josiah heard the law of the Lord, God's instructions were clear, not like stereo instructions and not in an unknown language. What the Lord wants from us today—both with respect to Him and in our dealings with others—is also clear, especially if we read and obey His Word.

DANIEL KEEPS COVENANT IN A FOREIGN LAND

BACKGROUND SCRIPTURE: Daniel 1
DEVOTIONAL READING: Psalm 141:1-4

KEY VERSE: But Daniel purposed in his heart that he would not defile himself with the portion of the king's meat, nor with the wine which he drank: therefore he requested of the prince of the eunuchs that he might not defile himself. Daniel 1:8.

KING JAMES VERSION

DANIEL 1:8 But Daniel purposed in his heart that he would not defile himself with the portion of the king's meat, nor with the wine which he drank: therefore he requested of the prince of the eunuchs that he might not defile himself. 9 Now God had brought Daniel into favour and tender love with the prince of the eunuchs. 10 And the prince of the eunuchs said unto Daniel, I fear my lord the king, who hath appointed your meat and your drink: for why should he see your faces worse liking than the children which are of your sort? then shall ye make me endanger my head to the king. 11 Then said Daniel to Melzar, whom the prince of the eunuchs had set over Daniel, Hananiah, Mishael, and Azariah, 12 Prove thy servants, I beseech thee, ten days; and let them give us pulse to eat, and water to drink. 13 Then let our countenances be looked upon before thee, and the countenance of the children that eat of the portion of the king's meat: and as thou seest, deal with thy servants. 14 So he consented to them in this matter, and proved them ten days. 15 And at the end of ten days their countenances appeared fairer and fatter in flesh than all the children which did eat the portion of the king's meat. 16 Thus Melzar took away the portion of their meat, and the wine that they should drink; and gave them pulse.

17 As for these four children, God gave them knowledge and skill in all learning and wisdom: and Daniel had understanding in all visions and dreams. 18 Now at the end of the days that the king had said he should bring them in, then the prince of the eunuchs brought them in before Nebuchadnezzar. 19 And the king communed with them; and among them all was found none like Daniel, Hananiah, Mishael, and Azariah: therefore stood they before the king. 20 And in all matters of wisdom and understanding, that the king enquired of them, he found them ten times better than all the magicians and astrologers that were in all his realm. 21 And Daniel continued even unto the first year of king Cyrus.

NEW REVISED STANDARD VERSION

DANIEL 1:8 But Daniel resolved that he would not defile himself with the royal rations of food and wine; so he asked the palace master to allow him not to defile himself. 9 Now God allowed Daniel to receive favor and compassion from the palace master. 10 The palace master said to Daniel, "I am afraid of my lord the king; he has appointed your food and your drink. If he should see you in poorer condition than the other young men of your own age, you would endanger my head with the king." 11 Then Daniel asked the guard whom the palace master had appointed over Daniel, Hananiah, Mishael, and Azariah: 12 "Please test your servants for ten days. Let us be given vegetables to eat and water to drink. 13 You can then compare our appearance with the appearance of the young men who eat the royal rations, and deal with your servants according to what you observe." 14 So he agreed to this proposal and tested them for ten days. 15 At the end of ten days it was observed that they appeared better and fatter than all the young men who had been eating the royal rations. 16 So the guard continued to withdraw their royal rations and the wine they were to drink, and gave them vegetables. 17 To these four young men God gave knowledge and skill in every aspect of literature and wisdom; Daniel also had insight into all visions and dreams.

18 At the end of the time that the king had set for them to be brought in, the palace master brought them into the presence of Nebuchadnezzar, 19 and the king spoke with them. And among them all, no one was found to compare with Daniel, Hananiah, Mishael, and Azariah; therefore they were stationed in the king's court. 20 In every matter of wisdom and understanding concerning which the king inquired of them, he found them ten times better than all the magicians and enchanters in his whole kingdom.

6

Monday, March 31	Psalm 141:1-4	*A Prayer for God's Support*
Tuesday, April 1	Daniel 1:1-2	*God's House Besieged*
Wednesday, April 2	Daniel 1:3-7	*The King's Plan*
Thursday, April 3	Daniel 1:8-10	*Daniel's Resolution*
Friday, April 4	Daniel 1:11-14	*The Ten-Day Test*
Saturday, April 5	Daniel 1:15-17	*Four Fine Young Men*
Sunday, April 6	Daniel 1:18-21	*Tested and True*

BACKGROUND

The Book of Daniel is simply titled in the Hebrew Bible, "Daniel," meaning "my judge is God." The reason for the name is twofold. First, Daniel is the chief character in the events unfolded. Second, it was Hebrew custom to identify a book by the name of the author. The author of this book is identified as *Daniel* (Dan. 12:4). He was born in the middle of good King Josiah's reign, and grew up under his religious reforms (see 2 Kings 22-23). During that time, Daniel probably heard Jeremiah, whom he later quoted (see Dan. 9:2).

When Judah fell and Josiah was killed in a battle with Egypt in 609 B.C., Josiah's eldest son, Jehoiakim, was made king of Judah by Pharaoh Neco. For four years, Judah was an Egyptian vassal nation until Nebuchadnezzar defeated Egypt at Carchemish in 605 B.C. That same year, the Babylonian king swept into Judah and captured Jerusalem (1:1). He had Jehoiakim, who was in the third year of his reign, carried off to Babylon. Nebuchadnezzar also ordered treasures from the temple in Jerusalem sent back home and placed in *the house of his god* (1:2). The *god* referred to was probably the chief Babylonian god, Bel, also called Marduk.

The majority of the greatest Middle Eastern empires of ancient times routinely deported or dispersed large segments of the population of conquered nations. Often, deportees from the upper classes were incorporated into the population of the ruling empire. This was done for a variety of reasons. First, it nourished the loyalty of subject peoples as they were gradually absorbed into the new culture. Second, it improved the conquering nation's pool of upper-class workers. Finally, and perhaps most importantly, it denied the lower-class citizens left behind in conquered countries the leadership of those most likely to plot rebellion.

NOTES ON THE PRINTED TEXT

In keeping with a common practice of the time, Nebuchadnezzar had the best educated, most attractive, most capable and talented among Judah's citizens sent back to Babylon. In essence, only the poorer, uneducated people were left behind to populate conquered lands (see 2 Kings 24:14). Included among those deported from Judah to Babylon were Daniel, Hananiah, Mishael, and Azariah (Dan. 1:3, 6). Most likely, they would have been about 14 or 15 years of age at this time. Nebuchadnezzar commanded Ashpenaz, who was in charge of the king's court officials, to bring in some of the Israelites. The king specifically wanted to see members of Judah's royal family and others who came from the ranks of nobility (1:3). Nebuchadnezzar was obviously looking for the "cream of the crop" (so to speak) among the captives. He wanted young men of such physical and mental superiority that they would be qualified for service to him (1:4).

Ashpenaz was charged with teaching the young men the Babylonian language (Akkadian) and literature. The latter was written in cuneiform (a complex, syllabic writing system made up of wedge-shaped characters) and mainly engraved on clay tablets. The intent was to assimilate the captives into their new culture. In addition to this, they were to undergo an intensive, three-year study program to prepare them for royal service. The course of study most likely included mathematics, history, astronomy, astrology, agriculture, architecture, law, and magic.

During this time, the young men would receive food and wine rations directly from the table of the king (1:5). But because Daniel was certain the monarch's provisions would bring ritual uncleanness, he made up his mind not to partake of them. Daniel's concern undoubtedly centered on the realization that the king's food was not prepared in compliance with the law of Moses. Even the simple fact that it was prepared by Gentiles rendered it unclean. The king's diet included pork and horseflesh, which were forbidden by the Mosaic law (see Lev. 11; Deut. 14). Furthermore, the Gentile monarch's food and wine would have been offered to Babylonian gods before they reached his table. Consuming anything offered to pagan deities was strictly forbidden in Exodus 34:15.

Accordingly, Daniel resolved not to defile himself by breaking the Mosaic law. The word translated *purposed* (Dan. 1:8) denotes a determined, committed stand. When Daniel took this position, it was simply the natural result of a life-long pledge to be obedient to God's will in every situation. With boldness and courage, Daniel asked Ashpenaz for permission not to eat the king's delicacies or drink his wine. Evidently, Daniel's three companions shared his resoluteness and made the same commitment as well. From this it is clear that the exceptional intelligence and physical appearance of the four young men from Judah were more than matched by their fidelity to God and devotion to divine principles.

Both Daniel 1:8 and 9 contain a phrase that can be rendered as "the commander of the officials" or "the chief of the eunuchs." The earliest-known eunuchs lived in Mesopotamia, where they worked as servants in the women's quarters of the royal household. They could also serve as palace or government officials, even generals. They were castrated in the belief that this would make them more compliant to their superiors. While the Hebrew term for "eunuch" appears 47 times in the Old Testament, it is used in the technical sense of a castrated man on only 28 of those occasions. The rest of the time, it appears to be used more broadly to refer to an official representative of the king. Its use in Daniel is probably meant to emphasize the official capacity of those who cared for Daniel, rather than their physical state.

As 1:3 states, Ashpenaz was in charge of the court officials. According to 1:9, God caused the overseer to be sympathetic to Daniel. Despite the respect, kindness, and compassion of Ashpenaz, he was afraid of violating the edict of his master, the king. Nebuchadnezzar had assigned the trainees a daily ration from his royal delicacies and from the wine he himself drank (1:5). Ashpenaz realized the monarch would hold him responsible if Daniel and his three Israelite associates looked malnourished in comparison to the other young men their age. The chief official also knew he would be decapitated for neglecting his duties (1:10).

Since Daniel got nowhere with Ashpenaz, the young Israelite captive turned his attention to the guardian or warden placed over him by the chief official (1:11). The petition was for the guardian to put Daniel and his friends on a 10-day trial diet. In the Old Testament, the number 10 was sometimes used as an ideal figure to denote completeness. Daniel proposed that the four be given nothing but vegetables to eat and water to drink (1:12). The Hebrew word rendered *pulse* meant "that which grows from sown seed." Thus, grains, bread made from grain, and even fruit would also have been included. Since no plants were designated unclean by the law of Moses, there was no danger of ceremonial defilement with this diet.

At the end of 10 days, the warden could compare the appearance of the test subjects with that of the young men who were eating the royal delicacies. Based on what the guardian saw, he would decide what to do with Daniel and his friends (1:13). The warden agreed to Daniel's proposal (1:14). Perhaps the guardian was reassured by Daniel's confidence that the Jews would fare better on the vegetarian diet than those who ate the king's food. In any case, the warden probably reasoned that 10 days was not enough time for the health of the four youths to suffer any permanent damage. At first, Ashpenaz worried that Daniel and his friends would become pale and thin compared to the other youths their age (1:10); but at the end of the 10 days, the four looked healthier in appearance and their bodies looked better nourished than the rest of the young men, who had been eating the royal delicacies (1:15). So after that, the warden removed the rich foods and wines from their diet and instead gave them only vegetables to eat (1:16).

While Daniel and his three friends were being groomed for service in the royal court, God was preparing them for service to Him and to His people. The Lord gave the four Israelites *knowledge and skill* (1:17). They had a special ability to reason clearly and logically, and to approach any subject with insight and discernment. Under royal tutelage and with divine assistance, the four youths excelled in a wide range of subjects in the arts and sciences. Daniel, however, surpassed all the other students in a special field. God gave him insight into all kinds of dreams and visions.

At the conclusion of the three-year educational program, Ashpenaz brought all the court trainees, including Daniel, Hananiah, Mishael, and Azariah, before the king for a final interview (1:18). When the Babylonian monarch spoke with the graduates, he discovered that none of the others were as outstanding as the four Israelite captives. Because they impressed him so much, Nebuchadnezzar appointed them to serve among his staff of advisers in his royal court (1:19). The Babylonian king found these four godly young men not only to be the best and brightest among the trainees, but also *ten times better* (1:20) than any of the magicians and enchanters throughout his empire. The phrase *ten times* was an expression in the Old Testament meaning "many times" (see Gen. 31:7; Num. 14:22; Job 19:3).

Daniel, Hananiah, Mishael, and Azariah achieved prominence even though forced to live in a foreign land and culture. They honored God by applying themselves to their studies and striving for excellence in everything they did. They honored Him most, however, by their dedicated prayer, unwavering trust, and steadfast loyalty to godly convictions. Daniel's service in the royal court continued until Cyrus overthrew the Babylonian empire in 539 B.C. (1:21). Other kings would come and go between Nebuchadnezzar and Cyrus; but it mattered little to Daniel which earthly monarch he was compelled to serve. His allegiance was to the King of all the earth. To God alone would Daniel kneel in prayer, bow in worship, and look for wisdom and guidance.

SUGGESTIONS TO TEACHERS

Although the king's servant commanded Daniel to eat food forbidden under the Mosaic law, he found a way to remain obedient to God. As Christians, we often find ourselves in complex situations that make it difficult for us to know how to be faithful to God. Yet we must obey Him, especially if we wish to please Him and live virtuously.

1. THE VALUE OF DISCERNMENT. The four Israelite youths knew exactly what was wrong with eating the king's food. Most likely, they learned this from pious parents (Deut. 6:4-9). Resisting temptation is easier and more effective if our principles are established ahead of time. The very moment at which temptation presents itself is a poor time to take a crash course in ethics.

2. THE COURAGE OF CONVICTION. Daniel and his friends were not afraid to speak up when their principles were challenged. But it was more than just talk. Their refusal to eat the king's food could have cost them their lives. The same courage of conviction was revealed later in a fiery furnace and a den of lions.

3. THE POWER OF PERSEVERANCE. Daniel and his companions were determined to overcome any obstacle in order to follow God. With respect and humility, Daniel presented his request to Ashpenaz that he not be made to defile himself with the king's food. But when Ashpenaz refused, Daniel, in quiet persistence, went to the guard and proposed a test that was both reasonable and feasible.

4. THE NEED FOR DIVINE WISDOM. Many Christians seem to believe that God has called them to be either meek and mild milquetoasts, or loud, obnoxious, "in your face" witnesses for Christ. Neither approach seems to be very effective. God wants us to hold to our convictions with courage, and to witness for Him with love, humility, and a healthy dose of common sense. The lives of Daniel and his friends proved that divine wisdom is the best possible guide. Daniel demonstrated what wisdom, coupled with quiet confidence and gentle persuasion, can accomplish.

FOR ADULTS	■ **TOPIC:** Holding to Your Convictions! ■ **QUESTIONS:** 1. Why did Daniel resolve not to defile himself by eating food and wine provided by Nebuchadnezzar?

2. Why would Daniel take the risk of approaching the guardian with the proposal of a vegetarian diet? 3. What was the basis for the superior intellectual abilities of Daniel and his three friends? 4. How was it possible for Daniel and his friends to be without equal among their peers? 5. How was Daniel's faith in God evident throughout the entire episode?

■ **ILLUSTRATIONS:**

Workplace Challenge. Cheryl wants to be a Christian at work. However, new rules at her office prohibit anyone from verbally sharing his or her religious beliefs with co-workers. Cheryl's boss has even frowned at a small poster with a Scripture verse Cheryl has hanging in her cubicle.

In the break room last week, Cheryl talked briefly with Jan, who told Cheryl about the difficulties in her life. Cheryl would like to invite Jan to her Bible study group, where Jan could find help and support. But Cheryl is unsure how to do that without causing problems for herself or Jan.

Cheryl's situation reminds us that being a Christian in a non-Christian society can create situations in which is difficult to serve God. Daniel faced similar circumstances. Yet, despite the possible negative consequences of his actions, he decided to obey God. The Lord calls us to demonstrate this same kind of obedience in difficult situations.

Lures. To aid you as you speak this illustration, you could ask an appropriate member of your class to bring in a variety of fishing lures. Holding several where the class can see them, remind the students that most lures don't look at all like food a fish would enjoy. They merely offer shiny or colorful surfaces that catch a fish's attention. Attracted by the novelty, the fish swims over to investigate. The fisherman knows there's nothing for the fish in his lures but danger and potential death. But the fish is not smart enough to figure that out.

Satan's temptations are like fishing lures. They catch our attention. But we end up getting hurt, sometimes seriously. In many situations we face, determining to follow the right course can be difficult, but like Daniel, we must be obedient to God in all things. And we have the assurance of Scripture that He will not allow us to be tempted more than we can stand. In fact, when we are enticed to sin, the Lord will show us a way out so that we can endure (see 1 Cor. 10:13).

Call for Public and Private Morality. In contrast to the immoral lives of many of our modern leaders, John Adams stands apart as a person who was convinced that public and private morality are interconnected. He speaks to self-indulgent baby boomers who prefer to use pundits and polls as their moral guides and divorce their actions from the traditional biblical moral codes. Adams was convinced that a corrupt people could not long remain free. An immoral person, he insisted, could not be free, but was instead a slave to unreasoning passion.

This great leader, who was a force behind the American Revolution and the establishment of our nation, demanded strict discipline, excellence, and integrity as the characteristics required in all persons, and especially in leaders. To attract and keep virtuous, disciplined people, Adams stated that society as a whole must foster virtue and discipline in its citizens.

"The best republics," Adams wrote, "will be virtuous and have been so." He noted that to remain virtuous, one must adhere to the rule of law and keep private passions in check. "A passion continually indulged feeds upon itself, eventually warping the owner's inherent capacity to judge right from wrong. People entrusted with unlimited power thrive upon their passions. The passion that is long indulged and continually gratified becomes mad; it is a species of delirium; it should not be called guilt, but insanity."

FOR YOUTH

■ TOPIC: Go Along to Get Along?

■ QUESTIONS: 1. What caused Ashpenaz to be sympathetic toward Daniel? 2. Why was Ashpenaz afraid? 3. What proposal did Daniel make to the guardian? 4. How did Daniel and his three friends look at the end of the 10-day period? 5. What did Nebuchadnezzar discover when he interviewed Daniel and his friends?

■ ILLUSTRATIONS:

Overcoming Obstacles. In 1921, an attack of infantile paralysis left Franklin D. Roosevelt crippled from the waist down. The experts at the time thought this would end his promising political career. Roosevelt, however, would not permit his illness to hinder him from pursuing his political goals. With determination he learned how to walk with artificial supports and a cane. By 1928, Roosevelt had made a successful comeback, becoming governor of New York. And in 1932, he was elected president of the United States, an office which he held until his death in 1945.

Many obstacles we encounter can deter us from living victoriously for Christ. With the Lord's help, however, we can overcome these problems and be triumphant in our efforts to behave in an upright manner.

Origin of the Word. True leaders and genuine Christians know that they must live disciplined lives of courage and conviction. The English word "true" has an interesting origin. It derives from the old English word "try." This term meant "firm and dependable, like a tree." What a significant way to define the type of individual who practices personal discipline! He or she is firm and dependable like a tree, standing strong and steady, useful and fruitful.

The Devil Is Ambidextrous. George Brushaber, a senior editor of the magazine *Christianity Today*, tells a story of a rainy day at summer camp when the program director was scrambling to keep the campers occupied. The director invited the local law enforcement officer to come. The officer wowed the audience with demonstrations of nightsticks and handcuffs. Finally, the officer called a camper up to help him demonstrate how to deal with a mugger.

The boy eagerly followed his stage directions. He slipped up behind the officer and jabbed his plastic water pistol into the officer's back. The bold hero lunged to his left, swung his right elbow fiercely, and was "shot" squarely in the back by the junior gunman. The huge water spot between the officer's shoulder blades was clear evidence of the failure of his supposedly safe maneuver. Red-faced and fumbling for words, the lawman scolded the junior gunman, "You're supposed to hold the gun in your right hand!" The left-handed robber, however, was not impressed.

Brushaber concludes, "I can, for example, deal successfully with temptations from the usual and expected sources—from the right side; but it is when I become too confident that I get gunned down from the left—any blind side, really—by the sins and failures I least expect. To make matters worse, Satan is ambidextrous, always ready to attack from either side; and so the price of moral growth is perpetual vigilance."

THREE REFUSE TO BREAK COVENANT

BACKGROUND SCRIPTURE: Daniel 3
DEVOTIONAL READING: Psalm 121

KEY VERSES: If it be so, our God whom we serve is able to deliver us from the burning fiery furnace, and he will deliver us out of thine hand, O king. But if not, be it known unto thee, O king, that we will not serve thy gods, nor worship the golden image which thou hast set up. Daniel 3:17-18.

KING JAMES VERSION

DANIEL 3:10 Thou, O king, hast made a decree, that every man that shall hear the sound of the cornet, flute, harp, sackbut, psaltery, and dulcimer, and all kinds of musick, shall fall down and worship the golden image: 11 And whoso falleth not down and worshippeth, that he should be cast into the midst of a burning fiery furnace. 12 There are certain Jews whom thou hast set over the affairs of the province of Babylon, Shadrach, Meshach, and Abednego; these men, O king, have not regarded thee: they serve not thy gods, nor worship the golden image which thou hast set up. 13 Then Nebuchadnezzar in his rage and fury commanded to bring Shadrach, Meshach, and Abednego. Then they brought these men before the king. . . . 16 Shadrach, Meshach, and Abednego, answered and said to the king, O Nebuchadnezzar, we are not careful to answer thee in this matter. 17 If it be so, our God whom we serve is able to deliver us from the burning fiery furnace, and he will deliver us out of thine hand, O king. 18 But if not, be it known unto thee, O king, that we will not serve thy gods, nor worship the golden image which thou hast set up. . . .

21 Then these men were bound in their coats, their hosen, and their hats, and their other garments, and were cast into the midst of the burning fiery furnace. . . . 24 Then Nebuchadnezzar the king was astonied, and rose up in haste, and spake, and said unto his counsellors, Did not we cast three men bound into the midst of the fire? They answered and said unto the king, True, O king.

NEW REVISED STANDARD VERSION

DANIEL 3:10 "You, O king, have made a decree, that everyone who hears the sound of the horn, pipe, lyre, trigon, harp, drum, and entire musical ensemble, shall fall down and worship the golden statue, 11 and whoever does not fall down and worship shall be thrown into a furnace of blazing fire. 12 There are certain Jews whom you have appointed over the affairs of the province of Babylon: Shadrach, Meshach, and Abednego. These pay no heed to you, O king. They do not serve your gods and they do not worship the golden statue that you have set up."

13 Then Nebuchadnezzar in furious rage commanded that Shadrach, Meshach, and Abednego be brought in; so they brought those men before the king. . .

16 Shadrach, Meshach, and Abednego answered the king, "O Nebuchadnezzar, we have no need to present a defense to you in this matter. 17 If our God whom we serve is able to deliver us from the furnace of blazing fire and out of your hand, O king, let him deliver us. 18 But if not, be it known to you, O king, that we will not serve your gods and we will not worship the golden statue that you have set up." . . .

21 So the men were bound, still wearing their tunics, their trousers, their hats, and their other garments, and they were thrown into the furnace of blazing fire. . . . 24 Then King Nebuchadnezzar was astonished and rose up quickly. He said to his counselors, "Was it not three men that we threw bound into the fire?" They answered the king, "True, O king."

7

BACKGROUND

Nebuchadnezzar became obsessed with his own power and grandeur and decided to have a golden statue made. The image was 90 feet tall (about the size of a nine-story building) and nine feet wide (Dan. 3:1). Most likely, the object was not solid gold, but made from a less valuable metal or wood and overlaid with gold (see Isa. 40:19; 41:7; Jer. 10:3-4). When placed on a pedestal, the statue's imposing height would have been a striking statement to the greatness of the king and his lofty achievements. Given the extremely narrow and high dimensions of the image, some have suggested it was an obelisk, that is, a pole-shaped tower of stone. Others think the statue represented either the king himself or a Babylonian deity. If the latter option was the case, it remains unclear which pagan god was honored by this object. Three possibilities include Marduk, Bel, or Nabu, with the third forming the first element of Nebuchadnezzar's name and being his patron deity.

Daniel 3:1 says that Nebuchadnezzar's dazzling image sat on the plain of Dura in the province of Babylon. It's unclear where this plain was located, but several sites have been suggested. One was the spot where the Harbor and Euphrates Rivers met. A second option is that Dura was located near Apollonia, north of Babylon and east of the Tigris River. A third possibility is that the location is to be associated with *Tulûl Dûra* (which means "tells of Dura"), which is about 16 miles south of Babylon. Some think the name *Dura* could also have referred to a circular enclosure or fortress. Despite these ambiguities, there is no doubt about the king's intent. He sent out a summons to assemble a variety of international delegates, seven categories of which are mentioned in 3:2 (see 3:3, 27). While the specific duties each of these groups performed is debated, their loyalty to Nebuchadnezzar is not questioned. They complied with his order to assemble for the dedication, stand before the image, and pledge their complete allegiance to the Babylonian monarch (3:3).

When all these important dignitaries had arrived, a herald made a loud proclamation. Those present represented the people of all races, nations, and languages whom Nebuchadnezzar had vanquished in order to establish his empire (3:4). The attendees learned that a variety of musical instruments would begin playing, including horns, flutes, zithers, lyres, harps, and pipes. (This indicates how important music was in the worship at ancient temples and palaces.) The sound of the music would be their signal to bow down to the ground and pay homage to the gold-plated colossus the king had erected (3:5). Falling prostrate in worship of the statue was not optional, either. Those who refused to obey would immediately be thrown into a furnace of blazing fire (3:6). Not surprisingly, as soon as the officials heard the music, they did exactly as they were told (3:7).

Imagine in the background a kiln with smoke roaring from its top. At once, a vast number of standing people bow in unison to the ground. It would not be difficult to spot any individuals who failed to comply. This proved to be the case with Daniel's three friends. Perhaps their Babylonian counterparts suspected they would refuse to fall prostrate before the statue. Also, some of the astrologers might have been jealous of the fact that Nebuchadnezzar followed Daniel's request to appoint Shadrach, Meshach, and Abednego as administrators over the province of Babylon (2:49).

Certain Babylonians used this as an opportunity to come forward and bring malicious accusations against their Jewish peers. In 3:8, some think the word rendered *Chaldeans* denotes an order of priests who looked to the stars to foretell the future (in other words, astrologers); but others note that the word can also be used to refer to a particular ethnic group. This would imply that the informants stigmatized the Jews simply because of their race (see Esth. 3:5-6). The word rendered *Jews* (Dan. 3:8) is a shortened form of "Judahite" and refers to the remnant of God's chosen people who once inhabited the southern kingdom of Judah.

The whereabouts of Daniel in this episode remain unclear. Some suggest that because of his high position within Babylon, he was exempted from demonstrating his loyalty. Previously, Nebuchadnezzar had promoted Daniel to be the governor over the entire province of Babylon and put him in charge of the other wise men (2:48). Others speculate that either sickness or official business elsewhere prevented him from being able to attend the dedication ceremony. Regardless of which explanation is preferred, Daniel's position of power and influence did not exempt his friends from experiencing the wrath of the king.

NOTES ON THE PRINTED TEXT

Before the Chaldeans pressed forward with their agenda, they addressed the Babylonian monarch with typical court greeting, *O king, live for ever* (Dan. 3:9). Following this prescribed protocol did not necessarily reflect the real sentiments of the informants. They reminded Nebuchadnezzar of the edict he issued in which he commanded everyone to bow down and worship the gold-plated statue when the music was played (3:10). He also decreed that anyone who was insubordinate would be burned alive in a fiery furnace (3:11). The Chaldeans brought to the king's attention three Jewish men he had appointed to high positions in the province of Babylon. Shadrach, Meshach, and Abednego were charged with failing to show proper respect to Nebuchadnezzar. Furthermore, the young men refused to serve his gods and pay homage to the golden statue he had erected (3:12).

Upon hearing the informants' report, Nebuchadnezzar became enraged at Shadrach, Meshach, and Abednego and ordered that they be brought before him (3:13). As the three Jewish officials stood in front of the monarch's throne, he questioned them sharply to be sure that his informers had told him the truth (3:14). It was incomprehensible to him that anyone would disobey him, especially his trusted administrators. He stated that if they refused to comply, they would be tossed at once into a flaming furnace. The king then threw down his final challenge. He dared them to even think that their God could save them from the wrath of his judgment; in other words, if they did not worship his god, they were doomed (3:15). Was Nebuchadnezzar really jealous for the worship of his gods, or was he outraged because the three had defied his order? Probably his authority was at stake.

Here is the beginning of a remarkable confession. Shadrach, Meshach, and Abednego were not daunted by the king's threats (3:16). Instead of defending themselves and trying to save their lives, they chose the path of unwavering faith. They testified that God was able to save them, and that if He so chose, He could rescue them (3:17). They also recognized the possibility that they may have misunderstood God's plans. Either way, their response would be the same. Whether it meant deliverance or death, they would never compromise in their faith (3:18). Perhaps Nebuchadnezzar had never before encountered such stiff resistance. Didn't these young Jewish officials understand what the powerful king could do with them? He was in no mood to back down, and in fact because of his pride and position he could not back down. He was so furious that his face became distorted with rage. To vent to his fury, he ordered his servants to heat up the furnace seven times hotter than usual (3:19).

To make sure that nothing could upset his plans, the king ordered his toughest soldiers to bind Shadrach, Meshach, and Abednego and hurl them into the fiery furnace (3:20). Perhaps even then, Nebuchadnezzar wasn't totally sure about his scheme. He certainly wasted no time on reflection or logic. He had put himself in a corner, and there was no way out. We don't know how long it was between the initial interrogation and the king's decision. While the monarch's face twisted with anger, no doubt the three young Jewish officials were deep in prayer, asking for God's intervention and for courage to remain true to their convictions. Faced with the prospect of certain death, they did not cave in, recant their faith, and beg for mercy.

Consequently, the three were tied up while still wearing their full court attire and tossed into the superheated oven (3:21). The king's command was so urgent and the furnace so hot that the flames leaped out and incinerated the soldiers as they threw the three men in (3:22). That Nebuchadnezzar was willing to sacrifice his strongest troops to carry out the execution shows the intensity of the king's fury. It was probably the monarch's anger, more than a sense of duty, that compelled the soldiers to endanger their lives in this way. Humanly speaking, nothing now seemed to prevent Shadrach, Meshach, and Abednego from experiencing a similar gruesome end. There is no indication in the narrative that the three Jewish officials had any kind of spiritual vision or revelation that they would be saved from the furnace. They simply trusted in God, even as they fell down into the roaring flames (3:23).

Nebuchadnezzar realized that something astounding had taken place. He had to check his arithmetic. He was sure that he had sentenced three men to die in the furnace, and his advisers said this was true. Even though the king's soldiers had cast three men into the fire (3:24), Nebuchadnezzar saw four unharmed, unbound men in the blazing furnace. The fourth figure looked *like the Son of God* (3:25). The monarch did not have a name for this person in the furnace, but he was sure the one he saw was not a mere mortal, but a supernatural being. According to 3:28, it was an angel. After the three walked out of the fire (3:26; the fourth had evidently disappeared), the king and the members of his royal court gathered around them and marveled that the ropes binding them were the only things scorched. Not a hair on the Jewish officials' heads was singed. There was not even the smell of fire on them (3:27). Instead of losing their ability to influence the king, Daniel's three friends were given a promotion, and God was honored throughout Babylon (3:29-30).

SUGGESTIONS TO TEACHERS

Shadrach, Meshach, and Abednego clearly understood that King Nebuchadnezzar would punish them if they refused to submit to his demand to commit idolatry. Yet despite the severe consequences, they were unwavering in their devotion to God.

1. FAITH'S HIGH COST. Christians around the world today are suffering and even dying for their faith. Most of us, however, will never face a deadly threat as a result of standing for our Christian convictions. But we are often in situations where we must pay some kind of price for our faith when we stand up for what the Bible teaches to be true and right. At times, the price may be as costly as losing a job or alienating a loved one, but more often we may suffer a smirk or a derisive laugh.

2. A WILLINGNESS TO SUFFER. When we put our religious beliefs on the line, we must always stand on our Christian principles, regardless of the consequences. After all, Jesus was resolute in saving us from God's wrath despite encountering every kind of hostility and indignation. Therefore, we must have the same kind of attitude as His apostles, who rejoiced in suffering for the risen Messiah (see Acts 5:41).

3. STRENGTH IN NUMBERS. When we are alone, keeping an unwavering faith in the Lord Jesus can be difficult. We need to remember that one straw can easily be broken, but many straws joined together are unbreakable. That is why God provides us with Christian brothers and sisters to strengthen us when we stand up for what is right in the Lord.

■ **TOPIC:** Holding on to Your Faith

■ **QUESTIONS:** 1. What was the consequence for disobeying the decree issued by Nebuchadnezzar? 2. Who brought the charge of insubordination against Shadrach, Meshach, and Abednego and why did they do so? 3. Why would the three refuse to defend themselves before the king? 4. What was the basis for the three deciding to defy the king? 5. How did God rescue the three from their fiery ordeal?

■ **ILLUSTRATIONS:**

Shallow Spirituality. Large majorities of Americans say they are religious and claim that spirituality is important. However, that does not seem to be translated into any form of Christ-centered commitment. Few show commitment to a single faith, a local congregation, or regular time of corporate worship. A MacArthur Foundation survey recently indicated that more than seven out ten Americans say they feel religious and consider spirituality to have a key role in their lives. But about half attend services either never or less than once a month.

Another study, this one done by the Barna Research Group, disclosed that nearly one-third of America's adults have not attended a worship service in the past six months, other than for a special event. This same study found that 31 percent of Americans—a proportion representing between 60 to 65 million adults—could be classified as "unchurched" because they were not present at any Christian worship service during the past six months (other than a wedding, funeral, or a holiday service such as Christmas Eve or Easter). Eighteen months earlier, researchers from the Barna Group found that 27 percent of adults could be called unchurched. The younger and more educated a person is, the study discovered, the less likely she or he would be attached to any congregation.

"Spirituality in the U.S. is a mile wide and an inch deep," reported David Kinnaman of the Barna Research Group. "Though there is an all-time high interest in spirituality," Kinnaman added, "people are beginning to develop a hybrid personal faith that integrates different perspectives from different religions that may even be contradictory. But that doesn't seem to bother them."

What a contrast this is to the God-centered faith we see in Shadrach, Meshach, and Abednego. They were clear about what they believed and the one they served.

Unwavering Faith. When new offices or shopping centers are built today, they can be "instantly" landscaped with bushes, rolls of sod, and even large trees. That kind of portable landscaping is not what the prophet Jeremiah described when he told his audience to "plant" themselves in God (Jer. 17:7-8). Like firmly rooted trees, those who trusted God could remain faithful to Him regardless of the circumstances.

Always standing for what is right challenges our faith. It is tempting to follow the crowd instead. Yet, just as a tree burrows its roots deep into the soil to brace itself against the storm and rain, so we believers can anchor ourselves in the Lord Jesus to withstand attacks against us. In this week's lesson, we see how three Jewish men stood against the wrath of King Nebuchadnezzar. Just as the Lord was with them, so He will be with us, especially as we honor Him in all that we say and do.

Undaunted Courage. The movie *Running Brave* tells the story of Billy Mills, who rose from poverty on an Indian reservation to win a gold medal in the Tokyo Olympics in 1964. Billy's victory came the hard way. He had to run in borrowed shoes, labor under the false charge of being a quitter, and battle back after being bumped off the track by a competitor. Billy showed the kind of courage and conviction that this week's Bible reading talks about in terms of faith in the Lord.

Toss-Up Commitment. There's an old story about a man who drove to his country club one Sunday morning. Breathlessly, he rushed into the locker room to change into his golf shoes. When someone asked why he was late, the man replied, "Well, it was a toss-up between whether I'd go to church or play golf this morning." He paused reflectively, then added, "And I had to toss up 15 times!" Is this what our commitment to the Savior should be like?

■ **TOPIC:** Standing Up to False Gods
■ **QUESTIONS:** 1. What was the decree that Nebuchadnezzar issued? 2. What were Shadrach, Meshach, and Abednego accused of doing? 3. In what way did the three display unwavering courage and faith? 4. Why would the king throw the three fully clothed into the furnace? 5. What prompted Nebuchadnezzar to leap to his feet in amazement?

■ **ILLUSTRATIONS:**

Assembly Line Art. Correspondent Barry Petersen of the television program *Sunday Morning*, filed a report from Defan Art Village in China. He noted that the country now has "factories for a popular new export: art." It isn't original, one-of-a-kind art, either. These are copies of such famous works as Van Gogh's "Starry Night." He may have "sold one painting in his lifetime," but today they "come off the line by the dozens."

"Mass reproduction" is the operational mandate of the factory where these pieces are churned out. One finds "gallery after gallery, painter after painter, art for the masses by masses of artists." For example, there's Cheng Pei, who took four days to copy the *Mona Lisa,* a piece that consumed four years of Leonardo Da Vinci's life. The replica Cheng will sell costs $36. Factory-workers such as this can "even take a small photo from a computer e-mail and turn it into fine art."

Thankfully, Daniel's three friends—Shadrach, Meshach, and Abednego—were not fooled by cheap imitations of the living God. They didn't settle for counterfeit, manufactured deities when they could know by faith the Creator of the universe.

A Masterful Forgery. According to correspondent Michele Norris of *National Public Radio,* a longstanding mystery had been solved. For decades experts were stumped by "inconsistencies in one of Norman Rockwell's most famous illustrations for *The Saturday Evening Post*." The picture is know as *Breaking Home Ties.* It portrays a "working-class father and his college-bound son," the latter beaming with anticipation. The problem, though, is that "something about [the painting] wasn't quite right." In particular, the "colors looked dull" and "the wrinkles in the clothing didn't fall quite the right way." It turns out the painting in question was a masterful forgery of the original. The owner of the artwork, Donald Trachte, Sr., "painted an almost perfect replica" and then "tucked away the original in a secret compartment behind a bookcase in his home."

Clearly, there are times when what seems authentic is phony. This even holds true in the spiritual realm. In Daniel's day, the false gods of Babylon were worshiped by countless people, who believed these pagan deities were the real thing. It took the courage of Daniel's three friends—Shadrach, Meshach, and Abednego—to distinguish the one true God from the idols of the day. Like other people of faith down through the centuries, they understood there is no other way to remain faithful to the Lord.

Say "Yes" to God. It's tough to make it to Broadway, but Krystal always knew that someday she'd be there. She had been comfortable with the spotlight from the first productions of civic theater that her mother had auditioned her for. It was all she had ever wanted—and now she was memorizing for her third successive part in a Broadway play. The producer said only the sky was her limit.

Krystal's father had been killed flying a Vietnam combat mission while Krystal was still in her mother's womb. Krystal loved the stories about this devoted man she'd never met, but she honestly felt that God had given her better parenting than many of her friends, under the care of a single, yet very spiritual, mother—Loren.

As Krystal thought about those "limitless" career opportunities ahead, she wondered if this producer knew what thunderstorms he was now bringing to her life, and to his play. He had just rewritten her script to include scenes that were a clear violation of the moral ethics that Loren had instilled in her daughter, and that Krystal willingly embraced in her life. Krystal had always tried to abstain from every appearance of evil, and this new part now called for something much more that just an appearance. This was definitely a time to have the courage to choose God's will above the demands of others.

DANIEL'S LIFE-AND-DEATH TEST

BACKGROUND SCRIPTURE: Daniel 6
DEVOTIONAL READING: Psalm 119:57–64

KEY VERSE: Now when Daniel knew that the writing was signed, he went into his house; and his windows being open in his chamber toward Jerusalem, he kneeled upon his knees three times a day, and prayed, and gave thanks before his God, as he did aforetime. Daniel 6:10.

KING JAMES VERSION

DANIEL 6:4 Then the presidents and princes sought to find occasion against Daniel concerning the kingdom; but they could find none occasion nor fault; forasmuch as he was faithful, neither was there any error or fault found in him. 5 Then said these men, We shall not find any occasion against this Daniel, except we find it against him concerning the law of his God.

6 Then these presidents and princes assembled together to the king, and said thus unto him, King Darius, live for ever. 7 All the presidents of the kingdom, the governors, and the princes, the counsellors, and the captains, have consulted together to establish a royal statute, and to make a firm decree, that whosoever shall ask a petition of any God or man for thirty days, save of thee, O king, he shall be cast into the den of lions. . . . 10 Now when Daniel knew that the writing was signed, he went into his house; and his windows being open in his chamber toward Jerusalem, he kneeled upon his knees three times a day, and prayed, and gave thanks before his God, as he did aforetime. . . .

16 Then the king commanded, and they brought Daniel, and cast him into the den of lions. Now the king spake and said unto Daniel, Thy God whom thou servest continually, he will deliver thee. . . .

19 Then the king arose very early in the morning, and went in haste unto the den of lions. . . . 21 Then said Daniel unto the king, O king, live for ever. . . .

25 Then king Darius wrote unto all people, nations, and languages, that dwell in all the earth; Peace be multiplied unto you. 26 I make a decree, That in every dominion of my kingdom men tremble and fear before the God of Daniel: for he is the living God, and stedfast for ever.

NEW REVISED STANDARD VERSION

DANIEL 6:4 So the presidents and the satraps tried to find grounds for complaint against Daniel in connection with the kingdom. But they could find no grounds for complaint or any corruption, because he was faithful, and no negligence or corruption could be found in him. 5 The men said, "We shall not find any ground for complaint against this Daniel unless we find it in connection with the law of his God."

6 So the presidents and satraps conspired and came to the king and said to him, "O King Darius, live forever! 7 All the presidents of the kingdom, the prefects and the satraps, the counselors and the governors are agreed that the king should establish an ordinance and enforce an interdict, that whoever prays to anyone, divine or human, for thirty days, except to you, O king, shall be thrown into a den of lions." . . .

10 Although Daniel knew that the document had been signed, he continued to go to his house, which had windows in its upper room open toward Jerusalem, and to get down on his knees three times a day to pray to his God and praise him, just as he had done previously. . . .

16 Then the king gave the command, and Daniel was brought and thrown into the den of lions. The king said to Daniel, "May your God, whom you faithfully serve, deliver you!" . . .

19 Then, at break of day, the king got up and hurried to the den of lions. . . . 21 Daniel then said to the king, "O king, live forever!" . . .

25 Then King Darius wrote to all peoples and nations of every language throughout the whole world: "May you have abundant prosperity! 26 I make a decree, that in all my royal dominion people should tremble and fear before the God of Daniel:

For he is the living God,
enduring forever.

BACKGROUND

In 539 B.C., Babylon fell and Darius the Mede took over the kingdom (Dan. 5:31). The exact identity of Babylon's new ruler remains debated (see 6:1, 6, 9). According to 9:1, he was the *son of Ahasuerus* (or Xerxes) and a Mede by descent (not to be confused with the person by the same name mentioned in Esther 1:1). Apart from Scripture, Darius is not referred to in the surviving historical sources. Some think *Darius the Median* (Dan. 5:31) was the throne name for Cyrus, the founder of the Persian empire (see 6:28). Others suggest the reference in 5:31 was a designation for Gubaru (or Gobryas), who was appointed governor over the territories the Persians had seized from the Babylonians.

When Darius came to power, he decided to divide the kingdom into 120 provinces, and he appointed *princes* (6:1) to rule over each region of the empire. Each of these officials answered to a supervisor, who similarly was accountable to Darius. Initially, the king appointed three administrators, one of whom was Daniel, to watch out for the monarch's interests and ensure that the government ran properly (6:2). This included minimizing any loss of territory due to insurrections and erosion of tax revenue due to corruption. From the earliest days of Daniel's career, he had shown considerable promise (see 1:17-21; 4:8; 5:12). Not surprisingly, then, this exceptionally gifted and morally upright statesman distinguished himself above the rest of his peers, regardless of whether it was the other administrators or the satraps. Darius took note of Daniel's exceptional qualities; and because he did his work so much better than the other government officials, Darius intended to appoint Daniel over the entire kingdom (6:3).

NOTES ON THE PRINTED TEXT

The king's plan did not sit well with the other administrators and satraps, who became envious of the positive turn of events for Daniel. They thought they could undermine his standing with Darius by trying to find damaging evidence of negligence or corruption against Daniel in his conduct of government affairs (Dan. 6:4). Yet despite their efforts (which we can assume were extensive and exhaustive), the courtiers were unable to find any pretext for charging Daniel with a crime. In every area of his professional and personal life, he proved to be faithful and honest.

Many years earlier, when Daniel was a younger Jewish captive being trained for a life of service in the government of Babylon, he resolved to follow the Lord whole-heartedly, regardless of the consequences; and God honored his devotion (see chap. 1). Now almost six decades later, the elder statesmen faced a new challenge from the ministers who served alongside him in the court of the Persian government. The administrators and satraps concluded that the only grounds for charges they could trump up against Daniel had to be in connection with the requirements of his religion, as expressed in the Mosaic law (6:5).

The idea of how to entrap Daniel met with the approval of all the courtiers, and they conspired together to petition the king (6:6). Perhaps a representative body of the ministers sought audience with Darius. After entering his presence, they followed the custom of the day by declaring their hope that the monarch would live forever. Then, the government officials concisely stated their proposal that a royal edict be issued, which would also be strictly enforced. They exaggerated, though, when they claimed that all the ministers were in unanimous agreement. Obviously, Daniel was not in collusion with the rest of his peers. The plan was straightforward. The king's loyal subjects were forbidden to pray to any god or human being, other than the monarch. Also, the duration was reasonable, lasting just 30 days, after which it would expire. Those who violated the decree would be thrown into a den filled with lions (6:7). Verse 17 suggests the latter would have been a pit below ground level with a modest-sized opening at the top that was covered by a stone. This would make it impossible for a detainee such as Daniel to escape from the den.

The collaborators petitioned Darius to issue and sign the decree, which would ensure that it could not be altered or revoked. This conformed to the practice of the day (as attested in extra-biblical ancient writings), in which no one could repeal or revoke a law of the Medes and Persians (6:8; see Esther 1:19; 8:8). Such a proposal would have met with the king's approval because he thought it would strengthen his political, military, and religious authority over the newly conquered territories once controlled by Babylon. Thus, he approved the request and signed the decree into law (Dan. 6:9). By doing so, he actually undermined his own power as king, for he allowed himself to be duped by subordinates who were manipulating him to achieve their own end.

Given Daniel's high-ranking status in the government, it probably did not take long for him to learn about the issuance of the decree (6:10). He returned to his home, went upstairs, and kneeled in prayer in front of the latticed window that faced Jerusalem. He repeated this practice three times a day, which involved offering petitions and thanks to the God of his ancestors. This customary practice finds its basis in other Old Testament passages (see 1 Kings 8:44, 48; 2 Chron. 6:37-39; Pss. 5:7; 55:17-18; 138:2). After more than eight decades of life under the Lord's care, there was no way that Daniel would suddenly now jettison his devotion. Not even the specter of death would prevent him from going before the Lord in prayer. Undoubtedly, his conspirators were familiar with the religious practices that characterized his piety and virtue; and sure enough, they found Daniel on his knees in prayer, asking God for help (Dan. 6:11).

The courtiers now had the evidence they needed to frame Daniel. The administrative officials approached the king and queried him about the seemingly innocuous decree he had enacted. He not only affirmed doing so, but also declared that it could not be revoked (6:12). Imagine how chagrined Darius must have felt when the entourage of subordinates mentioned Daniel, whom the king highly admired. The courtiers noted that Daniel was one of the captives from Judah (6:13). This might have reflected their own prejudice against his ethnic identity. Despite the presence of such, Daniel refused to compromise his Jewish heritage to achieve temporal gains.

The conspirators accused the elder statesman of refusing to obey the king or heed the royal edict he issued, as evidenced by Daniel's insistence on praying three times each day (most likely, early in the morning, then at midday, and finally at night). Rather than be enraged at his trusted subordinate, Darius became very upset and began thinking about how he might rescue Daniel. Evidently, the law mandated that the prescribed punishment be inflicted on a criminal the same day a transgression was committed. This meant the king had until sundown for his attendants to find any legal means of delivering Daniel from the predicament he faced (6:14). We can only imagine how even more agitated Darius felt when a bloodthirsty delegation reminded him of the irrevocable nature of the decree he had signed into law (6:15).

The king ordered Daniel to be arrested and thrown into a pit containing hungry lions. Darius tried to console the aged Jewish exile with the possibility that the God whom he continually worshiped and served might rescue him (6:16). Then, a stone was rolled over the opening of the pit. Also, the king sealed it with his signet ring and with those of his nobles (6:17). Darius was soon surrounded by the safety and comfort of his plush dwellings; but neither these nor his countless royal attendants could ease the anxiety he felt as his most trusted minister spent the night in a pit filled with ravenous beasts. Daniel 6:18 states that the king spent the night without eating and refused his usual entertainment. In fact, all night he could not sleep.

Very early the next morning, at daybreak, the monarch got up and rushed out of the palace to go to the lions' pit (6:19). At some point, he ordered the removal of the heavy stone from the mouth of the den. He cautiously made his way to the pit, his voice being filled with anxiety and distress as he called out to Daniel. Darius referred to the Jewish exile in the lions' pit as the *servant of the living God* (6:20). The king, hoping that Daniel was still alive, asked whether his God had rescued him from his predicament. Imagine the monarch's relief when he heard his most trusted minister respond with the customary wish that the king might live forever (6:21).

Then, Daniel explained that his God knew he was innocent of the charges his peers had maliciously brought against him. That is why the Lord sent His angel to keep the starved animals from devouring His faithful servant. Daniel ended with the assurance that he never did anything to defraud or harm Darius (6:22). Now that the stipulations of the royal edict had been fulfilled, it was permissible for Daniel to be hauled out of the pit by the king's attendants. Once they did this, they discovered he had no injury of any kind, for he had placed his trust in God (6:23). This ending contrasted sharply with the fate awaiting those who had used the king to achieve their diabolical goal. The custom of the day was to inflict punishment on both the criminals and the families members they represented. That is why the conspirators and their loved ones were tossed into the pit, where the half-starved beasts devoured them, bones and all (6:24).

Perhaps Daniel formally petitioned the king to issue a royal edict in which the God of the Jews was affirmed. We can only imagine how much of an encouragement this would be to the exiles returning to Judah from captivity in Babylon. The decree, which Daniel beyond question helped to draft, was directed toward all the peoples, nations, and language groups living in the Persian empire. After a customary opening in which the monarch wished peace and prosperity to his loyal subjects (6:25), he directed all inhabitants to tremble with fear before the *God of Daniel* (6:26). Such reverential worship and honor was appropriate, for Yahweh had proven Himself to be the living God, who endured forever. Moreover, no one could destroy His kingdom or bring His authority to an end.

SUGGESTIONS TO TEACHERS

Adults in your class probably consider themselves law-abiding citizens. At times, however, they are faced with situations in which they must obey God or submit to an authority that challenges their commitment to the Lord. When that occurs, they need to understand that they should set aside their desire to be "good" citizens, "good" employees, "good" adult children, or even "good" spouses if they are to be obedient children of God. This is neither easy nor pleasant, but with God's help it can be done. Daniel's life is proof of that.

1. MAKING THE RIGHT CHOICE. The issue of choosing to obey God goes far beyond mere legal matters. Many "laws" are unwritten—cultural expectations, prevailing attitudes in society, pressure from peers, the influence of traditions, and so on. All these weigh heavily upon believers, who must choose between the ways of people and the ways of God. When the ways of people are morally neutral, there's no problem. But when they violate God's principles, a choice is required.

2. MAKING PRAYER A PRIORITY. To choose for God in the face of popular opinion requires great courage and conviction. That is why we, like Daniel, need the indwelling power of the Spirit. And that is why we, like him, need to bath our circumstances in prayer. We may never be placed in a pit full of hungry lions, but every day we face other kinds of challenges to our faith. Also, every day we need the same devotion to God that motivated Daniel.

3. BEING EMPOWERED BY THE SPIRIT. Overcoming challenges to our faith is a two-stage process. It begins with a clear understanding of God's will as revealed in Scripture and exemplified in the Lord Jesus. This understanding clarifies our purpose in this world so that we can recognize our God-given task in any situation. Next, we experience victory by drawing upon the Holy Spirit's enabling power to fulfill God's purpose for us regardless of the opposition we encounter.

FOR ADULTS

■ **TOPIC:** Faith without Compromise!

■ **QUESTIONS:** 1. Why did Daniel's peers want to find a reason to bring charges against him? 2. Why did the conspirators try to frame Daniel in his religious practices? 3. Why did the king finally decide to have Daniel arrested and thrown into the lions' pit? 4. How did God rescue Daniel from the ravenous lions? 5. What was the nature of the decree the king issued?

■ **ILLUSTRATIONS:**

A Test of Faith. One of the most forgotten men in American history is James Otis. A devout Christian, Otis was educated by his pastor in his home church. He later studied at Harvard and read law with a leading attorney. In the mid-18th century, he was admitted to the bar in Plymouth County in New England. By 1761, James Otis was the Advocate General for the Crown, one of the highest-paying and most prestigious positions in the colonies. He had a safe, brilliant future and a comfortable, secure life as one of the king's leading officials.

When the English government insisted on presenting and enforcing a sweeping law called the Writs of Assistance, Otis found his faith severely tested. The Writs of Assistance, presented to the court where Otis presided, would have enabled English customs officials without a search warrant to go into any house, barn, hayloft, or shed on anyone's property to try to find goods suspected of being smuggled into the colonies. When the Crown came to Otis to have the case presented and approved, Otis resigned his post. Then he personally assumed the defense against the writs, without pay. His deep sense of justice was so offended that he was willing to have his faith tested to the point of losing everything.

The speech Otis gave so impressed the chief justice then representing the king that he was unable to decide the case on the spot, as was the custom. This was the first time an American stated the right of life, liberty, and protection against unwarrantable search and seizure. Historians note that this was also the first open assertion against the king and the first act of opposition to the arbitrary claims of the Crown. Some even think that the brave stand Otis took was the act that birthed the movement which culminated 15 years later in the Declaration of Independence. His willingness to have his faith tested cost him dearly, but brought future Americans great blessings.

Costly Commitment. It seems that a black man named Anthony, who came from St. Thomas in the Virgin Islands, somehow was deeply influenced by Count von Zinzendorf, the saintly German leader of the Moravians in the 18th century. Anthony, it turned out, had been a slave. He told how his fellow slaves wanted to hear the story of the kindly God from the lips of missionaries. However, he warned that the missionaries could gain entrance to St. Thomas and to the slaves only if they went as slaves. It seemed to everyone that the situation was hopeless. Who would be able to go to preach under such terrible restrictions?

Two Moravian men, however, stepped forward. Leonard Dober and Tobias Leopold had themselves sold as slaves and sent to the Caribbean, where they suffered and eventually died. Yet their uncompromising sacrifice of faith planted a strong Christian church in that area.

Faith's Unexpected Result. Mary Coburn struggled to become a singer and was about ready to give up in desperation when she grabbed a piece of music and began to sing it. The music happened to be Malotte's "The Lord's Prayer." Her courage returned. Jubilantly, she sang it five or six times as an expression of her vibrant faith.

A few days later, Mary saw a note being slipped under her door. The paper went something like this: "Dear Neighbor: Things have been so hard for me lately that I had no desire to live. But your singing helped me, for you sounded as if you had something to live for. The other night I decided to take my life. I turned on the gas. Just then you began singing 'The Lord's Prayer.' It made me realize what I was doing. I turned off the gas and opened the windows. You saved my life! I'll always be grateful." Imagine what unexpected things can result from our jubilant expressions of faith!

FOR YOUTH

■ **TOPIC:** Defiance!

■ **QUESTIONS:** 1. How did Daniel distinguish himself from his peers? 2. How did the conspirators try to frame Daniel? 3. What did Daniel do when he learned about the king's decree? 4. Why did the king hurry to the lions' den at the first light of dawn? 5. What truths about Daniel's God did the king's decree proclaim?

■ **ILLUSTRATIONS:**

An Extraordinary Person. Fourteen years ago this month, Juvenal Habyarimana, the Hutu president of the central African nation of Rwanda, was returning by plane to Kigali, the country's capital. But as the aircraft was about to land, it was shot down. In response, the political opponents of the deceased president were murdered. Then, over the next 100 days, members of the rival Tutsi clan were also slaughtered.

During this horrendous bloodbath, one extraordinary person stood out—Paul

Rusesabagina. He recounts in his book, *An Ordinary Man*, how he stood up to the insane actions unfolding around him by giving refuge to over 1,200 Tutsis and Hutus within the confines of the luxury hotel he managed. This was his way of defying the bands of murderers who hacked their victims to death with machetes. It is the same sort of ethical fortitude that believers should applaud, especially as they take a stand for justice and equity in our sometimes morally topsy-turvy world.

The Path of Faith. When Daniel's faith was put to the test, he resolved to obey God. Sometimes, we can also find ourselves in situations that challenge our willingness to do what is right. One cold November, Tommy Peluso was caught in the dilemma of having to choose between obeying his parents or caving in to the taunts of his friends. Tommy and his nine-year-old buddies had wandered out to an abandoned railroad bridge where some older youth hung out. Tommy's parents had forbidden him to play on the bridge because it was too dangerous.

The bridge crossed a river and had no walkway or guard railings. Tommy knew his parents' strict instructions about staying off the bridge. But his friends teased him about being afraid to cross the bridge on the rails. Tommy tried to resist, but the desire to please his buddies finally overcame his willingness to obey his parents.

Halfway across, Tommy's feet slipped on the ice-covered iron rails and girders. Tommy screamed as he tried to regain his balance, then plunged 15 feet in the chilly waters below. The stream was fairly shallow, and Tommy landed hard in the frozen mud below the surface of the river. He broke one leg in two places and shattered his ankle in the other leg. Thankfully, he was rescued and survived after a long and painful recovery. He also learned the hard way that the path of faith includes heeding the wise rules set down by one's parents.

Faith's Willing Sacrifice. Ron's sister, Pamela, was sick and needed a kidney transplant. Ron's kidney would be a perfect match. His parents knew that if Ron went through surgery and donated one of his kidneys, it would save his sick sister's life. Physicians carefully examined the procedure. Ron realized that he was being asked to give up something important to himself. His parents did all they could to keep him from feeling pressured.

Because of Ron's vibrant faith in Christ, the youngster agreed without any reservations. Ron saw the whole procedure as an opportunity to express his love for his sister, despite the sacrifice it entailed. Daniel also saw his decision as the best one because of his faith in God.

DANIEL'S PRAYER FOR THE PEOPLE

BACKGROUND SCRIPTURE: Daniel 9
DEVOTIONAL READING: Psalm 130

KEY VERSE: Now therefore, O our God, hear the prayer of thy servant, and his supplications, and cause thy face to shine upon thy sanctuary that is desolate, for the Lord's sake. Daniel 9:17.

KING JAMES VERSION

DANIEL 9:1 In the first year of Darius the son of Ahasuerus, of the seed of the Medes, which was made king over the realm of the Chaldeans; 2 In the first year of his reign I Daniel understood by books the number of the years, whereof the word of the LORD came to Jeremiah the prophet, that he would accomplish seventy years in the desolations of Jerusalem. 3 And I set my face unto the Lord God, to seek by prayer and supplications, with fasting, and sackcloth, and ashes:

4 And I prayed unto the LORD my God, and made my confession, and said, O Lord, the great and dreadful God, keeping the covenant and mercy to them that love him, and to them that keep his commandments; 5 We have sinned, and have committed iniquity, and have done wickedly, and have rebelled, even by departing from thy precepts and from thy judgments: 6 Neither have we hearkened unto thy servants the prophets, which spake in thy name to our kings, our princes, and our fathers, and to all the people of the land. 7 O Lord, righteousness belongeth unto thee, but unto us confusion of faces, as at this day; to the men of Judah, and to the inhabitants of Jerusalem, and unto all Israel, that are near, and that are far off, through all the countries whither thou hast driven them, because of their trespass that they have trespassed against thee. . . .

17 Now therefore, O our God, hear the prayer of thy servant, and his supplications, and cause thy face to shine upon thy sanctuary that is desolate, for the Lord's sake. 18 O my God, incline thine ear, and hear; open thine eyes, and behold our desolations, and the city which is called by thy name: for we do not present our supplications before thee for our righteousnesses, but for thy great mercies. 19 O Lord, hear; O Lord, forgive; O Lord, hearken and do; defer not, for thine own sake, O my God: for thy city and thy people are called by thy name.

NEW REVISED STANDARD VERSION

DANIEL 9:1 In the first year of Darius son of Ahasuerus, by birth a Mede, who became king over the realm of the Chaldeans— 2 in the first year of his reign, I, Daniel, perceived in the books the number of years that, according to the word of the LORD to the prophet Jeremiah, must be fulfilled for the devastation of Jerusalem, namely, seventy years.

3 Then I turned to the Lord God, to seek an answer by prayer and supplication with fasting and sackcloth and ashes. 4 I prayed to the Lord my God and made confession, saying,

"Ah, Lord, great and awesome God, keeping covenant and steadfast love with those who love you and keep your commandments, 5 we have sinned and done wrong, acted wickedly and rebelled, turning aside from your commandments and ordinances. 6 We have not listened to your servants the prophets, who spoke in your name to our kings, our princes, and our ancestors, and to all the people of the land.

7 "Righteousness is on your side, O Lord, but open shame, as at this day, falls on us, the people of Judah, the inhabitants of Jerusalem, and all Israel, those who are near and those who are far away, in all the lands to which you have driven them, because of the treachery that they have committed against you. . . .

17 "Now therefore, O our God, listen to the prayer of your servant and to his supplication, and for your own sake, Lord, let your face shine upon your desolated sanctuary. 18 Incline your ear, O my God, and hear. Open your eyes and look at our desolation and the city that bears your name. We do not present our supplication before you on the ground of our righteousness, but on the ground of your great mercies. 19 O Lord, hear; O Lord, forgive; O Lord, listen and act and do not delay! For your own sake, O my God, because your city and your people bear your name!"

9

Monday, April 21	Psalm 130	*The Assurance of Redemption*
Tuesday, April 22	Daniel 9:1-3	*Preparing to Pray*
Wednesday, April 23	Daniel 9:4-10	*A Righteous God*
Thursday, April 24	Daniel 9:11-14	*God's Response to Sin*
Friday, April 25	Daniel 9:15-19	*Hear, O God*
Saturday, April 26	Daniel 9:20-23	*A Word Gone Out*
Sunday, April 27	Daniel 9:24-27	*God's Strong Covenant*

BACKGROUND

The events of Daniel 9 took place during the first year of the reign of Darius the Mede (9:1). That began in 539 B.C., the year Babylon was conquered by the Medo-Persians. Daniel had been in captivity for 66 years, since 605 B.C. At this time, he would have been about 82 years old. The last date recorded in the Book of Daniel is 536 B.C., *the third year of Cyrus king of Persia* (10:1). Media was a region northeast of Babylon. Almost nothing is known about the origins of the ancient people known as the Medes, and only a few words of their language have survived. Persia, modern Iran, was located south of Media.

While the kings of Persia and Media had made joint military campaigns into southwest Asia in 559 B.C., 20 years later Darius overthrew Belshazzar to gain control of the Babylonian empire. Belshazzar knew about his own fall in advance because of a handwritten message inscribed on his palace wall (see chap. 5). The rise of the Medo-Persians was a providential act of God. Daniel apparently knew that the rise of Darius paved the way for the return of the Israelites to their homeland. Daniel also understood from Jeremiah's prophecies (which the elder statesman regarded as being verbally inspired) that the 70-year exile begun by the *desolations of Jerusalem* (9:2), was nearing its end (see Jer. 25:11-12; 29:10).

The writer of Chronicles saw those 70 years as the sabbath rest for the land, time accumulated during 490 years when the people had neglected to allow the land to rest every seventh year, according to the law (see 2 Chron. 36:20-23; compare Lev. 25:1-7). With no specific way to measure the 70 years, some interpret this as a round number, perhaps denoting either a complete generation or an entire human lifetime (see Ps. 90:10). Others see it as the time period extending from 605 B.C. (the first attack on Jerusalem) to 536 B.C. (when Jerusalem was resettled). Still others calculate the 70 years from 586 B.C. (when the temple was destroyed) to 516 B.C. (when Zerubbabel dedicated the new temple; Ezra 6:13-18; Zech. 1:12).

NOTES ON THE PRINTED TEXT

Daniel's expectation for his people concerning their release from captivity drove him to his knees in prayer (Dan. 9:1-2). Two distinct terms appear in 9:3. The first, simply rendered *prayer*, was a general word often used in intercessory entreaties. The second word, translated *supplications*, denoted a petition for mercy and compassion. In describing how he prayed, Daniel said that he turned his face to the Lord. This could mean that Daniel set aside his normal routine and devoted himself entirely to prayer. It may also allude to the practice of praying in the direction of Jerusalem. Earlier in this book, we read how Daniel prayed in his upstairs room, where the latticed windows opened toward Jerusalem (6:10). Daniel approached the throne of grace with fasting, adorned in sackcloth (a rough fabric similar to burlap) and ashes. All three of these were signs of deep repentance or personal grief and loss (Dan. 9:3; see Ezek. 27:29-31).

Daniel recognized that the exile in Babylon was God's judgment for Israel's sin. The prophet also understood what God's covenant with His people required if they were to receive forgiveness, restoration, and divine blessing. The nation had to confess its sin and obey the commands of God (Dan. 9:4-5). In this knowledge, Daniel confessed the sins of the people, not once but four times (9:5, 8, 11, 15). He included himself as if he were personally involved in Israel's wickedness, rebellion, and disobedience. Even though God had graciously sent the prophets to turn His people back, the nation as a whole had ignored their message. According to Daniel, all Israel was guilty before God (9:6, 8-11).

Daniel affirmed that God is great, awesome, and faithful to fulfill His covenant promises with those who loved and obeyed Him. In contrast, God's chosen people had sinned against Him by doing what is wrong and wicked. They also rebelled by turning away from His commands and scorning His teachings (9:5). The covenant community refused to listen to the Lord's prophets, who humbly served Him and spoke as His representatives in the authority of His name to a wide audience of people, including monarchs and princes who ruled the inhabitants of the promised land (9:6).

Daniel affirmed the righteousness of the Lord in His person and actions. His chosen people, though, suffered public disgrace as a result of their disloyalty to God. Because they transgressed His ways, He was in the right to scatter them far and wide (9:7). All the chosen people experienced the humiliation of being dragged away to foreign lands because of their sin (9:8). Yet despite their rebellion, the sovereign Lord remained merciful and forgiving (9:9). His compassion was evident when He gave the Mosaic law; but the recipients of His favor refused to heed His stipulations and listen to His teachings, as set before them through His prophets (9:10).

Before the destruction of Jerusalem by the Babylonians, many people of Judah did not believe that God would destroy His own temple and His holy city until it actually happened. They continued in their worship of other gods. The prophets repeatedly pointed out that the people's unfaithfulness would bring judgment, and it did, namely, their 70-year exile in Babylon. The rejection of the prophets confirmed the people's unfaithfulness. Although the Lord's representatives occasionally foretold future events, their primary responsibility was calling the nation to obey God in the present.

They spoke to Israel's leaders and, through them, to all the people.

Tragically, the entire nation was guilty of refusing to follow the Lord's will (9:11); and because God is just in everything He does (9:14), He had no other choice but to pour out on His people the judgment solemnly threatened in the Mosaic law (see Deut. 28:15-68). God had given His people a very simple choice: obey Him and be blessed or disobey Him and suffer terrible curses. Because Israel had chosen the latter course, the people were dispersed and Jerusalem fell (Dan. 9:12). These horrible calamities were meant to bring God's people back to Him, but they refused to respond. Yet even in spite of the unparalleled *evil* (9:13) brought upon the nation, the people still were not turning away from their sin and submitting themselves to God's *truth.*

Daniel's petition for divine favor was grounded in an awareness of how God had faithfully acted throughout the course of Israel's history. The premier example of this was the Lord's deliverance of His people out of the land of Egypt with great power. Because of that mighty act, God brought lasting honor to His name; but this did not prevent His chosen people from sinning and behaving wickedly (9:15). As a consequence of this sobering truth, the only thing Daniel could do was appeal to the Lord on the basis of His justice. In view of all God's faithfulness and mercy in connection with His covenant promises, the elder statesman humbly asked the Lord to turn His raging anger away from Jerusalem. It was the chosen city built on His holy mountain (9:16) and thus the place where God decided to dwell and reign (Pss. 43:3; 68:16; Isa. 24:23). As such, it was intended to be the sacred site where the people could enjoy a transcendent encounter with God, in addition to finding refuge, peace, and joy in His presence (Isa. 2:1-5; Mich. 4:1-5).

In short, Daniel was entreating the Lord to end Jerusalem's condition as an object of scorn among the surrounding nations. Suggested here is the idea that the fortunes of a country, whether good or bad, were an indicator of its deity's power and might. A positive outcome for Judah would require God to forgive the sins of the current generation of Jews and the iniquities committed by their ancestors (Dan. 9:16). With humility and courage, Daniel petitioned God to *hear* (9:17) the prayer of His servant. Expressed differently, the prophet asked the Lord to graciously accept the request to show favor on His devastated sanctuary. Daniel was convinced that God would bring honor to His name by smiling once again on His temple. Though it lay in ruins, the Lord could enable His people to rebuild it.

Daniel concluded with an entreaty for God to give ear to his prayer, as if the Lord would turn His ear to listen attentively to the prophet's request (9:18). Daniel also asked God to open His eyes and see the ruined condition of Jerusalem. The Hebrew word translated *desolations* usually describes devastation that results from divine judgment. Daniel was not implying that God was not listening or had closed His eyes to the exiles' problems. The Lord was fully aware of these issues. This prayer, however, came from the human perspective on the circumstances. It appeared to the Jews still in exile in Babylon as if God had stopped listening and had closed His eyes.

Daniel reminded God that both the city of Jerusalem and His people carried His *name* as a mark of ownership. The Hebrew word can signify reputation or renown, as in God's name being praised and known for what He has done (2 Sam. 7:25-26). The Lord's deliverance of His people from Babylon would show who He was to the people who were called by His name. Also, since God's reputation rested with His people and His holy city, the neighboring peoples would recognize who the Lord is by His deliverance of the Jews and restoration of Jerusalem and its temple. Daniel acknowledged that he was not basing his requests on his own righteous deeds or those of his fellow Jews, whether they were living in the past or present; rather, it was due to the Lord's abundant compassion (Dan. 9:18).

Daniel was not trying to manipulate God; rather, the prophet showed a concern for the glory of the Lord. Daniel realized that God's reputation was inevitably tied to the fortunes of His exiled people. Thus, the prophet was convinced that even though they had disowned God, He would not disown them. This truth emboldened Daniel to plead with the Lord to hear his request and forgive the sins of His people. The prophet entreated God to quickly act in restoring the exiles to the promised land and enable them to bring honor to His name by rebuilding their sanctuary and capital (9:19).

SUGGESTIONS TO TEACHERS

Daniel knew how to pray effectively. Unreserved confession of sin opened his heart to the Lord. Complete submission to God's will also prepared the prophet for divine direction. Like Daniel, we should first go to the Lord in confession, then listen with an attitude of submission and openness to hear what He wants to say to us.

1. ACKNOWLEDGING OUR SINS. Quite often God uses circumstances and other people to get our attention and draw us back to Him. In difficult times, we should be especially sensitive to how God may want to speak to us through them. Tragically, though, when trouble comes, it is all too easy for us to point the finger of blame and guilt toward others while excusing ourselves. It is difficult to imagine anyone among the Israelites more righteous and blameless than Daniel. Yet he was the one on his knees begging God's forgiveness for his sin and that of his people. If we want renewal and revival in our churches, the first step is for us to look into a mirror and ask the Lord to begin with the one we see.

2. RECOGNIZING GOD'S MERCY. Even when we go through the painful process of repentance, we must never forget that God shows mercy and graciously bestows blessings upon us because it pleases Him to do so, not because we deserve it. Many people, believers and unbelievers alike, act as if God is somehow obligated to grant any and all requests made of Him. But since sin placed all humanity under a death sentence, it would be unwise indeed to demand that a just and holy God give us what we deserve.

3. CLEARING THE WAY FOR OUR PETITIONS. The wonderful truth arising from this week's lesson is that God still answers the prayers of His children today. But there is a condition. He expects us to be walking in obedience to His will when we come to Him with our requests (see John 15:7). If there is unconfessed sin in our lives, the first prayer the Lord wants to hear from us is one of confession and repentance. Then the way is clear for prayers of petition. Indeed, that was Daniel's practice when he approached the throne of grace and God responded favorably to him. The same can also be our experience, if we so desire.

FOR ADULTS	■ **TOPIC:** Intercession in Crisis

■ **QUESTIONS:** 1. What understanding did Daniel have concerning Jeremiah's prophecy? 2. Why did Daniel begin his prayer by referring to the Lord as the *great and dreadful God* (Dan. 9:4)? 3. How had God's chosen people responded to His covenantal love? 4. In what sense were the Jewish exiles covered with shame? 5. What specifically did Daniel ask God to do for His people?

■ **ILLUSTRATIONS:**

The Power of Intercessory Prayer. Because Mork Eiwuley from Ghana had no visa, he would not be able to attend the leadership school for Christian publishers in Colorado Springs, Colorado. Then, to his surprise, he met a woman who was able to pull strings and get his visa at the eleventh hour. "That," Mork said, "never happens." It wasn't until Mork arrived at the institute that he found out the story behind his story. Patti, an employee of Cook Communication's U.S. ministry, along with most of her 250 colleagues, had agreed to pray for one of the publishers scheduled to attend. Her publisher was Mork. On the very day she started praying for him, he received his visa. "What never happens, happened," Mork smiled. "People at Cook were praying for me. That's how I got my visa."

The Advocate. Nancy Grace is an anchorwoman for *CNN Headline News* and *Court TV*. In *Guideposts*, she explained why she is so tough on crime and criminals. In the summer of 1981, her fiance, Keith, was at a "convenience store to buy sodas" when a mugger "shot him five times in the neck and head." Nancy relates that from that day on, the sheltered life she knew as a child growing up "on the outskirts of Macon, Georgia" had ended.

It would take months for Nancy to process the horrific murder of Keith and to figure out what to do next. Nancy sensed that God wanted her to study law at Mercer University. After graduating, she began working as an attorney. Eventually, she was "walking into courtrooms, staring down criminals, and badgering judges into meting out tough sentences." Nancy realized that as a result of Keith's death, God gave her a mission she could have never imagined on her own. Nancy had become an advocate for the innocent and vulnerable members of society, "their voice in a world that, though essentially good, is embattled by evil."

Daniel had a similar concern for those around him. He was so inundated by grief over the devastation of Jerusalem and exile of his people, that he made intercession and confession on their behalf for their sin against God. From the New Testament we learn that Jesus is the believer's Advocate. His intercession on their behalf before the throne of God enables them to experience divine mercy, grace, and forgiveness.

From Dream to Reality. In 2006, the Association of Baptists for World Evangelism (ABWE) reported that in Luís Eduardo Magalhães, Brazil, the intercessory prayers of believers turned a dream into a reality. The town is an agricultural-industrial center on "Bahia state's western frontier." At first, its residents doubted whether a new church building could be erected in four weeks. But according to ABWE, the people saw "God's hand and some of His choice volunteers at work" to bring about what seemed impossible.

In response to the petitions of many Christians, God provided for Emmanuel Baptist Church in Bahia "four one-week building teams from the Construction for World Evangelization ministry in Tampa, Florida." First came bricklayers, who got the work started. They were followed by carpenters, who covered the structure. Plumbers and electricians made the building functional, while painters and finishers brought the project to completion. At the end of the four-week period, the congregation moved from the "garage behind the missionaries' house to its new, permanent home." This was to "God's glory and the doubters' amazement!"

FOR YOUTH

■ TOPIC: Confess!

■ QUESTIONS: 1. How long did Jeremiah say the desolation of Jerusalem would last? 2. What was the nature of God's covenant with His people? 3. Why did the people of the covenant rebel against its stipulations? 4. In what way was God just in all His ways? 5. What was the basis for Daniel's confidence that God would respond quickly to his petitions?

■ ILLUSTRATIONS:

As Contrite As We Should Be? A Christian friend once declared to me that he had no fear of God because Scripture teaches that the perfect love of God expels all fear (see 1 John 4:18). Sadly, because he misunderstood this verse, his sins rarely disturbed him. Since he felt that God loved him so much, he also felt God would naturally and promptly forgive him whenever he sinned.

Most of us do not share my friend's attitude, but can we truly say we are as contrite as we should be when we ask for God's forgiveness? If not, then we need to learn from Daniel to be much more sincere and humble when we repent before our Lord.

Pray and Be Heard. Rev. E. M. Bounds led an eventful life. He studied to be a lawyer, but at age 26, he left law for the ministry. When the Civil War came, he served as a Confederate army chaplain until he was taken prisoner near the end of the war. After the war, he worked for a time as a Christian magazine editor but mostly served as a Methodist minister to churches in Missouri, Alabama, Tennessee, and Georgia.

But these are not the accomplishments for which E. M. Bounds is most remembered. He had a reputation for his passionate devotion to prayer. He regularly practiced the art of making supplication and petitions to God, rising at 4 A.M. and praying until 7 A.M. each day. His writings on prayer and its effects on the life of the believer (in books such as *Purpose in Prayer* and *Necessity in Prayer*) are still regarded as classics by many Christians.

Concerning the high value of prayer, Bounds wrote in *Prayer and Praying Men* that entreating God helps believers see beyond their own lives to heaven itself. Prayer gives people sweet visions of things beyond so that present things grow pale and unimportant in comparison. Daniel's sincere prayer for himself and his people allowed him to receive wisdom and understanding from the Lord. God still responds to our prayers if we come to Him with a humble and contrite heart.

Miracle at Dunkerque. When Adolf Hitler's armies were overrunning Europe in May, 1940, they trapped almost half a million British and French troops in the English Channel at Dunkerque, France. The British army estimated that they could safely evacuate no more than 30,000 to 40,000 of these troops to England. The rest would be captured or killed on the beaches by the German army and air force.

But then the situation changed. First, Hitler turned his tanks toward Paris, leaving the job of destroying Dunkerque mostly to his air force. Then, smoke from factories the Germans themselves had bombed began to blow across the beaches, hiding the escaping forces. Finally, the normally stormy English Channel became as calm as glass, and fog covered it for nine days. That grounded the German planes but allowed the armada of over 800 ships from England to rescue not 30,000, but over 338,000 troops to fight another day.

What was behind the "miracle" of Dunkerque? No one can say for certain. But perhaps the miracle came because in this time of crisis, Britain's King George VI called his country to a national day of prayer. The British people filled their churches, humbly asking God to save their troops and their nation from the Nazis.

THE TEMPLE REBUILT

BACKGROUND SCRIPTURE: Haggai 1, Ezra 5
DEVOTIONAL READING: Psalm 84:1-4

KEY VERSE: Go up to the mountain, and bring wood, and build the house; and I will take pleasure in it, and I will be glorified, saith the LORD. Haggai 1:8.

KING JAMES VERSION

HAGGAI 1:1 In the second year of Darius the king, in the sixth month, in the first day of the month, came the word of the LORD by Haggai the prophet unto Zerubbabel the son of Shealtiel, governor of Judah, and to Joshua the son of Josedech, the high priest, saying, 2 Thus speaketh the LORD of hosts, saying, This people say, The time is not come, the time that the LORD's house should be built. 3 Then came the word of the LORD by Haggai the prophet, saying, 4 Is it time for you, O ye, to dwell in your cieled houses, and this house lie waste? . . . 7 Thus saith the LORD of hosts; Consider your ways. 8 Go up to the mountain, and bring wood, and build the house; and I will take pleasure in it, and I will be glorified, saith the LORD. 9 Ye looked for much, and, lo, it came to little; and when ye brought it home, I did blow upon it. Why? saith the LORD of hosts. Because of mine house that is waste, and ye run every man unto his own house. 10 Therefore the heaven over you is stayed from dew, and the earth is stayed from her fruit. . . .

12 Then Zerubbabel the son of Shealtiel, and Joshua the son of Josedech, the high priest, with all the remnant of the people, obeyed the voice of the LORD their God, and the words of Haggai the prophet, as the LORD their God had sent him, and the people did fear before the LORD. 13 Then spake Haggai the LORD's messenger in the LORD's message unto the people, saying, I am with you, saith the LORD. 14 And the LORD stirred up the spirit of Zerubbabel the son of Shealtiel, governor of Judah, and the spirit of Joshua the son of Josedech, the high priest, and the spirit of all the remnant of the people; and they came and did work in the house of the LORD of hosts, their God, 15 In the four and twentieth day of the sixth month, in the second year of Darius the king.

NEW REVISED STANDARD VERSION

HAGGAI 1:1 In the second year of King Darius, in the sixth month, on the first day of the month, the word of the LORD came by the prophet Haggai to Zerubbabel son of Shealtiel, governor of Judah, and to Joshua son of Jehozadak, the high priest: 2 Thus says the LORD of hosts: These people say the time has not yet come to rebuild the Lord's house. 3 Then the word of the LORD came by the prophet Haggai, saying: 4 Is it a time for you yourselves to live in your paneled houses, while this house lies in ruins? . . .

7 Thus says the LORD of hosts: Consider how you have fared. 8 Go up to the hills and bring wood and build the house, so that I may take pleasure in it and be honored, says the LORD. 9 You have looked for much, and, lo, it came to little; and when you brought it home, I blew it away. Why? says the LORD of hosts. Because my house lies in ruins, while all of you hurry off to your own houses. 10 Therefore the heavens above you have withheld the dew, and the earth has withheld its produce. . . .

12 Then Zerubbabel son of Shealtiel, and Joshua son of Jehozadak, the high priest, with all the remnant of the people, obeyed the voice of the LORD their God, and the words of the prophet Haggai, as the LORD their God had sent him; and the people feared the LORD. 13 Then Haggai, the messenger of the LORD, spoke to the people with the LORD's message, saying, I am with you, says the LORD. 14 And the LORD stirred up the spirit of Zerubbabel son of Shealtiel, governor of Judah, and the spirit of Joshua son of Jehozadak, the high priest, and the spirit of all the remnant of the people; and they came and worked on the house of the LORD of hosts, their God, 15 on the twenty-fourth day of the month, in the sixth month.

10

287

HOME BIBLE READINGS

Monday, April 28	Psalm 84:1-4	*In God's House*
Tuesday, April 29	Haggai 1:1-11	*Time to Rebuild the Temple*
Wednesday, April 30	Haggai 1:12-15	*The Work Begins*
Thursday, May 1	Ezra 3:8-13	*Rebuilding the Foundation*
Friday, May 2	Ezra 4:1-4	*Help Rejected*
Saturday, May 3	Ezra 5:1-5	*The Rebuilding Questioned*
Sunday, May 4	Ezra 5:6-17	*The Decree of King Cyrus*

BACKGROUND

The devastation of Jerusalem in 586 B.C. forms the backdrop for the Book of Haggai. The Babylonians had overrun the holy city. When the invaders destroyed Jerusalem, they leveled the temple in the process. They then took many survivors captive, settling them in colonies throughout Babylonia. A generation after the city fell, the Jews were still in exile. By this time they had grown accustomed to their new homes and way of life. All but the aged had been born in exile and knew Judah only through stories. It was not God's plan, though, for the situation to remain that way. He wanted to repopulate Judah, rebuild Jerusalem, and restore the temple.

God knew it would take some prodding to get the Jews to leave their new land and return to Judah. He decided to use one man to get things rolling. That person was Cyrus, ruler of Persia, the empire that had replaced the kingdom of Babylon. In 536 B.C., with the permission of King Cyrus, the Jews began to rebuild the temple. The books of Ezra and Nehemiah present the history of God's people during the years following the destruction of Jerusalem and the temple (586 B.C.). They, together with the prophecies of Haggai and Zechariah (both dated about 520 B.C.) and Malachi (about 432 B.C.), comprise the main Hebrew records of those years.

NOTES ON THE PRINTED TEXT

Zerubbabel is identified as *governor* in the description of the return recorded in Haggai 1:1. The Persian government authorized this person of Davidic lineage to spearhead the return of the Jewish exiles and the restoration of Judah. Tragically, the rebuilding of the shrine was interrupted for a number of years due to opposition from the Samaritans and the indifferences of many of the returned exiles who had never worshiped in the temple of Solomon. In 521 B.C., King Darius Hystaspes ascended the Persian throne (ruling from 521–486 B.C.). After crushing a number of revolts, he consolidated his control over the empire and restored political stability. He also discovered the decree of Cyprus for rebuilding the Jerusalem temple and reactivated the mandate. Shortly thereafter, on August 29, 520 B.C., God raised up the prophet Haggai to exhort Zerubbabel, Joshua, and the people of Judah to resume the rebuilding of the shrine. Through the ministry of Haggai and Zechariah, his contemporary, the endeavor was completed in four years (516 B.C.).

The prophet began his message by stating, *Thus speaketh the LORD of hosts* (Hag. 1:2). Haggai did not want anyone to mistake his words; they came with the full authority of God Himself. The Jewish inhabitants of Jerusalem excused their apathy by declaring that the time had not yet come for them to rebuild the Lord's house of worship in the holy city. Some believed that the 70 years of captivity were not yet up (see Jer. 25:11-12; 29:10). Though they claimed to be waiting for a better time to proceed, the real problem was the people's lack of concern. Haggai exposed the reason why the work of rebuilding the temple wasn't finished by comparing the people's homes to God's house of worship (Hag. 1:3-4). If conditions weren't satisfactory for building the temple, then why were they able to remodel and beautify their own homes with cedar paneling or possibly a protective plastering? With God's sanctuary in ruins, the people should have given the rebuilding of their homes lesser priority. Haggai's penetrating question shows that the inhabitants put their own interests before God's.

Haggai did not wait for excuses or confessions. He forged ahead beyond the obvious answer and told the people to look at themselves and their circumstances (1:5). The prophet exhorted them to consider the results of the investment of their time and strength in meeting their own needs. The inhabitants had sown much seed, but harvested meager crops (such as grapes, figs, and pomegranates, which were picked at that time of year). They were eating and drinking without satisfaction. They had clothes, but were cold. They had money, but could not hold on to it (1:6).

It was proper for the Lord to withhold His blessings. After all, His people had lopsided priorities in which they crowded out God. In response, the Lord reversed the normal process of things, so that the harder the people worked for themselves, the less they got in return. Their crops, food, clothes, and wages seemed to disappear. In light of these facts, Haggai again told the people to consider their ways (1:7). Then he told them to swing into action. Once they admitted their unwise decisions, they would be ready to rebuild the temple. They would recognize that further delays would be self-defeating and dishonoring to God. The people had gone to the hills to get timber for their houses. Now it was time to gather lumber for the temple (1:8). Since the exterior of the shrine was primarily made out of large stones, the wood was probably used for the structure's interior paneling (see Ezra 5:8; 6:4). Gathering timber from the forests would show obedience and initiate the rebuilding process.

For emphasis, Haggai returned to his previous theme: because of the people's delay in rebuilding the temple, the all-powerful Lord had withheld His blessings. The people kept looking for abundance for themselves at the shrine's expense (Hag. 1:9). However, the greater their greediness, the more bitter was their disappointment because they were poorer than ever. As long as they remained unrepentant, the Lord would thwart their efforts to become more prosperous. They failed to recognize that God was judging them for their disobedience, in accordance with the stipulations of the Mosaic covenant (see Lev. 26:20; Deut. 11:8-15; 28:29, 38-40). The prophet's explanation of the people's hard times focused on their agricultural economy. When they brought their harvest home, God blew it all away (Hag. 1:9). This may be a reference to windstorms or possibly to the small size of the grain, which caused it to disappear with the chaff. This circumstance served as a reminder of the transitory nature of all human accomplishments (see Isa. 40:7). As long as the returnees to Judah continued to delay their rebuilding of the temple, it would prove to be costly.

During the dry summers, farmers in Judah relied on dew to water their crops (see 2 Sam. 1:21; 1 Kings 17:1). The air, full of moisture from the Mediterranean Sea, condensed during the cool nights, and usually provided enough water for the crops; and as good farmers, the people planted with high hopes of reaping an abundant harvest. God, however, kept back the dew, which in turn brought withered crops and widespread famine (Hag. 1:10). Moreover, the Lord sent a severe drought that affected everything—the fields and terraced hillsides; the grain (most likely, barley and wheat), the grapes (used to make new wine), the olives (used for food, ointment, and medicine), and all the other crops; and the people, livestock, and all that they labored to produce (1:11). This calamity occurred because the people put their homes first ahead of God's house of worship. The people had only to look at the ruins of the temple to find the reason for their devastated crops. Again, the contrast was plain. This should have been a signal to them to repent; but because they did not discern the will of God through the drought, He sent Haggai to make the connection clear (1:1, 12).

Haggai's message produced the desired result. Within a modest period of time, Zerubbabel, Joshua, and all the people recognized that God's hand was upon His messenger, the prophet. The Hebrew word translated *remnant* (1:12) here specifically denoted all the people who returned from exile in Babylon. More generally, it also referred to those among God's chosen people who remained loyal to Him despite widespread apostasy and disobedience. The survival of some of the people of Judah was God's gracious provision to avert the nation's complete disappearance (Isa. 1:9). If it were not for this group of survivors, Judah would have been utterly destroyed for its sin—just as the cities of Sodom and Gomorrah had been destroyed long before (Gen. 18:16—19:29; see Ezra 9:14; Isa 10:20-22; 11:11, 16; Jer. 23:3; 31:17).

All the old problems and obstacles persisted, but the people's attitude had changed. They gave priority to rebuilding God's temple over their concerns about their houses, crops, food and drink, clothes, and financial holdings. In response to this remarkable change of heart, mind, and will, God promised them His presence in the work that loomed ahead: *I am with you* (Hag. 1:13), He said. That was the most valuable component of all. Before the Exile, Ezekiel had seen a vision of the glory of the Lord leaving Jerusalem prior to the destruction of the city and its temple (Ezek. 10:1—11:23). Haggai's messages reassured the remnant that the Lord was indeed with them, and most importantly, His glory had returned to His temple (Hag. 1:13). Their obedience in rebuilding and His desire to honor the covenant He made at Mount Sinai had brought His blessings to them (2:4-5).

What a sense of relief the people must have felt as God's tone changed from reproof to tenderness. He hastened, as it were, to forget the remnant's previous unfaithfulness and to assure them that He was and would be with them. God's presence was the best blessing, because it included all the others. The civil and religious leaders, along with the entire remnant of God's people, moved from selfish excuses to sacrificial labor (1:14). The reason for the change in attitude was the stirring of God's Spirit in the hearts of His people. They were now energized and encouraged to undertake their divinely-appointed task. Haggai specified the day the work began was September 21, 520 B.C., namely, 23 days after he delivered his initial message (1:1, 15). Some suggest that the intervening days were spent in planning, obtaining building materials (such as wood), and getting a sufficient number of skilled artisans. The *sixth month* (1:15) was also the time when summer crops were harvested in the orchards and fields, so the people may have needed to complete that task first. Still, three weeks was remarkably fast, especially considering that the work had been halted for years.

SUGGESTIONS TO TEACHERS

The prophet Haggai spoke to people who were excited to be in their homeland but who had trouble settling in. They were relatively at ease but they still faced many obstacles, especially as they rebuilt their lives in Jerusalem. In some respects, Christians face similar challenges. We live in a world that is really not our permanent home. We are tempted to focus all our attention on the here-and-now while leaving the accomplishment of God's work to others. Because of that, we need to be careful how we listen.

1. BE CAREFUL TO LISTEN TO THE WORD OF THE LORD. The prophet Haggai gives us a strong incentive to listen, not to the whims of people around us, but rather to the rock-steady Word of God. The inspired message says that God is at work and wants us, His people, to be about His work. Others sometimes steer us wrong, but God never does.

2. BE CAREFUL TO LISTEN TO THE PEOPLE DOING THE WORK. The people listened to Haggai because he delivered God's message and was willing to be involved in the Lord's work. The old proverb is right—those doing the rowing don't have time to rock the boat. Some would-be leaders seem to want to speak from "on high" but not get involved in the nitty-gritty of serving God. Let that not be true of us.

3. BE CAREFUL TO LISTEN FOR THE RIGHT TIMING. Timing is essential to success in almost any enterprise. The prophet called the people to respond to the proper timing in rebuilding the temple. They had lived in relative luxury long enough. Today, too, timing is important in accomplishing God's work. When He gives the go-ahead, that is the proper time to act.

■ **TOPIC:** First Things First!

■ **QUESTIONS:** 1. What excuse did the people give for not rebuilding the temple? 2. In what way were the priorities of the people misplaced? 3. What was the result of the people's misplaced priorities? 4. How did the people respond to the exhortation of Haggai? 5. Why is it important for us to keep our priorities straight when it comes to the things of God?

■ **ILLUSTRATIONS:**

Maintaining Proper Priorities. Like many of his colleagues, Albert was a successful business executive climbing the corporate ladder. Albert's luxurious home, two late-model automobiles, mountain cabin, and membership in an executive club reflected his comfortable lifestyle. His wife added to this success as an established real estate agent. Albert's status had made him a pillar in the community. Who could ask for anything more?

Although surrounded by material and social achievements, Albert longed for meaning and purpose in life. His desire to go to seminary and become a missionary overrode his quest for success. Striving to be faithful to God's call, Albert and his wife sold all their worldly possessions and began to pursue their life's ambition. True happiness for Albert began when he exchanged his priorities for God's priority over his life.

Be Careful What You Get Attached To. We sometimes get too attached to our possessions, the way the returnees were attached to their houses. When Bill Bradley was U.S. Senator from New Jersey, he told this story about his days as a professional basketball player. During his time with the New York Knicks, they were in a playoff against their archrivals, the Boston Celtics. After they lost the first two games, the New York fans were upset. Senator Bradley said one fan wrote him a letter: "Bradley, if you guys lose one more game to the Celtics, I am personally coming over to your house and I'm going to strangle your dog." The guy signed his name—Joe Pell.

Bill Bradley wrote him back, "Dear Joe Pell: I don't have a dog." A few days later a delivery truck pulled up in front of Bradley's house and unloaded a crate. Inside were a dog and a note. The note said: "Bradley, don't get too attached to this dog."

Get a Life. John Wooden was a coach whose UCLA teams won 10 NCAA championships in 12 years. No one speaks more eloquently about Wooden than Bill Walton, who played for UCLA at a troubled time in America when young people were asking hard questions and when dissent was in style.

In a way reminiscent of the prophet Haggai, the answers never seemed to change for Wooden. "We thought he was nuts," Walton said. "But in all his preachings and teachings, everything he told us turned out to be true. His interest and goal was to make you the best basketball player but first to make you the best person," Walton said. "He would never talk wins and losses but what we needed to succeed in life. Once you were a good human being, you had a chance to be a good player. He never deviated from that."

Walton said that Wooden never tried to be your friend. "He was your teacher, your coach. He handled us with extreme patience." Walton recalls the old coach having thousands of maxims. Walton said, "He is more John Wooden today than ever. He is a man who truly has principles and ideas. He didn't teach basketball. He taught life."

"When you're touched by someone that special, it changes your life," Walton said. "You spend your life chasing it down, trying to recreate it. He stopped coaching UCLA years ago. Now he just coaches the world."

FOR YOUTH

■ **TOPIC:** Rebuild!

■ **QUESTIONS:** 1. What indictment did God bring against His people? 2. What lame excuse did the people offer in their defense? 3. What deprivation had the people experienced and why? 4. Why did the leaders and people respond so enthusiastically to Haggai's exhortation? 5. What should our response be to exhortations of the Lord?

■ **ILLUSTRATIONS:**

Does Anyone Care? A teacher once wrote the word *apathy* in large letters across the entire chalkboard of his classroom. One of his students broke his conversation with another student long enough to glance at the word on the board, slowly sounding the word out. Then the student turned to the guy slouched next to him and asked what the word meant. The classic response came: "Who cares!"

The story may be funny, but the truth it conveys is tragic. Apathy can be like a crippling disease among teens, especially believers. In fact, when it comes to doing the work of God in the church and surrounding community, too many Christians are apathetic. They would rather form "holy huddles" than do all that the Lord desires of them. Apathy might feel comfortable and safe, but it accomplishes little of value. The people of Haggai's day had grown apathetic about rebuilding the temple, and God used him to spur them to action. Once they overcame their complacency, they did a great work for God and experienced His blessing.

Nightmare in San Francisco. At 5:12 A.M. on April 18, 1906, the city of San Francisco was awakened to a 7.8-magnitude earthquake. According to Justin Ewers of *U.S. News & World Report*, the shifting of the "continental plate beneath California . . . split the ground for 300 miles." It also left a "visible scar down the state." Within three days, the "largest metropolis west of the Mississippi" was reduced to a "charred skeleton."

The natural disaster had burned more than 28,000 structures in 480 city blocks over more than three-quarters of the city. Also, more than 3,000 perished and 225,000 were left homeless. San Francisco native and newspaper magnate William Randolph Hearst wrote: "The hills rolled to the seas as bare as when the pioneers landed in '49. But now they are a blackened waste. North to the bay, west to the Mission—nothing but ruins. The wholesale district is destroyed, the manufacturing district, the financial district, and the waterfront section—all destroyed."

Despite the wide-scale destruction, the city devoted its energy to "quickly rebuilding—at any cost." Their success was evident in the hosting of a world's fair just nine years later. It was called the Panama Pacific International Exhibition and was "built on filled-in mudflats." The Jews making their way back to Judah after a long exile in Babylon also had high hopes for rebuilding their homeland—including Jerusalem and its temple. Too much was at stake for them not to succeed in their efforts to establish themselves once again in the land of promise.

From Relief to Recovery. On October 8, 2005, a 7.6-magnitude earthquake struck northwest Pakistan. In its wake, the natural disaster killed more than 80,000, injured an estimated 100,000, and left over 3.5 million homeless. About 200,000 went into camps, while the rest of the survivors sheltered in tents or tin-roofed shacks across the devastated region. According to *Twin Cities Public Television* correspondent Fred de Sam Lazaro, a "relatively warm winter and massive relief effort helped avert a second wave of deaths." Indeed, the region witnessed the "biggest humanitarian airlift" since the Berlin crisis after World War II.

With the arrival of spring, international government organizations and relief agencies turned their attention to help refugees return to their homes in Pakistan-controlled Kashmir. Officials pledged to give seeds and farm tools and initiate employment programs. Also, the Pakistani government promised to give money to returnees so they could build more permanent shelters in the towns and villages wiped out by the earthquake. The goal was to have the construction finished before the next winter came. By some estimates, 85 to 90 per cent of those displayed would eventually move back in the years ahead. One official said, "Out of the rubble of this tragedy is a unique opportunity to rebuild the region and its standard of living."

Thousands of years ago, the exiles who returned to Judah from Babylon also struggled to rebuild their temple, their capital, and their lives. At times, the difficult circumstances and ongoing opposition from antagonists left the returnees feeling dejected and wanting to quit. Thankfully, God gave them the courage to rebuild their community and the grace to work for a brighter future.

REBUILDING THE WALL

BACKGROUND SCRIPTURE: Nehemiah 1:1—2:20
DEVOTIONAL READING: Psalm 137:1–7; 138:1-5

KEY VERSE: Then I told them of the hand of my God which was good upon me; as also the king's words that he had spoken unto me. And they said, Let us rise up and build. So they strengthened their hands for this good work. Nehemiah 2:18.

KING JAMES VERSION

NEHEMIAH 2:1 And it came to pass in the month Nisan, in the twentieth year of Artaxerxes the king, that wine was before him: and I took up the wine, and gave it unto the king. Now I had not been beforetime sad in his presence. 2 Wherefore the king said unto me, Why is thy countenance sad, seeing thou art not sick? this is nothing else but sorrow of heart. Then I was very sore afraid, 3 And said unto the king, Let the king live for ever: why should not my countenance be sad, when the city, the place of my fathers' sepulchres, lieth waste, and the gates thereof are consumed with fire? 4 Then the king said unto me, For what dost thou make request? So I prayed to the God of heaven. 5 And I said unto the king, If it please the king, and if thy servant have found favour in thy sight, that thou wouldest send me unto Judah, unto the city of my fathers' sepulchres, that I may build it. 6 And the king said unto me, (the queen also sitting by him,) For how long shall thy journey be? and when wilt thou return? So it pleased the king to send me; and I set him a time. 7 Moreover I said unto the king, If it please the king, let letters be given me to the governors beyond the river, that they may convey me over till I come into Judah; 8 And a letter unto Asaph the keeper of the king's forest, that he may give me timber to make beams for the gates of the palace which appertained to the house, and for the wall of the city, and for the house that I shall enter into. And the king granted me, according to the good hand of my God upon me. . . .

11 So I came to Jerusalem, and was there three days. . . . 17 Then said I unto them, Ye see the distress that we are in, how Jerusalem lieth waste, and the gates thereof are burned with fire: come, and let us build up the wall of Jerusalem, that we be no more a reproach. 18 Then I told them of the hand of my God which was good upon me; as also the king's words that he had spoken unto me. And they said, Let us rise up and build. So they strengthened their hands for this good work.

NEW REVISED STANDARD VERSION

NEHEMIAH 2:1 In the month of Nisan, in the twentieth year of King Artaxerxes, when wine was served him, I carried the wine and gave it to the king. Now, I had never been sad in his presence before. 2 So the king said to me, "Why is your face sad, since you are not sick? This can only be sadness of the heart." Then I was very much afraid. 3 I said to the king, "May the king live forever! Why should my face not be sad, when the city, the place of my ancestors' graves, lies waste, and its gates have been destroyed by fire?" 4 Then the king said to me, "What do you request?" So I prayed to the God of heaven. 5 Then I said to the king, "If it pleases the king, and if your servant has found favor with you, I ask that you send me to Judah, to the city of my ancestors' graves, so that I may rebuild it." 6 The king said to me (the queen also was sitting beside him), "How long will you be gone, and when will you return?" So it pleased the king to send me, and I set him a date. 7 Then I said to the king, "If it pleases the king, let letters be given me to the governors of the province Beyond the River, that they may grant me passage until I arrive in Judah; 8 and a letter to Asaph, the keeper of the king's forest, directing him to give me timber to make beams for the gates of the temple fortress, and for the wall of the city, and for the house that I shall occupy." And the king granted me what I asked, for the gracious hand of my God was upon me. . . .

11 So I came to Jerusalem and was there for three days. . . .

17 Then I said to them, "You see the trouble we are in, how Jerusalem lies in ruins with its gates burned. Come, let us rebuild the wall of Jerusalem, so that we may no longer suffer disgrace." 18 I told them that the hand of my God had been gracious upon me, and also the words that the king had spoken to me. Then they said, "Let us start building!" So they committed themselves to the common good.

Monday, May 5	Psalm 137:1-7	*A Lament for Jerusalem*
Tuesday, May 6	Nehemiah 1:1-4	*Weeping and Fasting*
Wednesday, May 7	Nehemiah 1:5-11	*Nehemiah's Confession*
Thursday, May 8	Nehemiah 2:1-10	*Permission to Return*
Friday, May 9	Nehemiah 2:11-16	*A Secret Inspection*
Saturday, May 10	Nehemiah 2:17-20	*Determination to Rebuild*
Sunday, May 11	Psalm 138:1-5	*Giving Thanks to God*

BACKGROUND

After 20 years, in response to the urging of Haggai and Zechariah, the Jewish remnant managed to complete a small version of the former temple (see Ezra 6:14). During this time, Ezra strengthened the commitment of the exilic community in Judah to the Law of the Lord (see 7:14, 25-26). However, nearly a full century after the first exiles arrived in Judah, Jerusalem still lay unfortified, the spiritual reforms of Ezra were only skin-deep, and the powerful enemies surrounding Judah were committed to keeping the remnant weak and disgraced. At the time Nehemiah lived, the wall surrounding Jerusalem was completely destroyed. During the time of Ezra, attempts to rebuild the wall may have been started and then were stopped by orders from the king (4:21-23; 9:9). Perhaps any progress that had been made in restoring the city wall had been reversed.

The Book of Nehemiah begins by relating what happened in the city of Susa, the winter capital of Persia and the resort center of its kings. It was November–December, 445 B.C. Nehemiah's blood brother Hanani (7:2) and representatives from the territory of Judah came to Susa to see him. The Jewish patriot asked about the situation for the resettled Jews in their homeland (1:1-2). It was then that the Lord laid a burden for the welfare of Jerusalem on the heart of Nehemiah. He was so overwhelmed with grief by what he had heard that he sat down and wept (1:4). He also expressed his concern for days, through fasting and praying before the Lord, whose dwelling is heaven. In the address recorded in 1:5-11, Nehemiah affirmed both God's surpassing greatness and His involvement in the lives of His people. Nehemiah acknowledged that the Lord kept His covenant with those who loved and obeyed Him.

NOTES ON THE PRINTED TEXT

Nehemiah 2 brings us to the following spring, namely, April-May, of 444 B.C. (2:1; see 1:1). Artaxerxes I was the king of Persia (465–424 B.C.) and possibly hosting an opulent banquet. He had winter palaces in Susa and Babylon, and he may have been in Babylon during the four months of Nehemiah's fast. The latter was serving as the king's cupbearer (2:1; see 1:11). In this capacity, Nehemiah tasted all the wine before it was served to the king. Nehemiah certified that none of it was poisoned or contaminated. The position of cupbearer often included advisory responsibilities. As a trusted and loyal servant, Nehemiah had a considerable amount of influence in the imperial court.

On previous occasions, Nehemiah's appearance was pleasant, not depressed. Regardless of their personal problems, the servants of the king were expected to keep their feelings concealed and to appear cheerful in his presence. To do otherwise might leave the impression that a courtier was discontented with the monarch and planning a seditious act. In this situation, however, Artaxerxes I noticed a change in Nehemiah's countenance and asked why he seemed sad. The king surmised that Nehemiah was distressed about something. Nehemiah became even more concerned, for it was uncertain what the emotionally volatile ruler might do (2:2). As with most monarchies, Persian protocol required one to give the emperor a wish for a very long and prosperous reign (see 1 Kings 1:31; Dan. 2:4; 3:9; 6:21). Nehemiah gave this wish and then quickly but carefully connected his sadness, inappropriate as it was in the throne room, to the tragedy of knowing his ancestral city was desolate and defenseless. Without the protection of walls, it would be too difficult to rebuild Jerusalem, for such efforts were subject to attack and vandalism (Neh. 2:3).

Artaxerxes' blunt reply may have been more than the cupbearer hoped for so early in the conversation. In the space of a deep breath, Nehemiah's heart reached for God's hand even as his mouth started forming the words of his petition to the emperor. Perhaps he asked for wisdom about what to say and that God would grant him favor in his earthly master's sight (2:3-4). Nehemiah knew he needed the Lord to shape Artaxerxes' attitude toward the project and toward himself as a petitioner. In a masterstroke of diplomacy, Nehemiah did not mention Jerusalem by name but always tied the city to himself and his family. He did not waste the emperor's time with wishful generalities; God had helped him formulate a specific plan during those months of fasting and prayer. Indeed, Nehemiah used few words when he asked for permission to go back to Judah and to the city of his ancestors. He also asked for permission to rebuild the city, including its walls (2:5). It had been 71 years since the temple was rebuilt in 516 B.C. Now, to succeed in rebuilding Judah's capital signified an important aspect of restoring the Jewish remnant in their homeland.

At this point in his narrative, Nehemiah mentioned the presence of one of Artaxerxes' consorts. Perhaps the queen played a role in the emperor's decision in Nehemiah's favor. Artaxerxes I gave permission by asking how long it would take Nehemiah to get to Judah and when he would be back (2:6). Artaxerxes I was moved by Nehemiah's sincerity and perhaps by reasoning that the prosperity of Judah (at that time a province of Persia) would benefit the king; but the monarch's favorable response was a remarkable example of the power of prayer. Earlier, when the trouble had arisen over the first efforts to rebuild Jerusalem, Artaxerxes I himself had issued the decree that ended the exiles' efforts to completely restore their city (Ezra 4:17-23).

Nehemiah's faith in God and boldness to approach the king had effectively reversed that decree, an outcome that was highly out of the ordinary in a culture in which governmental policies were rarely repealed (see Esther 1:19; 8:8; Dan. 6:8, 12, 15). Because the king was amendable to dispatching Nehemiah, the cupbearer asked for official documents to present to the governors assigned in the Trans-Euphrates region of the empire (Neh. 2:7).

The papers Nehemiah requested would authorize whatever his rebuilding efforts required. In this situation, he would need permission to freely travel through various territories without any complications. Nehemiah also needed an escort to safeguard his journey. He requested a letter to Asaph (the keeper of the monarch's royal park or nature preserve) giving him access to the required building supplies he needed to restore Jerusalem. These included timber to make beams for the gates of the citadel on the north side of the temple, to construct the city wall, and to build a palace for the governor to live. While Nehemiah's words and actions suggest his careful thought and planning, he nevertheless acknowledged that the gracious hand of God upon him led to the king granting these requests (2:8).

Nehemiah presented his documents sanctioning his mission to the authorities in Trans-Euphrates (2:9). His status was enhanced by the presence of his armed imperial escort. Ominously, Nehemiah introduced into his narrative two characters who were upset that he had arrived to promote the welfare of the Jews (2:10). Sanballat's name was Babylonian; he was likely named after Sin, the moon god. He was probably from Upper or Lower Beth Horon, two villages about 12 miles northwest of Jerusalem on the main road to the Mediterranean coast. He was the governor of Samaria and a leader of the Samarian opposition. Tobiah was a Jewish name meaning "The Lord Is Good." He probably was a worldly Jew living in and controlling the territory associated with Ammon east of the Jordan River. These two men would be Nehemiah's bitter enemies for years to come.

After contacting the officials of the satrapy of Trans-Euphrates, Nehemiah went on to Jerusalem (2:11). As Ezra had done before him, Nehemiah rested three days before initiating any activity (see Ezra 8:32). Before telling anyone in Jerusalem what he had come to do, Nehemiah surveyed the most damaged portion on the city walls. As an outsider, he wanted to be able to give the leaders of Jerusalem an informed account of what needed to be done when he revealed his mission. Perhaps the greatest challenge Nehemiah faced was transmitting his conviction that rebuilding Jerusalem's walls at this time was God's idea—not the fantasy of a government official who would go home in a while and leave the locals to live with the trouble he had stirred up. Nehemiah took a few trusted associates—probably men who had accompanied him from Susa—and set out to inspect the walls at night perhaps by moonlight (Neh. 2:12-13). The governor knew there were enemies all around, and he needed to keep his plans a secret until they were fixed in his mind. Only when his plan was formulated would he disclose it to the residents of Jerusalem.

When the time was right, Nehemiah gathered everyone and surprised them all. First, he outlined the problem and then suggested the solution. The problem was that for about 130 years, much of the city lay in ruins, with only a broken-down wall and charred timbers for gates. The solution was to rebuild Jerusalem's wall and remove the residents' feeling of disgrace and defeat (2:17). In Old Testament times, the condition of a city's walls indicated its power and prosperity. Since the wall was the primary means of defense against an enemy, the quality of its construction and maintenance reflected the financial condition and vulnerability of the city's inhabitants.

Nehemiah challenged the people to rebuild the wall and thus restore the standing of the Jewish community in the holy city. As his clincher, the governor shared the amazing account of God's intervention with Artaxerxes I to secure official sanction for this task (2:18). The vision and decisiveness of Nehemiah were what the remnant had needed to get started. The response of the priests, nobles, officials, and ordinary people was profoundly united: *Let us rise up and build.* In the books of Ezra and Nehemiah, God is understood to be the influencing force behind everything that happens. Emperors, nations, and the people of God are all tools in His gracious hand.

SUGGESTIONS TO TEACHERS

Challenging tasks come in many forms. We meet them early in our school years, then in college, then in our jobs, and finally in our families and churches. Often it seems easier to accept new challenges when we are younger than when we are older. But we're never too old to take on hard tasks.

1. A BIG CHALLENGE. Nehemiah faced the prospect of leading his people to do something they had tried before but had failed at. Nearly every major challenge in life is met when one person recognizes what can be done. This is true today as well as in Nehemiah's day. Is there some major job you are facing? Are you up to a major challenge?

2. A BIG FAITH. Nehemiah saw what needed to happen in rebuilding the city wall, but he did not act alone. His faith in God led him to undertake the task of building. Nehemiah never thought it would be easy, but he did believe that God was larger than any difficulty he might face. Likewise, we may see a needed task ahead of us. Does it seem too big? Are we frightened? Like Nehemiah, we need a big faith.

3. A BIG CREW. Nehemiah was a visionary leader, but he could not do the work alone. He had to gather a crew to do the work under his supervision. Few things are more frustrating today than someone having a great vision that no one else joins in to accomplish. Is there something we need to lend our strength to?

4. A BIG EXPECTATION. Nehemiah was able to explain what he ultimately expected from the work he led. His expectation was huge—nothing less than rebuilding Jerusalem's wall. When we join in a large job, the expectation of the result can mean the difference between success and failure.

■ TOPIC: Following a Visionary Leader!

■ QUESTIONS: 1. Why was Nehemiah sad in the presence of Artaxerxes I? 2. Why was Nehemiah afraid when the king asked him about his dejected demeanor? 3. What difference do you think prayer made in Nehemiah's interaction with the king? 4. What did Nehemiah do after arriving in Jerusalem? 5. How did Nehemiah see the Jewish community removing the disgrace of their ruined city?

■ ILLUSTRATIONS:

Being Open to God's Leading. A veteran of many years in the U.S. Navy chaplains' corps retired. Instead of looking for a comfortable place where he could relax and take it easy, this visionary leader chose a run-down church in a tough urban neighborhood. When his friends asked him why, he said, "It was the toughest thing I could find to do."

That's the attitude with which we must always be open to God's leading. We need the Holy Spirit's guidance, as well as courage and faith, to follow the Lord, regardless of our ages and circumstances. The thrill of living for God is always there when we offer ourselves for His service.

A God-given Burden. Nehemiah was a man who had a burden—a God-sent desire—to restore the walls of Jerusalem. The circumstances, however, did not seem to warrant any hope of success. But Nehemiah overcame the obstacles with God's help—just as your students can if they will depend on Him.

Consider, for example, Henry Stenhouse, an ophthalmologist from Goldsboro, North Carolina. When he was 100 years old, he decided to run for the United States Congress. He was prompted to take such a bold step by his concern for the young children who attended his party. Stenhouse said he was distressed about the quality of life in the country, and he wanted to do something to make life better for the children.

Some of the adults in your class may think their options are closed when they reach a certain age; or they may feel closed in by confining circumstances. Yet here is the story of a man who proved that constructive action begins with a person who has a strong desire and a concern. If your students are willing to act on their ministry desires, God will give them the courage and ability they need to start new ventures, despite what may appear to be overwhelming obstacles.

One Person with Vision. A sports cover story headline in *USA Today* read, "Coale Resuscitates Oklahoma." In 1996, Sherry Coale was hired to coach the University of Oklahoma women's basketball team. She appeared an unlikely choice since she was a high school English teacher who was eight months pregnant with her second child and had no college coaching experience. She came into her interview with a 12-page plan to revitalize the program and a contagious excitement that convinced the search committee she was the person for the coaching job.

During Coale's first year, the team went 7-22 and drew less than 100 fans a game. In 2000, her Sooner team made the Sweet Sixteen for a second consecutive year, set school attendance records, peaking with over 11,000 fans for a NCAA second-round tournament game against Stanford. Coale says, "When people talk about turning things around, I'm always taken aback. I had all the tools. I landed in a fabulous place."

FOR YOUTH	■ TOPIC: Rebuild!

■ **QUESTIONS:** 1. What official function did Nehemiah perform for Artaxerxes I? 2. What was the first thing Nehemiah did when the king asked him what he wanted? 3. What enabled Nehemiah to be so specific in his response to the king's questions? 4. Why was Jerusalem in a state of ruin? 5. How did the people respond to Nehemiah's challenge to rebuild the city?

■ **ILLUSTRATIONS:**

Beacon of Freedom. On September 11, 2001, 19 hijackers simultaneously took control of four U.S. domestic commercial airliners. Within a span of 18 minutes, they crashed two of the planes into two of the tallest towers of the World Trade Center in Manhattan, New York City. Then, within two hours, both towers collapsed, resulting in the death of thousands.

It took several weeks to extinguish the fires burning in the rubble of the buildings; and the clean-up was not finished until May, 2002. It also took months for rescue and recovery efforts to be completed. Temporary, wooden platforms were set up for tourists to watch construction crews clear out the gaping holes where the towers formerly stood. On May 30, 2002, these platforms were closed. The government also established relief funds to assist victims of the terrorist attacks. The goal was to provide financial assistance to the survivors and the families of victims.

In 2006, a milestone was achieved in the effort to rebuild the World Trade Center. Work began on the construction of the Freedom Tower, a skyscraper located in the northwest corner of the 16-acre site in Lower Manhattan, New York City. According to city planners, the upper portion of the building will be visible by 2008, and the structure will be ready for occupancy by 2010.

The top of the spire will achieve a height of 1776 feet, making it the tallest structure in the city. It will also serve as a symbolic reminder of the year 1776, when the Declaration of Independence was signed. By 2012, the skyscraper will be joined by five more towers, a memorial, a transit hub, and a performing arts center. Officials from the government and private sector hope the entire complex will become an example of determination, resiliency, and resolve for freedom-loving people everywhere around the world.

Undoubtedly, this architectural tribute to liberty would have even been an inspiration to the inhabitants of Judah, especially as they struggled to rebuild their lives. Because they were people of faith, they had the assurance that God would enable them to move forward with their dreams.

Rebuilding Challenges. At the end of World War II, it is estimated that between 55 to 62 million soldiers and civilians had perished in the horrific conflict. Also, large parts of Europe and East Asia lay in ruins. Policymakers in the U.S. realized that if the devastated nations and economies were not rebuilt, the post-War era would be dominated by increased instability, destruction, and death. Consequently, the American government committed itself to an ambitious rebuilding program involving massive outlays of economic and military aid.

The path to full recovery was neither immediate nor easy. It took many years, huge sums of money, and untold hours of labor to overcome the challenges to rebuilding. The exiles who returned to Judah from Babylon also experienced problems as they tried to rebuild their lives in the promised land. There were delays, setbacks, and shortfalls. Yet, through it all, the Lord proved Himself faithful by enabling the covenant community to prevail in their efforts.

Remembering to Trust and Obey. "Racers, start your engines!" With that announcement the crowd roared and the race car drivers zoomed down the speedway. But before the event started, highly skilled engineers, mechanics, and drivers had spent many hours and lots of money in preparation.

How foolish it is to start a road race without adequate equipment and trained drivers. Yet sometimes that's how we try to get ahead in our spiritual lives. We think we know how to run the race of faith. We think we can jump in at any time and succeed with little preparation and effort. But we are incorrect. We cannot start and finish unless we trust in God and obey His Word.

Up Against the Wall

BACKGROUND SCRIPTURE: Nehemiah 4—6
DEVOTIONAL READING: Psalm 70

KEY VERSE: So built we the wall; and all the wall was joined together
unto the half thereof: for the people had a mind to work. Nehemiah 4:6.

KING JAMES VERSION

NEHEMIAH 4:1 But it came to pass, that when Sanballat heard that we builded the wall, he was wroth, and took great indignation, and mocked the Jews. 2 And he spake before his brethren and the army of Samaria, and said, What do these feeble Jews? will they fortify themselves? will they sacrifice? will they make an end in a day? will they revive the stones out of the heaps of the rubbish which are burned? 3 Now Tobiah the Ammonite was by him, and he said, Even that which they build, if a fox go up, he shall even break down their stone wall. . . .

7 But it came to pass, that when Sanballat, and Tobiah, and the Arabians, and the Ammonites, and the Ashdodites, heard that the walls of Jerusalem were made up, and that the breaches began to be stopped, then they were very wroth, 8 And conspired all of them together to come and to fight against Jerusalem, and to hinder it. 9 Nevertheless we made our prayer unto our God, and set a watch against them day and night, because of them. . . . 13 Therefore set I in the lower places behind the wall, and on the higher places, I even set the people after their families with their swords, their spears, and their bows. 14 And I looked, and rose up, and said unto the nobles, and to the rulers, and to the rest of the people, Be not ye afraid of them: remember the Lord, which is great and terrible, and fight for your brethren, your sons, and your daughters, your wives, and your houses. 15 And it came to pass, when our enemies heard that it was known unto us, and God had brought their counsel to nought, that we returned all of us to the wall, every one unto his work. . . .

6:15 So the wall was finished in the twenty and fifth day of the month Elul, in fifty and two days.

NEW REVISED STANDARD VERSION

NEHEMIAH 4:1 Now when Sanballat heard that we were building the wall, he was angry and greatly enraged, and he mocked the Jews. 2 He said in the presence of his associates and of the army of Samaria, "What are these feeble Jews doing? Will they restore things? Will they sacrifice? Will they finish it in a day? Will they revive the stones out of the heaps of rubbish—and burned ones at that?" 3 Tobiah the Ammonite was beside him, and he said, "That stone wall they are building—any fox going up on it would break it down!" . . .

7 But when Sanballat and Tobiah and the Arabs and the Ammonites and the Ashdodites heard that the repairing of the walls of Jerusalem was going forward and the gaps were beginning to be closed, they were very angry, 8 and all plotted together to come and fight against Jerusalem and to cause confusion in it. 9 So we prayed to our God, and set a guard as a protection against them day and night. . . .

13 So in the lowest parts of the space behind the wall, in open places, I stationed the people according to their families, with their swords, their spears, and their bows. 14 After I looked these things over, I stood up and said to the nobles and the officials and the rest of the people, "Do not be afraid of them. Remember the Lord, who is great and awesome, and fight for your kin, your sons, your daughters, your wives, and your homes." 15 When our enemies heard that their plot was known to us, and that God had frustrated it, we all returned to the wall, each to his work. . . .

6:15 So the wall was finished on the twenty-fifth day of the month Elul, in fifty-two days.

12

Monday, May 12	Psalm 70	*A Cry for Help*
Tuesday, May 13	Nehemiah 4:1-6	*Mocking Enemies*
Wednesday, May 14	Nehemiah 4:7-11	*A Plot to Confuse the Builders*
Thursday, May 15	Nehemiah 4:12-15	*The Plot Is Foiled*
Friday, May 16	Nehemiah 4:16-23	*Always at the Ready*
Saturday, May 17	Nehemiah 6:1-14	*Attempts to Stop the Building*
Sunday, May 18	Nehemiah 6:15-19	*The Wall Is Finished*

BACKGROUND

Last week, we learned how Nehemiah convinced the leaders and inhabitants of Jerusalem to join him in rebuilding city walls (Neh. 2:17-18). Their support was crucial for the undertaking to be successful. Opposed to the gracious hand of God were three potent human enemies (2:19). The company of Sanballat and Tobiah (who were first mentioned in 2:10) was joined by Geshem the Arab. Ancient sources reveal that Geshem led an assortment of Arab tribes that controlled the deserts south of Judah from Egypt to the Arabian peninsula. He was more powerful than Sanballat and Tobiah combined, but his hostility to the Jews (namely, the people of God living in Judah after the exile) appears to have been less intense.

Sanballat to the north, Tobiah to the east, and Geshem to the south forged a hostile boundary around Judah. Together, they launched a campaign of ridicule and mockery against the small Jewish community. Their initial charge was the old standby: rebellion against the emperor (see Ezra 4:11-16). Nehemiah shrugged off Sanballat, Tobiah, and Geshem as though they were minor annoyances (Neh. 2:20). He was used to dealing with the real heavyweights of Persia; comparatively speaking, these men were lightweights. On the other hand, Nehemiah looked at the situation in Jerusalem through a theological lens. The God of heaven wanted the walls built. Nehemiah and the Jews were the servants of the God of heaven by terms of a covenant. Sanballat, Tobiah, and Geshem had no covenant status. Jerusalem belonged to God and His people. The blustering nations around them had no part in God's plan for Jerusalem.

NOTES ON THE PRINTED TEXT

Nehemiah 4:1 picks up where 2:20 left off. Sanballat, the Samarian leader, assembled his army in his capital to agitate Nehemiah and his workers. Along with all the petty bureaucrats, Tobiah joined Sanballat on the speakers' platform as a visiting dignitary. The intensity of Sanballat's anger at the Jews exposed the lie behind his ridicule. Under the veneer of his propaganda, Sanballat was worried about what Nehemiah was doing. This tenacious exile threatened his power over Judah.

In a rapid series of five questions, Sanballat made Nehemiah and the Jews seem ridiculous in the eyes of the army of Samaria (4:2). Sanballat implied the Jews were powerless to do anything. He scoffed at the idea that such a bunch could fortify a city. He suggested they were religious fanatics trusting God to raise the walls in response to sacrifices. Sanballat claimed they had barely strength for one day, so they had better work fast. He mocked the wall as a fortress made of charcoal briquettes. The native limestone, when subjected to fire, turned brittle and crumbly. In time, Sanballat would find that the Jews had no trouble finding sound building stones. The Samarian army must have responded favorably to Sanballat's taunts, because Tobiah followed them up with the kind of joke that assumed his audience was ready to hear it (4:3). Allegedly, if a nimble fox jumped up on that ridiculous wall, the whole thing would totter and collapse from the shock. Imagine the clash of swords on shields and battle yells from the assembled army as they responded to the jibes and jeers of their leaders.

At this point in his memoir, Nehemiah inserted a prayer. He had no time to bother with the empty words of posturing opponents. He committed these hecklers to God, who alone has the right to take vengeance on those who oppose His purposes (see Deut. 32:35; Rom. 12:19). Nehemiah asked God to take note of the abuse hurled at His servants and to deflect that spite back on those who initiated it. The governor prayed that the enemies of God's people might know the horrors of the kind of captivity the Jews had survived (Neh. 4:4). Nehemiah also requested that their offense might never be forgiven, because they had opposed the purposes of God, the divine warrior, to protect His people (4:5).

While Sanballat and Tobiah waged a war of words, the Jewish laborers from Jerusalem and the surrounding towns were mounting stone on stone all around the two-mile perimeter of Jerusalem. Before the opponents knew what was happening, the wall had reached half its planned height all the way around. The wall went up quickly because the exilic community toiled hard (4:6). Perhaps to their dismay, Sanballat and Tobiah had to change their strategy, for their saber-rattling mockery clearly had discouraged no one. First, they recruited more allies. Sanballat and his Samarians to the north, Tobiah and his Ammonites to the east, and Geshem and his Arabs to the south were joined in angry opposition to Jerusalem's walls by the Ashdodites, people of the strongest Phoenician city on the Mediterranean coast to the west of Judah (4:7). Second, the alliance that ringed Judah and Jerusalem started planning attacks on Jerusalem. Nehemiah heard rumors about the impending raids; perhaps this was something Sanballat and Tobiah wanted him to hear. Their biggest problem was that Nehemiah had Artaxerxes' permission to rebuild the walls of Jerusalem. An actual attack would risk bringing Persian wrath on their heads. A threatened attack might do what taunts had not—demoralize the Jews (4:8).

In response to the threat of an attack, the Jews started praying (Neh. 4:9). Clearly, Nehemiah organized the prayer vigil, because it was accompanied by around-the-clock sentries to detect any raiders. Even as they prayed and watched, the builders were feeling the cumulative effect of the pressure of the task and the opposition. They were exhausted from the toil and discouraged by the rubble they had to work in. In response, the opponents engaged in psychological warfare by claiming they could use the cover of the rubble to send terrorists in among the builders to kill them before they knew the attackers were at hand (4:10-11).

When Sanballat and Tobiah sensed that rumors of war were affecting the morale of the builders, the antagonists planted more rumors in Jewish villages that bordered enemy lands (4:12). Soon, Nehemiah had repeated intelligence reports that together indicated attacks from every point of the compass. In response, the governor stopped the construction and posted heavy guards inside Jerusalem wherever the wall was still low or where there were open spaces. Nehemiah's "army" was his corps of builders, grouped by family units. Their armaments consisted of the weapons that were their personal property, namely, swords, spears (lances with long shafts), and bows (4:13). At this point, the governor took the time to look over the situation. Then, after completing his inspection, he mustered the nobles, officials, and the rest of the workers and gave them a three-part battle instruction. First, they were not to fear the enemy (see Exod. 14:13; Num. 14:9; Deut. 20:3; Josh. 10:25). Second, the Jews were to keep their minds fixed on the great and awesome Lord. Third, they were to fight for their families and homes (Neh. 4:14).

Nehemiah showed great organizational skill when he devised the initial plan for portioning out the work on the walls and gates among the labor crews. He displayed flexibility in the face of daunting opposition, especially as he anticipated and headed off the various schemes of the encircling foes. There came a time, however, when he needed to put in place a more robust approach that could handle a variety of threats. Otherwise, the rebuilding of the walls and gates wasn't going to get completed. After waiting an unspecified number of days for a surprise attack, Nehemiah somehow heard the news that Sanballat, Tobiah, Geshem, and the Ashdodites had given up on ambushing the workers. Nehemiah took no credit for the failure of the numerically overwhelming enemies. He knew only God could have frustrated their plans to attack (4:15).

After receiving the good news, Nehemiah encouraged everybody to get back to work. From this point on, until the walls and gates were finished, half the people worked, while the other half served as armed sentries (4:16). Officers ready to take charge in the event of a military emergency waited at intervals behind the workers and guards. The carriers who transported materials to the various work stations around the walls kept one hand free to carry their weapons. The builders wore swords on their belts (4:17-18). A trumpeter stayed with Nehemiah at all times so that he could signal everyone to gather at any point on the walls where trouble developed.

The opponents of Jerusalem's refortification abandoned their strategy of direct confrontation. They turned to attempts of subtle deception and betrayal. They made several attempts to lure Nehemiah out of Jerusalem into their hands at a "peace conference." They insinuated he was orchestrating a plot to rebel against the Persian Empire and eventually proclaim himself king. They hired false prophets to convince Nehemiah to do something damaging to his reputation. But the governor was too focused on what God wanted him to accomplish to fall for any of their ploys (6:1-14). Nehemiah told surprisingly little about building the wall of Jerusalem. He included an honor roll of the dedicated builders, but he told mostly about the obstacles overcome from without and within in the process of building. That's what he remembered. That's what God wanted every generation of His spiritual children to keep in mind as they do His work. Success comes after facing foes in the strength of His name.

All of the commotion reported in Nehemiah 4 through 6 occurred in the 52 days from the second of the month of Ab to the twenty-fifth of the month of Elul—approximately August 11 to October 2, 444 B.C. (6:15). Everyone in the coalition opposed to the construction of the walls was informed instantly by the intelligence network. They were awed because such an outcome was humanly impossible. In their hearts, they knew the God of Israel had been at work. Tinges of terror colored their thoughts of the future, and they doubted whether good things lay ahead for them (6:16).

SUGGESTIONS TO TEACHERS

This week's lesson helps us see that nothing of eternal good is accomplished easily. When God's people seek to serve Him, they will often run into obstacles that might include trickery, threats, lies, rumors, and coercion.

1. NO PAIN, NO GAIN. Nehemiah led his people in a project that seemed to be doomed from the beginning. But he clearly saw the benefits and kept urging his people to complete the job. Most people are tempted to give up when great difficulties arise. The phrase from physical trainers seems appropriate here: "No pain, no gain." If you want the results, you have to put up with the difficulty.

2. INTEGRITY STILL COUNTS. We are surrounded by lies and distortions of every manner. And we are regularly tempted to do what everyone else seems to do— distort the truth for our immediate personal advantage. Nehemiah shows us how to tell the truth and live with the short and long-term consequences. No matter what our circumstances might be, integrity still counts.

3. STAY ON TARGET. It's easy for us to allow events and problems to distract us from the core issues of life. Just as Nehemiah had to put up with the on-going distractions of his enemies' messages, we also have to stay on target in life and not allow ungodly influences to derail us. If we know where we are going, we have a better likelihood of getting there.

4. DO YOUR BEST AND COUNT ON GOD. Nehemiah called on God to help him be strong enough to do what he needed to do. That reminds us to do our best—to really put out our greatest effort to accomplish our God-given goals. It also reminds us to trust the Lord in the process. This means asking God to enable us to do our best for His glory.

■ **TOPIC:** Finishing the Task!

■ **QUESTIONS:** 1. Why was Sanballat enraged when he heard that the Jews were rebuilding the walls of Jerusalem? 2. What sort of sarcastic remarks did Nehemiah's adversaries use to demoralize the Jewish workers? 3. Why did Nehemiah and his associates resort to prayer in the face of intense opposition? 4. What plan did Nehemiah put into place to deal with the threat from the antagonists? 5. How was it possible for God's people to rebuild the Jerusalem wall in such a short period of time?

■ **ILLUSTRATIONS:**

Climbing for the Cure. Host Grant Goodeve of the television program *Northwest Backroads,* talked about a group of people who got together at Mount Hood National Forest in Oregon to climb "the state's highest peak" as way to "honor those lost to cancer." All the participants "share a bond," namely, each of them has lost a beloved family member or friend to some form of cancer.

During one particular outing, the group underwent "glacier training" before they began their climb at 1 A.M. Daylight finally arrived, but only after the team had been "climbing for hours in darkness." They continued their journey for a while, but they eventually realized that the weather wouldn't permit them to go all the way to the summit of the mountain. Some might think that their "months of preparation" were wasted because they did not make it to the peak. But as Goodeve notes, success is not measured in feet of elevation, but in the group's "devotion to the cause to raise money for cancer research." Their unwavering commitment reflects the same sort of devotion and determination required by believers to finish the tasks God has given them to do.

Staying on Target. A native ministry in Uganda reports that the Gospel is making headway in that central African nation. "This is a place where the devil has people bound," says the ministry's leader, explaining how the enemy has used the tribal system to keep the people divided. "They worship whatever god they know. But the power of the true God is breaking those barriers—the Gospel is making a difference." Recently, the number of churches rose from 14 just a few years ago to 50.

Self-professing Christians account for nearly 89 percent of the population, with evangelical Christians being 18 percent. This is almost three times the percentage of just 40 years ago. Many people in Uganda have opened their hearts to Christ, thanks in part to prayer and financial support from the United States, said a missionary. "I am convinced that we are all brothers."

"Many Ugandans are eager to hear the Word," the spokesperson added, "but there is a price the missionaries pay to accomplish this work, often being away from their families for two weeks out of each month. But that is a sacrifice we are willing to make—the results are so great."

The Courage to Continue. A large West Coast church was moved by the plight of the homeless in their city. After lengthy discussions about what they could do to help, several congregational members put forward the idea of buying the property next to theirs and opening a cafeteria that would offer meals to the poor at cost. The church moved ahead on the plan, never imagining that anyone would object to such a benevolent cause.

Nearby business owners, however, weren't pleased to learn that more transients would be coming into their neighborhood. The business owners banded together and filed a lawsuit, claiming that the church was opening a commercial restaurant and therefore should be required to pay taxes on the revenue. The congregation didn't have the money to fight a lawsuit or to pay taxes, so they gave up their plan to feed the homeless. In the aftermath of the incident, some wonder whether the church should have taken better measures to protect themselves from attack and enable them to complete the work God had given them to do.

FOR YOUTH

■ **TOPIC:** Keep on Building

■ **QUESTIONS:** 1. What was Sanballat's reaction to the news that the Jerusalem wall was being rebuilt? 2. Why do you think the enemies of the Jews mocked their rebuilding efforts? 3. Why were Nehemiah's adversaries upset when they heard that progress was being made on the rebuilding of the walls? 4. In what way did God frustrate the plot of Nehemiah's adversaries to undermine the rebuilding efforts? 5. How long did it take for the Jerusalem wall to be rebuilt?

■ **ILLUSTRATIONS:**

Rebuilding Churches. In late August 2005, Hurricane Katrina struck the Gulf Coast of the United States. At that time, it was the strongest hurricane ever recorded in the region. It has also become one of the costliest hurricanes in American history, destroying without discrimination homes, schools, and churches (among other things). In terms of the latter, Ray Suarez of the *NewsHour* on PBS noted that many congregational buildings, as a result of being "caked in mud," were "ready to be bulldozed with no hope of [a] . . . future."

Amazingly, though, the wholesale leveling of churches hasn't happened. This is because residents in "neighborhoods fighting for their survival" regard congregations to be an indispensable part of the infrastructure. It goes beyond churches being a "place for spiritual comfort" and a "place to mark the events of life, birth, death, and marriage." Congregational buildings are seen as being just as important as police stations, shopping centers, roads, and bridges, for they signify "the backbone, the lifeline of a community."

Pastor Danilo Digall said that his church was "under water for three days." He expressed gratitude for "all those partners across the country" who reached out to the church. He noted that apart from this help, his congregation and others would not have been able to reopen. The minister stated, "But thanks to the many helping hands who came together in our town, in our community, in our churches, in our homes, we have been able to rebuild our lives."

The exiles who returned to Judah from Babylon recognized the importance of the Jerusalem wall to their daily lives. They supported its rebuilding with their time, talents, and material resources. They were especially grateful that God remembered them and pledged to be with them in their rebuilding efforts.

Diligence Needed. Missionaries Eddie and Janice Ray said their hearts broke as the food was passed out to the 500 families registered for a Baptist relief project through local churches in Kuito, Angola. "The people are so hard off," said Ray, coordinator for International Mission Boards in Angola. "And when we handed out the food and clothes, you could see how grateful they were. They'd just light up!"

For close to three decades, civil war raged in Angola. Following the death of UNITA leader, Jonas Savimbi, in 2002, the war ended. But in its wake, over one million people died and four million others were displaced from their homes. Many of them streamed to Kuito for help.

While the attacks on Kuito ended years ago, still-hidden land mines keep people from rebuilding. After the land mines are removed, the Baptists of Angola plan to launch another major relief project—supplying hoes and seed to help Angolans in the countryside to become more self-sufficient. "They were forced to leave everything behind. They are willing to work, but don't have the means to get started," Ray advised. "Our goal is to help them both spiritually and physically."

Refusing to Give Up. The third verse of "Amazing Grace" says: "Through many dangers, toils, and snares I have already come." That verse is particularly appropriate for the hostility that Nehemiah and his colleagues encountered. And it is likewise true when we are doing God's work.

If we're content to let things go on in a routine sort of way, nobody bothers us. But when we dare to throw down the challenge of a great opportunity for God's glory, opposition suddenly appears. For example, if a church wants to buy property for a new sanctuary, suddenly people start to protest about the traffic, noise, pollution, and so forth.

Nehemiah knew what John Newton wrote about in "Amazing Grace." In this week's Scripture passage, we discover that the nature and intensity of the opposition were quite different than before. Nehemiah was not looking for trouble. He wanted to do God's will—build the wall. But Nehemiah's enemies would not let his project go uncontested. Thankfully, he refused to give up.

CALL TO RENEW THE COVENANT

BACKGROUND SCRIPTURE: Psalm 27:11-14; 19:7-14

DEVOTIONAL READING: Psalm 70

KEY VERSE: [Ezra] read therein before the street that was before the water gate from the morning until midday, before the men and the women, and those that could understand; and the ears of all the people were attentive unto the book of the law. Nehemiah 8:3.

KING JAMES VERSION

NEHEMIAH 8:1 And all the people gathered themselves together as one man into the street that was before the water gate; and they spake unto Ezra the scribe to bring the book of the law of Moses, which the LORD had commanded to Israel. 2 And Ezra the priest brought the law before the congregation both of men and women, and all that could hear with understanding, upon the first day of the seventh month. 3 And he read therein before the street that was before the water gate from the morning until midday, before the men and the women, and those that could understand; and the ears of all the people were attentive unto the book of the law. . . . 5 And Ezra opened the book in the sight of all the people; (for he was above all the people;) and when he opened it, all the people stood up: 6 And Ezra blessed the LORD, the great God. And all the people answered, Amen, Amen, with lifting up their hands: and they bowed their heads, and worshipped the LORD with their faces to the ground. . . .

13 And on the second day were gathered together the chief of the fathers of all the people, the priests, and the Levites, unto Ezra the scribe, even to understand the words of the law. 14 And they found written in the law which the LORD had commanded by Moses, that the children of Israel should dwell in booths in the feast of the seventh month: . . . 17 And all the congregation of them that were come again out of the captivity made booths, and sat under the booths: for since the days of Jeshua the son of Nun unto that day had not the children of Israel done so. And there was very great gladness. 18 Also day by day, from the first day unto the last day, he read in the book of the law of God. And they kept the feast seven days; and on the eighth day was a solemn assembly, according unto the manner.

NEW REVISED STANDARD VERSION

NEHEMIAH 8:1 All the people gathered together into the square before the Water Gate. They told the scribe Ezra to bring the book of the law of Moses, which the LORD had given to Israel. 2 Accordingly, the priest Ezra brought the law before the assembly, both men and women and all who could hear with understanding. This was on the first day of the seventh month. 3 He read from it facing the square before the Water Gate from early morning until midday, in the presence of the men and the women and those who could understand; and the ears of all the people were attentive to the book of the law. . . . 5 And Ezra opened the book in the sight of all the people, for he was standing above all the people; and when he opened it, all the people stood up. 6 Then Ezra blessed the LORD, the great God, and all the people answered, "Amen, Amen," lifting up their hands. Then they bowed their heads and worshiped the LORD with their faces to the ground. . . .

13 On the second day the heads of ancestral houses of all the people, with the priests and the Levites, came together to the scribe Ezra in order to study the words of the law. 14 And they found it written in the law, which the LORD had commanded by Moses, that the people of Israel should live in booths during the festival of the seventh month, . . . 17 And all the assembly of those who had returned from the captivity made booths and lived in them; for from the days of Jeshua son of Nun to that day the people of Israel had not done so. And there was very great rejoicing. 18 And day by day, from the first day to the last day, he read from the book of the law of God. They kept the festival seven days; and on the eighth day there was a solemn assembly, according to the ordinance.

13

Monday, May 19	Psalm 27:11-14	*Take Courage*
Tuesday, May 20	Leviticus 23:33-43	*The Festival of Booths*
Wednesday, May 21	Deuteronomy 16:13-17	*Do Not Appear Empty-handed*
Thursday, May 22	Nehemiah 8:1-6	*Hear the Word*
Friday, May 23	Nehemiah 8:7-12	*Teach the Word*
Saturday, May 24	Nehemiah 8:13-18	*Study the Word*
Sunday, May 25	Psalm 19:7-14	*Delight in God's Law*

BACKGROUND

It had taken over 80 years after the Exile for the Jerusalem wall to be completed (Neh. 6:15). Some of this delay was due to opposition from enemies, but the returnees were as much to blame for the delay as anyone else. They became discouraged when they faced hardship and they also easily fell into sin. Accordingly, while the first half of the Book of Nehemiah concentrated on the physical preservation of God's people, the second half focused on the spiritual preservation. Ezra plays a prominent role in this endeavor. He was a Jewish scribe and priest who traced his ancestry to Aaron (Ezra 7:1-5). In 458 B.C., he received permission from Artaxerxes I to travel to Jerusalem with 1,800 exiles and carry out religious reform.

While in the capital of Judah, Ezra wept bitterly over the sins of the people. In response, many Jews gathered to confess their sins and to weep alongside their spiritual leader. The people then made a covenant to obey God and to put away the foreign wives who had caused them to fall away from the Lord (10:1-4). The efforts of Ezra to initiate a spiritual renewal lasted for a short period; but by the time Nehemiah returned, the spiritual fire had fizzled. As a matter of fact, in the 13 years between the end of the Book of Ezra and the beginning of the Book of Nehemiah, the Jewish people once again fell into their sinful ways. They intermarried into foreign religions and neglected to support the temple.

Thankfully, God was at work in the hearts of His people. They had seen the Lord's hand on Nehemiah, and they knew that to survive, they needed God's help. To receive God's help, they needed to obey His commands. Rather than waiting for Ezra or Nehemiah to start another spiritual revival, the people started it themselves. The Jews assembled in Jerusalem on October 8, 444 B.C. The event was timed to coincide with the Feast of Trumpets, the New Year's Day of the Jewish civil calendar (later known as Rosh Ha-Shanah; Neh. 7:73—8:1). This was one of the most noteworthy seasons on Israel's religious calendar (Lev. 23:23-43), and it was celebrated by the blowing of horns or trumpets from morning until evening. After the Exile, the festival was observed by the public reading of the Law and by general rejoicing.

In the Hebrew canon, the Law (or Torah) comprise the first of three major divisions of the Jewish sacred writings. The other two are the Prophets and the Writings. Both

Jewish and Christian traditions assert that Moses was the human author of the Torah (which are also called the "Pentateuch" or five books). The Law is not only a compilation of the decrees of God entrusted to Moses, but also the history of humanity and the Israelites. Moses probably wrote these books in the fifteenth century B.C. A thousand years later, the Book of Nehemiah was being created as the wall of Jerusalem underwent rebuilding.

NOTES ON THE PRINTED TEXT

The people gathered in an open plaza in front of the Water Gate, an entryway leading to the Gihon spring (Jerusalem's primary source of water). The gate was located on the eastern side of the city, slightly south of the wall's midsection, and directly opposite the temple. This area was not considered sacred, which meant laypeople could participate with priests in the gathering. Women and children, who did not always attend temple ceremonies, were present in accordance with Moses' instructions in Deuteronomy 31:10-13 (Neh. 8:2; see 2 Chron. 20:13). The occasion for the assembly was Ezra's reading of the *book of the law of Moses* (Neh. 8:1), which the Lord had given Israel to obey. Several suggestions have been made concerning the identity of this document, but most likely it was a scroll containing the first five books of the Old Testament—Genesis, Exodus, Leviticus, Numbers, and Deuteronomy.

The purpose of having Ezra read from the Law was not only to preserve the Torah, but also to encourage every generation to revere and obey God's decrees and teachings. This public reading led the Jews to renew their commitment to God's covenant and to instruct their children to do the same. The Jews did not possess personal copies of the law. The main way they were able to become familiar with it was by hearing it read and explained. This is what Ezra had returned to Jerusalem to do; but during the 52 days when the wall of Jerusalem was being rebuilt, there was little time for an assembly. After the wall's completion, however, the people expressed a desire to hear more instruction in the Torah.

Ezra faced the open square just inside the Water Gate from early morning until noon and read aloud the Torah scroll to everyone who could understand. In ancient times, this was the customary practice. All the people, in turn, paid close attention to what they heard (8:3). Ezra the scribe was standing on a high wooden platform that had been built for this occasion. He wasn't alone, either. Standing next to him was Nehemiah, and they were flanked on their right and left by priests, Levites, and other Jewish leaders (8:4; see 8:9). They evidently stood alongside Ezra to assist in the long time that it took to read, translate, and interpret God's Word. When the people saw Ezra unroll the Torah scroll, they rose to their feet in unison out of respect for the reading and exposition of God's Word (8:5).

When Ezra gave praise to the Lord, *the great God* (8:6), the people chanted *Amen, Amen* and lifted their palms heavenward. Then the attendees bowed down and worshiped the Lord *with their faces to the ground*. In this way the people indicated their humble and willing submission to their God and Creator. A number of Levites instructed the people who were standing as Ezra read the law (8:7). Jewish tradition says the Levites were translating the words from ancient Hebrew to Aramaic, the international diplomatic and trade language of the day. Most likely, at intervals between the readings, the assistants circulated freely among the crowd and gave the sense of the text (perhaps paragraph by paragraph and sentence by sentence) so that the people could grasp what was being read (8:8).

The reading and teaching of the law took place under the watchful eyes of Nehemiah, Ezra, and the Levites, which indicated there was unity among the Jewish leaders. Unexpectedly, something quite remarkable happened. The people began to weep and mourn. The Holy Spirit used the words of the law to bring strong conviction of sin to their hearts and minds (8:9). Although the people's weeping and confessing of their sin (and possibly the transgressions of their ancestors) was an understandable response, this occasion called for a different reaction. The Jewish civil and religious leaders encouraged the people not to be sorrowful at this time. Because it was a sacred day before the Lord, the appropriate response was for the community of the redeemed to sing praises to the God of Israel. That's why Nehemiah, in concert with the other officials (8:11), urged the people to celebrate the occasion with rich foods and sweet drinks (8:10). The former reference is to festive, tasty morsels prepared with the fat of sacrificial animals. Nehemiah also encouraged the attendees to share gifts of food with those who had nothing prepared. This reflects the Jewish tradition of remembering the disadvantaged on joyous occasions (2 Sam. 6:19; Esth. 9:22).

The audience departed to do all that the leaders had said. They ate and drank at a festive meal, shared gifts of food with the disadvantaged, and celebrated the occasion with *great mirth* (Neh. 8:12) because they had both heard and understood the Word of God that had been read and expounded to them. The next day, the leaders of each family, along with the priests and Levites, assembled to meet with Ezra. He helped them understand the law better (8:13). They discovered that the Feast of Booths was celebrated during the fall season five days after the Day of Atonement (8:14).

The leaders announced in Jerusalem and Judah that the people were to observe the sacred day. This involved going out to the hill country and obtaining a variety of branches—from cultivated and wild olive trees, myrtle trees (evergreen shrubs that gave off a pleasant fragrance), date palms, and other leafy trees—to construct temporary shelters for living outside. This was done in accordance with the Law (8:15). The Feast of Booths (also called Tabernacles or Ingathering) was characterized by a week of celebration for the harvest in which God's people lived in booths and offered sacrifices. This observance memorialized the Israelites' journey from Egypt to Canaan and gave them an opportunity to thank the Lord for the productivity of the land (see Exod. 23:16; Lev. 23:33-43; John 7:37).

The people complied with the directive. They went out, cut branches, and used them to build shelters in every possible location of the city—on the flat roofs of their houses, in the courtyards of their homes, in the outer and inner courtyards of God's temple, and in the plazas around the Water Gate and the Ephraim Gate (the latter being on the north side of the city and facing toward the territory of Ephraim; Neh. 8:16). The people living in the surrounding villages also built temporary shelters. This holiday had not been observed in quite this way and with this much joy since the time of Joshua. The people were once again giving thanks to God for His blessings with the same enthusiasm and zeal as the Israelites of Joshua's day had done (8:17).

Understanding of biblical truth is dry without the joy that God produces. Likewise, feasting and joy are meaningless without the firm foundation of God's Word. That is why Ezra read from the law each day throughout the entire seven-day period of celebration. On the eighth day, a solemn assembly took place in accordance with the law (8:18). The purpose of the reading was not only to preserve the law, but also to encourage every generation to revere and obey God's Word. This public reading led the Jews to renew their commitment to God's covenant and to instruct their children to do the same.

SUGGESTIONS TO TEACHERS

If you're like me, you've learned to read the instruction manual when you've bought a new piece of equipment. The manufacturer knows how best to make the equipment run. Likewise, our Maker gives us instructions in His book, the Bible, that will help us lead better lives.

1. WE ALL NEED TO KEEP REFRESHING OUR MEMORY OF SCRIPTURE. Even if you've been reading the Bible for years, you need to keep reading it. Read it in a different translation. Study it with the aid of Bible reference works. Do whatever it takes to keep Scripture fresh in your mind. If you approach the Bible with the humble attitude that you can never come to the end of your need for it, God will honor you with new insights and new help for living.

2. COMBINE WORSHIP WITH BIBLE LEARNING. The Bible is not a mere text; it is God speaking to us. It is entirely appropriate, therefore, for us to offer prayers of thanks and praise to God when we approach Scripture.

3. TRY TO REALLY UNDERSTAND WHAT YOU'RE READING. Sometimes, people never get beyond a devotional reading of Scripture. But there is a time for study—for doing the hard work of trying to understand this ancient, complex, and unique set of books. As the Levites translated the law, so we must make sure we understand what Scripture says.

4. DON'T BE DISCOURAGED. The Bible will reveal your shortcomings. Face those shortcomings and realize that they displease God. But never forget the grace of God, which is able to forgive your sin and help you to overcome the bad habits you've developed. In obedience is freedom.

■ **TOPIC:** Restored and Renewed

■ **QUESTIONS:** 1. What do you think it would have been like to be a participant at the reading of the law? 2. What was the reaction of the people? 3. What connection do you see between the law of God and celebration? 4. Have you ever been through a phase of your life when you neglected to read the Bible? What effect did it have on you? 5. What can you do to renew a commitment to know and do God's will?

■ **ILLUSTRATIONS:**

Urban Renewal Program. On December 26, 2004, a 9.1 to 9.3-magnitude earthquake originated in the Indian Ocean, just off the western coast of northern Sumatra, Indonesia. A series of lethal tsunamis were triggered, which spread throughout the region. Approximately 230,000 people were killed in coastal communities of Indonesia, Sri Lanka, India, Thailand, and elsewhere. Experts regard this catastrophe as one of the deadliest disasters in modern history.

Correspondent Tom Hagler of the *NewsHour* on PBS noted that within a year, Thailand's Andaman Coast, which "suffered extensive casualties and damage," became a "vast construction site." All the laborers, who are survivors of the Indian Ocean tsunami, "start at first light and work past dusk, seven days a week." The Thai government sponsored the ambitious urban renewal program, resulting in over thousands of homes being constructed for "displaced families."

There were problems, though, with substandard housing and land disputes. According to one United Nations official, the difficulties related primarily to the "longer term recovery." For instance, in the area of shelter, some of the houses tended to be "the wrong size, the wrong place, and just the wrong design." Also, when some people returned to where they once lived, they found someone else already there "claiming the right to that land." The resolve of the government and people to restore communities proved to be the biggest asset, just as a similar level of cooperation made the renewal efforts of those living in Judah during the time of Ezra a success.

Responding to God's Law. We all accept the axiom that ignorance is no excuse when we break the law. Yet we tend to tolerate ignorance of God's decrees and wonder why our lives and our churches seem to lack spiritual authority and power. A researcher in church growth has noted that preaching is pretty much useless unless people first confess their sins. But why should they confess when they have no standard by which to measure their behavior? The stipulations in God's Word are that standard. Unless we know those decrees and respect them, there's not much likelihood for spiritual renewal to occur. Our task is to make God's Word clear and applicable to all of life, as Ezra did for the people in his day. Only then will we see tangible growth and strong discipleship in our lives and in our churches.

Road Map. In 1997, the Central American city of Managua, Nicaragua, adopted a program that most cities take for granted. The city named its streets and numbered its buildings. Larry Rohter writes in the *New York Times* that for 25 years, Managua, with a population of 1.5 million, had been without that basic necessity following a devastating 1972 earthquake, which relocated most residents. During that time, people learned to make do, wandering down the wrong streets, asking strangers where to go, and making one wrong turn after another until they hopefully found their destination.

Illogical is a good word to describe the system—if you can call it a system. "Formal addresses have come to be defined neither by numbers nor street names," writes Rohter, "but in relation to the nearest landmark, as in: 'From El Carmen Church, a block toward the National Stadium' or 'Across from Los Ranchos Restaurant.'

"That, in turn, has made it necessary to name the points of the compass in giving directions or addressing a letter, an issue that has been resolved in an equally baffling fashion. 'Toward the lake' has come to mean north, 'toward the mountain' means south, 'up' means east and 'down' means west.

"Furthermore, though some of the original guideposts still exist, many others have vanished, leaving all but pre-quake residents confused. A leading economic research institute, for instance, offers visitors the following address: 'From where the gate of El Retiro Hospital used to be, two blocks toward the lake, one block down.'"

Finding one's way in Managua sounds a lot like trying to spiritually revive one's life without the clear guidance of God's Word. One is dependent on directions from others who may not know the right way. One operates by trial and error. One wanders and feels lost. How much better to have a map! The Bible offers us clear direction to live by so we know where we are going—and can tell others how to get there too!

FOR YOUTH ■ **TOPIC:** Rebuilding the Relationship
■ **QUESTIONS:** 1. Why did Ezra read from God's Word to the people?
2. Why was it necessary for God's Word to be explained to the people?
3. Why did the people initially respond in sorrow to the reading of God's Word? 4. What did the civil and religious officials urge the people to do? 5. When the Spirit prompts us to heed the truths of Scripture, how should we respond?

■ **ILLUSTRATIONS:**
A Divine Send-Off. All of us use favorite send-off words to encourage our friends, like "Keep your chin in the wind." There must be a collection of these sayings somewhere. Right words do make a difference. The best words to remember are found in the Bible.

The joy of the LORD is your strength (Neh. 8:10) is one of those classic biblical promises. It means a lot more when we recall its original setting. When God's people wept for their sins, Nehemiah told them that it was now time for them to experience God's joy and let that be the foundation for rebuilding their relationship with Him and others within the faith community.

Scripture brings us to confession and joy. Divine words of truth are always the right and best ones for us. When we neglect them, it's like neglecting food and drink for our bodies. The Bible helps us to overcome our sins, to find joy, and to give joy to others.

Love Letters. My mailman and I often enjoy a humorous banter. When he comes by, I tell him, "Just bring checks and love letters." He laughs. Beyond the usual bills and junk mail, not many of us receive words of adoration and unbridled love through the mail any more.

I know someone who still sends love letters. In fact, He sends billions of them each day all around the world. I think the late Mother Teresa, the well-known servant to India's poor, put it best: "We are all pencils in the hand of a writing God, who is sending His love letters to the world."

What kind of reading do people get from you? Are you critical, judgmental, and sarcastic? Or are you loving, kind, and considerate? Do you take the time to help others, or are you so self-absorbed that you don't notice or care? God has something to say to the people around you. He will write His love letters of hope through you, if you are willing. In doing so, you can become, as one pastor says, "the visible expression of the invisible God." What does God want to say through you today to help rebuild a shattered relationship?

The Treasure of Truth. Have you ever been on a treasure hunt? You look all over for the treasure at the end because you know it is something worth finding. And what do you want to do when you find it? You call others over to see!

The Bible, God's Word, is our treasure. It is filled with words of hope, healing, and comfort. Although the Bible was written centuries ago, its truths are relevant to us today. What a gift to have God's promises to guide our lives!

In Christ, we have the treasures of wisdom and knowledge along with the riches of understanding. That's why we need to know the promises of the Bible, to live by them, and pass along the Gospel to others. Enjoy the treasure of truth that is yours in the Bible—and be sure to share the wealth with others. The great thing about this treasure is the more you give away, the more you have yourself!

JESUS AS GOD'S SON

BACKGROUND SCRIPTURE: Hebrews 1
DEVOTIONAL READING: Proverbs 8:22-31

KEY VERSE: Who being the brightness of his glory, and the express image of his person, and upholding all things by the word of his power. Hebrews 1:3.

KING JAMES VERSION

HEBREWS 1:1 God, who at sundry times and in divers manners spake in time past unto the fathers by the prophets, 2 Hath in these last days spoken unto us by his Son, whom he hath appointed heir of all things, by whom also he made the worlds; 3 Who being the brightness of his glory, and the express image of his person, and upholding all things by the word of his power, when he had by himself purged our sins, sat down on the right hand of the Majesty on high;

4 Being made so much better than the angels, as he hath by inheritance obtained a more excellent name than they. . . . 8 But unto the Son he saith, Thy throne, O God, is for ever and ever: a sceptre of righteousness is the sceptre of thy kingdom. 9 Thou hast loved righteousness, and hated iniquity; therefore God, even thy God, hath anointed thee with the oil of gladness above thy fellows. 10 And, Thou, Lord, in the beginning hast laid the foundation of the earth; and the heavens are the works of thine hands: 11 They shall perish; but thou remainest; and they all shall wax old as doth a garment; 12 And as a vesture shalt thou fold them up, and they shall be changed: but thou art the same, and thy years shall not fail.

NEW REVISED STANDARD VERSION

HEBREWS 1:1 Long ago God spoke to our ancestors in many and various ways by the prophets, 2 but in these last days he has spoken to us by a Son, whom he appointed heir of all things, through whom he also created the worlds. 3 He is the reflection of God's glory and the exact imprint of God's very being, and he sustains all things by his powerful word. When he had made purification for sins, he sat down at the right hand of the Majesty on high, 4 having become as much superior to angels as the name he has inherited is more excellent than theirs. . . .

8 But of the Son he says,
"Your throne, O God, is forever and ever,
  and the righteous scepter is the scepter of your
    kingdom.
9 You have loved righteousness and hated
    wickedness;
therefore God, your God, has anointed you
  with the oil of gladness beyond your companions."
10 And,
"In the beginning, Lord, you founded the earth,
  and the heavens are the work of your hands;
11 they will perish, but you remain;
  they will all wear out like clothing;
12 like a cloak you will roll them up,
  and like clothing they will be changed.
But you are the same,
  and your years will never end."

Monday, May 26	Proverbs 8:22-31	*From the Beginning*
Tuesday, May 27	Hebrews 1:1-5	*Appointed Heir*
Wednesday, May 28	John 1:1-5	*In the Beginning*
Thursday, May 29	Hebrews 1:6-9	*The Firstborn*
Friday, May 30	Hebrews 1:10-12	*The Work of God's Hands*
Saturday, May 31	John 1:14-18	*Full of Grace and Truth*
Sunday, June 1	Hebrews 1:13-14	*Heir of All Things*

Background

The writer of Hebrews began his letter by commenting on God's disclosure of Himself to humankind. Since the creation of the world (see Gen. 1:1), people have been aware of God's invisible attributes. In particular, they could infer His eternal power and divine nature through what He has made (Rom. 1:20; see Ps. 19:1-6). While this general revelation of God enables people to know that He exists, it does not impart divine truths leading to salvation. The latter is only made possible by God revealing Himself and His will in a special way. Hebrews 1:1 declares that during the era of the Old Testament, God spoke redemptively to His people through His prophets on a number of occasions.

In Bible times, a prophet was someone whom God called to speak on His behalf. Prophets used a variety of means to convey God's message to people, including oral, dramatic, and written forms. Prophets did not spend all of their time predicting the future. Much of their efforts went into observing what was taking place around them and declaring God's message concerning those situations. Prophets such as Isaiah had to deal with challenging religious, social, and political circumstances. In some difficult situations, they got the attention of people by speaking and acting in ways that were unconventional and riveting. For instance, Jeremiah placed around his neck a yoke made out of leather straps and wooden crossbars to symbolize the weak and fragile power of foreign nations (Jer. 27:1-11). Ezekiel took a large clay brick and sketched on it the city of Jerusalem to warn the inhabitants of a coming attack (Ezek. 4:1-8). Often, the prophets began their speeches with the declaration, "Hear the word of the LORD" (Isa. 1:10). These opening remarks signaled that the prophets were not speaking on their own behalf or for their personal benefit. Rather, they were God's messengers, whom He authorized to convey vital truths to others (see Amos 1:1-12; Hab. 1:1; Zech. 1:1).

Notes on the Printed Text

Hebrews 1:1 states that long ago the Lord spoke to His people in various portions and in a variety of ways (for example, through visions, dreams, and riddles). The idea is that His revelation was fragmentary, partial, and incomplete, though fully inspired and authoritative. The basis for God choosing to reveal Himself in progressive stages rests on the fact that He works with us according to the level of our understanding. At first, He revealed Himself only in shadows and symbols; but as people came to know more about Him and the way He works, He became more explicit in His dealings and revelations. It's important to acknowledge these ancient revelations for what they taught people about God, while simultaneously noting that they pointed to a time when God would reveal Himself more fully and finally in *his Son* (Heb. 1:2).

In these last days would carry a special significance for the readers, who probably interpreted the phrase to mean that Jesus, as the Savior, had ushered in the messianic age. He is not merely the end of a long line of Old Testament prophets, but also the one for whom the Hebrews had waited for centuries. He is the complete and distinct revelation of God. Even with the coming of the Savior, the inspired nature of God's communication has not changed. The messages He conveyed through the prophets to the community of faith were graced by His power and love; and this remains true now that the Son has revealed the Father to us. In fact, what the Messiah has unveiled is in harmony with all that appears in the Old Testament, for what the prophets foretold finds its fulfillment in the Messiah (see Rom. 1:2; 3:21).

The author of Hebrews proceeded to explain ways in which God's revelation through the Savior is superior to all other revelations of the Lord. To show this superiority, the writer made a number of statements describing the Son. First, the Father appointed His Son as *heir of all things* (Heb. 1:2). In Hebrew culture, the firstborn son was the highest ranked of all children. Therefore, he was also the family heir. Jesus is the heir, owner, and Lord of God's creation. Second, it is through the Son that the Father *made the worlds*. The Greek term rendered *worlds* refers to the temporal ages and includes the spatial realm, which exists in those time periods. Before time and matter were created, the Messiah eternally preexisted.

Third, the Son is the *brightness* (1:3) of the triune God's glory. This does not mean Jesus is merely a reflection of the Lord's majesty. The Messiah is God Himself, for the glory of God is His radiance. In Jesus' incarnation, He unveiled to humankind the majesty of the divine. Fourth, the Son is the *express image* of the triune God's being. The Greek word behind this translation originally referred to the die used in minting coins. The term later came to refer to the impression on coins. The writer of Hebrews was saying that who Jesus is corresponds exactly to that of the Godhead. Thus, He alone is the precise representation of God's essence. While the Son is one with the Father and the Spirit in terms of their being, there remains a distinction of the divine persons of the Trinity. Fifth, not only did the Son create the universe, but He also holds it together by His powerful word. Through His sustaining royal decree, He prevents the cosmos from destruction. Clearly, the Son has a continued interest in the world and loves it. Thus, He is carrying it toward the fulfillment of His divine plan.

Sixth, at the heart of the divine plan and revelation to humankind is making redemption available for the lost. This is why the Son died to wash us from the stain of our sins. The Greek verb for *purged* is *katharismon*, from which we derive the term *catharsis*, meaning a purging that brings about spiritual renewal. The idea is that through His atoning sacrifice at Calvary, Jesus accomplished cleansing for humanity's transgressions. The writer expressed his thoughts in the past tense to underscore that the Messiah's redemptive work on our behalf has already been accomplished. Seventh, because He completed the task for which He was sent, He was granted the place of highest honor, namely, to sit at God's right hand in a posture of rest (as opposed to endlessly ministering in a standing position; see 10:11). The Lord Jesus did once and for all what the Hebrew priests were required to do on a regular basis. Now, as our great High Priest, the Messiah continually applies to us the purification for sins He obtained at the cross. This enables us to worship in God's presence.

For the various reasons given by the writer of Hebrews, the Son is to be considered superior to all things, including *the angels* (1:4). The Hebrew people had long held angels in high esteem because these heavenly beings were instrumental in the giving of the law at Mount Sinai. The author told his readers that God's Son is absolutely above all angels. To emphasize Jesus' superiority, the writer of Hebrews said Christ's name (most likely, *Son*; see 1:5) is superior to that of the celestial beings in heaven. The idea is that Jesus' character and work—which were summed up in His name— were far superior even to those of God's cosmic messengers.

The author of Hebrews quoted a number of Old Testament passages to show how and why the Lord Jesus is superior to the angels. Apparently, the writer of the epistle intended to imply that the Messiah is to be seen throughout the Old Testament. This was a strategically important decision, for the Jewish readership of the letter highly regarded the Hebrew Scriptures. There was no better way to substantiate the superior-ity of Christ than by citing pertinent verses from the Old Testament. Those reading Hebrews would have to admit that even their sacred writings affirmed that Jesus is bet-ter than anyone else.

While the angels are God's servants (1:5-7), Jesus is God's Son and the divine King. This truth is stressed in 1:8-9, which contain a quotation from Psalm 45:6-7. Here we find one of the Bible's strongest affirmations of the deity of Christ. In Hebrews 1:8-9, the Son is addressed as God; and His royal status is alluded to in the words *throne*, *sceptre*, and *kingdom*. As the Father's representative and co-regent, the Son rules over all creation forever. His scepter symbolizes His regal authority, which is characterized by justice and equity. Because these virtues are the basis of His unending rule, He enjoys an infinitely exalted status as King.

The latter emphasis can be found in the phrase *oil of gladness* (1:9). The allusion is to an ancient Israelite practice of anointing the head of a king with olive oil at his coronation. The event was a time of great celebration and renewed hope. The ultimate focus, of course, is Jesus Christ, who reigns as King over the cosmos. Like the Father, the Son loves righteousness and hates wickedness. Because of these characteristics, the Father set His Son above all other people and beings, and anointed Him to carry out the most sacred function of all time—to bring people to salvation.

Hebrews 1:10-12 quotes Psalm 102:25-27. These verses declare that at the dawn of time, Yahweh (the covenant-keeping God of Israel) laid the foundations of the earth. Likewise, He made the heavens with His hands. We learn from Hebrews 1:10 that the Messiah acted as God's agent in Creation (see John 1:1-3; Col. 1:15-17). One day, the heavens and the earth will perish and disappear. The Son will roll up the Creation like a worn-out robe that is to be discarded, and replace this tattered garment with a new heaven and earth (see 2 Pet. 3:10-13; Rev. 21:1). In contrast, the Son (like the Father and the Spirit) will remain the same throughout all eternity (Heb. 1:11-12).

When Paul talked about *visions and revelations* (2 Cor. 12:1) he had from the Lord, the apostle disclosed that he had been caught up to *the third heaven* (12:2) or *paradise* (12:4). Contemporary Jewish writings subdivided the heavens into three or more layers. It is unclear how much of this thinking the apostle accepted, though his wording here suggests he embraced the Jewish belief in the plurality of the heavens. If we assume that the first heaven is the sky and the second heaven the more distant stars and planets, the third heaven refers to the place where God dwells. Paradise is the abode of blessedness for the righteous dead. For believers, it also signifies dwelling in fellowship with the exalted Redeemer in unending glory.

SUGGESTIONS TO TEACHERS

As the writer to the Hebrews opened his epistle, he must have been thinking that the most alluring temptations his readers faced did not involve obvious evils such as murder or adultery. Instead, they were tempted to overvalue the good (such as the Old Testament and angels) by elevating them to the level of the perfect (namely, God's Son). Christians today face similar temptations. Encourage your students to see the truth of the following statements.

1. ALL GOD'S GIFTS ARE VALUABLE. Just as the writer to the Hebrews valued the divine gifts of the Old Testament and the angels, so God's people today can appropriately enjoy all the good gifts God has given us. When God looked down on the world He had just made, He called it all very good.

2. BUT GOD'S GREATEST GIFT IS HIMSELF. God has given His people gifts such as natural beauty, the Scriptures, family and friends, and churches, but none of them can compare with His greatest gift—God Himself coming to earth in the form of His Son, Jesus Christ.

3. WE CAN ENJOY GOD AND HIS GIFTS. The writer wanted his readers to avoid worshiping the Old Testament and the angels. He thus instructed them to obey the teaching of the Old Testament and follow the example of the angels in worshiping the one true God (Father, Son, and Holy Spirit), the giver of all good gifts. The writer knew that, when God's people worship Him alone, they can best enjoy both God and all His many gifts.

<table>
<tr><td>

FOR ADULTS

</td><td>

■ **TOPIC:** Finding Deeper Meaning in Life

■ **QUESTIONS:** 1. What was the nature of God's revelation in the past

</td></tr>
</table>

through the Old Testament prophets? 2. In what sense is the Son heir of all things? 3. In what sense does Jesus sustain all things by His powerful command? 4. What virtues characterize the reign of the Son? 5. How does the existence of the Son contrast with that of Creation?

■ **ILLUSTRATIONS:**

Confused Eagle. Once upon a time, a man found the egg of an eagle. For some reason, it had been abandoned by its mother. But because it was still warm, the man took it and put it in the nest of one of his backyard chickens. It remained there along with the other eggs that the mother hen was incubating.

After a period of time, the eaglet was hatched. Then, along with the other chicks from the nest, he began to go about the backyard doing what the other chicks did. He scratched the earth for worms and insects. He looked for the corn that the man would throw into the yard. The eaglet clucked and cackled as best as he could. As he grew, he would, like the other chickens, thrash his wings and fly a few feet in the air.

Years passed in this way and the eagle grew very old. One day he saw a magnificent bird far above him in the cloudless sky. It glided majestically among the powerful wind currents, soaring and swooping, scarcely beating its long golden wings. The old eagle looked at it in awe and asked, "What's that?" "That's the eagle, the king of the birds," clucked one of his neighbors. "He belongs to the sky and to the high places. We belong to the earth, for we are chickens." The old eagle never doubted this statement. And so it was that he lived and died as if he were a chicken, for that is what he believed about himself.

How sad and limiting it would be if we who have trusted in Jesus for salvation continued to think of ourselves as condemned, hell-bound sinners. The Father has recreated us in the Son for grander purposes. We have our identity in Christ so that we might find deeper meaning and eternal significance to our existence.

Successful Operation. An irate woman approached the receptionist's desk at the ophthalmologist's office. "Yesterday, while I was having surgery, someone stole my wig," she said accusingly. The physician came out and tried to calm down the woman. "I assure you that no one on my staff would have done such a thing. Why do you think it was taken from here?" "Well," the woman huffed, "after the operation, I noticed that the wig I had on was ugly and cheap-looking." The surgeon gently remarked, "Ma'am, I think that means that your cataract operation was a success."

When we come to know Jesus by faith, it should serve as a lens through which to view our entire lives. In the light of our new birth, the truth of the Gospel functions like a new pair of eyeglasses through which we see ourselves and our world in a different light and with a fresh perspective. It's a light in which we find deeper meaning, especially as we recognize the love of God in every moment, in every place, and in every relationship.

Unusual Gifts Used for God. The opening paragraph of Hebrews offered its readers a wonderful example of using the Greek language with great stylistic effect. We don't know who wrote this epistle, but we do know that he must have been a highly educated person. When the writer became a Christian, God did not ask him to leave his education and talents behind. Instead, God called him to use his thinking and writing abilities for the glory of God and the growth of the church. Perhaps you know people who offer their skills and experience to God for His use.

Joy piloted a casino boat in Baton Rouge, Louisiana, before she heard God's call on her life. Today, she gives her time ministering to riverboat captains and crews. Joy knows what it's like to spend entire months away on the river. From her experience, she can minister empathetically to others who face that situation.

Barb was a computer web genius. She now gives half her time to building and maintaining a Christian website. Her site offers all kinds of information enabling Christians to minister better to nearby people of other ethnic groups.

FOR YOUTH

■ **TOPIC:** Here Comes the Son!
■ **QUESTIONS:** 1. How does the Father's revelation through the Son contrast with His revelation through the Old Testament prophets? 2. In what sense does Jesus radiate the glory of God? 3. When did the Son sit down at the right hand of the Father in heaven? 4. For how long will the kingdom of Christ endure? 5. What will the Son one day do to the heavens and the earth?

■ **ILLUSTRATIONS:**
Cracking the Code. In 2003, Dan Brown's novel, *The Da Vinci Code*, debuted and quickly became a publishing phenomenon. It sold over 60 million copies and was translated into 44 languages. In 2006, a heavily hyped movie by the same title was released. Both maintain the absurd premise that Leonardo da Vinci planted inside his famous works (including the *Mona Lisa* and *The Last Supper*) various codes and secret symbols about Jesus, the Bible, and the history of the early church.

Here are some other dubious claims made in Brown's novel: Jesus was only a man, not God; Mary Magdalene was the wife of Jesus and should be worshiped as a goddess; at the time of Jesus' crucifixion, Mary was pregnant with His child; for the child's safety, Mary fled from the holy land to France, where she gave birth to a daughter named Sarah; the daughter gave rise to a prominent family line that is still present in Europe today; a mysterious society called the Priory of Sion guards the secret of Jesus' royal bloodline; and long-suppressed Gospels (such as the Gospel of Mary, the Gospel of Thomas, and the Gospel of Philip) are finally revealing the truth.

Brown maintains that "all descriptions of artwork, architecture, documents, and secret rituals in this novel are accurate." But numerous scholars have documented the inaccuracies contained in his book. For instance, in *Cracking Da Vinci's Code*, James Garlow and Peter Jones note that there isn't any historical text which says Jesus was married to anyone. Also, within the entire body of ancient literature, there's not a scrap of evidence that Jesus and Mary Magdalene ever conceived a child. Garlow and Jones state that while Brown's novel might be a captivating work of fiction, it misrepresents the biblical truth about Jesus. According to Hebrews 1, He is fully divine and fully human. As such, He alone can cleanse us from our sins.

The Brilliant Light. Some of you have been blessed enough to observe a complete solar eclipse. During these events, the moon passes directly between the earth and the sun, blocking the sun's light. But even under these unusual circumstances, wise friends warned you not to look directly at the sun. Why? The sun still shines so brightly that even when its rays are blocked, you can be blinded by its radiance. Through the middle part of each typical sunny day, our eyes cannot distinguish the sun from its brilliance. In a similar way, we cannot separate God the Father and God the Son. Hebrews 1:3 reminds us that Jesus shines with the same brilliance of His Father.

CHRIST AS INTERCESSOR

BACKGROUND SCRIPTURE: Hebrews 7
DEVOTIONAL READING: Jeremiah 31:31-34

KEY VERSE: [Christ] is able also to save them to the uttermost that come unto
God by him, seeing he ever liveth to make intercession for them. Hebrews 7:25.

KING JAMES VERSION

HEBREWS 7:20 And inasmuch as not without an oath he was made priest: 21 (For those priests were made without an oath; but this with an oath by him that said unto him, The Lord sware and will not repent, Thou art a priest for ever after the order of Melchisedec:) 22 By so much was Jesus made a surety of a better testament. 23 And they truly were many priests, because they were not suffered to continue by reason of death: 24 But this man, because he continueth ever, hath an unchangeable priesthood. 25 Wherefore he is able also to save them to the uttermost that come unto God by him, seeing he ever liveth to make intercession for them. 26 For such an high priest became us, who is holy, harmless, undefiled, separate from sinners, and made higher than the heavens; 27 Who needeth not daily, as those high priests, to offer up sacrifice, first for his own sins, and then for the people's: for this he did once, when he offered up himself. 28 For the law maketh men high priests which have infirmity; but the word of the oath, which was since the law, maketh the Son, who is consecrated for evermore.

NEW REVISED STANDARD VERSION

HEBREWS 7:20 This was confirmed with an oath; for others who became priests took their office without an oath, 21 but this one became a priest with an oath, because of the one who said to him,
"The Lord has sworn
    and will not change his mind,
'You are a priest forever' "—
22 accordingly Jesus has also become the guarantee of a better covenant.

23 Furthermore, the former priests were many in number, because they were prevented by death from continuing in office; 24 but he holds his priesthood permanently, because he continues forever. 25 Consequently he is able for all time to save those who approach God through him, since he always lives to make intercession for them.

26 For it was fitting that we should have such a high priest, holy, blameless, undefiled, separated from sinners, and exalted above the heavens. 27 Unlike the other high priests, he has no need to offer sacrifices day after day, first for his own sins, and then for those of the people; this he did once for all when he offered himself. 28 For the law appoints as high priests those who are subject to weakness, but the word of the oath, which came later than the law, appoints a Son who has been made perfect forever.

Monday, June 2	Jeremiah 31:31-34	*Preparing for a New Covenant*
Tuesday, June 3	Hebrews 7:1-3	*The Old Order of Priests*
Wednesday, June 4	Genesis 14:17-20	*King Melchizedek*
Thursday, June 5	Hebrews 7:4-17	*Introduction of a New Order*
Friday, June 6	Hebrews 7:18-24	*The Permanent Priesthood*
Saturday, June 7	Hebrews 7:25-26	*Interceding for All Who Approach God*
Sunday, June 8	Hebrews 7:27-28	*Perfect Forever*

BACKGROUND

Humanity's need for a priesthood is rooted in people's consciousness of sin. Those whose hearts and lives had been stained by sin could not enter the presence of a holy God. They needed a mediator, a go-between, a representative—someone who could approach God with sacrifices and prayers on their behalf. The priest was authorized to come before God and intercede on behalf of the people. Prior to Moses' receiving the law at Sinai, the office of priest was filled by the family patriarch or head of the tribe. Abraham, Isaac, and Jacob built altars, offered sacrifices, and consecrated themselves and their households.

Once the Israelites had gained independence from Egypt, God gave laws governing every aspect of their life. His laws relating to worship defined the place, the forms, and the leaders (priests) of Hebrew worship. The priests were to be from among Aaron's descendants and were to be free of physical defects. Priests were required to dress in designated attire and live in strict obedience to the law. Besides upholding the civil and religious codes that applied to the Israelites, they had to execute those laws applying to their vocation as priests. The high priest was at the top of this religious hierarchy. While priests in general represented the people before God, the high priest was their supreme representative. He was uniquely set apart to God through the anointing of his head with sacred oil (Lev. 8:12; 21:10; Ps. 133:2). Other priests had oil sprinkled only on their garments, but the high priest became the "anointed priest."

Perhaps the Hebrew Christians were having a hard time believing that there could be any priesthood other than the one associated with Aaron. The writer of Hebrews revealed that the Lord Jesus is a priest forever in the order of Melchizedek (5:6, 10; see Ps. 110:4). Melchizedek is mentioned only three times in the Bible—in Genesis 14, in Psalm 110, and in Hebrews. The only biblical background for the life of Melchizedek is found in Genesis 14:18-20. The writer of Hebrews summarized the biblical data by noting that Melchizedek was not only the king of Salem, but also a priest of God Most High (7:1). The key factor is that he was both a king and priest. Here was a person outside the boundaries of God's revelation to Israel and yet he worshiped the Lord.

The author recounted how Melchizedek met with Abraham (probably before 2000

B.C.) when the patriarch was returning from his defeat of the kings of Elam, Goiim, Shinar, and Ellasar. During their meeting, Mechizedek blessed Abraham. The patriarch responded by presenting Melchizedek with a tenth of the spoils he had taken in his victory over the four kings (7:2). In ancient times, the person who collected the tithe was greater than the one who presented it. Also, the person who blessed was greater than the one who received the blessings (7:4-7). The implication is that Melchizedek was higher in rank than Abraham, along with all his descendants, including Levi and the priesthood originating from him (7:8-10).

The recipient of Abraham's gift was both a king of righteousness and peace (7:2). Interestingly, there is no record in Scripture of Melchizedek's parents and ancestors. It's almost as if his life and priesthood had no beginning or ending. In these ways, he resembled the Son of God (7:3). The implication is that Christ, the King-Priest in the order of Melchizedek (7:17), is superior to all Levitical priests. The latter, along with the Mosaic law, were unable to make anyone perfect in God's eyes (7:11). The law was also weak and useless (7:18). In addition, all the sacrificial rituals performed by the priests had really done little toward securing the peace of the souls of humanity (7:19). Consequently, God annulled the old system and replaced it with the high priesthood of Christ (7:11-15). Jesus did not attain His priestly status on the basis of the Mosaic law, but by the power of a life that cannot be destroyed (7:16). As a human being, He died on the cross, but He rose again to new life and now lives forever. He is the *better hope* (7:19) whom the Lord introduced to give people complete and lasting access to His heavenly throne. In essence, the Gospel of salvation through Christ is better than the ritualistic law.

NOTES ON THE PRINTED TEXT

The writer of Hebrews said that God did not make an oath when Levites became priests (7:20). On the other hand, God did make an oath in appointing Christ to His priesthood. Quoting from Psalm 110:4, the author showed his readers how this oath was worded: *The Lord sware and will not repent, Thou art a priest for ever after the order of Melchisedec* (Heb. 7:21; see 5:6, 10; 7:17). In Psalm 110:1, God the Father tells David's Lord (the Messiah) to occupy a kingly position at God's right hand. Therefore, God the Father is recorded as addressing God the Son in this passage. Thus, in 110:1, the Messiah is affirmed to be a king, and in 110:4, He is declared to be a priest. Expressed differently, Christ is the perfect combination of a king-priest in one person. Whereas the Levitical priesthood had as its inception God's command, the high priesthood of Christ had as its inception the promise God made to His Son. Unlike the Levitical priesthood, Christ's priesthood will not fall short of its goal, and thus will never come to an end.

Because of God's oath concerning Jesus' eternal priesthood, Christ is the guarantee of a new and better covenant (Heb. 7:22). This means the Savior takes full responsibility for ensuring that the divine promises associated with it will be fulfilled. What God specifically pledged can be found in the new covenant recorded in Jeremiah 31:31-34 (see Heb. 8:8-12; 10:16-17). In contrast with the old covenant inaugurated at Mount Sinai, the new covenant (ratified through Jesus' atoning sacrifice) bestows greater blessings on the righteous and executes more severe judgments on the wicked. In short, the final covenant is more complete in nature and comprehensive in scope.

The author explained that under the old system, there had been many high priests to serve the Israelites; but death prevented them from continuing in that office (Heb. 7:23). As a matter of fact, Josephus, the Jewish historian, claimed there had been 83 high priests from the time of Aaron until A.D. 70. By contrast, death cannot stop Jesus' service as our great High Priest. Because He lives forever, *he has an unchangeable priesthood* (7:24). The salvation that Christ offers is ongoing in extent and eternal in intent. Through His sacrifice, He is able to save completely those who come to God (7:25). No matter what the need of the sinner, the Messiah is capable of redeeming that person and making him or her worthy of entering into God's presence. And because He lives forever, His intercession for (or pleading on behalf of) humanity before God never comes to an end.

Our great High Priest is perfectly adapted to meet our temporal and eternal needs. His ability to do so is based on four characteristics. First, Jesus is *holy* (7:26). Second, Christ is blameless, meaning that He is innocent and without evil. Third, He is pure, in the sense that He is undefiled. Fourth, He is set apart from sinners in that He is exalted above the heavens. His sacrificial work on earth has been accomplished, and He now sits at the right hand of the throne of God. When taken together, these four characteristics imply that Jesus possesses the morally spotless character of God. Whether in motives, thoughts, words, or acts, the Messiah is upright and pure. He is free from all forms of evil, and also loves all goodness and truth. Accordingly, He abhors every aspect of wickedness, ethical impurity, and inauthenticity.

Hebrews 7:27 presents a bit of a problem for some interpreters because the Jewish high priests, strictly speaking, did not offer sin offerings on a daily basis. However, in 9:7 the author revealed that he was aware of the sacrificial regulations (see also 9:25; 10:1). Therefore, for the sake of argument, he must have been combining the annual Day of Atonement sacrifices with the daily burnt offerings (see Num. 28:1-8). Of course, any time a high priest himself sinned, he might offer a sacrifice for his sin, but rarely on a daily basis. Christ stands in stark contrast to the earthly priests. Unlike the high priests of Israel, He does not have to offer sacrifices for His own sins, because He is sinless. And He does not have to offer ritualistic sacrifices for our sins, because He offered a sacrifice once for all when He offered Himself for our transgressions (Heb. 7:27). Jesus' sacrifice for the sins of the world on the cross was final. No other sacrifices need follow it.

Two types (or orders) of priests are pinpointed in 7:28. Those appointed by the

Mosaic law the author called weak. The one High Priest sworn in by the oath of God the author called *consecrated for evermore.* The priests appointed by the law were limited, just as all ordinary people are limited. They were mortal and sinful and could only offer animals for sacrifices, which could never provide a real substitute for the sins of humanity. The High Priest appointed by divine oath, on the other hand, is unlimited. He is immortal and sinless. And He offered Himself as the perfect sacrifice for the sins of all human beings.

Hebrews 2:10 and 5:9 reveal that it was through Jesus' suffering on the cross that He was made perfect in connection with His divinely appointed mission of redemption. It's important to clarify that by saying the Father made the Son perfect, the author of Hebrews did not intend to imply that Christ was ever morally or spiritually imperfect. Rather, the writer meant that through suffering, Jesus was perfectly able to carry out the task God had given Him. Because Jesus so thoroughly identified with us—even with our pain—He became qualified to be sacrificed on behalf of sinful humanity.

SUGGESTIONS TO TEACHERS

In his commentary on the Letter to the Hebrews, entitled *Christ above All,* Raymond Brown uses four adjectives to describe the portrayal of Jesus' high priesthood. You can profitably use this material to take your students through this week's lesson text.

1. CHRIST'S PRIESTHOOD WAS VICTORIOUS. All other high priests offered their sacrifices in the Jerusalem temple. They then returned home, only to go back to the sanctuary on other days to offer still more sacrifices. In contrast, Jesus offered one eternally perfect sacrifice. After His resurrection, He *passed into the heavens* (4:14), returning to His eternal home. The other priests' sacrifices may have had some effect, but any benefit was temporary. In offering His sacrifice, Jesus defeated Satan, sin, and death once and for all.

2. CHRIST'S PRIESTHOOD WAS COMPASSIONATE. Perhaps God could have designed a world where a mere snap of His fingers offered forgiveness and salvation to people. Also, He who had created the world through His Word possibly could have redeemed it merely by speaking. But God willingly chose the costlier method that more fully revealed Himself, particularly His love for humanity. Hebrews 4:15 especially portrays how the God-man, Jesus Christ, made Himself vulnerable to demonstrate His compassion for the lost.

3. CHRIST'S PRIESTHOOD WAS SUBMISSIVE. Hebrews 5:7-8 describes how Jesus willingly accepted and fulfilled the Father's plan of redemption. Christ humbled Himself by taking on the role of a humble servant who learned obedience through the things He suffered. As a human being, He pled with His Father for some relief from the trauma He faced, but, when there was no other way to offer salvation, Jesus fully submitted to the Father's will.

4. CHRIST'S PRIESTHOOD WAS EFFECTIVE. Jesus achieved the goal of redemption. By offering Himself as a sacrifice in the manner the Father wished, Jesus *became the author of eternal salvation unto all them that obey him* (5:9). His submissive expression of love and obedience enabled a host of lost people down through the centuries to find new life in Him. We are wise to devote every aspect of our lives in adoration and service to Christ.

FOR ADULTS	■ **TOPIC:** Who Can Speak for Us? ■ **QUESTIONS:** 1. What point was the writer of Hebrews making when he noted that the high priesthood of Christ was established with an

oath? 2. In what sense is Jesus the guarantor of a better covenant? 3. How is it possible for Jesus to have a permanent priesthood? 4. Why is it important for our great High Priest to be sinlessly perfect? 5. Why did Jesus offer Himself on the cross?

■ **ILLUSTRATIONS:**

A Creative Inventor. We all remember the name of Thomas Edison for his successes, especially the invention of over a thousand devices we all have known and loved. These include the incandescent electric light bulb, the phonograph, the motion-picture projector, and key components of the first telephones. But behind any of these or other successes stood a number of failures.

Edison received his first patent for an electric vote recorder. But no one wanted to buy such a machine. Officials rejected his better way, choosing to stay with the tradition of paper ballots. Did Edison despair? He then began living the philosophy he later summarized, "Every wrong attempt discarded is a step forward." Each new insight and skill he gained contributed to his amazing record as an inventor.

Living in New York City to be near the center of action, Edison was there ready to help when the local Gold Exchange's telegraphic price indicator failed. He not only fixed the machine, but also found ways to improve it. Soon the Western Union Company asked him to refine their new, but primitive stock ticker machine. These successes started Edison on his way to fame. Yet none of his successes came without many preliminary failures.

In a similar but even greater way, our God met people's rejection of His first plan with creativity and determination. He went on to offer salvation through His intermediary, the Lord Jesus Christ.

The Need for an Intermediary. When I was younger, professional athletes negotiated their own contracts with team owners. Today that practice is quite rare. Most of the players feel they will end up with a better deal if an agent represents them.

Andrew Jones, after enjoying his first few years with the Atlanta Braves, wanted to stay with this team. He was even willing to sacrifice larger salaries he might have received from other teams to stay where he was. Because he knew the Braves would offer what he considered a fair amount of money, he did not employ an agent to work with him in his contract renewal. Only after signing a new contract did he realize that the new agreement omitted one crucial factor. It did not include a no-trade clause. Jones had sacrificed money out of loyalty to his team, but his team had made no similar agreement of strong loyalty to him. In this case, perhaps Jones would have been much better off had he worked through an intermediary.

The Most Important Question. In his book titled, *Is Jesus the Only Savior?*, James Edwards recounts a conversation he had with an acquaintance about whether Christ is indeed the sole Redeemer of the world. The person asked, "What are you writing about?" Edwards replied, "I'm writing a book about Jesus as the only Savior." He noticed that a "slight frown began to form" on the face of the questioner and that the "conversation was about to turn away from social courtesies."

The acquaintance next asked, "Is that the right question?" In response, Edwards said, "I think so. In fact, I think it is the most important question in life to answer correctly." But he could tell that the other person had a different view. He informed Edwards that "Buddha, Krishna, and the Dali Lama satisfy their followers as much as Jesus satisfies Christians." Perhaps the most significant (and shocking) aspect of this exchange is that the questioner was "well bred and well read in the Christian tradition." Even so, he was "annoyed at the subject of Jesus as the only Savior."

Edwards thinks this conversation exemplifies the "changing attitudes toward Christianity today." While it has become "fashionable to express . . . suspicion and doubt" about what Scripture teaches concerning the Messiah, it is absolutely imperative for twenty-first century believers to uphold historic Christian teaching. At the top of the list is the declaration that only Jesus is the way, the truth, and the life and that no one comes to the Father except through faith in the Son (John 14:6).

FOR YOUTH

■ **TOPIC:** We Have a Friend in High Places

■ **QUESTIONS:** 1. Where in Scripture did the Lord take an oath affirming Christ's high priesthood? 2. What prevented Israel's many priests from continuing in their office of service to the people? 3. How is it possible for Jesus to save us completely and forever? 4. How often did Israel's high priests offer sacrifices and for whom? 5. In what ways is Jesus' high priesthood perfect?

■ **ILLUSTRATIONS:**

The Best Coaches. Many young people play on athletic teams at their schools or in community leagues. If you have such experience, think about some of the people who have served as your coaches. Which ones have done the best job? It is likely the ones who both knew the game well and how to handle people. What experience does it take to know a game well? Reading books in a library doesn't provide adequate training. Most of the best coaches played the game themselves. What experience does it take to handle people well? You'd think that the best players might make good coaches. Sometimes they do, but more often, the best coaches are not the Hall of Fame players, but those who have struggled, who perhaps spent time sitting on the bench.

As a boy, I cheered for the Baltimore Orioles. Their manager, Earl Weaver, may have had a hot temper, but he led the team to several championships. What experience did Weaver bring to his role? It was years as a baseball player, but all in the minor leagues, where he struggled unsuccessfully to make it to the majors.

What qualifies Jesus to help us in our times of testing? He has lived in our world as a human being just like us. He is God, but that did not necessarily make His life easier. He struggled. He suffered. His facing the same kinds of testing and pain we face enables Him to offer us the instruction and strength we need.

Approaching Boldly. Perhaps you have seen or read Charles Dickens's *Oliver Twist*. Early in the story, Oliver's single mother had died. He ended up as an inmate of a barely livable Victorian orphanage. The children there received little love. Each child was allotted adequate food to survive, but never enough to fill his or her stomach.

After one meal of nothing more than oatmeal porridge, Oliver did what no child in memory had done before him. He bravely approached the master of the dining hall. As Oliver did so, he held his empty bowl before him, and asked, "May I have some more, sir?" The rest of the boys watched in utter amazement. Oliver's master reacted with rage, blatantly rejecting Oliver's wish. The writer to the Hebrews encouraged us to approach our heavenly Father boldly, knowing that He loves us and will give us what is best through His Son, our great High Priest, the Lord Jesus Christ.

Holding Fast to His Confession of Christ. When Martin Luther posted for public debate his first list of Reformation ideas, the church authorities initially did not do anything. They hoped Luther's ideas would disappear on their own. Then, after three years, one prominent leader felt he needed to respond. He labeled many of Luther's ideas heretical. When the reformer received the official document, he burned the decree on a public bonfire. "If they are going to burn my writings, I can burn theirs."

The other prominent church leader then took further action by excommunicating Luther. Luther faced the possibility of being burned at the stake, which was the fate of others who had suggested new theological ideas. While on trial before the authorities, Luther was asked to recant. He steadfastly refused. "My conscience is captive to the will of God," he announced. "I will not recant anything, for to go against conscience is neither honest nor safe. Here I stand; I cannot do otherwise. God help me."

CHRIST AS REDEEMER

BACKGROUND SCRIPTURE: Hebrews 9:11—10:18
DEVOTIONAL READING: John 4:21-26

KEY VERSE: Neither by the blood of goats and calves, but by [Christ's] own blood he entered in once into the holy place, having obtained eternal redemption for us. Hebrews 9:12.

3

KING JAMES VERSION

HEBREWS 9:11 But Christ being come an high priest of good things to come, by a greater and more perfect tabernacle, not made with hands, that is to say, not of this building; 12 Neither by the blood of goats and calves, but by his own blood he entered in once into the holy place, having obtained eternal redemption for us. 13 For if the blood of bulls and of goats, and the ashes of an heifer sprinkling the unclean, sanctifieth to the purifying of the flesh: 14 How much more shall the blood of Christ, who through the eternal Spirit offered himself without spot to God, purge your conscience from dead works to serve the living God?

15 And for this cause he is the mediator of the new testament, that by means of death, for the redemption of the transgressions that were under the first testament, they which are called might receive the promise of eternal inheritance. 16 For where a testament is, there must also of necessity be the death of the testator. 17 For a testament is of force after men are dead: otherwise it is of no strength at all while the testator liveth.
18 Whereupon neither the first testament was dedicated without blood. . . .

10:12 But this man, after he had offered one sacrifice for sins for ever, sat down on the right hand of God; 13 From henceforth expecting till his enemies be made his footstool. 14 For by one offering he hath perfected for ever them that are sanctified. . . . 17 And their sins and iniquities will I remember no more. 18 Now where remission of these is, there is no more offering for sin.

NEW REVISED STANDARD VERSION

HEBREWS 9:11 But when Christ came as a high priest of the good things that have come, then through the greater and perfect tent (not made with hands, that is, not of this creation), 12 he entered once for all into the Holy Place, not with the blood of goats and calves, but with his own blood, thus obtaining eternal redemption. 13 For if the blood of goats and bulls, with the sprinkling of the ashes of a heifer, sanctifies those who have been defiled so that their flesh is purified, 14 how much more will the blood of Christ, who through the eternal Spirit offered himself without blemish to God, purify our conscience from dead works to worship the living God!

15 For this reason he is the mediator of a new covenant, so that those who are called may receive the promised eternal inheritance, because a death has occurred that redeems them from the transgressions under the first covenant. 16 Where a will is involved, the death of the one who made it must be established. 17 For a will takes effect only at death, since it is not in force as long as the one who made it is alive. 18 Hence not even the first covenant was inaugurated without blood. . . .

10:12 But when Christ had offered for all time a single sacrifice for sins, "he sat down at the right hand of God," 13 and since then has been waiting "until his enemies would be made a footstool for his feet." 14 For by a single offering he has perfected for all time those who are sanctified. . . .

17 he also adds,
"I will remember their sins and their lawless deeds no
   more."
18 Where there is forgiveness of these, there is no longer any offering for sin.

Monday, June 9	John 4:21-26	*"I Am He"*
Tuesday, June 10	Hebrews 9:11-15	*Mediator of a New Covenant*
Wednesday, June 11	Hebrews 9:16-24	*On Our Behalf*
Thursday, June 12	Hebrews 9:25-28	*Once for All Time*
Friday, June 13	Hebrews 10:1-10	*A One-Time Sacrifice*
Saturday, June 14	Hebrews 10:11-14	*For Our Sanctification*
Sunday, June 15	Hebrews 10:15-18	*Forgiveness Forever*

BACKGROUND

The Book of Hebrews teaches that Christ, as the mediator between God and humanity, has established a new and better covenant than the old one based on the Mosaic law. The new covenant is better precisely because it is *established upon better promises* (8:6). If the first covenant had sufficiently met the needs of people and had adequately provided for their salvation, then there would have been no need for a new covenant to replace it (8:7). But the old covenant was insufficient and inadequate. It wasn't adequate in bringing people to God, and therefore a new covenant had to be established.

God had found fault with the people under the old covenant (8:8), primarily because they did not continue in that holy compact (8:9). In turn, human failure rendered the old covenant inoperative. Although Ezekiel had written about God's establishing an *everlasting covenant* (Ezek. 16:60), only Jeremiah had spoken of a *new covenant* (Jer. 31:31). Jeremiah did not say that the covenant God made with the Israelites would be renewed. Rather, the prophet said that a completely new compact would be established (Heb. 8:8).

As Hebrews 8:10-12 and 10:15-17 reveal (see Jer. 31:33-34), the new covenant would be inward and dynamic. God's Word would actually have a place inside the minds and hearts of His people. The old covenant had been inscribed on tablets of stone and was external. But in regard to the new covenant, God vowed that His teachings would be internalized by His people. The new covenant would also provide a way for believers to have an intimate relationship with God. Jeremiah echoed several Old Testament promises (see Gen. 17:7; Exod. 6:7; Lev. 26:12). But the life, death, and resurrection of the Lord Jesus opened a new avenue for human beings to relate to their heavenly Father. Because of the salvation the Messiah provided, all believers can enter into God's presence.

NOTES ON THE PRINTED TEXT

Under the old covenant, the main purpose of a priest was to sacrifice for sin. Therefore, as our High Priest, Christ too must offer a priestly sacrifice. Other priests offered animals as a sacrifice for sins, but those sacrifices were not able to cleanse the consciences of the people who brought them (Heb. 9:9). Christ sacrificed Himself by dying on the cross and so secured God's forgiveness and blessing for believing sinners. Jesus has now become the High Priest over all the good things that are already here (for example, eternal blessings such as direct access to God and the perfecting of the conscience). Indeed, Jesus has entered the greater, more perfect tabernacle in heaven. Humans did not make this celestial sanctuary and it's not part of this created world (9:11). We should not think of Christ as engaged in some elaborate ritual in heaven. Rather, those external, earthly elements in the tabernacle below find their spiritual and eternal counterpart in the reality of Christ and His work.

The Messiah was not counted worthy of entering God's presence—and making a way for all humanity to enter God's presence—by sacrificing animals such as goats and calves and sprinkling their blood on the mercy seat in the most holy place of the earthly tabernacle. This was, of course, how the Levitical priests were counted worthy, and they were required to offer such sacrifices year after year. Christ made His passage into the heavenly sanctuary by shedding His own blood on the cross. He does not have to offer sacrifices year after year because He gave His own life, once for all, to secure our redemption from sin forever (9:12). This means His sacrifice was decisive and final. It does not have to be repeated. After paying the ransom for people's sins, Christ ascended into the true heavenly sanctuary. From there, His salvation is continually offered to all human beings.

The writer briefly recounted how the high priests under the old covenant made atonement for the sins of the people, especially by means of two types of sacrifices (9:13). On the Day of Atonement, goats and calves were slaughtered and their blood was shed (see Lev. 16). But that annual ceremony was different from the ashes of a sacrificed calf (a young adult animal) being sprinkled on those who were ceremonially defiled (Heb. 9:13). This purification rite could take place any time during the year. In it the priest slaughtered a red heifer, burned its carcass, and stored its ashes. Whenever a person became ritually impure by touching a corpse or being in contact with a foreigner, he or she could be cleansed by being sprinkled with these ashes mixed into water (see Num. 19).

The effectiveness of these ceremonies was limited in duration and superficial in benefit. Jesus' atoning sacrifice, in contrast, was eternal in its saving benefit and provided inward spiritual cleansing. When compared to the many offerings sacrificed by the priests under the old covenant, the shed blood of Christ was infinitely more valuable. He offered Himself as a perfect sacrifice to the Father through the power of the *eternal Spirit* (Heb. 9:14). Another possibility is that the author was referring to Christ's own spirit (that is, His divine nature). This means Jesus gave Himself on the cross as an eternal and spiritual sacrifice to God. In either case, the greatness of Christ and of His offering is incomparable. Because His shed blood was unblemished and undefiled, He could purify our consciences from *dead works* (including useless rituals). Jesus' crucifixion at Calvary also enables us to serve God. No longer hampered by our sins, we are able to engage in service to our Lord with all our heart and soul.

The Redeemer alone mediates the new covenant between God and humanity (9:15). Like the arbitrator between two alienated factions, Jesus represents both sides. God, who is righteous, cannot accept unrighteous human beings into His presence. Therefore Christ, who is both God and man, lived a perfectly righteous life and then died as a ransom so that believers can be set free from the penalty of the sins they committed under the first covenant (see Rom. 3:23-26). So great is Christ's sacrifice that it enables all who are called to receive the eternal inheritance God has promised them (Heb. 9:15). These individuals, who will inherit salvation, are Jesus' spiritual brothers and sisters (see 1:14; 6:17).

The Greek word translated *testament* in Hebrews 9:16 is *diatheke*. Where it appears in other New Testament passages, however, this same Greek word is usually translated "covenant." The Greeks used *diatheke* when referring to a last will and testament. When the testator had died, his or her will was read to people who had no choice but to accept it. In that way the testator's words carried a sense of finality. Among Jews who spoke Greek, the word was also used to refer to divine covenants. In a compact, God issued the terms and the people accepted them. So just as in a last will and testament, in a covenant, God's words carry a sense of finality. The author may have used the term *diatheke* in Hebrews 9 as a rhetorical device to enhance the eloquence of his argument. He smoothly transitioned from using the word to mean *covenant* (9:15, NRSV) to using it to mean *will* (9:16).

It is a universally accepted idea that a will goes into force only when it can be confirmed that the testator has died. A will never goes into effect while the one who made it is still living (9:17). Accordingly, even the old covenant was put into effect with the blood of an animal (9:18). In essence, the writer meant that something living must die—which is what is really being emphasized by the author's use of the term *blood*— for a covenant to be inaugurated. Exodus 24:3-8 records the ceremony described in Hebrews 9:18-21. The presence of additional details not in the original account suggests the author relied on other dependable sources of information. Also, at times he changed the wording of the biblical text from what appears in the Septuagint (the Greek translation of the Hebrew Scriptures). The author wanted to stress that when Moses performed a sacrificial ritual to confirm the covenant, blood was shed for the sake of human purification. In fact, the Mosaic law required almost everything to be cleansed by the shedding of blood, for apart from this happening, there is no forgiveness (9:22).

Jesus, as our High Priest, shed His blood as the one-time-for-all-time sacrifice for our sins. With His great and perfect work accomplished, He *sat down on the right hand of God* (10:12). Jesus occupies the position of utmost power and the place of highest honor. As a result of His completed work, Christ is now waiting until an appointed time, when He will overthrow all His enemies (10:13). By the all-sufficiency of Jesus' single offering, He forever made perfect those who are being made holy (10:14). Most likely, this refers to all people who, at various intervals throughout the ages, are being added to the body of Christ, His church. They are the ones who trust in the Lord Jesus for salvation. They are also the ones being set apart forever for God's holy service.

The new covenant that Christ inaugurated would enable believers to have a deeper knowledge of God. An inclusiveness concerning knowing and learning about God will exist under the new covenant that was foreign to people under the old. No longer will this knowledge be limited to some people; all believers will have a personal knowledge of the Lord (10:15-16). Also, through the new covenant, the forgiveness of sins is an eternal reality (10:17). Amazingly, an omniscient God has amnesia when it comes to our transgressions! He will never again remember our sins and lawless deeds. Through Christ's sacrifice, our iniquities have been dealt with once for all. Because our sins have been finally and effectively dealt with through the sacrifice of Christ, there is no need for any other sacrifice (10:18).

SUGGESTIONS TO TEACHERS

We live today under the provisions of the new covenant. We continue to enjoy all its advantages. As you highlight these truths, you might want to contrast our present interaction with God with the less extensive level of fellowship enjoyed by those who lived under the earlier covenant. Lead your students in gratitude for God's generosity. One way we can show gratitude for God's new covenant gifts is to enjoy them to the fullest! In particular, there is . . .

1. GREATER INTIMACY WITH GOD. Through God's Spirit, all new covenant believers can know the Lord in a manner similar to, and even more personally than we know one another. In the days before Jesus came, the nation of Israel collectively could know God, but, with rare exceptions, individuals tended to know about God only through what they had heard. Under the new covenant, God has come to live not only with but also in His people.

2. GREATER KNOWLEDGE OF GOD. Through the incarnation of Jesus and the indwelling of the Holy Spirit, first century Christians could know more about God and also know God Himself. In addition to these blessings, later generations of Christians also gained access to the complete written New Testament (which was only gradually collected and distributed). From this we see that God has given us many ways to know Him.

3. GREATER FORGIVENESS FROM HIM. God offered forgiveness to Old Testament people, but the associated ritual of animal sacrifice dreadfully complicated the process. Now through Jesus, God's people have more direct access to Him and to His grace. Not only do we receive forgiveness, but through the Spirit, we can receive assurance of that forgiveness and our resulting relationship with God.

4. GREATER CERTAINTY OF GOD'S ETERNAL FAITHFULNESS. During the period of the old covenant, the Israelites struggled to know God. As the prophets began to speak about a new day coming, their hearers might have rejoiced in what God was going to do, but generations died, not seeing that new day. They might have heard God's promise of a new covenant, but they died under the old covenant. Today, we know we live in the days of God's new covenant. The covenant established through Christ will never change!

FOR ADULTS

■ **TOPIC:** Guilt Removed

■ **QUESTIONS:** 1. In what way is the heavenly tabernacle greater and more perfect than the one that formerly existed on earth? 2. How were the people of God in Old Testament times made outwardly clean? 3. When will Jesus finally vanquish His enemies? 4. What is the basis of believers being made perfect forever? 5. Why are the Old Testament sacrifices no longer necessary?

■ **ILLUSTRATIONS:**

An Outrageous Bill. According to the *New Straits Times*, Yahaya Wahab from northern Kedah state in Malaysia, "disconnected his late father's phone line" in January 2006. He then paid the $23 remaining on the bill. But in early April, Telekom, Malaysia's debt-collection agency sent Wahab a bill for $218 trillion! He was also "ordered to pay up within 10 days or face prosecution." Understandably, the "Malaysian man said he nearly fainted" upon receiving the notice. No one seemed to know whether "the bill was a mistake" or whether the phone line of Wahab's deceased father was used "illegally after his death." A spokesperson for the country's largest telecommunications company said the firm was "aware of Yahaya's case and would address it."

Every person has an infinitely greater debt they owe God for the sins they've committed. In fact, the liability is so great that the consequence is eternal separation from the Lord (see Rom. 6:23). Of course, none of us can ever wipe away the guilt associated with our transgressions. Thankfully, the Father has done this for us through the atoning sacrifice of His Son at Calvary. Through faith in the Son, our sins are forgiven completely, totally, and forever.

I've Forgotten. Craig Brian Larson tells the following story. After several years of marriage, Bert and Mary were still childless. They decided to adopt a boy they named John. Within months, Mary found herself pregnant. She gave birth to Larry. Some years later, a supposed friend was visiting the home. As the two women chatted, the visitor inquired, "Now which of these boys is yours, Mary?"

"Both of them," she quickly replied.

The friend was not satisfied. "Which of them did you adopt?"

In an answer that demonstrated overwhelming love for both her sons, Mary responded, "I have forgotten."

God, in adopting us as His children, forgave our sins. In heaven, we may ask God about one of our less desirable choices, asking how He could have forgiven that one. He may say, "Did you really do that? I don't remember that at all."

Open Now to All. Boston's Museum of Fine Arts includes a display unlike any I have seen in several major world art museums. When construction for a new shopping mall was about to condemn Oak Hill, a lovely home built in 1800, it needed to come down. The mall owners could have carefully photographed the mansion and displayed huge pictures throughout their new business establishment. That would have been one way to preserve the memory of the old place and allow throngs of visitors to experience it continually.

Curators at the museum decided they could do much better. They moved, and completely reconstructed within their museum, several entire rooms from the house. The original carpets, drapes, door jambs, fireplaces—everything but the space which these rooms had occupied—was moved to make a unique museum display. This is much better than photographs. People can see Oak Hill in three dimensions. The museum experience now, in effect, enables all people to walk into old Oak Hill itself.

God declared the need for a new covenant. And, through His grace, He opened a new and better covenant with the redeemed, one providing forgiveness and hope.

FOR YOUTH ■ **TOPIC:** Jesus to the Rescue
■ **QUESTIONS:** 1. What enabled Jesus to enter the tabernacle in heaven? 2. How is it possible for Christ's atoning sacrifice to make our consciences clear? 3. What is the implication of the Son sitting down at the Father's right hand in heaven? 4. What did Jesus accomplish by His once-for-all-time sacrifice? 5. How is it possible for God to never again remember our sins?

■ **ILLUSTRATIONS:**

Message of Grace. In 2003, a little girl named Kai Leigh Harriott was paralyzed by a stray bullet shot by Anthony Warren. According to Megan Tench of the *Boston Globe*, some think the family should have demanded "an eye for an eye" from the shooter. But in 2006, Kai Leigh said she had forgiven Warren. Tonya David, the girl's mother, was influential in encouraging her to respond in this way.

David noted that the world is filled with people who hold onto bitterness and anger. "But I don't want bitterness and anger in my life," she said, "and I don't want that for

Kai Leigh." David explained, "We are Christians. I tried very hard from the depths of my soul to hate Anthony, but it wouldn't come out." This willingness to forgive enabled Warren to apologize in court for shooting Kai Leigh. And when the mother went to shake Warren's hand, the forgiven fellon "surprised her when he pulled her in for an embrace." David, who had been "inspired by her daughter's strength," said she wasn't able to "let the man go."

Ultimately, it was the faith that Kai Leigh and her mother have in Christ that enabled them to absolve Warren of his crime. The decision of the mother and daughter honors the offer of forgiveness that Jesus makes available to all humanity as a result of His atoning sacrifice on Calvary.

Caught! One afternoon after school, Joe decided to do some target shooting with his father's shotgun. The lad had been allowed to use the gun for hunting game, but not for anything else. His father and mother were not at home, and so Joe felt it would not matter if he blasted away at some old metal cans along a tree line at the back of their lot. No sooner had he fired the weapon than his parents pulled into the driveway.

Joe became rigid. What should he do? Should he say he was hunting rabbits, for example? The lad decided to tell the truth. He admitted that he had been shooting at some metal cans. With this admission, Joe anticipated that he would lose his hunting privileges. But instead, his parents forgave him and asked him not to be irresponsible again.

To be forgiven is a wonderful feeling. It's one of the reasons for experiencing joy in the Christian life. When we sin, we should confess our wrongdoing to our loving and wise heavenly Father. God promises to forgive us and restore us to fellowship with Him. He can do this because of what Jesus did for us on the cross.

Declaration of Independence. Within a few weeks will be the 232nd anniversary of the signing of the American Declaration of Independence at the Continental Congress in Philadelphia. For decades, Great Britain had governed the people of the 13 colonies. Many within those locales thought it wisest for the people of Pennsylvania, Massachusetts, Georgia, and the other colonies to remain in agreement with King George III. Even if British rule restricted Americans' freedom a bit, some felt that economic advantages and the danger of war argued against moving toward freedom.

But as the representatives deliberated, they finally reached consensus. They would establish a new agreement, not with Britain, but with each other, among the colonies. They committed themselves, even if it required their death, to break free from the old ways and establish a brand new system. Aren't we glad that Jesus, at the cost of His death, chose to fulfill the old covenant and establish a new, better one?

CHRIST AS LEADER

BACKGROUND SCRIPTURE: Hebrews 12:1-13
DEVOTIONAL READING: Proverbs 3:5-12

KEY VERSE: Let us lay aside every weight, and the sin which doth so easily beset us, and let us run with patience the race that is set before us. Hebrews 12:1.

KING JAMES VERSION

HEBREWS 12:1 Wherefore seeing we also are compassed about with so great a cloud of witnesses, let us lay aside every weight, and the sin which doth so easily beset us, and let us run with patience the race that is set before us, 2 Looking unto Jesus the author and finisher of our faith; who for the joy that was set before him endured the cross, despising the shame, and is set down at the right hand of the throne of God. 3 For consider him that endured such contradiction of sinners against himself, lest ye be wearied and faint in your minds.

4 Ye have not yet resisted unto blood, striving against sin. 5And ye have forgotten the exhortation which speaketh unto you as unto children, My son, despise not thou the chastening of the Lord, nor faint when thou art rebuked of him: 6 For whom the Lord loveth he chasteneth, and scourgeth every son whom he receiveth. 7 If ye endure chastening, God dealeth with you as with sons; for what son is he whom the father chasteneth not? 8 But if ye be without chastisement, whereof all are partakers, then are ye bastards, and not sons. 9 Furthermore we have had fathers of our flesh which corrected us, and we gave them reverence: shall we not much rather be in subjection unto the Father of spirits, and live? 10 For they verily for a few days chastened us after their own pleasure; but he for our profit, that we might be partakers of his holiness. 11 Now no chastening for the present seemeth to be joyous, but grievous: nevertheless afterward it yieldeth the peaceable fruit of righteousness unto them which are exercised thereby. 12 Wherefore lift up the hands which hang down, and the feeble knees; 13 And make straight paths for your feet, lest that which is lame be turned out of the way; but let it rather be healed.

NEW REVISED STANDARD VERSION

HEBREWS 12:1 Therefore, since we are surrounded by so great a cloud of witnesses, let us also lay aside every weight and the sin that clings so closely, and let us run with perseverance the race that is set before us, 2 looking to Jesus the pioneer and perfecter of our faith, who for the sake of the joy that was set before him endured the cross, disregarding its shame, and has taken his seat at the right hand of the throne of God.

3 Consider him who endured such hostility against himself from sinners, so that you may not grow weary or lose heart. 4 In your struggle against sin you have not yet resisted to the point of shedding your blood. 5 And you have forgotten the exhortation that addresses you as children—

"My child, do not regard lightly the discipline of
    the Lord,
  or lose heart when you are punished by him;
6 for the Lord disciplines those whom he loves,
    and chastises every child whom he accepts."

7 Endure trials for the sake of discipline. God is treating you as children; for what child is there whom a parent does not discipline? 8 If you do not have that discipline in which all children share, then you are illegitimate and not his children. 9 Moreover, we had human parents to discipline us, and we respected them. Should we not be even more willing to be subject to the Father of spirits and live? 10 For they disciplined us for a short time as seemed best to them, but he disciplines us for our good, in order that we may share his holiness. 11 Now, discipline always seems painful rather than pleasant at the time, but later it yields the peaceful fruit of righteousness to those who have been trained by it.

12 Therefore lift your drooping hands and strengthen your weak knees, 13 and make straight paths for your feet, so that what is lame may not be put out of joint, but rather be healed.

4

BACKGROUND

The term rendered "witnesses" (Heb. 12:1) is loaded with significance. The Greek word is *martus* and comes from the verb *martureo*, which means "to testify" or "to bear witness." The idea is of one affirming what he or she has seen or experienced. The New Testament writers sometimes applied *martus* to those believers in Christ who were attesting to their faith while enduring persecution. Thus, in time such believers came to be known as *martyrs*, that is, those who voluntarily suffered death as the penalty for their allegiance to Christ.

The writers of the New Testament often used *martureo* to refer to believers who personally testified to Jesus' work on earth, regardless of whether suffering was present. John, in particular, noted the various witnesses who testified about Jesus. These included God the Father (John 5:31-32, 37; 8:18), the Holy Spirit (15:26), Jesus Himself (8:14, 18), Scripture (5:39), Jesus' own works (5:36), John the Baptist (1:34), and Jesus' disciples (15:27). The concept of witness is prominent not only in the New Testament but also the Old Testament. For example, Jacob used a pile of rocks to serve as a reminder that God was a witness to the patriarch's agreement with Laban (Gen. 31:45-50). In addition, the Mosaic law required that at least two witnesses had to support a charge of wrongdoing (Num. 35:30; Deut. 17:6).

NOTES ON THE PRINTED TEXT

Hebrews 12:1 refers to a huge crowd of witnesses testifying to the life of faith. From the perspective of runners in a stadium, the spectators all around them in the stands might look something like a cloud of people. In a sense, Christians also have a cloud of people watching us: the deceased saints in heaven. As *witnesses*, they watch us and cheer us on in our race. They are also motivating examples of faithfulness.

In the ancient world, runners in a long-distance race competed in the nude. They would strip themselves of anything that might weigh them down or entangle their arms and legs. Similarly, the Hebrew Christians were to rid themselves of every encumbrance that might prevent them from living for the Redeemer. While some of these hindrances were not inherently sinful (for example, longstanding religious traditions), others were. The latter included the fear of being persecuted, resentment toward others, and sexual immorality (10:38-39; 12:15-16). In mentioning *the sin which doth so easily beset* (12:1), the writer may have had in mind the danger of defection resulting from discouragement—in other words, apostasy. The presence of opposition from others tempted some first-century Christians to revert to their former way of life. In light of this possibility, the writer urged his readers to remain steadfast in their faith even when they encountered hostile forces.

Every race has a definite goal, a tape to break. The wise runner is one who keeps his or her eyes on the finish line and doesn't look back. As Christians, we too have a goal; we are heading for Jesus. And so the writer of Hebrews urged, *Looking unto Jesus* (12:2). After all, Christ is *the author and finisher of our faith*. While we must persevere in our running, it is Jesus who enables us both to begin and complete the race. One way Jesus helps us to start, continue, and finish our race is by being an example. He is the champion runner of the ages. As we struggle in our race, we can know that He has already been there and has shown that the race can be won.

Just as we are to focus our attention on Jesus, so He kept His eyes fixed on the joy of completing the mission the Father had given to Him. And just as we are to persevere in the race marked out for us, so Jesus *endured the cross, despising the shame*. The cross brought great suffering and disgrace, but Christ kept in mind that the glory of enduring the cross would be much greater. Despite facing the highest hurdle anybody ever has—the Cross—Jesus successfully completed His race. And instead of receiving the wreath of leaves awarded to a victorious runner in the ancient world, Christ was rewarded with supreme authority. He took His seat in the place of highest honor beside His Father's throne in heaven.

The writer of Hebrews, knowing that his readers would sometimes feel weary and lose heart because of opposition, urged them to reflect earnestly on what Jesus experienced (12:3). Throughout the course of His earthly ministry, the Lord had to endure terrible opposition from sinners, and yet He persevered until He won the victory. The writer reminded his readers that no matter how difficult their situation had become, it had not yet led to bloodshed; in other words, none of them had died for their faith (12:4). A schoolmaster was once asked what would be the ideal curriculum for children. He answered, "Any program of worthwhile studies, so long as all of it is hard and some of it is unpleasant." The original readers of Hebrews had been experiencing what was hard and unpleasant in their *striving against sin*. Thankfully, however, none of them had so far been martyred.

Despite the fact that their struggle was not as bad as it could be, the Hebrews were being tempted to look on their suffering in the wrong way. Once more, the author referred to some Old Testament Scripture to validate his point. This time he focused on Proverbs 3:11-12. This passage teaches those being disciplined by the Lord to respond properly. We are not to err by making light of it. Neither are we to err by losing heart, taking it too seriously. We should recognize that discipline from the Lord is a sign that He loves us and considers us His spiritual children (Heb. 12:5-6). And therefore, we should accept His discipline and pay attention to what He's trying to teach us through it.

The author's aim was to make his audience aware of suffering as a teaching tool used by God; in other words, discipline is pedagogical. This insight makes the writer's statement in the first part of 12:7 all the more forceful. Since the dawn of time, good parents have been actively involved in disciplining their children. Likewise, God disciplines all His spiritual children. When the Lord corrects us, it demonstrates that we are legitimate members of His heavenly family (12:8). Notice the way in which the writer argued from the lesser reality to the greater reality (*shall we not much rather*; 12:9)—from human parents upward to the heavenly Father. If we respect our earthly parents when they discipline us, we should much more *be in subjection unto the Father of spirits, and live.* Discipline by God should not cause us to think worse of Him, but rather to respect Him all the more. When He corrects us, His wise and loving purposes undergird His actions.

In human discipline, there is always the element of imperfection, even though our parents disciplined us as well as they knew how (12:10). By an upgraded contrast, divine discipline is always *for our profit, that we might be partakers of his holiness.* God's discipline is always prudent, and we can be sure it is needed and contributes to our spiritual growth. When we submit to the Lord's hand of correction, we experience greater moral fitness. We also become increasingly conformed in every aspect of our lives to the image of Christ. The author admitted that no discipline is pleasant while it's occurring; in fact, it's downright painful. The benefit appears only later, when it produces the fruit of righteousness and peace by allowing us to be spiritually trained in this way (12:11). The Greek verb rendered *exercised* is based on the word from which we get *gymnasium.* We could say discipline gives us a tough workout, but helps us get into shape.

On the surface, it might seem counterintuitive to imagine that the grief springing from tragedies, persecutions, and conflicts can have any temporal or eternal benefit. Yet Scripture teaches that God uses these hardships to prepare us to be at peace in all situations and to respond rightly to Him and other people in the face of difficulties. For instance, suffering can teach us humility and patience. Also, through hardships we learn to trust God more and draw upon His strength to endure the trials we're experiencing. Because God is our loving heavenly Father, He never disciplines us for sadistic reasons. And He does not enjoy seeing us experience pain. When God disciplines us, His intent is to help us grow and succeed in our walk with Christ. When we try to avoid God's discipline, we sacrifice long-term spiritual maturity for short-term ease. The real joys and victories of the Christian life will elude us, unless we yield to God's loving hand of discipline in our lives.

The writer of Hebrews, perhaps returning to the running imagery, exhorted his readers to strengthen their limp hands and feeble knees (12:12). Hebrews 12:13 extends the imagery by quoting from Proverbs 4:26. The Hebrews were to smooth out the racetrack so that even the lame could get around it without falling and hurting themselves. The idea is that, as we are running our own race, we should look out for our fellow believers and try to help them succeed in their race as well. By God's grace, the Christian life is one in which we all can eventually wear the wreath of victory— no matter what disabilities we start with.

Here we see that a holy response to God's discipline is realistic, not naive, about life. We should not minimize the pain and loss we or others are experiencing. Instead, we should remain confident that God will bring good out of evil and that He will not forsake us. We become more holy when we remain calm after being terminated from work. And we grow in holiness when we respond with kind words to those who hurl abusive comments at us. Furthermore, when we show love, not hatred, after being harassed by others, we become more holy.

SUGGESTIONS TO TEACHERS

The readers of the Letter to the Hebrews faced persecution. Many students in your class are also facing hard times of their own. The writer of the epistle used both historical facts and helpful analogies to encourage his followers toward steadfastness. Today, you can use these same images to encourage others to maintain hope and progress.

1. GOD'S PEOPLE BEFORE THEM HAD STRUGGLED AND WON. The writer opened chapter 12 by reminding his readers of the *great . . . cloud of witnesses* (12:1) that surrounded them. These witnesses were God's people from the past who had heard His promises and remained faithful to Him, despite not seeing the fulfillment of these pledges. But by the time Hebrews was written, all these witnesses had moved up into the grandstands of heaven. God's faithful people would ultimately join them in victory.

2. JESUS HIMSELF HAD STRUGGLED AND WON. *Jesus . . . endured the cross, despising the shame* (12:2). Because of His complete obedience to the Father, even to death, Jesus has taken His seat at the *right hand of the throne of God.* Contemporary believers find comfort in the fact that their God empathizes with their pain. God's Son faced it at its worst, and He enables Christians to be victorious today.

3. VICTORIOUS ATHLETES WILLINGLY STRUGGLE IN ORDER TO WIN. The writer used an athletic analogy to stress this point. The runners persevere in *the race that is set before* (12:1) them. Even when they sense themselves drooping, they forge on toward the finish line. They willingly challenge themselves. If their contest is worth all their energy and effort, how much more important it is for Christians to remain faithful to Jesus, especially as they press on toward their heavenly goal.

4. CHILDRENS' STRUGGLES WITH DISCIPLINE ENABLE THEM TO GROW. The middle portion of this week's Scripture passage employs the analogy of parents discipling their children. As loving parents allow their children to be stretched, they protect their children from anything that would truly harm them. Likewise, God always monitors our circumstances. If He chooses not to protect us from suffering, He allows only that testing that enables us to become holy as He is holy.

FOR ADULTS

■ **TOPIC:** Trustworthy Leadership

■ **QUESTIONS:** 1. In your opinion, what is the relationship between Hebrews 11 and 12? 2. What kind of weight do you think prevents believers from running their race well? 3. Why is it appropriate for God to discipline us as His spiritual children? 4. In what ways has God disciplined you? How have you responded? 5. What can you do to help other believers run their race of faith better?

■ **ILLUSTRATIONS:**

Businessman Turned Human Rights Activist. In 1990, an American businessman named John Kamm was the head of the American Chamber of Commerce in Hong Kong. A U.S. multi-national corporation also employed him. According to Correspondent Frank Langfitt of *Morning Edition*, Kamm's fringe benefits included a "chauffer-driven Mercedes and an apartment overlooking the South China Sea." But one evening at a Chinese government banquet, he "kissed that life goodbye."

The businessman told his hosts that their government "needed to improve its human rights record" and that a good starting point was "freeing a Hong Kong student held in Shanghai." While the approach seemed impertinent to the Chinese, it also proved effective, especially in conjunction with Kamm testifying in "Washington on China's behalf." Within six weeks, the Chinese government had freed the Hong Kong student. Since then, Kamm estimates he's either "helped free or improve the conditions of 400 political prisoners." He does it by presenting their "cases directly to Chinese officials." This advocate on behalf of the incarcerated explains that "showing mercy" is good public relations in the United States.

Kamm's "journey from businessman to human rights activist" is an account of courage and sacrifice on behalf of others. Indeed, over the course of his "second career," he has become a genuine example of trustworthy leadership. Surely, the Lord Jesus would applaud this humanitarian work. After all, He set the example by enduring the pain and shame of the cross to achieve the joy and victory of providing eternal life for all who trust in Him.

Nabbed Criminal. Richard Owen of *The Times* reported that police officers in Palermo, Italy, arrested an "elusive Mafia boss" named Bernardo Provenzano, who had been "on the run" for 43 years. According to the authorities, the police came close to capturing the 73-year-old criminal on six previous occasions. But he had "always escaped after being mysteriously tipped off."

In 2006, Provenzano's situation drastically changed when he was "betrayed by laundry sent to him by his wife." The end came "in an isolated, unheated, and run-down three-room stone farmhouse barely a mile from . . . his home town." The Italian authorities estimated the Mafia boss's personal wealth at $600 million, but in recent years he lived as if he'd taken "vows of poverty." The once-powerful individual "turned out to be an elderly, pink-cheeked man with thick lensed metal rimmed reading glasses."

What a contrast this legendary "boss of bosses" is to the Lord Jesus. He endured the shame of the cross so that we might be saved. And though the authorities executed Jesus as a criminal, the Father raised Him from the dead so that all who trust in Him can have eternal life. As the pioneer and perfecter of our faith, Christ alone demonstrates that He is a leader who can be trusted.

Diamond in the Rough. Years ago in a South African mine, workers dug up the Cullinan diamond. It was the largest diamond ever found, weighing one and one half pounds. The diamond was given as a gift to Edward VII of England.

The greatest stonecutter in Amsterdam studied the Cullinan diamond for weeks. He made drawings and models to better understand the inner structure of this jewel. Then the stonecutter, after notching the diamond, struck it with his hammer, which split the diamond in two pieces. Did the stonecutter make a mistake? Not at all. By splitting the diamond in two, he enabled others to see its shape and splendor.

Sometimes, God allows us to experience stinging blows. At first, we might think God has made a mistake, but then He knows hardships will reveal the beauty of our character.

FOR YOUTH

■ TOPIC: Supreme Commander

■ QUESTIONS: 1. How is the Christian life like a race? 2. In what sense is Jesus the *author and finisher* (Heb. 12:2) of our faith? 3. In what sense can one say that suffering is disciplinary? 4. What is the relationship between the discipline of God and the love of God in the lives of His children? 5. What can believers learn from the sufferings God allows them to endure?

■ ILLUSTRATIONS:

First Symphony Experience. An older man shared his experience as a small boy when he went to his first symphony orchestra concert. He marveled at the different musicians as they came onto the stage and sat down. They all seemed so different.

Some were young, while others were old. Some were thin and others were fat. Some had lots of hair, but others were bald. There were women and men.

One by one, the musicians picked up their instruments and began to play a few notes. It sounded like a dozen cats fighting on a hot night in the middle of the city. None of them were playing the same notes, let alone the same music. Then the boy saw a man in a long black coat walk to the center of the stage. When he raised a long, thin, black stick, the noise immediately stopped. With a sweep of this man's hand, the musicians began to play again and the sound this time was incredibly beautiful.

Jesus represents the supreme Conductor who gives order and meaning to our lives. He is our Leader and Guide, who watches over and provides for us throughout our life journey. He alone is sufficiently qualified, capable, and trustworthy to do this for us; and that is why He is to be the sole focus of our faith.

Remaining Courageous. On July 30, 1967, seventeen-year-old, Joni Eareckson, dived into Cheaspeake Bay and accidentally struck her head against a rock. That incident left her paralyzed from the neck down. At first, Joni was bewildered by what had happened to her. But then her confusion gave way to anger and despair. She tried to kill herself as a way to escape the prison of her body. However, she failed in her efforts.

Since her diving accident, Joni has become an artist, an author, a movie star in her autobiography, a spokeswoman for disabled Christians, and a gifted inspirational speaker. She has married and enjoys the company of friends and family. Despite her blessings, Joni has lived much of her life without being able to use her arms and legs. In fact, her loved ones must bathe, dress, and feed her every day.

There are times when Joni feels discouraged about her circumstances. But despite these times, her faith in Christ remains strong. He has enabled her to be courageous in the face of overwhelming obstacles.

Source of Spiritual Nourishment. One of the most famous American filmmakers is Cecil B. DeMille. On one occasion he said, "The greatest source of material for motion pictures is the Bible, and almost any chapter in the Bible would serve as a basic idea for a motion picture." In fact, his greatest achievement was *The Ten Commandments*, which starred Charlton Heston, who played the part of Moses.

DeMille, however, didn't find the Bible merely fascinating reading or an excellent source for movie ideas. More importantly, he valued how God's Word spiritually nourished him. "After more than 60 years of almost daily reading of the Bible," he said, "I never fail to find it always new and marvelously in tune with the changing needs of every day."

THE ETERNAL CHRIST

BACKGROUND SCRIPTURE: Hebrews 13:1-16
DEVOTIONAL READING: Psalm 118:5-9

KEY VERSE: Jesus Christ the same yesterday, and to day, and for ever. Hebrews 13:8.

KING JAMES VERSION

HEBREWS 13:1 Let brotherly love continue. 2 Be not forgetful to entertain strangers: for thereby some have entertained angels unawares. 3 Remember them that are in bonds, as bound with them; and them which suffer adversity, as being yourselves also in the body. 4 Marriage is honourable in all, and the bed undefiled: but whoremongers and adulterers God will judge. 5 Let your conversation be without covetousness; and be content with such things as ye have: for he hath said, I will never leave thee, nor forsake thee. 6 So that we may boldly say, The Lord is my helper, and I will not fear what man shall do unto me. 7 Remember them which have the rule over you, who have spoken unto you the word of God: whose faith follow, considering the end of their conversation. 8 Jesus Christ the same yesterday, and to day, and for ever. 9 Be not carried about with divers and strange doctrines. For it is a good thing that the heart be established with grace; not with meats, which have not profited them that have been occupied therein. 10 We have an altar, whereof they have no right to eat which serve the tabernacle. 11 For the bodies of those beasts, whose blood is brought into the sanctuary by the high priest for sin, are burned without the camp. 12 Wherefore Jesus also, that he might sanctify the people with his own blood, suffered without the gate. 13 Let us go forth therefore unto him without the camp, bearing his reproach. 14 For here have we no continuing city, but we seek one to come. 15 By him therefore let us offer the sacrifice of praise to God continually, that is, the fruit of our lips giving thanks to his name. 16 But to do good and to communicate forget not: for with such sacrifices God is well pleased.

NEW REVISED STANDARD VERSION

HEBREWS 13:1 Let mutual love continue. 2 Do not neglect to show hospitality to strangers, for by doing that some have entertained angels without knowing it. 3 Remember those who are in prison, as though you were in prison with them; those who are being tortured, as though you yourselves were being tortured. 4 Let marriage be held in honor by all, and let the marriage bed be kept undefiled; for God will judge fornicators and adulterers. 5 Keep your lives free from the love of money, and be content with what you have; for he has said, "I will never leave you or forsake you." 6 So we can say with confidence,

"The Lord is my helper;
   I will not be afraid.
What can anyone do to me?"

7 Remember your leaders, those who spoke the word of God to you; consider the outcome of their way of life, and imitate their faith. 8 Jesus Christ is the same yesterday and today and forever. 9 Do not be carried away by all kinds of strange teachings; for it is well for the heart to be strengthened by grace, not by regulations about food, which have not benefited those who observe them. 10 We have an altar from which those who officiate in the tent have no right to eat. 11 For the bodies of those animals whose blood is brought into the sanctuary by the high priest as a sacrifice for sin are burned outside the camp. 12 Therefore Jesus also suffered outside the city gate in order to sanctify the people by his own blood. 13 Let us then go to him outside the camp and bear the abuse he endured. 14 For here we have no lasting city, but we are looking for the city that is to come. 15 Through him, then, let us continually offer a sacrifice of praise to God, that is, the fruit of lips that confess his name. 16 Do not neglect to do good and to share what you have, for such sacrifices are pleasing to God.

5

Monday, June 23	Psalm 118:5-9	*Take Refuge in God*
Tuesday, June 24	Colossians 1:15-20	*Christ as Supreme and Eternal*
Wednesday, June 25	Hebrews 13:1-6	*Show Hospitality and Courage*
Thursday, June 26	Hebrews 13:7-9	*True Leaders to Imitate*
Friday, June 27	Hebrews 13:10-16	*Confess Christ's Name*
Saturday, June 28	Philippians 3:12-16	*A Leader Who Professes Christ*
Sunday, June 29	Philippians 3:17-21	*A Leader Looking to Christ Eternal*

BACKGROUND

Hebrews 13:2 mentions the prospect of entertaining angels without knowing it. The Bible relates many incidents in which angels visited both men and women. Sometimes these people did not realize they were talking to angels until they had time to ponder their encounters. During the Old Testament period, two angels accompanied the Lord when He called upon Abraham. The Lord told the patriarch that his wife Sarah would bear him a son, and God fulfilled the promise a year later (Gen. 18:1-2, 10; 21:1-2). After the Israelites had settled in Canaan, they turned away from the Lord, and their enemies oppressed them. An angel of the Lord visited Gideon and commissioned him to lead the Israelites in victory over the Midianites (Judg. 6:1, 11-16). On another occasion, an angel of the Lord twice visited the wife of a man named Manoah. Although this woman was barren, the angel promised she would bear a son. When the child was born, she named him Samson (13:2-21, 24).

During the New Testament period, the angel Gabriel told a priest named Zechariah that his barren wife, Elizabeth, would give birth to a son, whom the couple were to name John. Because Zechariah doubted this good news, he was not able to speak until his son was born (Luke 1:11-20, 64). God also sent Gabriel to Mary to tell her that though she was a virgin, she would give birth to the Son of God (vss. 26-38). When Mary's pregnancy became obvious, Joseph, who was pledged to marry her, decided to privately divorce her. An angel of the Lord appeared to Joseph in a dream, revealed that Mary's pregnancy was due to the work of the Holy Spirit, and encouraged Joseph not to be afraid of marrying her (Matt. 1:18-20).

NOTES ON THE PRINTED TEXT

In Hebrews 13:1, we learn that we should treat other believers as members of God's spiritual family. We also discover that travelers will visit our homes if we carry out the command of 13:2. But we ourselves will need to travel a bit in order to fulfill the command of 13:3. This directive is to remember two groups: prisoners and the mistreated. Probably with both groups the writer had in mind Christians who were being persecuted for their faith. Thus visiting and identifying oneself with such people, as the writer urged, could have entailed considerable risk. But it was important for the Christian community to present a united front—believers supporting one another and maintaining the links within the Body of Christ, regardless of the danger. The recipients of the letter had already suffered persecution and had stood with others who were being persecuted (see 10:33-34), so they knew just what the writer was talking about.

From relationships with individuals mostly outside the home (13:1-3), the author turned to the primary relationship within the home—marriage (13:4). Evidently some people were hawking the pleasures of sexual fulfillment outside of the spousal relationship. The author taught that marriage was to be honored by everyone in the Christian community, and adultery was to have no place among them. In warning, the writer said that God will one day judge fornicators (a general reference to those committing a wide range of sexually immoral acts) and adulterers (a specific reference to those violating their marital vows). Elsewhere, the New Testament warns against Christians becoming promiscuous and debased in their behavior (see Acts 15:28-29; 1 Cor. 5:9-11; Eph. 5:3, 5; 1 Thess. 4:3-7; 1 Tim. 1:10; Rev. 21:8; 22:15).

Just as there is a danger in wanting more than our mate, there is also a danger in always wanting more and more money. The Bible is never anti-money, but it does warn against the love of money (Heb. 13:5; compare 1 Tim. 6:10). The writer of Hebrews provided Old Testament quotes to show why Christians have every reason to be content. First, he quoted Deuteronomy 31:6 (see also Gen. 28:15; Deut. 31:8; Josh. 1:5; 1 Chron. 28:20), which contains a promise that God will never leave nor forsake His people. Why should we go crazy over dollars when God, who owns the whole universe, is our constant companion? Next, the author cited Psalm 118:6-7 (Heb. 13:6). This quote contains the psalmist's declaration that since he had God, he would not be afraid, because no person had the power to hurt him (unless it was God's will). Why should we look to money for our security when we have almighty God for our helper?

Hebrews 13:7-17 opens and closes with references to spiritual leaders. The reference in verse 7 appears to be to the Hebrews' past leaders, who had probably died. Verse 17 evidently refers to their present leaders. In the first case, the author urged the Hebrews to recall the leaders who had preached the Gospel to them, considering the results of how these people had lived (13:7). The Greek verb translated *remember* denoted calling to mind what one knew about a person, while the verb translated *considering* referred to carefully observing something.

The readers had evidently been blessed in the past with excellent Christian leaders. But just because these people were gone did not mean that one could no longer benefit from them. Alone or together, the Hebrews could recall these people, especially the Christlike character they had demonstrated and the good they had done for the Savior's cause. In this way, the departed leaders could still be heroes and models for the believers. Accordingly, the writer urged his readers to follow the example of their former leaders' faith. Human leaders come and go, but our great leader, the Lord

Jesus, never changes. Indeed, the Messiah is the contemporary of all the centuries, for He is the same yesterday, today, and forever (13:8). The Hebrews' leaders had undoubtedly made Christ the subject of their teaching, and the Hebrews were to cling to Him just as they had. They could do so for they knew that He remains faithful to His followers. They could also rely on Him even when circumstances seemed overwhelming. Even today, because Jesus is reliable, believers can remain faithful to Him and cultivate integrity in their lives.

With Christ as their spiritual anchor and eternal guide, the original recipients of Hebrews were not to be fooled by any kind of strange teachings (13:9). Most likely, this verse has Jewish practices in mind. Legalistic zealots maintained that because the Hebrew Christians did not participate in the ritual life of the Jerusalem temple, including the sacrificial feasts, they had no access to God. The writer responded that God's grace, not ritualistically prepared meals, strengthened the hearts of believers. And it was by grace that they participated in worship at the heavenly sanctuary where Jesus ministered.

In Old Testament times, the priests had the right to a portion of the animals sacrificed as fellowship (or peace) offerings (Lev. 3; 7:11-34). As long as those priests and others depended on the old system of animal sacrifices for atonement and peace with God, they couldn't benefit from what the Lord Jesus did at Calvary. The cross was the *altar* (Heb. 13:10) on which the Messiah, the believers' great High Priest, sacrificed Himself to atone for their sins. Through faith in Christ, they could partake of the benefits of His redemptive offering. The priests who ministered under the old covenant never enjoyed such a privilege. To put all this another way, Christians are not to be bound by the food laws of non-Christian religions (since many religions have dietary regulations). Instead, we are to eat the "food" of grace, which is ours because of the Cross. And this "food" is a privilege to eat, being even greater than the sacrificial food that the priests of the tabernacle ate.

The writer of Hebrews saw a parallel between Old Testament sacrificial practices and the way the Lord Jesus was sacrificed for people's sins outside the walls of Jerusalem (Heb. 13:12; see also Matt. 27:32; Mark 15:20; John 19:17, 20). His suffering outside the holy city served as a reminder that He bore the curse of sin. His death outside Jerusalem also meant that most of the Jewish religious establishment had rejected Him as the Messiah. The repudiation that Christ endured was mirrored in the lives of His followers. The leaders of the Jews had evidently expelled them from the synagogues and the temple. The writer of Hebrews summoned his readers to accept this situation with courage. In order to offer us grace, the Redeemer underwent great disgrace. Therefore, Christians should be willing to share Jesus' disgrace, in a sense following Him outside the camp (13:13).

While the Jews venerated their holy city of Jerusalem, that city wouldn't last forever. In fact, in A.D. 70, four Roman legions under the command of Titus sacked

Jerusalem, destroyed the temple, and either killed or dispersed much of the population. In contrast, believers long for the city that is to come (13:14). This is probably what the writer had referred to previously (see 11:10; 12:22; see also Isa. 65:17-25; Rev. 21). The fact that the "city" theme crops up several times in Hebrews implies some readers felt like rejects from their community because they had identified with Jesus as the Messiah.

Because of our relationship with Christ, we should give God glory. But instead of offering animal sacrifices, we are to offer to God a sacrifice of praise. And we aren't supposed to do this on our own. Rather, we offer such sacrifices through the Lord Jesus. The content of our offering is praise, namely, *the fruit of our lips giving thanks to his name* (Heb. 13:15). The latter refers to an open acknowledgment of our belief in Him as the Messiah (to be voiced even when we face public abuse and scorn). What we do with our lips is not the sum total of our commitment. Our sacrifice also includes what we do with our lives (13:16). First, we are to *do good*. The English word *good*, when the letters are reordered, becomes *go do*. To *do good* we must *go do*; in other words, activism is required. Second, we must share with others as part of our Christian sacrificial system. This was also the way of life in God's eternal city.

SUGGESTIONS TO TEACHERS

It's much easier for the students to focus on having *passed from death unto life* (John 5:24) through faith in Christ, than it is to reflect His values in their treatment of others. But the members of your class cannot ignore the biblical mandate to live out the teachings of Christ in their relationships. Such a lifestyle includes doing good to others. Use the following points to stress the importance of honoring the Lord by doing good to others.

1. REMEMBERING TO DO GOOD. Hebrews 13:16 reminds us of the importance of doing good to others. How could we ever forget something so basic? Yet many of us do. Sometimes we can become so preoccupied with meeting our own needs—whether physical or spiritual—that we forget to meet the needs of others. And sometimes we can become so absorbed in our worship of God that we can forget to show His love to others. For us as Christians, doing good to others cannot be torn from the context of spiritual reality. Our faith in Christ should never be a matter of "pie in the sky by and by." The teaching and example of the Savior demand a practical outworking of faith in our relationships with others.

2. TAKING TIME TO DO GOOD. Just as travelers can bounce from city to city without really getting involved in the lives of others, so we can rush through life without taking the time to do good to others. We can bounce from relationship to relationship and from experience to experience without making the effort to see how God can use us in meeting the needs of others. A number of years ago, a popular song urged us to "stop and smell the roses." Jesus would want us to stop, take an interest in others, and do good things for them.

3. WAYS TO DO GOOD. How can we do good to others? We can show love to those whom others have rejected and open our homes to people who have nowhere else to go. We can visit those in halfway houses, prisons, or nursing homes and share God's love with them. We can affirm the value of our loved ones and be supportive of our church leaders.

| **FOR ADULTS** | ■ **TOPIC:** Finding Stability and Permanence Today |

■ **TOPIC:** Finding Stability and Permanence Today
■ **QUESTIONS:** 1. Why do you think the writer of Hebrews stressed the importance of showing brotherly love? 2. How would the truth that Jesus never changes have encouraged the Hebrew Christians? 3. How far should they have gone in following their leaders? 4. Why did the writer of Hebrews draw a sharp contrast between Christ's sacrifice and that of animals? 5. Why did the writer of Hebrews say that praising God and doing good works were sacrifices?

■ **ILLUSTRATIONS:**

From One Fad to the Next. Joel Best, the author of *Flavor of the Month: Why Smart People Fall for Fads*, noted that every major discipline has its fads. In medicine, "there are fad diagnoses and fad treatments." In elementary and secondary education, "faddish teaching methods abound." And in business, the shelves of bookstores groan under the weight of new "titles explaining this month's revolutionary management scheme."

Best says at their inception, "fads follow a parallel trajectory." Consider the hula hoop craze of the 1960s. At first, not many people had them. But then, "the number of people using hula hoops rises rapidly to a peak." After this, the "decline begins." This pattern indicates that each fad is characterized by "short-lived enthusiasm." Best observes that "while any novelty is spreading, it is always possible for its advocates to insist that this innovation will endure." In most instances, however, they prove to be wrong.

The presence of fads reminds us that we live in a world filled with rapid change. So where can we go to find stability and permanence? The answer is Jesus Christ. The Father gave us His Son so that through faith in Him, we could have a firm foundation for living in relationship with Him and others.

Gracious Winner. The Dallas Cowboys and the Buffalo Bills met in 1994's Super Bowl XXVIII, in which the Bills suffered their fourth straight Super Bowl loss. The Bills' great player, Thurman Thomas, had fumbled three times, contributing to Buffalo's defeat. After the game, Thomas sat on the bench with his face buried in his hands.

Walking up to him, and carrying his little daughter, was Emmit Smith of the

Cowboys. The Dallas Cowboy running back had just been named Most Valuable Player of the Super Bowl. Emmit Smith said to the little girl in his arms, "Honey, I want you to meet the greatest running back in the National Football League, Mr. Thurman Thomas." That kind gesture by Smith brought comfort to Thomas, and reflected a Christian way to do good to others, even when it wasn't required.

Doing the Right Thing. Perhaps you remember the movie, *Schindler's List*. During World War II, as the Nazis were gathering Jews to send them to the gas chambers, a businessman named Oscar Schindler chose to take action. Although not otherwise known for his morality, before the war was over, Schindler had given his large fortune to save the lives of all the Jews he could. He established a factory near a work camp. In that factory, he provided food, health care, and ultimately safety for hundreds of Jews. He wished he could have rescued more, but he did what he could.

Did the particular Jews whose lives he protected do anything to earn Schindler's mercy? They had little, if anything, to offer. Yet, after the war, none of them ever forgot the man who had saved them from death. They repaid his kindness by showering him with many kindnesses and supporting him with material objects he needed.

FOR YOUTH

■ TOPIC: Someone You Can Count On

■ QUESTIONS: 1. What does it mean to love our fellow believers as brothers and sisters in Christ? 2. What are some ways we can show hospitality to strangers and reach out to those who are mistreated? 3. Why would covetousness have been a problem among the Hebrew Christians? 4. What encourages believers to submit to their church leaders? 5. What are some sacrifices of praise that Christians can offer to the Lord?

■ **ILLUSTRATIONS:**

A Model Mom. Who served as the greatest model for Theo Ratliff, a 1995 first round NBA draft choice and center for the Atlanta Hawks? It was his mother. When her boys were young, she supported the family by driving an hour each way to her job in a garment factory. When she came home each evening, she spent time, alongside her children, doing her own homework—toward a college degree. She reached her goals—providing food and shelter for her children, her own college graduation, and raising her sons well.

Theo said, "Without that type of influence from within their families, a lot of our friends went astray." Even today, Camillia Ratliff could probably live off her son's income. But she did not earn that college degree for nothing. She currently manages elder-care programs in 10 Alabama counties, and demonstrates to these residents that she, like the Lord Jesus, is someone they can count on.

Taking Aim at Despair. Her shoulders slumped as she waited to talk with me after church. Deep worry lines tugged her face into a furled, forlorn expression of grief. A three-year-old swung from her coat sleeve like a pint-sized Tarzan, whining so loudly that I could hardly hear the "secret" spoken from her despondent lips: "My husband is an alcoholic." Crushing despair overwhelmed Barb. She was trapped in a meaningless vortex. Life had become dismal, depressing, and seemingly hopeless.

As I listened to Barb's story, I realized that the eternal Christ, who is the same yesterday, today, and forever (Heb. 13:8), alone could give Barb the hope to dispel her heavy clouds of gloom. Later, I shared with her that hopeful believers live today in the light of tomorrow. They know why they are in this world. They know where they are going, and they sense the excitement of being part of the emerging, eternal kingdom of their Lord. Hopeful believers are a people who lean ahead to take hold of that for which God has called them heavenward in Christ Jesus (see Phil. 3:12).

This kind of hope opens the door of an eternal future to those whose horizons are limited to the present, the mundane, and the monotonous. Hope anchored in Christ lifts sullen and discouraged faces heavenward for the rays of tomorrow's glory to brighten them. It strengthens feeble arms and weak knees to make them useful to the King.

Love for the Homeless. One day, I walked a mile or so to our local public library. In just that short walk, I was approached twice by homeless men, asking me for money. As a believer committed to loving others as Christ loves them, I never know quite how to respond.

In one similar situation a few years ago, I gave money, but later regretted my choice. A man approached me in a gas station asking for money supposedly for gas. He gave me a long story about taking his wife home after surgery and his leaving his wallet at the hospital. His story sounded so convincing that I gave him $10. As I drove on, I realized that details in his story did not fit together well. He had "taken me." Regrettably, that one bad experience has skewed my vision of all people asking for money. At least some of these people truly are needy. How would Christ have us respond?

My cynical self suggests that I should tell beggars to go get a job, to work as I do. But then I know that many of them have mental and emotional issues that hinder them from living a normal life. What should I do? Perhaps I could at least go with these people to a fast food restaurant and buy them a hamburger. In that situation, I would know that money was not being dreadfully abused. But I would also receive the joy of obeying God's Word. I would, in this manner, devote myself to *do good* (Heb. 13:16) to others.

CHRIST AS TEACHER

BACKGROUND SCRIPTURE: Luke 4:31-37; 20:1-8
DEVOTIONAL READING: Isaiah 11:1-3

KEY VERSE: [The people] were astonished at [Jesus']
doctrine: for his word was with power. Luke 4:32.

KING JAMES VERSION

LUKE 4:31 And came down to Capernaum, a city of Galilee, and taught them on the sabbath days. 32 And they were astonished at his doctrine: for his word was with power. 33 And in the synagogue there was a man, which had a spirit of an unclean devil, and cried out with a loud voice, 34 Saying, Let us alone; what have we to do with thee, thou Jesus of Nazareth? art thou come to destroy us? I know thee who thou art; the Holy One of God. 35 And Jesus rebuked him, saying, Hold thy peace, and come out of him. And when the devil had thrown him in the midst, he came out of him, and hurt him not. 36 And they were all amazed, and spake among themselves, saying, What a word is this! for with authority and power he commandeth the unclean spirits, and they come out. 37 And the fame of him went out into every place of the country round about. . . .

20:1 And it came to pass, that on one of those days, as he taught the people in the temple, and preached the gospel, the chief priests and the scribes came upon him with the elders, 2 And spake unto him, saying, Tell us, by what authority doest thou these things? or who is he that gave thee this authority? 3 And he answered and said unto them, I will also ask you one thing; and answer me: 4 The baptism of John, was it from heaven, or of men? 5 And they reasoned with themselves, saying, If we shall say, From heaven; he will say, Why then believed ye him not? 6 But and if we say, Of men; all the people will stone us: for they be persuaded that John was a prophet. 7 And they answered, that they could not tell whence it was. 8 And Jesus said unto them, Neither tell I you by what authority I do these things.

NEW REVISED STANDARD VERSION

LUKE 4:31 He went down to Capernaum, a city in Galilee, and was teaching them on the sabbath. 32 They were astounded at his teaching, because he spoke with authority. 33 In the synagogue there was a man who had the spirit of an unclean demon, and he cried out with a loud voice, 34 "Let us alone! What have you to do with us, Jesus of Nazareth? Have you come to destroy us? I know who you are, the Holy One of God." 35 But Jesus rebuked him, saying, "Be silent, and come out of him!" When the demon had thrown him down before them, he came out of him without having done him any harm. 36 They were all amazed and kept saying to one another, "What kind of utterance is this? For with authority and power he commands the unclean spirits, and out they come!" 37 And a report about him began to reach every place in the region. . . .

20:1 One day, as he was teaching the people in the temple and telling the good news, the chief priests and the scribes came with the elders 2 and said to him, "Tell us, by what authority are you doing these things? Who is it who gave you this authority?" 3 He answered them, "I will also ask you a question, and you tell me: 4 Did the baptism of John come from heaven, or was it of human origin?" 5 They discussed it with one another, saying, "If we say, 'From heaven,' he will say, 'Why did you not believe him?' 6 But if we say, 'Of human origin,' all the people will stone us; for they are convinced that John was a prophet." 7 So they answered that they did not know where it came from. 8 Then Jesus said to them, "Neither will I tell you by what authority I am doing these things."

6

BACKGROUND

Sometime after Jesus' baptism and victory over temptation (Luke 4:1-13), He returned to Galilee. Luke didn't provide details about what Jesus did in Galilee, but we know He ministered in the power of the Spirit and taught in the synagogues (4:14-15). People who saw and heard Jesus spread the news of what He was doing. Eventually, Jesus returned to His hometown of Nazareth, and following His custom, He went to the synagogue on the Sabbath. His reputation had mushroomed, and the locals turned out to hear the homegrown boy who had made good. But no doubt many were skeptical. They came doubting He could be as good as the stories painted Him to be.

As a visiting rabbi and hometown celebrity, Jesus was invited to be the guest speaker. At the appropriate time in the service He was handed the scroll of Isaiah, which He unrolled and from which He read in Hebrew (4:16-17). Presumably, He then translated the passages into Aramaic, which was the common language of the people. Jesus read Isaiah 61:1-2, which was a messianic prophecy. The passage predicted that the era of the Messiah would be a time of liberation and change. Then Jesus gave the scroll back to the attendant and sat down to teach (Luke 4:18-20). Most Jews hoped for a powerful leader to arise and deliver them from the Romans, who dominated them. So when Jesus announced that this messianic prophecy was now being fulfilled (4:21), He had the worshipers' full attention. Some were impressed. But others were not so sure.

Amazed by Jesus' message, the audience began to talk among themselves (4:22). Jesus knew He had a skeptical bunch on His hands. But He met their doubts head-on. He acknowledged that they would want Him to prove Himself, to see dramatic evidence of His power. But because they couldn't imagine God raising up one of their own to be a prophet, He would not show them God's power (4:23-24; see Matt. 13:58). Jesus drove His point home, reminding the skeptical worshipers that because God's chosen people doubted, they had missed blessings that the Gentiles then received. Jesus cited an instance in the time of Elijah and another in the time of Elisha (Luke 4:25-27; see 1 Kings 17:8-16; 2 Kings 5:1-14).

Hearing about the widow of Zarephath and the leper from Syria infuriated Jesus' hearers. It was bad enough for Jesus to say He was the fulfillment of messianic prophecy. Now He was saying that His audience was unworthy of God's blessings! The people surged toward Jesus. They pushed and shoved, moving Him toward a bluff at the edge of town, intending to toss Him over the side. But He slipped away from the mob and escaped (Luke 4:28-30). Luke doesn't say this escape was a miracle, but it probably was. By rejecting Jesus, the Nazarenes allowed the blessings of God to slip away from them. They showed they were unworthy by refusing to listen. In obstinate pride, they thought they knew better than Jesus.

NOTES ON THE PRINTED TEXT

Jesus descended from the elevated region where Nazareth was located to the town of Capernaum (Luke 4:31). As was Jesus' custom, He taught on the Sabbath in the synagogue. As in Nazareth, the people of Capernaum were amazed at His teaching, for He spoke with authority (4:32). The Greek word rendered *power* denotes the ability and right to perform an action. Permission could be obtained from a government official, a court of law, or one's master (to name a few possibilities). As Jesus proclaimed the imminence of God's kingdom, He exercised the divinely given right and power to forgive sins, expel demons, and teach. In His day, it was typical for rabbis to appeal to tradition and a list of experts to support one's point. What impressed Jesus' audience is that He spoke directly to the issues at hand, basing His remarks solely on His own understanding (see Matt. 7:28-29). He could do so, for His authority came directly from God.

Once when Jesus was in the synagogue at Capernaum, a man possessed by a demon began shouting at Him (Luke 4:33). In a display of defiance, the evil spirit forced its victim to demand that the Savior go away. Only one entity shrieked, though it spoke for *us* (4:34), perhaps as one spirit speaking for all the demons whom Jesus ultimately defeated on the cross. The unclean spirit reasoned that *Jesus of Nazareth* was interfering in matters that supposedly were none of His concern. The idea is that Christ and the demon really had nothing to do with one another. Thus, Jesus should leave the evil entity alone. The demon feared the Son of God had come to *destroy* it. Expressed differently, the unclean spirit realized that the Messiah sent from God would cause it to perish by bringing it to eternal ruin. As the *Holy One* (see John 6:69), Jesus was filled with God's Spirit and lived in holiness. Likewise, Jesus was uniquely qualified and empowered to deal with all forms of moral and spiritual impurity.

The demon who called Jesus the *Holy One of God* (Luke 4:34) was trying to gain control of the Messiah, in keeping with the ancient belief that to know a person's name gave one power over him. The attempt failed, however, for Jesus was not intimidated by the evil entity. The Son of God ordered the unclean spirit to be quiet and leave its victim. This command was appropriate, for Jesus did not need the forces of darkness to bear witness to His status as the Messiah. Neither did He want such testimony from demons to give people an incorrect impression of His identity as the promised Redeemer of Israel (for example, that He was a revolutionary seeking to free the Jews from the control of Rome). The demon responded by throwing the man to the ground in front of everyone. Then, the unclean spirit departed without further hurting its victim (4:35).

This incident is an example of Jesus' ability to completely deliver and protect an individual oppressed by the evil one. In contrast with the exorcists of the day, the Messiah did not resort to rituals or incantations. Nor did He conjure up someone else's name to bring about the cure. He simply gave the command and expelled the demon from its host. All the people in the synagogue were amazed at the authority and power Jesus' words possessed. In fact, it was so great that He could rebuke an unclean spirit and expel it from its tormented victim (4:36). Understandably, the news about Jesus spread throughout every village in that part of Galilee (4:37).

The authority that Jesus displayed in places such as Nazareth and Capernaum was challenged by the religious leaders of the day. One episode occurred in the Savior's final week before His crucifixion. It was Sunday when He entered Jerusalem triumphantly and surveyed the temple (Matt. 21:1-11; Mark 11:1-11; Luke 19:28-44). Then, on Monday, the Savior cursed a fig tree and cleared the temple (Matt. 21:12-22; Mark 11:12-19; Luke 19:45-48). The challenge to Jesus' authority took place on Tuesday of Passion Week, while He was teaching the people and proclaiming the Good News in the temple courts (Luke 20:1). The Jewish religious leaders resented what Jesus was doing. They thought He had overstepped His bounds. Since Jesus had challenged the religious leaders' authority, they now challenged His. They demanded that He tell them who had given Him permission to act as He did in the temple (20:2). Apparently, they hoped His response would expose Him as a fraud with no legitimate authority.

The Savior knew His interrogators had sinister motives. He thus responded to their question with one of His own (20:3). In so doing, He was using a common debating technique of the rabbis. His query also put the religious leaders on the defensive. Their attitude toward John the Baptist had revealed that these men would not recognize anyone's authority unless it served their own purposes. So Jesus forced the religious leaders into an impossible position by asking them about the authority behind John's baptism. If they answered Jesus' question, He said He would reveal who had given Him permission to act as He had. In particular, He wanted to know whether they thought John's authority to baptize came from heaven or was merely human in origin (20:4).

The delegation from the Sanhedrin found themselves in the same type of bind with which they had tried to trap Jesus. They discerned that they could not answer His question without either alienating the crowd or supporting His position. Despite their contempt for the common people, the religious leaders feared them. The multitudes had held John in high esteem as a prophet during his lifetime, and still did. So the leaders were afraid to say anything against John. But if they acknowledged that John's authority came from heaven, then they would also have to acknowledge Jesus' authority, for John had told the nation to accept Jesus as the Messiah. In turn, the Savior would ask the leaders why they had refused to believe the message John had declared (20:5-6).

In the end, the religious leaders were too duplicitous and cowardly to answer Jesus' question. By professing ignorance and conveying an attitude of indifference (20:7), they revealed that they were not interested in the truth, only in eliminating Jesus. Ironically, their response discredited them in the eyes of the people. Since the Jewish authorities had refused to answer the Savior's question, He refused to reveal the source of His authority (20:8). If He had revealed it, He undoubtedly would have been accused of blasphemy. We should never read of the hostile leaders without being concerned about making the same mistake they did. When God's will does not match up with our ideas or wishes, we should not question His right to do as He pleases. We should look for the fault in ourselves rather than question His sovereignty. We must trust the Lord, for He is God.

SUGGESTIONS TO TEACHERS

How do you respond when someone challenges your authority? Most of what we would do is just the opposite of what Jesus did. Scripture reveals that throughout the Son's earthly ministry, He kept His focus on the redemptive mission the Father wanted Him to complete. This truth can be further developed in class by emphasizing the following points.

1. JESUS DID NOT GET ANGRY AND YELL. During Jesus' earthly ministry, He experienced many potentially stressful confrontations, whether from a demon in the synagogue at Capernaum or the religious leaders in the precincts of the Jerusalem temple. Regardless of the situation, Jesus did not lose His temper, hurl abusive remarks at His opponents, or become violently oppositional. Instead, He remained godly and virtuous in all His responses. Too often, we respond first with anger and later repent of what we said. Sometimes we can wind up being as sinful as the ones who attacked us.

2. JESUS DID NOT SEEK REVENGE. At any point during His earthly ministry, Jesus could have summoned a legion of angels to bring retribution on His detractors. Instead of doing this, the Son submitted to the will of the Father, even to the extent of dying on the cross for our sins. Sometimes, we will not even pause when attacked. We will speak or act automatically, and make the situation worse. Instead, as someone once said, "It is better to suffer an injustice than to commit one."

3. JESUS DID NOT SINK INTO SELF-PITY. When Jesus' authority as the Messiah was challenged, He did not cry to His Father, or anyone else, about the unfairness of the situation. In other words, Jesus did not wallow in self-indulgent pity.

Instead, He calmly and bravely faced the reality of His situation. In contrast, we can easily think, *Why is everybody always picking on me?*

4. JESUS DID NOT RUN AWAY. Although the Messiah had the ability to entirely avoid tough situations, He didn't. We can all learn from that. Whenever times get hard, we can be assured that Jesus is there, helping us face whatever is happening.

■ **TOPIC:** Teaching That Transforms

FOR ADULTS

■ **QUESTIONS:** 1. What was the significance of Capernaum to Jesus' earthly ministry? 2. Why did the demon want Jesus to go away? 3. How was it possible for Jesus to expel the unclean spirit from its victim? 4. Why were the religious leaders upset with Jesus for His activities in the Jerusalem temple? 5. Why did Jesus respond to the query of the religious leaders with a question about John the Baptizer?

■ **ILLUSTRATIONS:**

Disregard for Others. Jean Rhys was the author of a series of popular novels during the 1920s and 1930s, but then fell into obscurity. She was re-discovered and showered with fame after the publication of her fifth and last novel, *Wise Sagasso Sea*, in 1966. She died in 1979. Her unfinished autobiography, which appeared in 1980, revealed an intensely self-centered woman. Critics and readers had suspected that Rhys was herself the subject of her fiction, but the depth of her egotism was disclosed in her candid remarks about herself. "People have always been shadows to me," she wrote. "I have never known other people. I have only ever written about myself."

Contrast this person to Jesus. He always regarded others, not as mere "shadows," but as beloved fellow members of the human race. Unlike people such as Rhys, Jesus would never arrogantly disregard others and focus on His own comfort and security. Though He is the Lord of heaven and earth, Jesus cared about the blind, the mute, and the distressed. He did not hesitate to help others in need so that they might come to a life-transforming knowledge of the truth.

Short-Sighted Reflections. In the village of Bedford, Ohio, lived two young women. To one of these, future president, Rutherford Hayes, had become an ardent suitor. However, the parents of the young lady vigorously opposed their courtship, on the grounds that young Hayes was poor and gave no evidence of future promise.

Incredibly, the other young woman's suitor was future president James Garfield. The woman's parents, however, also objected, noting Garfield's poverty and anything but bright prospects for his future. Similarly, in the eyes of the religious leaders of Jesus' day, He didn't "make the grade" for Israel's Messiah. They rejected Him because He was too unconventional.

Skewed Perspective. The religious leaders had their minds made up about Jesus, and no amount of evidence would change their point of view. Their stubborn resistance to the new insight Jesus brought is not unlike a group that exists today in England. They call themselves the "Flat Earth Society."

This social group firmly believes that the earth is flat and that Christopher Columbus and all of the astronauts have suffered from the same kind of delusion. Supposedly, astronauts only think they circle the earth. What really happens is that they fly in ellipses parallel to the earth, like a phonograph needle going around on a record. And when a ship disappears below the horizon, it is a trick of perspective, not a sign the earth is round.

FOR YOUTH	■ **TOPIC:** Christ Tells It Like It Is! ■ **QUESTIONS:** 1. What activity did Jesus routinely do on the Sabbath? 2. What amazed the people about Jesus' teaching? 3. How did Jesus

back up His teaching with authority and power? 4. What was Jesus doing in the Jerusalem temple when the religious leaders interrogated Him? 5. Why did the religious leaders decide not to answer Jesus' question concerning John the Baptizer?

■ **ILLUSTRATIONS:**

Courage to Speak Out. The *Kansas-Nebraska Act* of 1854 was designed to open the new western territories to slavery. It was championed by Stephen A. Douglas. Standing in opposition was a new politician, Abraham Lincoln. He wanted to check the extension of slavery and to preserve the Union, which was rapidly dividing over the issue of slavery.

In 1858, Lincoln accepted the Republican nomination for the Senate. His acceptance reiterated his desire to preserve and defend the Union, amidst rumblings of secession from various southern states. His speech began, "A house divided against itself cannot stand. I believe the government cannot endure permanently half slave and half free."

Abraham Lincoln was right. The United States could not withstand division. His quote, which was based on the teachings of Jesus, proved to be tragically correct. Both men were not afraid to declare the truth as it is, regardless of how unpopular doing so might prove to be.

No Greater Opportunity. James C. Dobson has said, "There is no greater opportunity to influence our fellowman for Christ than to respond with love when we have been unmistakably wronged. Then the difference between Christian love and the values of the world are most brilliantly evident."

Jesus was "unmistakably wronged" by the religious leaders, high priests, and

Pilate. Jesus had every right to respond in any way except with love. But what an impact Jesus made in this world when He showed love instead of hatred, revenge, anger, or bitterness to those who so wrongfully accused and abused Him. We need to remember Jesus' response when we are faced with those who try to harm us, either intentionally or unintentionally.

Proof of Authority. Sally was a casualty of the "too-many-hypocrites-in-the-church" phenomenon that has afflicted so many. Sally's uncle lived a life of such phony religiosity that she had been turned off to God for as long as she could remember. Uncle Jerry was the pastor of a small church in a rural Southern community.

By the time Sally was a high school senior, she and her sisters and brothers were creating skits that mocked the weird and empty traditions that dominated the lives of Uncle Jerry and Aunt Shirley. It wasn't that Sally was against God or His church. Sally simply couldn't stomach the duplicitous life that she observed when her uncle was away from his pulpit.

In the spring of Sally's 33rd year, she met Rob. Sally sat on the board of a philanthropic foundation that was reviewing grant requests, when Rob's application caught everyone's attention. Not only did the board decide that Rob would receive all the money he requested for his work with HIV-infected children in Chicago's inner city, but his sincerity and honest Christian character also engendered Sally's admiration and affection. They eventually married, and Sally finally found a man whose faith matched his actions.

CHRIST AS HEALER

BACKGROUND SCRIPTURE: Mark 1:29-45
DEVOTIONAL READING: Isaiah 61:1-4

KEY VERSE: [Jesus] healed many that were sick of divers diseases, and cast out many devils. Mark 1:34.

KING JAMES VERSION

MARK 1:29 And forthwith, when they were come out of the synagogue, they entered into the house of Simon and Andrew, with James and John. 30 But Simon's wife's mother lay sick of a fever, and anon they tell him of her. 31 And he came and took her by the hand, and lifted her up; and immediately the fever left her, and she ministered unto them. 32 And at even, when the sun did set, they brought unto him all that were diseased, and them that were possessed with devils. 33 And all the city was gathered together at the door. 34 And he healed many that were sick of divers diseases, and cast out many devils; and suffered not the devils to speak, because they knew him. 35 And in the morning, rising up a great while before day, he went out, and departed into a solitary place, and there prayed. 36 And Simon and they that were with him followed after him. 37 And when they had found him, they said unto him, All men seek for thee. 38 And he said unto them, Let us go into the next towns, that I may preach there also: for therefore came I forth. 39 And he preached in their synagogues throughout all Galilee, and cast out devils.

40 And there came a leper to him, beseeching him, and kneeling down to him, and saying unto him, If thou wilt, thou canst make me clean. 41 And Jesus, moved with compassion, put forth his hand, and touched him, and saith unto him, I will; be thou clean. 42 And as soon as he had spoken, immediately the leprosy departed from him, and he was cleansed. 43 And he straitly charged him, and forthwith sent him away; 44 And saith unto him, See thou say nothing to any man: but go thy way, shew thyself to the priest, and offer for thy cleansing those things which Moses commanded, for a testimony unto them. 45 But he went out, and began to publish it much, and to blaze abroad the matter, insomuch that Jesus could no more openly enter into the city, but was without in desert places: and they came to him from every quarter.

NEW REVISED STANDARD VERSION

MARK 1:29 As soon as they left the synagogue, they entered the house of Simon and Andrew, with James and John. 30 Now Simon's mother-in-law was in bed with a fever, and they told him about her at once. 31 He came and took her by the hand and lifted her up. Then the fever left her, and she began to serve them.

32 That evening, at sundown, they brought to him all who were sick or possessed with demons. 33 And the whole city was gathered around the door. 34 And he cured many who were sick with various diseases, and cast out many demons; and he would not permit the demons to speak, because they knew him.

35 In the morning, while it was still very dark, he got up and went out to a deserted place, and there he prayed. 36 And Simon and his companions hunted for him. 37 When they found him, they said to him, "Everyone is searching for you." 38 He answered, "Let us go on to the neighboring towns, so that I may proclaim the message there also; for that is what I came out to do." 39 And he went throughout Galilee, proclaiming the message in their synagogues and casting out demons.

40 A leper came to him begging him, and kneeling he said to him, "If you choose, you can make me clean." 41 Moved with pity, Jesus stretched out his hand and touched him, and said to him, "I do choose. Be made clean!" 42 Immediately the leprosy left him, and he was made clean. 43 After sternly warning him he sent him away at once, 44 saying to him, "See that you say nothing to anyone; but go, show yourself to the priest, and offer for your cleansing what Moses commanded, as a testimony to them." 45 But he went out and began to proclaim it freely, and to spread the word, so that Jesus could no longer go into a town openly, but stayed out in the country; and people came to him from every quarter.

HOME BIBLE READINGS

BACKGROUND

Mark 1:14 notes that after the authorities had arrested and imprisoned John the Baptizer, Jesus went into Galilee, where He proclaimed the good news that comes from God and is about God. In particular, the Messiah declared that the time promised by the Lord had finally arrived. Indeed, His kingdom was already at hand. Jesus was referring to God's sovereign rule over His creation. This involved bringing His plan of redemption to completion through the Savior. Here we see that a new era had begun. And when that era reaches its completion, the kingdom of God will have come in all its fullness. History is not in the unbroken grip of evil. Satan is powerful and active now, but his doom is certain. Neither is history moving in pointless circles, with all things being as they always have been and always will be. God is moving history toward a just conclusion. In light of these truths, Jesus urged everyone to turn back to God in repentance and believe the Good News (1:15).

After announcing the start of a new era, Jesus set out to call His disciples. First, He called Simon (Peter) and Andrew (1:16). These brothers certainly were not perfect. But Jesus did not call them because of who they were. He called them because of who they could become. Such people are the raw material with which Christ builds His kingdom. Jesus spoke to the brothers in language they could understand. They knew how it feels to catch fish—the thrill of hauling in a full net. Now they were being called to a task that offered deeper fulfillment: fishing for people (1:17). Jesus' words went straight to the hearts of Peter and Andrew. Here was what the brothers had been longing for! So they immediately followed Jesus, laying aside the nets they had used in their daily work as fishermen (1:18). Jesus continued walking until He found James and John at work with their father, Zebedee (1:19). Jesus called this pair of brothers too and they followed Him (1:20). Zebedee had the help of hired servants, and therefore presumably was able to maintain his fishing business without his sons.

NOTES ON THE PRINTED TEXT

Mark 1:21-28 spotlights the episode we studied last week, in which Jesus expelled a demon from a man in attendance at a synagogue service in Capernaum. Next, after leaving the synagogue, Jesus walked with James and John to the home of Peter and Andrew to eat a Sabbath meal, which was customarily served at that time (1:29). Part of the reason for this visit was the illness of Peter's mother-in-law. She was lying down in bed, being sick with a high-grade fever (1:30; see Luke 4:38). At that time, a fever was considered to be an illness itself, rather than a symptom of many kinds of illness. We don't know precisely what was wrong with Peter's mother-in-law, but Jesus knew what to do. He went over to her bedside and ordered the fever to go away (4:39). Here the woman's malady is personified as an entity that held her captive and that Jesus rebuked and cast out by the power of His command. Next, He took Peter's mother-in-law by the hand and gently helped her up. In the process, Jesus healed her. With her fever now gone, the grateful host prepared an evening meal for her guests (Mark 1:31).

Later that Saturday evening, many local people came to Jesus, bringing the sick and the demon possessed (Mark 1:32). The widespread occurrence of the latter might have been due to the presence of pagan occult practices in Galilee. According to Jewish law, now that the Sabbath was over (having ended at sunset), the people could travel and carry a burden. The crowd was so large that it looked as though the entire town had turned out (1:33). Jesus healed the sick and drove out demons. Here we see a distinction made between healing and exorcism, which implies that Jesus was dealing with two separate issues—one physical and the other spiritual in nature.

The Savior would not allow the demons to identify Him, for they knew He was the Messiah (1:34; see Luke 4:41). After all, He didn't need the testimony of the demonic world to establish His credibility. He also did not want unclean spirits to leave people the false idea that He had any political aspirations to liberate Israel from their Gentile taskmasters. It would be incorrect to assume from Jesus' growing popularity that He was widely received as the promised Messiah of the Jews. Most of those who came to Him at this stage were not seeking Him because they appreciated who He is. Some just wanted to be healed, while most of the others likely were curiosity seekers. Jesus was calling them to His eternal kingdom, but they were chiefly interested in a comfortable existence within the kingdoms of this world.

Jesus knew the value of renewing His spiritual vitality. That's why, before daybreak the next morning, He got up, went out to an isolated place, and spent time in prayer (Mark 1:35). The demands of His ministry were already pressing upon Him, so it made sense for Him to commune alone with the heavenly Father. Perhaps the Son focused on the holiness of the Father, the advent of His kingdom, and the fulfillment of His will throughout creation. Possibly, Jesus also entreated the Lord to provide the disciples with sufficient food to eat, strength to endure temptation, and protection from all forms of evil (see Matt. 6:9-13; Luke 11:2-4). Eventually, Peter and the other disciples got up. When they noticed that Jesus had left the house, they decided to track Him down (Mark 1:36). When the disciples found Jesus, they interrupted His prayer, exclaiming, *All men seek for thee* (1:37). They could not understand why He would ignore the call of the crowd, even for prayer. Undoubtedly, they assumed the success of His mission required approval from the masses. But Jesus knew better. The success of His mission required approval from the Father.

Jesus stated that it was imperative for the group to go on to the nearby villages (1:38). His mission was to confront the people living in those places with the Good News. For this reason, He did not want to see the Gospel confined to one place. Consequently, Jesus traveled throughout the region of Galilee. As He made His way from town to town, He preached in the synagogues and expelled demons from their victims (1:39). These are just some of the signs that Jesus performed in the presence of His disciples. And while the four Gospels do not record every miracle, what they do report is intended to convince everyone to believe that Jesus is the Messiah, the Son of God. In so doing, they will have life in His name (John 20:30-31).

In Mark's continuing presentation of Jesus the Messiah (see Mark 1:1), we next find Him encountering a leper. This man had heard of Jesus' power, but evidently knew little about His compassion. The leper came to the Savior, knelt in front of Him, and begged Him for help. The leper reasoned that if Jesus was willing to do so, He could cleanse the leper of his affliction (vs. 40). The wording of the Greek text indicates that the leper was not presuming that Jesus would heal him, only that the Messiah had the power to do so.

Leper refers to several types of inflammatory skin diseases. Judging by the excitement that followed the healing (1:45), the leper who approached Jesus was probably suffering from true leprosy (Hansen's disease), not just a mild skin ailment. Old Testament laws addressed how to treat people with many skin diseases like leprosy (Lev. 13:1-46; 14:1-32). But what we label leprosy was distinct from other skin diseases because some rabbis taught that it was a punishment for sin. To them, leprosy was the visible sign of inward corruption. The Jews feared leprosy, not only because it was disfiguring, but also because lepers were treated as outcasts. Lepers lived in communities outside the city gates and were not allowed contact with others.

Jesus, being filled with compassion (Mark 1:41), was willing and able to heal the leper. Thus, Jesus stretched out His hand, touched the leper, and made him clean. The man probably had not been touched by a nonleper in months or even years. Religious law declared that a person became "unclean" by touching a leper. Jesus could have healed the leper without touching him, but He did touch him, instantly healing him (1:42). Here we see that Jesus' compassion ignored ritual defilement. As He had been with the crowds in Capernaum, Jesus was moved by kindness at the sight of suffering and willingly removed its cause.

Jesus did not waste any time sending the former leper on his way with a stern warning to tell no one about the healing (1:43). In the time of Jesus, the Jews wanted freedom from Rome. Expectations ran high that God would raise up a warrior-prince who would throw off the yoke of pagan rule and usher in a Jewish kingdom of worldwide proportions. John 6:15 and Acts 1:6 show traces of this hope among the people. This explains why Jesus was careful not to give false impressions about the exact nature of His messiahship (John 18:33-37). He saw His destiny in terms of service to God and sacrificial suffering (Mark 8:31; 9:31; 10:33-34; Luke 24:45-46).

Jesus told the former leper to go to a priest, let him examine the once afflicted bodily area, and verify that a genuine healing had occurred. Jesus also directed the man to take along the offering required in the Mosaic law for those who had been cleansed from leprosy (Mark 1:44; see Lev. 13:6, 13, 17, 23; 14:2-32). Not only would such verification fulfill a requirement of the Mosaic law, but it would also testify to the religious establishment of Jesus' authority and His respect for the law. Indeed, the sight of a fully healed leper would attest to the religious leaders that Jesus is the Messiah, for the Jews believed only God could cure such a disease (2 Kings 5:1-7).

The former leper may have obeyed the priestly verification part of Jesus' orders, but he did not obey the Lord's command to remain silent. He proclaimed to everyone what had happened, which led large crowds to swarm around Jesus wherever He went. The presence of so many miracle seekers (along with the intensifying opposition of the religious leaders) hindered Jesus' ability to publicly enter a town or synagogue anywhere in Galilee. Instead, He had to confine Himself to *desert places* (Mark 1:45), that is, secluded, remote areas. Even then, the people were so desperate that they kept coming to Him from everywhere to be healed.

SUGGESTIONS TO TEACHERS

Like the needy and afflicted people who came and were brought to Jesus, we, too, experience pain and difficulty in our lives. Jesus is still the right source of comfort and healing for our afflictions. We need to remember that only He can make us whole.

1. THE PHYSICAL AND THE SPIRITUAL. In all the episodes highlighted in this week's lesson, physical needs mirrored deeper spiritual needs. For instance, in the case of those who were possessed by unclean spirits, their behavioral problems were a direct result of their spiritual bondage. And even in the case of the man with leprosy, his ailment was a result of the fallen condition of all creation. In fact, his physical condition reflected his spiritual helplessness.

2. THE NEED FOR DELIVERANCE. Every person needs the deliverance and forgiveness only the Lord Jesus can provide. Those who have never placed their trust in the Messiah for salvation are as helpless as the large number of sick and demon-possessed who came to Jesus for assistance. Unsaved men and women need to be rescued from the terrible effects of Satan, just as those afflicted by evil spirits needed deliverance and healing.

3. THE GOD WHO HEALS. Christian men and women stand in need of situational deliverance and forgiveness. Even though the eternal issue of salvation has been dealt with, physical disease and personal sins are still realities of life. Believers need to look to the Lord for help in time of sickness, and for forgiveness of the transgressions that damage fellowship with the heavenly Father.

FOR ADULTS	■ **TOPIC:** Finding Healing and Wholeness

■ **QUESTIONS:** 1. What did Jesus do to heal Peter's mother-in-law? 2. Why did the crowds seek out Jesus? 3. Why was prayer important to Jesus? 4. How did Jesus respond to the leper's request to be healed? 5. Why did Jesus sternly warn the former leper not to tell anyone else about the healing?

■ **ILLUSTRATIONS:**

A Real Touchdown. In 2006, the Seattle Seahawks made it to the Super Bowl, which was played in Detroit, Michigan. The entourage included the football team's coach, Mike Holmgren. But according to columnist Robert L. Jamieson of the *Seattle Post-Intelligencer*, Mike's wife, Kathy, was on the other side of globe in the "violent, far-away place" of the Democratic Republic of Congo for 17 days of "medical and missionary work." Some quipped that the coach's wife had "gone nuts." But others think her decision symbolized a "refreshing reordering of priorities in a culture that likes to get drunk on pop culture."

Kathy explained that her vibrant Christian faith was the basis for her trip. She believes that "God has a purpose for every life." In her case, it was to support humanitarian work in the Congo with Northwest Medical Teams, a non-profit relief group based in Oregon. The organization, which was founded in 1979, strives to help meet the physical and spiritual needs of devastated people in countries like Cambodia, Mexico, Honduras, Romania, and Albania. Unlike the Seahawks, who lost to the Pittsburgh Steelers in the Super Bowl, it's hard to dispute that Kathy's trip was a real "touchdown" for time and eternity!

Jesus Cares. In his book, *What Americans Believe*, national pollster George Barna released a survey of values and religious views in America. His study found that "the two most important elements in life to people are their family (considered very important by 94 percent) and their health (87 per cent)."

Most, if not all, your students have probably put a lot of thought into their own health and the health of their loved ones. They have also probably thought about who to go to with their health concerns. As we see in this week's lesson, Jesus miraculously healed a number of different people. Many individuals in Jesus' day sought His help. But how seriously do we go to Him in prayer about our health problems?

As much as we are concerned about our health, and as much as we believe in Jesus' power to heal, we still may find it difficult to go to Him first. Maybe it's because we have so much trust in modern medicine, or maybe it's because it doesn't seem as though Jesus heals as He did two thousand years ago.

Regardless of whether the Savior heals our physical afflictions or delivers us from suffering, we should always bring both our spiritual and physical needs to Him. We might feel as though the Lord Jesus has abandoned us when He has not removed the source of our pain, but the truth is, He hasn't left us alone.

Healing Touch. Katie is young, married, and the mother of two children. Not long ago, during a prayer time at a Bible study she attends, another Christian began praying for her. This believer did not know Katie's life situation, yet his prayer was specific to her needs. Katie had been hospitalized with a dangerous blood clot in her chest. This believer placed his hand on her shoulder and prayed that Jesus would cleanse her vessels and arteries. Katie reported that she experienced immediate physical relief from lingering symptoms of that condition.

Not only did Jesus work through this man for Katie's physical healing, but this man also prayed that she would feel forgiven for whatever happened four and a half years earlier. He did not know that Katie had become pregnant out of wedlock four and a half years prior and had struggled with guilt and shame ever since. Experiences such as Katie's are rare. Nevertheless, just as Jesus reached into Katie's life in a tender yet powerful way that day to heal her, so He longs to touch and mend each of His spiritual children where they are torn and broken.

FOR YOUTH

■ TOPIC: The Doctor Is In!

■ QUESTIONS: 1. What issue confronted Jesus when He went to the home of Peter? 2. How did Jesus respond to the crowd of people who wanted to be healed by Him? 3. What attitude did Jesus' disciples have toward the Savior's decision to pray? 4. How did the leper present his request to Jesus to be healed? 5. How did the former leper respond to Jesus' stern warning?

■ ILLUSTRATIONS:

Physicians to the World. In 1996, Scott and Sally Harrison began CURE International to provide physical and spiritual healing for disabled children in the developing world. In its effort to minister to the largest number possible, the organization targets the poorest countries with the greatest medical needs.

By 1998, CURE began operating their first hospital in Kenya, Africa. Since then, they have established hospitals in Honduras, the Dominican Republic, Uganda, Malawi, and Afghanistan. The organization also has plans to open three more facilities in Egypt, Ethiopia, and Zambia. In its efforts to meet the needs of children with physical handicaps, the organization creates opportunities to spread the Good News of Christ. As a result, many have an opportunity to find healing and wholeness through the Savior.

One success story involves a child named Patrick. According to CURE, his life had been "riddled with mocking and laughter from others living in the Kirinyaga district in the Eastern Province of Kenya." The reason was the child's physical disability. From the time of his birth, one leg was "shorter than the other." He also had a "knee that bent backward rather than forward."

These issues prevented Patrick from being able to walk and run "like his six brothers and sisters" and his "friends and schoolmates." His disabilities also decreased the likelihood he would have a successful future in an area where "physical labor capability is critical for survival." In September 2005, Patrick and his mother went to CURE Bethany Crippled Children's Centre. Orthopedic and neurosurgeons operated on the child to "correct his deformity." And what was the outcome of the surgery? A photo showing Patrick smiling "says it all."

Searching. In May, 1998, Robert Ballard found the *USS Yorktown*. Ballard, who 10 years before had discovered the lost ocean liner, *Titanic*, had been searching for the *Yorktown*, a World War II aircraft carrier that sank 56 years earlier, after a Japanese torpedo attack.

The expedition was the largest and most technologically challenging undersea search ever mounted by the United States Navy and the National Geographic Society. For several weeks while aboard the research vessel, *Laney Chouset*, Ballard and his crew crisscrossed 300 square miles of the Pacific Ocean north of Midway Island. They watched and waited as a towed mapping device and an underwater drone scanned the ocean bottom miles below. The wreckage was finally discovered 16,650 feet down, which is nearly one mile further down than the wreckage of the *Titanic*.

If people will go to such extremes to find an old sunken aircraft carrier, imagine the extent to which God has gone to seek and save us! Though lost, we can be found and and spiritually healed by trusting in Christ.

Showing Care and Compassion. At the end of August, 1997, Princess Diana was killed in an automobile accident in Paris. People of all ages were stunned at her senseless death. Emotion surged and was evidenced by the thousands who brought flowers to Buckingham Palace. While Great Britain mourned, the royal family seemed aloof and uncaring. Public sentiment rose as the nation stingingly criticized Queen Elizabeth II for her seclusion and her lack of compassion. She was finally forced to speak to her nation's people.

Contrast this queen's response with that of King Jesus. Far from being indifferent and unconcerned, He got involved in the lives of people. Jesus showed genuine care and compassion.

CHRIST AS SERVANT

BACKGROUND SCRIPTURE: John 13:1-20
DEVOTIONAL READING: Isaiah 53:4-6

KEY VERSE: [Jesus said,] For I have given you an example, that ye should do as I have done to you. John 13:15.

KING JAMES VERSION

JOHN 13:1 Now before the feast of the passover, when Jesus knew that his hour was come that he should depart out of this world unto the Father, having loved his own which were in the world, he loved them unto the end. 2 And supper being ended, the devil having now put into the heart of Judas Iscariot, Simon's son, to betray him; 3 Jesus knowing that the Father had given all things into his hands, and that he was come from God, and went to God; 4 He riseth from supper, and laid aside his garments; and took a towel, and girded himself. 5 After that he poureth water into a bason, and began to wash the disciples' feet, and to wipe them with the towel wherewith he was girded. 6 Then cometh he to Simon Peter: and Peter saith unto him, Lord, dost thou wash my feet? 7 Jesus answered and said unto him, What I do thou knowest not now; but thou shalt know hereafter. 8 Peter saith unto him, Thou shalt never wash my feet. Jesus answered him, If I wash thee not, thou hast no part with me. . . . 12 So after he had washed their feet, and had taken his garments, and was set down again, he said unto them, Know ye what I have done to you? 13 Ye call me Master and Lord: and ye say well; for so I am. 14 If I then, your Lord and Master, have washed your feet; ye also ought to wash one another's feet. 15 For I have given you an example, that ye should do as I have done to you. 16 Verily, verily, I say unto you, The servant is not greater than his lord; neither he that is sent greater than he that sent him. 17 If ye know these things, happy are ye if ye do them.

18 I speak not of you all: I know whom I have chosen: but that the scripture may be fulfilled, He that eateth bread with me hath lifted up his heel against me. 19 Now I tell you before it come, that, when it is come to pass, ye may believe that I am he. 20 Verily, verily, I say unto you, He that receiveth whomsoever I send receiveth me; and he that receiveth me receiveth him that sent me.

NEW REVISED STANDARD VERSION

JOHN 13:Now before the festival of the Passover, Jesus knew that his hour had come to depart from this world and go to the Father. Having loved his own who were in the world, he loved them to the end. 2 The devil had already put it into the heart of Judas son of Simon Iscariot to betray him. And during supper 3 Jesus, knowing that the Father had given all things into his hands, and that he had come from God and was going to God, 4 got up from the table, took off his outer robe, and tied a towel around himself. 5 Then he poured water into a basin and began to wash the disciples' feet and to wipe them with the towel that was tied around him. 6 He came to Simon Peter, who said to him, "Lord, are you going to wash my feet?" 7 Jesus answered, "You do not know now what I am doing, but later you will understand." 8 Peter said to him, "You will never wash my feet." Jesus answered, "Unless I wash you, you have no share with me." . . .

12 After he had washed their feet, had put on his robe, and had returned to the table, he said to them, "Do you know what I have done to you? 13 You call me Teacher and Lord—and you are right, for that is what I am. 14 So if I, your Lord and Teacher, have washed your feet, you also ought to wash one another's feet. 15 For I have set you an example, that you also should do as I have done to you. 16 Very truly, I tell you, servants are not greater than their master, nor are messengers greater than the one who sent them. 17 If you know these things, you are blessed if you do them. 18 I am not speaking of all of you; I know whom I have chosen. But it is to fulfill the scripture, 'The one who ate my bread has lifted his heel against me.' 19 I tell you this now, before it occurs, so that when it does occur, you may believe that I am he. 20 Very truly, I tell you, whoever receives one whom I send receives me; and whoever receives me receives him who sent me."

8

Monday, July 14	Isaiah 53:4-6	*The Suffering Servant*
Tuesday, July 15	John 13:1-2a	*To the End*
Wednesday, July 16	John 13:2b-11	*Unless I Wash You*
Thursday, July 17	John 13:12-17	*An Example*
Friday, July 18	John 13:18-20	*Whoever Receives Me*
Saturday, July 19	Matthew 20:20-23	*What Do You Want?*
Sunday, July 20	Matthew 20:24-28	*Not to Be Served*

BACKGROUND

The farewell meal that Jesus ate with His disciples probably followed a well-established Jewish pattern for celebrating the Passover feast. During an opening prayer, the first of four cups was blessed and passed around. Each person at the table then took herbs and dipped them in salt water. Next, the host took one of three flat cakes of unleavened bread, broke it, and laid some of it aside. Typically, the youngest member of the group then asked the question "What makes this night different from all others?" The host responded by recounting the events of the Passover. This was usually followed by the singing of Psalms 113 and 114 and by the filling and passing around of the second cup.

Before the actual meal was eaten, all the participants washed their hands. Thanksgiving to God was prayed, and more of the bread was broken apart. The host dipped bread in a sauce usually made of stewed fruit, and then distributed a portion to each person gathered at the table. Finally, the time for the meal arrived. Eating a roasted lamb was the high point of the evening. It was after Jesus and His disciples had eaten the Passover meal that He instituted the Lord's Supper. Jesus took the third cup, which was known as the "cup of blessing," and uttered a prayer of thanks to God. He then instructed each of His disciples to take the cup and share its contents among themselves. Then He took a flat cake of unleavened bread, broke it, and passed it around so that each of His disciples could eat a portion of it.

NOTES ON THE PRINTED TEXT

The events in this week's lesson took place on the night before the official start of the Passover celebration (John 13:1). Jesus knew the time had come for His departure from the world. This was the time appointed by the Father for His Son's saving work to be completed. Throughout Jesus' earthly ministry, He loved those entrusted to His care. His compassion for the disciples was was unselfish, unconditional, and unbounded. Jesus demonstrated His love completely and to the very end of His life. He knew that after His crucifixion and burial, He would be resurrected from the dead and exalted to the right hand of the Father (John 13:1).

Prior to the start of Jesus' farewell meal, Satan had put it into the mind of Judas

Iscariot to betray his loyalty to the Savior (13:2). Judas is identified as the son of Simon (see 6:71). Most likely, the term *Iscariot* refers to the town of Kerioth, which was located near Hebron in southern Judah (Josh. 15:25). Among Jesus' 12 disciples, Judas was their treasurer. He carried the moneybag and would sometimes steal from it (12:6). The three Synoptic Gospels detail how Judas plotted with the Jewish leaders to bring about Jesus' arrest. Judas received a payment of 30 silver coins (Matt. 26:14-16; Mark 14:10-11; Luke 22:3-6) for leading the authorities to Jesus (John 18:1-2). It is unlikely that Jesus felt any personal sense of defeat about this, for He was aware that the Father had given Him authority over everything. Jesus also knew that nothing could happen to Him apart from the will of God, from whom He had come and to whom He was returning (13:3).

Without warning, Jesus rose from the table during the farewell meal. Perhaps His disciples were preoccupied with eating and talking when they saw the Lord stand a short distance from them and remove His outer robe. Undoubtedly, they were shocked by this action. But even more unexpected was Jesus' decision to tie a towel (a long piece of linen cloth) around His waist (John 13:4). As the disciples watched in complete silence, they saw the Lord pick up a basin and a jar of water, which He then set down on the ground near the table. Next, He filled the large bowl with water, washed the feet of every disciple, and dried their feet with the towel around His waist (13:5).

When Jesus knelt down in front of Peter, he asked the Lord whether He intended to wash the feet of His disciple (13:6). The Savior, perhaps looking directly at Peter, explained that even though he failed to grasp the significance of the foot-washing episode, he would later (after Jesus' resurrection) understand the meaning of what had been done (13:7). Because Peter was unable to fathom the Messiah's intent, he strongly protested what his Lord was doing. The Greek literally says, "You will never wash my feet forever." Jesus, while maintaining His composure, replied matter-of-factly that if Peter did not permit Him to wash his feet, Peter would no longer really belong to Him. Expressed differently, Peter would not be Jesus' disciple (13:8). Christ's reply probably referred to His gift of cleansing in His blood, of which the foot washing was a symbol.

Perhaps at this point there was considerable tension and anxiety among the rest of the disciples over the exchange that had occurred between Jesus and Peter. The mood may have lightened up considerably as the group heard Peter beg the Lord to wash not just his feet, but also his hands and head (13:9). This reaction showed not only Peter's respect for Jesus, but his devotion as well. Most likely, Peter wanted to show Jesus that he was one of His loyal followers. Jesus responded by describing a situation in which a person went to a feast after having taken a bath. This person did not need to wash again, except for his feet, which had gotten dirty on the way to the feasting place (13:10). In a spiritual sense, Peter had already been cleansed of sin through faith in Christ. Thus, the disciple did not need to be cleansed from sin again. At this point, none of those present understood the meaning of Jesus' words about who was *clean* and who was not. He meant that, except for the betrayer, Judas (13:11), all the disciples had experienced spiritual cleansing through faith in Him (15:3). Jesus' explanation implies that the foot-washing incident was more than just an example of humble service. It also pointed to His atoning sacrifice at Calvary. Those who accepted Jesus' act of humiliation also embraced by faith His redemptive work on the cross.

After Jesus had washed the feet of His disciples, He stood up, put on His outer garment, and returned to His place at the table. Once Jesus was seated, He took the opportunity to explain the significance of His actions. He asked His followers whether they grasped the import of the foot-washing incident (13:12). Jesus referred to the typical terms with which His disciples respectfully addressed Him. Jesus fully approved being recognized as their Teacher and Lord (13:13). Yet, even though they rightfully submitted to His authority and instruction, He was willing to serve them. If Jesus voluntarily ministered to His subjects in this most unassuming and sacrificial way, what should be their response? The Redeemer said they were morally obligated to follow His example (13:14). He had given them a demonstration of humility by washing their feet. Likewise, a generous and sacrificial attitude should characterize His followers in their relationships with each other (13:15). Because the foot washing also symbolized the spiritual cleansing that comes through Jesus' blood (which He was about to shed on the cross), He was urging His disciples to be willing to lay down their lives for one another, if necessary, as an act of sacrificial love (see 15:13).

Jesus solemnly assured the Twelve (and all who trust in Him for eternal life) that slaves are not greater than their master. Likewise, messengers are not greater than the person who sends them (13:16). Jesus' use of the word *sent* reminded His disciples that He had been sent to them by the Father. In turn, Jesus was sending His followers out to serve others, beginning with the proclamation of the Gospel (see 20:21-23). The Lord Jesus, by example as well as by precept, introduced to His followers this principle of servanthood toward one another. Therefore, He is the believers' model of unselfish service. Those who willingly, consistently, and wholeheartedly follow His example are promised blessings (13:17). Thus, the only way for believers to be truly fulfilled and satisfied in their relationship with Christ is for them to be willing to accept and perform the role of a servant.

It is unclear how Judas felt as Jesus talked openly about the importance of humble and sacrificial service. Perhaps Judas reacted with calloused indifference, especially as Satan took control of him (see 13:27). In any case, Jesus explained that His statements were not directed to all of those present at the farewell meal (13:18). He knew that Judas would hand Him over to the authorities. Jesus also knew the ones whom He had chosen to receive eternal life. Jesus stated that the decision made by Judas to betray Him was foretold in Scripture. Next, Jesus quoted Psalm 41:9. In this prayer for mercy, David noted that a trusted associate who served in his royal court and ate at his table had lifted up his heel against the king. There are differing views concerning the meaning of this idiom. Most likely, the idea is that one of David's closest friends had acted treacherously by taking cruel advantage of him. What Israel's monarch lamented found its ultimate fulfillment in Jesus, the Son of David, when Judas Iscariot became His enemy by turning against him. The Savior was predicting this act of betrayal before it ever happened so that when it occurred, His disciples would believe that He is the Messiah (13:19).

The Messiah solemnly declared that anyone who welcomed His messengers also welcomed Him. In turn, those who welcomed Him were welcoming the Father, who had sent the Son (13:20). Earlier, in the episode involving the nighttime visit that Nicodemus made to Jesus, we learn that God sent His only Son to die for our sins (3:16). God calls us to believe in Jesus—not just assenting to what Jesus said as true, but entrusting our lives to Him. Those who believe in the Messiah will not suffer eternal separation from God, but enjoy a reconciled, deeply satisfying relationship with Jesus and His heavenly Father that will last forever.

SUGGESTIONS TO TEACHERS

One of the most vivid illustrations in Scripture is found in this week's passage from John, which describes Jesus' dropping to His knees and washing the filthy feet of His beloved disciples. Jesus showed them—and us—the power of love. This illustration of humility and love is pertinent for all Christians. We realize, of course, that it is not easy for us to set aside our pride and express love by being a servant to others. But since the Lord of the universe could do it, we can do so as well.

1. IMPACT OF SERVICE. Peter tried to resist having the Lord wash his feet. But Jesus insisted that Peter first had to receive love before he could show loving service to others. Peter's protests were finally overcome as the impact of the Savior's example sunk in. Talk with the class about how we must first receive from Jesus before we can give. Only when we are served by Him in grace are we able to serve others graciously.

2. INSIGHT INTO SERVING. Emphasize the theme of John 13:12-20 by quoting Jesus' command to carry out acts of service in humility: *For I have given you an example, that ye should do as I have done to you* (13:15). Jesus insisted that we, as His followers, must be willing to humble ourselves. We must forget about obtaining honors and recognition, and seek to serve rather than be served.

3. INFAMY OF BETRAYING. That evening during the farewell meal, Jesus willingly washed the feet of Judas Iscariot. The Messiah knew that Judas had already conspired with the authorities to arrest Jesus later that night. The traitor's act of self-serving was the opposite of Jesus' act of self-giving. What a contrast of lifestyles! John's account seems to suggest that those who are found by the Redeemer must respond either by betraying Him for selfish reasons or by imitating Him by serving others.

Instead of trying to fathom the reasons for the decision of Judas to betray Jesus, hold up the account of the traitor's unfaithfulness as a way of contrasting worldly wisdom with the godly, self-giving wisdom of the Son.

FOR ADSULTS	

FOR ADULTS

■ **TOPIC:** To Be a Servant

■ **QUESTIONS:** 1. In what way did Jesus show that He loved His followers to the very end? 2. Why did Judas Iscariot decide to betray Jesus? 3. How do you think the disciples felt as they saw Jesus washing their feet? 4. What explanation did Jesus give for wanting to wash the feet of His disciples? 5. What did Jesus say was the significance of the foot-washing episode?

■ **ILLUSTRATIONS:**

After-School Fun. In the *Statesman Journal*, Pastor Chris Haydon of Trinity Covenant Church in Salem, Oregon, described the congregation's after-school program for children. The endeavor is called the Community Corner and especially targets "latchkey children and others in first to fifth grades" who need a "safe, fun environment in which to gather with friends." When the program began in 2003, there were only four children who came. In the years since, community interest has become so strong that a decision was made to "limit daily enrollment to 55."

A volunteer named Ruth Motley noted that her involvement in the program "has been a privilege." And it's her hope that the children's participation in games, crafts, computer lab, and Bible stories (among other activities) will be a "positive experience toward faith and the church" and remain an "anchor for them as they grow." According to Reverend Haydon, Ruth and other church members have "embraced this outreach ministry as a loving service to the community." Opening the doors of the church to offer hope and help to those in need is part of what it means to be a servant of the Lord Jesus.

Love in Action. When the downtown merchants of Lansing, Michigan, learned that a minor-league baseball stadium would be built in their midst, they were ecstatic. Like many other older downtowns, Lansing had seen its share of closed businesses, shuttered warehouses, and decaying city blocks. The new stadium, offering inexpensive family entertainment, would bring thousands of people—and their entertainment dollars—to the area.

The merchants were correct. Along with the stadium came a number of new businesses and restaurants that brought money back into the heart of the city. But all was not perfect. Less than one block away from the stadium gates, nestled between two trendy, upscale restaurants, was a very public eyesore: the Lansing City Rescue Mission.

"Can't we do something about this?" one person wrote the newspaper. "Maybe we could move the mission to another part of the city," another suggested. But one person wrote back with a different perspective altogether: "I would not want to do business at one of the area's new businesses if I thought that business was closing its eyes to the very real needs of the people in its community," he wrote. "Let the mission stand where it is, for everyone to see. No, it's not pretty or trendy. But the mission is shining the light of God in a needy part of our world."

Pride could have sent the mission packing. But, as this week's lesson explains, Christian love sometimes requires us to reach out in ways that our pride would tell us to avoid.

When Understanding Is Not Enough. In the 1950s, Jonas Salk discovered a vaccine that could immunize children from the crippling disease of polio. As millions of children received the vaccine, the disease almost disappeared. Now, as we pass through the early years of the new century, physicians fear that polio is staging a comeback. Why? Many parents fail to have their children vaccinated. Protection from polio is available only to those who receive the necessary immunization.

In a similar way, Jesus provides protection from condemnation and death. He defeated sin. No one has to perish. Yet salvation is not automatic, and the new birth is not universal. To have eternal life, we must trust in Christ, not spurn Him as Judas Iscariot did.

FOR YOUTH

■ **TOPIC:** Stooping Down to Lift Up
■ **QUESTIONS:** 1. Why was Jesus planning to leave this world and return to the Father in heaven? 2. Who prompted Judas Iscariot to betray Jesus? 3. What was Peter's initial reaction to Jesus' desire to wash his feet? 4. What did Jesus mean by the reference to some, but not all, His disciples being clean? 5. What example had Jesus demonstrated in the presence of His disciples?

■ **ILLUSTRATIONS:**

Presidential Servanthood. For years, Henry Sloane Coffin was the esteemed president of Union Theological Seminary in New York. One September, the day before classes began, Coffin was in shirtsleeves near the entrance of the students' residence at 120th and Broadway, when a young man stepped out of a cab and put two large suitcases on the sidewalk. After eyeing President Coffin, the young man asked, "Do you work here?" Coffin said that he did. Thinking Coffin was a janitor, the young man rather rudely commanded, "Take these pieces of luggage up to Room 319 for me!"

Coffin said nothing. Instead, he took the two large suitcases and trudged up to the third floor of the building. The young man followed, and at the door of Room 319, handed Coffin two quarters. Coffin thanked him and put them in his pocket.

The following day, the young man attended the opening convocation and saw the man he had ordered to carry his bags presiding as the distinguished head of the illustrious institution. Rushing up to the president afterward, the young man stammered apologies for his behavior the day before. President Coffin merely smiled and quietly quoted the text, "If any would be first, he must be last of all and servant of all." His example of humility and servanthood echoed Jesus' example.

The Towel Test. A young university student in China became a Christian. Someone from the western world asked him why he did so. The Chinese student disclosed that his reasons did not stem from a belief that Jesus was the greatest philosopher. The student acknowledged that China had known outstanding philosophers such as Confucius. Nor was it because of Jesus' miracles. The Chinese had heard about miracle workers in their long history. And it wasn't because Jesus was the greatest teacher the student had encountered. The Chinese civilization had seen numerous illustrious teachers.

The student stated he had become a Christian because Jesus had taken a towel. The questioner looked puzzled. The student explained, "You don't know Asia as I do. I know that anywhere in the East only one who is God among us could do that!" The "towel test" of religion, as this young Chinese student learned, revealed that the God who came among us is one who serves. Only when we realize that God stoops to serve and care do we begin to comprehend who this gracious one is.

What It Means to Serve. "We try hard. We fail. We are sure we can succeed if we try harder tomorrow. We fail again. And if we succeed, it is only half success, half of what it would have been with God. We are all guilty. . . . The world has yet to see what God can do with one person wholly committed to Him."

Those words, spoken in the 1860s by Henry Varley in a prayer meeting, burned into the heart of ex-shoe salesman, Dwight L. Moody. He was already involved in ministry in Chicago, but Varley's words helped to change the self-sufficient Moody into a humble, God-directed evangelist and servant who went on to preach the Gospel to more people than anyone else in his time. And even though his crusade hymnbook royalties amounted to a million dollars, Moody lived on $120 a year, donating the rest to Christian charity and education. Moody followed his Redeemer's example of being a Christian servant to others.

CHRIST AS MESSIAH

BACKGROUND SCRIPTURE: Matthew 16:13-23
DEVOTIONAL READING: Isaiah 43:1-7

KEY VERSE: [Jesus] said unto [the disciples,] "But whom say ye that I am?" Matthew 16:15.

KING JAMES VERSION

MATTHEW 16:13 When Jesus came into the coasts of Caesarea Philippi, he asked his disciples, saying, Whom do men say that I the Son of man am? 14 And they said, Some say that thou art John the Baptist: some, Elias; and others, Jeremias, or one of the prophets. 15 He saith unto them, But whom say ye that I am? 16 And Simon Peter answered and said, Thou art the Christ, the Son of the living God. 17 And Jesus answered and said unto him, Blessed art thou, Simon Barjona: for flesh and blood hath not revealed it unto thee, but my Father which is in heaven. 18 And I say also unto thee, That thou art Peter, and upon this rock I will build my church; and the gates of hell shall not prevail against it. 19 And I will give unto thee the keys of the kingdom of heaven: and whatsoever thou shalt bind on earth shall be bound in heaven: and whatsoever thou shalt loose on earth shall be loosed in heaven. 20 Then charged he his disciples that they should tell no man that he was Jesus the Christ.

21 From that time forth began Jesus to shew unto his disciples, how that he must go unto Jerusalem, and suffer many things of the elders and chief priests and scribes, and be killed, and be raised again the third day. 22 Then Peter took him, and began to rebuke him, saying, Be it far from thee, Lord: this shall not be unto thee. 23 But he turned, and said unto Peter, Get thee behind me, Satan: thou art an offence unto me: for thou savourest not the things that be of God, but those that be of men.

NEW REVISED STANDARD VERSION

MATTHEW 16:13 Now when Jesus came into the district of Caesarea Philippi, he asked his disciples, "Who do people say that the Son of Man is?" 14 And they said, "Some say John the Baptist, but others Elijah, and still others Jeremiah or one of the prophets." 15 He said to them, "But who do you say that I am?" 16 Simon Peter answered, "You are the Messiah, the Son of the living God." 17 And Jesus answered him, "Blessed are you, Simon son of Jonah! For flesh and blood has not revealed this to you, but my Father in heaven. 18 And I tell you, you are Peter, and on this rock I will build my church, and the gates of Hades will not prevail against it. 19 I will give you the keys of the kingdom of heaven, and whatever you bind on earth will be bound in heaven, and whatever you loose on earth will be loosed in heaven." 20 Then he sternly ordered the disciples not to tell anyone that he was the Messiah.

21 From that time on, Jesus began to show his disciples that he must go to Jerusalem and undergo great suffering at the hands of the elders and chief priests and scribes, and be killed, and on the third day be raised. 22 And Peter took him aside and began to rebuke him, saying, "God forbid it, Lord! This must never happen to you." 23 But he turned and said to Peter, "Get behind me, Satan! You are a stumbling block to me; for you are setting your mind not on divine things but on human things."

9

HOME BIBLE READINGS

BACKGROUND

In Matthew 16:13, Jesus referred to Himself as the *Son of man*. This phrase was His most common self-description. He wanted to teach that, as the Messiah, He combined two Old Testament roles: Son of Man (Dan. 7:13-14) and Servant of the Lord (Isa. 52:13—53:12). Daniel described a Son of Man to whom God gives an everlasting kingdom, while Isaiah described a Servant of the Lord who suffers on behalf of others. Jesus knew that He must perform the role of the suffering Servant. But He also knew that eventually He would receive glory as the Son of Man.

At the heart of Jesus' reference to Himself as the Son of Man is the presence of divine authority. God the Father had chosen and commissioned His Son to bring about His plan of redemption, which included having authority to forgive sins (Mark 2:10) and exercise lordship over the Sabbath (2:28). The Father also gave the Son of Man the authority to judge and the power to grant eternal life (John 5:27; 6:27). Jesus' redemptive mission as the Son of Man involved serving others and giving His life as a ransom for many (Mark 10:45). One day the Son of Man will be seen sitting at the right hand of almighty God (14:62). Indeed, the Savior will return in the clouds with great power and glory, accompanied by the holy angels (8:38; 13:26). Those who put their faith in the Son of Man (John 9:35) must be willing to endure the deprivation and derision He experienced during His earthly ministry (Matt. 8:20; 11:19).

NOTES ON THE PRINTED TEXT

The episode narrated in this week's lesson marks a dramatic change in Jesus' earthly ministry and a turning point in Matthew's Gospel. With opposition increasing, Jesus began to repeatedly withdraw with His disciples in order to begin preparing them for His departure so that they could carry on His work after He left. If Jesus had intended only to amaze people with sensational miracles and lofty ideals, His purpose would have been fulfilled. But astonishment was meaningless unless it led to faith in Him and to salvation. Because of this, His followers needed to understand who He was. Thus, Jesus left Galilee and went north to the region around the city of Caesarea Philippi so that He could privately quiz His disciples about popular opinions of His identity (16:13).

Caesarea Philippi was a city located in the upper Jordan Valley and along the south-western slope of Mount Hermon. Behind the town, which was about 1,150 feet above sea level, rose bluffs and rugged mountain peaks. The area was one of the most lush in Palestine, with an abundance of grassy fields and groves of trees. The city was also strategically located, standing as a sentinel over the plains in the area. For many years, a cave and spring there had been associated with the worship of Canaanite gods. Later, a shrine was built on the site and dedicated to the Greek nature gods. Herod the Great built a temple to Rome and Augustus in the town, and later Herod's son, Philip the tetrarch, refurbished the city and named it Caesarea Philippi. Jesus may have chosen this spot to ask His disciples who He was so that He could draw a stark contrast between Himself and the pagan worship for which this area was famous.

Jesus undoubtedly knew what the people were saying about Him, but He used the question as a prelude to helping the Twelve obtain a clearer understanding of His identity. The disciples reported a variety of opinions concerning who Jesus was. It seems that popular opinion had it that Jesus was one of the great figures of the past reincarnated, though there was no agreement on which great figure. Some thought He was John the Baptist, while others thought He was an earlier prophet, such as Elijah or Jeremiah (16:14). Next, Jesus put the same question to His disciples, *whom say ye that I am?* (16:15). Peter responded (perhaps for the Twelve) with an affirmation of Jesus' identity that revealed greater insight than that of the people at large. Peter answered correctly, *Thou art the Christ* (16:16). The title *Christ* comes from the Greek term *christos*, which means "anointed (with ointment or oil)." It is equivalent to *Messiah*, a word derived from the Hebrew term *mashiach*. Peter also called Jesus the *Son of the living God*. This phrase draws attention to the divine, exalted status of Jesus as the Messiah (Matt. 1:20-23; Luke 1:31-33; Acts 13:33; Rom. 1:3-4).

Jesus declared that Peter was *blessed* (Matt. 16:17); in other words, he was highly favored by God because his spiritual awareness did not come to him through any human agency or power, but from the heavenly Father. In light of Peter's blessing, Jesus commented on his name. The Savior made a play on words when He declared, *thou art Peter, and upon this rock I will build my church* (16:18). *Peter* translates the Greek word *petros*, which means "stone." *Rock* translates *petra*, which refers to a massive formation of bedrock. *Church* renders the Greek word *ekklesia*, which literally refers to those who are "called out." In 16:18, the term denotes the global community of Christians, while in 18:17 it refers to a local congregation of believers.

There are differing views concerning what Jesus meant by His statement in 16:18. One option is that Peter's confession of Jesus as the Messiah, is the *rock* upon which the church is built. A second option is that Jesus Himself is the *rock* (see Acts 4:11-12; 1 Cor. 3:11; 1 Pet. 2:5-8). A third option is that Peter, as a representative and leader of the Twelve, is foundational to the church (see Eph. 2:20-21). Regardless of which view is preferred, there is no ambiguity to Jesus' declaration that the *gates of hell*

(Matt. 16:18) will not *prevail against* His church. *Hell* renders the Greek word *hades*, which is used to denote the the place of the dead. The Greek verb translated *prevail against* refers to one entity winning the victory over another entity. Through this figure of speech, Jesus was promising that not even the forces of evil and death will vanquish the community of the redeemed. More broadly speaking, while the apostles played a foundational role in the spiritual construction of the church, Jesus is the most important stone of the edifice. Also, those who affirm Jesus as the Messiah and trust in Him for salvation (as Peter did in his confession) represent the type of spiritually regenerate people on which the church is built. In turn, the Savior enables them to prevail against the forces of darkness.

In 16:19, the Lord promised to give the *keys of the kingdom of heaven* to Peter. In Jesus' day, keys were a symbol for authority and power. In this verse, *keys* probably refers to the exercise of spiritual authority in God's kingdom. The nature of this spiritual authority is elaborated upon in terms of binding and loosing. There would be a correspondence between binding and loosing on earth and binding and loosing in heaven. But what, exactly, is the binding and loosing? One possibility is that as Peter heralded the Gospel, he would play a part in determining who would not believe in Jesus (binding) and who would believe (loosing). Another possibility is that Peter would have authority in church discipline cases to determine whether a sinner had not repented (binding) or had repented (loosing). A third possibility is that Peter would have the authority to tell Christians what they could not do (binding) and what they could do (loosing).

The question of the meaning in 16:19 is complicated by uncertainty over the proper way to translate the verse. Some render it as the KJV does (*shall be bound . . . shall be loosed*), which might imply that God will ratify decisions made on earth. Others translate the verse as the NASB does: *Whatever you shall bind on earth shall have been bound in heaven, and whatever you shall loose on earth shall have been loosed in heaven.* This rendering implies that decisions made on earth would be in keeping with decisions already made by God. The ideas of binding and loosing are referred to again in 18:15-18. That connection implies that Peter and the other disciples had the authority to confront sin among the members of the church. Put another way, God sanctioned the leaders of a congregation to discern (based on the teaching of Scripture) and declare who had repented of a sin that had been committed (and was therefore loosed) and who had not repented (and was still bound; see John 20:23). This observation suggests that the *keys* (Matt. 16:19) Jesus gave to Peter were also given to all other believers.

Jesus strictly warned Peter and the rest of the Twelve not to tell anyone that He was the Messiah (16:20). Why? Possibly because Jesus knew His followers needed additional time to learn more about Him before they could accurately declare the truth of His messiahship. Also, Jesus may have wanted to avoid drawing excessive attention to Himself at this time, the kind of attention that might make people think He would free them from the control of Rome. Furthermore, Jesus probably wanted to avoid intensifying the opposition of the religious leaders against Him, for doing so might lead to His arrest before the divinely appointed time. Should that happen, Jesus' enemies probably would have openly denounced Him as a heretic and tried to kill Him before He had intended.

It is true that Jesus was the fulfillment of Old Testament prophecies concerning Israel's Savior. In addition, He was the suffering Servant—something His disciples did not yet understand. Jesus thus moved swiftly to tell them why He had come to this world. He came to die. This was Jesus' first specific teaching about His death. It was not a brief speech; rather, it gave particular details surrounding His crucifixion. In this regard, Jesus made five points about His future: (1) He would go to Jerusalem, (2) He would suffer, (3) He would be rejected by the religious leaders, (4), He would be executed by the authorites, and (5) He would rise from the dead (16:21).

Peter was so shocked by Jesus' prediction of His suffering, rejection, and death, that the statement concerning His resurrection apparently meant nothing to the disciple. In Peter's mind, Jesus had violated all he understood about the mission of the Savior. Along with the majority of the Jews, Peter evidently was looking for a Messiah who would defeat Rome and establish Israel as the dominant power in the region (if not the entire world). As a result, Peter took upon himself the role of counselor. As Jesus talked openly about the future with His disciples, Peter took Him aside and *began to rebuke him* (16:22). As Peter was in the process of chastising Jesus, the Savior did an amazing thing. He turned and declared that Peter's words were satanic. In fact, Peter was behaving as Jesus' adversary. Thus, Jesus referred to him harshly as *Satan* (16:23). Expressed differently, Satan was using Peter to tempt Jesus to abandon the Father's will. Peter's ideas about the career of the Messiah were worldly, not godly. Indeed, Peter's words echoed the same kind of temptation Satan used in the wilderness to try to get Jesus to stumble (4:1-11).

SUGGESTIONS TO TEACHERS

Many people think of Jesus as a wise philosopher, a social revolutionary, or a kind healer, but their knowledge makes no difference in the way they live. They neither love the Lord nor serve Him. In fact, they don't really see Jesus with biblical clarity. We will have difficulty understanding Jesus' teachings—especially about His suffering messiahship and heavenly glory—if we are not committed to obeying Him.

1. CLEARLY RECOGNIZING JESUS. Have we strengthened our commitment to Jesus so we can see Him clearly with the eyes of faith? We may have known about Jesus since we were young children, but do we recognize Him as the Son of God so we can follow Him more devotedly? Being committed to Jesus does not mean being loyal to Him once in a while. It does not come and go like the wind. No, full commitment affects every phase of our lives. Such commitment to Jesus illumines His teachings more and more, day by day.

2. UNDERSTANDING JESUS MORE. As we become more committed to Jesus, we desire to spend more time studying God's Word, are more attentive when God's Word is taught, and discuss God's Word with family and friends. The more interaction we have with God's Word, the more we understand Jesus' teachings. In addition, our commitment to Jesus deepens, and our experiences make Jesus' teachings more clear. We gain new, God-given insights into the same teachings.

3. COMMITTING OURSELVES TO SERVE JESUS. Oswald Chambers said, "Our Lord's making of a disciple is supernatural. He does not build on any natural capacity at all. God does not ask us to do the things that are easy to us naturally. He only asks us to do the things we are perfectly fitted to do by His grace." In short, we can commit to knowing and following the Lord Jesus, but not by trusting in ourselves to keep that commitment. We need His grace. The apostle Paul had this truth in mind when he noted in Philippians 2:13 that God is working in us, giving us both the desire to obey Him and the power to do what pleases Him.

| **FOR ADULTS** | ■ TOPIC: Getting to Know a Person |
| | ■ QUESTIONS: 1. What popular views existed concerning Jesus' identity? 2. What view of Jesus' identity did His disciples voice? 3. Why |

was it necessary for Jesus to die? 4. Why would Peter rebuke Jesus for predicting His death? 5. What did Jesus imply by referring to Peter as Satan?

■ **ILLUSTRATIONS:**

Look for the Hallmark. On one episode of the *Antiques Roadshow*, an owner brought a large, colorful, porcelain plate for the appraiser to examine. Immediately, the expert turned the item upside down to look at its hallmark. I learned that this is an identifying stamp used by manufacturers to certify an object's authenticity. Such items as pots, dishes, trays, utensils, and jewelry typically have a distinctive imprint painted, etched, or engraved on them.

Hallmarks serve two purposes. First, they show whether an item is actually what it appears to be. Experts can tell whether an artifact is genuine or phony. The antique will be noted for its age, quality, and craftsmanship, while the imitation will have indicators pointing to its relative newness, cheapness, and slipshod construction. Second, hallmarks indicate where an item came from and who made it. Regardless of whether the mark consists of letters, initials, or a crest (to name a few possibilities), one can distinguish what is bona fide from what is a sham imitation.

In the spiritual realm, there are false messiahs called antichrists, who try to deceive others into believing they are the Savior (see Matt. 24:23-24; 1 John 4:1-4). There are also demons who masquerade as servants of righteousness, even though they are the lackeys of Satan, who himself pretends to be an angel of light (see 2 Cor. 11:14-15). Believers must not be duped by these frauds, but follow only the Lord Jesus. He bears the true hallmark of messiahship, which certifies that He alone is who He claims to be—*the Christ, the Son of the living God* (Matt. 16:16).

Who Is Jesus? Benji Bruneel tackled this all-important question in *Kindred Spirit* magazine. The author noted that down through the centuries, the church has affirmed seven key truths about Christ: 1) Jesus was eternally preexistent (John 1:1-2; 8:58; 17:5). 2) Jesus was born of a virgin (Isa. 7:14; Matt. 1:22-23; Luke 1:26-38); 3) Jesus performed literal miracles (John 2:1-11; 6:1-13, 16-21; 9:1-11; 11:17-44); 4) Jesus was conscious of His divine Sonship (Matt. 28:18-20; John 10:30); 5) Jesus knew His destiny led to Calvary (Matt. 20:28; Mark 8:31; 9:31; Luke 9:22; John 3:16-18; 10:14-18); 6) Jesus experienced bodily resurrection (Matt. 28:1-10; Luke 24:36-49; John 20; 1 Cor. 15:3-7); and 7) Jesus will physically return to earth (Rev. 1:7; 19:11-16).

Learning His Name. Helen Keller grew up without being able to see or hear. Despite her visual and auditory handicaps, she became one of America's most famous women. She graduated from college and had an illustrious career as a writer and speaker. As a young girl, she was told the good news about Jesus for the first time. It was reported that upon hearing the Gospel, Helen Keller exclaimed, "I already knew that such a God existed. I simply did not know His name!"

In the life, death, and resurrection of the Lord Jesus, we learn the name and personality of the eternal, living God.

FOR YOUTH

■ **TOPIC:** What's My Line?
■ **QUESTIONS:** 1. Why did Jesus ask His disciples what the people thought of Him? 2. Why was this a pivotal moment in the life and ministry of Jesus? 3. Why was it important for Jesus to teach His disciples about His upcoming suffering, death, and resurrection? 4. What does Peter's rebuke of Jesus say about Peter's character at this time? 5. How was it possible for Peter to misunderstand the necessity of Jesus having to die on the cross?

■ **ILLUSTRATIONS:**
False Views of Christ. In 1975, the first annual Yoga and Meditation Conference was convened in Chicago, Illinois. Yogis, swamis, lamas, Zen masters, and other religious leaders from the East spoke at this conference, which attracted thousands of Americans. These speakers all praised the teachings of Jesus. In fact, they quoted the

Bible more than they quoted their own sacred writings. What they said beguiled most of their listeners, many of whom did not understand to what extent these religious leaders presented a distorted view of Christ.

Sun Myung Moon is the founder and leader of the Unification Church, which has millions of members worldwide. He is another religious leader who speaks highly of Jesus. Indeed, Moon's followers assert that they are Christians and that Jesus is their savior. Yet again, a faulty view of Christ is taught. Moon claims that Jesus' work on the cross has only partially redeemed humanity and that a second messiah must come to complete the work Jesus left unfinished.

These false views of Christ represent countless ways people have distorted the biblical teachings about the Savior. Even in the church, some people have tried to promote these views, and sadly, in some cases they have been successful.

Knowing Jesus' True Identity. *The Empire Strikes Back* is the follow-up movie to the blockbuster *Star Wars*. When the sequel opened, the waiting crowds in many cities were treated to an extravaganza: searchlights piercing the sky, vendors hawking programs, and a parade of costumed characters, including the villainous Darth Vader.

Every *Star Wars* fan knew Vader: powerful, mysterious, and evil. They also knew his young nemesis, Luke Skywalker: brave, honest, and good. Two characters could not be more opposite. Yet, the crowds waiting for the empire to strike back were about to be struck themselves. During the movie, Darth Vader revealed that he was Luke's father. Knowing his father's identity changed Luke's outlook on everything.

As this week's lesson describes, it is like that when we know Jesus' true identity. For centuries, historians and theologians have put labels on Him, ranging from "prophet," "priest," and "Savior" to "rebel," "heretic," and "madman." Today the debate about who Jesus is rages on. Why? Because knowing His true identity does change everything: our past, our present, and our future. Thankfully, He has already answered the questions about His identity in the pages of the Bible, and in the hearts and minds of people transformed by His power.

Just Who Is He? Have you ever noticed how Jesus is portrayed in literature, on stage, or on screen? In *Jesus Christ Superstar*, He is an idealistic, but deluded, would-be Messiah. In *Godspell*, Jesus is a lovable innocent who becomes a crucified clown. Jesus is a well-intentioned charlatan in *The Passover Plot*, while He is a fierce champion in the film titled *The Gospel According to Saint Matthew*. And in *The Last Temptation of Christ*, Nikos Kazantzakis portrays Jesus as a man who did not want to be the Messiah.

So, who is Jesus to the teens in your class: a superstar, a sap, or a Savior? Peter had no difficulty whatsoever in affirming Jesus as the Messiah. Hopefully, your students can say the same.

DOERS OF THE WORD

BACKGROUND SCRIPTURE: James 1
DEVOTIONAL READING: Psalm 92:1-8

KEY VERSE: Be ye doers of the word, and not
hearers only, deceiving your own selves. James 1:22.

KING JAMES VERSION

JAMES 1:17 Every good gift and every perfect gift is
from above, and cometh down from the Father of
lights, with whom is no variableness, neither shadow of
turning. 18 Of his own will begat he us with the word
of truth, that we should be a kind of firstfruits of his
creatures.

19 Wherefore, my beloved brethren, let every man be
swift to hear, slow to speak, slow to wrath: 20 For the
wrath of man worketh not the righteousness of God.
21 Wherefore lay apart all filthiness and superfluity of
naughtiness, and receive with meekness the engrafted
word, which is able to save your souls. 22 But be ye
doers of the word, and not hearers only, deceiving your
own selves. 23 For if any be a hearer of the word, and
not a doer, he is like unto a man beholding his natural
face in a glass: 24 For he beholdeth himself, and goeth
his way, and straightway forgetteth what manner of
man he was. 25 But whoso looketh into the perfect law
of liberty, and continueth therein, he being not a forgetful hearer, but a doer of the work, this man shall be
blessed in his deed. 26 If any man among you seem to
be religious, and bridleth not his tongue, but deceiveth
his own heart, this man's religion is vain. 27 Pure religion and undefiled before God and the Father is this,
To visit the fatherless and widows in their affliction,
and to keep himself unspotted from the world.

NEW REVISED STANDARD VERSION

JAMES 1:17 Every generous act of giving, with every
perfect gift, is from above, coming down from the
Father of lights, with whom there is no variation or
shadow due to change. 18 In fulfillment of his own purpose he gave us birth by the word of truth, so that we
would become a kind of first fruits of his creatures.

19 You must understand this, my beloved: let everyone be quick to listen, slow to speak, slow to anger;
20 for your anger does not produce God's righteousness. 21 Therefore rid yourselves of all sordidness and
rank growth of wickedness, and welcome with meekness the implanted word that has the power to save
your souls.

22 But be doers of the word, and not merely hearers
who deceive themselves. 23 For if any are hearers of
the word and not doers, they are like those who look at
themselves in a mirror; 24 for they look at themselves
and, on going away, immediately forget what they were
like. 25 But those who look into the perfect law, the
law of liberty, and persevere, being not hearers who
forget but doers who act—they will be blessed in their
doing.

26 If any think they are religious, and do not bridle
their tongues but deceive their hearts, their religion is
worthless. 27 Religion that is pure and undefiled before
God, the Father, is this: to care for orphans and widows
in their distress, and to keep oneself unstained by the
world.

10

Monday, July 28	James 1:1-4	*The Full Effect of Endurance*
Tuesday, July 29	James 1:5-8	*Ask in Faith*
Wednesday, July 30	James 1:9-11	*How to Boast*
Thursday, July 31	James 1:12-15	*Endure Temptation*
Friday, August 1	James 1:16-21	*Everything Is from God*
Saturday, August 2	James 1:22-27	*Blessed in Doing*
Sunday, August 3	Psalm 92:1-8	*How Great Are Your Works*

BACKGROUND

Law (Jas. 1:25) translates the Greek noun *nomos*. In some contexts, it refers to a formalized set of rules that prescribe what people must do. In the New Testament, *nomos* usually refers to the Pentateuch (the first five books of Moses), but it can also denote the Old Testament as a whole. While *nomos* primarily refers to that which regulates behavior, it can also denote the promise of God (see Luke 24:44). Additionally, *nomos* refers to a word of instruction that is divine, not human, in origin and that indicates the path of righteousness and blessing.

James 1:25 specifically uses *nomos* to denote the moral and ethical teachings of the Old Testament, especially as expressed in the Ten Commandments (2:10-11; see Ps. 19:7). This is the same law that Jesus said He came to fulfill, not abolish (Matt. 5:17), and which finds its culmination in Him (Rom. 10:4). He perfectly obeyed the law and brought to pass its types and prophecies. Also, in Him, the law finds its significance and continuity. Through the Savior's ministry of teaching and His redemptive work on the cross, those who are united to Him by faith are able to understand and apply the precepts of Scripture, as expressed in the law.

Before trusting in Christ, believers were slaves to sin (John 8:34). God used the law to make them aware of their transgressions and their need for a Savior (Gal. 3:19-24). Thus, rather than being an agent of sin, the law gives perfect expression to God's holiness, righteousness, and goodness (Rom. 7:7-12). It is true that believers are no longer under the condemnation of the law (Rom. 6:14; 7:4, 6; 1 Cor. 9:20; Gal. 2:15-19; 3:25). Nevertheless, the law continues to disclose whether believers are living for God as much as they should. They can do so when they allow the Spirit, rather than the sinful nature, to control them (Rom. 8:4). Indeed, believers who are genuinely led by the Spirit and manifest the love of Christ fulfill the intent of the law (13:9-10). For them, heeding the precepts embodied in the law results in spiritual freedom, not bondage (Jas. 1:25; 2:12).

NOTES ON THE PRINTED TEXT

Some of the early Christians to whom James wrote blamed God for their troubles. The author sternly rebuked this idea as false. God's divine and absolute goodness as the sovereign Lord renders evil powerless before Him. Thus, He is never tempted to do wrong; and because He acts in accordance with His holy nature, He never tempts anyone else (Jas. 1:13). The blame for temptation that produces sin rests squarely upon the evildoer's own shoulders (1:14). Notice that James did not blame the devil here. If Satan and his cohorts didn't exist or were rendered powerless, evil could still exist in the world. First and foremost, temptation comes from within. James used a fishing metaphor when he referred to a person being dragged away and enticed. Like a glimmering lure that attracts a fish from the deep, dark waters, the inner desire to sin entices the person to do what he or she knows is wrong. Sin results when a person is snared by a trap built and baited by his or her own hand.

James shifted from a fishing metaphor to that of the reproductive cycle. The process leading to sin begins with an enticement to transgress. If the temptation is entertained, then those evil desires conceive and the embryo of sin develops. After the sin is born, it matures and then produces its own terrible offspring—physical and spiritual death (1:15). In light of this, James admonished his readers not to be deluded by the false notion that God is the source of temptation (1:16). Instead, He is the origin of *every good gift and every perfect gift* (1:17). Without question, the needs sin promises to fulfill can be met, without guilt, by the provisions God sends. This same generous God is the Father, or sovereign Creator, of the celestial lights (namely, the sun, moon, and stars). Since He was able to create these magnificent sources of illumination and life, surely He can provide every other good gift. But unlike the variations of light and darkness produced by those heavenly bodies, God's virtue and goodness never fluctuate. The same power the unchanging Lord demonstrated at Creation is available to believers today to enable them to resist enticements and bear fruit for His glory.

Our Creator has provided redemption through the Lord Jesus. Indeed, by God's sovereign plan, He chose to give us spiritual birth through the message of truth (Jas. 1:18). The Spirit inwardly recreates our fallen human nature (John 3:5-8) so that we become a kind of *firstfruits* (Jas. 1:18) of God's redemptive plan for all of creation (see 1 Cor. 15:20). In Old Testament times, the firstfruits were both the initial and best portion of the entire harvest (Exod. 23:19; 34:26; Lev. 23:9-14; Ezek. 44:30). Metaphorically speaking, the redeemed are God's most prized possessions in all creation. They also are the guarantee of God's plan to liberate the entire creation at the second advent of Christ (Rom. 8:19-21; Col. 1:20). The regeneration of believing hearts gives a snapshot picture of what the new heavens and the new earth will be like when touched by the redeeming hand of God.

James instructed his fellow believers that even in the midst of trials, they should be quick to listen and slow to speak (Jas. 1:19). In the middle of a heated exchange, it is natural for us to begin forming our response to the other person even while he or she is still talking. Consequently, we tune out what this person is really saying. Patience and deference in speech takes concentrated effort, but in the long run pays great dividends in relationships. We usually walk away from such conversations feeling as if we've been understood and appreciated.

James also exhorted his readers to be slow to get angry. Human anger is a volatile emotion that can easily get out of control, especially in tense situations. When inappropriate forms of anger erupt, whether toward evildoers or unwanted circumstances, it does not accomplish God's *righteousness* (1:20). This means that the aftermath of human anger falls short of God's righteous moral standard, does not reflect the upright standing He gives believers in Christ, does not result in any of the good things God wants done, and is contrary to the equity and justice He will establish in His future eternal kingdom. In short, human anger does not produce the righteousness God desires, regardless of its form.

Inappropriate anger is just one example of immoral behavior and evil excess that arise when believers follow the desires of their sinful nature (see Gal. 5:19-21). James told his readers to set aside such vices. The phrase *lay apart* (Jas. 1:21) was often used of casting off burdensome clothing. Only a humble heart that acknowledges its own sinfulness and God's holiness is ready to accept and fully appropriate the message of His saving truth. It is like a seed that the Lord has been planted deep in the soil of our hearts. If we allow the Good News to take root and grow, we will spiritually thrive and experience the fullness of our redemption in Christ.

James told his readers that passively listening to God's Word was not enough to promote spiritual growth. It was just as important for them to obediently act upon what it says (1:22). To hear the Good News without implementing its teachings is nothing but self-deception. Those who hear but do not heed the Gospel are like people who observe what they look like in a mirror, walk away, and quickly forget the image they saw (1:23-24). In Bible times, a typical mirror was made of polished metal (such as copper, bronze, silver, or gold). Due to imperfections on the surfaces of these mirrors, they gave a distorted image of what they were reflecting. James exhorted his readers to look carefully into and fix their attention on the *perfect law of liberty* (1:25). They were to live out, not forget, what the law that gives freedom taught. The sustained and thoughtful study of God's Word would bring them true liberty, spiritual vitality, and abundant blessing in whatever they undertook.

James continued the theme of active Christianity with a look at the meaning of true religion. The Greek word translated *religious* (1:26) denotes the practice of external rituals and observances of a spiritual tradition, such as attendance at worship, prayer, fasting, and giving to the poor. Merely doing these things does not in itself constitute true religion. Those who are genuinely pious demonstrate their faith by controlling what they say. On the other hand, failure to bridle the tongue betrays the self-deception in those who regard themselves as religious and exposes a form of spirituality that has no eternal value.

James 1:27 shifts the focus from outward observances to service for others, particularly *the fatherless and widows*. In Scripture, widows, orphans, and aliens are usually depicted as the most helpless among the people. Often, they had none but God as their patron and protector (see Exod. 22:22-23; Deut. 10:18; Isa. 1:17). Moreover, in Bible times, there was no social safety net to catch the dispossessed and homeless when their source of support was suddenly gone. Widows, orphans, and foreigners were frequently reduced to begging, especially if there was no friend, relative, or benefactor to care for them (see Gen. 38:11; Ruth 1:8). Often, the disadvantaged were ignored by their neighbors, but Job rebuked those who *sent widows away empty, and the arms of the fatherless have been broken* (Job 22:9). The psalmist reminded widows and orphans that God cared for them (Ps. 146:9). And the law made provision for widows to glean grapes, grain, and olives out of the bounty of others (see Deut. 14:28-29; 24:19-21). In the end, according to Malachi 3:5, God's judgment will include those who oppress the disadvantaged.

James 1:27 reflects this biblical perspective when it focuses attention on orphans and widows who are living in a state of distress. The writer maintained that pure and undefiled religion is demonstrated, not just in rituals and observances, but in upright conduct and in righteous character. Examples of this type of behavior include caring for those in anguish and keeping oneself clean in a morally polluted world. The writer's intention in this passage was not to give a formal definition of religion. Rather, his aim was to draw a contrast between religion as mere ritual and observance and faith in action that pleases God. Religion that demonstrates genuine spirituality and Christian maturity is an active faith motivated by love.

SUGGESTIONS TO TEACHERS

James always connected truth and behavior. Scripture was to be obeyed, not just formulated into propositions for analysis and assent. The author stood in the line of the theology of the Old Testament in which law, or "torah," meant instruction for living and wisdom meant skill in living.

1. HEARING AND DOING. James believed that the Word of God has not been heard until it has been obeyed. Comprehending the meaning of the Word in the abstract without making concrete application of it is dangerous. A person can deceive himself or herself into thinking intellectual agreement with the Word impresses God.

2. LAW AND LIBERTY. When Paul wrote about the law, he had in mind an approach to salvation based on the efforts of the sinful nature to achieve the righteousness of God. James used the term "law" to represent God's moral principles inherent in human character and relationships. From James' perspective, living in harmony with God's law spiritually liberates believers, while living in opposition to God's law produces bondage to sin.

3. FAITH AND ACTIONS. James denied that inactive faith is real faith within the Body of Christ. James would agree with Paul that we are God's masterpiece, whom He created anew in the Messiah to accomplish many good things for His glory (Eph. 2:10). At the same time, the actions prompted by faith do not save. Faith in Christ alone saves. Actions validate the vitality of a person's saving faith.

■ TOPIC: Committed Living

■ QUESTIONS: 1. In what sense does God never change? 2. In what sense are believers a kind of firstfruits of all God has created? 3. In what way is the word planted within us able to save us? 4. In what sense is God's law perfect and a source of freedom? 5. What sort of religion does God accept as pure and faultless?

■ ILLUSTRATIONS:

Conforming to Culture. In *The Scandal of the Evangelical Conscience*, Ronald Sider analyzes why Christians live just like the rest of the world. He notes that popular American culture is "sick unto death" and that not even "the evangelical community has effectively resisted" this "corrosive influence." According to "numerous national polls conducted by highly respected pollsters," while evangelicals affirm the lordship of Christ, they demonstrate by their actions "allegiance to money, sex, and self-fulfillment."

What are some of the vices that plague contemporary Christians? According to Sider, these are the same ones lauded in Hollywood. Whether its television or radio, movies or magazines, the message is the same, namely, that "two-day marriages, constant divorces, and adulterous affairs" are the ethical standard by which to live. It's little wonder that many who claim to be Christians regard "sexual fidelity and lifelong marriage" to be "boring, old-fashioned, and silly."

James 1 contains a sorely needed prescription for the ethical cancer ravaging evangelical churches in the West. For instance, believers are urged to get rid of all the moral filth and evil in their lives and become doers of God's Word (1:21-22). Moreover, true spirituality is evident in a life characterized by virtue, especially as seen in caring for orphans and widows in their distress and refusing to be corrupted by the world (1:27).

Getting the Right Fit. According *NBC News* correspondent Rosiland Jordan, Ginger Dosedel of Beavercreek, Ohio, has turned "her living room into a makeshift military depot." In 2005, she established Sew Much Comfort, a non-profit group to "provide clothing for thousands of injured U.S. soldiers around the world." Dosedel's not alone in her efforts, either. More than one thousand people from across the U.S. have donated their "time, money, and talent to create street clothing for servicemembers with combat injuries."

The output of the group is impressive. Over 10,000 pieces—"everything from casual shirts to pants and shorts"—have been altered and sent to "20 military clinics and hospitals." The clothing items "provide easy access to burns and amputations that need regular cleaning and monitoring." Also, each piece is "adapted so that an injured soldier, airman, or marine can get dressed without help." This is a noteworthy way of caring for the distressed and neglected, especially as an expression of vital faith.

Concern for the Distressed. James 1:27 states that religion applauded by our heavenly Father includes looking after those in distress. Samaritan's Purse is one international relief organization providing spiritual and physical aid to hurting people around the world. For instance, in the spring of 2006, killer tornadoes struck northwestern Tennessee. Dozens of lives were taken and the roofs on over 400 homes were damaged or destroyed. Disaster officials said it was one of the deadliest storms in Tennessee history.

The organization reported that they "sent two truckloads of heavy-duty roofing plastic, material otherwise not available in the two hardest-hit counties, Dyer and Gibson." Volunteers from Samaritan's Purse were also "working alongside church teams to repair roofs." What an example this is for all believers to help meet the needs of people who are victims of war, poverty, natural disasters, disease, and famine with the purpose of sharing God's love through His Son, Jesus Christ.

FOR YOUTH

■ TOPIC: Right on Living
■ QUESTIONS: 1. Who is the source of every good and perfect gift? 2. How does God bring about spiritual rebirth? 3. What does human anger typically produce? 4. How do we deceive ourselves when we passively listen to the Word? 5. What sort of religion is worthless?

■ **ILLUSTRATIONS:**

Scriptural and Social Holiness. The Methodist movement began as a meeting to bring renewed devotion and spiritual holiness within the Church of England. John and Charles Wesley, its founders, met with a small group derisively called the "Holy Club" on the campus of Oxford University to engage in a disciplined pattern of worship, prayer, and Bible study. Here we see that true Christianity for the Wesleys involved both word and deed in promoting the kingdom of God on earth. Their ultimate goal was to practice scriptural and social holiness. As James 1:26-27 teaches, our personal relationship with Christ must also be translated into acts of love and service toward others.

Seven Deadly Sins. Thomas Benton, in an editorial appearing in *The Chronicle of Higher Education*, lists seven "deadly sins" he's observed among college students throughout a decade of teaching: sloth, greed, anger, lust, gluttony, envy, and pride. He says these transgressions "spring from thoughts and behaviors that, over time, become habits." These are individuals who have chosen "self-indulgence instead of self-denial and self-esteem instead of self-questioning." Also, these students fail to recognize that the misguided choices they make will ultimately cause them "more unhappiness than the more difficult paths they chose not to walk."

Benton advocates replacing these vices with "seven contrary virtues": diligence, generosity, patience, chastity, moderation, contentment, and humility. He notes the path to moral reform begins with recognizing "how little one really knows" about oneself. It involves fighting "unmerited pride" and spotting the "smallness of one's ambitions in the context of human history." For believers, this process of transformation begins with faith in Christ. He enables His followers, regardless of their age, to turn away from their sinful ways and live in a manner that is good and pleasing to God.

A Sterling Example. In 1962, Dolores Hart was a rising star in the film industry. The actress was 24 and had almost a dozen films to her credit, including two roles opposite Elvis Presley. But then she stunned the entertainment world by walking away from it all to devote herself to religious work. Over four decades would pass before she visited Hollywood again in 2006. According to Bob Thomas of *The Mercury News*, Hart was doing more than simply "renewing friendships from her studio years." She wanted to "spread awareness about a largely mysterious neurological disorder that afflicts countless Americans," including herself.

Hart told one group at an upscale hotel in Beverly Hills about her "ordeal with the disease." She also "testified at a congressional hearing" in Washington, D.C. In particular, she cited the "need for research into a cause and cure for the painful and crippling disease." Hart is a sterling example of committed living. She not only knows the truth of the Gospel, but also has responded to it throughout much of her adult life with transforming action.

Speed Demon. It was early afternoon when a police officer pulled over a teacher for speeding near the high school where he worked. While the officer checked the driver's license and registration, the lights on the police cruiser were flashing. Soon students passing by recognized the teacher sitting in his car. His embarrassment increased when some of the adolescents honked their car horns as they drove by, whistled, and yelled, "Way to go, speed demon!" Other teenage drivers slowed down and chided the teacher in a mocking tone of voice for speeding.

Eventually, the officer returned to the stopped car and asked the driver if he was a teacher at the high school. The driver, now feeling quite ashamed, admitted that he was. Just then, the police officer smiled and said, "I think you've learned your lesson about speeding!" And with that, the officer let the teacher go without issuing him a ticket. From that experience he learned the importance of setting an example in deed, not just in word. James 1:22 would wholeheartedly affirm this sentiment!

IMPARTIAL DISCIPLES

BACKGROUND SCRIPTURE: James 2
DEVOTIONAL READING: Matthew 25:31-46

KEY VERSE: Hath not God chosen the poor of this world rich in faith? James 2:5.

KING JAMES VERSION

JAMES 2:1 My brethren, have not the faith of our Lord Jesus Christ, the Lord of glory, with respect of persons. 2 For if there come unto your assembly a man with a gold ring, in goodly apparel, and there come in also a poor man in vile raiment; 3 And ye have respect to him that weareth the gay clothing, and say unto him, Sit thou here in a good place; and say to the poor, Stand thou there, or sit here under my footstool: 4 Are ye not then partial in yourselves, and are become judges of evil thoughts? 5 Hearken, my beloved brethren, Hath not God chosen the poor of this world rich in faith, and heirs of the kingdom which he hath promised to them that love him? 6 But ye have despised the poor. Do not rich men oppress you, and draw you before the judgment seats? 7 Do not they blaspheme that worthy name by the which ye are called?

8 If ye fulfil the royal law according to the scripture, Thou shalt love thy neighbour as thyself, ye do well: 9 But if ye have respect to persons, ye commit sin, and are convinced of the law as transgressors. 10 For whosoever shall keep the whole law, and yet offend in one point, he is guilty of all. 11 For he that said, Do not commit adultery, said also, Do not kill. Now if thou commit no adultery, yet if thou kill, thou art become a transgressor of the law. 12 So speak ye, and so do, as they that shall be judged by the law of liberty. 13 For he shall have judgment without mercy, that hath shewed no mercy; and mercy rejoiceth against judgment.

NEW REVISED STANDARD VERSION

JAMES 2:1 My brothers and sisters, do you with your acts of favoritism really believe in our glorious Lord Jesus Christ? 2 For if a person with gold rings and in fine clothes comes into your assembly, and if a poor person in dirty clothes also comes in, 3 and if you take notice of the one wearing the fine clothes and say, "Have a seat here, please," while to the one who is poor you say, "Stand there," or, "Sit at my feet," 4 have you not made distinctions among yourselves, and become judges with evil thoughts? 5 Listen, my beloved brothers and sisters. Has not God chosen the poor in the world to be rich in faith and to be heirs of the kingdom that he has promised to those who love him? 6 But you have dishonored the poor. Is it not the rich who oppress you? Is it not they who drag you into court? 7 Is it not they who blaspheme the excellent name that was invoked over you?

8 You do well if you really fulfill the royal law according to the scripture, "You shall love your neighbor as yourself." 9 But if you show partiality, you commit sin and are convicted by the law as transgressors. 10 For whoever keeps the whole law but fails in one point has become accountable for all of it. 11 For the one who said, "You shall not commit adultery," also said, "You shall not murder." Now if you do not commit adultery but if you murder, you have become a transgressor of the law. 12 So speak and so act as those who are to be judged by the law of liberty. 13 For judgment will be without mercy to anyone who has shown no mercy; mercy triumphs over judgment.

11

399

Monday, August 4	Matthew 25:31-46	*Sheep or Goats?*
Tuesday, August 5	James 2:1-4	*Acts of Favoritism?*
Wednesday, August 6	James 2:5-7	*God's Favored*
Thursday, August 7	James 2:8-11	*The Royal Law*
Friday, August 8	James 2:12-17	*The Law of Liberty*
Saturday, August 9	James 2:18-20	*Faith and Works*
Sunday, August 10	James 2:21-26	*An Active Faith*

BACKGROUND

James 2:8 refers to the *royal law* of Scripture. Within both Judaism and Christianity, the Ten Commandments (as found in Exod. 20:1-12 and Deut. 5:6-21) hold a premier status. Many consider them to be the moral law, or the basic list of God's universal, ethical norms for proper human conduct. Some also think the Ten Commandments are the theological foundation for all other ordinances and directives in Scripture. During the first century A.D., specialists in Judaism debated which of these commandments was the greatest. When an expert in the interpretation of the law asked Jesus for His opinion, He declared that loving God with all one's heart, soul, and mind was the foremost commandment (Matt. 22:37-38; see Deut. 6:5). The second premier directive was to love one's neighbor as oneself (Matt. 22:39; see Lev. 19:18). Jesus noted that the entire Old Testament was based on these two commands.

In a similar vein, Paul asserted that every directive recorded in Scripture was summed up in the command to love others as much as we love ourselves (Rom. 13:9). Verse 10 states that when we make every effort to treat others with the sensitivity and compassion of Christ, we do what is prescribed in the law. In short, love is the essence and fulfillment of the law. The apostle repeated the same truth in Galatians 5:14, when he wrote that believers, by loving and serving others, satisfied what the law required. Expressed differently, God's people are closest to pleasing Him when they are unconditional and unreserved in their compassion and kindness toward others.

NOTES ON THE PRINTED TEXT

The author of James, in addressing his friends in the faith, literally referred to the Savior as "our Lord Jesus Christ of glory" (2:1). The focus is on Jesus having the divine attribute of glory. The latter refers to the indescribable majesty and splendor of God (Isa. 6:3), as well as His moral perfection, especially in connection with His righteousness (Rom. 3:23). Jesus, as the *brightness of [God's] glory* (Heb. 1:3), is ever-present to deal with the problem of sin in the faith community. Concerning the readership of James, some believers were guilty of showing favoritism and partiality toward the wealthy among them (2:1). James made it clear that all forms of prejudice had to stop. The construction of the original sentence and his accusation in 2:6 indicates that this discrimination had been an ongoing problem.

The scene that follows James 2:1 serves as an illustration to drive home a point. The author asked his readers to imagine two people who visited the Christian *assembly* (2:2). This term renders the Greek noun *synagogue*, which originally referred to a Jewish place of worship. In this verse, it denotes a gathering of the church, possibly in a home or even in a synagogue (which is where some early Christians may have met). One person at the assembly was wealthy, for he was well-dressed and wearing gold jewelry. In those days, it was a common practice to wear gold rings as a sign of economic success (see Luke 15:22) and high social status (such as being a politician or important official). The other person in filthy, old rags was poor.

The seating arrangement at gatherings indicated the honor and respect extended to those present. For example, imagine the hypothetical congregation giving special attention and a good seat to the rich person. Meanwhile, the impoverished beggar had only two options: either remain standing or be seated in the lowliest spot in the house, namely, out of sight on the floor (Jas. 2:3). Perhaps the author knew about such a situation taking place among his readers. In any case, James labeled this behavior as discrimination, and it showed that the judgments being made were guided by evil motives (2:4). In brief, it was unjust to say that some people (such as the rich) were better than others (such as the poor).

The author asked several pointed questions to show why all forms of prejudice are morally wrong and make no sense. Against the backdrop of the first question is the faulty assumption that the presence of great wealth in one's life was evidence of God's approval. Oppositely, those who were impoverished supposedly were languishing under the searing gaze of God's disapproval. James 2:5 shatters these mistaken notions by maintaining that God has deliberately chosen the poor of the world to be rich in faith. They also are the ones who will inherit the divine kingdom.

These truths mirror Jesus' declaration in Luke 6:20, where He revealed that God will bless those who are poor with His kingdom. Scripture teaches that God has extended His free gift of salvation to people of all economic classes. The poor, however, tend to be more aware of their need for God. Also, the security often associated with wealth is a spiritual barrier that the poor don't have to overcome. Consider Proverbs 30:8-9, where Agur prayed that God would not make him excessively rich lest he be tempted to abandon his faith for lack of want. There's also the rich young ruler, who rejected Jesus' invitation to follow Him because the young man's security was too wrapped up in his wealth (see Matt. 19:16-26).

In the early years of the church, the Gospel was primarily spread throughout the lower classes in the Roman Empire. Tragically, these were the very ones self-appointed judges had dishonored and disdained. It was even more incongruous to favor the wealthy, for they had exploited and persecuted Christians (Jas. 2:6). The oppression of the rich involved using the court system to intimidate and harass believers. The wealthy had also spoken disrespectfully and irreverently of the noble name of the glorious Messiah (2:7). *Which ye were called* is more literally rendered "which has been called upon you." Some think this phrase refers to the time when new converts were baptized and affirmed their devotion to Christ (see Matt. 28:19; Acts 2:28; 8:16, 36-38; 16:30-33). During the church ritual, participants confessed their faith in the Savior. Then, the leaders of the congregation invoked the honorable name of the Lord Jesus over these believers to signify His ownership of them as His people (see 2 Chron. 7:14; Isa. 63:19; Jer. 14:9; 15:16; Dan. 9:19; Amos 9:12; Acts 15:17).

According to James 2:8, the directive recorded in Leviticus 19:18 is the supreme commandment in terms of defining how people should treat one another. This dictum is also royal, for among all the commandments given by God (who is the sovereign King of the universe), it sums up the entirety of the law. James 2:8 builds on this truth by stressing that the royal law will become the guiding principle in the future messianic kingdom. The author observed that believers are doing well when they love others as much as they love themselves. The point is that they could not heed the most important directive in Scripture and discriminate against others at the same time.

The author set up a sharp contrast between treating others the way we would like to be treated and showing favoritism toward somebody for any reason (Jas. 2:9). Doing the first pleases God, while doing the second is sin. Accordingly, failing to observe the royal law—the most liberating, relationship-building command of God—makes one a lawbreaker. Perhaps James thought that some among his readers would look upon showing favoritism as more a social convention than as sin. How, they might ask, could such a custom compare to sins like adultery and murder (2:11)? The answer James provided is clear and direct. If we transgress any part of the law, we are guilty of breaking all of it (2:10).

The author seems to have associated obedience to the law with fellowship with God, the one who gave the law. From this perspective, striving to obey is a display of faith and springs from love. Disobedience to God's law, on the other hand, is a breach of faith that disrupts fellowship with God, the lawgiver. In 2:12, the author placed an equally strong emphasis on talking and acting as if one is going to be judged by the liberating law of God. There is also an emphasis in the original language to make this behavior a matter of habit. Because of the wise counsel contained in God's law, James could say that it gives spiritual freedom (see 1:25)—but only if it is respected and obeyed. Disobedience results in bondage and restricted living.

According to 2:13, the believer who has been merciful will be shown mercy when his or her character flaws and weaknesses are exposed on the final day. In contrast, those who have shown little mercy to others will receive little themselves. Furthermore, the believer who has demonstrated mercy to others will have nothing to fear at the time of divine assessment, for the mercy shown to him or her will triumph over that judgment (see 1 John 4:17). As Jesus' followers strive to become more merciful, there is hope. The liberating power of Christ working within them makes it possible for them to obey God more fully and completely.

In addition to James 2:12-13, the writings of Paul teach that a future day of evaluation awaits believers. Sometime after Jesus' return, He will preside over the judgment (1 Cor. 4:5). In relation to believers, the issue at the judgment seat of Christ will not be our spiritual status (a determination of whether we are saved or lost), but rather the bestowal of rewards (see 2 Cor. 5:10). All that a believer has thought and done will be scrutinized at that time. Jesus' bestowal of rewards will be conducted in a fair and impartial manner. Whatever was done contrary to God's wishes will be regarded as worthless and will not be rewarded. Whatever was accomplished through the power of the Holy Spirit will be regarded as worthy of praise and will be rewarded (see 1 Cor. 3:10-15). Clearly, one of the qualities assessed in this judgment is the degree of mercy shown by the Christian.

SUGGESTIONS TO TEACHERS

The church gathering in this week's passage reflected the values of the world: economic accumulation, social status, and outward appearance. When the church reflects God's priorities, however, it will usually value the opposite of what our overall culture applauds.

1. VALUING THE POOR. God has always valued the poor in a way our world does not. For example, the people whom God chose to use in history were slaves in Egypt. When God became human, He came as a poor Galilean with no influence. Jesus identified so closely with the hungry, thirsty, naked, and estranged that He said that to mistreat them was to mistreat Him (Matt. 25:31-46). And the early church was not populated with the elite of society (see 1 Cor. 1:26).

2. RECOGNIZING A PLACE FOR THE RICH. Admittedly, God can use rich people. Abraham was rich and owned a lot of land and flocks. Moses lived in the luxury of Pharaoh's court for 40 years. Paul and Luke were well-educated. But God also seems to delight in using the underdog, the unexpected person, so that His power is made visible through their weakness (2 Cor. 12:9-10). The temptations for the rich are great: enticements to become proud, to trust in what is untrustworthy and uncertain, and so on (1 Tim. 6:7). At one point in history, the church rented favored pews to people who could pay for them. This practice was abolished, but Christians must root out all favored treatment of people based on money.

3. REFUSING TO BE ENAMORED BY WEALTH. Political parties give special privileges to generous benefactors, but this should not happen in the community of faith. Money must never be a bargaining chip or a way to gain status or leadership in the church. Within any congregation, leadership and respect are given to those who honor and obey the royal law of love: to be as compassionate and kind to others as they want others to be to them. With the Spirit's help and the encouragement of one another, it is possible for this to become a consistent reality throughout Christ's Body.

■ TOPIC: Honoring All People

■ QUESTIONS: 1. What does it mean to show favoritism? 2. What example did James describe to illustrate what he meant by showing favoritism? 3. Why would God chose the poor of this world to be rich in faith? 4. Why is it illogical to favor the rich over the poor? 5. How is possible that one transgression of God's law makes one guilty of violating all of it?

■ ILLUSTRATIONS:

Accommodating the Elderly. According to a report appearing in *USA Today*, a motorcycle officer ticketed 82-year-old Mayvis Coyle for "taking too long to cross a street." When the light turned green at Foothill Boulevard in San Fernando Valley, California, the elderly great-great-grandmother "began shuffling with her cane," but failed to complete the crossing before the lighted turned red. Her fine for allegedly "obstructing traffic" was $114.

Coyle said she thought receiving the ticket was "completely outrageous." Others have noted that the "light in question doesn't give people enough time to cross the busy, five-lane boulevard." For instance, Edith Krause, who is 78, has to use an "electric cart because she has difficulty walking." Even then, she noted, "I can go halfway, then the light changes." It's not much different for high school students. Unless they run across the boulevard, the light changes before they can get to the other side.

Being more sensitive to the needs of the elderly concerns Wendy Greuel, a councilwoman. She said, "We should look at those areas with predominantly seniors and accommodate their needs in intersections." Honoring all people, particularly those with special needs, finds support in James 2:5, which says that God has chosen those who are nobodies from the world's perspective to be heirs of the kingdom.

Who Are the Poor. How many poor people do you know personally? Unfortunately, as adults grow older, our circle of friends often becomes more homogeneous. It becomes more difficult to bridge our socioeconomic strata. When asked about the poor, many adults respond with "Hey, it's not my fault. . . . They aren't really trying hard enough. . . . I could get a job if I were them. . . . Let them pull themselves up by their own bootstraps. . . . We're just weakening them by helping them all the time."

Do any of those comments sound familiar? Many of us think that way, even if we haven't made the overt statements. Adults also use an interesting criterion to establish exactly who is "poor." Ask your students what is their definition of "poor." Adults may find that those just above the poverty line are ignored or treated worse than those below it. Regardless of the social and economic circumstances of the people we encounter, the Letter of James summons us to honor them unconditionally with the kindness, compassion, and respect that Christ offers.

Are We Among the Poor? This week's lesson focuses on an attitude that treats all people according to their socioeconomic status. The fact is, most adults are only a few paychecks away from financial disaster. North America seems to run on credit, and most adults get sucked into debt beyond their limit.

A woman came into my office and shared with me that she and her husband had run up a $16,000 bill on one credit card and $8,000 on another! The interest was killing them and I could sense the panic in her voice. Unfortunately, that is fast becoming a common scenario. Loving the poor? Given the right circumstances, any of us might quickly be part of that group!

FOR YOUTH

■ **TOPIC:** No Bench? Don't Judge!
■ **QUESTIONS:** 1. Why is it morally wrong to show favoritism? 2. How is discrimination evident in the illustration James gave? 3. Why would God give His future kingdom to the poor of this world? 4. What is the royal law found in Scripture? 5. How is it possible for mercy to triumph over judgment?

■ **ILLUSTRATIONS:**

With the Judgment You Make. Bill had wild hair, wore jeans and a T-shirt with holes in it, and had no shoes. That was his wardrobe for his entire four years of college. He was kind of esoteric and extremely bright. Also, he had become a Christian while attending college.

Across the street from the campus was a very traditional church. The congregation wanted to develop a ministry to the college students, but the members weren't sure how to go about it. Then one day Bill decided to attend the church. He entered the building in his customary wardrobe.

Since the service had already started, Bill walked down the aisle looking for a seat. The church was packed, and Bill couldn't find a seat. As he moseyed around, the people were growing a bit uncomfortable, but no one said anything. Bill moved closer and closer to the pulpit and, when he realized there were no seats, he sat down on the floor in front of the first pew. By now, the congregation was really uptight, and the tension in the air was thick.

It was then that the minister realized that, from the back of the church, one of the older deacons had begun slowly making his way toward Bill. The deacon was in his eighties, had silver-gray hair, and was wearing a three-piece suit. He was a godly man, very elegant, very dignified, and very courtly. He shuffled down the aisle with a cane. As he slowly inched toward the college student, the congregation was thinking that they couldn't really blame the deacon for what he was about to do.

It took well over a minute for the deacon to reach Bill. The church was completely silent except for the clicking of the man's cane. All eyes were focused on him. Even the minister had held off on his sermon until the deacon had finished what he had planned to do.

Finally, the deacon reached the front of the sanctuary. Then the congregation watched in utter amazement as the elderly man dropped his cane on the floor. With great difficulty, he lowered himself and sat down next to Bill so that he wouldn't be alone. When the minister stepped behind the pulpit, he said, "What I'm about to preach, you will not remember for very long. But what you have seen here, you must never forget."

Blurry Spiritual Vision. Have you ever tried to remove a speck of dirt or a tiny insect from your eye by yourself? It's hard because you can't see well enough to do it. Jesus said that often some things in our lives blur our spiritual vision. Without clear vision, we cannot give help to others, we cannot choose the right moral path, and we cannot discern what is true from what is false.

Jesus made it clear that blurry spiritual vision is caused by pride, self-righteousness, hypocrisy, and a failure to love others. The result can be the kind of judgmental attitude that James condemned in his letter. How important it is to have our spiritual eyes free of obstructions.

Sin clouds our judgment and keeps us from following God's ways. The first step in obtaining clearer spiritual vision is to confess our sin. When we come to Jesus in repentance and faith, we are asking Him to give us clearer vision. The moment we make this our prayer request, our relationships with others will improve.

Changed Baseball and Changed America. On April 15, 1947, a 28-year-old rookie named Jackie Robinson started a professional baseball game as the first baseman for the Brooklyn Dodgers at Ebbets Field against the Boston Braves. He was the first African American to appear in a major league baseball game since well before the turn of the century.

The game and the nation would never be the same. The young athlete suffered intense discrimination from other players, many coaches, and fans. But Robinson, son of a sharecropper and grandson of a slave, was not only a skilled player, but also a mature leader. Accepting and enduring the slurs and curses day after day, he lead the nation through its national pastime, the game of baseball, in a sociological revolution. His sacrifice helped to integrate sports everywhere.

Today, a steady stream of visitors comes daily to the Cypress Hills Cemetery in New York, near the Brooklyn-Queens border, to visit the grave of Jackie Robinson. A stone bearing his family's name identifies the plot. Underneath, carved into the granite, are the words of one of Jackie Robinson's favorite sayings: "A life is not important except in the impact it has on other lives." There is no better description of true leadership!

WISE SPEAKERS

BACKGROUND SCRIPTURE: James 3
DEVOTIONAL READING: Proverbs 15:1-4; 16:21-24

KEY VERSE: Out of the same mouth proceedeth blessing and cursing. My brethren, these things ought not so to be. James 3:10.

KING JAMES VERSION

JAMES 3:1 My brethren, be not many masters, knowing that we shall receive the greater condemnation. 2 For in many things we offend all. If any man offend not in word, the same is a perfect man, and able also to bridle the whole body. 3 Behold, we put bits in the horses' mouths, that they may obey us; and we turn about their whole body. 4 Behold also the ships, which though they be so great, and are driven of fierce winds, yet are they turned about with a very small helm, whithersoever the governor listeth. 5 Even so the tongue is a little member, and boasteth great things. Behold, how great a matter a little fire kindleth! 6 And the tongue is a fire, a world of iniquity: so is the tongue among our members, that it defileth the whole body, and setteth on fire the course of nature; and it is set on fire of hell. 7 For every kind of beasts, and of birds, and of serpents, and of things in the sea, is tamed, and hath been tamed of mankind: 8 But the tongue can no man tame; it is an unruly evil, full of deadly poison. 9 Therewith bless we God, even the Father; and therewith curse we men, which are made after the similitude of God. 10 Out of the same mouth proceedeth blessing and cursing. My brethren, these things ought not so to be. . . .

13 Who is a wise man and endued with knowledge among you? let him shew out of a good conversation his works with meekness of wisdom. 14 But if ye have bitter envying and strife in your hearts, glory not, and lie not against the truth. 15 This wisdom descendeth not from above, but is earthly, sensual, devilish. 16 For where envying and strife is, there is confusion and every evil work. 17 But the wisdom that is from above is first pure, then peaceable, gentle, and easy to be intreated, full of mercy and good fruits, without partiality, and without hypocrisy. 18 And the fruit of righteousness is sown in peace of them that make peace.

NEW REVISED STANDARD VERSION

JAMES 3:1 Not many of you should become teachers, my brothers and sisters, for you know that we who teach will be judged with greater strictness. 2 For all of us make many mistakes. Anyone who makes no mistakes in speaking is perfect, able to keep the whole body in check with a bridle. 3 If we put bits into the mouths of horses to make them obey us, we guide their whole bodies. 4 Or look at ships: though they are so large that it takes strong winds to drive them, yet they are guided by a very small rudder wherever the will of the pilot directs. 5 So also the tongue is a small member, yet it boasts of great exploits.

How great a forest is set ablaze by a small fire! 6 And the tongue is a fire. The tongue is placed among our members as a world of iniquity; it stains the whole body, sets on fire the cycle of nature, and is itself set on fire by hell. 7 For every species of beast and bird, of reptile and sea creature, can be tamed and has been tamed by the human species, 8 but no one can tame the tongue—a restless evil, full of deadly poison. 9 With it we bless the Lord and Father, and with it we curse those who are made in the likeness of God. 10 From the same mouth come blessing and cursing. My brothers and sisters, this ought not to be so. . . .

13 Who is wise and understanding among you? Show by your good life that your works are done with gentleness born of wisdom. 14 But if you have bitter envy and selfish ambition in your hearts, do not be boastful and false to the truth. 15 Such wisdom does not come down from above, but is earthly, unspiritual, devilish. 16 For where there is envy and selfish ambition, there will also be disorder and wickedness of every kind. 17 But the wisdom from above is first pure, then peaceable, gentle, willing to yield, full of mercy and good fruits, without a trace of partiality or hypocrisy. 18 And a harvest of righteousness is sown in peace for those who make peace.

12

HOME BIBLE READINGS

BACKGROUND

The phrase *full of deadly poison* (Jas. 3:8) brings to mind Psalm 140:3. *They have sharpened their tongues like a serpent; adders' poison is under their lips.* Like a poisonous snake concealed in the brush beside a hiking trail, the tongue is loaded with deadly venom and poised to strike. Though the viper is a small serpent, it has a particularly mean disposition. It strikes swiftly and holds fast to its victim with great tenacity. The fact that it hisses each time it breathes in and out gives it the appearance of being an adder with an attitude. It is no wonder James admonished in 1:19, *be swift to hear, slow to speak.*

In the eastern Mediterranean area, there are some 20 poisonous snakes. Several of these are true vipers (called "adders" in some translations of the Bible). The class of vipers are poisonous snakes with curved, retracted fangs that extend forward when the serpent strikes. One snake in this class, called the horned viper, though only 12 to 18 inches long, has been known to strike at large animals like horses and bears (Gen. 49:17). This snake often buries itself in the sand. With only its eyes and the hornlike protrusions on its head visible, it lies in wait to ambush an unsuspecting victim. Viper poison attacks the central nervous system and destroys red blood cells. Jesus and John the Baptizer both made reference to the viper (Matt. 3:7; 12:34; 23:33). Luke also recorded an incident in which a viper struck Paul (Acts 28:3).

NOTES ON THE PRINTED TEXT

Perhaps there was great eagerness among many early Christians to teach. It was a ministry that carried considerable rank and honor, like that of rabbi in Jewish circles. Even today, Bible teachers are some of the most admired people in the church. Those who explain the meaning of Scripture to others in formal settings come across as being more knowledgeable than and perhaps even a notch above other Christians. As we consider James 3:1, however, we are forced to reassess this notion. We discover that knowing divine truth is not necessarily the same as living it. Expressed differently, it is one thing to have an intellectual grasp of the Bible, but it is quite another matter to practice what it teaches.

Perhaps that is why James issued a warning to Christians. While it is noble to aspire to a teaching ministry, we should also be ready to be judged more strictly. Put another way, God will evaluate our lives more rigorously and stringently based on our increased awareness of the truth and influence over the lives of others. This sobering admonition is not intended to discourage teachers in the church who are gifted and called by God. Providing biblical instruction continues to be an essential part of carrying out Jesus' Great Commission to make disciples (Matt. 28:19-20). But the responsibility of teaching carries with it a degree of power and authority, and regrettably, this often attracts people who are not called by God to instruct others in Scripture, but rather who desire the esteem and influence the position seems to offer.

James 3:2, in affirming that all of us make many mistakes, used a verb that describes active sin, not simply human error. According to the context, much of this moral stumbling occurs because of harmful forms of speech (including lying, slander, and gossip, to name a few examples). The writer revealed that if people can control their tongue, they can control their entire body and are perfectly self-controlled people. The Greek adjective rendered *perfect* denotes those who are fully developed in a moral sense and meet the highest ethical standards in their conduct (see Matt. 5:48). The emphasis is on the maturity of one's behavior. The idea is that believers who do not sin with their tongues will probably show themselves mature in other areas of their lives. The simple truth is that there can be no spiritual maturity while the tongue remains untamed and out of control.

James 3:3-4 offers two illustrations to demonstrate how a small device can positively or negatively control the destiny of a much larger vehicle. First, an eight-ounce metal bar placed in the mouth of a 1,000-pound horse allows the rider to dictate to the large animal where it will go (3:3). Second, a ship's rudder (a wooden blade about the size of a person's arm) determines the course of its many-times-larger vessel. The pilot steering the 500-foot vessel needs only to change the direction of the rudder and, despite harsh winds, can keep the ship on course (3:4).

James 3:5 says that though the tongue is a small member of the human body, it can do a great deal of good or evil. Also, despite the tongue's pretentious claims, it can wreck untold havoc in the lives of its victims. To illustrate his point, James noted how a small spark, which by itself is extinguished in the blink of an eye, can reduce acres of forest to a charred rubble. In a sense, the tongue is like a flame of *fire* (3:6), because a few ill-chosen words can do a vast amount of damage in little time. And like an incendiary device, the tongue can set a person's entire life on fire. In short, the tongue is a source of *iniquity*. When the tongue goes unchecked, it spews forth wickedness that spiritually defiles the whole person as well as the entire direction of one's existence. Perhaps the writer was thinking of Jesus' teaching that a person's words reflect what is really in his or her heart (see Luke 6:45). These blunt statements should not surprise us when we realize that the tongue is *set on fire [by] hell* (Jas. 3:6). The implication is that the tongue, when left uncontrolled, could become a tool for vice, rather than virtue. For instance, under the influence of the devil, people can say things that are quite destructive in nature.

In 3:7-12, the writer continued his description of the tongue. He had just compared this small organ to an out-of-control fire. Next, he compared it to an untamed animal. The author pointed out that while all kinds of animals—birds, reptiles, and even sea creatures—had been tamed and were continuing to be domesticated, one entity, the tongue, was not included among them (3:7-8). Humankind has successfully carried out God's command to rule over virtually every aspect of creation (Gen. 1:26). But the tongue has remained beyond the control of God's crowning creation. To subdue that entity, nothing less than the power of God Himself is required. The reason the author gave his readers for their lack of success in taming the tongue was blunt. James 3:8 says the human instrument of speech is *unruly* and *evil*. The Greek word translated *unruly* suggests a staggering, unsteady, and uncontrollable kind of wickedness. The implication, perhaps, is that the tongue could strike anytime, without warning or even rational cause.

The tongue—representing intelligent human speech—shows its deadly nature in its erratic and inconsistent behavior. One moment it blesses God; the next it curses a human made in God's image (Jas. 3:9; see Gen. 1:26-27). Even within fallen humanity, though the image of God has been defaced through sin, people still bear the divine likeness to some degree (Gen. 5:1; 9:6), and this sets them apart from the rest of earth's creatures. James despaired that the same mouth could spout blessings and cursings in almost one breath. Such inconsistency does not occur in the natural world. A spring gives either fresh or brackish water, not one now and the other later. Also, fruit trees and vines bear their natural harvests, never unnatural ones. The tongue, by contrast, is perverse (Jas. 3:10-12).

We can imagine some Bible teachers claiming they were wise and understood God's ways. James 3:13 admonished them to prove their moral insight and intellectual perception by living in an honorable manner. They were also to show their expert knowledge by doing good works with the humility that comes from godly wisdom. Wisdom may be defined as the ability to handle matters skillfully, to exercise sound judgment, and to apply biblical truths to one's conduct. Divine wisdom guides the believer to live in an upright, virtuous, and well-pleasing manner. The wise person is committed to God, devoted to His will, and obedient to His Word.

Against the backdrop of humility and graciousness that characterizes a truly wise person, it is easier to spot the cheap imitations. The worldly wise (the so-called "street smart") are characterized by bitterness, envy, and selfish ambition. The trail of deceit and strife they leave behind is nothing to boast about; in fact, their bragging and lying are used to cover up the truth (3:14). James 3:15 spotlights the real source of worldly wisdom. The jealousy and selfishness it spawns originate from below, not from heaven. In this light, we can appreciate more fully the emphasis being placed here on seeking divine wisdom.

James 3:16 explains that where envy and selfish ambition are present, the natural result is confusion and a variety of immoral behaviors. These vices, of course, are in direct opposition to the unity, peace, and righteousness God intends to be at work in the relationships His people have with one another. A person focused on nothing but his or her own advancement is less likely to be concerned with the "troublesome" issue of ethics. Moral boundaries are usually perceived by such people as obstacles in the way of their success. Since the Lord is neither a God of disorder nor receptive toward evil, the worldly wisdom that produces such bitter fruit cannot come from Him (see 1 Cor. 14:33; 1 John 1:5).

After being exposed to the unwholesome images associated with earthly wisdom, it is refreshing to learn more about heavenly wisdom. First of all, divine prudence is known for its purity and compassion. Such, in turn, promotes tranquility and harmony, gentleness and humility (Jas. 3:17). The wisdom from above is furthermore characterized by sensibility and kindness, mercifulness and charity, impartiality and sincerity. None of these virtues comes about immediately; rather, the Spirit cultivates them as believers yield to God's will. The emphasis in 3:18 is on being peacemakers, rather than peace-breakers. James compares peace to seeds that the godly plant. The harvest is an abundance of righteousness, goodness, and justice. These graces are worth cultivating!

SUGGESTIONS TO TEACHERS

Taming the tongue is a discipline rarely achieved by most adults. How many of your students have wished to take back something they blurted out? Most adults have to consciously guard their tongues. Why is this so incredibly difficult? Apart from God's wisdom, we are helpless to counter the destructive effects of our speech on our relationships with God and other people.

1. POWERFUL SPEECH. Leaders in the church will give an account for how they handle the authority they exercise. Perhaps the greatest burden a teacher bears is the responsibility to govern his or her tongue. Our words wield enormous power in the lives of those to whom we speak. The little tongue may be the most powerful member of the body.

2. DEVASTATING SPEECH. Thoughtless or malicious speech lays waste to lives, reputations, and careers like a fire consuming a forest and leaving it a blackened, smoking wasteland. No human power is able to exercise effective, lasting control over the tongue.

3. INCONSISTENT SPEECH. The tongue can alternately bless and curse, build up and tear down. Its potential for good is limitless; so is its power for evil. The Jekyll and Hyde nature of human speech is unparalleled in the natural world where animate and inanimate beings have consistent characters. The tongue is frightening in its power, destructive capacity, and inconsistent, unpredictable character.

4. TWO WISDOMS. There are two wisdoms at work in the world. They reveal themselves in radically different ways of behaving. Their contrast explains the schizophrenia of our speech. The wisdom of the earth is based on envy, expresses itself in selfish ambition, and results in turmoil and sin. Its spiritual nature is demonic. The wisdom from above is based on purity, expresses itself in sweet reasonableness, and results in peace and righteousness. Its spiritual nature is godly.

FOR ADULTS

■ **TOPIC:** Thoughtful Speech

■ **QUESTIONS:** 1. Why do you think James encouraged those who taught in the church to be careful about what they said with their tongues? 2. In what ways is being able to control one's tongue, or speech, an indication of spiritual maturity? 3. In what ways can an uncontrolled tongue bring great harm and sadness to oneself and others? 4. Why is earthly wisdom so prone to brag about how much it supposedly knows? 5. What is the fruit of godly wisdom, and why is it to be preferred over that of earthly wisdom?

■ **ILLUSTRATIONS:**

The Boomerang Effect. Our words are like boomerangs. They come back either to haunt us or bless us. In this week's lesson about speech, we find many moral boomerangs. Some of them warn us about the serious repercussions and troubles that will come upon us if we do not control our tongues. Others promise us the rich blessings of proper speech, directed by the Word of God and controlled by the Holy Spirit.

Every person could probably tell stories filled with regrets of when their "big mouth" caused them to sin, as well as deep satisfaction when the Lord gave them just the right words to say. The sins of the tongue are many, and each one warrants our study because we need to know the consequences of our failures to heed these warnings.

On the other hand, people need to be encouraged to practice blessing others with their words. We don't need instructions in how to sin with our tongues, but we do need help in guarding our lips, giving gentle answers, and ministering "pleasant words" to others. We can help each other by telling stories of how we have learned to do better.

Furor over Words. James 3:5-6 deals with the incendiary power of the tongue. We learn that this organ of speech has the ability to set ablaze the course of human existence, oftentimes with disastrous results. Correspondents Emily Taguchi and Lee Wang of *Frontline World* reported on one such episode involving China and Japan in which, at one juncture, "diplomatic relations" between the two nations reached "a breaking point."

It began in April 2005, when a seemingly innocuous "Japanese junior high school textbook" became the catalyst that sparked a furor between the two economic rivals of east Asia. The publication focused on the Nanjing Massacre, which took place more than six decades earlier during World War II. According to historians, it was "one of the most infamous instances of Japanese war-time atrocities in China." The textbook, however, down-played the event by calling it an "incident."

News of this "sent thousands of Chinese onto the streets." Three weeks of "what amounted to a rare instance of state-sanctioned protest" ensued. Government officials even allowed protesters to besiege "the Japanese embassy with bottles and rocks" and scrawl "threats of boycott on the storefronts of Japanese businesses." Eventually, the furor subsided, but "China and Japan remain bitterly divided over how to move forward from the past."

Words and Anger Burn. In the spring of 1894, the Baltimore Orioles went to Boston to play a routine baseball game. But what happened that day was anything but routine.

The Orioles' John McGraw got into a fight with the Boston third baseman. Within minutes, all the players from both teams had joined in the brawl. The warfare spread to the grandstands. Among the fans, the conflict went from bad to worse. Someone set fire to the wooden stands and the entire ballpark burned to the ground. Not only that, but the fire spread to 107 other Boston buildings as well.

Folly of Selfish Wisdom. Two Texans were trying to impress one another with their ranches. One asked the other, "What's the name of your spread?"

The second rancher boasted, "Why, it's the Rocking R, ABC, Flying Q, Circle C, Bar U, Staple Four, Box D, Rolling M, Rainbow's End, Silver Spur Ranch."

The first rancher was impressed. "Go-olly! What a handle! How many head of cattle do you run?"

"Actually, not many," the second rancher admitted. "Very few survive the branding."

■ **TOPIC:** Put a Sock in It!

■ **QUESTIONS:** 1. What words of caution did James offer regarding the tongue? 2. What harm did James say could come through the inappropriate use of speech? 3. Why should we shun ungodly forms of wisdom? 4. Why is it sometimes hard for people to control their speech? 5. What can we do to promote peace through the things we say?

■ **ILLUSTRATIONS:**

Heated Words. A waitress carrying a two-gallon container of dressing to the salad bar paused for a second while coming through the swinging doors from the kitchen. Bad idea. The doors whacked her backside, knocked her forward, and launched two gallons of dressing over a well-dressed customer. It was 12:30 on a Sunday afternoon. Where had a guy in a suit and tie come from at 12:30 on Sunday afternoon?

The customer leaped to his feet with dressing oozing from his hair, covering his glasses, coating his face, drenching his jacket, shirt, tie, and trousers, and puddling around his smeared shoes. Two gallons of it.

The diner spluttered and swore. Then he found his tongue. "You're so stupid! I can't believe you could do such a stupid, stupid thing. This is a brand-new suit. It cost me $300. I want to see the manager!"

The shaken waitress hurried off to get the manager, who remembered his training and asked blandly, "Is there a problem?"

The man ranted, "Is there a problem? She's ruined my $300 suit. It's brand new. I want a new suit!"

The manager says, "We'll be glad to get your suit cleaned. We are terribly sorry about this dreadful accident."

"No! No!" the man objected. "I don't want my suit cleaned. I want a brand new suit. I demand a check for $300 right here and now."

To avoid a bigger scene, the manager went to his office, and wrote out a check for $300. Restaurant employees wiped off as much salad dressing as they could, and the irate diner fumed out the door with his check.

Where had a guy in a suit and tie come from at 12:30 on Sunday afternoon? I wonder what the sermon topic was?

The Power of Peace. Christmas Eve 1914 brought an eerie halt to the carnage of World War I on the western front. Trenches lay within 50 miles of Paris. The war was only five months old but had killed or wounded 800,000 combatants. What would happen Christmas Day?

British soldiers raised Merry Christmas signs. Here and there, sounds of carols wafted from both lines. Frequently, unarmed British and German soldiers left their trenches against the orders of their superiors and met in no-man's land to sing, talk, and exchange candy and cigars. At one spot, an impromptu soccer game broke out, and the German team won three to two.

In some places, the Christmas truce stretched on through the next day. Neither army wanted to fire the first shot. But new troops kept arriving, eager for battle, and fighting resumed from the English Channel to the Swiss Alps. The high command of both armies ordered that further "informal understandings" with the enemy be treated as treason.

A Time to Speak. Albert Einstein was asked to say a few impromptu words at a dinner given in his honor at Swarthmore College. He stood and said, "Ladies and gentlemen, I am very sorry, but I have nothing to say," and sat down. Shortly he rose again and added, "If I do have something to say, I'll come back."

Six months later, Einstein wired the president of Swarthmore to say, "Now I have something to say," Another dinner was hosted, and Einstein made a notable speech.

PEOPLE OF GODLY BEHAVIOR

BACKGROUND SCRIPTURE: James 4
DEVOTIONAL READING: Proverbs 3:13-18

KEY VERSE: Draw nigh to God, and he will draw nigh to you. James 4:8.

KING JAMES VERSION

JAMES 4:1 From whence come wars and fightings among you? come they not hence, even of your lusts that war in your members? 2 Ye lust, and have not: ye kill, and desire to have, and cannot obtain: ye fight and war, yet ye have not, because ye ask not. 3 Ye ask, and receive not, because ye ask amiss, that ye may consume it upon your lusts. 4 Ye adulterers and adulteresses, know ye not that the friendship of the world is enmity with God? whosoever therefore will be a friend of the world is the enemy of God. 5 Do ye think that the scripture saith in vain, The spirit that dwelleth in us lusteth to envy? 6 But he giveth more grace. Wherefore he saith, God resisteth the proud, but giveth grace unto the humble. 7 Submit yourselves therefore to God. Resist the devil, and he will flee from you. 8 Draw nigh to God, and he will draw nigh to you. Cleanse your hands, ye sinners; and purify your hearts, ye double minded. 9 Be afflicted, and mourn, and weep: let your laughter be turned to mourning, and your joy to heaviness. 10 Humble yourselves in the sight of the Lord, and he shall lift you up.

11 Speak not evil one of another, brethren. He that speaketh evil of his brother, and judgeth his brother, speaketh evil of the law, and judgeth the law: but if thou judge the law, thou art not a doer of the law, but a judge. 12 There is one lawgiver, who is able to save and to destroy: who art thou that judgest another?

NEW REVISED STANDARD VERSION

JAMES 4:1 Those conflicts and disputes among you, where do they come from? Do they not come from your cravings that are at war within you? 2 You want something and do not have it; so you commit murder. And you covet something and cannot obtain it; so you engage in disputes and conflicts. You do not have, because you do not ask. 3 You ask and do not receive, because you ask wrongly, in order to spend what you get on your pleasures. 4 Adulterers! Do you not know that friendship with the world is enmity with God? Therefore whoever wishes to be a friend of the world becomes an enemy of God. 5 Or do you suppose that it is for nothing that the scripture says, "God yearns jealously for the spirit that he has made to dwell in us"? 6 But he gives all the more grace; therefore it says,

"God opposes the proud,
 but gives grace to the humble."

7 Submit yourselves therefore to God. Resist the devil, and he will flee from you. 8 Draw near to God, and he will draw near to you. Cleanse your hands, you sinners, and purify your hearts, you double-minded. 9 Lament and mourn and weep. Let your laughter be turned into mourning and your joy into dejection. 10 Humble yourselves before the Lord, and he will exalt you.

11 Do not speak evil against one another, brothers and sisters. Whoever speaks evil against another or judges another, speaks evil against the law and judges the law; but if you judge the law, you are not a doer of the law but a judge. 12 There is one lawgiver and judge who is able to save and to destroy. So who, then, are you to judge your neighbor?

13

Monday, August 18	Proverbs 3:13-18	*Understanding and Peace*
Tuesday, August 19	James 4:1-3	*Ask Rightly*
Wednesday, August 20	James 4:4-7	*Yearn for God's Spirit*
Thursday, August 21	James 4:8-10	*Humble Yourselves*
Friday, August 22	James 4:11-14	*Do Not Judge*
Saturday, August 23	James 4:15-17	*Seek God's Wishes*
Sunday, August 24	Ephesians 5:8-11	*Living in the Light of God*

BACKGROUND

It remains unclear which specific Old Testament passage is being referenced in James 4:5. Perhaps the general teaching of a broad range of verses is in view—for instance, Exodus 20:3, 5; 34:14; Deuteronomy 6:15; 32:21; Joshua 24:19; and Nahum 1:2. In these passages, the Lord's exclusive claim on His people is being addressed. The teaching of the Old Testament is that God maintained a burning zeal and passion for the covenant community and would deal with all rivals firmly. Thus, any believer who was spiritually unfaithful to the Lord would experience His hand of discipline (see Prov. 3:11-12; Heb. 12:5-6).

There are three primary ways James 4:5 has been rendered. First, the KJV says, *the spirit that dwelleth in us lusteth to envy.* This refers to the individual human spirit that God placed within Adam at creation (Gen. 2:7). With the fall of humankind into sin (Rom. 5:12-14), the individual human spirit is filled with envy; put another way, the jealous yearning refers to the covetous desires of people. Second, the NRSV rendering for James 4:5 says that *God yearns jealously for the spirit that he has made to dwell in us.* The idea is that when God's people become unfaithful in their commitment, He zealously desires to have them return to Him in faithfulness and love. A third rendering is that "the Spirit he caused to live in us longs jealously." In this case, the Holy Spirit, who dwells in us, cares for us deeply and wants us to be faithful to the Lord. Regardless of which rendering is preferred, the overall thrust of the verse is clear. When we opt for friendship with the world, it provokes God to anger. Indeed, He will not permit us to have divided loyalties between Himself and the world.

NOTES ON THE PRINTED TEXT

James 4 deals with the presence of conflict among the first recipients of the letter. The author asked what was causing the discord among them (4:1). The question was framed in the language of military conflict. In effect, the Christians to whom James wrote were clashing with each other. They were warring among themselves about things they wanted but could not acquire. James stated that the source of these conflicts was not circumstances or personalities, but selfish passions that battled within their own hearts. The Greek word rendered *lusts* in 4:1 and 4:3 are both translations of *hedonon*, the root from which our English term *hedonism* comes. *Hedonism* is the pursuit of pleasure merely for the sake of the sensual satisfaction it brings.

The readership of James, in their shortsightedness, strongly desired what they did not have and thus resorted to scheming and injustice to get it. The more envious they became, the more they tried to obtain through worldly, underhanded means what others had (4:2). The writer was possibly using exaggeration when he said that Christians committed murder in the pursuit of pleasure. Since James had previously used war imagery when there was no actual physical battle, the Greek word he chose for *kill* might also be translated "hate." The Lord Jesus and the apostle John made it clear that harboring hatred toward another person was a spiritual form of murder (see Matt. 5:21-22; 1 John 3:15).

The displays of jealousy and greed among believers led only to futility and frustration. The solution was to pray to God about these and other pressing matters. James explained that his readers did not receive what they desired because they left God out of their pursuits. Perhaps these believers recognized the selfish or immoral nature of what they craved, so they felt that asking God's assistance would be futile. Of course, if so, they would have been correct. Some of those who did make their requests known to God used prayer as a means of self-gratification. Their motives were impure because they sought pleasure for its own sake—not the joy and satisfaction one derives from implementing the will of God (Jas. 4:3). When someone's motives are outside the will of God, the Lord is not going to grant that person's requests.

The envy, rivalry, and violence previously described are widespread in fallen human society. When they also appear among Christians, it is because believers have jettisoned loyalty to God for friendship with *the world* (4:4). This means believers have embraced the outlook of the unsaved and decided to operate by their twisted logic. Put another way, Christians are guilty of drinking deeply from the cesspool of the world's way of thinking and acting. The author used strong language when he labeled compromising believers as adulterous people. The idea is that they had become spiritually unfaithful to God by embracing the values and aims of the world (see Jer. 3:6-10; Ezek. 16:38; 23:1-49; Hos. 2:2-5; 3:1-5; 9:1). Those who are a friend of the world also are the enemy of God. Nothing less than enmity can exist when one's aim is to enjoy the world rather than to love and serve God.

Sometimes when we talk about God's love, we misconstrue it to be merely static and willful in nature; but James 4:5 suggests that there is also a strong affective dimension to God. He longs to be in relationship with us and is displeased when we stray from Him. Thankfully, God in His *grace* (4:6) does not abandon us in our spiritual waywardness; instead, He is ready to shower us with His kindness to overcome our envy and greed. In fact, we need His strength to turn from the world and back to Him. As the quote from Proverbs 3:34 teaches, God opposes all who are arrogant, but manifests His grace to the lowly. The author's remedy for conflict among believers, then, is a humble spirit energized by the grace of God. With this, harmony can be restored to the Body of Christ, which in turn enables a cease-fire among warring factions within a congregation.

James 4:7 calls upon believers to reject their unrighteous conduct and to draw near to God with repentant hearts. In turn, this would promote a harmonious relationship with God and one's fellow believers, both of which are essential for growth and development toward spiritual maturity. The first part of the process of renewal and recommitment is like the two sides of a coin: *Submit . . . to God* and *Resist the devil*. The initial readers were doing the opposite—they were resisting the will of God and cooperating with the powers of darkness! The word *therefore* refers back to Proverbs 3:34, which was quoted in James 4:6. Since the Lord gives grace to the humble, it only made sense that an attitude of submission would be the most beneficial way to relate to God. The act of submission carried the idea of subordinating oneself to a superior. Submission is not simply obedience, but the humble attitude that makes obedience possible. The act of resisting, on the other hand, meant to take a stand against something. In this case, the stand was against the devil and his pervasive influence in the world.

As the readers of this letter drew near to God, they had the assurance that He would reciprocate by drawing near to them. But such close communion with God required divine cleansing. Put another way, clean hands (signifying outward conduct) and a pure heart (signifying inward thoughts and motives) were necessary prerequisites to intimacy with a holy God (4:8). In this verse, James made reference to concepts drawn from the Old Testament. In ancient Israel, the priests would wash their hands before approaching God (Exod. 30:19-21). This process of external cleansing symbolized the internal purification of the worshiper's thoughts, motives, and desires (Ps. 23:3-4; Jer. 4:4; 1 Tim. 1:5). The need for cleansing was highlighted by the writer's description of his readers as *sinners* (Jas. 4:8) and *double minded.* Their evil conduct warranted the label *sinners*, and their double-mindedness stemmed from their attempts to be close to God while pursuing the selfish and immoral pleasures lauded by the world.

In light of the severity of the sins these believers were perpetually committing, the writer called for a response of grief, mourning, and wailing (4:9). There was no room here for a lighthearted attitude. They couldn't just brush these actions off as social conventions. The author further admonished his readers to turn their empty laughter into mourning and their artificial joy into gloom. The meaning of the Greek word rendered *heaviness* was to cast one's eyes down. It is a picture of a contrite heart that in shame and sorrow confesses grievous wrongdoing. James was not describing a long-term Christian disposition here, but rather an appropriate short-term emotional response to failing God.

In 4:10, the writer turned once again to the theme of humility. In order to be lifted up, one must follow the path of humility before God. Humility is the key that unlocks the treasure of God's grace. The exact opposite of humility is the attitude that leads a believer to speak harshly to fellow Christians. James called upon his readers to stop their mean-spirited verbal attacks. In effect, they were being unjustly critical and judgmental toward one another. Moreover, to spread falsehoods about other believers or to censure them unfairly was equivalent to sitting in judgment over the law of God. When the self-appointed critics placed themselves above the law, they treated it with contempt and transgressed its commands (4:11).

God's law was intended to govern people. But those who dared to assume a superior stance over this divine legal code were attempting to take a position that belongs only to God. After all, He alone is the righteous Lawgiver and Judge (4:12), and only He has the authority to overrule or change His edicts. This is true because as the Lawgiver, God is the author of the law. Also, as the Judge, He is the administrator of the law. In short, He is both the legislator and enforcer of His eternal decrees. Accordingly, only He has the right and power to save and destroy. While the law given by the Lawgiver brings condemnation to transgressors, the righteous Judge is the only one with the authority to save the condemned offender. In light of this truth, James rebuked his readers for setting themselves up as judges of their neighbors.

SUGGESTIONS TO TEACHERS

James identified greed as the source of constant strife among his readers. Selfish cravings for pleasure and the things of the world battled inside them and eventually led to acrimony and strife. When anything but God becomes the center of our lives, it will never satisfy. Instead, it becomes part of a downward spiral that only keeps us longing for more.

1. WORLDLY ANTAGONISM. James forcefully stated that our cravings for pleasure and happiness easily take the place in our hearts and minds that belongs only to God. When they do, we find ourselves in antagonistic relationships with people who might block our pleasures and happiness.

2. SPIRITUAL ADULTERY. Devotion to our desires is a worldly attitude and, therefore is friendship with the world. God will not accept a rival for the devotion of His covenant people. He expects undivided loyalty and provides His grace to enable us to be true to Him.

3. SUBMISSIVE CONFIDENCE. Humility involves choosing God over the devil and then choosing to be intimate with God. Humility realizes that intimacy with God demands moral purity and is willing to repent to experience it. Just as Jesus promised (Matt. 23:12), self-abasement leads to exaltation by God.

4. ARROGANT CONFIDENCE. We live in a culture obsessed with planning and goal setting. "If you can visualize it, you can achieve it," is a mantra of our age. James taught that all planning and goal setting must be tentative. It must be contingent on God's will. Only His will is deserving of the trust and confidence our culture teaches us to place in our plans and goals.

■ **TOPIC:** Living Responsibly

■ **QUESTIONS:** 1. What was the origin of the conflicts and disputes to which James referred? 2. In what way does God give grace to the humble? 3. Why is it important to relate to God with an attitude of humility? 4. How can believers submit all their plans to God? 5. Why is God displeased when we go through our lives with an attitude of arrogance?

■ **ILLUSTRATIONS:**

Transforming Skid Row. These days, the phrase "skid row" refers to the rundown area of a city where alcoholics and vagrants congregate. There is such a place in Los Angeles, California. An expansive, 50-square-block area known as Central City East is home to thousands of vagrant men, women, and children. Visitors are shocked to find that against the backdrop of shiny, glass-covered skyscrapers, many streets, sidewalks, and alleyways are lined with cardboard box shelters and camping tents used by transient persons.

Correspondent Farai Chideya of *National Public Radio* noted that Skid Row has become a "growing irritation to downtown business owners." It has not only hindered a "luxury apartment boom in the city center," but also serves as a "daily reminder of a huge need unmet." Thankfully, there are people who care enough to make a difference.

Chideya reported that a "core group of counselors, volunteers, health workers and police officers toil around the clock to create pockets of stability amid the chaos." For example, there's the "School on Wheels," which provides a refuge for homeless children to use "coloring books, toys and even computers." It is efforts such as these that represent the generosity and kindness God wants to see present in the life of His people.

Moral Failure. An editorial appearing in *Christianity Today* dealt with the issue of church leaders who succumb to moral failure. The magazine noted that the problem of "pastors snared by sexual transgression" transcends church affiliation and belief. The phenomena is worsened by a culture inundated by "sensuality and disregard for communal accountability." Also, there's the "availability and anonymity" of the Internet, which has made it all too easy for clergy to obtain pornography and get caught up in "clandestine sexual encounters."

The editorial stated that a "wise church response" is needed to help ministers resist these enticements to sin. One recommendation is to "enact clear and enforceable standards that will guard against temptation." A second piece of advice is for congregations to "implement plans for discipline and restoration when possible." The so-called *Modesto Manifesto* is a sterling example. In 1948, evangelist Billy Graham met with his associates in Modesto, California, to discuss ways to "protect themselves against smearing the gospel of Christ." The rigorous standards they established included not meeting, traveling, or eating alone with "any woman but their wives."

Regardless of what code of professional ethics is adopted, the goal is to prevent moral failure among church leaders and encourage them to model upright behavior before God's people. As ministers become less inclined to give in to their "ignoble impulses," it will help "rehabilitate the image of gospel preachers." Additionally, when the threat is understood and preemptive action is taken, it will "protect our pastors, their families, their churches, and the appeal of the gospel."

Humility's Perspective. Several years ago, shortly after Tom Brokaw was promoted to co-host the "Today" show, he was picking up some things in Bloomingdale's. That promotion capped a series of career advances that started with *NBC* in Omaha and progressed through Los Angeles and Washington, D.C., to New York. Brokaw noticed a man watching him closely and prepared for some fan adoration. Finally, the man stepped up, pointed, and said, "Tom Brokaw, right?"

"Right," Brokaw nodded.

"You used to do the morning news on KMTV in Omaha, right?"

Brokaw was impressed with how much the fan knew about him. "That's right."

"I knew it the moment I spotted you," the tourist went on. After a pause, he asked, "Whatever happened to you?"

Humility recognizes that we aren't as impressive as we might like to think we are.

FOR YOUTH

■ TOPIC: Greed Is Out!

■ QUESTIONS: 1. In what ways can Christians become embroiled in disputes and conflicts with one another? 2. What does it mean to be a friend with the world? 3. Why is it arrogant to make plans without submitting them to the will of God? 4. What can believers do to cultivate an intimate relationship with God? 5. How can we, as Christians, refrain from sinful forms of boasting?

■ ILLUSTRATIONS:

Unparalleled Generosity. For 2005, *Time* magazine named Bill Gates as one of three persons of the year. The other two were his wife, Melinda, and Irish rock star, Bono. Bill Gates is the co-founder (along with Steve Ballmer) of the computer giant, Microsoft Corporation. According to *Reuters*, Gates' "personal fortune of $46.5 billion topped Forbes magazine's list of the world's richest." But that's not why he made the *Time* magazine list. It's because he, his wife, and Bono have made a difference in the world as "Good Samaritans."

Bill Gates has been especially effective at "finding ways to eradicate such calamities as malaria in Africa, HIV and AIDS, and the grinding poverty that kills 8 million people a year." This is one reason why he established the Gates Foundation, "the world's biggest charity" with a $30 billion endowment. In 2006, that charity received a huge boost from Warren E. Buffett, the chairman of Berkshire Hathaway, Inc. This industrialist and entrepreneur plans to donate $31 billion (the bulk of his fortune) to the Gates Foundation. The combined assets of $61 billion will be used to fund "hundreds of projects around the world." Improving public health is one area of concern, including the vaccination of children and the development of new drugs. Another area of focus is "educational programs and scholarships in the United States and abroad."

For people such as these, greed is out and living responsibly is in. Clearly, this is at the heart of the decision of Bill Gates to make 2008 the year he ends his day-to-day role at Microsoft in order to devote more time to his global health and education work. The Book of James would applaud such a mindset and urge all who love God to do what they can to show favor to the humble and oppressed.

Where Conflict Originates. One day, the lion was feeling especially good about himself, so he set out to feed his ego. He approached the bear and asked, "Who is king of the jungle?"

"Why you are, of course," the bear answered quickly.

The lion roared his approval and stalked off to find the tiger. "Who's the king of the jungle?" he demanded.

"Everyone knows that you are," the tiger said with a low bow.

The lion checked the tiger's name from his list and went looking for the elephant. "Who is king of the jungle?" the lion snarled at the hulking pachyderm.

The elephant, who suffered from a painfully inflamed tusk, grabbed the lion with her trunk, whirled him around six times in the air, slammed him against a tree, dribbled him on the ground, held him under the surface of the waterhole five minutes, and tossed him contemptuously under a bush.

The lion—battered and bruised—struggled to his unsteady feet. "Look," he said, "just because you don't know the answer, you don't have to get mean about it."

When we focus on ourselves and what makes us happy, we end up in conflict with other people who are doing exactly the same thing. Everybody can't get his or her own way at the same time.

Loyal Love. A college man took a portrait of his new girlfriend to a photography studio. He wanted copies of her picture so he could post them in strategic places at school and at home. When the studio owner removed the photograph from its frame, he noticed an inscription on the back: "My dearest John, I love you with all my heart. I love you more and more each day. I will love you forever and ever. I am yours for all eternity." It was signed, "Marsha." Beneath the signature was a P.S.: "If we ever break up, I want this picture back."

God expects greater faithfulness than that.

PRAYERFUL COMMUNITY

BACKGROUND SCRIPTURE: James 5
DEVOTIONAL READING: 1 Thessalonians 5:16-22

KEY VERSE: Is any among you afflicted? let him
pray. Is any merry? let him sing psalms. James 5:13.

KING JAMES VERSION

JAMES 5:13 Is any among you afflicted? let him
pray. Is any merry? let him sing psalms. 14 Is any sick
among you? let him call for the elders of the church;
and let them pray over him, anointing him with oil in
the name of the Lord: 15 And the prayer of faith shall
save the sick, and the Lord shall raise him up; and if he
have committed sins, they shall be forgiven him.
16 Confess your faults one to another, and pray one for
another, that ye may be healed. The effectual fervent
prayer of a righteous man availeth much. 17 Elias was
a man subject to like passions as we are, and he prayed
earnestly that it might not rain: and it rained not on the
earth by the space of three years and six months.
18 And he prayed again, and the heaven gave rain, and
the earth brought forth her fruit. 19 Brethren, if any of
you do err from the truth, and one convert him; 20 Let
him know, that he which converteth the sinner from the
error of his way shall save a soul from death, and shall
hide a multitude of sins.

NEW REVISED STANDARD VERSION

JAMES 5:13 Are any among you suffering? They
should pray. Are any cheerful? They should sing songs
of praise. 14 Are any among you sick? They should call
for the elders of the church and have them pray over
them, anointing them with oil in the name of the Lord.
15 The prayer of faith will save the sick, and the Lord
will raise them up; and anyone who has committed sins
will be forgiven. 16 Therefore confess your sins to one
another, and pray for one another, so that you may be
healed. The prayer of the righteous is powerful and
effective. 17 Elijah was a human being like us, and he
prayed fervently that it might not rain, and for three
years and six months it did not rain on the earth.
18 Then he prayed again, and the heaven gave rain and
the earth yielded its harvest.

19 My brothers and sisters, if anyone among you
wanders from the truth and is brought back by another,
20 you should know that whoever brings back a sinner
from wandering will save the sinner's soul from death
and will cover a multitude of sins.

14

423

BACKGROUND

Some interpretors have understood James 5:15 to teach that complete physical health is always assured through prayer. Whenever illness strikes, the Christian should pray in faith as a guarantee for healing. If illness persists (in this view), then the prayer must not have been offered in genuine faith. Others see the verse as teaching cooperation between prayer and medicine (the anointing with oil), between God and a physician. According to this view, just prayer or just medicine alone is less than a full prescription for renewed health. Together, they are a powerful remedy for serious illness.

An important question concerns what is meant by the Greek word rendered *sick*. In 5:14, the term literally means "to be weak" and is used in the New Testament for physical illness as well as for weakness of faith or conscience (see Acts 20:35; Rom. 6:19; 14:1; 1 Cor. 8:9-12). Thus, it would seem that James could have been referring to either sicknesses of the body or sicknesses of the spirit. This reminds us that there are times when physical illness might have a spiritual cause, namely, sin. The remark in James 5:15 about forgiveness of sin might be a reference to an illness brought on by personal sin in the believer's life. In this case, the writer assured the sick that the prayer of faith would result in forgiveness and spiritual restoration. Of course, the use of the word *if* implies that sometimes illness is not the result of personal sin. Irrespective of the details, God is not limited as to the methods He may employ in restoring ailing believers. Also, with regard to prayer, God answers only according to His will. Sometimes, God's will does not include physical healing (see 2 Cor. 12:7-9).

NOTES ON THE PRINTED TEXT

In James 5:12, the author warned his readers not to make frivolous oaths. Not all pledges are necessarily forbidden by this verse. Only vows made lightly or in a blasphemous and profane way are forbidden. Many people invoke flippant oaths in an attempt to increase their credibility. Admittedly, there are examples of the use of oaths in Scripture to validate the truth of one's claim (see Exod. 22:11; Matt. 26:63-64; Rom. 1:9). But the point in James 5:12 is that if a person trusts the Lord, there is no need for invoking any type of oath by making reference to heaven (the throne room of God), earth (the footstool of His feet; see Isa. 66:1), or any other aspect of creation. When a person appealed to any of these entities while making an oath, they became as binding as if the individual had invoked the name of the Lord. If a person's word is truthful and honest, then a simple *yes* or *no* (which reflects unambiguous language) should be all that is necessary. James was clearly referring to the teaching of Jesus in this matter (see Matt. 5:33-37). Ignoring this command will result in the condemnation of the flippant oath taker.

James concluded his letter with an emphasis on prayer. Prayer is the most potent action a believer can take in time of trouble. Prayer ought to be a Christian's reflexive response to all of life's problems—accompanied with praise to God for His bountiful gifts. The English word *prayer* comes from the Latin word *precarious*, which means to be in a vulnerable position. In prayer, we are acknowledging our vulnerability and deepest needs before an all-powerful and holy God. The author employed a series of questions as springboards for conveying some important principles of prayer to his readers. The Greek word rendered *afflicted* (Jas. 5:13) in the first question refers to suffering that comes from any source. The author used the same word in 5:10 when describing the trials of the prophets.

The matter of offering songs of praise (a type of prayer) in response to happiness is easy to understand. The difficulty, however, comes in times of sickness and affliction. Earlier, in 1:2, the author told his readers to *count it all joy* when they faced hardships. He was not telling these Christians that trials bring joy in a person's life. Instead, he meant that we are to cultivate a joyful attitude in the midst of life's difficult times. Trials serve as tests of our faith by which we develop patience. Mature believers are the result of responding properly to this testing. This spiritual maturation makes us fit to do God's work in the world. In 1:12, James said that God blesses those who patiently endure afflictions. In turn, He is glorified when we persevere under trials. James did not say "if" but "when" we face temptations. Nevertheless, God promises to reward with an eternal *crown of life* those who love and serve Him despite life's obstacles.

In times of illness, God should be the first healer to whom a Christian turns. It is also a faith action to turn to other members of the church body. The elders should be available for counsel and comfort, and willing to help the afflicted in any way possible (Jas. 5:14). Elders were leaders in the early church. They are first mentioned in Acts 11:30 as the recognized leaders of local congregations (see 1 Tim. 3:1-7; 5:17; Titus 1:6-9). Once called, the elders were to pray over the sick and anoint them with oil in the Lord's name. The oil symbolized the presence of God (see Ps. 23:5). But in Bible times, it was also thought to contain some medicinal properties (see Luke 10:34).

Since olive trees, which grew even in rocky places, produced much oil, olive oil came to be regarded as a special gift from God. This oil was also associated with the outpouring of God's Spirit. Anointing with oil customarily accompanied the consecration of individuals to God's service. It was used to set apart prophets (1 Kings 19:16), priests (Lev. 8:12), and kings (1 Sam. 16:13; 1 Kings 1:34). The use of oil for healing is seen in Jesus' parable of the Good Samaritan. While binding the wounds of the man who had been mugged, the Samaritan poured in oil and wine (Luke 10:34). Apparently, it was for the same purpose that the 12 disciples took oil for healing when Jesus sent them out two by two on a ministry mission (Mark 6:13).

James 5:15 says that if the elders have faith when they pray for the sick, they will get well. In fact, the Lord will restore the afflicted to health. *Faith* primarily refers to a person's belief or trust in God. The term is also used in the New Testament to refer to the body of truths held by followers of Christ. This second use became increasingly prevalent as church leaders and scholars defended the truths of the faith against the attacks of false teachers. Faith can be understood as having four recognizable elements. First is cognition, an awareness of the facts; second is comprehension, an understanding of the facts; third is conviction, an acceptance of the facts; and fourth is commitment, trust in a reliable object. As James made clear in his epistle, genuine faith is evidenced by more than mere words. It leads to a transformed life in which the believer reaches out to others in need with the Savior's love.

All of us need some kind of healing, whether physical, spiritual, or emotional; and we should be able to turn to other believers for help. This includes confessing our sins to each other as well as praying for each other (5:16). The acknowledgment of sins among believers helps to promote wellness and wholeness of individuals and relationships. In particular, believers draw their fellow Christians toward a deeper, more mature walk with the Savior. Members of the community of faith also deepen their commitment to one another in the bonds of Christian love. This verse does not signify a call for indiscriminate airing of a believer's every shortcoming. The Holy Spirit should always be given complete charge over the matter of conviction and confession of sin. He will lead the believer in the knowledge of which sins to confess in private prayer and which to confess in the company of other believers.

In any case, whether public or private, one truth is clear, namely, that prayer is a powerful and effective means of accomplishing the will of God. The Lord especially uses the earnest prayer of righteous believers (those who are characterized by virtue and integrity) to produce wonderful results in the lives of believers. As was his practice, James offered an illustration to support his point. This time it was Elijah, an Old Testament prophet with the same human frailties that we have. This man, who was just like us, prayed earnestly that no rain would fall, and none fell for three and a half years (5:17; see Luke 4:25). Then, when he prayed again, rain fell from the skies and made the crops grow (Jas. 5:18; see 1 Kings 17:1; 18:41-46). Because prayer is our most powerful tool, it should be our first option in responding to a crisis, not a last resort. It only makes sense to rely on God's power, which is infinitely greater than our own.

The author's final appeal to his readers concerned individuals who had wandered from the way of truth. Some think James 5:19 refers to those who claimed to be Christians but whose faith was spurious (see Heb. 6:4-6; 2 Pet. 2:20-22). Others think James 5:19 is dealing with genuine believers who have strayed into sinful patterns. In either case, when anyone belonging to a congregation wanders from the path of moral rectitude, it is the duty of God's people to seek out the wayward and bring them back into the fellowship—through prayer, counseling, friendship, or whatever it takes. When sinners are turned back from their error-prone ways, it means they have been rescued from the path of destruction.

In some cases, the *death* (5:20) being averted is eternal separation from God (see Rev. 21:8). For others, James 5:20 denotes avoiding the experience of premature physical death (see 1 Cor. 11:29-32; 1 John 5:16). When the wayward are spiritually restored, it signifies the forgiveness of many sins (Jas. 5:20). Often, the process includes godly sorrow that leads to repentance and salvation (2 Cor. 7:10). Most likely, there will also be the confession of sin, which brings about divine pardon and cleansing from all unrighteousness (1 John 1:9). James provided his readers with the valuable instruction necessary for progress on the road to spiritual restoration and growth. Whether the issue was taming the tongue or persevering in persecution, all that a believer needed to grow in holiness was found in the One who answered the prayers of the faithful.

SUGGESTIONS TO TEACHERS

Prayer works. Anyone who prays regularly would agree. It is our strongest communication link with the God who created us. It is a powerful means for giving our voice to our faith. Most important of all, God can use our prayers to change our world. Clearly, our petitions matter.

1. THE PARTNERS OF PRAYER. Hands, feet, back, and pocketbook—these are some of the means that come to mind when we think of helping our fellow Christians. They enable us to comfort, carry, accompany, and contribute. They are solid, tangible realities. Beside them, the ethereal act of prayer can seem like little more than nice words spoken more to comfort the person doing the petitioning than to actually accomplish anything tangible. In reality, though, God uses these external means to "partner" (in a manner of speaking) with prayer to accomplish His eternal good.

2. THE POWER OF PRAYER. James 5:16 points out that a committed believer's prayer can produce powerful results. Powerful is hardly the way to describe nice words whose sole purpose is to offer psychological comfort to those who pray them. No, prayer changes things. Instead of being the last thing we do—when all other avenues are exhausted—it should be the first thing we do in every situation.

3. THE WONDER OF PRAYER. Prayer can be power-producing and effective in more ways than we might realize at first. For instance, while prayer may not change our circumstances, it can indeed alter our response to those circumstances. On the other hand, prayer very well may change our circumstances. As we pray, our lives will reflect our prayerful hearts. We will find ourselves more in tune with the needs of others and better able to meet them because of our deeper walk with God. Our spiritual maturity will enrich our own lives even as it extends to those to whom we minister, bearing fruit in many ways as it touches many lives.

FOR ADULTS	■ **TOPIC:** Powerful and Effective Living

■ **QUESTIONS:** 1. Why is prayer appropriate in times of trouble? 2. Why are ailing believers encouraged to summon the elders of the church? 3. What is the purpose of anointing an ailing believer with oil in the name of the Lord? 4. In what way is Elijah an example of someone who prayed humbly and earnestly? 5. How can concerned believers restore the wayward to the truth?

■ **ILLUSTRATIONS:**

The Need for God's Power. During Haddon Robinson's tenure as president of Denver Seminary, lawsuits were brought against the school. Because he was named in one of the suits, Robinson had to give a deposition. For two days, prosecutors relentlessly grilled him as they questioned his motives and tried to cast everything he said in a negative light.

Robinson not only faced legal problems, but he also had to deal with attacks against his sterling reputation as a minister. For example, a disgruntled former employee of the seminary spread false statements about Robinson throughout the community. Robinson and his wife responded to the devastating emotional pain they experienced by bathing their circumstance in prayer.

Looking back on this trying ordeal, Robinson wrote, "If anything good for me came out of this painful time, it was the overwhelming sense of my need of God. I felt completely vulnerable. Although I was not guilty of any legal negligence or failure, I felt more in need of grace than ever."

As God did with Robinson, He also upholds us during the difficult periods of our lives and ministries. As we spend time with Him in prayer, He gives us the strength to remain faithful to the work He has called us to do.

Just in Time. A Christian woman, Joan (not her real name), married an unbelieving husband, Brian. He was a salesman who often traveled during the week, so Joan had lots of time to pray for her husband's salvation. Joan had great joy in her heart knowing that God was hearing her pleas as she lifted Brian in continuous prayer. But Joan was devastated the day she received news that Brian had been instantly killed in a highway accident. Joan's faith was deeply shaken, that is, until nearly five years later, when she received a surprise visit from a young man who came looking for Brian.

As it turned out, this young man, Josh, was the last person to see Joan's husband alive. Brian had picked him up as Josh was hitchhiking on a country highway. When Brian dropped off Josh, Brian gave him his address and said if he was ever in Indianapolis to look him up. Josh was shocked to hear Joan report that Brian had been killed only five miles beyond the place that Josh had last seen Brian. But that tragic news felt less dreadful when Josh informed Joan that 10 minutes before the fatal crash, he had prayed with Brian, and that Brian had repented of his sins and asked God to give him a personal relationship through faith in Jesus Christ.

Down, But Not Out. When Rick and Sandy married 25 years ago, Rick was energetic and healthy. But for the last four years, he has struggled with chronic fatigue syndrome. Extreme tiredness, forgetfulness, difficulty concentrating, and irritability are symptoms to which Rick and his family have had to adjust.

Rick's role as the pastor of a busy church seemed to compound the problem. For health reasons, he considered leaving the pastorate. *Should I give up ministry altogether? he wondered. Can God use someone so spent? Perhaps a different kind of job—or even disability—is what God wants.*

Then the Lord seemed to confirm He could still use Rick in ministry. His denominational superintendent met with him to say, "Rick, we value your gifts and abilities. We will find another church for you to serve." As Rick and Sandy started out on this new road, Sandy wrote, "We can either rail against circumstances, questioning God's wisdom, or we can pour ourselves into Bible study and prayer and faithfully allow the all-powerful Lord to work in us."

FOR YOUTH	■ **TOPIC:** Knee Theology Works! ■ **QUESTIONS:** 1. Why is prayer appropriate in times of joy? 2. What are the elders of a church instructed to do for ailing believers? 3. Why

and when should believers confess their sins to each other? 4. How did Elijah demonstrate his earnestness in prayer? 5. What incentive is there for believers to restore the wayward to the truth?

■ **ILLUSTRATIONS:**

Under the Gallows. Back in 1738, London's main detention center was Newgate prison. Charles Wesley (later to be the great Christian hymn writer) frequently went there, preaching to those prisoners sentenced to death. On one occasion, Charles was even locked in overnight in order to pray with and comfort prisoners.

In his *Journal,* Wesley wrote about a poor man who was condemned to die. Wesley told him about "one who came down from heaven to save the lost and him in particar." Wesley led this man to faith in Christ. After Wesley served this man communion, he accompanied the man to the gallows. The assurance of salvation was etched on the new convert's face. Because of his new friend's faith, Wesley penned, "That hour under the gallows was the most blessed hour of my life."

Prayer Is Work. Oswald Chambers (1874-1917) was a Scottish minister whose teachings on the life of faith have endured to this day. He observed that prayer is hard work. "There is nothing thrilling about a laboring man's work but it is the laboring man who makes the conceptions of the genius possible; and it is the laboring saint who makes the conceptions of the Master possible. You labor at prayer and results happen all the time from His standpoint. What an astonishment it will be to find, when the veil is lifted, the souls that have been reaped by you, simply because you had been in the habit of taking your orders from Jesus Christ."

The Blessing of "Unanswered" Prayers. A copy of the following prayer was found in the pocket of an unidentified Confederate soldier at the notorious "Devil's Den" in Gettysburg, Pennsylvania. On July 2, 1863, he became a casualty of the battle fought there during the United States Civil War.

> I asked for strength that I might achieve;
> I was made weak that I might learn humbly to obey.
> I asked for health that I might do greater things;
> I was given infirmity that I might do better things.
> I asked for riches that I might be happy;
> I was given poverty that I might be wise.
> I asked for power that I might have the praise of people;
> I was given weakness that I might feel the need of God.
> I asked for all things that I might enjoy life;
> I was given life that I might enjoy all things.
> I got nothing that I had asked for,
> but eveything that I had hoped for.
> Almost despite myself, my unspoken prayers were answered;
> I am, among all people, most richly blessed.